SOUTHERN POLITICS

SOUTHERN POLITICS
IN STATE AND NATION

V. O. KEY, JR.

With the Assistance of

ALEXANDER HEARD

A New Edition

THE UNIVERSITY OF TENNESSEE PRESS
KNOXVILLE

Reprinted by arrangement with Alfred A. Knopf, Inc., by
The University of Tennessee Press, Knoxville, 1984;
Second printing, 1986.
Copyright 1949 by Alfred A. Knopf, Inc., Published October 3, 1949;
Second printing, May 1950.
Copyright 1977 by Asalie Key Price, W. Cecil Key, Luther S. Key, and
Marion T. Key.

Frontispiece: V. O. Key, Jr.
Photograph by John Brook, courtesy of Marion T. Key.

The paper in this book meets the guidelines for permanence and durability of
the Committee on Production Guidelines for Book Longevity of the Council
on Library Resources. Binding materials have been chosen for durability.

Library of Congress Cataloging in Publication Data
Key, V. O. (Valdimer Orlando), 1908–1963.
    Southern politics in state and nation.

    Reprint. Originally published: New York: Knopf,
1949. With a new introduction and profile.
    Includes bibliographical references and index.
    1. Southern States—Politics and government—1865–
1950. 2. Political parties—Southern States—History.
I. Heard, Alexander.   II. Title.
F215.K45 1984   324.975'04   84–3665
ISBN 0–87049–434–1
ISBN 0–87049–435–X (pbk.)

CONTENTS

CONTENTS

ILLUSTRATIONS

ALL PHOTOGRAPHS BY WIDE WORLD PHOTOS

TABLES

FIGURES

INTRODUCTION
TO THE NEW EDITION

BY ALEXANDER HEARD

My envy rises when the modern interviewer unpacks his microphone, murmurs his assumption that I understand, and begins his questioning on the record, his record. I think of V. O. Key, Jr., and 1946 when Professor Key sent forth two associates to interview participants in southern political life—538 of them, it turned out, in sessions averaging seventy minutes each—with instructions to learn subtleties and secrets that political practitioners would surely not reveal to a note-taking stranger, much less one with a recording machine.

It was Key's conviction that confidential conversations with persons closest to southern political power, or most ardently aspiring to it, would give a deeper understanding of the region's political behavior than would be derivable from official records and printed words alone. In those years of a racially sensitive, one-party South, he correctly felt that informal talk might breed trust, and trust might breed candor, and candor might lead to subjects seldom discussed—and never discussed for attribution.

Nowadays, when the visitor plunks down his microphone and pulls out his written schedule of queries, I think of that earlier time when long outlines of questions and then their much longer answers had to be memorized, and then of the pressure to get quickly to that heavy Ediphone dictating machine with its large wax cylinders. The extreme case was a six-hour unbroken conversation with the maverick Democrat Edward W. Carmack of Tennessee. It was reported in twenty thousand words on thirty-seven single-spaced pages under fourteen file categories.

The study of southern politics was launched September 9, 1946, at
the University of Alabama in Tuscaloosa. Key immediately drafted a thirty-
two page outline of topics to be explored, suppositions to be tested, data
to be gathered, and hints on how to proceed. (Later we learned the term
"research design.") In the margin I entered in red pencil a numerical
classification system. Some 240 filing categories were thus created. Each
segment of an interview report was coded with one or more numbers.
Other items were similarly classified—e.g., state constitutional provisions;
session laws; political party rules; registration figures; poll tax data; clip-
pings from a daily newspaper in each southern state, plus others; excerpts
from the literature of political science and other disciplines; and county-
by-county primary and general election returns. In some states those returns, essential for our research, were extraordinarily difficult to obtain.
They were so difficult to come by that my colleague Donald S. Strong
and I put together a volume of them called *Southern Primaries and Elections, 1920–1949*, published by the University of Alabama Press in 1950.

Key attached great value to the interviews. I reported on the interviewing process in the December 1950 *American Political Science Review*.
Professor Strong interviewed in two states and I in nine. Thirty percent of
the time of the project's senior staff was spent in the field, and 40 percent
of the $40,000 grant from the Rockefeller Foundation went to the salaries
and expenses of the two interviewers and for transcribing their reports.

In writing *Southern Politics in State and Nation*, Key drew on all
the resources of political analysis he could find. What he drew on most,
however, and what made the work distinguished, was himself. He grew
up in Lamesa, west Texas, where his father was active in local politics.
Young Key spent much time around the courthouse square. He once said
that sensitivities to political phenomena developed there underlay his
later capacity for interpretation when studying politics in more complex
settings. It was part of his remarkable talent that he could sit in his office
in Tuscaloosa or Baltimore (or later, in New Haven or Cambridge) and
feel actualities that another person could sense only by being on the scene.
His unusual interpretative instincts were bred in those early experiences
in Texas.

Key's capacity to analyze at a distance did not mean he had no personal
political feelings. In 1948, Henry Wallace ran for President of the United
States on a minor party ticket and was subjected to the then politically
potent charge of being under Communist influence. The Wallace train
stopped in Tuscaloosa one night when Key was in town. We went to the
station. A man was circulating with a large, round basket of fruit, offering
it to those who wanted to throw at whoever might show his head, preferably
the former Vice President. Key was mild-mannered and normally held
events in perspective. But there we were. He put his hand into the middle
of the basket as though to take a tomato. But his other hand went below

the rim of the basket and somehow the whole thing tipped up. That was an uncharacteristic bit of political activism. Key held no brief for Wallace, but he did believe in giving an unpopular fellow a fair hearing.

Key went first to MacMurray College in Abilene, Texas, and then to the University of Texas to earn a bachelor of arts degree in 1929. One of his instructors was Roscoe C. Martin. Martin encouraged him to go for graduate study to the renowned political science department of the University of Chicago. There he received the Ph.D. degree in 1934 under Charles Merriam.

By the time *Southern Politics* appeared, Key had a strong reputation. His published doctoral dissertation on "The Techniques of Political Graft in the United States" examined graft as a form of social influence. *The Administration of Federal Grants to States* was published in 1939 and *The Initiative and Referendum in California,* written with W. W. Crouch, two years later. A small work on *The Problem of Local Legislation in Maryland* came out in 1940. And in 1942 appeared the first of what became five editions of his textbook, *Politics, Parties, and Pressure Groups*— widely used, much quoted, sometimes cited as if it were a technical monograph instead of a textbook.

V. O. Key was the right person to analyze southern politics as the nation emerged from World War II and as the place of blacks in American society, the root of southern Democratic one-party politics, began to change.

The concept of a study originated with Martin, who had become Chairman of the Department of Political Science and Director of the Bureau of the Public Administration at the University of Alabama. Martin started with the conviction that the poll tax needed searching analysis. The poll tax was a timely, controversial, cardinal regional issue, seen to strike at the heart of American political doctrine by disfranchising people, white and black. The proposal to examine the poll tax easily evolved into a broader ambition to study southern regional politics in its entirety.

Martin came to believe that Key was not just the best person to undertake the study, but the only one. Having money in hand, Martin asked Key to lead a study of "the electoral process in the South." He relished telling how he induced a protesting Key to do so. Key was self-deprecating, and he often wore a mantle of skepticism. He said he could not do it. He had worked in Washington during the war while on leave from Johns Hopkins and must now give full attention to his university.

But Martin was tenacious. Shortly, Key received a letter from Isaiah Bowman, President of Johns Hopkins. President Bowman said the proposed study at Alabama had special importance for Johns Hopkins, and he hoped Professor Key would undertake it.

Key now told Martin he had agreed to work a day a week as consultant to the U. S. Bureau of the Budget. He could not pull out of the obligation.

A letter soon arrived from Harold B. Smith, Director of the Bureau of the Budget, telling Key that his obligation to the Bureau should not stand in the way of the more important opportunity to study southern politics.

Now Key told Martin he was not sure the study was worth doing in the first place. What could be accomplished? The nation had many problems; the national interest was broad and varied; politics was very complex; he doubted the undertaking was worthwhile.

Key next received a letter from Harry S. Truman, Thirty-Third President of the United States. The President understood Key had an opportunity to serve the nation by studying the politics of the South. The President hoped Key would do so. At that point, Key wrote Martin saying he supposed the Pope would be next.

Martin, undeterred, went to Baltimore. Here appeared the devil's most potent weapon, a pint of spirits, Old Crow it was said. The two men went to a restaurant near the railroad station and Martin pressed his case. Key signed on. Later, in reminiscence, Key said, "With Roscoe, liquor is an instrument of national policy."

The division of work prescribed by Key in writing *Southern Politics* required that I edit what Key wrote. Key gave stern instructions. When you read what I write, don't give general criticisms. Don't write in the margin "wordy" or "vague" or "please amplify." Give alternative language. If you think the paragraph is no good, write it the way it should be. I learned a lot that way. Key similarly edited the four or five chapters I drafted. I learned a lot that way, too.

In one of Key's chapters, there was a long paragraph—I called it then and think of it now as "poetic." It had great flavor, but I thought that the impressionistic language was technically unclear. It carried impact, but I wasn't sure why. True to my charge, I rewrote the paragraph, organizing it systematically and making the reasoning, such as I could discover, explicit. I sent it back to Key. When the next draft came down, I eagerly looked for his reaction. He had used minor suggestions, but held basically to his original intuitive prose. He noted in the margin of my rewrite that the changes made the target too visible. In fact, Key was trying to communicate more than simple rational prose would convey. He was trying to convey a spirit, something beyond factual information. I twitted him later, saying that he didn't really know what he wanted to say. I was wrong; he always did.

Key once asked my opinion of an hypothesis he was formulating. (He often used the words "hypothesis" and "research design" when he was poking fun at academic jargon and pronounced them with deliberately mischievous emphasis.) He gave forth a highly convoluted proposition. When he finished, I stated what I gathered he meant to say. Right away he responded: "It sounds less plausible when you simplify it." He promptly abandoned the thought. He was self-confident and undeceived.

Key had efficient work habits along with his capacious mind and reliable memory. In completing a manuscript, he did not feel it necessary to check the accuracy of footnotes. Make the citations correct as you go along, he said, and you don't have to worry about them later. In my experience, he was infallibly accurate.

He was also invariably pragmatic. He kept front and center, every day, the need to send *Southern Politics* to the publisher on schedule. The book is 675 pages long. Key worked on it full time two summers and part-time two academic years—the latter while teaching courses and serving actively in professional organizations. He worked abnormally fast. And he worked all the time.

Luella Gettys Key was a political scientist with a Ph.D. earned at Chicago in the same period V. O. was there. They were married in 1934. The two collaborated in some early work, but by the time of *Southern Politics* Luella confined herself to making the indexes for his books, offering an occasional comment on a draft manuscript, keeping an impeccable house, and cooking superb meals. She fretted that Key overworked.

They would have a short time together before dinner, but after dinner Key went back to work. *Southern Politics* has many charts and maps. Key made them all himself, mostly sitting in bed. He said it relaxed him.

Key did not have outside interests in the usual sense, but he had professional interests outside his daily routine that were the spice in his life. *Southern Politics* was followed by a spate of writings and honors that brought Key to the forefront of American political science. He was long the dominant member of the Political Behavior Committee of the Social Science Research Council and in 1958 became President of the American Political Science Association. He was constantly in demand. He was admired and popular in the circles that meant most to him, those of professional political scientists. I think he found more joy in these off-campus professional activities than in anything else he did, excepting the basic satisfaction of recognizing the quality of his own work.

Key's personal standing with other political scientists, junior and senior, was a significant source of his influence. It was also a crucial element in his sense of personal worth. He helped students and colleagues, nearby and far away, giving time, energy, and insight with extraordinary generosity. His help was compassionate as well as critical. Most of all, it was prompt—always prompt—no matter what the pressures of his own work. Across a quarter of a century he helped dozens of persons who believe that his interest in them aided decisively the development of their abilities and the enhancement of their careers. We all lost in 1963 when V. O. Key, Jr., never in robust health, died at age fifty-five.

V. O. KEY, JR.: A BRIEF PROFILE

BY WILLIAM C. HAVARD

Innovative scholars often suffer more from the embraces of their devotees than from the attacks of their severest critics. Poor imitation is less a problem for them than the tendency of their followers to turn complex, carefully qualified conclusions into simplistic doctrine, or even dogma. The so-called "New Critics," for instance, are still trying to explain that their notion of considering a literary work as a whole (or what it is in itself) does not absolutely preclude the appropriate use of biographical perspective and social and historical context in the evaluation of a poem or a story. If such things can happen in the humanities and be a point of contention for more than forty years, it is easy to see why social scientists who avidly seek to imitate the natural sciences, and to exclude from consideration virtually everything that cannot be verified with mathematical precision, would want to ignore such apparently extraneous considerations as the effect of personality, character, and historical circumstance on what is supposed to be pure empirical evidence.

But the fact that we have not been able to reduce the study of human activities entirely to the conditions prescribed for the sciences of external phenomena by their most rigid interpreters is amply revealed by the recent appearance of works of psychobiography and psychohistory.

Reprinted from *South Atlantic Urban Studies,* Vol. 3, 1979, pp. 279–288, by permission.

It may be that in the physical sciences the pure experimentalist's work can be explained without resort to the terms of the human activity involved, but it is doubtful that a satisfactory explanation of a highly imaginative theoretical advance, even in the mathematized sciences, can be given without considering the contributor's habits of mind and the context in which he works.

All of this is a rather elaborate apology for saying that I think any discussion of the work and influence of the late V. O. Key, Jr., needs to be accompanied by some understanding of the man himself. And this is important not only because of Key's eminence as a political scientist, but also because a good many things that are implicit in the corpus of his work cannot be grasped fully without some appreciation of the person who put so much of himself into that work.

Lest my own bias be thought to intrude too much in what follows, I should make plain at the outset that I regard V. O. Key as the most astute and comprehensive professional student of American politics over the past fifty years. Furthermore, I think *Southern Politics* was by far his best work, and in my view it remains the most impressive book published in the general area of American politics since World War II. Largely because of *Southern Politics*, Key probably had a greater impact on American political science than any other individual of his time or since. At the same time, I do not think his breadth of understanding of the generic nature of politics was as great as many other political scientists of this era, nor do I think his philosophical gifts came near to matching his keen powers of observation and almost visceral understanding of his political environment. Because of these strengths and limitations I do not think he made a general theoretical contribution that compares with a number of comprehensive theorists who never came close to attaining his reputation.

In many ways, V. O. Key was so much a product of his political era that he may be said to be a sort of institutional embodiment of American political science from the 1930s on. Key was born in Texas in 1908, the son of a smalltown lawyer and farmer of progressivist-populist intellectual leanings. He took his first two degrees at the University of Texas, and then moved on to the University of Chicago, where he completed his Ph.D. in 1934. By the time he had embarked fully on his career in teaching and research (which mainly consisted of a fairly long stint at Johns Hopkins, followed by a short period at Yale, and the final move to Harvard in 1951), the formative influences had already worked their effect on his choice of areas of interest in research and the general perspective from which he viewed them.

Although the Political Science Department at the University of Chicago has had a long and distinguished career, with many notables on its faculty, the period when Key was there was one in which the influence of Charles E. Merriam was at its height. Merriam is too often remembered now as belonging entirely in the category of those who advocated a pure "science" of politics, and thus were forerunners of behavioralism, but he was actually much broader than this retrospective attitude towards him implies. In many ways Merriam was one of those academicians whose influence on his profession came more through his stimulation of others and his promotion of the discipline than from the seminal nature of his published work. Although he was a prolific writer and covered a spectrum that was almost as broad as the discipline itself, none of his books can be considered a historical classic; in fact, the totality of his work does not point in any particular direction. He did advocate more empirical study of the political and administrative processes, and he really merged what today would be considered normative theory with his observations on the workings of pragmatic politics. To top it all, he was an activist in the progressive reform spirit which led from the legal and organizational changes of the early part of the century through the programmatic adaptations of the New Freedom and the New Deal. Much of Merriam's reputation may be attributed to the attachment that many of the important scholars who studied with him at Chicago felt (and still feel) to him, and the major part of his appeal was based on his commitment to an active role in politics and the consequent projection of a strong sense of the reality of politics as an object of study. Much of this inspiration came from Merriam's persistent attachment to what is now considered an old-fashioned notion of "citizenship training" as a fundamental goal of political science.

When carefully studied, many elements of Key's reflections on politics are related to this combination of attributes displayed by Merriam: the political scientist as scientist, the reformer as advocate of institutional change, and the activist as responsible citizen engaged in the practice of politics as an avocation, if not as a vocation. Key was, of course, a far better scholar than Merriam, and far less of an activist, but he did serve his turn in the bureaucracy at the beginning of his career, and it is typical that one of his earliest articles should have been on methods of evasion of civil service requirements. Furthermore, one can find many examples in his books and articles of prescriptive suggestions for institutional and program reform, and a number of little homilies on the proper role of the informed and responsible citizen.

Key's personal style and manner tended to reflect his background and, to some extent, his approach to his discipline. I do not remember having seen him until he was in his middle forties, and by then he had taken on the appearance of a middle-aged, southern farmer—his frame was thin and angular, his shoulders were stooped, and he had a pale, freckled complexion and thinning sandy hair that must have been red in his younger days. His teeth had a coloration that suggested an upbringing in that area of Texas in which the natural water supply contained substantial quantities of fluoride. If one could use the term in an application that reflects the honorable sources of hard work from which its literal quality was derived, rather than in the cruel, discriminatory sense the appellation now connotes, one might even say that Key looked like a redneck. One regularly heard him referred to in a rather affectionate way as "old" V. O. His appearance of listlessness and premature age was almost certainly due to poor health. Key apparently suffered most of his life from a chronic illness which, although never completely diagnosed, led to his death while he was still in his mid-fifties.

If Key sometimes appeared to be infirm, his mental and physical capacity for sustained intellectual labor can hardly be called into question. He was a twenty-four-hour-a-day political scientist. His wife, Luella Gettys Key, whose contributions to Key's work are probably underestimated by all but a very few people, was also a political scientist, and one of the first, if not the first, woman to take a Ph.D. in the subject. As a teacher, Key was at his best in a one-to-one relationship with graduate students. Although he did not produce a large number of Ph.D. students, the ones he did supervise have turned out exceptionally well, and have almost invariably reflected his intense commitment to political inquiry based on commonsense hypotheses drawn from familiarity with the literature and direct observation of the political processes, and pursued by methods commonly referred to among themselves as "barefoot empiricism," rather than the application of formularized methodologies that tend to evade the most interesting questions.

As an undergraduate lecturer, Key by all accounts left a great deal to be desired. He was the type of scholar who was less interested in a stirring didactic performance than in thinking problems through on his feet in the lecture room, as well as in the chair in his study. A student in his class was not likely to be able to maintain the kind of systematically organized notebook that would enable him to regurgitate doctrine on his examination papers. The rambling tendency of this lecture style was exaggerated by hesitant speech patterns and a broad, somewhat nasal, southwestern drawl. According to graduate student legend, Key prefaced so many statements with the phrase "generally speaking," and dragged the two words out to such an extent, that the in-house joke became, "Who is this General Raleigh who is always speaking for Key?"

The pattern of Key's career conforms to many of the characteristics suggested here. His early reputation was made by the favorable reception of his comprehensive text *Politics, Parties, and Pressure Groups* when it first appeared in 1942. Except for the initiative of Professor Roscoe Martin (then at the University of Alabama, and another major promotional contributor to the development of American political science), Key might very well have become known primarily as a writer of distinguished textbooks in several areas of American politics. In 1946 Martin secured a grant from the Rockefeller Foundation that enabled the Bureau of Public Administration at the University of Alabama to undertake a study of the electoral process in the South; and after considerable persuasion on Martin's part, Key was induced to accept the directorship of the project. At first Key was inclined to restrict the study to the effect of the poll tax on elections in the South, but as the staff was built up and the documentary collection on the subject accumulated, the idea of covering southern politics generally became too compelling to resist. It is still difficult to see how this book —so complete in its coverage, involving so many fundamental ques-

tions to which answers were sought in so many methodologically cre-
ative ways, relying for its depth on over 500 interviews throughout the
South, and written in a clear and lively style that can be read with intellectual profit and pleasure by political scientists and laymen alike—
could have been produced and brought into print within the short span
from 1946 to 1949. In addition to solid institutional support, widespread cooperation from his colleagues throughout the South, an excellent staff, and his own organizational capacity and diligence, one
must look for an explanation of this feat to some of the more general
assumptions and patterns of inquiry identifiable throughout Key's entire career.

   In the first place, Key worked from his own sense of what was important and what was not, and he had no qualms about expressing the
values that he thought inherent in the institutions and practices of
American politics and that also formed the standards against which he
measured his empirical findings. One does not need to look for hidden
biases in Key simply because he states his premises openly. In the
preface to *Southern Politics*, for instance, he notes the "predispositions
that color the book," as follows: "One . . . is a belief in the democratic
process as it is professed in the United States. Another is a belief that
Southerners possess as great a capacity for self government as do citizens elsewhere in the country. Yet another is the conviction that the
best government results when there is free and vigorous competition at
the ballot box in contests in which genuine issues are defined and candidates take a stand."

   Extrapolating from these and other statements in *Southern Politics*
and other places, one may say that Key's pragmatic approach to political science rests solidly on these foundations:

   1. An openly expressed "belief" in the tenets of liberal constitutional democracy as practiced in the United States.
   2. The assumption that openness to the broadest possible citizen
   participation tends to foster competition, and that effective competition is a sort of drive-wheel that powers everything else.
   3. Such competition is best pursued through a two-party system
   of the American type, which opens clear choices between candi-

dates and their stands on issues in ways that are understandable
to the voting public.

4. Acceptance of the idea that issue-based politics flows freely
from such a competitive system in a manner that tends to bring
fundamental political problems to the surface where they can be
resolved to the relative satisfaction of the participant public or
publics. Here I think Key's attitudes reflect his own experience
with the pluralistic side of American politics, and the ways in
which pluralistic conflict is settled through the mediating institutions of pressure groups and political parties as these relate to the
formal constitutional institutions. The pragmatism of New Deal
politics and the flexibility of the coalitional alignments within the
parties were obviously deep rooted in his consciousness.

5. The faith that the elimination of what he observed as the major
southern barriers to competition—disfranchisement, segregation,
malapportionment, and one partyism—would lead the South
into a pattern of liberal democratic politics that would bring the
region much closer to what he regarded as the more effective
national system.

If there were certain underlying rational assumptions in Key's mental constitution as a political scientist that may not have been subject
to incontrovertible proof, it is important to note that there were also
certain things that he was not. First of all, he was not a theorist, either
of the purely normative or the absolutely causal persuasion; at the outside, one might refer to him as a tentative explanatory theorist who
used broad-based hypotheses as guides to inquiry, and in turn allowed
the inquiry to refine or redirect the hypotheses. Perhaps because of the
pragmatic way he approached the subject, he did not like the term
"theory" very much, although he used it in the title of his well-known
1955 article, "A Theory of Critical Elections," and in some other places
in his writing.

For a "nontheorist" he was a most suggestive hypothesis maker, and
he tested his deductions on a grand scale—through intuition, empirical
historical knowledge, and carefully worked out quantitative measures,
mainly of a rather simple statistical nature. *Parsimonious* is a term that
has been incorporated into the jargonistic lexicon of the social sciences,
and it is used to characterize a piece of research as having established

propositional proofs in the most direct way possible, and through the use of the least complicated methodological tools capable of doing the job. The term could be appropriately applied to Key's methods. He obviously wanted to be as precise as possible in the areas in which he thought political science could be precise, but he did not pretend to more definitiveness of knowledge than the subject would allow by applying elaborate methodologies to problems of no consequence. His influence has been substantial precisely because he offers a challenge to others to accumulate and disseminate knowledge through cooperative critical efforts.

In the second place, it may be said that if Key was not a theorist, he was also not a behavioralist. Some graduate students who were close to him have told me that they never remembered hearing him use the terms, *behavioral* or *behavioralist*, although he did note on occasion that he was *describing political behavior*. Nevertheless, he had an enormous influence on the development of a more quantitatively oriented political science. Although aggregate data methods had been used for many years prior to the appearance of *Southern Politics*, Key's diversification of earlier techniques and the immediate academic success of *Southern Politics* stimulated a quantum expansion of work of that type. Key himself wrote his book on comparative state politics and a primer on statistics for political scientists in direct succession to his earlier initiatives along these lines. But he never went so far as to assume that all political science had to be translated into quantitative proofs or measures, and he never followed the lead of his own bad imitators who failed to understand that simplicity often triumphs over the artificial complexity of the scientistic Voodoo Doctors of Philosophy.

Although some would say that Key's anticipation of behavioralism was almost entirely on the aggregate data side, his interest in the other major pillar of that "persuasion's" foundation—survey research—led to the preparation of his second comprehensive text, *Public Opinion and American Democracy*, which came out in 1961. One might go so far as to say of that book that Key used it to pioneer the whole area of secondary analysis of accumulated social survey data by reworking material previously collected and initially analyzed by the Survey Re-

search Center at the University of Michigan. In reevaluating the re-
sponses to these polls in relation to the larger questions about the
ambiguities in the whole concept of "public opinion," he went well
beyond the analysis of the psychological foundations of voting tendencies and electoral trends that had been done by the Center's staff. In
some respects he might be said to have informed the Center about the
deeper meanings of its raw materials in the context of the institutions
and processes by which the American democracy is sustained. And
here again, he never abandoned those basically moral assumptions that
underpinned his view of American politics. On the very last page of
the book, he reasserts his general faith in popular democracy, and af-
firms the necessity for a substantial public leadership, which is both
competent and virtuous, if public order is to remain uncorrupted.

In the third place, it follows from what has been said above that
Key did not engage in reductionism, either in its sociological or psychological form. As the title of his posthumously published book, *The
Responsible Electorate*, indicates, Key was not a determinist. Politics
for him was open and, in the most complete sense of the term, was
"rational," provided its processes and policies were not corrupted by
ideology or barriers to participation and competition.

In the decade since Key's death, enormous changes have taken place
in American politics, and an almost complete transformation of southern politics has occurred since the appearance of his masterpiece on
the subject. It is not surprising, therefore, that these changes in practice
and circumstance should have led to an intensive questioning of many
of the hypotheses set forth in *Southern Politics*. Perhaps the most important doubts have been raised about the idea that a reorientation of
issues—mainly produced through state legislation of a liberal nature
—would follow the disappearance of segregation, malapportionment,
disfranchisement and the one-party system in the South. Another major
notion—that competition would take the form of nationally prevailing
two-party politics after removal of the barriers to popular participation—has been put through enough wringers to become dry and thread-
bare. Numerous lesser suggestions in the book have also been examined
and found wanting. Perhaps Key did not take sufficiently into account
the complexities of the political system, including such intangibles as

the uncertainties of even short-range historical circumstance and the intractability of historical political cultures. But he never claimed to have developed a complete and closed system, and his prescriptions were based on moral expectations in conjunction with as careful an empirical analysis of the existing political order as that object of study permitted.

On the whole, then, Key's achievements in advancing our understanding of American politics seem to me to remain the most impressive attained by any single individual of the current era, and to have exerted more influence on the directions set for the discipline in recent years than those of any other political scientist. And *Southern Politics* still stands out as the brightest star in his firmament. Those of us who pick away at him do so in most cases with an unqualified respect for what he was able to do, and he would be the last among us to protest the need to make corrections and additions to the interpretations of what he observed. But he would undoubtedly still urge on us the importance of those assumptions that go beyond the observational part of his work. Overall, his political science holds up extraordinarily well, particularly if one gives due consideration to two things: the change in circumstance that inevitably occurs with the passage of time, and the extent to which Key allows for the ability of ordinary citizens to affect, if not completely control, their own political destinies. No eagle has torn V. O. Key apart as yet, but if he were still alive, he would almost certainly be entitled to feel that he is being intellectually pecked to death by ducks. And those flat bills are awfully dull.

SOUTHERN POLITICS

FOREWORD

BY ROSCOE C. MARTIN

THE study of public administration is often confined to problems which arise in the organization and operation of government agencies. Without questioning the highly important character of such problems or the value of the numerous and intensive inquiries which have been devoted to them, many students are coming increasingly to believe that public administration cannot adequately be considered apart from the other processes of government. The staff of the Bureau of Public Administration of the University of Alabama have generally been of the belief that public administration cannot be viewed as a thing apart, cannot be understood out of context.

A most important element in the context of public administration is politics. The Bureau has published a goodly number of monographs on problems of public administration more or less narrowly defined. It was inevitable that eventually its attention should be turned to the setting in which public administration functions in the southern region. Fundamental to an understanding of the democratic process and to the successful fulfillment of its purposes is the study of the selection of elective officials and the resolution of public controversies at the ballot box. Through the study of politics the cause of good government may be advanced, a purpose wholly appropriate to the Bureau of Public Administration as a division of a state university.

The politics of the South has a regional unity which necessitates its study over a broad area if there is to be maximum opportunity for understanding. With this in mind, an inquiry was projected which resulted in the present volume. The conception of such a project developed over a number of years beginning in 1944. It reached the stage of action in 1946 when the Rockefeller Foundation made a grant to the University of Alabama for a study of "the electoral process in the South." The Bureau was fortunate to secure the services of V. O. Key, Jr., Professor of Political Science at The Johns Hopkins University, as director of research. On September 1, 1946, the offices of the project were opened on the campus of the University of Alabama at Tuscaloosa, and shortly thereafter Mr. Key had a staff at work.

Research into contemporary politics early and inevitably introduces problems of method. The acquisition of reliable basic data was a first need. The staff began by assembling election statistics, statutes and constitutions, party rules, court decisions, and newspapers and periodicals. It was realized that no matter how complete the collection of legal, statistical, and other documentary data, there could be no genuine understanding of the electoral process without intimate acquaintance with the day to day practice of politics; consequently it was planned from the beginning to engage in extensive field interviewing. It was thought that the raw material for interpreting the political process could best be obtained from those active in public life. Over a period of fifteen months 538 southerners were consulted in interviews. Approximately six weeks were spent by a field investigator in each of eleven states. Alexander Heard did this field work in nine states and Donald S. Strong in two.

The persons whose testimony was sought were in large measure active or retired politicians, including congressmen, governors and other state officials, state legislators, campaign managers, Democratic and Republican party officials, precinct leaders, and individuals charged with the administration of the poll tax, registration, and elections. A large number of other persons, participants in the political scene or close observers, were consulted. These included, among others, publishers, editors, newspaper reporters, leaders in labor and industry and farm organizations, plantation owners, small farmers, influential Negroes, leading spirits in reform movements, and students of government and politics. To all these people, scattered in large communities and small over the whole South, a great deal of gratitude is due. Almost invariably persons whose help was solicited responded cooperatively, and in many cases with enthusiasm and generosity of spirit which reflected an appreciation of the efforts of a group of southerners (for the principal staff members were all southerners) to arrive at an understanding of their own problems. Most of the interviews were granted on condition that the person interviewed not be quoted. For that reason specific acknowledgments have not been made. It is hoped that the many people who provided this essential assistance will accept this expression of the deep appreciation of the staff.

Professor Key, with the consent of his University, carried on the work of directing the study through three years, and during the summers of 1947 and 1948 spent his full time in the project offices. In the execution of all phases of the project, from the initial collection of data to the preparation of final manuscript, Mr. Key had the assistance of Mr. Heard. Mr. Strong, Assistant Professor of Political Science at the University of Alabama, served for two summers in field work and in the preparation of manuscript. Merrill R. Goodall and Frederic D. Ogden, Instructors in Political Science at the University of Alabama, worked one summer each in the preparation of special studies which were used by the author as the bases for certain chapters. Mary Helen Crawley and Katherine Wade Thompson served for extensive periods as research assistants. To them is due a yeoman's reward for the tireless efforts needed to keep the project moving during the long absences of other members of the staff. Margaret Bittner and Samuel Strang worked for shorter periods in a similar capacity. There was in addition a faithful corps of clerical and stenographic assistants to whom the author has asked that special appreciation be expressed.

Throughout the life of the study York Willbern gave generously of his counsel and assistance far beyond the requirements of his position as Assistant Director of the Bureau. The author and I wish to join in extending him special thanks.

In an undertaking that is dependent on the cooperation of a large number of persons, obligations are incurred which cannot be acknowledged individually. There are, nevertheless, certain debts of gratitude which must not go ignored. Foremost is that to the trustees and officers of the Rockefeller Foundation, whose recognition of the usefulness of a scholarly study of southern politics made possible the financing of the project. While the enterprise was yet in embryo I made a trip around the South and consulted some twenty prominent newspaper editors about the desirability and method of procedure of such a project. To these persons a note of particular appreciation is due for their counsel in the formative stage. Also always ready with wise advice and a helping hand in the planning stage was Ellis Arnall, then Governor of Georgia. During the field interviews numbers of people lent hospitable and courteous assistance which greatly facilitated the collecting of information and smoothed the way of the travelling inquirer. That they are too numerous to list individually in no way lessens the sense of indebtedness which the staff feels toward them.

After the manuscript was prepared, two or three persons in each state read and commented on the chapter on that state which appears in the first part of this volume. They sometimes dissented in part from the views expressed, and this acknowledgment of their assistance is not intended to saddle them with responsibility for what is said anywhere in the book. Among these readers were Henry M. Alexander, Harry S. Ashmore, George A. Buchanan, Jr., W. G. Carleton, Hodding Carter, David A. Cheavens, Brainard Cheney, Virginius Dabney, Manning J. Dauer, Rowland Egger, Hallie Farmer, C. E. Gregory, Robert J. Harris, Noble B. Hendrix, Charles Houston, Herman Jones, John Blount MacLeod, Edward J. Meeman, Allen Morris, H. C. Nixon, Alden Powell, Forrest Rozzell, Albert B. Saye, Kenneth Toler, O. Douglas Weeks, Josephine Wilkins, and Bryan Willis.

Professor E. E. Schattschneider, Chairman of the Department of Political Science of Wesleyan University and Chairman of the Committee on Political Parties of the American Political Science Association, read the entire manuscript and contributed numerous helpful suggestions. The author and I join again to thank him most cordially for his constructive comments.

Research in the field of politics, no matter how scholarly or detached, inevitably touches the heart of many matters of controversy. This is especially true in the South, where deep and long standing emotional strains run through political affairs. In the preparation of this work Mr. Key enjoyed complete freedom. The Rockefeller Foundation imposed no restrictions on scope, methods, or findings. As a public educational institution, the University of Alabama is pleased to maintain the Bureau of Public Administration for the study of public problems, but no conclusions concerning University policies or views are to be drawn from this volume. The materials presented and the opinions expressed are exclusively those of the author, who accepts full responsibility for them.

ROSCOE C. MARTIN
Director of the Bureau of Public Administration
University of Alabama

PREFACE

OF books about the South there is no end. Nor will there be so long as the South remains the region with the most distinctive character and tradition. Yet in all the writing about the South there exists no comprehensive analysis of its politics. Instead we have relied on a pair of caricatures for our understanding of southern politics. On one hand, regional leaders are described as statesmen of the old school, sound in their economics, devoted to the Constitution, and ever alert against subversive and foolish proposals. The contrary picture is of a southern ruling class dedicated to reaction, intent on the repression of little people, both black and white, and allied with northern finance in a conspiracy to grind down the masses.

In both caricatures there is a grain of truth; yet each is false. The South, to be sure, has its share of scoundrels, but saints do not appear to be markedly less numerous there than on the other side of Mason and Dixon's line. Rather, the politics of the South is incredibly complex. Its variety, its nuances, its subtleties range across the political spectrum. The richness and diversity of the subject make an attempt to present a panoramic view more an act of brashness than of boldness. Nevertheless, the broad outlines of the structure and character of southern politics are here sketched out with the full realization that more prolonged examination would bring modification. Further, the South is changing rapidly. He who writes about it runs the risk that change will occur before the presses stop, no matter how he strives, as I have done, to identify and emphasize elements of continuity.

These special hazards give more than ordinary justification to the usual expressions of diffidence with which a book is offered to the world. There is no illusion that the whole story has been told or that solutions

1

have been found. It is only hoped that some better understanding of the politics of the South is promoted, for the subject, though not without its rollicking aspects, is of the gravest importance. The South is our last frontier. In the development of its resources, human and natural, must be found the next great epoch of our national growth. That development, in turn, must in large measure depend on the contrivance of solutions to the region's political problems. A first step toward solution is identification; this study can claim to offer no more than a part of the first step.

A word about the structure of the book is in order. In telling the story of southern politics the objective has been to deal, insofar as possible, with the common characteristics that give the South its peculiar qualities. For that reason state boundaries have been leaped wherever possible and subject matter treated as southwide phenomena. The section with which the book opens is concerned with the nature of factional competition in the internal politics of the states. It was impractical to handle this subject except by analysis of the politics of each state. The book commences, therefore, with a series of chapters describing the alignments within the Democratic party in each state. In these descriptions the predominating characteristic of each state has been accentuated, not only to present it in clear relief but to illustrate a condition which usually runs throughout the South but may exist in less discernible form elsewhere. The reader who dips into only one or two state chapters, therefore, will gain only a part of the interpretation this book intends to convey.

It should also be said that certain predispositions color the book. One of them is a belief in the democratic process as it is professed in the United States. Another is a belief that southerners possess as great a capacity for self-government as do citizens elsewhere in the country. Yet another is the conviction that the best government results when there is free and vigorous competition at the ballot box in contests in which genuine issues are defined and candidates take a stand.

A work of this scope must necessarily be a team product. In his foreword Roscoe C. Martin has recorded my extensive obligations. A special word is in order concerning the contribution of Alexander Heard, who bore the brunt of interviewing and assisted in every phase of the project. To him should go a major share of the credit for whatever merit the book may have. I also must express my appreciation to Mr. Martin, Director of the Bureau of Public Administration of the University of Alabama, for the opportunity to do this work and for aid and assistance in many ways. To the authorities of the University of Alabama, I am deeply indebted, but they should not be taxed with what I have said. They gave no intimation of what I should say or should leave unsaid; the responsibility for what follows rests with me.

V. O. KEY, JR.

Chapter One | **O F   T H E   S O U T H**

$\mathbf{T}$HE South may not be the nation's number one political problem, as some northerners assert, but politics is the South's number one problem.

From afar, outlanders regard southern politics as a comic opera staged on a grand scale for the amusement of the nation. They roared when Texans elected "Ma" Ferguson as their governor to serve as proxy for her husband, barred from office by an earlier impeachment and conviction. They shuddered when Louisiana was ruled by Huey Long, a flamboyant advocate of the subversive doctrine of "Every Man A King." Yet he put on a good show. The connoisseurs of rabble-rousing relished the performance of Gene Talmadge, he of the "red galluses" and the persuasive way with the wool-hat boys. Bilbo's artistry in demagoguery excited, if not admiration, attention from beyond the hills of Mississippi. Alabama's "Big Jim" Folsom, the "kissing governor," Texas' W. Lee O'Daniel, flour salesman and hillbilly bandsman, South Carolina's "Cotton Ed" Smith, eloquent exponent of the virtues of southern womanhood, and other fabulous characters have trod the southern political stage to the accompaniment of hilarity—often derisive—from the other side of the Mason and Dixon line.

That not all the actors in the southern political drama have been clowns or knaves may be dismissed as a detail obscured by the heroic antics of those who were. That the South's spectacular political leaders have

3

been indiscriminately grouped as demagogues of a common stripe, when wide differences have actually separated them, may likewise be regarded as an excusable failing of the Yankee journalist insensitive to the realities of southern politics.

Nor does the fact that, as southerners are wont to say, "the North is just as bad" give ground for complacency about the political plight of the South. It may be conceded that Illinois' Republican party is an evil combination of North Shore plutocracy and downstate, rural backwardness; that Pennsylvania's Republican party has been unbelievably corrupt; and that Boston's Democratic party has about it little of the attar of roses.

When all the exceptions are considered, when all the justifications are made, and when all the invidious comparisons are drawn, those of the South and those who love the South are left with the cold, hard fact that the South as a whole has developed no system or practice of political organization and leadership adequate to cope with its problems. In its shortcomings the South has all the failings common to the American states. The South after all is a part of the United States, and everywhere state governments have a long way to go to achieve the promise of American democracy. The states, often dominated by the least forward-looking elements and always overshadowed by Washington, only infrequently, North or South, present inspiring performances as instruments of popular government.

Southern politics labors under the handicaps common to all states. Southern politicians are also confronted by special problems that demand extraordinary political intelligence, restraint, patience, and persistence for their solution. The South's heritage from crises of the past, its problem of adjustment of racial relations on a scale unparalleled in any western nation, its poverty associated with an agrarian economy which in places is almost feudal in character, the long habituation of many of its people to nonparticipation in political life—all these and other social characteristics both influence the nature of the South's political system and place upon it an enormous burden.

Thus southern politics is no comic opera. It is deadly serious business that is sometimes carried on behind a droll façade. By the process of politics we determine who governs and in whose interests the government is run. Politics embraces far more than campaigns and elections. Actions by legislature, by governors, and by all agencies of government between campaigns are readings of the balance in a continuous competition for power and advantage. The management of government is as much a part of politics as is campaign oratory. Moreover, the political process extends beyond the operations of those formal mechanisms that we usually call government. Custom, the organization of the economic system, and, now and then, private violence have a role in determining who governs and who gets what.

In its grand outlines the politics of the South revolves around the position of the Negro. It is at times interpreted as a politics of cotton, as a politics of free trade, as a politics of agrarian poverty, or as a politics of planter and plutocrat. Although such interpretations have a superficial validity, in the last analysis the major peculiarities of southern politics go back to the Negro. Whatever phase of the southern political process one seeks to understand, sooner or later the trail of inquiry leads to the Negro.

Yet it is far from the truth to paint a picture of southern politics as being chiefly concerned with the maintenance of the supremacy of white over black. That dominance is an outcome, but the observer must look more closely to determine which whites and which blacks give southern politics its individuality. The hard core of the political South—and the backbone of southern political unity—is made up of those counties and sections of the southern states in which Negroes constitute a substantial proportion of the population. In these areas a real problem of politics, broadly considered, is the maintenance of control by a white minority. The situation resembles fundamentally that of the Dutch in the East Indies or the former position of the British in India. Here, in the southern black belts, the problem of governance is similarly one of the control by a small, white minority of a huge, retarded, colored population. And, as in the case of the colonials, that white minority can maintain its position only with the support, and by the tolerance, of those outside—in the home country or in the rest of the United States.

It is the whites of the black belts who have the deepest and most immediate concern about the maintenance of white supremacy. Those whites who live in counties with populations 40, 50, 60, and even 80 per cent Negro share a common attitude toward the Negro. Moreover, it is generally in these counties that large-scale plantation or multiple-unit agriculture prevails. Here are located most of the large agricultural operators who supervise the work of many tenants, sharecroppers, and laborers, most of whom are colored. As large operators they lean generally in a conservative direction in their political views.

If the whites of the black belts give the South its dominant political tone, the character of the politics of individual states will vary roughly with the Negro proportion of the population. The truth of that proposition will be abundantly illustrated as the story progresses. At this point it is only necessary to call attention to the marked differences in the composition of the population of the southern states. Over a third of all Mississippi whites live in counties over half Negro, while only 2.4 per cent of Florida whites reside in such counties. Equally striking differences prevail between the two states in their politics.

The black belts make up only a small part of the area of the South and—depending on how one defines black belt—account for an even smaller part of the white population of the South. Yet if the politics of the South revolves around any single theme, it is that of the role of the black belts. Although the whites of the black belts are few in number, their unity and their political skill have enabled them to run a shoestring into decisive power at critical junctures in southern political history.

Two great crises have left their imprint on southern political behavior: The War of the 'sixties and the Populist revolt of the 'nineties. Both these social convulsions had an impact on political habit whose influence has not worn away even yet, and in both of them the black-belt whites played a determining role. In the maneuvers leading to The War those

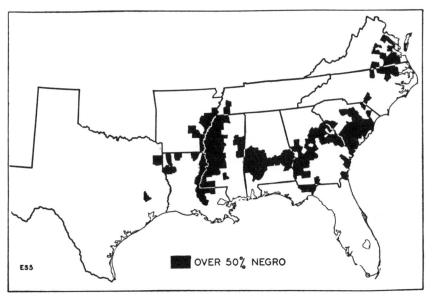

FIGURE 1

Bedrock of Southern Solidarity: Counties of the South with 50 Per Cent or More
Negro Population, 1940

with most at stake—the owners of large numbers of slaves—were to be found roughly in the same areas as present-day black belts. They recruited allies wherever they could find them; their allies were fewest in the regions of few Negroes. Opposition to The War was most intense in the highlands and in the upcountry, where the soil would not support a plantation economy and where independent yeomanry had no overwhelming desire to take up arms to defend the slave property of the lowland planters.

The impressive—and unfortunate—political victory of the large slaveholders came in their success, despite their small numbers, in carrying their states for war. Within the South the scars of the dispute over whether to go to war remain in persistent Republican enclaves in the highlands of eastern Tennessee, western North Carolina, northern Georgia, northern Alabama, and in isolated pockets elsewhere over the region. West Virginia, which was torn away from the Commonwealth, stands as an even more impressive reminder of the lack of unanimity within the South over a policy of war. Yet even more significant for the practical politics of the South of today is the fact that The War left a far higher degree of southern unity against the rest of the world than had prevailed before. Internal differences that had expressed themselves in sharp political competition were weakened—if not blotted out—by the common ex-

TABLE 1

Proportion of White Population of Each Southern State Residing in Counties with Specified Percentages of Total Population Negro, 1940

STATE	PERCENTAGE OF STATE'S WHITE POPULATION RESIDING IN COUNTIES		
	50 PER CENT OR MORE NEGRO	40 PER CENT OR MORE NEGRO	30 PER CENT OR MORE NEGRO
Mississippi	36.6	50.3	69.9
South Carolina	20.2	46.8	61.1
Alabama	11.6	16.9	49.4
Georgia	11.3	28.3	58.8
Louisiana	8.2	25.2	71.6
Arkansas	8.1	14.9	26.9
Virginia:			
Counties	5.1	10.5	18.3
Independent Cities	0.0	1.9	16.4
North Carolina	4.5	17.7	38.9
Florida	2.4	8.4	33.1
Tennessee	0.8	9.2	12.6
Texas	0.5	2.2	7.8

periences of The War and Reconstruction.[1] And, however unreasonable it may seem, it follows—as even a sophomore can see from observing the European scene—that a people ruled by a military government will retain an antipathy toward the occupying power.

In the second great crisis whose influence persists—the Populist revolt—political cleavages often fell along the same lines as in the dispute leading to The War. The details of the pattern differed, of course, from state to state as did the timing of the great upsurge of agrarian radicalism. Yet everywhere the most consistent, the most intense rural re-

---

[1] It may also be noted that The War left quite as permanent an imprint on parts of the rural North as on the South. In many rural northern counties Republicanism can be quite as clearly attributed to The War as can southern Democracy.

sistance to Populists and like radicals of the day came from the black-belt whites. They had valiant allies in the merchants and bankers of the towns and in the new industrialists. Against these defenders of the status quo were arrayed the upcountrymen, the small farmers of the highlands and other areas where there were few Negroes and where there was no basis for a plantation economy. And they were joined by many of the workers of the cities which were beginning to grow, as well as by many poor white farmers of other regions.

The black-belt whites, the townsmen, and all the allied forces of conservatism staved off radical agrarianism, although not without leaving a residue of a belligerent attitude that for decades found expression in support for leaders who at least talked, if they did not always act, against the "interests." And in crucial campaigns even now the counties of several states divide about as they did in the elections of the agrarian uprising.

The battle of Populism left a habit of radicalism in the upland areas; fortuitously it also strengthened the position of the black-belt whites. Intense agitation over Negro voting came as an aftermath of the Populist crisis. In some states the Negro had been disposed to go along with the coalition of upcountry white Democrats and Republicans under the Populist or fusion banner. Everywhere the plantation counties were most intense in their opposition to Negro voting; they raised a deafening hue and cry about the dangers to white supremacy implicit in a Negro balance of power. The Populists, with the death of their party on the national scene, dispiritedly returned to the Democratic party which offered them more than the party of McKinley and Hanna. And in the disillusionment brought about by Populist defeat, the black belts were able to recruit enough upcountry support to adopt poll taxes, literacy tests, and other instruments to disfranchise the Negro. Even on Negro disfranchisement, however, almost everywhere the battle was close. While the upcountryman had no love for the Negro he suspected, at times rightly, that the black belt was trying to disfranchise him as well as the black man.

In the fight against Populism and in the subsequent agitation about the place of the Negro, the black belts strengthened their position by reenforcing the South's attachment to the Democratic party. The raising of a fearful specter of Negro rule and the ruthless application of social pressures against those who treasonably fused with the Republicans under Populist leadership put down for decades the threat of the revival of two-party competition.

Two-party competition would have been fatal to the status of black-belt whites. It would have meant in the 'nineties an appeal to the Negro vote and it would have meant (and did for a time) Negro rule in some black-belt counties. From another standpoint, two-party competition would have meant the destruction of southern solidarity in national politics—in presidential elections and in the halls of Congress. Unity on the national scene was essential in order that the largest possible bloc could be mobilized to resist any national move toward interference with southern authority to deal with the race question as was desired locally. And the threat of Federal intervention remained, as the furore over the Lodge force bill of 1890 demonstrated.

This sketch of the broad outlines of the foundations of southern politics points to an extraordinary achievement of a relatively small minority —the whites of the areas of heavy Negro population—which persuaded the entire South that it should fight to protect slave property. Later, with allies from conservatives generally, substantially the same group put down a radical movement welling up from the sections dominated by the poorer whites. And by the propagation of a doctrine about the status of the Negro, it impressed on an entire region a philosophy agreeable to its necessities and succeeded for many decades in maintaining a regional unity in national politics to defend those necessities.

If the interpretation is correct—and there are many deviations in detail—the political prowess of the black belts must be rated high. The thesis, however, runs counter to the idea that many top-drawer southerners firmly believe, viz., that the poor white is at the bottom of all the trouble about the Negro. The planter may often be kind, even benevolent, towards his Negroes, and the upcountryman may be, as the Negroes say, "mean"; yet when the political chips are down, the whites of the black belts by their voting demonstrate that they are most ardent in the faith of white supremacy as, indeed, would naturally be expected. The whites of the regions with few Negroes have a less direct concern over the maintenance of white rule, whereas the whites of the black belts operate an economic and social system based on subordinate, black labor.

The critical element in the structure of black-belt power has been the southern Senator and his actual, if not formal, right to veto proposals of national intervention to protect Negro rights. The black belts have had nothing to fear from state governments on the race question, although control of state governments by hill people with their Populist notions might mean heavier taxation for schools and other governmental services. On the fundamental issue, only the Federal Government was to be feared. The black belts became bulwarks of Democratic strength. Their common attachment to the Democratic party gave them security of sorts against Republican meddling in the South. In the great apostasy of 1928 it was not the black belts that went Republican; they stood stalwart in the Democratic ranks. By the same logic, in 1948, after the Democratic party had abandoned the black belts, it was not the South as a whole that deserted the party. The seat of rebellion was the delta of Mississippi, the home of great planters, few whites, and many Negroes, as well as the last vestige of ante-bellum civilization. In the Dixiecrat standard-bearers, Governor Thurmond of South Carolina and Governor Wright of Mississippi, there was neatly symbolized the roots of a southern solidarity that was in process of erosion. As chief executives of the two states with the highest proportions of Negroes in their population, they spoke fundamentally for the whites of the black belt and little more, at least if one disregards their entourage of professional Ku Kluxers, antediluvian reactionaries, and malodorous opportunists.

Perhaps 1948 marked the beginning of an even sharper rate of descent in the long curve recording the decline in the power of black-belt whites. Yet their success—in conspiracy with the grand accidents of history—in cementing the South to the Democratic party will for a long time exert a profound influence on the politics of the South. Attachments to partisan labels live long beyond events that gave them birth.

If the critical element in the southern political system has been solidarity in national politics, there is logic in defining the political South—as it is here defined—in terms of consistency of attachment to the Democratic party nationally. Eleven states and only eleven did not go Republican more than twice in the presidential elections from 1876 to 1944 (both inclusive). These states constitute the South for the purposes of this study. They are: Alabama, Arkansas, Florida, Georgia, Louisiana, Mississippi, North Carolina, South Carolina, Tennessee, Texas, and Virginia. Of these states only two went Republican twice in the period 1876–1944: Florida in 1876 and 1928 and Tennessee in 1920 and 1928. Five went Republican only once: South Carolina and Louisiana in the disputed election of 1876 and North Carolina, Texas, and Virginia in 1928. Alabama, Arkansas, Georgia, and Mississippi maintained an unbroken record of Democratic loyalty.[2]

A high percentage of Negro population is associated with the Democratic voting tradition of those states we call "the South." In nine of them one-fourth or more of the population was Negro in 1940. Tennessee and Texas are marginal to "the South" by the criterion of Negro population. Tennessee in 1940 was 17.4 per cent Negro and Texas, 14.4. Maryland, which we exclude from the South, was 16.6 per cent Negro, but its voting habits diverged markedly from those of Tennessee and Texas. The range of Negro population—from 49.2 per cent in Mississippi to 14.4 in Texas—

[2] Over the same period border states that might be considered southern went Republican more than twice: Missouri, 5 times; West Virginia, 8; Maryland, 7; Delaware, 9; Kentucky, 3. Oklahoma, since its admission to the Union in 1907, has gone Republican twice, in 1920 and 1928. It has strong southern characteristics in its politics, but it leans more strongly Republican than any of the eleven states included in the South. In 1940, for example, Oklahoma, along with Kentucky, Missouri, West Virginia, Maryland, and Delaware, gave more than 40 per cent of its popular vote to the Republican presidential candidate. In none of the eleven states did the Republican strength reach the 40 per cent level.

suggests that even "the South" is by no means homogeneous and that if the Negro influences the politics of the South, there ought to be wide variations in political practices from state to state. That supposition will amply be borne out as the analysis proceeds.

Much labor could be expended on a definition of the South. Indices of illiteracy, maps of the distribution of cotton production, averages of per-capita income, and scores of other statistical measures could be used to delimit the region. Some writers have tried to delimit the South in terms of psychological attitude and have spoken of "the mind" and "the spirit" of the South. For the immediate purpose no better delimitation can be devised than one based on political behavior. And it can be contended, of course, that the regional cast of political attitude has a reality and a being over and beyond all the underlying social and economic characteristics that can be pictured in endless tabulations, correlations, and graphic representations.

Incidentally—and not without importance—it may be noted that the eleven states that meet the test of partisan consistency also are the eleven states that seceded to form the Confederacy.

The chapters that follow are not dedicated solely to the elaboration of the introductory proposition, which, in its unvarnished form, runs to the effect that the fundamental explanation of southern politics is that the black-belt whites succeeded in imposing their will on their states and thereby presented a solid regional front in national politics on the race issue. The main burden of the chapters that immediately follow lies not in the support of this thesis—to which exceptions and modifications in detail are admittedly in order—but rather in the consequences of solidarity in national politics on political life within the individual states.

The coin of southern politics has two sides: on one is seen the relations of the South as a whole with the rest of the nation; on the other, the political battle within each state. And the two aspects are, like the faces of a coin, closely connected.

Consistent and unquestioning attachment, by overwhelming majorities, to the Democratic party nationally has meant that the politics within southern states—the election of governors, of state legislators, and the settlement of public issues generally—has had to be conducted without benefit of political parties. As institutions, parties enjoy a general disrepute, yet most of the democratic world finds them indispensable as instruments of self-government, as means for the organization and expression of competing viewpoints on public policy. Nevertheless, over a tremendous area—the South—no such competing institutions exist and the political battle has to be carried on by transient and amorphous political factions within the Democratic party, which are ill-designed to meet the necessities of self-government. By yielding to their black belts in their desire for solidarity in national politics, the states of the South condemned themselves internally to a chaotic factional politics. A survey of the factional arrangements in each of the eleven states will lay the basis for an understanding of the variations within the South, as well as a foundation for a treatment of elements common to all states of the South.

PART ONE

Political Leadership:

The One-Party System in the States

Rulers have always found foreign wars useful to blot up discontent, to repress opposition, and to promote "unity" at home. In domestic politics sectionalism represents a sort of sublimated foreign war in which one part of the country acts as a unit against the rest of the nation. That unity is, of necessity, to some extent achieved by the repression of dissident groups. In the American South the discipline necessary to maintain sectional unity on the race question has by no means completely repressed dissent on other questions; nevertheless, it first crushed and then prevented the rebirth of political parties—institutions essential for the conduct of a normal democratic politics.

Political parties provide leadership for the expression of discontent —or satisfaction—with the current state of affairs. These institutions of democracy consist in their essence of little groups of leaders and sub-leaders bound together at least by the ambition to control the machinery of government, and this party core ordinarily counts as its loyal followers a substantial number of voters. In the Anglo-American democracies the notion prevails that the public weal is best served by the existence of two major political parties that compete on more or less even terms for control of the state. The groupings called parties possess extraordinary durability and vitality. They persist over long periods and survive many a reverse. Moreover, in what is usually deemed a healthy party life, party leaders possess at least a rudimentary collective sense of responsibility for the party's welfare. In turn this sense of responsibility induces a degree of group discipline among the leaders who, although they may have their fraternal differences, unite to battle the enemy for control of the government.

Normally a political party has its foundation in sectional, class, or group interests. One party draws its strength principally from certain sectors of the population; another depends for its support (in the main) on other groups within the population. The differentiation in the interests of these groups produces a differentiation in the policies that the parties seek to effectuate through government. Even when divergencies are by no means sharp, there often remains a fairly cohesive group of party leaders held together by the ambition to retain or to win office. To gain office they must criticize the "ins," manufacture a new issue to attract votes, or put forth a candidate superior to the champion of the opposition.

15

The South, unlike most of the rest of the democratic world, really has no political parties—at least as we have defined them. A single party, so the saying goes, dominates the South, but in reality the South has been Democratic only for external purposes, that is, presidential and congressional elections. The one-party system is purely an arrangement for national affairs. The legend prevails that within the Democratic party in the southern states factional groups are the equivalent of political parties elsewhere. In fact, the Democratic party in most states of the South is merely a holding-company for a congeries of transient squabbling factions, most of which fail by far to meet the standards of permanence, cohesiveness, and responsibility that characterize the political party.[1]

The restriction of all significant political choices in the South to the Democratic primaries enables the South to maintain its constancy to Democratic presidential candidates, but it has not enabled the South to maintain social groupings equivalent to political parties within the Democratic party. In the conduct of campaigns for the control of legislatures, for the control of governorships, and for representatives in the national Congress, the South must depend for political leadership, not on political parties, but on lone-wolf operators, on fortuitous groupings of individuals usually of a transient nature, on spectacular demagogues odd enough to command the attention of considerable numbers of voters, on men who have become persons of political consequence in their own little bailiwicks, and on other types of leaders whose methods to attract electoral attention serve as substitutes for leadership of a party organization.

The peculiar organization or disorganization of political leadership characteristic of the South undoubtedly leads to results of profound import for its public affairs. Those results stare one in the face, yet they can best be evaluated only after an analysis of the kinds of factions that develop within the nonparty South. Technically the description of the politics of the South amounts to the problem of analyzing the political struggle under a system of nonpartisan elections, i.e., a system in which no party nominations are made and no party designation appears on the ballot. What kinds of leadership develop in the absence of a party system? What kinds of cleavages and groupings arise among the voters?

Although most states of the South have common elements in their pattern of factional politics, each state also has its peculiar characteristics which need to be understood. Before looking at the factional structure of individual states, a panoramic view of the entire South may furnish a guide for our expectations. If something approaching a two-party system existed within the Democratic party of the South, most voters in the Dem-

---

[1] In the chapters that follow the term faction is used to mean any combination, clique, or grouping of voters and political leaders who unite at a particular time in support of a candidate. Thus, a political race with eight candidates will involve eight factions of varying size. Some factions have impressive continuity while others come into existence for only one campaign and then dissolve.

ocratic primary would be lined up in support of the two leading candidates for nomination, which is, of course, the equivalent of election. On
the other hand, if the popular vote distributed itself more or less evenly
among more than two candidates, a multifactional system would prevail.
The proportion of the popular vote won by the two high candidates, of
course, tells us nothing about the viewpoints of the factions within the
party. The distribution of the vote, however, gives a general clue to broad
differences in the nature of political life from state to state.

The extent to which the Democratic party divides into two party-like
factions or veers toward a splintered factional system in the various states
is suggested by the following figures on the percentage of the total vote
polled jointly by the two high candidates for governor in the first Democratic primary: [2]

	MEDIAN [a]	HIGH	LOW
Tennessee	98.7	100.0	76.0
Virginia	98.3	100.0	82.8
Georgia	91.6	100.0	70.4
North Carolina	77.4	100.0	54.0
Alabama	75.2	100.0	52.9
Louisiana	69.1	99.7	62.4
Arkansas	64.2 [b]	99.4	46.7
South Carolina	63.2	100.0	45.4
Texas	63.2 [b]	97.1	48.3
Mississippi	62.9	86.0	59.0
Florida	57.0	93.7	30.0

[a] Medians computed on the basis of gubernatorial primaries, 1920–48.
[b] In Texas and Arkansas primaries at which sitting governors sought renomination
for a second term are excluded from the calculations, since a renomination is ordinarily
granted as a matter of course.

In Tennessee, Virginia, and Georgia, at one end of the scale, the
battle within the party appears to be between two, and only two, major
factions. At the other extreme is Florida, where the two leading candidates
for the gubernatorial nomination do well to poll together as much as 60
per cent of the vote. From these figures alone one would expect to find in
Florida a multifactional politics quite different from that of Virginia and
Tennessee. Arkansas, South Carolina, Texas, and Mississippi manifest
multifactional characteristics, although not quite to the same degree as
Florida. North Carolina, Louisiana, and Alabama occupy intermediate

[2] In nine states a second primary is held at which the two leading candidates in the
first, provided that none had a majority, run for the nomination. The distribution of
the vote in the first primary (where many candidates seek the nomination) is more
revealing of the factional structure of the party than the vote in the second or run-off
primary (in which there are only two candidates).

positions. They have not developed to the same extent as Tennessee a bi-factional division within the party; nor have they gone so far as Florida in spawning a multiplicity of factions contending for state control.

Another way to look at the data on factionalism is to determine the proportion of the primary vote received by the leading candidate for governor. This method gives a measure of the popular strength of the strongest faction or leader within the party. As might be expected, it reveals disparities among the political systems of the South similar to those brought to light by the preceding tabulation. The figures are as follows:

	MEDIAN	HIGH	LOW
Virginia	72.6	86.0	61.4
Tennessee	58.8	87.3	39.2
Georgia	51.7	100.0 [a]	27.3
Alabama	43.4	78.7	27.7
Louisiana	41.5	67.1	34.9
North Carolina	40.2	100.0 [a]	31.4
Arkansas [b]	36.3	55.7	26.0
South Carolina	35.1	100.0 [a]	25.9
Texas [b]	33.9	68.5	27.5
Mississippi	33.5	55.3	31.4
Florida	29.5	59.4	15.7

[a] Unopposed candidates, omitted in determining median.
[b] With the exclusion of the same primaries excluded in the preceding tabulation.

These figures suggest an extraordinary diversity in the character of factionalism among the one-party states of the South. From them one might infer, and correctly, that Virginia stands alone as a state in which one Democratic faction consistently commands the support of about three-fourths of those who vote—almost a one-party system within a one-party system. At the other end of the scale, from the figures alone it might be surmised that in Arkansas, South Carolina, Texas, Mississippi, and Florida there occur wide-open political battles in which even the strongest factional leader cannot usually be certain of the support of much more than a third of the primary vote.

Only the most general contours of Democratic factionalism within the one-party states are defined by the foregoing type of analysis. Yet the diversities suggested by this simple analysis indicate that there may be no single type of one-party system. Examination of the one-party politics of the eleven southern states will reveal, if not eleven types of factionalism, at least great variation.

Chapter Two | **V I R G I N I A :**

POLITICAL MUSEUM PIECE

O<small>F</small> all the American states, Virginia can lay claim to the most thorough control by an oligarchy. Political power has been closely held by a small group of leaders who, themselves and their predecessors, have subverted democratic institutions and deprived most Virginians of a voice in their government. The Commonwealth possesses characteristics more akin to those of England at about the time of the Reform Bill of 1832 than to those of any other state of the present-day South. It is a political museum piece. Yet the little oligarchy that rules Virginia demonstrates a sense of honor, an aversion to open venality, a degree of sensitivity to public opinion, a concern for efficiency in administration, and, so long as it does not cost much, a feeling of social responsibility. Senator Harry F. Byrd heads the governing oligarchy; he is less than a tyrant, a good deal more than a front. Nevertheless, he is not the machine, and he created it only in the sense that he gave it its present form. Political oligarchy is firmly rooted in the social structure of Virginia whose history is rich with political organizations, some sectional in character, like that inherited by Harry Byrd from his uncle, Hal Flood. Byrd pulled together elements all over the state to form, under conditions made favorable by his own reorganization of the state government, an autocratic machine which may live long after him.

Withal, the Virginia machine is an anachronism. With its cavalier and aristocratic outlook, it can boast, quietly, of an eighteenth-century tone. With its tightly articulated hierarchy of power, it resembles the highly organized state machines that prevailed in some states toward the end of the nineteenth century. Their crudeness, however, it carefully avoids and parades its honesty, a virtue for which, its enemies assert, no honorable man should claim reward.

The Byrd machine owes its existence both to competent management and to a restricted electorate. A smaller proportion of Virginia's potential electorate votes for governor than does that of any other state of the South. On the average, over the years 1925–45, only 11.5 per cent of those 21 and over have voted in Virginia Democratic primaries. Smallness of voter turnout alone does not necessarily ease the job of controlling the outcome of elections; campaigns for the favor of small electorates may be fought quite as bitterly as those for large electorates. Under the conditions prevailing in Virginia, however, the small number of voters definitely contributes to the manageability of elections. The organization, by various stratagems, keeps opposition leadership weak, and unimpressive opposition itself tends to restrict the active electorate to organization supporters. Further, formal suffrage restrictions undoubtedly remove from the electorate many persons who, with adequate leadership, would oppose the machine.

Turnout at the polls is so small that the Byrd organization has had to win the support of only from five to seven per cent of the adult population to nominate its candidate for governor in the Democratic primary; its candidate usually has more votes than are necessary. Approximate percentages of the adult population supporting the winning organization candidate in recent gubernatorial primaries have been as follows:

1925	8.6
1929	8.1
1933	8.5
1937	11.2
1941	6.7
1945	6.2

By contrast Mississippi is a hotbed of democracy. Over a similar period, its Democratic nominees for governor won the votes of from 12.4 to 16.4 per cent of all adults. When one allows for the nonvoting Negroes of Mississippi, the interest of white Mississippians in public affairs dwarfs that of white Virginians.[1]

1. Anatomy of the Machine

Unlike most southern states, Virginia has had within the Democratic party two fairly well-defined factions. The "organization" or "machine"

[1] For a comparative analysis of levels of voting, see chap. 23.

is the dominant faction. The antiorganization group, which constitutes the opposition, is extraordinarily weak, has few leaders of ability, and is more of a hope than a reality.

Instead of the usual tenuous relations between southern state factional leaders and county courthouse crowds, the Virginia organization binds tightly to the state leadership its outposts in almost all the counties and cities. A competent and shrewd state board of strategy, under the leadership of the Senator, maintains a high degree of discipline over the local political leaders affiliated with the organization, which thus has a well-co-ordinated state-wide machine to bring out the vote in support of its candidates. By contrast factional organization in the Democratic party in most other southern states is fluid, amorphous, primitive. Virginia's machine, old-fashioned in its effectiveness, is manned, in the main, by highly respectable citizens.

Although many Virginians are too genteel to use the term, Senator Byrd is the boss of the machine and of the state. Associated with him in the high command is E. R. Combs, chairman of the state board of compensation, clerk of the state senate, and, until 1948, Democratic national committeeman. Governor William Tuck plays a powerful role, and Virginians speak mysteriously of unknown private persons who participate in the deliberations of the "high command."

Mr. Combs' compensation board, in repute, whether or not in reality, plays an important role in maintaining organization cohesion. It fixes the compensation of the principal county officials and makes allowances for the salaries and expenses of their offices. Charges are occasionally made that the board has punished local officials who declined to accept the orders of the high command; the more general opinion, however, among Virginia observers is that the board need not exert its power to command political obedience. Power in the hands of the Senator's field marshal, as one informed observer puts it, keeps local goverment officials in "an understanding and sympathetic frame of mind."

County officials usually manage the local outposts of the organization, although in some counties a nonofficial person serves as the local leader. The chief elements in the county machine are five elected administrative officers: commonwealth's attorney, treasurer, commissioner of revenue, clerk of circuit court, and sheriff. These officials usually outrank in political potency the county supervisors who represent subdivisions of the county. The clerk of the circuit court, perhaps because of his eight-year tenure of office, often becomes the kingpin of the county organization. Another figure in the background who sometimes overshadows all these officials is the circuit judge, who possesses important appointing powers. He (and his counterpart in the independent cities, the judges of the corporation or hustings courts) appoints the electoral board, which assures organization control over the machinery of elections. He designates the school trustee electoral board, which in most counties names the school boards. He appoints the local board of public welfare and exercises other administrative duties.[2] Since the judge is always Democratic, his appointive power assumes special importance in keeping the electoral machinery and other perquisites in Democratic hands in counties with Republican majorities.

The circuit judge ties into the state organization through his election by the General Assembly. The high command maintains the closest surveillance over the choice of circuit judges. Mr. Combs, as clerk of the senate and as secretary of its Democratic caucus, is in a position to put in a helpful word. The Senator is not a man to neglect detail. On one occasion the machine candidate for a judgeship faced opposition in the legislature from a candidate who had openly differed with the Senator on a matter in days gone by. The Senator, reputed never to forget, appeared on the scene, inquired how the battle was going, and was told that the organization candidate needed two votes to win. Two men, already committed otherwise, yielded to the Senator's pressure and saved the day.

In each county, owing in part to the small local electorate but also to a tradition of re-election, local officers affiliated with the organization usually manage to stay in office for extremely long periods. Occasionally factions of a county organization become involved in a fight for office. The state high command infrequently meddles in these local squabbles, but if local candidates who have been particularly co-operative are in trouble, the state organization will use its influence in their behalf. Or if a "particularly obnoxious candidate" seeks a county office, the state organization will marshal its forces in opposition. Only rarely in other southern states would such interposition in local affairs be tolerated. The local citizenry would bury the hatchet and escort out of town on a rail any "boss man" from the statehouse with the temerity to meddle in a purely local squabble.

Local leaders thus are bound to the state organization by the Senator's leadership, by the compensation board's control of the pursestrings, by the intimate tie of the circuit judge with both Richmond and the local government. State patronage also pyramids power. The Commonwealth of Virginia performs directly functions that many states leave to local governments. What the state does within a county and whom the, state appoints there concern the county organization, and the state customarily clears with the local organization its appointees to posts within the locality. While the arrangement furnishes limited opportunity for local patronage, especially in highway work, even in patronage matters decorum prevails in Virginia. An unmitigated spoils system does not reign nor do state employees ordinarily engage in blatant electioneering.

---

[2] For a listing of the powers of the circuit judge, see *Report of the Virginia Commission on County Government* (January, 1940, House Document No. 9), chap. 8.

2. Give-and-Take Within the Oligarchy

Dictatorship is hardly the word to apply to the relations between the high command and its local subsidiaries. Apparently the high command permits, and even survives because of, a degree of "democracy" within the organization on candidacies. Loyal organization men, that is, men who have not differed with Senator Byrd, may compete for the support of local leaders for state-wide office. Such competition may go on for a year or more before the primary. The high command gets "the feel of the situation" by its reports from its local leaders. Once it puts its stamp of approval on a candidate, the courthouse machines accept him almost unanimously and he is virtually assured of the nomination in the Democratic primary. Local leaders, however, do not risk their necks by public endorsements of aspirants for nomination for state-wide office until the high command gives "the word." One can go from courthouse to courthouse today and the officials will not know who will be the next governor. Tomorrow, after the "nod" has been given, one can travel the same route and observe a remarkable unanimity of prediction.

The vitality of the machine and its long record of electoral success may rest in part on the hesitancy of the high command to outrage the sensibilities of the rank and file of the machine—that is, about 1,000 persons—by forcing the nomination of unacceptable persons for state office. The high command usually accepts those that it probably could not defeat; yet all must meet the test of organization loyalty.

The high command's sensitivity to organization sentiment was demonstrated in the election of James H. Price as governor in 1937. In 1935, Mr. Price, then lieutenant-governor, announced that he would seek the Democratic nomination in 1937. Mr. Price, an active Mason, had an impressive network of personal friendships over the state. Nevertheless, an arctic silence from the high command greeted his announcement. About six months went by, during which time presumably the organization leaders were sounding Price's strength and considering whether to put up a candidate. About eighteen months before the primary, Mr. Combs announced his support of Mr. Price and a rain of endorsements immediately followed from big and small politicians over the entire state. Mr. Price, a person more in sympathy with the policies of the national Administration than Senator Byrd, in due course was nominated and elected. The organization, through its control of the legislature, acceded to as much of Governor Price's program as his public support demanded. It delayed or killed the rest.[3]

[3] For an account of Governor Price's troubles with the legislature, see George W. Spicer, "Gubernatorial Leadership in Virginia," *Public Administration Review*, 1 (1941), pp. 441–57.

Usually for state-wide nominations the rivalries of organization men
are settled amicably within the family. An aspirant tours the counties,
finds himself without followers, and deems it futile to seek the "nod."
Another so clearly represents organization sentiment that the choice is
made long in advance of the primary. On rare occasion, the high command permits a pair of organization men to fight out their differences
in the primary. Such an event occurred in the nomination of a candidate
for lieutenant-governor in 1945. The high command, as organization leaders later ruefully admitted, made a mistake and told the aspirants,
Charles R. Fenwick and L. Preston Collins, to fight out their contest
publicly. From this conflict a scandal developed. The organization abhors
scandal and prides itself on its honesty and respectability. Late in the
race, so the gossip goes, the high command concluded that the contest
was becoming too hot and a last-minute word went down the line for Mr.
Fenwick. The Wise County organization in southwestern Virginia took
the "word" too seriously. In any event 3,307 votes were reported for Mr.
Fenwick and 122 for Mr. Collins. In an election contest brought by Mr.
Collins, it developed that the poll books containing the names of those
who had voted had disappeared. The Richmond City Circuit Court concluded that in this "primary election, Wise County was impregnated with
political crooks and ballot thieves. . . ." [4] The court threw out the Wise
County votes. So close was the race in the state as a whole that the loss of
3,307 votes from Wise County for Fenwick gave the nomination to
Collins.

Only infrequently does the high command permit a free and open
battle for a nomination. More generally it will accept a second-choice
candidate rather than subject the organization to the strain of internal
strife. Thus, in the 1946 Democratic convention to nominate a successor
to fill the unexpired senatorial term of Carter Glass, it was believed in
some quarters that Senator Byrd desired the nomination of Representative Howard Smith, of Alexandria, who was even more extreme than the
Senator in his dislike of the New Deal. But the convention was not well
managed and the high command acquiesced in the nomination of Willis
Robertson. The delegates believed that Robertson could be elected with
less outcry from the antiorganization element. A long story lay behind
the sidetracking of Howard Smith. In August, 1946, at Covington in Alleghany County in far western Virginia, several CIO unions brought their
members to the mass meeting to elect delegates to the state Democratic
convention. They caught the local machine unprepared, controlled the
meeting, and elected the delegates. The county Democratic chairman,
doubtless fearful of a loss of face in the state organization, "declared with

---

[4] The text of the court's opinion is quoted in the *Sunday Star* (Washington, D. C.),
September 30, 1945.

emotion that he didn't believe a meeting had ever been held in Alleghany county 'that has hurt the party more than this meeting tonight.' " [5]

Came the convention. The Alleghany delegates, occupying a strategic place on the alphabetical roll, yielded to the Nansemond County delegation which put in nomination former Governor Colgate W. Darden. The Governor was no crusader, no antiorganization man, but he enjoyed an enormous personal popularity and great respect throughout the state. His nomination threw the convention into an uproar, caused confusion, and gave opportunity to demonstrate the unacceptability of Representative Smith. Although Governor Darden did not desire the nomination,[6] the maneuvers of the labor delegation from Alleghany and the restiveness of other delegations induced the high command to acquiesce in the nomination of its second choice. Or, at least, such is the story of those who believe that they blocked the high command.

In most southern states individual Senators and Representatives avoid entangling alliances and look out for themselves. In states with an atomized political structure it is every man for himself, but in Virginia the organization encompasses all, or at least nearly all. It seeks to control congressional nominations in every district. In state legislative nominations the local prongs of the machine usually designate the organization candidates, while the high command concerns itself with congressional nominations, to the end that the state will have a solid organization delegation in the House. Yet the organization does not always have its way. It has had to tolerate, for example, Representative John W. Flannagan, Jr., of the "Fighting Ninth," the district at the southwestern tip of the state. Flannagan's personal popularity enabled him to carry a district with a heavy Republican vote. From a district with strong railroad brotherhoods and with a considerable mining population, the Congressman's voting record has been far less in agreement with that of the Republicans than Senator Byrd would have liked.[7] Although the organization accepted him, in 1946 it viewed with some satisfaction the announcement that Representative Flannagan would retire in 1948. The organization will probably have to remain flexible in its principles in the "Fighting Ninth." In this area, a fairly genuine Republican-Democratic competition prevails in contrast to some localities in the state where the Republican and Democratic rings mitigate the risks of partisan warfare by an agreed division of local offices.

Through its control of candidatures (and incidentally through its rumored influence over private rewards, such as corporate retainers), the organization constitutes a remarkable system for the recruitment and ad-

[5] AP dispatch from Covington, Virginia, August 10, 1946.
[6] He was later made president of the University of Virginia.
[7] See below pp. 379–80.

vancement of political leaders. While state elective offices are prizes sought by men rising in the organization, so careful is the management of the organization that the claims of those within it are nicely balanced by the allocation of rewards. On the other hand, individuals who, in the legislature or other lower office, demonstrate "unpredictable" qualities, that is, fail to follow the organization line, find their way blocked to further political preferment. In almost the manner of a churchly order, or the Communist party, the machine tests the loyalties and abilities of its neophytes. Those with unquestioned faith in the organization and belief in its doctrine are advanced. Those found wanting, either in ability or doctrine, remain in a lowly status. Thus, skilled management alone does not produce the well-disciplined oligarchy. Selection, advancement, and reward of those who conform to the machine place in positions of power those who almost instinctively act according to the machine's unwritten code. Careful selection and indoctrination make unnecessary the crude and spectacular disciplinary measures used, for example, by a Huey Long.

The practical monopoly that the organization enjoys in public affairs brings into its fold most of the able men of political ambition, who must conform to the machine mold. Virginians, whether as exponents of state pride or as accurate reporters, conclude that to succeed in high-level politics a person must enjoy a relatively high social status commanding at least a measure of respect. In a word, politics in Virginia is reserved for those who can qualify as gentlemen. Rabble-rousing and Negro-baiting capacities, which in Georgia or Mississippi would be a great political asset, simply mark a person as one not to the manner born. A public attitude favorable to this type of leadership combined with organization discipline represses most of the crudities commonly thought to be characteristic of southern politics. Virginia leadership is ingenious in stratagems to maintain political decorum. Thus, in 1948 Henry Wallace met eggs and tomatoes and antisegregation laws in many parts of the South in his campaign tour. Virginians calmly construed his political meetings to be private gatherings to which antisegregation laws did not apply.

The organization's skill in corralling within its ranks most persons of political ability leaves the antiorganization group relatively weakly led, and machine leaders and supporters regard with some disdain the chief figures in opposition. Thus, a high organization leader spoke with mild, perhaps unconscious, disdain of the fact that M. A. Hutchinson, antiorganization candidate for the Senate in 1946, had been employed around the state capitol for fifteen or twenty years and had obtained his law degree far beyond the usual time by going to night school.

In essence, Virginia is governed by a well-disciplined and ably managed oligarchy, of not many more than a thousand professional politicians, which enjoys the enthusiastic and almost undivided support of the business community and of the well-to-do generally, a goodly number of whom are fugitives from the New York state income tax. Organization spokesmen in Congress look out for the interests of business, and the state government, although well managed, manifests a continuing interest in the well-being of the well-to-do. The quid pro quo for support of the organization is said to be taxation favorable to corporations, an antilabor policy, and restraint in the expansion of services, such as education, public health, and welfare. The organization pursues a negative policy on public services; if there is an apparent demand it will grudgingly yield a bit here and there, but it dedicates its best efforts to the maintenance of low levels of public service. Yet it must be said that the organization gives good government; while the school system is inadequate it is about as good as the money appropriated will buy. The organization, however, has an "adding machine mentality"; attached to the fetish of a balanced budget, it takes a short-run view that almost invariably militates against the long-run interests of the state. Men with the minds of tradesmen do not become statesmen.[8]

The machine is more than an oligarchy of officeholders. Though it has its following of voters, the traditional concepts of democracy have no marked relevance in the discussion of Virginia politics. Of necessity the state practices the rituals of primaries and elections. Their outcome is usually predictable. The organization for years has carried state-wide primaries by ample majorities, but its majorities in the counties usually far exceed its urban majorities. Its relative strength in the cities and counties appears in the analysis in Table 2. In 1946, Senator Byrd won 68.4 per cent of the county vote, but only 55.2 of the city vote. The Senator has the distinction of being the weakest vote-getter among recent state-wide organization candidates. A rural concentration of strength would be expected, given the conservatism of the organization. County officials are also keenly aware of the advantages that the counties enjoy as against the cities under state financial legislation, a factor that reenforces their loyalty to the organization and stimulates their efforts on behalf of its candidates.

3. The Liberal Wing

Within the Democratic party of Virginia the organization constitutes a faction with a tightly knit, well-defined group of leaders that maintains an existence from election to election. Among the one-party states of the South such an institution within the party is exceptional. But what

[8] A state senator, musing over the record of the machine, reflected that though he had supported the organization's pay-as-you-go road program, he now believed it had been a mistake. Neighboring North Carolina, by floating a bond issue, built roads right and left and paved the way for the development of rural industry. Virginia, with its pay-as-you-go policy, postponed the same kind of development twenty years.

of the opposition? Has there developed in Virginia another "party" within the Democratic party to give the state in effect a bipartisan system within the dominant party?

The unity of the organization results in a rudimentary two-party system. All those against the organization rally to the antiorganization banner, which, however, is not always visible, and the battalions behind it are practically without leaders, almost completely lacking in patronage,

TABLE 2

Virginia's Machine Is Weakest in the Cities: Proportion of Vote Polled by Organization and Antiorganization Candidates in Democratic Primaries in Counties and Independent Cities of Virginia, 1933–48

YEAR	OFFICE	CANDIDATE	PER CENT OF TOTAL VOTE	PER CENT OF COUNTY VOTE	PER CENT OF CITY VOTE
1933	Governor	*Peery* [a]	61.6	69.7	49.4
		Smith	17.1	15.7	19.3
		Deal	21.3	14.6	31.3
1937	Governor	*Price*	86.0	90.2	79.8
		Page	14.0	9.8	20.2
1941	Lieutenant-Governor	*Tuck*	81.3	86.2	73.7
		Plunkett	18.7	13.8	26.3
1945	Governor	*Tuck*	69.9	76.7	58.2
		Plunkett	30.1	23.3	41.8
1946	Senator	*Byrd*	63.5	68.4	55.2
		Hutchinson	36.5	31.6	44.8
1948	Senator	*Robertson*	70.3	74.4	63.4
		Hart	29.7	25.6	36.6

[a] Organization candidates in italics.

and poorly disciplined. The fact is, as organization leaders admit privately, many antiorganization people are disfranchised, a matter that, incidentally, contributes to organization discipline. Ambitious organization men disgruntled by actions of the high command, cannot carry their case to the people; the people do not vote.

The nature of the antiorganization faction emerges from an examination of campaigns since 1940. Persons generally favorable to national Democratic leaders and their policies, persons desirous of improving the state's educational and other social services, and others have formed a loose alliance to combat the organization. In 1941 Moss Plunkett, of

Roanoke, ran as an antiorganization candidate for the lieutenant-governorship. In 1945, he opposed Tuck, the organization man, for governor. In 1946, Martin Hutchinson led the antiorganization forces in a campaign for the senatorial nomination against Senator Byrd. At each of these primaries, as may be seen in Table 2, the proportion of the total vote against the organization increased. In 1946, in the face of a country-wide swing to the right, the Byrd machine polled a smaller proportion of the vote than it had in the governor's primary of 1945.[9]

In 1940 a few liberal Democrats laid plans for a long-run fight against the Byrd machine: the objective was not so much to win elections as to bring about an expansion of public services and poll-tax repeal. In furtherance of the general strategy Moss Plunkett ran for lieutenant-governor in 1941. Mr. Plunkett, a man of crusading zeal, regarded as a bit erratic by conservative Virginians, had developed a concern about the Byrd oligarchy in the course of his professional employment by the state teachers' association. Inquiry into the status of public education in Virginia and comparison of Virginia's performance with that of other states led him to the conclusion that the Byrd organization concerned itself more with the tax burden of the wealthy than with the needs of most of the people. Mr. Plunkett's 1941 race for lieutenant-governor resulted in no impressive antiorganization vote; he polled only 18.7 per cent of the total vote. In his race for the gubernatorial nomination in 1945 he developed greater strength, although at no time did he endanger the organization. Nevertheless, as the campaign wore on the high command revised its initial plan for its candidate, Tuck, to conduct a quiet campaign from the front porch of his home in South Boston.

The centers of antiorganization strength in the electorate in 1945 appear on the map in Figure 2, which reveals the geographical concentration of the opposition and, obversely, the location of the organization strongholds. In far southwestern Virginia, where, it will be recalled, the organization, faced by Republican competition, tolerated deviation from the organization line, Mr. Plunkett's vote was heavy in Scott and Washington counties. Slightly farther to the east in Alleghany County and in Clifton Forge, an area of labor alertness, he polled a heavy vote as he did in his home city, Roanoke. The principal area of antiorganization strength, however, was in the counties from Richmond to Norfolk and in the cities of the tidewater area. In Chesterfield County, Henrico County, Prince George County, James City County, Warwick County, Charles City County, Portsmouth, Richmond, Hopewell, Norfolk, Newport News,

---

[9] In 1948 Mr. Hutchinson abandoned an early intention to oppose Senator Willis Robertson for renomination. James P. Hart, Jr. entered the primary against Robertson, but full antiorganization strength was not mobilized in his behalf and the turnout was only about half that of the 1946 senatorial primary. Robertson, who, incidentally, had differed with Senator Byrd on several important roll calls, won handily.

and Williamsburg, Mr. Plunkett polled more than 40 per cent of the votes.

Citizens of the tidewater area have long felt that the organization ignores their interests—an attitude that accounts for some antiorganization votes in this region; but the primary source of antiorganization strength in the area from Richmond to the sea apparently came from workers. Norfolk, Portsmouth, Newport News are centers of industrial employment, and the counties contributing antiorganization strength in this region are not primarily rural. Most of them have a high proportion of rural nonfarm population, a population that has spilled over from the industrial cities or that is locally employed in semirural industrial enterprise.

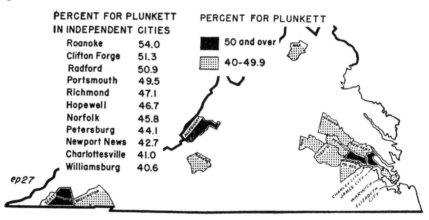

PERCENT FOR PLUNKETT
IN INDEPENDENT CITIES

Roanoke	54.0
Clifton Forge	51.3
Radford	50.9
Portsmouth	49.5
Richmond	47.1
Hopewell	46.7
Norfolk	45.8
Petersburg	44.1
Newport News	42.7
Charlottesville	41.0
Williamsburg	40.6

PERCENT FOR PLUNKETT

50 and over

40-49.9

FIGURE 2

Antiorganization Strength in Virginia, 1945: Counties and Cities Voting 40 Per Cent or More for Plunkett in 1945 Democratic Gubernatorial Primary

In Mr. Hutchinson's 1946 race against Senator Byrd for the senatorial nomination the antiorganization proportion of the total vote increased; in general its geographical distribution resembled that polled in Mr. Plunkett's 1945 campaign. In southwestern Virginia Mr. Hutchinson drew heavy support in Buchanan, Dickenson, Lee, Scott, Tazewell, and Wise counties, all counties with considerable employment in mining. Alleghany County, where paper manufacturing and other industries are centered, again delivered a heavy vote to the antiorganization candidates as did its independent city, Clifton Forge. Again the tidewater cities and adjacent counties came through with heavy votes for the liberal candidate. The suburbs of Washington—Fairfax and Arlington counties and Alexandria City—registered a protest vote as they had in 1945, and thus demonstrated that the antiorganization vote was by no means entirely a "labor" vote.[10] The race made by a newcomer to state politics, James Hart, against Senator Robertson in 1948 was not regarded seriously by either the organization or the opposition, but Mr. Hart's greatest strength centered in the same general areas as had Mr. Hutchinson's.

In all three primaries—1941, 1945, and 1946—an ineradicable residue of history appeared in the rebelliousness of the people of the southwestern mountain counties. They had been mainstays of the Readjuster movement, Virginia's agrarian radical uprising of the past century. All over the South the voters of the highlands tend to respond when the interests and powers-that-be are baited.

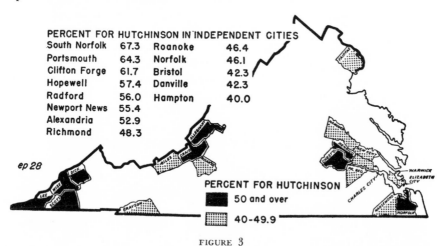

PERCENT FOR HUTCHINSON IN INDEPENDENT CITIES

South Norfolk	67.3	Roanoke	46.4
Portsmouth	64.3	Norfolk	46.1
Clifton Forge	61.7	Bristol	42.3
Hopewell	57.4	Danville	42.3
Radford	56.0	Hampton	40.0
Newport News	55.4		
Alexandria	52.9		
Richmond	48.3		

PERCENT FOR HUTCHINSON

■ 50 and over

▦ 40-49.9

FIGURE 3

Antiorganization Strength in Virginia, 1946: Counties and Cities Voting 40 Per Cent or More for Hutchinson in 1946 Senatorial Primary

The antiorganization faction possesses no solid network of local officials or other organizational apparatus extending over the entire state. It must depend on individuals here and there and on nonparty groups held together by a common opposition to the organization. Nor can anti-

[10] A note for the technician: The antiorganization vote, while drawn in large part from urban areas, from areas of industrialization, and from counties with considerable rural nonfarm population, does not show a high correlation from county to county with any of these factors. In some cities and in some industrialized areas the anti-organization vote is relatively low. The explanation probably is that antiorganization effort has been applied quite unevenly from place to place; that the anti-Byrd leaders are able to make most headway in the urban industrialized areas. In each of the three races by antiorganization candidates—1941, 1945, and 1946—there fell into the upper quartile of antiorganization strength (ranking counties and independent cities together) the following counties: Alleghany, Charles City, Chesterfield, New Kent, Prince George, and Roanoke. The following independent cities fell in the upper quartile in all three races: Alexandria, Clifton Forge, Hopewell, Newport News, Radford, Richmond, Roanoke.

organization candidates draw on the business community, as can organization leaders, to finance their campaigns. When Mr. Hutchinson ran for the Senate in 1946, for example, he managed his own campaign, tried to keep his law practice going, and furnished more than half the cost of the pitifully financed campaign. He received, it is reliably reported, no contribution from any business enterprise.

The money honesty of the organization, too, deprives the opposition of support. In Virginia, we are assured, a state contractor does not have to make a pay-off; he has to make a low bid. Even distilleries selling to the state liquor board, the almost incredible report is, do not concede a percentage to the organization. In most southern, and perhaps most northern, states a man with political ambition—and some political prospects—can always find a disgruntled or hopeful contractor or supplier willing to help finance a campaign. And these businessmen are often not concerned about political ideology: they want to do business with a winner, be he right, left, center, or monarchist. The Virginia opposition can enlist no such financial support.

Among the groups that have rallied around antiorganization candidates are the Committee for Virginia, an affiliate of the Southern Conference on Human Welfare, the CIO-PAC, and various—but not all— Negro organizations.[11] The CIO-PAC often works undercover, for it realizes that its public endorsement may be the kiss of death to a candidate. The 1946 senatorial campaign, for example, gave Senator Byrd opportunity to indulge in a bit of genteel demagoguery: he rang the welkin, with warnings about the CIO, Communism, and the imminent revolution in Virginia. All this was, of course, hokum unworthy of the Senator. The CIO at the time had no more than 40,000 members in the state and probably no more than 10,000 voters. In unionized areas, however, labor votes added to the antiorganization vote from other classes gave the antiorganization candidates a respectable showing. The railroad brotherhoods, in their few areas of concentrated strength, as in Roanoke, apparently deliver a considerable anti-Byrd vote, although in some congressional races the brotherhoods are driven to support Republican candidates who may be more favorable to their interests than the Byrd candidate.

All in all, the opposition forces are weakly organized. A ragtag miscellany of nonparty groups can be relied upon to back an antiorganization

---

[11] Southern Negro voters generally align themselves with candidates and factions opposing the status quo. This tendency is less marked in Virginia and Tennessee where Negroes have voted longer and in larger numbers than farther south. In the cities, where Negroes vote in highest proportions, they have often been allied with the local arms of the Byrd organization, which in turn has protected their right to the suffrage. Virginia's white citizens in and out of the machine have demonstrated a relatively acute sense of responsibility toward the Negro—an attitude that may account in part for the fact that its race relations are perhaps the most harmonious in the South.

candidate. He can usually line up a few personal friends in some counties and cities of the state to aid in his campaign. By and large, however, the minority faction is without organization.

In the form and continuity of its factions Virginia comes quite close to having a two-party system within the Democratic party. Yet the regular organization dominates the situation thoroughly, and there ought to be no nonsense about its methods. "Liberals" and other political amateurs often decry the methods of an organization like that headed by the Senator, but any group that seeks to challenge the organization or to maintain a continuing opposition must utilize similar methods or at least assume a similar form. The business of recruiting people and organizing them to work together consistently and fairly harmoniously over the years to achieve electoral victory is a problem that has to be solved by any group that wishes to compete with the Byrd machine.

The crux of the problem of developing a healthy political life in Virginia lies in the creation of a nucleus of leaders that can compete with the regular organization on fairly equal terms. The Byrd methods are responsible in part for the difficulties of erecting a competing organization. For a two-party system to operate effectively each party must, almost of necessity, have a territorial stronghold in which it can win legislative elections and control local governments. The powers exercised by the central government of Virginia over local officials make it difficult to found an opposition faction on control of local governments. The punitive powers of the organization, through its control of the perquisites of local officials and its ability to obstruct local bills in the legislature, can discourage competing factions territorially segregated.

Probably more fundamental in explanation of the weakness of the opposition than peculiar governmental arrangements is the success of the regular organization in allying with itself the business and financial interests of the state. It has in effect brought into camp most of the people who might furnish opposition leadership. In the counties usually the local banks and other businesses, such as retailing, are allied with the local organization, while larger enterprises have their connections with organization leaders higher in the hierarchy. Virginia, like many another commonwealth, presents an example of the extraordinary success of the corporations and of the wealthy in persuading the upper middle class that their interests are identical. The small group of citizens earning, say, $5,000 or more annually, from which community leaders must come, have been persuaded by and large that their interests lie with individual and corporate wealth.[12] Thus, the leading citizens of each community—the banker, the preacher, the lawyer, the doctor, the merchants and often the

[12] The distribution of Virginia Federal income tax returns according to net income in 1941 follows: Under $3,000, 198,796; $3,000–$5,000, 33,892; $5,000–10,000, 9,458; $10,000–$20,000, 3,014; $20,000 and over, 1,235.

newspaper owners whose self-interest dictates a deep concern about the way in which the government is fulfilling its responsibilities to the community in which they live—surrender their self-interest and follow the Senator in his pursuit of New Dealers, Communists, the CIO-PAC, et cetera. The principal source of opposition leadership thus reduces itself to a few lawyers willing to buck the organization, labor leaders whose sustenance cannot be readily cut off through organization influence, and now and then a substantial citizen of more courage than discretion.

Not to be regarded lightly as another factor in keeping down opposition is the absence of competition for the state's electoral vote in presidential elections. The state's considerable Republican vote could be used as the nucleus for an opposition party in state affairs, but the state Republican organization dedicates itself to the high purpose of wangling patronage when the Republicans are in power nationally and lives in hope when the Democrats are in power. National patronage could aid mightily in keeping an opposition nucleus alive within the state by creating career opportunities outside the Byrd organization. The dilemma, of course, is that by all rules of rationality and consistency, which have little application in politics, the Senator and his chief associates ought to be Republicans, whereas the Republican highlanders ought, by the same rules, to be Democrats.

4. Is the Machine Immortal?

It is in the nature of political machines that they must periodically undergo a reorganization. Leaders grow old—and careless. Public demands change, and political hierarchies have difficulty in adjusting themselves to the new requirements for political survival. Able though the leaders of the Virginia machine are, it is unlikely that they can manage a frictionless succession to produce a high command canny enough to keep the organization in power in perpetuity. In 1948 there was talk that Senator Byrd would retire in 1952 and, more serious, that his political judgment had become impaired. His first lieutenant, Mr. Combs, was growing old. A shake-up in the organization seemed to be in the cards.

The high command weakened its position by a serious miscalculation of the sentiment of the organization rank and file on the civil rights issue. In February, 1948, Governor Tuck proposed to the legislature that the state Democratic convention be permitted to lodge with a party committee, such as the Senator and a few cronies, the right to determine for whom Virginia's Democratic electors would cast the state's electoral vote. Presumably the proposal would have permitted a party committee before the election to instruct the party's electors for a candidate other than the nominee of the national convention, but there was some fear that the plan would also permit the committee to alter its instructions after the election. Senator Byrd, on the floor of the Senate, acclaimed Governor Tuck as a great statesman but John Flannagan, from the "Fighting Ninth," immediately proclaimed the Governor's proposal to be nonsense. Not only the press but the machine's legislature took up arms, and in a face-saving maneuver, the Governor was allowed to suggest "amendments" that completely wrecked his scheme and left the anti-Truman people in a weaker position than before. Unsatisfied with one blunder, the high command rammed through the Democratic state convention in July resolutions critical of the national administration, with no opportunity for debate. Faithful organization men, especially those who had to fight Republicans, went home soured on the leadership.

All these high jinks gave Messrs. Hutchinson, Plunkett, and other antiorganization leaders an opportunity to make hay. They challenged the right of the organization to call itself "Democratic," and their candidate for the governorship in 1949, Francis Pickens Miller, set to work. Meanwhile, aspirants for the blessings of the machine for the 1949 gubernatorial nomination angled for the "nod." Even early in 1947, high organization leaders were suggesting that Mayor Horace H. Edwards of Richmond was too "unreliable" a person to carry the organization banner in the primary. In 1948, after he had resigned as state Democratic chairman, Edwards announced for the nomination and began to talk at variance with the high command on such questions as Federal aid for education. By August, 1948, it was widely believed that state senator John S. Battle, of Charlottesville, had organization blessing for the governorship. Unless the organization could compose its inner differences before August, 1949, Virginians looked forward to the unusual spectacle of a real battle in the primary. That the top leadership of the organization would eventually change was a certainty; whether August, 1949, would be the time was another question.[13] Yet when a change occurred, it seemed certain that Virginia's politics would retain a character all its own, a character fixed perhaps by a pervading belief that the upper orders should govern. That belief, incidentally, also infects the Negroes who take pride in being Virginians and look down on lesser peoples.

[13] Before the August, 1949 primary observers punned that the machine might lose the Battle and still win the war. Even if Senator Battle should lose, the machine would certainly control the legislature and live to fight another day.

Chapter Three | # ALABAMA:
PLANTERS, POPULISTS, "BIG MULES"

THE political distance from Virginia to Alabama must be measured in light years. Virginian deference to the upper orders and the Byrd machine's restraint of popular aberrations give Virginia politics a tone and a reality radically different from the tumult of Alabama. There a wholesome contempt for authority and a spirit of rebellion akin to that of the Populist days resist the efforts of the big farmers and "big mules"— the local term for Birmingham industrialists and financiers—to control the state. Alabamians retain a sort of frontier independence, with an inclination to defend liberty and to bait the interests.

Illustrative of the spirit of Alabama politics was the reaction of the late Julian Hall, editor of the Dothan *Eagle,* to a 1935 antisedition act that made it a misdemeanor to advocate overthrow of the government. He urged the citizens to equip themselves "with shillalahs, set out for Montgomery, and whale hell out of the members of the Alabama legislature." The legislature recanted.[1] In 1947, when the legislature was up in arms over appointments by Governor "Big Jim" Folsom to the Board of Trustees of the Alabama Polytechnic Institute, one car of a motorcade of students demonstrating in support of the governor carried a poster bearing the expressive but unoriginal inscription: "To Hell with the Legislature."[2] While all this rebelliousness tends toward the inelegant, it indi-

[1] *Alabama, American Guide Series* (New York: Richard R. Smith, 1941), p. 384; *General Laws of Alabama,* 1935, Nos. 161 and 330.
[2] Photograph in *Birmingham News,* March 5, 1947.

36

GOVERNOR "BIG JIM" FOLSOM: "THE LITTLE MAN'S BIG FRIEND"

The people must take their leaders where they find them.

GOVERNOR "HUMMON" TALMADGE, SON OF "OLD GENE"

*In a one-party system the magic of a name may be a political heritage
of uncommon value.*

cates the robustness of Alabama political life. Clearly a state that produces a Senator (and Justice) Hugo Black, a Senator Lister Hill, a Senator John Sparkman scarcely merits application of the conventional stereotype of the South as a region of hidebound reaction.

The most cursory contrast of Virginia and Alabama quickly confirms the earlier forecast that a broad range of variety would be found in the factional systems (or "subparties") within the Democratic party in the southern states. Unlike Virginia, Alabama has not been dominated over a long period by a single well-disciplined machine. Nor have there been in recent years well-organized competing machines. Political factions form and reform. Leadership in state-wide politics tends to be transient. New state-wide leaders emerge, rise to power, and disappear as others take their places. Voters group themselves in one faction and then in another in the most confusing fashion. No orderly system prevails—as under Virginia machine rule—for the recruitment, development, and advancement of political leaders. Rather the political process appears as a free-for-all, with every man looking out for himself.

Yet within the anarchy of competing factions and leaders, elements of continuity are perceptible. A progressive-conservative cleavage persists, and from time to time the issues become so clear that this split among leaders of opinion projects itself into the divisions among the voters in the form of a sectionalism. More generally, however, disorganization handicaps the voters—both conservative and progressive—in grouping themselves about leaders committed to their cause. The turnover in the ranks of state-wide leaders alone prevents the crystallization and solidification of voter loyalties around particular banners or groups of politicians. A tenuous and impermanent factional organization confuses the voters and makes for electoral decisions based on irrelevancies.

1. Friends and Neighbors

A powerful localism provides an important ingredient of Alabama factionalism. Candidates for state office tend to poll overwhelming majorities in their home counties and to draw heavy support in adjacent counties. Such voting behavior may be rationalized as a calculated promotion of local interest, yet it also points to the absence of stable, well-organized, state-wide factions of like-minded citizens formed to advocate measures of common concern. In its extreme form localism justifies a diagnosis of low voter-interest in public issues and a susceptibility to control by the irrelevant appeal to support the home-town boy. In some instances, of course, localism may reflect concern about some general state issue bearing on the area.

If the factions within the Democratic party of Alabama amounted to political parties, a candidate's strength in the vote from county to county would not be influenced appreciably by his place of residence. A well-knit group of voters and leaders scattered over the entire state would deliver about the same proportion of the vote to its candidate wherever he happened to live. A concern for issues (or at least for group success) would override local attachments. In well-developed two-party situations localism is minimized, if not erased, by a larger concern for party victory. The classic case is that of Duchess County, New York, the home of Franklin D. Roosevelt, a Democrat of some note. The county, traditionally Republican, stubbornly held to its partisan attachments and repeatedly failed to return a majority for even its most distinguished son.

TABLE 3

Friends and Neighbors: Home-County Strength of Candidates for Democratic Nomination in Alabama's Eighth Congressional District, September 24, 1946

CANDIDATE	HIS HOME COUNTY	PER CENT OF HOME COUNTY VOTE FOR LOCAL BOY	PER CENT OF DISTRICT VOTE FOR HIM	PER CENT OF COUNTY VOTE TO OUTSIDER WITH HIGHEST VOTE
Johnson	Limestone	65.1	15.0	22.0
Jones	Jackson	97.5	22.7	0.9
Meadows	Morgan	47.4	8.5	24.7
Pounders	Lauderdale	40.2	4.5	28.7
Smith, Jeff	Madison	70.1	17.8	14.4
Smith, Jim	Colbert	62.1	19.5	2.9
Twitty	Colbert	30.1	12.0	2.9

Radically different voting behavior characterizes battles within the Alabama Democratic primaries. A candidate for governor normally carries his own county by a huge majority, and the harshest criticism that can be made of a politician is that he cannot win in his own beat or precinct. If his friends and neighbors who know him do not support him, why should those without this advantage trust a candidate?

A special primary held in Alabama's eighth congressional district in September, 1946, provides an extreme illustration of the friends-and-neighbors effect. Each of six of the district's seven counties was represented by at least one candidate for the nomination. Each home-town candidate led the polling in his own bailiwick in the first primary. In one county the local candidate was credited with 97.5 per cent of the vote. The other counties manifested less of an urge toward unanimity but in every instance outsiders fared poorly against the local candidate. The details are set out in Table 3. In this district it is plain that no dual system of district-wide factions existed. The controlling factors in voting were local pride and patriotism, reinforced perhaps by county machines and by the candidates' personal followings.

The same type of localism appears in state contests. In a sense the battle of state politics is not a battle between large party factions. It is rather a struggle of individuals—perhaps with the support of their county organizations—to build a state-wide following on the foundation of local support. This localism appears most clearly in the so-called "first primary," which is a contest to determine the two strongest contenders who "run off" the race for the nomination in the second primary. In these first races, usually involving a multiplicity of candidates, the fluidity of factions shows itself most sharply. In the second primary, limited to two candidates, voters are compelled to divide into two camps and the underlying localism becomes blurred.

The pattern of localism emerges vividly in the pair of maps in Figure 4, which identify the counties of peak strength of "Big Jim" Folsom and Judge Elbert Boozer in the first gubernatorial primary of 1946. "Big Jim's" strength clustered around two counties: Coffee and Cullman. Born in southeastern Alabama in Coffee County, he spent his young manhood there and married the daughter of the probate judge, a functionary of great political importance in Alabama. In later life he lived in Cullman County, in northern Alabama, and in traveling the surrounding counties as an insurance salesman built up a wide acquaintance. In the 1946 primary, he polled 72 per cent of the popular vote of Cullman County, a remarkable tribute by his fellow citizens. In the surrounding counties his strength tapered down, and in the state as a whole he drew only 28.5 per cent of the vote.[3]

The second map in Figure 4 delineates geographically the popular strength of Judge Elbert Boozer, a self-made man of wealth who, having become probate judge of Calhoun County, aspired to the governorship. In the state he polled only 15.9 per cent of the total vote, running fourth in a field of five candidates. In his own county and a couple of adjacent

---

[3] The friends-and-neighbors spirit colors the following letter to the editor of the *Birmingham News* (February 9, 1947); "It seems that some persons don't know Mr. Folsom, our governor, well enough to wait and see how he will do. . . .

"I happened to be born on one side of the road and Jim Folsom on the other side. My father and Jim's father were old pals. I lived in sight of five Folsom families, Jessie, Frank, Thomas, Mrs. Millie and Marion Folsom, Jim's father. The first school teacher I went to was Miss Ola Folsom (deceased). I want to say to the citizens of Alabama and elsewhere that there is no better community in Alabama than is the Folsom community about 16 miles northeast of Elba.

"I have worked in the fields with the Folsoms. There are no better managers than the Folsoms. There are no better neighbors than the Folsoms. (No, I am not related to them.)

"When I saw Jim's picture and that he was in the race for governor, I put one of his large pictures up in my shop and began speaking my knowledge of the Folsoms and won him many friends, of which some were business men. . . . I just knew there was a man from a good family seeking a place where he could serve many people the best way."

counties, he managed to attract more than 50 per cent of the vote, and
his highest popular strength appeared mainly in counties clustered about
his home bailiwick.

An endless number of illustrations of the friends-and-neighbors effect
could be presented. Another pair of examples is mapped in Figure 5. In
keeping with an Alabama custom, Chauncey Sparks in 1938 ran for
governor presumably with the hope that he might make enough of a
showing to try again in 1942 and win. The good people of Barbour

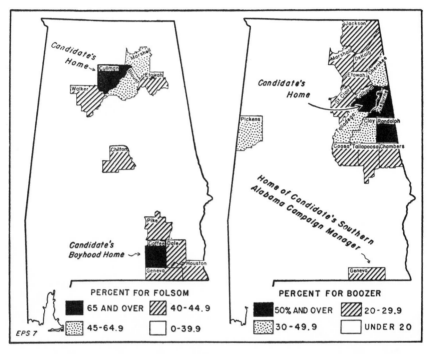

FIGURE 4

Friends and Neighbors: Areas of Concentration of Popular Strength of Folsom
and Boozer in First Alabama Gubernatorial Primary, 1946

County gave their fellow-citizen Sparks 84.7 per cent of the vote, a truly
heroic performance when viewed against the 23.7 per cent of the vote he
received in the state as a whole. R. J. Goode, another candidate at the
1938 primary, attracted 71.6 per cent of the vote of his home county and
only 22.4 per cent of the state vote.

Not every candidate for state-wide office profits from a heavy friends-
and-neighbors vote, but nearly always such a following constitutes a
nucleus around which an aspirant for a state-wide office attempts to build
a faction. The voters of the larger cities apparently do not have the same
sense of loyalty toward a local candidate as do those who dwell in small

towns and in the rural areas. The frequency of the friends-and-neighbors pattern points to the personal factor in the transient factions of southern state politics. At times it also points to control of a local machine or perhaps to incapacity of election officials to restrain from slanting their arithmetic for the benefit of the home-town boy. More important than all these factors, the friends-and-neighbors pattern reflects the absence of well-organized competing factions with stable and state-wide followings among the voters. Almost any local leader with any prospects at all who aspires for state office can cut into the strength of established state leaders or factions within his own immediate bailiwick. He gains support, not

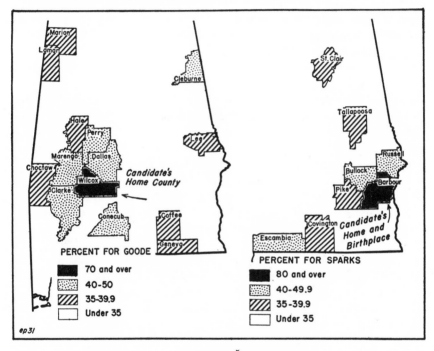

FIGURE 5

Friends and Neighbors: Areas of Concentration of Popular Strength of Sparks and Goode in Alabama Gubernatorial Primary of May 3, 1938

primarily for what he stands for or because of his capacities, but because of where he lives. A more or less totally irrelevant appeal—back the home-town boy—can exert no little influence over an electorate not habituated to the types of voting behavior characteristic of a two-party situation.

2. Sectionalism Emergent from Localism

It is not a long step from localism to a sectionalism based on a genuine diversity of interest. Sectionalism amounts to localism on a larger scale,

but divisions of voters along sectional lines may represent a rational sort
of grouping of voters bound together by common interest and common
policy objectives rather than a neighborhood loyalty. Within the Alabama
Democratic party there emerges from time to time a sectional cleavage
that party lines would probably follow if the state had parties. In this
sectional pattern north Alabama and southeastern Alabama are usually
allied against the black belt, a strip across the south center of the state so
named because of the color of the soil. The black belt, a region of large
farms and of many Negroes with the accompanying socio-economic system, tends to ally itself with the "big mules" of Birmingham and the
lesser "big mules" of Mobile. The north Alabama region, an area in
which smaller farmers are more typical, retains to this day a strident
radical agrarian tone in its politics and tends to be the source of movements disturbing to the "big mules."

The most recent clear-cut manifestation of this sectional division
occurred in the run-off gubernatorial contest of 1946 between "Big Jim"
Folsom and Handy Ellis. "Big Jim" conducted a campaign in the tradition of southern rabble-rousers. A man of huge proportions, "The Little
Man's Big Friend," he toured the state with a hillbilly band, "The Straw-
berry Pickers," and promised to use his "suds bucket" in cleaning out the
statehouse. Into the "suds bucket" went contributions from those aroused
to enthusiasm at his rallies. "Big Jim" had something more than a colorful
show. He proposed more adequate care for the aged, better salaries for
school teachers, a road-building program, and threatened generally to be
tough with the interests, all in a spirit reminiscent of the agrarian radicals
of an earlier day.

This kind of a program—by no means radical but certainly progressive as politics goes in the state—aroused the fears of big business, of
big farmers, and of people of substance generally. Any expansion of public
functions requires taxation, which is perhaps the major question of concern to the more prosperous citizenry and especially to corporations.
Hence, most of the conservative leaders of the state rallied around Ellis—
a man of considerably more experience and maturity in public affairs
than Folsom. The press, many local machines, business generally, and the
black belt organized in his support. Although Ellis drew most of the big-
business support, Folsom benefited from the aid of a few types of business.
As one unsuccessful candidate for governor in Alabama puts it, businesses
with a stake in politics fall into two groups: first, those who wish to be left
alone; second, those who wish to do business with the state. Mr. Folsom
attracted some support from the second group.

In the voting, division fell along lines of cleavage that appear in
Alabama when progressive-conservative issues are raised in a compelling
manner. Ellis had his greatest popular strength in the black-belt counties,

which are black both in soil and in a majority of their people, whereas Folsom's strength tended to be higher in the northern and southern parts of the state where the Negro population is relatively less numerous.[4] The dominant elements of the black belt bracketed Folsom with the CIO as a threat to the established order. The *Hale County News,* for example, saw little support for this "CIO-endorsed" candidate in a "county of farmers, business and professional men." [5]

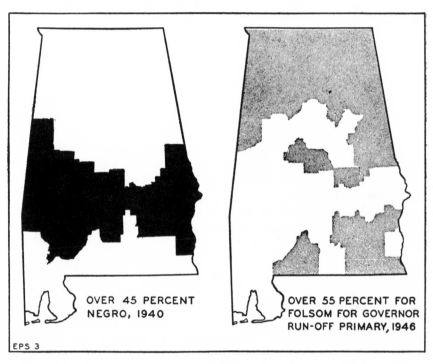

OVER 45 PERCENT
NEGRO, 1940

OVER 55 PERCENT FOR
FOLSOM FOR GOVERNOR
RUN-OFF PRIMARY, 1946

EPS 3

FIGURE 6

Black-Belt Conservatism: Relation between Vote for Folsom for Governor in Alabama Democratic Primary of 1946 and Distribution of Negro Population

The split between the black belt and the remainder of the state in the Folsom-Ellis contest suggests that the backbone of southern conservatism may be found in those areas with high concentrations of Negro population. For decades the Alabama black belt has been a stronghold of conservative agricultural strength which has frequently allied itself

[4] The coefficient of correlation between county percentages of Negro population and percentages of vote for Folsom was minus 0.74. If one omits from the calculation Shelby County, Ellis' home, which gave him a larger proportion of the vote than might be predicted on the basis of its Negro population, the coefficient becomes minus 0.80.

[5] *Hale County News,* May 9, 1946.

with the business interests of the state.[6] The presence of a large proportion of Negroes in the population alone may induce a degree of conservatism. To maintain its own status the ruling group must oppose any political program that tends to elevate or excite the masses, black or white. Beyond the racial influence, however, probably the whites of the black-belt counties are disproportionately represented in the upper economic strata. In the predominantly white counties the lesser persons of the community are white and have the vote; in the black-belt counties the lesser orders are black and do not vote. Consequently the black-belt electorate is probably loaded with persons of upper socio-economic status in contrast with the more normal composition of the electorate of the white counties.

If the black counties are the backbone of southern conservatism, a partial explanation for the recurrent progressive outbursts in Alabama politics rests in the fact that over considerable areas of the state the population includes comparatively small proportions of Negroes. The whites in these areas can act radically without fear of any involvement in the race question. In fact, apart from the restraint imposed by that question, the South ought, by all the rules of political behavior, to be radical. A poor, agrarian area, pressed down by the colonial policies of the financial and industrial North and Northeast, it offers fertile ground for political agitation. The overshadowing race question, in which the big farmers have the most immediate stake, blots up a latent radicalism by converting discontent into aggression against the Negro.

Whether the foregoing explanation is correct, developments after Folsom's election supported the expectations of all concerned. The governor soon made himself even more unpopular with those groups that had opposed his election. He proposed $57,000,000 new revenue per year for educational purposes, for increased old-age assistance, and for highway construction. Business interests inaugurated a campaign in opposition, under the leadership of the director of public relations of the State Chamber of Commerce.[7] The governor's revenue commissioner boosted the assessment of the Southern Railway Company, with a statement that the assessment had been kept low through "political pressure." [8]

The legislature's reluctance to enact Folsom's program points to an important consequence of the one-party system. Without a continuing state-wide organization with a perceptible program orientation, legislators may be elected entirely without regard to their attitude on the program advocated by the winning candidate for governor. The transient, factional followings of candidates preclude the existence of a state-wide organiza-

---

[6] Of interest in this connection is the fact that in the 1946 senatorial primary most of the counties of high popular strength of James A. Simpson, a leading Birmingham lawyer generally regarded as an able spokesman for the business interests of the state, were in the black belt.

[7] *Birmingham News-Age-Herald,* March 16, 1947.

[8] Ibid., August 9, 1947.

tion to designate and back legislative candidates, and thus leave much to chance in the legislature.[9] Further, the absence of a party label or a definite "organization" or "antiorganization" designation for local candidates contributes to the voters' confusion. There is much to be said for voting a straight ticket, provided that it represents the work of a group well enough organized to put more or less like-minded candidates in the field. Without the benefit of party organization, then, the majority of the people of a one-party state are confronted by special difficulties in making their will effective. Dual party organization can be a means of confronting the voter with effective choices for all offices; factional struggle within a single party may make the alternatives obscure or even lead to default in the presentation of alternatives. Moreover, after the election no disciplined factional group exists to carry out a program in the legislature. A great advantage goes to those who seek to obstruct action.

The alignment of the Folsom-Ellis campaign was only a recurrence of a cleavage of interest that has long persisted in the state's history. A natural antagonism of sectional interests strives for expression in the confused factionalism of the Democratic party, but at an earlier time it took form in a two-party system. In the 1840's the Whig party, the "broadcloth party," was the party of the slaveholders and the men of means, while the Democratic party won most of its support from the whites without slaves in the northern and southeastern parts of the state.[10] The conservative black-belt Democrats of today are the heirs of the Whigs of a century ago.

In the debates over secession a party realignment occurred. The slaveholders of the black belt became Democrats and eventually carried the state for secession, but the northern and southeastern whites went along only reluctantly. After The War, the black-belt counties had to appeal to the whites of northern Alabama to aid in throwing off Negro and carpetbag rule. The *Montgomery Advertiser,* in November, 1874, put their problem and their plea: "South Alabama raises her manacled hands in mute appeal to tht mountain counties. The chains on the wrists of her sons and the midnight shrieks of her women sound continually in their ears. She lifts up her eyes, being tormented, and begs piteously for relief from bondage. Is there a white man in north Alabama so lost to all his finer feelings of human nature to slight her appeal?" [11]

[9] The lack of co-ordination of campaigning of governor and legislator probably has the most marked significance when a governor comes into office committed to a program that upsets apple carts. Before Folsom, Alabama governors managed to exert strong legislative leadership. See Hallie Farmer, *The Legislative Process in Alabama* (University, Ala.: Bureau of Public Administration, University of Alabama, 1949). The woes of an Alabama governor who speaks for the hills and for the branch heads are also compounded by legislative malapportionment giving the black-belt counties overrepresentation.

[10] A. B. Moore, *History of Alabama and Her People* (Chicago and New York: American Historical Society, 1927), pp. 216–17.

[11] Quoted, ibid., pp. 645–46.

Once an end had been put to Reconstruction the old party lines reappeared. In the 'eighties and 'nineties rivalry between the black belt and the predominantly white counties again flared up as the agrarian uprising got under way. The agrarian forces under the leadership of Reuben Kolb in 1892 and 1894 threatened black-belt and conservative Democratic supremacy. In 1892 Kolb was credited with 47.5 per cent of the popular vote of the state. It seems to be conceded that in 1894 he was counted out in the black belt and the state was saved from the dire results of Populism.

Although in moments of crisis—generated either by objective conditions or the exhortations of a colorful leader—Alabama voters divide along lines that parallel their conflicting hopes and aspirations in state policy, this type of division is exceptional. The transient factions within the Democratic party do not provide the organization with leadership necessary for a consistent politics of issues. Without the leadership of competing cliques of politicians bound together election after election by the hope for electoral victory, the voters go willy-nilly into the camp of this and that leader, influenced by considerations of localism, by the prompting of local bosses, and in no small measure by sheer chance. Such leadership as exists in state politics is furnished by individuals who rise from primary to primary on their own motion and attempt to construct a personal following.

3. The Transient Nature of Personal Factions

The kaleidoscopic alignment and realignment, combination and recombination of Alabama voters differ markedly from electoral behavior in two-party states where each party attracts and holds the support of a bloc of voters that remains relatively stable from election to election. Paralleling these cohesive blocs of loyal Republican and Democratic voters in two-party states are relatively cohesive groups of leaders who work more or less in concert from election to election. They provide a somewhat orderly and systematic means for the development and grooming of candidates and a continuity of personnel that encourages at least a germinal sense of group responsibility for party action. In contrast, each leader of a personal faction in a state such as Alabama must build his own coterie of leaders from the ground up—having no party machinery on which to rely. State-wide leaders do not emerge from the competition within a coterie of party leaders. They are self-appointed and self-anointed and attract to themselves sub-leaders by favor, chance, or demagogic skill. Perhaps a clue to the picturesque quality of many southern political leaders lies in the fact that attention-attracting antics function as a substitute for party machinery in the organization of support.

Personalization of leadership fractionalizes the electorate. It results in a multiplicity of citizen groupings, each around its own leader. Broad movements of citizen opinion cannot make themselves felt through any group that works to control all offices. The common leadership concerned with both state and Federal offices characteristic of Virginia, for example, has little parallel in Alabama. Temporary alliances of convenience arise, but each officeholder has his own personal following, which he is careful not to compromise by entangling commitments.

Even candidates of quite similar general political views attract different popular followings. The confusing elements of localism, of personal followings, and perhaps of local vote manipulations appear in a comparison of the county-by-county vote for "Big Jim" Folsom in the gubernatorial primary of June 4, 1946, and that for John Sparkman in the special senatorial primary held on July 30, 1946. Sparkman, like Folsom, hailed from northern Alabama and expressed generally a progressive point of view. Many of Folsom's campaign workers moved over to labor in the Sparkman cause and in general the same crowd supported both. If the factional alignments among the voters had any consistency, it would be expected that Sparkman would be strong in the areas in which Folsom had been strong, weak where Folsom had been weak in the voting of sixty days earlier. The relation between the county-by-county popular strength of the two candidates is charted in the scatter-diagram in Figure 7.[12]

The chart aids in comprehending the nature of factionalism under a one-party system. In the senatorial primary, Sparkman opposed Frank W. Boykin, Congressman from Mobile, and James A. Simpson, Birmingham corporation lawyer. Under a politics of principle, Sparkman would be expected to inherit the Folsom vote of two months earlier, with the Ellis vote of the earlier campaign divided between Boykin and Simpson. While

---

[12] For the general reader, an explanation of the scatter-diagram is obviously in order. The diagram provides a simple way to show graphically the relation between two sets of figures. Each tiny circle on the diagram in Figure 7 is located to show the percentage of a county's vote going to Sparkman and the percentage going to Folsom. That is, the circle is placed at the intersection of lines drawn from the lower and left scales of Sparkman and Folsom strength. If both candidates had had precisely the same popular strength in every county in the two primaries, all the tiny circles would have fallen along a straight line. The strength of one candidate would have varied, from county to county, directly with that of the other. The inference from such a diagram would have been that a tight, state-wide organization existed which could deliver about the same vote everywhere to one candidate as to another. (See the diagram in Figure 9 on p. 51 showing the relation from county to county in the vote for two Democratic gubernatorial candidates in Indiana.) On the other hand, when the counties are dispersed on the diagram, a less close relation between the strength of two candidates prevails and it is a fair inference that a loosely organized factionalism prevails. In the Folsom-Sparkman diagram the chart itself contains some explanation of why particular groups of counties showed markedly different degrees of popular support for the two candidates. To the technician, it should be said that this simple and crude sort of statistical device is used on the assumption that it is both adequate for the present purpose and more comprehensible to the general reader than a conventional technical presentation.

a rough correspondence existed in the distribution of the Folsom and Sparkman strength, extraordinary exceptions also manifested themselves. Folsom carried the counties within his friends-and-neighbors sphere by huge majorities, but this strength could not be transferred intact to

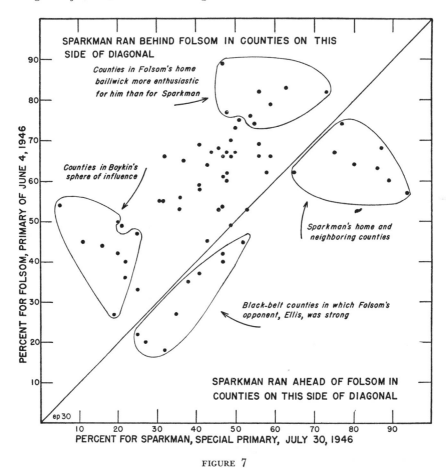

FIGURE 7

Fluidity of Conservative-Progressive Groupings of Voters: Relation between Percentages of Vote Polled in Alabama Counties by Folsom in Gubernatorial Primary of June 4, 1946, and by Sparkman in Senatorial Primary of July 30, 1946

Sparkman. Similarly, in the counties in Boykin's congressional district Folsom attracted much heavier support than Sparkman could. It is an indication either of vote manipulation or of the influence of completely irrelevant considerations when Washington County casts 54.5 per cent of its vote for Folsom, a progressive candidate, and sixty days later marks only 5.4 per cent of its ballots for Sparkman, a like-minded candidate, because of its preference for Boykin, known generally as a conservative.

The same tendency, to a lesser degree, made itself felt in the other counties in Boykin's local sphere of influence.

In certain counties Sparkman made a stronger showing than Folsom had. Again elements of localism provide the explanation. In his home county and in the other counties of the congressional district that he had served for ten years, Sparkman drew a heavier vote than Folsom had drawn. Similarly, he ran ahead of Folsom in a handful of black-belt counties in which Folsom's opponent, Handy Ellis, had been strong. Ellis had been able to command an extremely heavy vote for himself in these counties, but the same general forces of conservatism could not deliver the vote in the same degree to nonlocal candidates against Sparkman, the progressive candidate.

Personal followings cohere so weakly that the leader can only within severe limits hold his following together from election to election for himself, much less transfer his support to some other candidate. The looseness of factional ties is illustrated by the vote for Frank Dixon for governor in the primaries of June 12, 1934, and of May 3, 1938. He polled 46.3 per cent of the total vote in the 1934 primary and lost the nomination to Bibb Graves, while in 1938 he drew the ballots of 48.6 per cent of those voting and won the governorship.[13] In general, he was strong in 1938 where he had been strong in 1934, as may be seen in the scatter-diagram in Figure 8. Yet the correspondence in distribution of strength in the two primaries was not extremely close and in some counties his proportion of the popular vote was cut in half or more from 1934 to 1938. In these counties in 1938 he encountered the competition of Goode and Sparks whose candidacies induced their friends and neighbors to renounce their 1934 affections for Dixon.[14] When a county goes 40 per cent for a candidate at one election and four years later casts only 10 per cent of its vote for him, factions are built upon something other than persistent attachment either to principle or personality.

The amorphous character of Alabama factions emerges graphically by contrast with the behavior of voters in a two-party state. Dixon's followers, as demonstrated by the data in Figure 8, manifested in some cases an extreme fickleness and in others a fair degree of loyalty over a four-year period. Contrast the scatter-diagram in Figure 9 comparing the county-by-county distribution of strength of two different Democratic candidates for the governorship of Indiana, Henry Schricker in 1940 and Samuel D. Jackson in 1944. An extremely close relation prevailed between the Democratic strength in every county in 1940 and 1944. The traditional party affiliations of voters and party organization coherence in such a state far

[13] Although he lacked a majority in 1938 by a narrow margin, no run-off primary was held.

[14] See the geographical distribution of the 1938 vote for Goode and Sparks in Figure 5, p. 41.

exceed in durability the groupings of voters in Alabama personal factions.

Of all the personal machines or factions of this century in Alabama, the one built up by the late Bibb Graves has won the greatest renown. Graves, an able man but not notable as the exponent of any particular

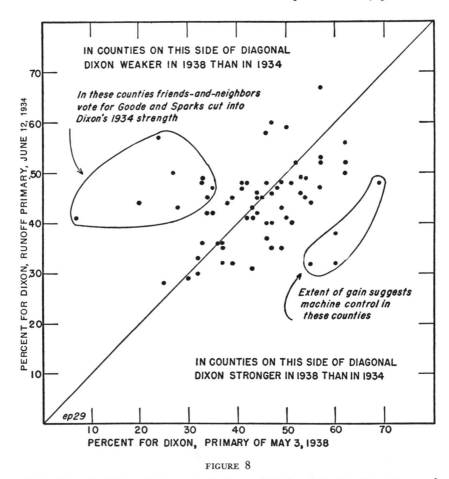

FIGURE 8

Amorphous Qualities of Personal Factions: Relation between Percentages of Vote Polled in Alabama Counties by Frank Dixon in Gubernatorial Primaries of June 12, 1934, and May 3, 1938

philosophy or point of view in politics, served as governor from 1927–31, and from 1935–39, and would have been elected again in 1942 had death not overtaken him during the campaign. In his long political career he gathered about himself a popular following that coincided with no apparent natural grouping of voters. The area of his highest popular strength wove in and out of the black belt—with its center of gravity there—and in and out of northern Alabama in a manner completely at variance with the way Alabama voters divide when the chips are down in a battle over issues comprehensible to them.

"A natural-born dealer"—thus he is described by his friends and associates. "He would deal with anybody on anything," one of them

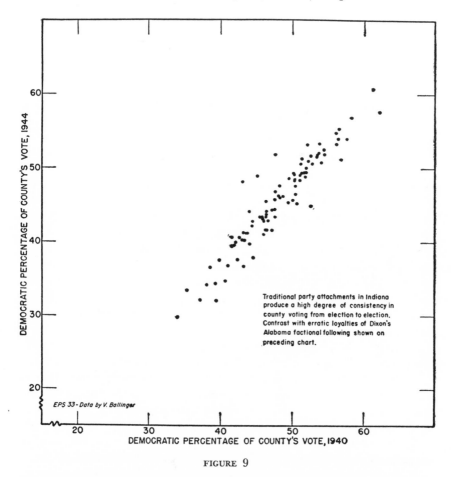

Traditional party attachments in Indiana produce a high degree of consistency in county voting from election to election. Contrast with erratic loyalties of Dixon's Alabama factional following shown on preceding chart.

EPS 33 - Data by V. Ballinger

DEMOCRATIC PERCENTAGE OF COUNTY'S VOTE, 1940

FIGURE 9

Two-Party Stability and Consistency in Party Affiliation: Relation between Percentages of County Vote Polled by Democratic Candidates for Governor of Indiana in General Elections of 1940 and 1944

reports but with no suggestion of personal dishonesty. Unencumbered by ideological fixations, he impressed local politicians over the state as a practical man who could and would do business with them to meet the immediate practical problems of governing with mutually beneficial results. With the friends produced by favors and the expectation of favors, he bound to himself an essentially personal following. Graves served as state adjutant-general from 1907 to 1911 and as the colonel of an Alabama regiment in World War I. He endeared himself to his men. Campaigners in later years were amazed by the number of his erstwhile comrades in arms who idolized the colonel and talked him up in their communities. He ran for governor in 1922 and made a poor showing. In 1926, with the support of the Ku Klux Klan added to his veteran following, he became governor and proceeded to organize a following that re-elected him in 1934.[15]

In campaigning he guided himself by the advice of his local friends. His speeches began with generalizations about his program but soon got down to specifics: the ten-mile stretch of road in the county over which a crow couldn't fly. He was not unwilling to divert a road from a bee-line course so that it would go by the home of a legislator or through the land of citizens influential in the locality. He lent a sympathetic ear to requests for pardons and paroles. A legislator or other local leader would explain to the Governor the great pressure on him to get old Bill out of the pen. The local bigwig might admit that old Bill probably belonged in the pen, but after all Aunt Sue was a pretty respectable citizen and old Bill was up for only a year and had already served six months. On all such questions Graves leaned heavily on his lieutenants and advisers in the localities immediately concerned, and thereby tied them to himself. By all the standard methods a personal following was pieced together, but the faction thus formed had a life little longer than that of its leader. In 1938 it divided between Goode and Sparks, and Dixon—with exceptions—was strong where Graves had been weak in 1934. By 1946 the Graves faction had dissolved.

Friends and favors, perquisites which are everywhere the usual practices of politics, take on a special significance in one-party states. In a two-party state a nominee for governor, say, has a ready-made machine of sorts; he has a following among the voters that will support him, as the nominee of the party, through thick and thin. He has only to strengthen an organization that already exists, to enlarge the loyal party following by the recruitment of the independent and wavering vote. In a one-party state, such as Alabama, the building of a faction by a state-wide leader must start almost at the bottom, and an especially heavy reliance probably has to be placed on the dispensation of favors, on the promise of favors, and on the appeal of individual personality.

4. Channels to the Voter

In a factional politics in which party organization plays no role in the appeal for voter support in primary campaigns, political leaders must

---

[15] The fact that an Alabama governor cannot succeed himself perhaps contributes to the chaos of factionalism. After a governor has served his four years, everyone has to choose up sides again and start the battle over.

improvise machinery for reaching the voter and consolidating their support. This informal machinery naturally takes on a highly complex form; it consists in essence of all the centers of influence within the electorate that can be attached to the cause of a particular leader. Factional machinery is generally of two broad kinds: first, that created for other purposes which is converted to campaigning purposes, such as governmental organizations and private nonparty associations; second, the essentially personal organization built up by each candidate among his acquaintances, admirers, and followers. No generalizations can be made about the second type; it differs enormously from faction to faction. However, several nonparty associations and governmental organizations often constitute important cogs in factional machinery.

According to the usual interpretation of southern politics, each state has a state-wide machine firmly based on county rings. Virginia fits the conventional stereotype. The state leaders of the Byrd machine keep firmly in hand the activities of county machines which accept its leadership in state politics. Alabama presents a more complex, and more usual, situation. No continuing or dominant state boards of strategy seem to exist; the county machines, such as they are, play a more independent role.

The chief figure in the governments of about two-thirds of the counties of Alabama is the probate judge, who serves as chairman of the governing board. In the other counties a chairman is either popularly elected or designated by the board. The probate judge generally is the leader of the dominant faction within the county and often becomes the patriarch of the county. In many counties the potency of the probate judge demonstrates itself by a long string of re-elections.[16]

As the principal factotum in local affairs, the support of the probate judge is eagerly sought by candidates for state-wide office. Although the Association of County Commissioners, to which the probate judges belong, officially endorses no candidates, its meetings provide occasion for intense politicking by the friends of aspirants. Yet only within limits can the probate judge openly ally himself with a state-wide candidate; probably within lesser limits he can swing the vote of the county, although it must be said that his position differs greatly from county to county.[17]

[16] Writing of a black-belt county in 1941, Karl Bosworth reported: "In the important position of probate judge there have been only four incumbents since 1886. Since 1904 no clerk of the circuit court has left that office except to become probate judge, two having followed that channel of succession. . . . Tax collectors have left office in the last 36 years only with the discovery of shortages in their funds, and in each of the two such cases the person appointed to fill out the unexpired terms has been elected and reelected."—*Black Belt County* (University, Ala.: Bureau of Public Administration, University of Alabama, 1941), p. 11. In another county that came to our attention the probate judge was retiring at the end of 42 years' service. Tenure of county officials tends to be shorter outside the black belt.

[17] Within the black-belt county analyzed by Bosworth, the voter cleavage resembled somewhat the cleavage within the state in the Folsom-Ellis contest commented on

When county officials attempt to swing the local vote for a candidate for governor, a prime consideration is their forecast of which candidate will win. Probate judges are the ambassadors of their counties in dealing with the governor and state departments. Quite apart from obtaining favorable treatment for their counties, it is important for their local prestige that they be on good enough terms with the governor to be received with promptness and deference. To guess right on the outcome of a gubernatorial campaign will bring kudos to the probate judge in his ability to obtain action on highway questions, local appointments, and other matters by state departments. The governor's intervention may be helpful on questions of local legislation, which are important for Alabama county government.

Some probate judges are so strongly entrenched that they can go all out for a candidate for governor; others either work quietly or not at all. They fear that they will suffer in their local contests by the criss-crossing of lines in the balloting for state and local office. If they endorse Dixon, or Graves, or Folsom, they may antagonize their own supporters among the opponents of such state candidates. In Alabama the election calendar creates special conditions governing the activity of county officers in state campaigns. The probate judge serves for six years; the governor, for four years. When the races for the two offices coincide, the probate judge must watch carefully his entanglements with state candidates. When the probate judge is not seeking re-election, he has greater freedom in his support of a gubernatorial candidate. Sheriffs, who serve for four years and must always seek re-election at the time of the gubernatorial campaign, more generally than the probate judges cannot afford to cross themselves up locally by taking an active part in a state campaign.

Alabama, on the whole, appears to occupy a mid-position among southern states with respect to the place of courthouse rings in state politics. In a few states local officials have so tenuous a hold over their local constituents that they are fearful of involving themselves in state campaigns. At the other extreme, county rings are closely integrated with a state faction. Probably the strength and role of county rings in state politics has been generally misinterpreted. The control of a county determines which individuals of the political class—planters, lawyers, merchants, professional politicians—enjoy the perquisites available locally. But in state elections it may be that the county machine tends to "swing" the vote in the way the voters would go anyway. In exceptional instances, of course, local machines can swing the vote at will. It is probable that in

---

earlier in this chapter. Within even a black-belt county there are, of course, variations in the types of soil and in the proportions of Negro population. The probate judge of the county, a spokesman for the conservative, planter-official class, in one county election analyzed "got 78 per cent of the vote in the black belt beats, 62 per cent in the midlands, and only 29 per cent in the uplands."—Bosworth, *Black Belt County*, p. 14.

all counties their capacity to swing the vote increases as the issues in state campaigns are blurred.

Each Senator and Representative, through long tenure and the consequent opportunity to build a following piece by piece, has an organization of sorts independent of factions and organizations developed in battles for the governorship. Occasionally the leaders of these "Federal" factions attempt to deliver their following to a candidate for some other office, but more generally they are, like county leaders, wary of alliances that might split their own following.

Some Alabama cities and towns have had political machines, the most notable being that of Montgomery. Town politicians have much the same relation to state-wide campaigns as their county counterparts. The secretary of the Alabama League of Municipalities has managed several state-wide races, but the League does not officially endorse candidates.

A ready-made group that can be used in state campaigning consists of state employees. They often take a hand in campaigns, but they are not ordinarily integrated into a single machine. Practice and attitude differ from department to department. The State Agricultural Extension Service has a reputation for a more continuous activity in campaigns for Federal and state office than any other state agency. Its network of county agents provides a channel to the farmers, especially the more prosperous farmers. Its political work, carried on in close collaboration with the Alabama Farm Bureau Federation whose membership is recruited in considerable measure by the farm agents, has to be conducted discreetly because of Federal rules against political activity. Those familiar with the Service report that the political word sometimes, but not always, in the past has gone down from Auburn, the Service headquarters. In 1946, for example, extension workers supported Joe Poole, State Commissioner of Agriculture, for governor but he failed to win a place in the run-off primary. The Extension Service and Farm Bureau team seems to exert more compelling power in lobbying and in campaigns on constitutional amendments than in campaigns for office.

In 1947 the Extension Service demonstrated its political potency by administering defeat to Governor Folsom. The Governor—a spokesman of the branch-heads rather than of big farmers—appointed trustees to fill vacancies in the Board of Trustees of Alabama Polytechnic Institute, the governing authority of the Service. He won from the board unanimous approval of a resolution critical of the Service for failure to co-operate with other agricultural agencies, for failure to aid farmer-owned co-operatives, for manipulation of the Farm Bureau, and for political activities.[18] The Farm Bureau, generally reputed to be in this state a tool of the Extension Service rather than vice versa, rose to the defense of the Service and charged that the Governor sought to "destroy the force

[18] *Birmingham News*, February 22, 1947.

of the Farm Bureau and to establish in its stead the philosophy of the
Farmers Union-CIO." [19] The Farmers Union, unconnected with the CIO,
had few members in Alabama; the Extension Service organization
drummed up members only for the Farm Bureau, whose president sued
to challenge the right of the governor's interim appointees to the board
of trustees to serve until confirmed. In subsequent maneuvers the Extension Service forces licked the governor hands down in the legislature
on confirmation of his appointees. "It is common knowledge," the *Birmingham Age-Herald* commented, "that the extension service has been
up to its neck in factional politics." [20]

The Extension Service-big-farmer amalgam, which covers the entire
state but is most potent in the black belt, usually teams up with the big
money interests, according to most participants and observers of Alabama
politics. The "big mules"—steel, coal, iron, insurance, utilities—possess
few votes of their own, but they control campaign funds and command
the loyalties of many individuals influential with the electorate. The
"interests" apparently possess no formal organization for political action
in gubernatorial campaigns, but they gravitate in each campaign toward
a candidate likely to be favorable to their point of view. Among the corporate interests, as among county rings, informed observers conclude,
there is a tendency to back the person most likely to win. This sort of
band-wagon behavior, of course, makes sense only when the issues are not
drawn and you can do business with whoever wins. The "big mules" probably exert their strength far more effectively in the politics of legislation
than in gubernatorial campaigns. And it is mainly in the legislature that
questions of concern to them are settled: measures of taxation and regulation. In the legislature the points of local contact by the "big mules"
with the electorate—local attorneys on retainer and the like—may reflect
themselves in favorable votes.

In a few scattered localities labor unions perform the party functions
of arousing the voter and getting him to the polls. Thus, in the unsuccessful campaign for the re-election of Luther Patrick to Congress from the
Birmingham district in 1946 the PAC carried almost the entire burden
of the campaign. In the 1946 gubernatorial campaign the PAC bought

[19] Ibid., February 23, 1947. At its 1946 state convention the Farmers Union "went
on record for abolition of the poll tax, reapportionment of the state legislature, a
broad health program within the reach of all classes, a $40 per month old age pension
without the 'pauper' requirement to qualify, an increase in teachers' salaries and employment of teachers on a 12-month basis, and a fair wage and social security program."
These resolutions, the *Limestone Democrat* (Athens, Ala.), December 4, 1946, argued,
"should allay some of the fears of that group of Alabamians to whom the mere mention" of the Farmers Union "conjures up Communist boogey-men under the nearest
bed."

[20] *Birmingham Age-Herald*, March 5, 1947. The new president of the Alabama
Polytechnic Institute in 1948 announced a policy of nonintervention in factional politics
for the Extension Service.

radio time to use in support of Folsom, and in a few localities unions can deliver their vote in county and city campaigns. In a state predominantly rural and agricultural, labor organizations can play only a limited role in state politics, and in the areas of working population its potential political strength has not been realized because of Alabama's suffrage limitations. Further, mobilization of the labor vote has been comparatively ineffectively conducted, although the CIO-PAC has introduced new standards of efficiency.

Although the Alabama Education Association officially endorses no candidates, teachers constitute a significant bloc in state politics and their support is sought by candidates for state-wide office. The principal concern of the teaching group is compensation levels and related questions of educational policy. Their interest in these matters has perforce thrown them on the progressive, higher-expenditure side. "Big Jim" Folsom in 1946 won the support of many teachers through his promise of a minimum salary of $1800, which was coupled with a program for old-age pensions of $45 per month. Subsequently a wedge was driven into the teachers-old folks coalition when the legislature proposed and the electorate approved an amendment to give more funds to schools. The old folks were left out in the cold and Folsom was left stranded with them. He opposed the measure to benefit teachers only.

In the final analysis, the organizational structure of the amorphous factions of Alabama politics defy general description. Absence of the pooling of organization that prevails for virtually all candidates of each party in a two-party state multiplies factional organization. And each state-wide organization takes on a different form and consists of a combination of persons different from that of any other organization. In intrastate politics absence of the organizing influence of party probably compels a heavier reliance than in two-party states on the use of private associations and of persons of prestige in nonparty groups as the unit cells of factions and as avenues to reach the voter.

Chapter Four

TENNESSEE:

THE CIVIL WAR AND MR. CRUMP

HAVE said before, and I repeat it now," wrote E. H. Crump in an advertisement in Tennessee's 1948 campaign, "that in the art galleries of Paris there are twenty-seven pictures of Judas Iscariot— none look alike but all resemble Gordon Browning; that neither his head, heart nor hand can be trusted; that he would milk his neighbor's cow through a crack in the fence; that, of the two hundred and six bones in his body there isn't one that is genuine; that his heart has beaten over two billion times without a single sincere beat." [1] Thus did the boss of Memphis and of Tennessee characterize Gordon Browning, the opposition candidate for governor. In speaking of the opposition senatorial candidate, Estes Kefauver, Crump was more temperate. He likened Kefauver to a pet coon "that puts its foot in an open drawer in your room, but invariably turns its head while its foot is feeling around in the drawer. The coon hopes, through its cunning by turning its head, he will deceive any onlookers as to where his foot is and what it is into." [2] The allegory introduced the campaign charge that Kefauver was in reality a "darling of the Communists" who was "desperately trying to cover up his very bad record." Kefauver put on a coonskin cap, honorable badge of the pioneer, and made political hay. He might be a pet coon, he conceded, but he was not Crump's pet coon.

[1] Political advertisement in *Memphis Press-Scimitar,* July 21, 1948.
[2] Political advertisement in *Memphis Press-Scimitar,* June 10, 1948.

The pet coon charge boomeranged and Crump's candidates, for the first time in many years, went down to defeat. The papers, with some extravagance, called it "the end of an era." Perhaps it was, but more fundamently the 1948 primaries marked the defeat of Crump's coalition by a combination resembling the faction he had ousted from control of the state in 1932.

Tennessee's factional politics has a character all its own. The peculiar form of the coalitions and combinations that struggle for control of the state grow out of geographical diversity and the powerful influences of long-past events on the voting behavior of its citizens. Tennessee is a narrow ribbon of real estate stretching from North Carolina to the Mississippi. From Bristol, in the far northeast, to Memphis, in the southwest, about equals the distance from Hartford, Connecticut, to Cleveland, Ohio. Tennessee's far western counties are but northward projections of Mississippi; its eastern mountain counties share both the topography and spirit of western North Carolina and southwestern Virginia. Between West Tennessee and East Tennessee lies Middle Tennessee, a fertile bowl, sometimes called locally the "dimple of the universe," whose principal city is Nashville. To the problems of political management inherent in three distinct geographical sections are added patterns of political behavior deposited by the Civil War. In 1861 East Tennessee had few slaves and was unionist; West and Middle Tennessee held slaves and Confederate sentiments. Today East Tennessee harbors many Republicans while Middle and West Tennessee are Democratic strongholds.

1. Matrix for Minority Rule

For a decade and a half prior to 1948 the boss of one county, E. H. Crump of Shelby, dominated the politics of Tennessee. For an even longer period his influence was great, and his 1948 defeat by no means assured his political demise. He still controlled every important office in Memphis and Shelby County, at least one Congressman, one United States Senator, and had political allies all over the state. A canny old fox, who had overcome many a setback in the past, his age offered far more hope to the opposition than his loss of a campaign. Unlike Virginia, where the machine is deeply rooted in the social fabric of the state, the Tennessee organization is a highly personal operation of Mr. Crump. He heads no well-ordered hierarchy that will, through the normal processes of indoctrination, testing, and advancement, produce a successor to himself.

Tennessee's division into geographical-historical blocs provides an explanation of how Crump was able to pyramid his dominance of Memphis into control of the state. An important element in the political arithmetic by which Memphis became the keystone of the controlling coalition consisted of the political inertness of from three-fourths to four-fifths of the potential electorate. Rarely does more than one-fourth of Tennesseans of voting age participate in the choice of a governor. When over a million politically inert citizens are written off, Tennessee political leaders have to worry about only 450,000 persons, more or less, who vote either in the Democratic primary or the general election.[3] The details of fluctuations in the number of voters appear in Table 4. Of the 400,000

TABLE 4

Voting for Tennessee Governors: Estimates of Maximum Number of Citizens Voting in Either the Democratic Primary or the General Election

YEAR	ESTIMATED CITIZENS 21 AND OVER	MAXIMUM NUMBER VOTING [a]	PER CENT VOTING
1920	1,208,228	417,146 [b]	34.5
1922	1,249,264	265,647	21.3
1924	1,290,300	283,230 [b]	21.9
1926	1,331,336	233,246	17.5
1928	1,372,372	342,405	24.9
1930	1,413,414	331,873	23.5
1932	1,471,390	404,963	27.5
1936	1,587,342	436,279	27.5
1938	1,645,318	477,134	29.0
1940	1,703,299	448,720 [b]	26.3
1942	1,693,206	348,317	20.6
1944	1,631,581	441,191 [b]	27.0
1946	1,744,363	386,027	22.1

[a] The estimate was arrived at by the following method: If the total Democratic primary vote exceeded the Democratic vote in the general election, the number participating in the Democratic primary was added to the Republican vote for governor in the general election. Otherwise, the total vote in the general election was used.

[b] Total votes for all candidates for governor in the general election. The figures not so designated were derived by the method stated in the note above.

plus who vote at one step or another in the process of choosing a governor, the Republicans normally can be dismissed, for they usually have no effect on the outcome.

If the Republicans are regarded as of no consequence most of the time in state-wide elections, around 100,000 voters can be eliminated from the calculations of those seeking to control the state government. The political impotence of Republicans in state affairs reduces the size of the effective electorate. More important, by simply being Republican these 100,-000 or so citizens may load the dice in favor of one or the other Democratic faction. If they were either all in the Democratic party or if there were a straight-out two-party battle, the nature and relative strength of the competitors for control of the state might be quite different. Repub-

[3] For comparative analyses of voter participation in elections, see chaps. 23 and 24.

licanism has had, at least for over two decades, about the same effect for gubernatorial politics as abstention from voting. And these "abstainers," as inspection of Table 5 will show, have been numerous enough to tip the scales in battles between Democratic factions had they participated on one side or the other of the real politics of the state.

After making allowance for nonvoters and for Republicans, the strategy of control of the state becomes a problem of winning a majority of 300,000 voters, more or less, of the potential electorate of 1,600,000 or more. The factional division of these 300,000 voters in the Democratic primaries has, over the years, given Crump a pivotal position through his control of the vote of Memphis. In most Democratic counties of Tennessee, according to old-time politicians, at least two factions compete for

TABLE 5

Political Eunuchs: Republicans in Tennessee Gubernatorial Campaigns

YEAR	TOTAL VOTF IN DEMOCRATIC PRIMARY	VOTE FOR DEMOCRATIC NOMINEE	PLURALITY OF DEMOCRATIC NOMINEE	REPUBLICAN VOTE IN GENERAL ELECTION
1920	113,972	67,886	23,033	229,143
1922	163,061	63,940	4.018	102,586
1924	158,230	125,031	91,832	121,228
1926	187,008	96,545	8,097	46,238
1928	217,672	97,333	5,316	124,733
1930	246,275	144,990	43,705	85,598
1932	283,566	116,022	9,572	121,397
1936	357,987	243,463	134,293	78,292
1938	394,103	231,852	72,998	83,031
1940	284,549	237,319	193,197	125,244
1942	297,197	171,259	47,222	51,120
1944	151,635	132,466	120,807	158,742
1946	312,806	187,119	66,584	73,222
1948	431,596	240,676	56,728	179,957

control of the county government. When state offices are at issue, one county faction is almost honor bound to support the state-wide candidate opposed by its local enemy. Consequently each of any two candidates for state-wide nomination with any prospect or hope of victory will poll a considerable vote. When candidates compete on more or less even terms outside Memphis and it is necessary to amass only a little more than 150,-000 votes to win the Democratic nomination, the man with 50,000 votes from Memphis' Shelby County in his vest pocket holds more than a balance of power.

For a long series of elections Crump had so thoroughly intimidated opposition in Memphis that his candidates for state office received 85 per cent or more of the Shelby County vote. In practice, his candidates did not depend entirely on the vote of Memphis. They usually polled more than 51 per cent of the primary vote and received less than a third of their vote from Memphis.[4] The mere existence of a large block of votes—almost a third of the primary total—that could be manipulated at will constituted a powerful weapon for the demoralization of the opposition.

In 1948, when a few Memphis citizens of substance dared oppose Crump's candidates, the critical role of Memphis became apparent. The opposition outside Memphis took heart when the organization was challenged on its home grounds and when there was promise of a free and fair election there. Although Crump's candidates led in Shelby County, they led by reduced majorities. The assault on Memphis struck at the keystone of Crump's structure of state-wide power, and even a modicum of success in attack there brought the entire structure tumbling down. Yet, given Memphis' tradition of machine rule, it would be rash to predict that the same power combination could not again be built on the ruins.

2. Mr. Crump's Organization

Although secure in Memphis and Shelby County, the roots of Crump's power within the state have never been deep. Long before the 1948 upset even the weakest opposition candidate for state office always made a respectable showing against his organization. The country boy who subdued Memphis simply outsmarted the opposition in the state. Even Crump's opponents, as fellow professionals, express admiration for his technical virtuosity as a politician. Essentially, however, his state-wide power rested on a system of shifting alliances with local leaders outside Memphis, alliances that often became relations of subordination.

Crump's bargaining power with these leaders came basically from his control of Memphis.[5] In delivering overwhelming votes from Shelby County to his candidates for governor and Senator, Crump did not simply ride the popular wave; he steered the Memphis vote as he wished. Consider the history of Gordon Browning. In 1934 he ran for the Senate and in all of Shelby County 5,444 votes were recorded for him. In 1936, in favor with Crump, Shelby gave him 59,874 votes in his successful gubernatorial campaign. In 1938, out of favor with Crump, Browning ran again and only 9,315 of the fickle citizens of Memphis voted for him.

How much fraud has entered into the Memphis vote is a moot point. Many Tennesseans believe that the Shelby organization has exercised some discretion in counting the ballots, although the chances are that

[4] The percentage of the vote of the candidate winning the Democratic gubernatorial nomination that came from Shelby County in recent primaries has been as follows: 1946, 24.3; 1944, 16.6; 1940, 16.7; 1938, 24.7. Even in 1948 Crump's candidate for governor polled 70 per cent of Shelby's vote.

[5] On Memphis politics, see G. M. Capers in R. S. Allen's symposium, *Our Fair City* (New York: Vanguard Press, 1947), chap. 10.

arithmetical enthusiasm is of less importance than the herding of the voters to the polls. Illustrative of the popular belief is a legend of the 1926 primary between Peay and Crump's candidate, McAllister. A Nashville organization adviser "talked with Memphis" about midnight of election day and reported that, on the basis of returns from the rest of the state, a 15,000 majority from Shelby for McAllister would turn the trick.[6] Shelby was so reported, but around 7 o'clock the next morning returns from the remote hill counties gave Peay enough votes to overcome his deficit in Memphis. In 1948 opposition leaders attributed their "success" in Memphis—about 30 per cent of the vote—to the wholesome influence of alert and unintimidated watchers at the polls.

Control of Memphis has given Crump a powerful persuader in the recruitment of allies. Senator Kenneth D. McKellar, for example, once enjoyed a degree of independence, but Crump's Memphis votes and tactical skill converted the senior Senator into a junior partner. In 1936 Senator McKellar sponsored Burgin E. Dossett for the Democratic gubernatorial nomination without obtaining Crump's approval. Gordon Browning then entered the contest. Crump, playing his role of a wily old fox, withheld indication of his preference. He waited and he waited. People all over Tennessee worked themselves into a state of suspense. What would Crump do? What he did, they came to believe, would determine the outcome. Crump bided his time, and perhaps sounded sentiment a bit while waiting. Finally, he announced for Browning. Dossett's headquarters took on the hush of a funeral parlor and some of his county campaign offices closed up. He could not raise a dime for campaign expenses. A reporter remarked to him that Crump's announcement sort of left him out on a limb. "Limb, hell!" was the reply, "Out on a twig." In Shelby County Mr. Dossett received 825 of over 60,000 votes. In Senator McKellar's home precinct in Memphis, Dossett got three votes.[7]

Although his Memphis machine was the key to Crump's control of Tennessee, it merits no special attention. Its only special characteristic is its insistence that it does not steal from the public till, and, indeed, evidence to the contrary would be difficult to find. Crump's critics—who have been few in Memphis—generally concede that they have efficient government, a clean city, and other blessings, but all without freedom or liberty. Crump's assiduous dissemination of a picture of himself as the provider of a reform administration undoubtedly adds to his strength in the city,

[6] Persons who supported Governor Peay claim credit for planting the seeds of optimism in McAllister headquarters. They arranged for telegrams from several eastern Tennessee cities to the McAllister headquarters in Nashville reporting that Governor Peay was leading by smaller majorities than was actually the case. These reports stimulated high glee in McAllister headquarters and also formed the basis for the estimate of the required majority from Shelby.

[7] Jennings Perry, *Democracy Begins at Home* (Philadelphia: J. B. Lippincott Company, 1944), p. 28.

but his organization supplements the high moral appeal with most of the standard machine techniques. Business gets what it wants—unless it crosses Crump—and has been counted as a cog in his organization. But businessmen—big and little—have scarcely been able to call their souls their own. The fear of the boosted tax valuation, the overly technical enforcement of some obscure city ordinance, the loss of city business, and any one of a dozen other weapons to discipline—whether ever used— have made the citizens of Memphis speak with pride of Crump.

A breach in business solidarity came in 1948 when a handful of business and professional men dared to support Kefauver for the Senate in opposition to Crump's candidate. Historically, however, potential opposition was silenced and control of the city boiled down to the routine task of qualifying the voters and getting them out to the polls. A machine, manned in large measure by city employees, performed these duties as efficiently as it managed primaries and elections. In 1946, for example, the CIO trained a couple of hundred watchers in Shelby County. By the end of primary day the CIO had watchers at two voting places. Some did not show up at the polls; others were chased away; still others wound up in jail. The organization's coolness toward the CIO makes for it no enemies among the middle and upper classes of Memphis.

In the whole scenario Crump personally is portrayed as a political anachronism—an old-time political boss dispensing largesse to the poor and downtrodden. Annually he stages a boat ride for orphans and shut-ins. Free candy, apples, cookies, and soda pop are featured. When the circus comes to town Mr. Crump takes with him the same boys and girls. "And I'll have more fun than all the rest of them together," he said in 1946 as he reserved 361 seats.[8] Let a home burn and Crump will send checks to the unfortunate. An indubitably genuine spirit of beneficence redounds to organization advantage.

Crump was boss in Memphis long before he extended his domain over the state. During the 1920's he lost state campaigns to Luke Lea's organization which was based on Nashville. Finally, however, Crump almost entirely liquidated his opposition in Memphis, the city's voting population grew more rapidly than that of the rest of the state, and Luke Lea got into trouble. In 1930 a bank in which Lea was interested closed with state deposits of over $3,000,000. The ensuing revelations discredited the Lea organization and Crump moved in. His candidate, Hill McAllister, who had been unsuccessful in 1926 and 1928, won the Democratic gubernatorial nomination in 1932 as a "reform" candidate.[9]

Simultaneously with Crump's victory in the state in 1932, the Demo-

---

[8] *Memphis Press-Scimitar*, October 15, 1946.

[9] An excellent account of the political background appears in John Berry McFerrin, *Caldwell and Company, A Southern Financial Empire* (Chapel Hill: University of North Carolina Press, 1939), chaps. 11 and 17.

cratic party won control nationally. Kenneth McKellar, of Shelby County, the senior Senator, thereby gained access to a large store of patronage. He had a disposition to make the most of it. After some essays toward independence, he accepted a role as the number-two man in Tennessee, and the Crump organization had both state and Federal patronage with which to cement local organizations into a powerful state faction.

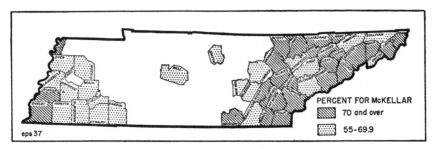

FIGURE 10

The Memphis–East Tennessee Coalition: Popular Vote for McKellar in 1946 Democratic Primary

The Crump faction, as it eventually took shape, had two main centers of heavy voting strength: Shelby and neighboring counties in western Tennessee and the Republican counties of eastern Tennessee. The common explanation of Crump strength in eastern Tennessee is that McKellar controlled these counties through Federal patronage. The state government, too, had means of winning friends and influencing people in these counties. Patronage in East Tennessee can exert exceptional influence, for here Republicans generally control local governments and local Democratic leaders must look to Nashville or Washington for their sustenance. A minority locally is always far more susceptible to central control than is the local majority, which can maintain itself on the spoils of local office. In only a few East Tennessee counties do Democrats win local elections. The exceptions, as often as not, are victories compounded of fraud and force: McMinn County, site of the battle of Athens, Tennessee, usually followed Crump in the Democratic primaries.[10] Polk County, province of the now twice defeated Biggs machine, regularly turned in incredible majorities for Crump candidates.

The traditional areas of greatest organization strength appear in the map in Figure 10, which identifies the counties with the highest vote for McKellar in the Democratic primary of 1946. The counties of Governor

[10] Politics is a hazardous calling in East Tennessee. The Cantrell machine of McMinn County, allied with Crump in the state, was ousted by a GI force equipped with superior fire power.—See T. H. White, "The Battle of Athens, Tennessee," Harper's Magazine, January, 1947. Three election-day killings in Polk County in August, 1948, necessitated mobilization of the National Guard to restore order.

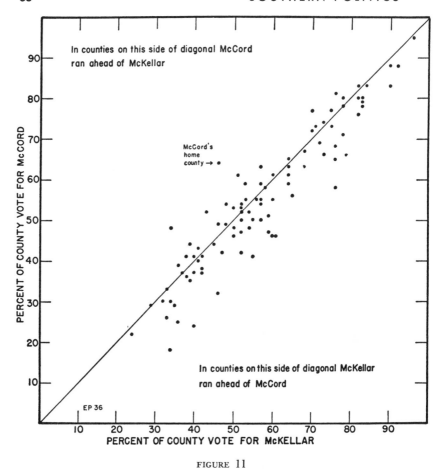

FIGURE 11

Machine Discipline in Tennessee: Correlation between Percentages of Popular Vote of Democratic Primary of 1946 Polled in Each County by Crump Candidates, McKellar and McCord

McCord's greatest strength in his unsuccessful 1948 race were, though fewer, similarly located in the east and west.

The degree to which the Crump organization became able to deliver its voters for its slate of candidates is suggested by Figure 11, which shows the relation between the per cent of the total vote in each county in the Democratic primary of 1946 for McCord, for governor, and the per cent for McKellar, for Senator. McCord is described by a fellow Tennessean as a former auctioneer with "a voice like a golden gong. A wonderful speechmaker. He never says a damn thing that means anything, but it certainly sounds good." McKellar at the time prided himself on having more people on the public payroll than any other man in Congress. Even his enemies conceded that he was indefatigable in his labors for Tennessee. Two such diverse characters might be expected to have different popular followings, but the Crump organization delivered fairly similar votes to each in most counties. In some places McCord ran ahead of Mc-Kellar; in others, McKellar was stronger. Yet withal a relatively high degree of factional discipline prevailed, less impressive than party attachments in two-party states but far tighter than prevails in states with loose factional systems, such as Alabama.[11]

Although the organization has had centers of consistent strength in Memphis and in East Tennessee, there has been considerable variation from primary to primary in the location of peaks in the organization vote. Fluctuations in organization strength in particular counties make it apparent that the system of alliances with county leaders has undergone frequent alteration. And the 1948 senatorial campaign spotlighted the fundamental character of the Crump following as an alliance-system rather than an ordinary organization. No "coalition campaign," as the Tennessee term goes, was conducted for McCord and Mitchell, the Crump gubernatorial and senatorial candidates, respectively. Rather they campaigned more or less independently. In a pattern much more common in other states, the strategy was to avoid entangling McCord with Mitchell, the weaker of the two. Organization lines held fairly well in the gubernatorial race but in the three-way senatorial campaign traditional voting patterns were shattered. Crump, in ditching Senator Stewart, aroused animosities by his desertion of an ally. Crump probably brought defeat onto himself. Kefauver won the senatorial nomination with less than a majority of the vote.[12]

In the analysis of political groupings of citizens the normal supposition is that some common interest binds one group together against another of antagonistic interest. Thus, in Alabama, the predominantly white, poor farm, and industrial area of northern Alabama is aligned against the big-farmer, conservative black belt when significant questions of public policy are at issue. It is true that Tennessee business has supported Crump, but his state organization was held together largely by the perquisites of office, the desire for office, the disciplinary tools inherent in the control of government and party machinery, and the capacity to trade with East Tennessee Democrats—and Republicans. It is difficult to identify any other tie to bind Memphis and East Tennessee together against Middle Tennessee.[13]

---

[11] Compare Figure 11 with Figure 7, page 48, and Figure 9, page 51.

[12] Another evidence of the comparatively loose nature of the organization is provided by the position of Representatives. Crump control over these posts has been much less extensive than, for example, that of the Byrd machine of Virginia.

[13] If the analysis is correct, Governor Browning, who dethroned Crump in the state in 1948, would be expected to shift East Tennessee from its alliance with Memphis and West Tennessee to a combination with the traditionally anti-Crump counties of Middle Tennessee.

In addition to the usual perquisites of the executive departments, legislative control in Tennessee is of peculiar importance as a means both to bludgeon and to reward local political leaders. The conduct of local governments requires the adoption of an unusually large volume of local legislation. Each county's legislative delegation has a keen interest in obtaining the passage of its local bills. The organization, by its control of the legislative processes and through the governor's veto, has been able to delay or expedite local bills. It could thus trade for support on general measures and also strengthen or weaken local leaders who could help or hinder the organization in the next primary.[14] The Shelby organization customarily maintained an agent or two—in one session, for example, the chairman of the state Democratic committee—to monitor the stream of legislative proposals on behalf of the top leadership. Such centralization of guidance of the flow of legislation facilitated the administration of factional discipline and the distribution of rewards.

Those in power can utilize their authority to buy off, to discourage, or to intimidate opposition and potential opposition, as well as to reenforce the loyalties of their own followers. These are ancient political practices, but they probably assume exceptional significance when used systematically by a faction in power over a long period. Some opposition leaders or potential leaders could be kept at least neutral by jobs or other favors. Others, beyond reach by these methods, could be neutralized by the fear of outright physical injury. Although Crump has no organized forces of Brown Shirts, some of his critics in the state have stayed away from Memphis in fear that a visit there would endanger their lives. An insult, a scuffle, a planted gun, a verdict of justifiable homicide in self-defense—all these expectations have been worked up in the minds of such persons by events in Memphis. After it has been pricked a balloon appears less formidable, but these fears existed. When Estes Kefauver invaded Memphis on primary day of 1948 to speak and tour the polls, he aroused anxiety among his friends for his safety.[15]

Some county factions have been tied to the Crump organization chiefly by cash sluiced into the county during campaigns. Thus, recently a county shifted allegiance and returned majorities for the organization candidates. "Our voters mostly are interested in boodling," a county leader observed. In a "free" election the county would be anti-Crump, he says, but a contribution from state headquarters of $1,000 in a quiet race,

[14] The possibilities are suggested by a 1947 bill put through by the Knox delegation to abolish the council-manager plan in Knoxville shortly after the voters of the city had recalled a mayor and two councilmen who had "attempted to wreck" the manager system.—*Memphis Press-Scimitar*, February 10, 1947.

[15] When Gordon Browning spoke in Memphis after the 1948 primary it had been ten years since his last public speech there. At the time of his 1938 appearance the United States marshal interrupted his speech to read a lengthy court order enjoining him from sending state troops to Memphis and a switch engine "puffed up and down noisily nearby" while he spoke.—*Memphis Press-Scimitar*, August 9, 1948.

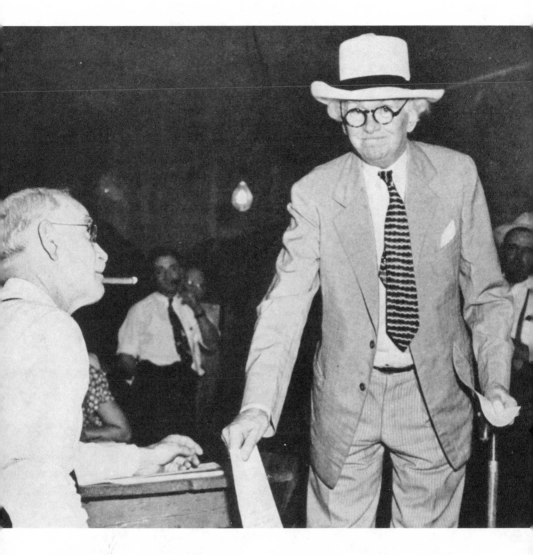

MISTER CRUMP

The country boy who came to rule a commonwealth.

ELECTRIC FURNACE AT MUSCLE SHOALS

Industrialization is altering the politics of a plantation economy.

or of $2,500 in a hard-fought race, will buy the support of enough key leaders of the poor rural county to carry the day. Even in such a county, however, there are limits to the influence of money: the relative appeals of candidates and other factors have a bearing. Yet within these limits state candidates with money can get the local leaders to string along with them.[16] Counties side by side differ. One will require money and another will not. The differences are regarded in part as a matter of tradition. "Some counties," reports a person experienced in the management of campaigns, "have gotten into the 'habit' of requiring money during a campaign." This conclusion parallels the observations of experienced managers of campaigns in other states that particular counties develop persistent patterns of demand toward the central dispensers of campaign funds.

Commonly in the South the Democratic party machinery adopts a more or less neutral attitude between party factions, but in Tennessee the Crump organization until 1948 controlled the party machinery to its advantage.[17] The principal advantage is control of the conduct of primaries. Electoral irregularities are reported to be most prevalent in East Tennessee. In these counties, the Democrats are in a minority and, it will be remembered, have cleaved to the state administration for succor. In part because of their control of the machinery for the conduct of the Democratic primary locally they have been able to make a good showing for state-wide organization candidates in their area.

It would be naive to conclude that Crump's power has rested on standard machine practices alone. True, these practices contributed to the cohesion of his organization and demoralized the opposition, but, as all his opponents concede, Crump is a shrewd politician. At critical moments he outmaneuvered the opposition. Thus, a movement by veterans after World War II held some threat to the organization. The possibility existed of rebellion in the legislature because of the presence in its membership of GI's elected on antimachine tickets. Shortly before the legislature convened, the "administration" announced its support of two "fine young veterans," as Governor McCord described them, to preside over the house and the senate. Mr. Crump declared: "The ex-service man played a great part for four years in world affairs. They are entitled to great consideration, and I am sure Memphis and Shelby County will accord them the honors they so richly deserve in future politics." [18] Somewhere along the line the threat of revolt subsided.

[16] A trustworthy Tennessee politician estimates that there are about twelve such counties in the state.

[17] The Crump organization won a majority of the state executive committee in 1948, but the chairman announced that he would not seek re-election since he believed that the party machinery should be controlled by the faction that won the primary nominations.

[18] *Memphis Press-Scimitar,* January 4, 1947.

3. The Antiorganization Faction

A cohesive and continuing majority faction tends to force most opposition elements into at least the semblance of a united minority faction. All those opposed to Crump, for whatever reason, have usually rallied around an antiorganization candidate in each campaign. Until Estes Kefauver and Gordon Browning led the opposition coalition to victory in 1948, it consisted of a little band of faithful souls who valiantly but futilely broke lances with Crump every two years. Whether a single victory is enough to convert a loosely knit opposition into a cohesive faction remains to be seen. Former Governor Browning polled 55.8 per cent of the vote in a race against the Crump-backed incumbent governor, Jim Nance McCord. In the senatorial primary Representative Kefauver polled 42.2 per cent of the vote, and thus won by a plurality over Senator Tom Stewart and a third candidate, Judge John A. Mitchell, an unknown who had been picked by Crump sight unseen, on the recommendation of Roane Waring, president of Memphis Street Railways and former National Commander of the American Legion.[19]

Over the years the opposition has maintained some continuity in its leadership as well as in its following of voters. The result has been, within the Democratic party, a rough sort of bi-factionalism which differs radically in form from the multifactional systems of such states as Alabama and Florida and lacks the rigidity and tenacity of the dual factionalism of Virginia. In most southern states voters divide into transient groupings around individual candidates, whereas in Tennessee the political battle is ordinarily fought between only two major groups, the Crump and anti-Crump factions. Rarely does a third candidate attract a considerable percentage of the vote.[20] Tennessee's dual factionalism is in all probability induced in large measure by the considerable Republican minority. That state-wide minority places the majority Democrats in a local minority in many eastern counties and thereby compels the Democratic organizations of such counties to accept state-wide factional leadership from Crump—or whoever looks like a winner. Other Democratic groups, faced by such a coalition, are impressed enough by the futility of a multiplicity of independent candidacies to unite against the organization.[21]

The antiorganization faction is in general heir to the political following of Austin Peay, who won the governorship in 1922, 1924, and 1926.

[19] Stewart received 31.9 per cent and Mitchell 23.7 per cent of the vote.

[20] There are, of course, minor candidates who poll a minuscule vote. Perennially John Randolph Neal turns up on the ballot as a candidate for one office or another. He is described as an eccentric man of wealth, economical in his tonsorial and sartorial expenditures. In 1946 he ran simultaneously for governor and United States Senator in both the Democratic primary and the general election.

[21] For a discussion of the hypothesis that a Republican minority induces bi-factionalism within the Democratic party under certain conditions, see below, pp. 223–28.

The line of political descent has, of course, been blurred by movements both ways across factional lines. The elder statesman in the Crump opposition has been Lewis Pope, of Nashville, who made unsuccessful races for governor in 1932 and 1934. In the 'twenties Mr. Pope was prominent in the Peay ranks, but by 1948 he was largely inactive in politics. Silliman Evans, publisher of the *Nashville Tennessean*, although never a candidate himself, has played an important role in the Crump opposition both in the inner circles of campaign management and through his paper. Edward Ward Carmack, of Murfreesboro, carried the banner against Crump in the senatorial primaries of 1942 and 1946 after he had offered to support any other likely candidate. Mr. Carmack has kept up a running fire against the Crump organization and is the bearer of an honorable and influential name in Tennessee politics.[22]

Even before his victory in 1948 Gordon Browning was the strongest anti-Crump candidate. He had been elected governor in 1936 with Shelby support. In office he fell out with Crump and pushed through the legislature a county-unit law to deprive Memphis and other cities of the weight in state-wide nominations to which their voting population entitled them. This step led to his defeat in 1938.[23] While on military duty in Germany, Browning was on the ticket as a candidate for the nomination for governor in 1946. No campaign of any consequence was made for him, but he received 38.5 per cent of the vote. On his return from Germany he began speaking around the state and was immediately regarded as a prospective 1948 candidate.

He was suggested for both the Senate and the governorship, with Representative Kefauver as a running mate. Kefauver had made a name for himself in the House, to which he was first elected in 1939. He had not been much involved in state politics but in 1946 announced that he would not vote for McKellar and gained prominence among anti-Crump leaders. Kefauver finally emerged as the senatorial candidate and Browning ran for governor.

These, and other less prominent persons, make up the leadership of the anti-Crump faction. It would be in error to say that they constitute a well-disciplined core of opposition. Elements of jealousy and mutual distrust have colored their relations in the past and no single person is recognized as the chief. The looseness, discontinuity, and weakness that long marked the anti-Crump leadership point to a feature of political

[22] Mr. Carmack's father, also named Edward Ward (1858–1908), served in the House, in the United States Senate, edited the *Nashville American*, predecessor of the *Tennessean*, and as a prohibitionist opposed, both politically and editorially, with the vigor and invective characteristic of his times, the policies of Governor M. R. Patterson. In 1908 the elder Carmack was killed by Duncan B. Cooper and his son, Robin Cooper, partisans of Governor Patterson. The elder Cooper was given a sentence of twenty years but the Governor immediately pardoned him. The younger Cooper was granted a new trial but was not further prosecuted.

[23] The law was held void in *Gates* v. *Long*, 113 S. W. (2d) 388 (1938).

organization inherent in a one-party system, viz., the extreme difficulty of maintaining an organized opposition. In a state with a two-party system it is difficult enough to maintain a going opposition organization, but that difficulty is compounded in a one-party state where the minority has no formal organization, no party name, no support or sympathy from fellow partisans in other states. In Tennessee Crump's strength has induced a degree of unity in the opposition. In one-party states that lack a continuing, dominant faction, the function of opposition, both in campaigns and within the legislature, is left mainly to the initiative of lone individuals completely unsupported by an organization.

Although the centers of the peak voting strength of the antiorganization faction move about from primary to primary, depending on the candidates and the pattern of deals by both state-wide groups with local leaders, the major area of persistent opposition strength is Middle Tennessee. The vote for Carmack for the senatorial nomination in 1946 was heaviest in Middle Tennessee, with McKellar drawing his concentrated support from West and East Tennessee. Browning's greatest strength in 1948 was in Middle Tennessee but in the senatorial voting of that year the usual pattern did not appear. With Crump's desertion of Senator Stewart and his endorsement of a candidate not widely known, elements of localism unusual in Tennessee showed up. Judge Mitchell received a majority in no county outside his judicial district except Fentress, which adjoins it, and Shelby. Stewart, who had built a personal following during his two terms in the Senate and whose treatment by Crump attracted a sympathetic support, was strongest in the western half of the state, including many counties in the middle grand division. Kefauver had strongest support in his old congressional district, including Chattanooga, and he also cut into the organization vote in many other East Tennessee counties.

Why Middle Tennessee should have been the center of antiorganization strength is by no means clear. Local explanations cite the rivalry of Memphis and Nashville; the feeling of Middle Tennesseans that Memphis and the East combined to obtain preferential treatment in patronage and policy; resentment that the governor, although often a Middle Tennessean, has been controlled from Memphis; and a general sectional competition between the West and the Middle.

In Middle Tennessee, Mr. Evans' *Nashville Tennessean* plays no mean political role. In a sense the anti-Crump faction has been built around the *Tennessean*, although in 1948 Edward J. Meeman's *Memphis Press-Scimitar* got in some powerful licks against Crump. The *Tennessean* has been a consistent and strident critic of Crump and, through its publisher's participation in the designation of anti-Crump candidates and in the financing and planning of their campaigns, it has tended to be the spearhead of the antiorganization faction. The circulation area of the *Tennessean* coincides roughly with the area voting most consistently anti-

Crump; hence its staff attributes the vote to the paper's influence.[24] Whether the *Tennessean* guides Middle Tennessee or is merely its voice, the newspaper plays a role of unusual significance in state politics. Its long-time rival, the less influential but highly important Nashville *Banner*, commonly takes a position opposite that of the *Tennessean*. It was the *Tennessean* that loudest and longest hammered the organization for the sponsorship of the sales tax, which, with the labor vote, was credited by Crump for his 1948 defeat.

Apart from their geographical concentration, the anti-Crump voters have had no readily identifiable characteristics setting them off from organization supporters. Prior to the Browning-Kefauver campaign, however, few businessmen of importance were in the anti-Crump ranks, or, at least, they feared to play a prominent role. Antiorganization leaders generally had no ready sources to tap for campaign funds. Even contractors at outs with the state administration were not a source of cash. During the war and the immediate postwar years, they were busy on Federal and private projects and had no need of a friendly state administration.

Crump blamed labor in large measure for his defeat in 1948. In view of the Crump organization's labor record, unions might be expected to be solidly against him. Perhaps over half the weight of labor has been in opposition all along, but labor has also been extremely weak. The AFL leadership is often divided; the CIO has been more consistently against Crump. The mass of labor does not vote; those who vote are divided.

In Memphis, the AFL has strung along in the main with Crump who has followed the standard machine practice of infiltrating his men into this as well as other private groups.[25] The weight of the building trades in the AFL make it particularly susceptible to machine capture. Union leaders are eligible for jobs as building inspectors and in various capacities on public works. Building trades unions also have to get along with public authorities in their normal business dealings. Further, the AFL has had a measure of gratitude to Crump because of his coolness toward the CIO. Senator McKellar, mainly because of his prewar pro-labor record, was able in 1946 to obtain an endorsement from the state AFL executive committee by a 5–4 vote, a score that probably roughly indicates the cohesiveness of the AFL in state politics at that time. The AFL became less devoted to Crump after the 1947 legislature enacted an anticlosed-shop bill sponsored by the Tennessee Business Men's Association. On this bill Crump had worked both sides of the street. His Shelby legislators divided. The "best speeches against the bill" came from his Shelby dele-

[24] For example, see Jennings Perry, *Democracy Begins at Home* (Philadelphia: Lippincott, 1944), pp. 175–84.

[25] In 1948 the Tennessee League for Political Education (AFL) endorsed Gordon Browning for governor. "Lev Loring, president of the Memphis Trades and Labor Council, commented that the action 'hasn't anything to do with Memphis.'"—*Memphis Press-Scimitar*, July 12, 1948.

gation and, on the other hand, "the most effective and vitriolic speeches against labor and in behalf of the bill" were also made by members of his delegation.[26]

The CIO has leaned more definitely toward collaboration with the antiorganization faction than the AFL. In 1946, for example, the CIO-PAC endorsed Carmack for the Senate against McKellar, contributed a modest sum to the campaign, and carried on an organizing and publicity campaign of its own. The announcement of the CIO-PAC position gave Carmack a pink tinge and perhaps, on balance, damaged his cause. The CIO's political effectiveness has not been impressive, but it makes a more earnest political effort than the AFL. Few of its members vote, and CIO leaders recognize that they have before them a long and arduous task of educating the rank and file in political action. Nevertheless, the CIO made powerful medicine in 1948 and is potentially a key factor in the anti-Crump faction.

A potential source of support for the antiorganization faction is the Negro. Generally in the South Negroes, insofar as they participate in politics, tend to line up with the more progressive white faction. In Tennessee, however, anti-Crump leaders have not won undivided Negro support. Negroes, as a group, play no important role in state politics. In Shelby County Negroes, like whites, have voted as Crump desired. In other West Tennessee counties, according to one observer, Negroes usually vote for whatever candidate the "boss man" says, when they vote. In Middle Tennessee, Negroes divide, in the opinion of several politicians, with the majority in the anti-Crump camp as do the whites in this area. Before FDR, Tennessee Negroes leaned Republican, but the New Deal drew them preponderantly into the Democratic ranks.[27]

Why the antiorganziation faction does not attract more solid Negro support in Tennessee is puzzling. Negro votes for Crump candidates in Memphis can be explained. The Shelby organization controls their votes just as it does those of the whites, but it ought to be remembered that Crump sees that Memphis Negroes get a fairer break than usual in public services. His organization, of course, follows through and takes specific measures to hold Negro leaders in line. Outside Memphis, Negroes vote chiefly in the cities, and, although a majority may be anti-Crump, the Negro community is rife with factionalism. In Nashville, for example, Negroes continually fight among themselves [28] and do not usually unite

---

[26] *Joint Legislative Report* (by Joint Tennessee Labor Legislative Committee on 1947 General Assembly), p. 16.

[27] One Negro political leader found it amusing to see Negroes sitting as delegates to a state or county Republican convention one day and to see them voting in the Democratic primary the next. He asserts that a great many Negro Republicans vote in the Democratic primaries, a practice that is doubtless not limited to black Republicans.

[28] Thus, a Negro political leader described a couple of Nashville groups: "Their officers would rather go to jail than attend a meeting with each other."

in support of candidates, although occasionally they are credited with a "balance-of-power" position in local elections.

The minor place of the Negro in state politics is suggested by the absence of any state-wide organization for political action. In the amorphousness of the Negro group in Tennessee politics there may be a lesson. In the cities there has long been no serious obstacle to Negro voting. Disunity of Tennessee Negroes may be attributable in part, at least, to the absence of the unifying effect of a common concern about winning the right to vote. In most of the South, Negroes must pull together to establish the right to vote. Perhaps the substantial disappearance of the common obstacle to voting in Tennessee removes an incentive to cohesiveness and makes way for cleavages among Negroes. Whatever the reasons may be, Tennessee Negroes do not seem to constitute so cohesive a block against the incumbent organization as might be expected, although they probably lean against Crump outside Memphis.

4. Tennessee Republicanism

Tennessee in a sense has not one one-party system but rather two one-party systems. In East Tennessee Republicans win local elections and customarily two congressional seats. In Middle and West Tennessee the Democrats rule. Within their respective strongholds neither is seriously challenged by the other. At the obvious point for conflict—campaigns to choose governors and other state-wide officials—the contest has gone to the Democrats apparently by default.

Tennessee's Democratic-Republican cleavage stands as a monument to the animosities of Civil War and Reconstruction. Even before The War a sense of separatism set off East Tennesseans from their fellow citizens to the west, although partisan divisons did not follow closely geographical lines.[29] The dispute over slavery and secession, however, forged Tennessee partisan alignments into a form that has persisted to this day. Slavery was both unprofitable and unpleasing to the people of the mountains of East Tennessee. The plantation system never flourished in the hills and the small farmer who tilled his own land could take no stock in the theory of slavery as a divinely ordained institution. Even less was he disposed to defend the slave property of his planter neighbors to the west.

East Tennesseans, staunch unionists, resisted secession. Twice—in February and June, 1861—they voted against secession, but the slave interests of West and Middle Tennessee took the state out of the union. The unionists of East Tennessee gave trouble to the Confederate government and in turn they suffered. The more outspoken went to prison and others endured less-drastic repression. All this was not without provoca-

[29] See the maps in A. C. Cole, *The Whig Party in the South* (Washington, 1914).

tion from the unionists. They joined the Federal armies by the thousands; others conducted private warfare. Once the Federal Government regained Tennessee, the unionists of East Tennessee got in the saddle. Reprisals against secessionists followed and the vindictiveness of war and reconstruction left an indelible mark. In the state there was reproduced, on a small scale, the consequences for party loyalties of the war for free and slave territories in the nation as a whole.[30]

The extraordinary durability of voting habits fixed by war and reconstruction reflects itself in the series of maps in Figure 12. The vote on secession, shown in the first map, set a pattern of behavior for the next century. This vote, in turn, roughly paralleled the distribution of slave ownership. The areas that voted against secession became centers of Republican strength; the secessionist counties became steadfast in their Democracy.

The exceptions from the correlation between slavery and secession sentiment that appear in the map forcibly demonstrate the strength of partisan attachments. Note, for example, Sullivan County in northeastern Tennessee. Although it had few slaves and was surrounded by counties that voted against secession, it favored the South in 1861 and has consistently remained Democratic in its loyalties.[31] The other exceptions to the slavery-secession-Democratic correlation occur in West Tennessee chiefly in counties of the Highland Rim. In some of these counties the proportion of slaves in the population was relatively high but the counties were loyal to the Union. Similarly, they maintain a staunch Republicanism nine decades later.[32]

Persistence of partisan loyalties in Tennessee should give pause to those who predict drastic party realignments in the short run. Social mechanisms for the transmission and perpetuation of partisan faiths have an effectiveness far more potent than the political issue of the day. And the consequences of the projection of the past into the present for Tennessee politics are great. The relegation of Republicans to a role of impotence in state affairs probably deprives the state of the kind of influence exerted, for example, in Alabama politics by its northern, white

[30] See J. W. Patton, *Unionism and Reconstruction in Tennessee, 1860–1869* (Chapel Hill: University of North Carolina Press, 1934); Philip M. Hamer, *Tennessee, A History, 1673–1932* (New York: American Historical Society, 1933).

[31] At the census of 1860, 7.9 per cent of the population of Sullivan County was slave. The slave percentages of the population of the surrounding counties were: Johnson, 4.6; Washington, 6.4; Carter, 5.2; Greene, 6.8; Hawkins, 11.9. It is probable that the pattern of partisanism of Sullivan County, and perhaps others also, became set in antebellum days. It was then Democratic in contrast with the Whigism of many East Tennessee counties. See the maps in Cole, *The Whig Party in the South*, Appendix.

[32] Time has not permitted determination of the causes for the departure of these counties from expectation based on the extent of slave ownership in 1860. Their deviation from expectation is significant, but as significant is the fact that once their partisan attachments were fixed they remained as stable as did those counties that acted according to the formula that interest determines political attitudes.

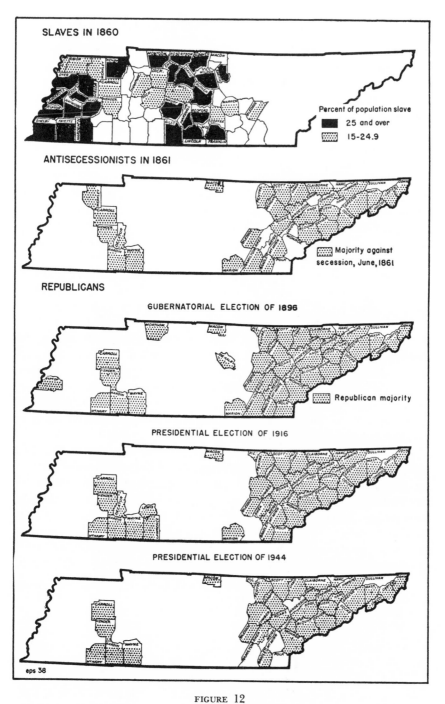

SLAVES IN 1860

Percent of population slave
- 25 and over
- 15-24.9

ANTISECESSIONISTS IN 1861

Majority against
secession, June, 1861

REPUBLICANS

GUBERNATORIAL ELECTION OF 1896

Republican majority

PRESIDENTIAL ELECTION OF 1916

PRESIDENTIAL ELECTION OF 1944

eps 38

FIGURE 12

The War and Tennessee Party Lines: Distribution of Republican Popular
Strength, 1861–1944

counties. By its loyalty to Republicanism, East Tennessee—in popular legend the home of the mountaineer, the independent yeomanry—cannot become an effective bloc or party in state politics that would be as a rebellious wind, or at least a breeze, blowing down out of the mountains on Nashville.

The forces of history, by not making them numerous enough, may have destined Republicans to a minority position, but, if what one hears in Tennessee has any truth in it, the present heirs of the past have helped along the inevitable. Political reporters, candid Republican leaders, and others conclude that the Tennessee Republican high command contemplates victory in state races with a shudder. Election of a Republican governor or a Republican United States Senator would probably alter the leadership of the Republican party of the state. The current leaders, so the prevailing interpretation goes, look forward to Republican victory nationally, with themselves in charge of the distribution of Federal patronage locally. If a strong party developed in the state, it probably would have new leaders who would at least share in the Federal patronage.[33]

In addition, the political gossip of Tennessee runs to the effect that the Democrats in East Tennessee make no earnest fight for county and district offices. In turn, the Republicans stay in their own territory and do not strive to reach out for control of the state. Thus, the first congressional district, in northeastern Tennessee, is usually represented by a Republican. Carroll Reece, who became Republican national chairman in 1946, was first elected from this district in 1920; his only defeat in thirteen campaigns came in 1930 when he lost to an independent Republican.[34] "Carroll has an arrangement up there," was the usual observation. The belief is widespread that the Democratic-Republican bargain involves a trading of votes, with Democrats supporting Republican candidates locally and Republicans voting for organization candidates for state-wide office in the Democratic primaries.[35] The intimation is even heard that state and Federal patronage has been given to Republicans to dampen such urges as they might have toward determined political warfare.[36] Others point to a few Republican legislators who train with Crump Dem-

[33] Thus, the manager of the successful campaign for governorship of Alf Taylor, Republican, in 1920 made a bid for votes in every county of the state. Later top Republican leaders avoided campaigning in Democratic counties on the assumption that such efforts would only bring more Democrats to the polls.

[34] In five of his thirteen races he had no Democratic opponent. In those elections in which he had Democratic opposition he won usually by a ratio of about two to one.

[35] The calendar of elections would make such an arrangement feasible. The primaries for the nomination of state-wide candidates are held on the same day as the general election for local officials. The primaries for state-wide nominations for the two parties are also conducted by different sets of election officials.

[36] An East Tennessee Republican county judge was probably nearer the truth when he reported that it was his observation that Senator McKellar usually made sure that his appointees were not only Democrats but also that they were McKellar Democrats and sometimes even carried the inquiry back at least a generation.

ocrats in the State legislature and note that Democrats by their control of local legislation keep Republicans in their place.

Good political stories become embellished in the telling, and the truth of the alleged Republican-Democratic armistice is elusive. The Republicans usually do not put up much of a fight for state office and often do not offer impressive candidates. Probably the most able, recent gubernatorial candidate, John Wesley Kilgo, who ran in 1944, was regarded with misgiving by the old guard in the party.[37] Cursory inspection of the election statistics provides little evidence on vote trading although the figures on elections of county officers are not available.[38] The election figures suggest, however, that some local Republican prosecuting officials probably wink when the Democratic primary election commissioners "write up" the totals for organization candidates for nominations for state-wide office.[39]

Whatever the nature of interparty arrangements may be—and they probably occur most frequently between leaders at the sub-county level —[40]the position of the Republican party requires more fundamental explanation. The Republicans in East Tennessee usually do not have to have an "understanding" to win. The Democrats could put up a more vigorous fight, but the Republicans simply have the votes by inheritance. The greenest carpetbagger, provided he had the Republican nomination, could win. But why do not the parties join battle in the state as a whole? We may have an equilibrium not unlike what the economists call "monopolistic competition." Industrial enterprises sometimes follow a "live and let live" policy. Maximum competitive power is not exerted, and spheres of influence develop within which each enterprise has a place for operation. Politicians, also, under some circumstances make war against the opposition only with reluctance. If each of two groups of potential competitors for power is in possession of offices that it can hold without

[37] Mr. Kilgo, of Greene County, has published an account of his campaign as *Campaigning in Dixie* (New York: Hobson Book Press, 1945).

[38] From several sources the story came that Mr. W. I. Davis, the Republican state chairman in 1944 traded with the Democrats in his home county, sacrificing his gubernatorial and presidential candidates in return for Democratic support of Republicans for local office. Inspection of the election returns shows that Dewey and Kilgo both carried the county and thus, as often happens, a good story is ruined.

[39] Suggestive are three counties which in 1944 returned a larger vote for McCord in the Democratic primary than in the general election.

[40] If election returns were available for sub-county units, it would be possible to identify prima facie instances of interparty deals. For example, a story current in East Tennessee is that state senator Brooks, facing a tough fight for re-election in 1944, arranged for a block of Democratic voters in Butler (a town in Johnson County) to vote for Dewey, McCord, and Brooks. The returns for the county as a whole suggest that something unusual happened. The vote was: For President, Roosevelt, 450; Dewey, 2,699; for governor, McCord (D), 1,032; Kilgo (R), 1,701; for state senator, Laws (D), 790; Brooks (R) 1,907. Evidently party lines did not hold tightly up and down the ticket, although analysis of the vote by precincts would be more indicative of what happened.

fighting and that it might risk by fighting, why fight? Politicians, like other people, desire security. By establishing an equilibrium between the two parties, commonly accepted whether explicitly or tacitly, both groups of politicians enjoy a measure of certainty.

Republicanism in Tennessee is, of course, also paralyzed by the dilemma that the party faces in the entire South. The Crump Democratic organization has had the support of the conservative element. The Republican party, to make headway in the state, would have to adopt a line in Tennessee out of harmony with the national conservative tenor of the party. Indeed, in Tennessee the party would have to take such a line to be representative of the mass of its voters in the hills. The logical sort of realignment would be a liberal combination of the Republicans and anti-Crump Democrats. In the 1934 governor's race this type of coalition arose around an independent candidate, Lewis Pope. A few Republican leaders, such as John Wesley Kilgo, the 1944 gubernatorial candidate, seem to be aware of the possibilities.[41] Kilgo, a prosperous "poor man's lawyer," was not regarded with enthusiasm by the old guard of his own party. The Republican dilemma in Tennessee perhaps has in reality produced two Republican factions in the state. One includes most of the state leadership and is conservative in tone, closely linked with urban business, and not displeased with Crump policies. The other, of which Mr. Kilgo has been one leader, consists of mountain agrarians and others with interests different from those of the prevailing state and national leadership. The schizoid character of Tennessee Republicanism suggests the problem of conversion of the Republican party in the South into an effective political force.

In 1948 Tennessee Republicans took on life by infection from the revitalized national Republican party and from competition within their own ranks. Carroll Reece, no longer safely ensconced in his House seat, ran for the Senate and was fighting to maintain his supremacy in the state party organization. He and his running mate, Roy Acuff, candidate for governor noted for his "Grand Old Opry" hillbilly radio program, campaigned with hope that a national swing to Republicanism would give them a fighting chance for victory in the state. Democratic candidates feared defeat, as they saw crowds gather to listen to Roy's Smoky Mountain Boys give out such ballads as "Night Train to Memphis" and "The

41 "We believe it proper to mention," the legislative chairmen and representatives of Tennessee labor unions said in reporting on the work of the 1945 legislature, "the fact that" Governor McCord's state "platform was considerably less liberal and progressive than the platform of his Republican opponent, Hon. John W. Kilgo, but on the whole it is safe to say that the overwhelming majority of Tennessee's working population supported McCord, because the majority of the workers, organized and unorganized, are members of the Democratic Party."—Joint Legislative Report of Legislative Chairmen and Legislative Representatives (of various unions on the work of the 1945 general assembly), p. 2.

Great Speckled Bird." There were also signs that some Democrats, high in the defeated state organization, were viewing prospects of a Republican victory with something less than disfavor. The chances are that the 1948 show of activity inaugurated no lasting activation of Republicanism in Tennessee.

Chapter Five | # F L O R I D A :

E V E R Y   M A N   F O R   H I M S E L F

THE salient features of political organization in Virginia, Alabama, and Tennessee indicate that the one-party system includes as many types of factional arrangements as there are states. Florida's political structure, an incredibly complex mélange of amorphous factions, only confirms the impression of diversity within the Democratic party of the South.

Florida ranks high in political atomization. In its politics it is almost literally every candidate for himself. Ordinarily each candidate for county office runs without collaboration with other local candidates. He hesitates to become publicly committed in contests for state office lest he fall heir to all the local enemies of the state-wide candidate. Each candidate for the half dozen or so minor elective state offices tends to his own knitting and recruits his own following. Senators and Representatives hoe their own row and each of the numerous candidates for governor does likewise. With each successive campaign different divisions within the electorate develop. Few politicians exert real influence beyond their own county, and those who can deliver their home county are few. Florida is not only unbossed, it is also unled. Anything can happen in elections, and does. On the same day—in 1944—the state nominated, i.e., elected, as its United States Senator, Claude Pepper, a man tending leftward, and as its Attorney General, Tom Watson, a labor baiter of the first order.

Factional lines, in the Tennessee fashion, simply do not exist. Nor does there seem to be any clear-cut, fundamental cleavage within the state that reveals itself starkly in times of political tension, as in Alabama. And the state's mutable political structure is at the opposite pole from the stable and well-defined hierarchy of Virginia. Whether Florida's political unorganization is a blessing or a curse is another question,[1] but the fact remains that the state is a political curiosity. Before examining its one-party system in detail, let us identify some of the state's characteristics that contribute to its political structure.

1. Florida Is Different

What makes Florida different politically is a difficult question. Plausible partial explanations flow from the state's peculiarities in geography and social composition. Florida is unlike other states of the South in many ways and, in truth, it is scarcely a part of the South. It votes Democratic, it is geographically attached to Georgia and Alabama, it occasionally gives a faintly tropical rebel yell, but otherwise it is a world of its own.

Florida's huge area and its peculiar geographical configuration obstruct the formation of state-wide political organizations. While great weight should not be assigned to this factor, the physical inconvenience of assembling persons from all parts of the state for factional collaboration needs to be pointed out. From Miami to Pensacola, as the crow flies, is about the same distance as from Atlanta to Washington, from Indianapolis to Lincoln, Nebraska, or from San Francisco to Portland, Oregon. It is twice as far as from Memphis to Chattanooga. From Jacksonville to Miami the road stretches about as far as from Springfield, Illinois, to Columbus, Ohio. Or, if a person travels from Tallahassee to Key West, he might have in the same mileage gone from Montgomery, Alabama, to Springfield, Missouri. Even the lesser distances impress. From Miami to Tampa the distance is about the same as from New York to Boston.

Florida distances become more important in view of the uneven distribution of population over the peninsula. The counties with the five largest cities contained more than 43 per cent of the state's 1940 population. The centers of population in which more than four out of ten Floridians live are widely separated: Escambia (Pensacola) in the far

---

[1] One should not leap to the conclusion that a loosely organized politics invariably produces undesirable results in governmental action. An undisciplined politics in effect creates (regardless of the formal administrative structure) semi-autonomous spheres within which those concerned with specific public services and institutions enjoy freedom and discretion. Under some circumstances individual units in this pluralism of authority exercise their prerogatives to maintain high standards of performance, striking illustrations of which may be found in Florida. On the other hand, dispersion of authority in an amorphous politics complicates the enforcement of political accountability.

western tip of the northern panhandle; Duval (Jacksonville) in the far
northeastern corner; Pinellas (St. Petersburg) and Hillsborough (Tampa)
at the middle of the west coast; and Dade (Miami) at the southeastern tip
of the peninsula. For political organization the significance of this dispersion may be grasped by superimposing a map of Florida on a map of the
United States, with Jacksonville over Lansing, Michigan. The problem of
organizing for state political action becomes in terms of geography something like that of rallying for common action the citizenry of Lansing,
Michigan, Dubuque, Iowa, Muncie, Indiana, and Huntington, West
Virginia. When Bernarr Macfadden piloted his plane over the state in his
1940 senatorial campaign, he might have been charged with theatrical
affectation but he was only meeting the necessities imposed by geography.

While dispersion of urban centers makes for political localism, urbanization itself makes for a politics differing from that of predominantly
rural states. Florida is the most highly urbanized of the southern states
and its city population consists mainly of residents of relatively large
cities. In 1940 its fifth city, Pensacola, had more than 37,000 inhabitants
and Jacksonville and Miami each had more than 170,000. The political
characteristics of such cities differ from those of smaller communities,
although both are classified as urban by the census authorities. In 1940,
55 per cent of Florida's total population lived in urban areas, but about
four-fifths of this 55 per cent was in the five counties containing the largest
cities. Moreover, Florida's rural population includes a considerable proportion of non-farm population; consequently the state has by far the
smallest proportion of farm population of the southern states. Only 16.1
per cent of the population, or one out of eight persons, lived on farms in
1940. The next-ranking southern state, Texas, had relatively twice as
many people living on farms, 33.7 per cent. At the opposite extreme, was
Mississippi, whose farm population was 64.3 per cent of its total population. Florida's ranking in urbanism is paralleled by a relatively high
average per-capita income. The details of Florida's comparative position
within the South on these matters may be seen in Table 6.

Florida's urbanization undoubtedly conditions its politics and contributes to its political differentiation from the South generally. A small
farm population—and much of it engaged in a specialized agriculture
requiring both skills and capital—means that the rustic demagoguery
often associated with southern politics must play a lesser role in Florida.
The numerous company of southern politicians equipped with spectacular command of invective and with an earthiness, appealing to the wool-
hat boys and to the voters at the branch heads, currently includes no
Floridian of state-wide potency.[2] Florida politicians have to adapt their

[2] Former Congressman Lex Green has sported a ten-gallon hat and a flowing black
tie as political trademarks. As a rural thumper he is not in the same class with "Big Jim"
Folsom or "Hummon" Talmadge.

appeals to urban dwellers, who, of course, are not beyond reach of demagoguery, but a calculated rusticity is not the appropriate appeal. Apart
from screening out some types of political leaders, urbanization introduces all the peculiarities of urban political behavior. In urbanization,
for example, may be found a major explanation of Florida's relative
unconcern about the Negro. While the state's politics is by no means
free of Negro-baiting, the dominant attitude on the race question is comparatively mild.

Another ingredient contributing to Florida's amorphous political
structure is the rapid increase of its population by immigration from

TABLE 6

Florida is Different: Comparison with other Southern States in Proportion of Population Urban, Proportion of Population Living on Farms,
and Average Per-Capita Income

STATE	PER CENT POPULATION URBAN, 1940	PER CENT POPULATION FARM, 1940[a]	AVERAGE PER-CAPITA INCOME, 1944[b]	AVERAGE PER-CAPITA INCOME, 1947[c]
Florida	55.1	16.1	$1013	$1104
Texas	45.4	33.7	947	1128
Louisiana	41.5	36.1	815	892
Virginia	35.3	36.8	944	1064
Tennessee	35.2	43.7	796	916
Georgia	34.4	43.8	766	885
Alabama	30.2	47.2	756	837
North Carolina	27.3	46.5	698	890
South Carolina	24.5	48.2	655	778
Arkansas	22.2	57.1	604	710
Mississippi	19.8	64.3	546	659

[a] The difference between urban and farm populations and 100 per cent
consists of rural non-farm population.
[b] *Survey of Current Business*, September, 1947, p. 24.
[c] Ibid., August, 1948, p. 19.

other states. Through the nineteenth century Florida remained sparsely
populated in its lower half. Here was a sort of a pocket-edition frontier
susceptible of development by a more diverse lot than the hardy folk who
settled the west. The attractions of St. Petersburg to the old people, of
Palm Beach to the wealthy, of Miami to those in search of the diversions
of Miami, and of the agriculture of the state to farmers elsewhere harried
by boll weevil and drought—all these and other drawing features have
about quadrupled the population since 1900. From 1900 to 1910 the state
gained 42 per cent in population, exactly twice the national rate. Its rate
of growth declined in the next decade, although Florida continued to
grow at twice the national rate. From 1920 to 1930—the decade of William Jennings Bryan's orations about Florida real estate and the decade

of the great real estate bubble—migration to the state spurted upward and its population increased at four times the national rate. By 1930 the state had 51 per cent more people than it had in 1920. From 1930 to 1940 the rate of growth declined to a mere 29 per cent, still about four times the national rate. In twenty years—from 1920 to 1940—the population of the state almost doubled.

What are the political consequences of a veritable flood of new-comers? The chances are that the rate and character of population acquisition have been a fundamental short-term influence towards a politics without form and without issue. Almost half of Florida's people were born in other states; half the people have no roots in the state or perhaps are in the process of putting down roots. The consequence may be what the sociologist calls a relatively uncrystallized social structure. Individual

TABLE 7

Rate of Growth of Florida Population, 1900–40

YEAR	POPULATION	PER CENT INCREASE OVER PRECEDING DECADE	
		FLORIDA	U. S.
1900	528,542		
1910	752,619	42.4	21.0
1920	968,470	28.7	14.9
1930	1,468,211	51.6	16.1
1940	1,897,414	29.2	7.2
1948	2,356,000	24.2 [a]	10.0 [a]

[a] Estimated per cent increases over 1940.

status is perhaps less fixed by family connections and by community accordance than in an old society that projects its structure through generation after generation. In politics loyalties have not been built up, traditional habits of action with respect to local personages, leaders, parties, and issues have not been acquired. Social structure, to use a phrase of perhaps ambiguous meaning, has not taken on definite form in the sense of well-recognized and obeyed centers of political leadership and of power. Flux, fluidity, uncertainty in human relations are the rule. Whether it can be proved, there is plausibly a relation between a diverse, recently transplanted population and a mutable politics.

Add to all these elements, a highly diversified economy and you have another base for the deviations of Florida political practices from those of neighboring states. Florida escaped the curse of cotton and its associated social phenomena: the hazards of a one-crop economy, the blight of tenancy and share-cropping, and the poverty of a primitive and inefficient agriculture. In a few northern counties the Old South seeped over into

Florida from Georgia and Alabama, but the plantation region is overshadowed by the diversified agriculture and ranching of the most recently
settled sections of the state. To a diversified farming, add lumbering,
phosphate mining, fishing, cattle raising, and—the greatest of them all—
the tourist industry, and the sum is an economic structure of far greater
vitality, with many more centers of initiative than are to be found in a
state such as Georgia or Mississippi.[3]

TABLE 8

Native Floridians Are Few: Per Cent of 1940 Population of each Southern
State Born outside the State

STATE	PER CENT	STATE	PER CENT
Florida	48.1	Georgia	10.7
Arkansas	22.3	North Carolina	9.7
Texas	18.3	Alabama	9.4
Virginia	16.8	Mississippi	9.1
Tennessee	15.8	South Carolina	8.7
Louisiana	12.9		

2. Multiplicity of Factions

Florida's peculiar social structure underlies a political structure of
extraordinary complexity. It would be more accurate to say that Florida
has no political organization in the conventional sense of the term. Several characteristics of its political "system" catch the eye: (a) a multiplicity
of state factions, (b) a dispersion of leadership, which is inherent in multifactionalism but exists in exaggerated form in Florida, and (c) a discontinuity or lack of persistence in the grouping of voters into factions.
These characteristics, which occur in lesser degree in other states, are
difficult to disentangle but, on the assumption that they can be disen-
tangled, each of them will be examined.

The skeptic may ask why the nature of political organization matters.
Mr. Byrd and Mr. Crump have organizations of voters, of leaders, and
of sub-leaders, differing in almost every respect from Florida factions. One
may not like their programs either in content or tempo, yet Byrd and
Crump provide leadership, their programs go through, and the voters
know whom to blame or to praise. The question is whether a government
propped by so tenuous a political underpinning as that of Florida's can
act, on a broad front at least, either for good or for ill.

The nature of Florida's factional system manifests itself in the

[3] A convenient source of information on the geography, people, and resources of
Florida is the handbook, *Florida: Wealth or Waste?*, prepared and published by the
State Department of Education in 1946.

numerous candidates who offer for governor in the first Democratic primaries. Any individual who has an itch to be governor, the filing fee, and perhaps some political standing in his own locality enters the race. So many candidates make the first-primary race, on the chance they might get into the run-off, that it has come to be regarded as a lottery. Its outcome has been influenced by such fortuitous elements as the home-town strength of a candidate who ran last in a field of six. He drew votes from the third-ranking candidate who might otherwise have gotten into the run-off.

In 1936 Florida achieved its highest degree of political pulverization. In that year 14 men contended in the first primary, and the leading candidate attracted the support of only 15.7 per cent of the voters. In 1940 a mere 11 candidates entered the race and the highest two polled a larger percentage of the total vote than did the two leading candidates in 1936. In 1944 the field narrowed to six and the three leading candidates polled almost four-fifths of the total vote. In 1948 the three leaders, in a field of nine, again attracted almost four-fifths of the vote. A tendency away from the scattering of the votes among a large number of local favorites may be under way. Nevertheless, the distribution of the primary vote among several contenders reflects the absence of a dual system of factions organized to compete for control of the state.[4] The fractionalization of the electorate into something resembling European multiparty systems— except that Florida factions lack sharply defined programs or doctrines —is illustrated by the data in Table 9, showing the division in recent campaigns of the first-primary vote among gubernatorial aspirants.

In the search for the bases of the many factional groups that reveal themselves in the primary an obvious hypothesis is that they may be "friends-and-neighbors" followings of the type that exists in Alabama. Support for this view comes from the map in Figure 13, which shows the counties of highest popular strength of four of the fourteen 1936 contestants for the gubernatorial nomination. Each of the four candidates achieved his peak strength in his home county and in nearby, although not always adjacent, counties. Another map, for the 1944 primary, Figure 14, shows the same concentration of popular strength around the home of each of the candidates.

The intensity of attachment to local candidates is usually far lower in Florida than in Alabama where, it will be recalled, a candidate for governor commonly received from 75 to 90 per cent of the vote of his own

[4] Inspection of the table at page 89, indicates that the maximum scatter of the popular vote among candidates occurred in 1936. Apparently in 1920 some sort of dual division of the electorate existed which gradually dissolved into a multifactionalism. Since 1936 a move toward the condition of 1920 has been under way. The coincidence of these political developments with the period of the most rapid growth of population suggests the hypothesis that the political assimilation of the mass of immigrants of the 1920's was beyond the digestive capacities of Florida's social order.

TABLE 9

Fractionalization of Florida's Electorate: Proportion of Total First Democratic Primary Vote Polled by Leading Candidates for Gubernatorial Nomination, 1936–48

1936		1940		1944		1948	
CANDIDATE	PER CENT OF TOTAL VOTE	CANDIDATE	PER CENT OF TOTAL VOTE	CANDIDATE	PER CENT OF TOTAL VOTE	CANDIDATE	PER CENT OF TOTAL VOTE
Petteway	15.7	Holland	24.7	Caldwell	28.6	Warren	32.5
Cone	14.2	Whitehair	19.8	Green	27.9	McCarty	28.7
Hodges	14.1	Warren	17.3	Graham	22.4	English	15.8
Carter	10.8	Paty	15.7	Upchurch	7.5	Shands	11.0
Paty	10.4	Fraser	7.6	Sheldon	6.9	Watson	9.1
Chappell	9.0	Barbee	7.0	Baker	6.7	Cooper	1.4
Eight others	25.8	Five others	7.9	Others	0.0	Three others	1.5
Total	100.0		100.0		100.0		100.0

county. So close an approach to unanimity is infrequent in Florida and, sample tests suggest, is most nearly achieved when a candidate hails from a predominantly rural county. Thus, in the first 1936 primary Governor Cone's fellow citizens of Columbia County gave him 65.3 per cent of their votes, not a high figure in Alabama but high for Florida. A more usual local response is that received by Paty, of Palm Beach County, in the same

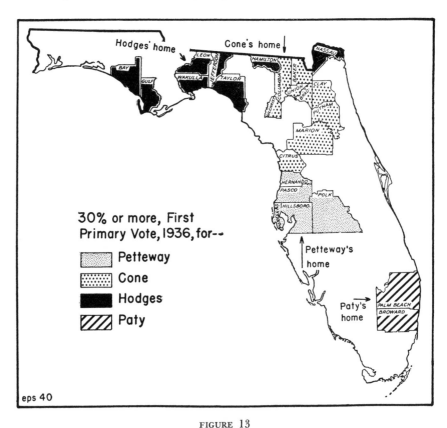

FIGURE 13

Localism in Florida's First Democratic Gubernatorial Primary of 1936

campaign. He won 51.9 per cent of the vote of his county. This example points to another difference between the localism of Alabama and Florida. In the latter state a candidate from a large urban community may draw a friends-and-neighbors support, whereas in Alabama the city is more likely to vote against the home-town boy.

Localism may be in reality a mask for a substantial interest geographically concentrated that seeks its objectives through the championship of a local candidate. One editor concludes that with the state's diversity of economic interests, many persons offer themselves as candidates in the hope that they can gain the financial backing of one or another of these groups. A man with connections in the cattle business may attract the financial support of a few wealthy cattlemen; a fruit grower may have an especial appeal to that important economic group; the gambling interests are reported to be always eager to finance a candidate; the limestone people may encourage a candidate favorable to the

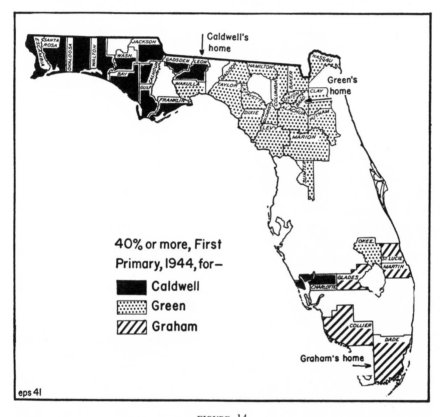

FIGURE 14

Localism in Florida's First Democratic Gubernatorial Primary of 1944

use of limestone in highway construction. While these kinds of relations have prevailed between particular interests and particular candidates, it is doubtful that diversity of economic activity inevitably produces multiplicity of faction. Although in many two-party states diversity prevails, each party manages to bring into its fold a variety of economic interests. Partial explanation of the Florida situation may be that in the absence of an institutionalized party system informal private groups sometimes take on the function of stimulating candidacies. Some observers conclude, however, that the more typical pattern is that particular interests will pick from the many candidates who offer on their own motion the one most favorable to them.[5]

In view of state policies towards the larger population centers it might be expected that an urban faction would develop. The counties of small population dominate the legislature. The seven most populous senatorial and house districts contain one-half the population but elect only one-seventh of the senators and one-fifth of the representatives.[6] The consequence is discriminatory policy, such as the equal division among the 67 counties of about half the proceeds from taxation of race gambling—a pecuniary unguent for pious rural consciences seared by the wickedness of the cities.[7] The big cities have been unable to get together in gubernatorial politics. Undoubtedly, the city vote for home-town candidates reflects the viewpoint of each urban community, but no faction has been constructed around the cities generally.

An imperfect sort of sectionalism can be perceived dimly in Florida from time to time; it lacks, however, the durability of the sectionalism of Alabama or Tennessee. The long-settled, rural northern section of the state has some attitudes that conflict with those of the more recently developed southern half of the peninsula. Between the two regions there is a tremendous gap in tempo epitomized in the contrast between a sleepy, rural, Old South county of northern Florida and the bustling city of Miami. In no small measure the political differences between the two areas are not ordinary sectionalism; they are in fact rural-urban differences. A candidate for governor from northern Florida must persuade the people of southern Florida that he will not upset race-track betting and other tourist attractions. A candidate from southern Florida must convince the people of northern Florida that he will not upset the distribution of revenues from gambling. Although south-north sectional differences are identifiable, they do not consistently appear in the division of the popular vote. An approximation of such a division occurred in the second gubernatorial primary of 1936 (Figure 15) and in the 1946 senatorial primary (Figure 16). Each of the candidates who attracted heaviest strength in the northern counties of the state was himself from that section, while his opponent hailed from lower down the peninsula. In both races the vote probably represented in part sectional attachment to a favorite son rather than a pure expression of regional interest or ideology.

Another somewhat similar division of the popular vote appeared in

    [5] See discussion of pre-primary nominations, below, pp. 410–16.

    [6] J. E. Dovell, "Apportionment in State Legislatures: Its Practice in Florida," *Economic Leaflets* (University of Florida), February, 1948.

    [7] For the season 1947–48, each county's share was $83,667; two years earlier it was $98,000. Such sums go far toward eliminating local property taxation in the less-populous rural counties.

the gubernatorial run-off primary of 1948 between Fuller Warren, of Jacksonville, and Dan McCarty, of Fort Pierce. (Figure 17.) Warren's peninsula strongholds, save for Tampa, were mainly the more rural and less-populous counties, while McCarty, the more conservative candidate, made a clean sweep of the east coast save for Warren's home county of Duval and others adjacent to it. All these vague manifestions of section-

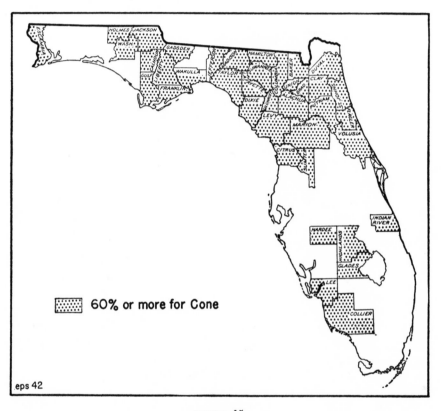

60% or more for Cone

eps 42

FIGURE 15

Sectionalism?: Counties Giving 60 Per Cent or More of their Vote to Cone in Second Florida Gubernatorial Primary, 1936

alism depart in a sense from the expectation that the more rural, older-settled sections would tend toward conservatism, the new, urban populations toward progressivism.[8] It may be that Florida's northwestern rural counties retain a tinge of old-time Populism.

[8] Geographical interpretations of Florida votes, however, have to be hedged because of the large vote of the metropolitan counties. The maps cannot reveal the nature of cleavages among the voters of individual cities. See the additional maps on Florida voting, prepared by Allen Morris, in Fuller Warren's *How to Win in Politics* (Tallahassee, 1948).

Patient probing of the minds of many Florida politicians fails to reveal among them a consciousness that the factional groupings of the voters represent clusters formed around deep and continuing issues. The attitude of the great bulk of practitioners of the art of vote-getting is about like that of a north Florida county judge, elected and re-elected many times. "Issues? Why, son, they don't have a damn thing to do with

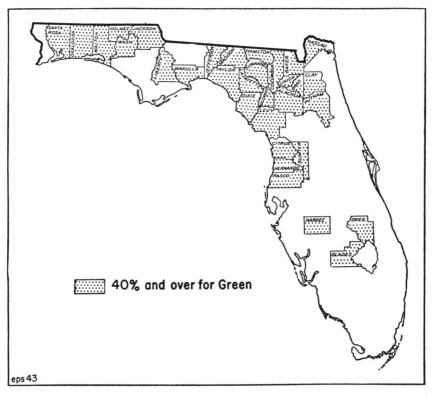

FIGURE 16

Sectionalism?: Counties Giving 40 Per Cent or More of their Vote to Green in Florida Senatorial Primary, May 7, 1946

it." Nevertheless, in the multifactional melee that is the first gubernatorial primary there are usually candidates representing several shades of opinion. The differences among them are by no means always readily discernible save to the most sophisticated politically. Yet at times candidates offer who hold the most extreme views—more often to the right than to the left of center. The electorate, with its usual good sense, tends to screen out the extremists in the first primary. Down the homestretch, in the run-off, the electorate is confronted by two contenders, one of whom is usually

more of a progressive than the other. Yet it is indicative of Florida's political disorganization—in contrast with Tennessee, for example—that
neither the conservatives nor the liberals possess enough cohesion within
themselves to center on a candidate before the primary. Absence of a
factional or a party system with a real function in the narrowing of
alternatives poses difficult choices for the electorate. Even in the run-off,

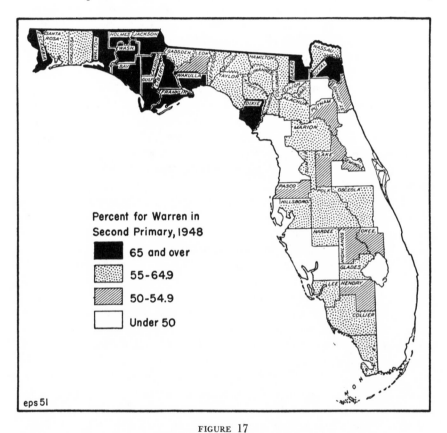

FIGURE 17

Sectionalism?: Distribution of Popular Vote for Warren in Second Florida
Gubernatorial Primary, 1948

the nature of the alternatives, except to the best-informed voters, must
be by no means clear.

The vague liberal-conservative cleavage has appeared in recent gubernatorial run-offs. In 1936 the economic and "moral" liberals supported
Cone in preference to Petteway. In 1944 Green rather than Caldwell
attracted more liberal support, and in 1948 Fuller Warren was thought
less conservative than Dan McCarty. In Senator Pepper's races the divi-

sion has been most concretely drawn. There is never much doubt about
where Claude stands.[9]

3. Dispersion of Leadership

Florida's factional multiplicity differs only in degree from that of
Alabama, Texas, and South Carolina. It reflects a dispersion of political
leadership in contrast with the concentration of leadership characteristic
of the bi-factional systems of Virginia and Tennessee and of two-party
systems. Beyond the disorganization inherent in multifactionalism, however, Florida shares with such states as South Carolina a pulverization of
politics in which it is every man for himself. The leader of a state faction
does not head a disciplined group that seeks control of state, Federal, and
local offices after the fashion of a political party. In fact, collaboration
among candidates for different offices is the exception, and the sort of
joint candidacies that are the rule under Louisiana's "ticket" system are
alien to Florida.

The place of county officials in state-wide politics illustrates the
atomization of the state's politics. The potency of the courthouse ring in
state races is usually greatly exaggerated. In Florida its influence is probably at the lowest point in the South. Although in a few counties fairly
well-defined factional groups compete for control of county governments,
generally there seems to be no "courthouse ring." It is, rather, each county
official for himself. The factional discipline, loyalty, and mutual enmity,
built up during generations of political feuding, as in Tennessee, is replaced in Florida by a bland sort of politics in which an elective career
service often develops. Nor is there a single official who tends to dominate
county politics, as does the probate judge in many counties of Alabama.

The structure of local politics provides no effective base for the construction of a state factional organization composed of local rings. To a
marked degree local officials decline to become publicly involved in races
for state office. Campaign managers generally conclude that only a few
local officials have a following they can deliver to a candidate for state
office. Further, local officials and candidates hesitate to endorse candidates
for state office lest they themselves suffer by losing the votes of those
opposed to the state candidate. The extent to which this sort of self-
insurance goes is suggested by the neutrality of Polk County officials
during the 1940 gubernatorial campaign. They were urged to come out

[9] Curiously enough the liberal-conservative cleavage appears most sharply in Florida
in battles for control of the state Democratic committee. Recently Frank D. Upchurch,
a bitter opponent of Senator Pepper, has led the conservatives, while Alex D. Littlefield,
committee chairman, has headed the liberal Pepper forces. In the absence of significant
power in the hands of the state committee, it would seem that the contest for its control
is primarily one of prestige.

for Holland because Polk was his home county. All feared to do so except the county judge who finally endorsed the home-town boy.[10] Similarly state candidates tread warily in local negotiations, lest they lose votes because of their allies.

There are, of course, exceptions. In a few counties factional lines are fairly tightly drawn and leaders attempt to deliver the vote to particular state candidates. Campaign managers say that most of these counties are in north and west Florida, the older and more "southern" part of the state. Collier County, a large Everglades area with few people, has also for many years, under the leadership of the local manager of the Collier Corporation which owns most of the county, turned in a lopsided vote for this or that candidate.[11]

In the large urban communities machines have from time to time been able to deliver a considerable vote in state races, but Florida politicians speak of these city organizations in the past tense. A former police and fire commissioner of Jacksonville had a machine of sorts. At one time Volusia County (Daytona Beach) had a potent organization and it remains faction-ridden. Tampa had an organization that drew many of its voters from controlled Latin precincts, but the machine was routed by a newspaper campaign, and voting machines put a different cast on the count in the "hot" precincts, in the local terminology. Although former state senator Ernest Graham, unsuccessful candidate for governor in 1944, has had a reputation for influence in Dade County (Miami), recent election returns indicate that his reputation exceeds his ability to deliver, even when he is a candidate himself.

The unorganized condition of Florida politics manifests itself also in the fact that candidates for the national House and Senate operate independently of each other and of candidates for the governorship and other state offices. This political individualism gives great weight to factors such as personality and skill on the stump. In the confusion of individual candidacies, consistency by the electorate is purely fortuitous. In fact, the more general consequence is that the only genuine choice is between personalities who struggle simply to make themselves known, and not disagreeably. When opportunity for meaningful choice arises its existence is often concealed.

A striking example of the strange results of the nonparty system oc-

[10] The reticence of local officials may be explained in part by the fact that Holland lost the county because of active labor opposition. Incidentally Polk had earlier been the home of Holland's opponent, Whitehair.

[11] Of course, there are, says one manager of state campaigns, some county leaders or would-be leaders who are "chiselers." "They come up to headquarters and want $1000 to deliver the county and you will tell 'em you don't have that kind of money and you talk around awhile and end up giving 'em $300 or $400 which they either use for their own purposes in local campaigns or, usually, keep. You hate to do it and you are sorry after you have done it but you are afraid not to do it. And it is the same counties that make this kind of approach in campaign after campaign."

curred in the simultaneous victories in the 1944 primary of Claude Pepper
and Tom Watson,[12] who sought renomination as Senator and attorney
general, respectively. Mr. Pepper had a national reputation as a progressive while Mr. Watson had a local reputation for his antilabor views.
Watson had first annoyed organized labor by hiring, in union argot, a
"rat" contractor to refurbish his offices. He carried on from this to the
sponsorship of a "right-to-work" amendment to the state constitution.
Here were two candidates with antithetical views, yet the voters of Florida
gave majorities to both of them on the same day. Thirty-seven of the 67
counties gave majorities to both candidates.[13]

Florida politicians explain this sort of conflicting behavior by the
electorate primarily on the basis of Senator Pepper's superb performance
on the stump. He first gained recognition for his talents as an orator in
the legislature and soon came to be in demand over the state as a speaker
on ceremonial occasions. His acquaintance with politicians was supplemented by ties with business interests when he moved his law offices to
Tallahassee to represent them there. In the 1934 senatorial race it was
generally conceded that Pepper was counted out in the Latin precincts
in Tampa. His sportsman-like acceptance of defeat helped him win the
next Senate vacancy. After a while in Washington he became a whole-hog
New Dealer but he did not neglect Florida. New Deal projects and later
defense and war projects came to the state in generous measure and the
Senator received the credit. Perhaps more important, businessmen among
his constituents found him able to move wheels in Washington. They
found him energetic in pursuit of their interests, although a particular
action might not neatly fit with his views on some grand issue of policy.
There are those who remark somewhat sadly that "Claude is not the same
Claude that we knew when he started out back here in Florida." Yet the
professional politicians look with great admiration on his ability to come
back to the state for a few weeks and wipe out the opposition in a whirl-
wind campaign.[14]

Nor does he lack admirers among businessmen. A politician-business-
man—the combination is not rare in Florida—says that he tells people

[12] No relation to Georgia's late Senator and Populist leader, though some Floridians
assert he does not object to a confusion of identity.

[13] In general, a negative relation, from county to county, might have been expected
between the strength of Pepper and Watson but no such pattern develops from a scatter-
diagram. Watson's strength was generally greater in the non-metropolitan counties
than it was in the major cities, probably in reflection of rural and small town antipathy
toward labor. Pepper might have been expected to do uniformly better in the cities
than elsewhere but he did not do so. In Tampa and St. Petersburg (Pinellas and Hillsborough counties) he was strong; in Jacksonville (the home of his opponent, Judge
Edmunds) he was weak. In Dade County (Miami) he ran only slightly ahead of Watson
(58.0 and 54.3 per cent of the total vote, respectively).

[14] His principal opponent in 1944 was Ollie Edmunds, county judge of Duval
(Jacksonville) County. Edmunds lacked Pepper's histrionic skills and his managers handled his campaign ineptly.

if they don't want to vote for Pepper they "had better not (1) listen to him talk or (2) ask him to do something for them in Washington. He is a whingdinger at both!" As smart and as sharp as he is, even Claude's most ardent admirers, as 1950 approached, were wondering whether he was going to be able to talk himself into another term in the Senate. Yet, no matter how good a spellbinder Pepper is, the fact that Florida's voters sent him to the Senate twice points to the existence of a powerful strain of liberalism within the state.

Fragmentation of political leadership appears again in the election of Florida's so-called "cabinet" officers. Six lesser state officials are elected: the secretary of state, the attorney general, the comptroller, the state treasurer, the superintendent of public instruction, and the commissioner of agriculture. Collectively, with the governor, they have certain functions in addition to those pertaining to their respective offices; hence Floridians refer to their "cabinet" form of government.[15] Each of these officers conducts his campaign quite independently of other candidates. There are no slates of candidates for the cabinet offices, which, in fact, constitute something of an elective career service. An official dies in office; his successor is appointed by the governor and thereby gets his name before the public. He runs at the next election and is almost invariably re-elected so long as he desires to retain the office. These officials, with perhaps one exception, have no machine, in the strict sense of the word, but they have their circles of friends and the advantage that comes from public familiarity with their names. Continuity in the cabinet offices gives the state government a degree of stability. On the other hand, the existence of the "cabinet" weakens the governor and obstructs the development of executive leadership.

The search for coherent, organized political leadership in Florida seems futile in whatever direction one looks. The situation is neatly illustrated by the reply of three state senators to an inquiry by Allen Morris, a well-informed Florida capital correspondent. He asked each to prepare independently, a list of the ten most effective men in Florida campaigns, the men they would want on their team in running, say, for governor. The most names that any of the three could list was eight.

[15] The Florida "cabinet" is an institution the like of which is not to be found elsewhere in the South. The governor and the cabinet members, or some of them, are members ex officio of numerous state boards and commissions, such as the Budget Commission, the State Board of Conservation, and the Board of Commissioners of State Institutions. Although some departments are under more direct gubernatorial control than others, a considerable part of the state government is, in effect, under the direction of a collegial executive consisting of the governor and the elective "cabinet" officials. In newspaper reports and public discussion "the cabinet" is recognized as a corporate entity of great importance in state affairs. It may not be mere coincidence that such an institution developed in the southern state with the most disintegrated and least-stable structure of political organization. Some sort of law of institutional compensation may be operative in the stimulation of substitute mechanisms to assure a degree of stability and of integration when the political parties or factions fail to do so.

Only two persons appeared on all three lists and they were newspaper publishers, not politicians. "Some might argue," Mr. Morris opined, "from the disagreement revealed by those three lists that we have achieved a boss-less democracy in Florida, with no individual actually able to claim much for himself as a kingmaker." [16]

With weak political organization and leadership, vocational and economic groups of one sort or another probably take on more electoral importance. Mr. Morris' quiz of the state senators also included an inquiry on organizations whose members as a rule stood together in politics. On this list were the beauticians (but not the barbers), road contractors, cattlemen, the Farm Bureau, and the insurance industry. Of the correctness of their evaluation, Mr. Morris had some skepticism but he reported the judgment of practicing politicians for what it was worth. Even the nonparty organizations, however, seem to be weak in contrast with their counterparts in other states. The Florida Farm Bureau, for example, was formed as late as 1941 and had in 1947 only 7,000 members. It officially endorses no candidates; other techniques are used to make its influence felt. Thus, its president resigned in 1947 reputedly to be free to campaign, presumably chiefly among Farm Bureau people, for a candidate for governor. The bureau, whenever the situation is clear enough for it to see what it is doing, lines up, as elsewhere, on the conservative, business side of the fence. Yet politically the Florida bureau amounts to little in comparison with the organizations in Georgia and Alabama.

Organized labor, although relatively more numerous in Florida than in the more rural southern states, plays the same ineffectual role. The AFL membership far outnumbers that of the CIO. Although from time to time in local races the AFL meets with success, it is not a cohesive force in state-wide politics. In 1940, for example, its executive board endorsed Francis P. Whitehair for governor, but the rank and file of the membership went along with Mr. Holland, the winner. "It was," a member of the executive board said, a "90–10 situation with the top 10 going one way and the bottom 90 another." The presence in the electorate of a considerable body of organized workers undoubtedly conditions candidates' attitudes; it cannot be said, however, that the workers pull together effectively. Yet their cohesion in primary campaigns probably goes up and down with labor effectiveness in the country as a whole. In 1948 labor is said to have delivered a good vote to Fuller Warren.

4. Mutability of Factions

Florida's politics is not only characterized by a multiplicity of faction and by a dispersion of leadership through the independence of candidates

[16] *Jacksonville Journal*, November 22, 1947.

SENATOR CLAUDE PEPPER

Florida is different.

Oil

A new and important ingredient in the politics of the South.

for different offices; such factions as exist among the voters also have a high degree of mutability and impermanence. Observers of Florida politics profess to see among its political leaders small cliques lasting over a good many years.[17] They also report that the superficial independence of candidacies conceals a good deal of undercover collaboration. Thus, the Pepper forces may quietly support a gubernatorial candidate to their liking, and in turn the governor's lieutenants may support Pepper. The fact of undercover support—rather than open and avowed collaboration among leaders as occurs in Louisiana or in an ordinary party system—is not peculiar to Florida, but is indicative of a loose and curious organization of political activity. Campaigns are fought between what appear to be new factions formed around new candidates for each campaign. They are essentially personal factions in contrast with the institutionalized factions of an organized politics. Although there may be some continuity among the inner cliques in campaigning from primary to primary, the voter has, on the surface at least, a choice from among individual candidates rather than from among aspirants clearly identified as the champions of well-established, recognized and continuing groups, as, for example, the "organization" and "antiorganization" candidates in Virginia.

Consequently the electorate is not divided into groups with relatively constant attachment to well-known factions. Voters shift and the shape and membership of factions change. And political leaders also cross the dimly drawn factional lines. The continual formation, dissolution, and re-formation of factions suggests the relation of a politics without clearly defined issues to the nature of factional organization. When substantial policy is at stake, leaders of like interests and views might be expected to work together campaign after campaign. "Oh, maybe they do a little bit along Pepper and anti-Pepper lines," concedes one politician; often, however, the allies of one campaign find themselves enemies in the next. When only prestige and patronage are the prizes, political leaders are obstructed by no principle in changing alliances. Even the politics of a Pepper has introduced no sharply defined continuity of alignment of leaders.

An index of the amorphousness of Florida politics is provided by the state of the professional campaign organizer. Florida has extremely few professional or semiprofessional politicians who have a state-wide acquaintance among local professionals. In Georgia, in Mississippi, in

[17] Thus, one categorization of leaders places in the liberal group, Pepper, Littlefield, Jerry Carter; then there is a group of the Upchurch, Associated Industries of Florida, Watson leaning; midway is found a moderate group in the Doyle Carlton-Holland-Caldwell tradition, whose members often wander in and out of the other two camps. Such a categorization of leaders, however, is paralleled only by the most vague constancy in voter cleavages. The streams of attitude, personified by a few leaders, appear not to be institutionalized in organization with corporate identity or spirit.

Alabama there are professionals who work for first one candidate and then another and who have affiliated with themselves a corps of local leaders scattered over the state. In Florida one must search long for persons who have a comprehensive knowledge of local political situations and who can command the co-operation of local professionals. Among Florida politicians there are perhaps two individuals who have enough of a following to put together a campaign organization by telephone.

The discontinuity inherent in a system of personal factions reveals itself in the nontransferability of state-wide followings. In a two-party state normally an outgoing governor, along with other party leaders, supports the party's nominee for the succession. In Florida the general belief is that the governor, who is ineligible to succeed himself, can only within narrow limits bring his followers to vote for any particular candidate for the succession, and he normally does not try to. An official with long service in the statehouse explains the matter in this way: A candidate would not want the governor's endorsement because it would give his opponents a "cudgel" with which to charge an attempt to create a dynasty. Further, a governor usually goes out of office with many enemies. He can control his first legislature with patronage and favors, but the second is often beyond his control. As his term wears on even his own appointees become independent. Whatever the governor does to influence the succession, he usually does behind the scenes. Among the enemies of the administration, those seeking to organize a group powerful enough to take over the governorship find their most willing recruits.

A governor ordinarily cannot even deliver his own vote to himself when he runs for another office. The so-called gubernatorial machine has amounted to little as a vote producer. For fifty years outgoing governors have often tried for election to the Senate. They have generally failed.[18] Exceptions are few. Florida politicians regard with awe Governor Holland's growth in popularity during his term as governor. In 1946, the year after leaving office, he won the senatorial nomination.[19] His accomplishment is belittled by those who say that as wartime governor he had nothing to do save sit and watch Federal money flow into the state. Thereby he made no enemies. More generally, according to participants

[18] Governor Jennings (1901–05) failed to win the senatorial nomination in 1904. Governor Broward (1905–1909) lost the senatorial nomination in 1908 but won in 1910. Governor Trammel (1913–17) succeeded in the 1916 senatorial primary. Governor Catts (1917–21) lost the senatorial race in 1920. He failed to win the gubernatorial nomination in 1924 and 1928. Governor Hardee (1921–25) unsuccessfully sought the gubernatorial nomination in 1932. Governor Martin (1925–29) lost the senatorial race in 1928 and was likewise defeated in the gubernatorial primary of 1932. Governor Carlton (1929–33) lost the 1936 senatorial primary. Governor Sholtz (1933–37) failed of nomination for the Senate in 1938. Governor Cone (1937–41) could not make the grade to the Senate in 1940.

[19] Holland polled a vote of 118,962, or 24.7 per cent of the total vote, in the first gubernatorial primary of 1940; his vote in the second primary was 272,718, 57.1 per cent of the total. In the 1946 senatorial primary his vote was 204,532, 60.7 per cent of the total on the first balloting.

and observers of Florida politics, a governor has made so many enemies by the end of his term that his following has evaporated.[20]

Even the small group of personal supporters that a politician builds up is apt to be bound to him by the loosest ties. Consider the case of Lex Green, unsuccessful candidate for the governor in 1944 and for the Senate in 1946. Mr. Green served in the House for many years. As a Congressman he spent much of his time, a political correspondent reports, trying to build up a following over the state, "giving away cook books outside his own district and that sort of thing." After the 1940 reapportionment, Florida had a Congressman-at-large and Green won that post. The pay-off of a sustained program to build a state-wide following failed in 1944 when he lost the governorship. He ran for the Senate in 1946, again without success. A comparison of his popular strength from county to county in these two campaigns, shown in Figure 18, illustrates vividly the looseness of the typical Florida personal faction. In most counties Green lost strength between 1944 and 1946; in others, he gained. In general he was strong in 1946 where he had been strong in 1944, yet the great variation in the faithfulness of his followers from county to county contrasts sharply with the tight lines maintained among the voters in a two-party state even when the candidates are different. The personal faction is radically different in nature, and probably equally different in its impact on government, from a true political party.[21]

Reliance on personality (however it may be associated with policy) as an organizing point for voters inevitably produces impermanence in factional systems. Institutionalization of political leadership in a party system carries with it virtual immortality. And only the most able—or spectacular—personality can function effectively in the organization of a stable following. The Florida governor most influential in the creation of a factional group was Napoleon Bonaparte Broward. Before election to the governorship in 1904, he had won fame as a leader of filibustering expeditions to aid Cuban revolutionists. In state politics his progressive

[20] Thus, in 1940 Governor Cone, whose term was expiring, ran for the Senate and failed even to win a place in the run-off primary. Bernarr Macfadden also made the race for the Senate in 1940 and, writing later, spoke of "the Cone influence through his powerful state road department machine." (*Confessions of an Amateur Politician*, p. 107). Cone in the first primary in 1936, without benefit of the state highway department machine, polled 14.2 per cent of the total vote. In 1940, after four years control of the state government, he drew 15.6 per cent of the vote in his senatorial race. One is justified in considerable skepticism about the potency of Florida gubernatorial "machines."

[21] The correlation between Green's 1944 and 1946 vote was relatively close in comparison with the correlation between different candidates at different times who were popularly supposed to appeal to about the same people. One element—indicative of incohesiveness of factions among voters—is that differences in the vote pattern between two races is often attributable in part to the friends-and-neighbors following of other candidates. In the first primary of 1944 one tactic employed against Green, who was "the man to beat," was to enter futile candidates with a local appeal to divert support from Green. The tactic in this instance failed to keep him out of the second primary.

program and personal qualities generated loyalties and antipathies so intense that even after his death in 1910 political divisions were for several years along pro- and anti-Broward lines. An anticorporation man, in the Florida terminology of the time, he urged with great courage and per-

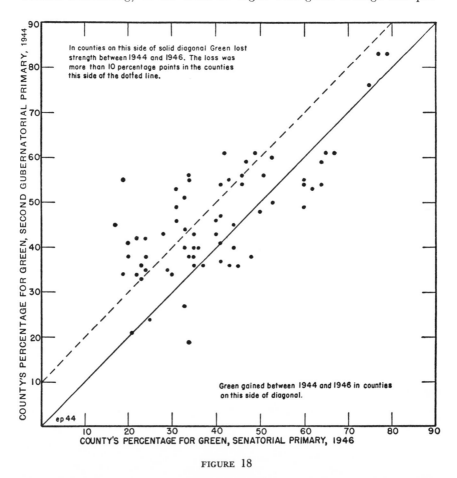

FIGURE 18

Looseness of Personal Factions: Relation between Percentage of Vote in each Florida County for Green in Second Gubernatorial Primary of 1944 and Senatorial Primary of 1946

suasiveness all the tenets of the progressivism of the day and added a few planks of his own. One of his greatest achievements was the beginning of Everglades drainage. He campaigned on the straightforward proposition that water runs down hill. The water to be drained was higher than the ocean. To drain, all you had to do was to dig a ditch. With a broad positive program, he attracted to himself a coterie of lieutenants who acted together for a time, and over the years many of them achieved prominence in state politics.[22]

The Broward and anti-Broward factions, if institutionalized, would have provided a party system based on genuine issues, but the conditions of factional, rather than party, politics seem to be such that impermanence is the rule. The chance rise of personalities and their peculiarities mightily condition the nature of the shifting divisions among the voters. Thus, the next outstanding Florida leader was Sidney J. Catts. A Baptist minister, he made political capital of an anti-Catholic sentiment built up by Tom Watson, of Georgia, and others. In his 1916 campaign he played on fears of the state fish and oyster conservation law. New issues and new personalities brought an alignment of voters unlike that of the Broward era. Catts ran for office several times after his governorship, without success. His following, too, gradually disappeared. The moral of the tale, of course, is that the kaleidoscopic alteration of voter-groupings that can develop within the one-party system magnifies the confusion through which the voter must find his way.

[22] W. T. Cash, *History of the Democratic Party in Florida* (Tallahassee: Florida Democratic Historical Foundation, 1936), chap. 15.

Chapter Six | # GEORGIA:
RULE OF THE RUSTICS

Sოutherners object to the assumption that their politicians enjoy a monopoly of demagoguery. The uniform linkage of the adjective "southern" with the noun "demagogue," they maintain, is a mistake. Demagoguery assumes many forms, of which homespun hoopla from the rural stump is only one. Class-conscious harangues by urban labor leaders and pontifical pronouncements by Republican Congressmen are equally designed to play on the emotions and esthetic sensibilities of their listeners. And with the same purpose: to win votes.

The "southern demagogue" is, nevertheless, a national institution. His numbers are few but his fame is broad. He has become the whipping boy for all his section's errors and ills—and for many of the nation's. His antics have colored the popular view of a region of the United States. Yet in all the diverting publicity about him one important aspect of his influence has been ignored. The colorful demagogue possessed of an intensely loyal personal following can introduce into the disorganized politics of one-party states elements of stability and form that are of the utmost importance.

Eugene Talmadge has been Georgia's demagogue. He was a candidate in every state-wide Democratic primary save one between 1926 and 1946. He ran three times for commissioner of agriculture, twice for United States Senator, and five times for governor. He won the agriculture post three times and the governorship four times. He led a cohesive, personal faction that, with his death in 1946, transferred its allegiance to his son, Herman Talmadge, who was elected governor in 1948. The Talmadge personality and the vividness of his race and class appeals divided the Georgia electorate into two camps, whose struggles created a strong tendency toward bi-factionalism. For a decade and a half Georgians have been faced with a series of political campaigns in which the voters have had positive and passionate reactions to the candidates, a privilege denied many one-party states.

In our exploration of Florida politics the political anarchy possible in the absence of a party system became evident. Constant realignment among voters and leaders makes the politics of that state a free-for-all in marked contrast to the continuity of Georgia's personal factionalism. Also in sharp contrast to Georgia is the highly integrated machine politics of Virginia. The division of that state into continuing organization and antiorganization factions gives it a semblance of responsible, if not popular, government. Georgia's one-party politics stands between the extremes of Florida and Virginia. The highly personal nature of Georgia's Talmadge faction probably diverts attention from needs that might find expression and relief through party government. Yet it is possible, too, that the Talmadge following itself represents a genuine interest of some sort. To the extent that it does, and the interest is not betrayed, an important deficiency of one-party government has been remedied.[1] The study of Talmadge's influence on the multifactionalism of Georgia may provide clues to the significance of "southern demagogues" in other states.

1. Talmadge as the Issue

A fiction in the rationalization of southern one-party politics is that there are competing "parties" within the Democratic party. Early in this century a dual division grew up in Georgia in the long fight between Hoke Smith of the *Atlanta Journal* and Clark Howell of the *Atlanta Constitution*. By the 1920's, however, there had developed a wide-open competition and splintered leadership, such as we have observed in Alabama and Florida. After Talmadge's entry into gubernatorial politics in 1932, multifactionalism declined sharply as the bulk of the voters began to coalesce in each race around two candidates. The proportion of the vote

[1] Undoubtedly behind Georgia's factions there exist powerful economic aggregates that play with whatever faction looks like a winner. Without exaggerating the importance of Georgia's bi-factionalism, it may be noted that a first step in the conduct of a politics for the people is the development of competing aggregates of political leaders with some discipline and continuity who will, in the long run, bid against each other for popular support.

received by the two top contenders in the Democratic primary shot up. With Talmadge or his personal candidate in a race, the opposition tended to consolidate against the common enemy. Few would try to beat Talmadge unless assured of major combinations of support. The voters were given much clearer alternatives than when forced to choose among a confusing melee of candidates. The details of Talmadge's impact on the form of the state's factional struggle appear in Table 10.

TABLE 10

Impact of Talmadge on Georgia Factionalism: Distribution of Vote among Candidates in First Democratic Primary for Governor. Years in which Incumbent not Seeking Re-election for Two-Year Term, 1926–46

YEAR	PERCENTAGE OF TOTAL POPULAR VOTE RECEIVED BY:					
	1ST CAND.	2ND CAND.	TOTAL OF 1ST TWO	3RD CAND.	4TH CAND.	REMAINING CANDS.
1926	37.3	35.1	72.4	16.8	10.8	—
1930	27.2	25.2	52.4	22.9	21.5	3.2
1932	42.0 [a]	28.4	70.4	12.7	7.1	9.8
1936	60.0	31.6 [b]	91.6	8.4	—	—
1940	51.5 [a]	36.0	87.5	12.5	—	—
1942	57.6	42.4 [a]	100.0	—	—	—
1946	45.3	43.0 [a]	88.2	10.0	1.8	—
1948	51.8 [c]	45.1	96.9	1.9	0.7	0.5

[a] Eugene Talmadge.
[b] Talmadge's personal candidate.
[c] Son Herman.

Talmadge not only compelled the bulk of the opposition to unite against him, but he could, under certain conditions, deliver his own following to another candidate. In 1936 he opposed the re-election of United States Senator Richard B. Russell, and at the same time he put forward his lieutenant, Charles Redwine, for the governorship. County after county gave virtually the same proportion of its vote to Redwine as to Talmadge. Their popular votes differed markedly in only about a dozen of the 159 counties, mainly because the friends-and-neighbors influence of opposing candidates outweighed loyalty to Talmadge.

The cohesiveness of the Talmadge following implied by the scatter-diagram in Figure 19 made Old Gene an exception to the rule laid down by many politicians of the one-party South that no candidate can "transfer his vote" to a political ally. The correlation in the 1936 vote points not only to the loyalty of Talmadge followers but also to an awareness by voters that the issue of Talmadgism transcended the personal candidacy of the man himself. Nevertheless, his influence did not pervade the entire elective politics of the state, as would that of a political party. Only a few statehouse officials have been clearly aligned for or against him. The choice of Congressmen has, as in most southern states, been independent of the turmoil over state government. State legislators lined up for and

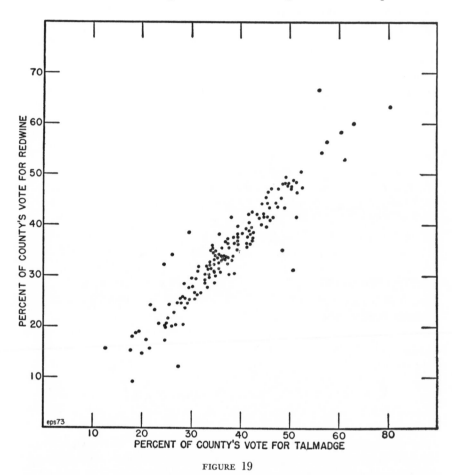

FIGURE 19

Deliverability of the Talmadge Vote: County-by-County Relation between Vote for Talmadge for Senator and Vote for Redwine for Governor, Georgia Democratic Primary, 1936

against the governor's program, but these groupings could not be described as responsible coalitions elected because of their members' inclusion on a pro- or anti-Talmadge ticket. Legislative alignments rested on personal or other grounds as was dramatically shown in 1947.

The critical test of factional cohesion in the legislative battle of that year occurred on the election of Herman Talmadge to the governorship to replace his father who died before inauguration. A bitter controversy arose in the legislature over the succession. Talmadge partisans maintained that the legislature could elect a new governor, meaning Herman, while the opposition held that M. E. Thompson, the lieutenant-governor-elect, should succeed. If the Talmadge influence had extended to legislative races, supposedly those counties that cast their unit votes for Talmadge in July, 1946, would have at the same time sent Talmadge partisans to the legislature. Yet, in January, 1947, legislators from almost a fifth of the counties that had supported Talmadge in July failed to give unanimous support to the Talmadge cause. On the other hand, legislators from about half the counties that opposed Talmadge in July failed to vote solidly against Herman in January.[2] The frequent election of Talmadge legislators from anti-Talmadge counties suggests the inadequacy of even so cohesive a personal faction as Talmadge's as a means for holding together chief executive and legislature in the manner of a political party.

Talmadge's influence caused voters to tend to cluster around two candidates in the primary. Another evidence of his influence on the form of factional division among the voters is provided by a parallel decline in the significance of localism. In a southern multifactional system the normal expectation is that the vote in the first Democratic primary will divide among a goodly number of candidates and that each will draw his most intense support from his home county and the neighboring territory. On the other hand, the rise of a bi-factional structure tends to reduce both the number of candidates and the intensity of the friends-and-neighbors influence. The two propositions are illustrated by the maps in Figure 20. The 1930 gubernatorial primary revealed the usual friends-and-neighbors pattern, although Russell, who came from a political family of prominence, drew a relatively heavy vote in scattered counties far from home. By the time of the 1942 primary the shape of the political dispute had changed into a bi-factionalism and, as may be seen from the map, the division of the voters was only mildly associated with the residence of the candidates.

The replacement of localism by a different type of cleavage within the electorate reflects a change of fundamental importance in the nature of the political struggle. The chances are that the friends-and-neighbors appeal can assume overriding importance only in an immature politics in which issues are either nonexistent or blurred. When there emerges a factional system of competing politicians whose differences provide opportunity for the expression of cleavages of sentiment latent in the elec-

[2] Of the 152 county delegations recorded in the lower house vote on the election of Herman Talmadge, 98 were from counties that had been for Eugene Talmadge in the July primaries. Of the 98, 79 stood by Herman, 17 were against him, and 2 legislative delegations split. Fifty-four of the recorded delegations were from counties that had been against Talmadge in July. Of these, 28 remained anti-Talmadge, 20 cast their votes for Herman, and six delegations split. The legislature is said to have been influenced by trading, another evidence of the nature of factional allegiance.

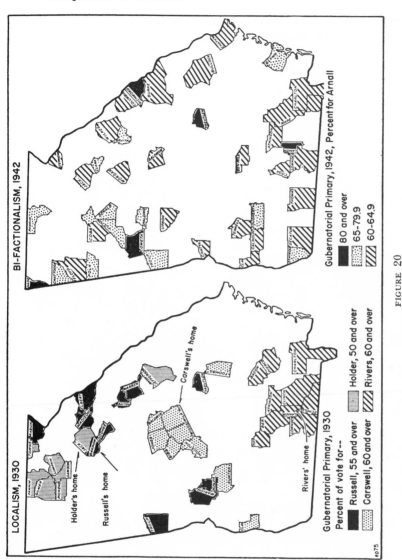

FIGURE 20

Localism and Bi-Factionalism: Friends-and-Neighbors Pattern in Georgia's First Gubernatorial Primary of 1930 and Distribution of 1942 Vote for Arnall for Governor

torate, localism is apt to decline in significance in the face of the divisive effects of a politics of substance.

2. Sectionalism and Urbanism

Talmadge built an enduring following and forced the politics of the state into the semblance of a bipartisan mould. Who were the Talmadge men? What sorts of people composed the anti-Talmadge faction?

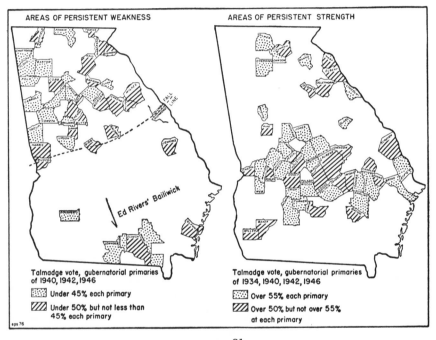

FIGURE 21

Areas of Talmadge's Durable Strength and Persistent Weakness

What interests or areas lined up in the two camps to fight out their political differences? The Talmadge and anti-Talmadge cleavage divides the counties with large cities and those that are completely rural or have only small towns. The areas of most consistent strength and most persistent weakness of Talmadgism appear in the maps in Figure. 21. One map identifies the counties in which the older Talmadge received more than 50 per cent and more than 55 per cent of the popular vote in each of the primaries of 1934, 1940, 1942, and 1946. The other map indicates those counties in which he received less than 50 per cent and less than 45 per cent of the vote in each of the primaries of 1940, 1942, and 1946.[3]

[3] In the map showing areas of consistently high strength the 1932 race, Talmadge's first for the governorship, is omitted because his faction did not take shape until

While the two maps show the centers of Talmadge strength and opposition, they tell nothing about the differences, if any, between the two antagonistic groups. The highest degree of attachment to Talmadge, in the south-central part of the state, suggests a crude sort of sectionalism, with the south against the north. The sectional pattern is marred by the curious behavior of about ten counties in north Georgia that have consistently joined the irregular pattern of counties in middle and south Georgia to form the backbone of Talmadgism.[4] One factor that might account for Talmadge's strength in the south-central part of the state and his weakness in the north is the location of Georgia's Negroes. His anti-Negro rantings might be expected to appeal to black-belt whites. The counties with highest Negro percentages are scattered mainly across the center of the state. They include many Talmadge strongholds, although detailed analyses do not support a general conclusion that Talmadge's strength increases from county to county with the proportion of Negroes. Even in the 1946 primary in which racist invective was his principal campaign weapon, such a relationship did not prevail.[5]

The tendency of a great many counties north of the fall line to oppose Talmadge produces the semblance of a north-south sectionalism.[6] Though the pattern does not appear clearly in each of the contests, an especially marked sectionalism showed up in the vote of Talmadge's principal 1946 opponent, as may be seen in Figure 22. The political cleavage along the fall line may not be mere coincidence. The proportion of the labor force engaged in manufacturing is higher above the fall line.

---

after his first victory. The 1934 vote is not used in the map of areas of consistent weakness because the feeble opposition encountered in a race for a second term permits no gauge of areas of weakness. The two maps, thus, show the locations of the extremes of pro- and anti-Talmadge feeling as developed by Eugene Talmadge. In 1948 Herman Talmadge made headway in a number of counties in which his father had been weak.

[4] A diligent examination of census data reveals no characteristics in common between the main southern bloc of Talmadge counties and the northern group. Nor do they suggest any plausible explanations for the differences in behavior of neighboring Talmadge and anti-Talmadge counties in north Georgia.

[5] One might argue that the rural votes of Negroes in 1946, virtually all of which would be against Talmadge, offset the pro-Talmadge white vote in some counties with heavy Negro populations. While this may have been true in a few instances it is doubtful that Negro voting was extensive enough in rural counties to upset the general conclusion. It is possible, however, that Georgia's county-unit system makes correlational analysis of county votes meaningless. The intensity of campaign appeal differs enormously from county to county, with the greatest effort being concentrated in doubtful counties. A quite different pattern of voting behavior may result than under an electoral system that requires candidates to appeal to all voters.

[6] The sectional interpretation becomes stronger when the seven southern counties in which Talmadge was consistently weak are explained away. Dougherty, Ware, Lowndes, and Glynn contain large towns, and towns generally resist Talmadge. Lanier and Clinch are in the home bailiwick of former Governor Rivers, a bitter antagonist of Talmadge. The seventh weak Talmadge county barely made the criteria for inclusion in the list of such counties. It did not give him less than 48 per cent of its vote in any of the primaries.

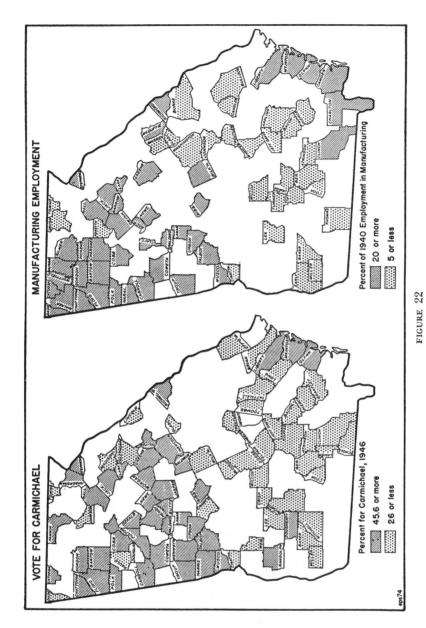

FIGURE 22

The Anti-Talmadge Vote and Manufacturing Employment: Vote for Carmichael in 1946
Georgia Gubernatorial Primary and Distribution of Manufacturing Employment

Carmichael, a north Georgia lawyer, served during World War II in a management position in the Bell bomber plant in his home, Cobb County. The connection did not necessarily endear him to labor but it differentiated him from Talmadge, a candidate with a strong rural appeal and little friendliness toward organized labor.[7]

It is not in sectionalism, however, but in an urban-rural cleavage that the most persuasive interpretation of Talmadgism is found. All over the South actual or fictional antagonisms between urban and rural areas are exploited for political purposes. In Georgia, the advantage that counties of small population enjoy under the county-unit system has encouraged candidates to irritate the already sensitive attitudes of rural voters toward their big-city brethren. Table 11 reveals the remarkable

TABLE 11

Relationship between Talmadge Strength in Georgia Gubernatorial Primaries and Ruralism

| | COUNTIES WITH TOWNS (1940) OF— | | |
	13,000 AND OVER	2500– 12,999 [a]	UNDER 2500 [b]
Total number of counties in group	14	53	92
Number voting less than 50% for Talmadge in 1940, 1942, and 1946	12	16	12
Per cent of counties in group	85.7	30.2	13.0
Number voting 50% or more for Talmadge in 1934, 1940, 1942, 1946	0	10	44
Per cent of counties in group	0	18.9	47.8

[a] That is, the county has a town of at least 2500 but none over 12,999.
[b] That is, the county has no town of 2500 or over.

aversion of city voters to the "Wild Man from Sugar Creek," the sobriquet early acquired by Gene. Of 14 counties containing towns of 13,000 or more population in 1940, 12 cast a majority of their votes against him in 1940, 1942, and 1946.[8] Of 53 counties with towns between 2500 and 12,999,

[7] The relation between Talmadge's opposition and manufacturing employment also prevailed in races before 1946. Of the 32 counties with highest percentage of their labor force in manufacturing, 20 gave Talmadge less than half their vote in 1940, 1942, and 1946. Of the 29 low counties in manufacturing employment, 16 cast a majority for him in 1934, 1940, 1942, and 1946. At the extremes on each end of the scale the relation between anti-Talmadge vote and manufacturing employment is sharper. Of the eight counties with 40 per cent or more of their labor force in manufacturing, seven gave Talmadge less than half their vote in 1940, 1942, and 1946. Of the nine counties with less than three per cent of their labor force in manufacturing, eight gave Talmadge at least a majority each of the four times he ran for governor after 1932.

[8] The two large-town mavericks were Chatham County (Savannah) and Richmond County (Augusta). The former gave Talmadge a majority in 1940 and 1946 and the latter in 1940. The explanation is found in the well-organized political machines of both cities, the only urban machines of consequence in the state.

16 were similarly perverse. And yet of 92 counties with no town over 2500 only 12 were consistently in opposition. A reading of the scale the other way yields a like result. In no county with a town of over 13,000 did he consistently receive a majority in the four gubernatorial races that he entered after 1932. In only 10 of 53 counties with medium-sized towns (for Georgia) did he receive consistent support. But in almost half the counties without incorporated places over 2500 he could count on a majority in all four elections.

There were reasons why the town and country counties split over Talmadge. He often bragged that he did not want to carry a county that had a streetcar. He spoke plainly in the rural idiom for what he said were the farmers' interests and, more important, for what many of them believed were their interests. In his first campaign for commissioner of agriculture, in 1926, he assailed the state department of agriculture and its inspection of fertilizer and other supplies used by farmers. His lambasting of the corporations was reminiscent of the Populists. Then and ever after his colloquialisms on the hustings and a pair of bright red galluses marked him as a man of the farming people. And indeed he was a country lawyer who had fought many a farmer's cause at court, and his listeners knew that the calluses on his hands came from work in the fields.[9]

Talmadge, like many professed champions of the forgotten man, in the showdown turned up on the side of the fellows who did the forgetting. He found himself intellectually and temperamentally at odds with the New Deal, including the AAA. He bitterly resented Federal control over the administration in Georgia of federally financed relief, welfare, and public works. He failed to co-operate in the passage of state legislation to enable Georgia to participate fully in the New Deal. It is not astonishing that Talmadge was warmly supported by a large segment of the business community of Georgia. Atlanta bankers and corporation executives soon learned that he was "safe." He might frighten them at first with his bluntness and calculated lack of gentility but he understood the businessman's viewpoint. He was a practical man, in favor of a balanced budget, a low tax rate, and not much public regulation of private enterprise. He showed little sympathy for organized labor. Although he talked about the needs of his rural constituents, he in fact did little in their behalf. He dramatically ousted a set of public service commissioners to obtain a reduction in utility rates but agreed shortly thereafter to a reduction in the ad valorem tax which, some have wryly estimated, more than compensated for the rate reduction. His slicing of license-tag costs to three

[9] Without detailed inquiry into sub-county election performance it is difficult to know what class of farmers Talmadge appealed to most. Reliable informants in two widely separated counties reported that he found greater support among poor farmers than their better-off neighbors. Some indication that he may have thought this, too, can be read into his advocacy of poll-tax repeal.

dollars profited trucking and bus companies infinitely more than the owners of jalopies.

Talmadge showed his basic sympathies in 1936 when he became the central figure in a so-called "grass roots" convention held in Macon, Georgia. Anti-New Dealers from many states attended the convention as a protest against the policies of the national Administration. Talmadge was the principal speaker. The financial backers of the meeting included northern industrialists, as well as southerners of high economic brackets who had little in common with poor farmers in streetcarless counties.[10]

Talmadge played the ends against the middle. His strength was drawn from the upper and lower reaches of the economic scale. Industrialists, bankers, corporation executives provided funds. Poor farmers provided votes. Both are necessary to win campaigns. That he could not be true to one without betraying the other seemed never to be discovered by the wool hat boys.[11] Probably in the absence of a highly competitive system of parties it is easier for politicians to build a self-contradictory combination. The record and traditional policies and composition of parties probably limit the kinds of allies an individual candidate can recruit.

Talmadge, the demagogue, is often linked in condemnation with such politicians as Theodore Bilbo and Huey Long. The basis for the association seems to be little more than unruly conduct and an uninhibited tongue. Talmadge had little sympathy for the heavy-taxing, free-spending ways of Huey. He would have looked askance at the New Deal voting record of Bilbo. In outlook he was more like some northern governors, John W. Bricker, for example, than either Long or Bilbo.

3. Rural Hegemony and the County-Unit System

Antagonism between populous centers and rural counties extends far back in Georgia history. Populism fed on rural-urban frictions, and Populist candidates did not fare so well in urban counties as in rural sections.[12] Although the bitterness of feeling stirred by Populism gradually

[10] Stetson Kennedy, *Southern Exposure* (Garden City: Doubleday & Company, Inc., 1946), pp. 128–29.

[11] Edna Cain Daniel, editor of the South Georgia *Quitman Free Press*, got to the heart of the matter when she wrote in the *Atlanta Journal*, March 2, 1947: "The wool hat boys . . . are not the rulers of Georgia politics. They are for the most part honest, sincere people, who, when the game is played out to the end, find that they have been pawns but never real winners. . . ." O'Daniel in Texas had a winning combination somewhat like that of Talmadge, but the voters finally caught up with him. Talmadge perhaps had a special advantage in that he could obfuscate the voters by playing on the race issue.

[12] A. M. Arnett, *The Populist Movement in Georgia* (New York: Columbia University Press, 1922), p. 184.

died down in most southern states, Georgia's agrarian crisis aroused a deeper and more lasting rural distrust of cities. Moreover, great Populist leaders lived on to keep rural antagonisms alive. In such endeavors they were aided by Georgia's peculiar system of nomination, which gives disproportionate weight to rural counties in the choice of state officials and accords great advantage to rabble-rousers with a rustic appeal.

The special imprint of Populism on Georgia may be accounted for by the extraordinary zeal with which the state turned to commercial and industrial development after Reconstruction and the corresponding neglect of its agrarians. The principal political leaders had all the trappings of Confederate respectability, yet their eyes were turned toward a new day. The new day for the "New South" involved the construction of railroads and expansion of manufactures. Henry Grady preached a doctrine of "progress," which was applauded in most quarters including eastern investment circles. While the attention of men of affairs and of government was directed toward the new day, the serious plight of plain farmers went unattended.

Tom Watson, Georgia's, and perhaps the nation's, ablest Populist leader, lived on long beyond the day of great Populists in other states. His invective was uncompromising. Bankers, merchants, owners of railroads, corporation executives, prosperous, cautious, and respectable souls of all descriptions fought back. Most such people lived in the towns, and city distrust of rural plainness seemed completely confirmed by the wild rantings of this man of the country. And so Watson, like his fellow spirits elsewhere, turned the towns into whipping boys.

Watson was elected to Congress early in his career; after defeat in 1892 he did not again hold public office until he was elected to the United States Senate in 1920. Though he became a national figure, he continued active participation in Georgia politics. Watson never let the self-awareness of the farmer fade. He addressed himself to the "men of the country" and pitted them against their iniquitous, slick brothers in the cities. He appealed, viciously in his later years, to sectional, race, class prejudices. Through his hold on underprivileged white farmers he was able to exert powerful and sometimes decisive influence in state primaries until his death in 1922.

Thus, down to the time of Talmadge, rural voters of Georgia were continuously reminded of their common differences with the towns.[13] Tom Watson's and Gene Talmadge's solicitude for the farmer may be regarded as a noble championing of the underprivileged, or it may be viewed as a calculated and cynical play for votes. In the choice of governors, under Georgia's county-unit system small, rural counties wield an influence far disproportionate to their population. The candidate with

---

[13] C. Vann Woodward, *Tom Watson* (New York: Macmillan Company, 1938), *passim*; Arnett, *The Populist Movement in Georgia, passim.*

the greatest following in the rural areas is almost certainly the winner. Great is the incentive to incite antagonism toward the cities.

The county-unit system largely accounts for the accentuation of rural-urban differences in Georgia. Unquestionably it is the most important institution affecting Georgia politics and has been a subject of continuous controversy. In recent years it has attracted attention elsewhere as another southern institution inspired by the devil to thwart the processes of democracy.[14] In essence, it is an indirect system of nomination under which each county has a specified number of unit votes. Nominations are determined, not by popular votes, but by unit votes. The unit votes of a county go to the candidate with a popular plurality in the county. The loading of the dice occurs in the allocation of unit votes. The Neill Primary Act of 1917, which enacted previous Democratic practice into law, gives to each county twice as many unit votes as it has members in Georgia's House of Representatives. The eight most populous of the 159 counties are entitled to three representatives each; the next 30, two each; and the remaining counties, one each. The manifest underrepresentation of the populous counties gives the small, rural counties a commanding voice in the choice of governors, Senators, and others nominated through the county-unit system.

The effect of the unit system in deflating the popular vote of the larger counties and ballooning the influence of the small counties can be judged from the data in Table 12. The weight of the white vote of

TABLE 12

Proportion of the Total Unit Vote Cast by Six, Four, and Two Unit-Vote Counties in Georgia Democratic Primaries Compared with the Proportion of 1940 Population in those Counties

COUNTY GROUPS ESTABLISHED BY LAW	UNIT VOTES EACH	PER CENT IN EACH GROUP OF COUNTIES OF STATE'S		
		TOTAL POPULATION	ADULT WHITE POPULATION	TOTAL UNIT VOTES
8 Most Populous Counties	6	30.1	34.1	11.7
30 Next Most Populous Counties	4	26.4	26.0	29.3
121 Remaining Counties	2	43.5	39.9	59.0

[14] The unit system applies to nomination of candidates for United States Senator, governor, statehouse offices, justices of the supreme court, and judges of the court of appeals. It may apply to the nomination of United States Representatives if the congressional district Democratic committee so determines. A plurality of the unit vote is required to nominate except for governor and Senator. In the absence of a majority in those races a run-off primary is held. In case of a unit-vote tie the candidate with the highest popular vote is nominated.

the smaller counties is also compounded by the fact that these counties have a disproportionate share of the Negro population which votes least in the rural areas. The 121 two-vote counties contain 43.5 per cent of the total population but only 39.9 per cent of the state's adult white population. They have 59.0 per cent of the unit votes. Table 12 conceals instances of extreme disparity between population and unit vote of individual counties. Examples of the grosser inequities appear in Table 13.

TABLE 13

Popular Votes Cast per Unit Vote, Democratic Primary for Governor of Georgia, 1940–46, Selected Counties

COUNTY	1940	1942	1946
Fulton	6062	5857	14,092
Chatham	1639	1265	6,751
DeKalb	1717	1911	4,462
Cobb	1554	1174	2,933
Hall	1128	1008	2,184
Laurens	1184	720	1,967
Quitman	218	247	299
Towns	387	321	296
Chattahoochee	145	113	132

Source: 1940 and 1942, *Georgia Facts in Figures* (Athens: University of Georgia Press, 1946), 152–53.

The disparity between popular vote and unit vote makes it possible for a candidate with only a popular plurality to receive a majority of the unit vote. During the past two decades a governor, a state treasurer, a public service commissioner, and a judge of the court of appeals have won unit-vote majorities although an opponent polled more popular votes. In 1946 three Democratic nominees for Congress failed to receive a plurality of the popular votes.

    An arrangement so patently calculated to thwart majority rule invites attack. Its defenders contend that the system permits each county to act as an entity in the choice of officials, an argument not unlike the defense of the electoral college for the election of the President. They rest their case principally, however, on the unblushing assertion that the best government flows from the rural areas, which are free from the "pinkness" that they associate with cities. The yeoman farmer, with his stable attachment to the basic virtues, should be given a greater say in state government than such urban classes as workers. Running throughout discussion of change is the cry that Atlanta would have complete control. Such a forecast ignores the fact that Birmingham does not run Alabama, that the cities of Florida have not ganged up on the farmers of that state, that Richmond and Norfolk do not run Virginia. It also ignores the fact that the two cities in Georgia with machines of any consequence, Savannah and Augusta, are the only cities that strung along at times with the farmers' candidate, Eugene Talmadge.

Actually none of the argument is pertinent. The simple truth is that those who gain political advantage by the system do not wish to surrender their vested interest. Genuine reform of the system by legislative action is virtually impossible because the legislators themselves are the beneficiaries of the malapportionment that would have to be altered. There is considerable sentiment, even in some rural areas, for increasing the voice of the larger counties. The demand for full equality is confined to the impotent cities, and even there politicians with state-wide ambitions find it expedient to indulge in the piety of self-denial. Talmadge forces in the 1947 legislative session barely lost in a move to propose a constitutional amendment to extend the unit principle to the general election. The house vote was 129 for and 49 against: a two-thirds majority of the entire membership was constitutionally required. On the "must" list of Herman Talmadge after his election in 1948, the 1949 session submitted the amendment to the people.

Opponents of the county-unit system have unsuccessfully attacked its constitutionality. After Eugene Talmadge won the nomination in 1946 by a minority of the popular vote, private citizens sued to invalidate the Neill Primary Act on the ground that it violated the equal protection clause of the Fourteenth Amendment. A Federal court held that equal protection was not denied, in view of the classification of the counties on the basis of population and of the constitutional provisions for readjustment after each census.[15] Although the Supreme Court refused to review the lower court's action, possibilities of constitutional attack may not be exhausted.

So long as the system prevails it will exert a profound influence on the character of the state's politics. Fundamentally its effect is that only those candidates for state office who can win pluralities in the small, rural, two-unit-vote counties have a reasonable expectation of success. The necessity for a specialized sort of rural appeal deprives the state of a great body of potential leadership and places the election of governing officials in the hands of a segment of the population presumably no better qualified to govern than any other. In a state with a large effective vote in urban as well as rural areas a candidate must tailor his campaign to suit both. A hillbilly like Governor "Big Jim" Folsom of Alabama, for instance, rallied the support of organized labor the best he could in 1946 and was the candidate of the downtrodden in the cities as well as at the forks of the creeks. In Georgia, however, the only effective vote lies in the

15 *Turman* v. *Duckworth*, 68 Fed. Supp. 744 (1946).

country. There is not only the positive need to be an effective rural campaigner but there is the absence of need to be solicitous of city voters. It
then becomes possible to use the cities as whipping boys, to inflate rural
pride and prejudices, including that against the Negroes who vote most
frequently in the cities, and to perpetuate the frictions between country
and city.

Another feature of critical importance in county-unit voting is its
effect on methods of campaign organization and management. In normal
campaigns a vote anywhere is a vote gained or lost. It is always to the
candidate's advantage to win a vote anywhere; hence the campaign is
fought in every quarter with equal vigor. In Georgia every state-wide
campaign is made up of 159 separate races, one for the unit votes of each
county. Practical politicians emphasize that the man who knows what
he is doing diagnoses every county individually. He classifies the counties
into three groups: those in which he is sure of a plurality; those in which
he has no chance of a plurality; those which are doubtful. He forgets
about the first two groups except for routine campaign coverage.[16] He
concentrates his resources in the third group: expenditures, appearances
by the candidate, negotiations, all the tricks of county politicking. These
maneuvers can only be executed through politicians native to the county.
A tremendous premium is therefore placed upon the political chieftain
acquainted with local leaders in all counties.

A candidate must appeal to voters of the rural, two-unit counties and
be familiar with the intricacies of their factionalism. By the same token
the system aggrandizes the importance of the local leaders in the small
doubtful counties. In the small counties a few popular votes may determine which candidate receives the unit vote. In such counties the number
of county officeholders is high in relation to the number of voters. Hence
the importance of the county ring, if there is one, is correspondingly increased. Two or three local politicos may be able to determine who wins
the county plurality. The extraordinary importance of coming to terms
with local leaders who control even a handful of votes is suggested by
the 1946 primary. In that year in each of 27 counties a shift of 75 popular
votes would have given a plurality to a candidate other than the one who
received it. A shift of 25 rural, two-vote counties from Talmadge to Carmichael would have changed the outcome.

The unit system, thus, requires that candidates deal with local patriarchs and also probably provides a stimulus for the construction of local
rings and perhaps for electoral irregularities. Moreover, all these pressures
tend to be concentrated on the close counties. Campaign effort is con-

---

[16] An editor in a north Georgia county was much perplexed at the behavior of his
county. Talmadge never did much for the county, especially in the way of roads, yet it
always supported him with large majorities. Ellis Arnall came along and put in two
roads and a bridge and the county still preferred Talmadge.

centrated within about a third of the counties where there is a great premium on controlled blocs of votes. Whether such a bloc is under the thumb of a single official, or subject to a courthouse ring, or responsive to the behest of a leading citizen of economic and civic prominence, it can often spell the difference between victory and defeat. The boss of the bloc must be dealt with, a fact that increases the importance of political contacts and of the ability to operate smoothly with local-level politicos in all sections of the state. Few individuals have the acquaintance in every county necessary for conducting a state-wide campaign. Experienced observers say the best qualified in this regard are Roy Harris, former speaker of the house, and Ed Rivers, former governor. Either of them can "get on the telephone and organize a campaign."

Organization work in the critical counties reaches the stage sooner or later of simple, unvarnished horse trading. A politician of wide experience states that his usual practice is to put roughly $10,000 into the fifty or so doubtful counties on "election day," or from one hundred to three hundred dollars per county,[17] which, he says, goes to spruce the enthusiasm of bosses and petty heelers who may be wavering (often deliberately in order that they will have to be spruced) and to provide a little loose money for the inevitable expenses of last-minute electioneering. It would seem essential in Georgia to possess not only the attributes of stump speaking effective in rural areas but also the wherewithal—money and a willingness to pledge governmental favors—to reach those who control the critical blocs of votes in marginal counties. The readily demonstrable relation that may prevail under the unit system between outlays and the delivery of votes may operate to enhance the power of campaign contributors. "Atlanta money" may exert greater influence through the county-unit system than it would in a system of popular election.

Georgians talk of the importance of county machines. Those who lament the unit system maintain that the hold of small-county rings bought with corporation funds is as nefarious in state affairs as any large urban machine could ever be. Few political observers in Georgia deny that some counties can be "bought and sold." The widespread talk that precedes and follows every campaign about the "buying" of counties finds its origin in the negotiations between campaign managers and county leaders for the necessary narrow margin of plurality. In some areas it is doubtless unnecessary that local leaders muster support among the voters to "deliver" a county. Election administration is extremely lax in some Georgia counties and overtly corrupt in others. Controllers of election

---

[17] This last-minute pittance is not to be confused with the total expenditures of a major candidate or to be considered as indicative of the total sums placed in individual counties during a campaign. One former candidate speaks of amounts as high as $10,000 being sent into a doubtful county during a hot race.

machinery can at times deliver the margin of plurality as effectively as a boss whose followers respond to the snap of his fingers.

4. The Opposition

The county-unit system invariably works to the advantage of a candidate of Talmadge's proclivities and personality. It not only yields maximum results for his particular campaign appeal but by the controversy over its retention encourages an exploitation of the issues on which he can be most telling. One may well wonder what form the opposition forces take in the face of this strong combination of institution and individual.

Characteristically in one-party politics, as we have observed in Virginia and Tennessee, a strong political combination tends to force rival political elements to associate in an opposition faction. Strong political leadership, be it personal or organized, seems to produce counterorganization. In a state with an established political organization ambitious politicians find the surest road to political success via the organization. In other one-party states the story is different. Cohesive, political forces with lasting power usually consist of the personal followings of an individual leader. The basis of the faction is loyalty to an individual. There is no room in it for the professional who wants to ascend to the top, for the top place is taken and when it becomes vacant with rare exception the faction itself disintegrates. In consequence the professional who wants top honors must place himself in opposition, must become an "anti"— be it anti-Graves, anti-Bilbo, or anti-Talmadge. While it is an opportunistic sort of opposition and often lacks cohesiveness, the battles between the two camps serve as stabilizing influences on the composition of the factions.

In Georgia the leadership and the composition of the anti-Talmadge faction have changed as new candidates have come to the fore. In their political youth, as legislators, both Ed Rivers and Ellis Arnall, later the principal anti-Talmadge politicians, wore the political galluses of Old Gene. The practice is best illustrated by Georgia's most prominent and energetic political manager, Roy Harris, former speaker of the house and the closest adviser of Governor Herman Talmadge. His journeying from one political camp to another is illustrative of a political amorality that takes little cognizance of ideological preferences. He was an early Rivers supporter and did heavy work in three of that gentleman's campaigns, 1928, 1936, and 1938. He was a floor leader for Talmadge during the 1935 legislative session. He played a large part in Senator George's 1938 victory. His assistance to Ellis Arnall during the 1942 race was of major importance in defeating Gene Talmadge. Yet when 1946 came around he was again in the Talmadge fold, opposing both Rivers and Arnall. The prevailing view in Georgia is that these maneuvers were brought about by Harris's personal ambitions and frustrations. He is said to have aspired to the governorship, feeling that he had made two governors himself, and when he failed to gain the support of Rivers and Arnall to this end he turned against them.

Along with their more prominent colleagues, other Georgia politicians of county, sectional, and state importance have migrated from one alignment to another. There is, however, a constant agglomeration of sentiment on which to build any anti-Talmadge campaign. A candidate of Talmadge's audacity, occasional uncouthness, iconoclasm, disrespect for established process always aligned against him a healthy number of Georgians who are usually damned with the designation "respectable." Persons objectively favoring good government for its own sake have usually found themselves opposing him. Talmadge's first terms in office, 1933–37, were distinguished by a blunt unfriendliness to the New Deal, which antagonized those Georgians desiring to have their state take full advantage of Federal programs.

In 1936 discontent with the kind of government that held Georgia up to the ridicule of the nation found expression in what was known as the "Weltner movement." Philip Weltner had been Chancellor of the University System of Georgia. He resigned his post and traveled the state to stimulate a concerted anti-Talmadge effort for the 1936 campaign. A state convention was held in Macon to which delegates unsympathetic with Talmadge came from most counties. Judge Blanton Fortson won the contest for the convention's "nomination" for governor. Shortly thereafter E. D. Rivers, one of the contestants for the convention's favor, announced his own candidacy and in the subsequent primary defeated Judge Fortson and Talmadge's candidate, Charles Redwine.

A surge of public opinion similar to the Weltner movement took place spontaneously during the 1947 controversy over the succession to the governorship. After the death of his father, the governor-elect, Herman Talmadge was "elected" governor by the legislature, an action later invalidated by the state's supreme court. Outgoing Governor Ellis Arnall insisted on relinquishing his office to the new lieutenant-governor, whereupon the new Talmadge stormed the gubernatorial offices and set himself up as governor in the manner of a Central American general.

Georgians were chagrined by the national spotlight thrown upon their state, as well as infuriated and frightened by the forceful, extralegal seizure of the government. Mass meetings were held over the state at which outraged persons banded together in groups known as the Aroused Citizens of Georgia. The sentiment took the semblance of a movement when Judge Fortson and Mayor Harvey J. Kennedy of Barnesville were called upon to serve as co-chairmen for the state.

Another locus of anti-Talmadge sentiment has been urban labor, though organized labor has not been consistently in the opposition camp. Early in his career Eugene Talmadge used the militia to evict workers from company-owned homes, as an incident to an AFL textile organizing drive. Before it was all over the strikers and their families were behind barbed wire in what labor sympathizers called a "concentration camp." Organized labor, however, like business, finds it expedient to be in the good graces of whoever is in power, and that has often meant a Talmadge. Further, the Talmadge exploitation of the race issue has attracted many labor votes that would otherwise have gone to a more liberal candidate. Even the CIO, which in Georgia as elsewhere propounds a more militant political program than the AFL, has suffered dissensions in its own ranks which have qualified its effectiveness in opposing Talmadge.

Perhaps Negroes are the most cohesive group opposing Talmadge. An estimated 85,000–100,000 actually cast ballots in 1946 when they voted for the first time in numbers. Except for mild defections to Rivers in a few counties they voted almost solidly for Carmichael. Following the decision of the Federal courts in a local case,[18] their registration as voters had been facilitated by the Democratic state committee under the leadership of Governor Arnall. A program to encourage Negroes to register and vote was pushed forward under the leadership of A. T. Walden, a Negro attorney of Atlanta. Walden, as head of the Georgia Association of Citizens' Democratic Clubs, is the chief Negro political leader in the state. Through a large number of county and city clubs Negroes have a means for concerted political action.

The urban press constitutes another element of the anti-Talmadge forces. The *Atlanta Journal* has consistently maintained an enthusiastic opposition to Talmadge. The *Atlanta Constitution* has been milder and after the 1948 primary was considered by many to have joined with Herman. Both papers have supported Ellis Arnall. Neither, however, exerts the same political leadership it did thirty years ago or equals that of the *Nashville Tennessean* in its own state today. The press of the state has been predominantly anti-Talmadge in recent elections though, as is generally true, such editorial support has not been a major influence on the voting.

The problem of a political faction is not only one of votes, which naturally are essential, but of greater importance is leadership that can hold the multifarious elements of the faction together and give power and direction to their efforts. Demands on leadership are especially great in a faction born of opposition. The Talmadge faction, by definition, has leadership. The anti-Talmadge faction is likely not to have effective leadership. So it is with "anti" groups everywhere. Their inability to develop and choose their own leadership by orderly and binding processes is another evidence of their distinctness from organized parties.

[18] *Chapman* v. *King*, 154F. (2d) 460 (1946).

The inevitable consequence of lack of factional discipline was made abundantly clear in 1946. The two most influential anti-Talmadge leaders were former Governor Ed Rivers and incumbent Governor Ellis Arnall. Rivers aspired to be governor again. He claimed he had a promise of support from Governor Arnall. When Arnall declined to back him, Rivers announced his own candidacy and ran against both Talmadge and Carmichael, the candidate brought into the field by Arnall around whom virtually all the anti-Talmadge sentiment in the state rallied. Rivers had no chance of winning but he satisfied a yearning for vengeance, some said, by diverting enough support from Carmichael to defeat him. The inability of political factions of one-party states to resolve personal rivalries and preserve unity is a major weakness. In 1946 there were no influences that could be brought on Rivers or Arnall to suppress their differences.

It is always to the advantage of a man like Talmadge to have several opponents. His basic vote is assured. If he can split the opposition he can carry enough counties under the unit system to win. The utility of futile candidacies does not go unrecognized. In the 1940 gubernatorial primary Abit Nix and Columbus Roberts were Talmadge's chief opponents. When Nix showed signs of dropping out because of lack of money, a large and timely contribution came to his headquarters. The rumor circulated that the money had come from the Talmadge camp and Roberts so charged from the stump. Nix was drawn into rebuttal and the two of them spent much of the rest of the campaign fighting each other—to the assurance of a Talmadge victory.[19]

The 1946 primary marked a critical juncture in Georgia political history, certainly the most important contest in a generation. A victory for Carmichael (who, as it was, received the most popular votes) would have given the elder Talmadge his second successive defeat. After four more years of opposition government, Herman Talmadge's future would not have been assured. The 1946 outcome gave Talmadgism a new lease on life. The potency of the young Talmadge was recognized as the 1948 primary approached. Acting Governor M. E. Thompson became the standard bearer against him. The possibility of a Talmadge victory was so apparent that Arnall and Rivers publicly patched up their differences and were designated by Thompson as his joint campaign managers. Only under dire necessity or the most favorable circumstances can such unity be maintained.[20] Talmadge won a resounding victory: 51.7 per cent of the popular vote; 76.1 per cent of the unit vote.

[19] A. L. Henson, *Red Galluses* (Boston: House of Edinboro, 1945), pp. 215–16.

[20] Even in 1948 there was an independent candidate in the person of Joe Rabun, a former navy chaplain and former pastor of Talmadge's church, who took issue with Talmadge's race baiting and was asked to seek another pastorate. In his 1948 gubernatorial candidacy he was backed by certain labor elements disappointed in both Talmadge and Thompson, both of whom had failed to veto the anti-closed shop bill. He

By 1949 the anti-Talmadge faction was sorely in need of leadership. Ed Rivers had been so discredited by the exposés following his last term that it is doubtful that he can ever again be elected governor. M. E. Thompson is widely considered to lack the tenacity of viewpoint and intellectual conviction necessary for political leadership. Many believe that his 1948 defeat marked the end of his political career. Ellis Arnall accepted the presidency of the Independent Motion Picture Producers Association, which, with his other business and professional interests, would leave him little time for local politicking.

The case of Ellis Arnall is a telling commentary on Georgia and on much of the South. Many Georgians and most outsiders consider his administration (1943–47) the most competent given the state in several decades. He brought to office administrative reforms, constitutional revision, and a dignity refreshing to many of his fellow citizens. He acquired a national reputation for liberalism, and, most remarkable of all, he dared to be fair on that nemesis of southern liberals, the rights of Negroes. After leaving office he wrote two successful books, made a nation-wide lecture tour, and identified himself with the liberal wing of the Democratic party in the presidential campaign of 1948. A native son's popularity all too often varies inversely with his prestige in the rest of the land. This is especially true when he excites the admiration of the "northern press" and draws plaudits from commentators who annoy the folks at home with meddling observations on southern life. Arnall was accused by his opponents of "smug snobbery" and portrayed as having traded his loyalty to Georgia for the pottage of outside approval.

Factional division of the electorate around a powerful personality is characteristic of southern politics. It exists in its most exaggerated form in Georgia where a fairly consistent bi-factionalism persists, dependent on the militancy and cohesiveness of the Talmadge faction. Unity in the opposition faction is maintained with great difficulty. The differences that have divided the two factions have been primarily issues of personality and method. Where substance has entered the controversies, Talmadge generally favored restricted state services and a limited use of governmental powers. These attitudes and his low-tax beliefs found him favor with the highest economic forces in the state. He viciously exploited ancient prejudices against Negroes and cities in appealing to the rural constituency which kept him in office.

The bi-factionalism produced by Talmadgism has effected a clear definition of some issues for decision by the public at the polls. A few of them represented genuine conflicts of interest, such as the tilts with the New Deal in the 'thirties and the battle over Negro voting in 1946. The heart of the contest has always remained the fight for office. The bitter

---

received only one-half of one per cent of the votes, and his campaign served only to weaken Thompson.

division of the state's electorate produced by the demagogue has thus facilitated in some measure the resolution of conflicts and the waging of elections along lines of genuine conflict. It has not produced, however, substitute mechanisms for a party system, with the paraphernalia necessary for the continuous effective association of individuals and groups with common political interests.

Chapter Seven | # SOUTH CAROLINA:
THE POLITICS OF COLOR

O UTSIDE the South the misconception prevails that all southerners are equally concerned about the race problem. Tension and anxiety about white supremacy, however, are sharper and more continuous in some states than in others. The degree to which the race issue influences political life varies almost directly with the proportion of Negro population. Seldom do any political leaders speak up for Negroes, but in states with the highest proportions of Negroes, white-supremacy demagogues seem to be most strident. In states with fewer blacks, Negro-baiting, to be sure, occurs, but it seems that leaders most unrestrained in denunciation of the Negro rise in the states with many blacks. South Carolina has had a succession of spectacular race orators who almost blanket out the achievements of its abler and more temperate leaders, such as James F. Byrnes. While others shared their views, the politicians of South Carolina —and Mississippi—have put the white-supremacy case most bitterly, most uncompromisingly, most vindictively. "Pitchfork Ben" Tillman, Cole Blease, and "Cotton Ed" Smith used the floor of the United States Senate as a rostrum for white-supremacy oratory, matched in virulence mainly by such Mississippi spokesmen as Vardaman, Bilbo, Rankin.

The harshness and ceaselessness of race discussion in South Carolina are not matters of coincidence. It is but a short time, as time must be measured, since the state had three Negroes for every two white persons.

In 1900, the population was 58.4 per cent Negro; in 1910, 55.2; in 1920, 51.4; in 1930, 45.6. In 1940 the state's population was 42.9 per cent colored, a ratio exceeded only by Mississippi's 49.2 per cent. The next ranking states clustered around 35 per cent: Louisiana, 35.9; Georgia, 34.7; Alabama, 34.7. Furthermore, only nine South Carolina counties—seven of them in the extreme northwest—had less than 30 per cent Negro population while 22 of the state's 46 counties were more than 50 per cent Negro. Thus, the state has no considerable region—such as Tennessee, Virginia, North Carolina, and even Georgia and Alabama—in which political life can proceed without unbroken concern over the race question.

South Carolina's preoccupation with the Negro stifles political conflict. Over offices there is conflict aplenty, but the race question muffles conflict over issues latent in the economy of South Carolina. Mill worker and plantation owner alike want to keep the Negro in his place. In part, issues are deliberately repressed, for, at least in the long run, concern with genuine issues would bring an end to the consensus by which the Negro is kept out of politics. One crowd or another would be tempted to seek his vote.[1] In part, the race issue provides in itself a tool for the diversion of attention from issues. When the going gets rough, when a glimmer of informed political self-interest begins to well up from the masses, the issue of white supremacy may be raised to whip them back into line. And, in the simple strategy of self-advancement, leaders possessed of an artful invective or chancing upon a timely opportunity may raise the issue and thereby place themselves in unassailable positions as skilled defenders of the highest value, almost without regard to their position on other matters. Perhaps South Carolina's record, since it is an extreme case, illuminates the real effects of race over the entire South.

1. Localism: "Friends and Neighbors" Again

The high pitch of feeling on race is only one factor giving character to South Carolina politics. This element adds overtones, shrill overtones

[1] How much "deliberateness" is involved in the repression of issues may be debatable. The mechanism for the suppression of issues is closely related to local unity in national politics. That unity, historically induced by resistance to national intervention in racial relations locally, prevents division on questions of national politics. These questions, far more than state and local issues, provide the basis for a politics of issues. Thus, the "repression" of issues may not be so much "deliberate" as it is the inevitable consequence of local, white unity vis-a-vis the national government. The situation is put by a South Carolina editor as follows: "All white persons in South Carolina are not of one mind on the great national issues. But by making the Democratic party of South Carolina the white party, South Carolinians have smothered these differences and disfranchised for every practical purpose everybody who didn't go along with the national Democratic party. And also sacrificed have been the disagreements among white South Carolinians concerning the proper policy to be pursued in state affairs."—*Columbia Record* (Columbia, S. C.), April 26, 1948.

to be sure, to a loose multifactional system that the state has in common with those southern states that have no durable bi-factional system. By now it has become clear that in the absence of well-organized politics, localism will play a powerful role in the orientation of voters' attitudes in state-wide politics. South Carolina is without a well-organized factional

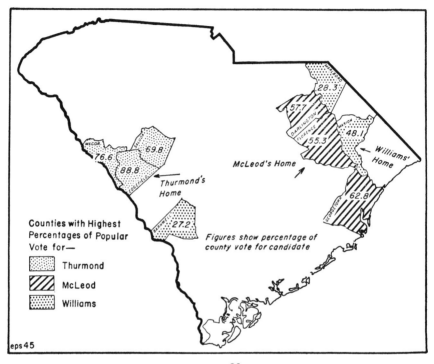

FIGURE 23

Friends and Neighbors: Counties Giving Highest Percentages of their Popular Vote to Leading Candidates for Governor, First Democratic Primary, South Carolina, 1946

system. In its gubernatorial politics, localism provides the electoral nucleus to which candidates hope to add a sufficient number of votes to carry the day. South Carolina localism, however, has peculiarities unto itself. In so small a state with so few counties it is a short step from localism to sectionalism. When a few counties are annexed to a local friends-and-neighbors following, a candidate has organized about himself, for the moment at least, a sectional faction.

The character of localism in South Carolina is suggested by the maps in Figures 23 and 24, which locate the counties ranking highest in the percentage of vote cast for the leading candidates for the gubernatorial nomination in the first primaries of 1938 and 1946. Although the intensity of local support for most of the candidates was comparatively low, the

THE LATE SENATOR "COTTON ED" SMITH

With the disappearance of the old-style spellbinder this will be a duller world.

MECHANICAL COTTON PICKER

Its perfection will accelerate political change.

persons who eventually won in the second primaries in the two campaigns piled up impressive leads in their home bailiwicks in the first primary. J. Strom Thurmond in 1946 polled 88.8 per cent of the vote in his home county of Edgefield, a rural county with a small vote. He had served as county superintendent of education, county attorney, state senator,

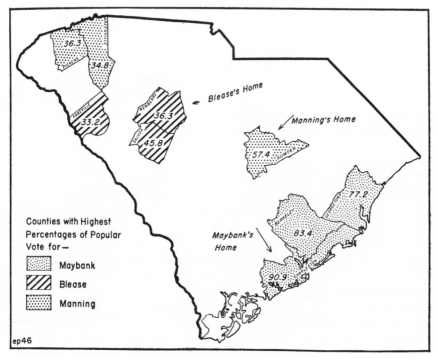

FIGURE 24

Friends and Neighbors: Counties Giving Highest Percentage of their Popular Vote to Leading Candidates for Governor, First Democratic Primary, South Carolina, 1938

and circuit judge from the county. On his return from military service, he ran for governor on a generally progressive platform. In South Carolina, as elsewhere, the small, rural county with a fairly homogeneous population probably offers most fertile ground for localism.

City dwellers, except under machine rule, tend more than rural people to divide their vote. The 1938 Charleston County vote for Burnet Rhett Maybank for governor provides one of these exceptions. The election officials certified that he received 90.9 per cent of the vote cast in Charleston County. Mayor of Charleston from 1931 to 1938, he headed a political machine equipped for the efficient management of the vote. The Charleston machine, however, fluctuates in effectiveness, and in recent years Maybank has been the only candidate for state office to whom it has delivered overwhelming majorities. It has been far less consistent over the past two decades than the Memphis machine in delivering a heavy vote to state-wide candidates. The local explanation is that the machine has had discretion enough not to report 90 per cent of the vote for its candidate when only 60 per cent would serve. In quite recent primaries, discretion has been supplemented by one of the organization's periodic slumps and by the introduction of voting machines.[2]

Whatever the explanation in particular instances, localism tends to be associated with a multifactional system rather than with the sort of dual division found in Virginia and Tennessee. In the fractionalization of its electorate, South Carolina approaches Florida's high degree of political granulation. Although, as we shall see, underlying forces drive South Carolina toward a two-sided fight in politics, no continuing dual organization has developed in its elective politics. Many groupings of voters exist in each campaign, each group ordinarily formed around a local political potentate.

For lack of whatever circumstances might force political leaders and voters into two camps, South Carolina gubernatorial races start out as a free-for-all among three or four principal contenders. In 1930, 1934, and 1938, there were eight candidates. In 1942 there were only two, while in 1946 the number rose to eleven. Many candidacies are not regarded seriously by either the candidate or the electorate. Usually the four leaders poll over three-fourths of all votes. (Aggregate percentages recently polled by the four leading candidates have been: 1930, 75.7; 1934, 94.9; 1938, 89.5; 1946, 82.4.) The top candidate draws the support of from one-fourth to one-third of all voters, with the result that the first-primary vote is dispersed somewhat less widely among different candidates than in Florida. Detailed data on the division of the first primary vote are set out in Table 14.[3]

[2] In recent first senatorial primaries, the percentages of the Charleston County vote polled by the candidate leading in the county have been: 1930, 61.4; 1938, 66.7; 1941, 78.4; 1942, 83.5; 1944, 53.4. In recent first gubernatorial primaries, the percentages of the vote polled by the leading candidate in the county have been: 1930, 56.6; 1934, 26.5; 1938, 90.9; 1942, 58.8; 1946, 37.3. The common belief is that state-wide candidates on occasion have been counted out by the local organization. Thus, in 1930 Johnston came to Charleston in the lead but the vote for Blackwood there (10,636 to 2,656) gave the governorship to Blackwood by 118,721 to 117,752. Similarly, in 1938 Charleston reported an extremely high total vote with a lop-sided victory to Maybank (21,864 to 1,374 for Manning), enough to cover the margin of victory in the state, 163,947 to 149,368. One erstwhile gubernatorial candidate reported that the Charleston leaders had asked him at the time of his campaign what size vote he wanted from Charleston. He recalled, with a mild astonishment persisting after several years, that these leaders "were not embarrassed at all" by these conversations.

[3] The high degree of atomization of South Carolina gubernatorial politics may knock into a cocked hat the earlier attempt to get at the underlying causes of the similar state of affairs in Florida. South Carolina is small in area and has no social disorganization attributable to a mass of recent migrants as in Florida. The similarities between the politics of the two states, however, may be more apparent than real. As

The multiplicity of candidacies points to the function of a two-party system—or of a strong bi-factional system—in narrowing the range of choice offered the voter by limiting major contestants to two. A party system performs a negative function in repressing candidacies, as well as the positive role of choosing and putting forward candidates. The loose factional politics in South Carolina blocks few persons with an inclina-

TABLE 14

Fractionalization of South Carolina's Electorate: Percentage of Total Vote Polled by Leading Candidates for Governor in First Democratic Primaries

1946		1938		1934	
CANDIDATE	PER CENT OF TOTAL VOTE	CANDIDATE	PER CENT OF TOTAL VOTE	CANDIDATE	OF TOTAL PER CENT VOTE
Thurmond	33.4	Maybank	35.1	Johnston	35.2
McLeod	28.8	Manning	22.1	Blease	28.8
Williams	12.4	Blease	18.1	Manning	18.7
Taylor	7.8	Bennett	14.2	Pearce	12.2
7 others	17.6	4 others	10.5	4 others	5.1

tion to run for governor. Under a two-party system, of course, minor candidates appear on the ballot but without fractionalizing the electorate as in a one-party state. In the first 1946 primary eight minor candidates for governors polled together about one-fourth of the total vote. One of them entered the race because he felt the New Deal viewpoint ought to be expressed and that someone ought to try to offset the anti-Negro talk. Another was a bitter anti-FDR man. One was a former Congressman, with a following around the state and an illusion that he had a chance. Another, the local explanation is, was a rich old man with nothing much better to do than run for governor. Another was a big liquor dealer and ran as a wet. Still another was even more anti-Negro than any of the leading candidates.[4] All such dilettantes are, of course, by and large frozen out by the professionals in a state with genuine political organization. In a multifactional system they confuse the process of choice.

2. Piedmont vs. Low Country

In a factional system organized around friends-and-neighbors nuclei, it is but a short step to larger groupings of voters formed along sectional

the description of South Carolina proceeds it will become apparent that there has existed a clearer tendency toward a bi-factional division than in Florida.

[4] A fact not widely known is that time after time the electorates of southern states have killed off candidates with the most extreme views on the race question.

lines by the addition of nearby counties to local followings. The many-sided first-primary contest reveals the multiplicity of personal and local followings; in the second primary, however, the voters are compelled to line up with one or the other of two candidates. In South Carolina this dual division often shapes up along low-country-upcountry lines, though voter consciousness of such differences is not sharp.

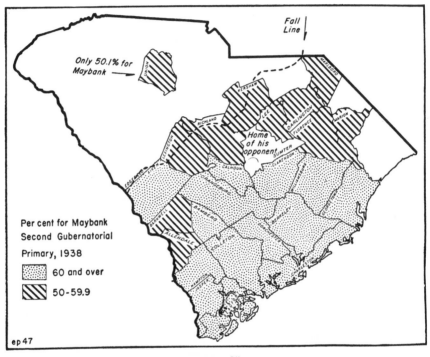

FIGURE 25

Coastal Plain vs. Piedmont: Popular Vote for Maybank in Second South Carolina Gubernatorial Primary, 1938

The northwestern third of the state lies on the Piedmont Plateau, whose elevation ranges from about 400 feet at the fall line to 1200–1500 feet at the foothills of the Blue Ridge, which edges over into the state's three northwestern counties. The "low country" consists of the lower two-thirds of the Coastal Plain, the Coastal Terraces, which include the great swamps and marshes of the state. Between the Coastal Terraces and the fall line, elevation rises from 100 to 400 feet. In most counties of both the Plain and the Piedmont cotton is king. These geographic provinces do not differ sharply enough to produce radically different systems of agriculture. Cotton-mill workers, concentrated in the upper Piedmont, would furnish the basis for a sharper sectionalism if they were more alert politically, but even over most of the Piedmont agriculture outranks manufacturing. In an earlier day Ben Tillman inflamed the upcountry-men in his crusade against the aristocrats of Charleston; since his time, however, the sharpness of sectional animosities has been mitigated.

Regardless of the blandness of sectionalism in South Carolina, differences between the Piedmont and the Coastal Plain frequently divide the state's voters. The line between Piedmont and Coastal Plain, for example, closely paralleled the line between the regions of highest popular strength of Burnet Rhett Maybank and of Colonel Wyndham Manning in the 1938 gubernatorial race. Maybank polled a majority of the vote in most of the counties below the fall line. In the Piedmont he won a bare popular majority only in Union County. (See Figure 25.) In his victory, Maybank overcame the long-standing antipathy to Charlestonians in the governorship, a prejudice attributed to the animosities kindled by Tillman.

Maybank won by the vote of the Coastal Plain, although in South Carolina as elsewhere, practicing politicians hesitate to attribute significance to a correlation between a popular vote and geographical, economic, or social factors. Indeed, geographical concentration of strength may represent a pseudo-sectionalism in that a friends-and-neighbors vote rallies around the regional champion, who is no regional champion at all in the sense of being a spokesman for regional interest. Working politicians, in explanation of Maybank's vote, point rather to particular political situations. The Charleston machine, at a peak in its power, delivered a heavy vote to Maybank. In adjoining Berkeley County the Santee-Cooper power project was under construction and Maybank was chairman of the South Carolina Public Service Authority which controlled it. Many individuals thought they had jobs and when the campaign was over found that they did not. In other counties the vote is explained by alliances between Maybank and local leaders.

Regardless of the disposition to explain a sectional vote in terms of patronage, deals, arrangements, alliances, the chances are that the sectional groupings manifest in the 1938 Maybank vote represents a deeper sectional unity that provided a framework within which alliances could be made. Charlestonians confess to a sense of isolation, shared with them by the citizens of the other coastal counties, which creates a common psychological bond. On the other hand, the uplanders perhaps still feel an antipathy toward aristocratic Charleston, as it was pictured in the agrarian crusade, an antipathy kept alive by persistent evangelical condemnation of that city as the symbol of all sin. Then, too, Charleston has always insisted on home rule, and its neighboring counties, with a lesser approach to unanimity, oppose prohibition. In fact, the vote for Maybank's opponent Colonel Manning, whose platform included a law-enforcement plank, matched the county-by-county dry vote in 1940 on an advisory referendum on the question, "Are you in favor of discontinuing the legal sale of intoxicating liquors, wines, beers or other intoxicating beverages, and the imposition of new taxes to replace lost revenues as a result of repeal of present liquor laws?" Lowlanders voted no and they were most wet in Charleston and the adjoining coastal counties. The

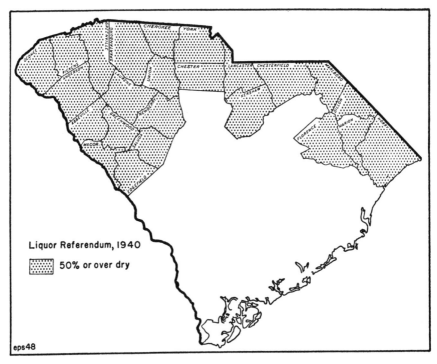

FIGURE 26

South Carolina Counties Voting in Favor of Prohibition, 1940

uplanders, as may be seen in Figure 26, followed the usual southern highland practice of voting dry.

Sectional alignment is not the invariable rule. Such divisions have cropped up frequently in campaigns in which Maybank, of Charleston, and Olin D. Johnston, of Spartanburg at the opposite end of the state, have been candidates. When these men have not been candidates divisions have often not been along sectional lines. Nevertheless, at bottom solid foundations exist for the organization of political factions, with their centers of gravity in the uplands and in the lowlands. Its cotton mills differentiate the Piedmont from the rest of the state. In ten northwestern counties more than 30 per cent of the 1940 labor force was employed in manufacturing. In eight of these counties manufacturing employment exceeded that in agriculture. Here is a compact area potentially the basis for a political grouping with a labor orientation.

This potential labor grouping has not been well organized politically, although from time to time issues and candidates are joined in a manner to consolidate the labor vote. Johnston's vote in the first gubernatorial primary of 1930 probably illustrates the rock-bottom basis and extent of Piedmont factionalism. In 1930 Johnston was, in the words of a low-country politician, "a young squirt from Spartanburg with a labor background." In the first primary his popular strength coincided roughly with the counties of high manufacturing employment, as may be seen in Figure 27. While his "friends and neighbors," too, coincided with manufacturing employment, it is important what kinds of friends and neighbors one has. Johnston, years later after he had gone to the Senate, was the only member of the South Carolina delegation to vote against the Taft-Hartley Act. It cannot be said, however, that northwestern industrial workers constitute a cohesive block in state politics. South Carolina's textile operatives are in large degree engaged in less-remunerative types of textile work, and their organization into unions and their political education have a long way to go.[5]

The fundamental basis for the latent unity of the Coastal Plain perhaps rests in its more complete dependence on agriculture than the Piedmont and in the fact that its counties have the highest proportions of Negroes. Then, too, in the rural, low-country counties the situation is ideal for the development of strong banker-planter-lawyer bourbon rings.[6] Low-country politicians note the difference when they observe that machines do not flourish in the upcountry, whose individualistic and independent people "look you in the eye and tell you to go to hell no matter who you are." The opinion is reported for what it is worth and not as an established fact. Nevertheless, the bourbon-controlled counties ("feudal" is the local word for them) are down toward the coast.

Perhaps all these and other elements of unity expressed themselves in the vote for "Cotton Ed" Smith for the Senate in 1944, his last race, which he lost to Olin Johnston. "Cotton Ed," unrivalled as a critic of the New Deal, unmatched as an exponent of white supremacy, and without peer as a defender of southern womanhood, had all the qualities to appeal to the lowland complex of attitude. His opponent, on the other hand, had,

---

[5] South Carolina politicians conclude that workers politically hold together better in the counties where they are most completely unionized. Such general conclusions by politicians and other "informed" citizens are wrong so much of the time that one becomes skeptical of all such remarks. This one, however, seems to be true. Note in Figure 27 Johnston's relative weakness in Greenville County, a county with far less unionization than other textile counties. Johnston, as a citizen of Spartanburg, may have suffered from the rivalry between his home town and near-by Greenville, although in several primaries examined Greenville deviated in its voting behavior from near-by counties.

[6] Even these low-country rings, in their endeavors in state campaigns, can never be sure who will win. The local crowd may support a candidate, but it will designate one of its number to back another candidate with a chance to win. If their favorite does not win, the local group will have a man with access to the victor to plead local matters.

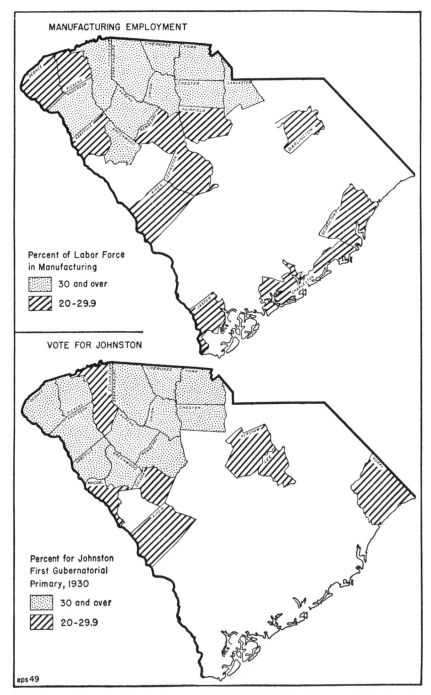

MANUFACTURING EMPLOYMENT

Percent of Labor Force
in Manufacturing

30 and over

20-29.9

VOTE FOR JOHNSTON

Percent for Johnston
First Gubernatorial
Primary, 1930

30 and over

20-29.9

eps 49

FIGURE 27

Bedrock of Piedmont Sectionalism: Employment in Manufacturing and Vote for
Johnston in First Democratic Gubernatorial Primary, 1930

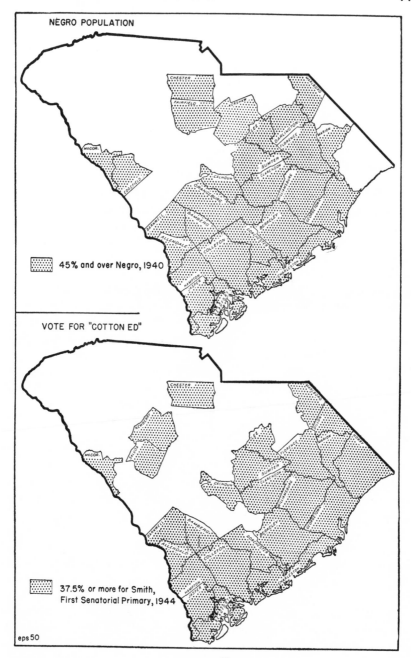

FIGURE 28

Backbone of Coastal Unity: South Carolina Counties with More than 45 Per Cent
Negro Population and Countries Polling 37.5 Per Cent or More of Total Vote
for Smith in 1944 Senatorial Primary

at least earlier, toyed with the advancement of the underdog. In John-ston's first term as governor, a lowland politician recalls, he wanted "to appeal to the rag tags, lintheads, and poor farmers." Old and crochety, Smith no longer had his old-time fire on the stump. And Johnston wooed away some of his bourbon support and won the day. Nevertheless, Smith retained his bed-rock support, located mainly in the counties with the most Negroes.[7]

3. Latent Bipartisanism Smothered by Racism?

The recurrence of the cleavage between Plain and Piedmont makes it clear that a basis exists for a bipartisanism, which, however, cannot develop because of racism. True, in all southern states bipartisanism is stifled by racism in the sense that attachment to the Democratic party nationally has been dictated by a common determination to resist the rest of the nation on the Negro question. Beyond this, however, the Negro question hampers the maintenance within the Democratic party of factions that amount to political parties. A common illusion of southerners is that they have the equivalent of parties for state matters in the sub-divisions of the Democratic party. South Carolina experience demonstrates the falsity of the belief. The confusions and ambiguities inherent in the one-party system make for splits of voters along lines quite irrelevant to issue, such as localism. The race problem in exaggerated form adds a weapon that can be used at times to destroy all semblance of a rational politics. Throughout the South that question can be used to smother conflict over other issues; its effect in South Carolina only reveals graphically the consequences that occur in less-perceptible degree elsewhere.

The Negro question suppressed the tendency of the two-party pattern to reassert itself in South Carolina after Reconstruction. Military occupation and government by carpetbaggers, scalawags, and Negroes set in train powerful forces of cohesion within the white population, but ineradicable cleavages of political interest soon began to appear. The dominant conservative interests came to be challenged by the embattled farmers led by Ben Tillman, of upcountry Edgefield County. Whether Tillman led the "common man" against the "aristocracy" is open to doubt. That he did so is ridiculed by William Watts Ball, irreconcilable conservative editor of the Charleston *News and Courier*. "Tillmanites said that, it was their slogan—and slogans are often nonsense. This one was nonsense." Tillman, perhaps unaware of the conflicts of interests

[7] A lurking caveat remains about the whole argument of sectional divergence. In view of the potency of the friends-and-neighbors influence, would the division of the vote have been the same had Smith's opponent lived somewhere other than in Spartan-burg?

among farmers, succeeded in fusing owners, tenants, farm workers into a ramrod for use against the city. "Intense vindictiveness of the country against the town was the defining characteristic of Tillman." [8]

Tillman may have been a spurious radical, yet the financial, business, and professional men took him seriously. Indeed, he had a program that, for the time, was radical, although perhaps his principal claim to radicalism was his threat to the position and perquisites of those who had monopolized office. The anxieties of conservatives were stirred by Tillman's early agitations, and his candidacy for the governorship in 1890 brought into existence a dual factionalism that almost amounted to a party system. In that year the conservatives refused to abide by the convention nomination of Tillman and put into the field as an independent, A. C. Haskell, Columbia lawyer and bank president. Here was a campaign between leaders of apparently antithetical groups. People felt deeply about the issues and inevitably the Negro came into the debate. Haskell, the low-country candidate, sought the support of Negroes and promised them "fair play." [9]

After his election Tillman set about to disfranchise the Negro. The low-country aristocrats had brought the Negro into the argument, and probably the Tillmanites calculated that the aristocrats had a better chance to win and hold the Negro vote. Disfranchisement brought immediate political advantage. It turned out also to bring long-term advantage. Tillman soon moved on to the Senate and became the most noted exponent of white supremacy. His brutal and frank presentation of the South Carolina viewpoint attracted large Chautauqua audiences over the country. [10] By Negro-baiting and by a picturesque stump technique, he welded to himself a following, which remained loyal even though as the years went by his general political position shifted markedly. In the Senate the fire-eating radical became a conservative of the conservatives, yet he was still a Democrat and a Negro-baiter. By 1912, hard pressed in his campaign for reelection, the old hero of the common man won by appealing to the conservatives. In victory, "He had joined forces with the very persons it had been his mission in life to teach the common people to despise. In peril, he had frantically asked for Conservative votes. . . . He had, in a sense, surrendered to the Haskellites. . . ." [11]

Cole Blease, after Tillman went to the Senate, came on the stage of South Carolina politics as a highly effective demagogue. Blease drew his support largely from the same classes that followed Tillman. He had been

[8] W. W. Ball, *The State That Forgot, South Carolina's Surrender to Democracy* (Indianapolis: Bobbs-Merrill Company, 1932), p. 206.

[9] W. A. Mabry, "Ben Tillman Disfranchised the Negro," *South Atlantic Quarterly*, 37 (1938), p. 172.

[10] Francis Butler Simkins, *Pitchfork Ben Tillman* (Baton Rouge: Louisiana State University Press, 1944), chap. 26.

[11] Ibid., p. 499.

Governor Tillman's floor leader in the legislature. By the time of his election as governor in 1910, after several unsuccessful campaigns, the mill workers had increased greatly in number although they were often the same farmers and farm workers who had supported Tillman transplanted to mill towns. Blease not only inherited Tillman's following, he also inherited "Tillman's enemies—the corporations, the aristocrats, the newspapers, the preachers, the political rings—all who by reason of superior culture or craft had made themselves into the better classes." [12] Blease excelled even Tillman as a demagogue and Negro-baiter, but his "original contribution is found in his ability to make a class appeal without offering a class program." [13] He mesmerized the mill workers, the tenant farmers, and the poor whites, while at the same time opposing governmental programs to benefit them. He fought affiliation of textile unions with national labor organizations. He wanted no Yankees interfering in South Carolina labor unions and he resisted further regulation of conditions of work. He drew cheers and votes from the white mill workers (who held a virtual monoply of mill jobs) by his extraordinary appeals to race prejudice, and at the same time drew quiet and effective support from mill owners.[14]

Perhaps so nonrational a politics can be practiced only when some diversionary issue, such as race, lies handy for use. "Indeed," says Cash, "Blease could not have functioned as the active advocate of the cotton-mill workers had he wanted to—and there is no evidence that he ever did want to. For there before him was the fateful lesson of Populism. To attempt to carry through a tangible program in their behalf would inevitably be to raise class conflict, and to raise class conflict would inevitably be to split the Democratic party into irreconcilable factions. And that, again, would be to threaten the Proto-Dorian front and lay the way open to the return of the Negro in politics. Which, in its turn, would be perfectly sure to alienate a great part of the mill people themselves." [15]

It may be that it took a little more than the race issue for Blease to oppose all social welfare measures and also command the support of the mill workers. And that additional ingredient may have been the ignorance of farm folk turned mill operatives overnight. Old Bleasites note the decline of their hero's popularity over the years. His "southern unions" became less popular as outside textile organizers filtered in and as workers through their new unions and through the gradual impact of education became better able to see what the score was. Further, perceptive coastal politicians, viewing the mill worker from afar, credit his disposition to

[12] Ibid., p. 488.

[13] Rupert B. Vance, "Rebels and Agrarians All," *The Southern Review*, IV (1938–39), p. 34.

[14] Blease served in the South Carolina house of representatives, 1890–98; in the state senate, 1904–08; as governor, 1911–15; as United States Senator, 1925–31.

[15] W. J. Cash, *The Mind of the South* (New York: Alfred A. Knopf, 1941), p. 245.

political self-immolation to the overlying cast of his own local brand of protestantism. When the mills were built, often a first act of the new mill owner was to build a church, put the pastor on his payroll, and reap the profits of a theology propagating the doctrine that the meek shall inherit the earth. The people are changing, slowly, to be sure, and far-seeing politicians recognize that in the long pull they must reckon with a people less naive politically than the simple clodhopper that Blease held in the palm of his hand.

The followings of Tillman and Blease might be regarded as personal factions rather than groupings equivalent to political parties and the issues raised may have been spurious; nevertheless, these powerful personalities were potent organizing forces in the politics of the state. Old-timers recall that in the days of Tillman and Blease pro- and anti-factional lines were tight and that each faction usually put out a slate of candidates in the primary for every office. Legislative candidates, for example, were pro- or anti-. These sharp lines have been replaced by a much looser political system in which each candidate avoids identification with other candidates and all is confusion compounded.[16]

Senator Olin Johnston, the "millboy-attorney" in the words of the choleric Charleston News and Courier, is regarded in the line of descent from Tillman and Blease. Although Johnston's popular strength in his early campaigns centered in the upper Piedmont,[17] in a series of state races he broadened his political base by winning allies in other sections. Unsuccessful in his race for the governorship in 1930, he tried again in 1934 and won. In 1938, the year of the abortive purge, he ran for the Senate as a New Dealer, with the blessings of FDR, against "Cotton Ed" Smith and lost.[18] In a special primary in 1941, he again lost the Senate race. In 1942, he made a comeback by winning the governorship. By this time, like his predecessors, he had gone the full cycle. Conservative elements had come to regard him with less hostility; perhaps they had taken him into camp to a degree. And the Negro question popped up opportunely to aid him in fulfilling the ambition, nurtured by many South

[16] It may be that the full fruits of uni-partisanism are achieved only with the lapse of time. Tillmanism and Conservatism in South Carolina represented a powerful surge toward bipartisanism. Factional structures and combinations were established and as primitive sorts of political institutions they had a powerful capacity for survival. Gradually, however, they eroded under the impact of the confusion inherent in the one-party system until finally the state had a multiplicity of factions. Something of the same sequence of events has been followed in other states of the South. In later years the New Deal projected itself into state politics and threatened, as Populism had, to become the grand issue around which state factions might be aligned. Again the race issue was used—without such universal success as three or four decades earlier—to blot up class antagonisms by diverting frustrations and aggressions against the hapless black.

[17] See the map in Figure 27.

[18] A part of the explanation, as it is related in South Carolina, is that some of FDR's advisers on South Carolina matters double-crossed him and used both their personal influence and Federal patronage under cover to back Smith.

Carolina governors, to go to the Senate. In 1944, the Supreme Court outlawed the white primary. Governor Johnston, running for the Senate like a jackrabbit, immediately convened a special session of the legislature to cope with the situation. His message to the special session, if it lacked the virulent artistry of Tillman, identified him indubitably as an exponent of white supremacy. A few months later he was elected to the Senate, winning over the ailing "Cotton Ed" Smith.

Johnston's career may point to a significant consequence of the one-party system. Time after time, wild-eyed men with stirring slogans get a start in politics by appealing to the common man, not, it should be said, that Johnston qualified on all these scores. Yet he built on the foundation of a mill following. Gradually, as had his predecessors, he reached out and won the support of other classes. In fact, he moved so far to gain support in the lowlands and in the upper brackets that his mill following became restive and he had to backtrack to hold their support. On the other hand, Maybank, of Charleston, had to make gestures in the other direction to build himself up in the Piedmont and in the process lost some low-country support. Uni-partisanship may make it possible for a politician to shift his general orientation with far less risk to personal political survival than under two-party conditions. Lack of party labels and of party lines means that there are no institutional obstacles to collaboration with erstwhile enemies. Free and easy transfer of affections, by both politician and follower, may be accomplished without treason to party. Sooner or later the mass of voters catch on to what has happened and retire the unfaithful servitor; there may be, however, a considerably longer lag in adjustments between constituency and representative than is the rule in two-party situations.

An electorate that lacks party guideposts and traditions and that is also susceptible to manipulation by Negro-baiting, can be whipped into groupings quite contrary to what might be expected on the basis of rational political behavior. The mention of the underlying significance of Piedmont and Plain in voter alignments will leave an erroneous impression of South Carolina politics unless it is corrected by reference to other campaigns in which different kinds of divisions arose. Two campaigns by Colonel Richard Wyndham Manning, of Sumter County, neatly illustrate the volatility of electoral affections possible under one-party circumstances. In 1938 and in 1942 the Colonel unsuccessfully sought the governorship. His father had been South Carolina's World War I governor and he had family connections with at least five other governors of the state.[19] Generally he stood for a conservative viewpoint. A principal plank

[19] No outlander unversed in genealogy should get into the question, but it all goes back to one General Richard Richardson, of Virginia, who settled in what is now Clarendon County. Three of his descendants—all Richardsons—became governor. A Richardson married Richard Irvine Manning (governor, 1824–26). John Lawrence Manning became governor in 1852; Richard I., in 1915. "Obviously, there has never

of his platform in both campaigns was "law enforcement." Now, in South Carolina, law enforcement is an elusive sort of proposition. It means something or another about home rule, i.e., local discretion in enforcement of the liquor laws. Law enforcement carries with it some intimation of interposition of the state constabulary in local areas when local officials neglect to enforce the law.

The maps in Figure 29, showing the counties that gave Colonel Manning 45 per cent or more of their votes in the 1938 and 1942 campaigns, reveal the striking shift in the centers of the Colonel's highest strength between the two campaigns. Such a radical realignment rarely happens in a state with a two-party tradition.

Factions in a one-party state are much more fluid than parties, and such crosscurrents as localism force alignments out of the pattern indicated by fundamental cleavages of interest. In 1938, Manning opposed Maybank of Charleston, and drew heaviest support in the Piedmont. Even counties with concentrations of mill workers returned majorities for Manning, a conservative of impeccable aristocratic background whose views on law enforcement coincided with upcountry attitudes. Came the 1942 primary and a radical shift in the Colonel's strength occurred. He ran against Johnston, of Spartanburg, and most of the mill counties returned majorities for their champion, although Manning held his strength in Greenville and in some of the more rural upcountry counties. The low country, with its regional champion Maybank not in the running, gave Manning much stronger support than in 1938. Charleston, with its libertarian views, went for the advocate of law enforcement in preference to upcountry Johnston. Even Berkeley County, locale of the Santee-Cooper power project which Colonel Manning had opposed in the legislature, gave him 47.5 per cent of its votes, while in 1938 it had reported only 8.4 per cent for the Colonel. Beaufort County, another coastal county, gave him 81.7 per cent in contrast with 19.5 in 1938.

Another example of the odd combinations of voters possible in the loose politics of South Carolina comes from the 1946 gubernatorial campaign between J. Strom Thurmond, of Tillman's county of Edgefield, and Dr. James C. McLeod, of Florence County. Thurmond campaigned as a mild progressive, and the conservative forces tried to stem the tide by backing Dr. McLeod, who was described as "anti-Roosevelt, anti-New Deal, anti-organized medicine, and anti-all the rest." [20] The conservatives darkly hinted that huge sums of CIO money were behind Thurmond.

been an individual identified with the history of South Carolina who has been so closely related to so many governors as the wife of Richard Irvine Manning, the first of that name. She was the wife of a governor, the mother of a governor, the aunt and foster mother of a governor, the sister of a governor and the niece of a governor."—Yates Snowden, *History of South Carolina* (Chicago: Lewis Publishing Company, 1920), I, p. 530.

[20] The state AFL, although it does not "publicly" endorse candidates, sends word down the line and in this instance the word is said to have been for Dr. McLeod.

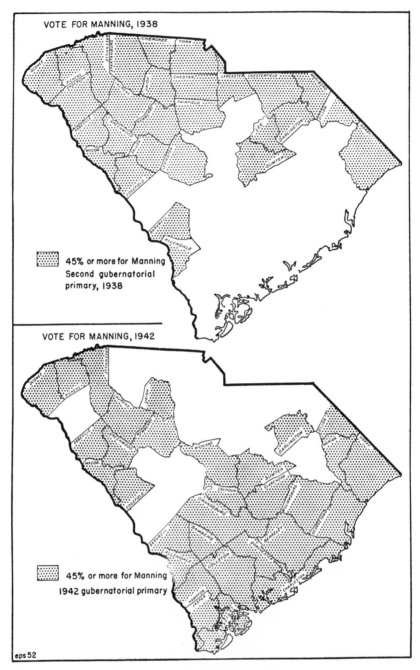

VOTE FOR MANNING, 1938

45% or more for Manning
Second gubernatorial
primary, 1938

VOTE FOR MANNING, 1942

45% or more for Manning
1942 gubernatorial primary

eps 52

FIGURE 29

Fluidity of Factionalism: South Carolina Counties Casting 45 Per Cent or More
of their Popular Vote for Manning for Governor in Primaries of 1938 and 1942

"We thought it was so," a banker later said who has long functioned as a collector of campaign funds from businessmen, mill owners, and large economic operators generally. That "they" thought it so, whether true, was in itself important. While no radical, Thurmond's general attitude of

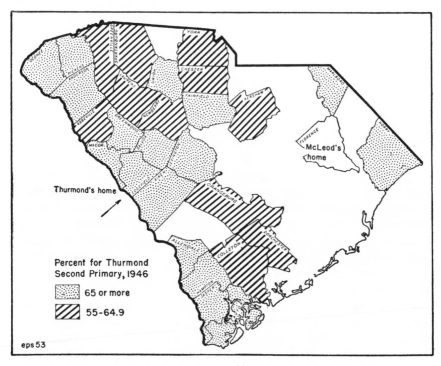

FIGURE 30

Confusion of Alignment: Distribution of Peak Popular Vote for Thurmond in South Carolina Gubernatorial Primary, 1946

"unreliability" may be suggested by a speech made after he was governor to the National Association of Real Estate Boards in which, to the embarrassment of the hosts, South Carolina realtors, he urged retention of rent controls "until some degree of sanity returns to profiteering real estate owners." [21] Even Negro leaders were favorably disposed toward Thurmond because he did not indulge in the usual type of Negro-baiting. On the other hand, Thurmond had the support of Eugene Blease, former chief justice of the state, a candidate for Senator in 1942, who advocated the racial views of his late brother, "Coley."

Observe the curious distribution of Thurmond strength as shown on the map in Figure 30. Although he was generally strong in the upcountry, some Piedmont counties were receptive to the conservative appeal of

[21] *Atlanta Journal,* September 16, 1947.

McLeod. Some extreme northwest counties in which Manning, an earlier conservative candidate, had been strong were counties of extremely high Thurmond strength. The "radical" Thurmond, in contrast with the "radical" Johnston, attracted a high degree of support in some of the low-country "feudal" counties. McLeod's greatest strength appeared in a tier of counties from the coast to the northern boundary running through his home county of Florence. All of which points again to the significance of localism in disturbing alignments of voters that might be expected to appear in a politics of interest.

By 1948 the wheel had made a complete turn. The southern civil rights revolt got under way. Governor Thurmond, in the tradition, got on the band wagon early and played a prominent role in the organization of the South to defend its right to interpret the bill of rights. Sage South Carolina politicians nodded and concluded that Strom was running for the Senate.

At times of dissatisfaction with the national leadership of the Democratic party, South Carolinians, as do southerners elsewhere, begin to talk about the great virtues of a two-party system and to express some sort of hope that they are moving toward such a system. Few of them, however, realize what a genuine two-party system would mean in the way of raising issues and of activating the masses politically. By the same token, few of them realize the capacities of a one-party system for muffling protest, postponing issues, preserving the status quo. Yet South Carolina still has its philosophers in politics. One of them concludes that no matter what is said, no person who makes more than $20,000 a year wants a two-party system in South Carolina. If there were two strong parties, each would compete for the lower-level vote. With the present Democratic party structure, the $20,000-a-year men can keep control of the situation.

4. "Legislative Government"

South Carolina politics cannot be understood by analysis of gubernatorial politics alone. Its government is, as its politicians are wont to say, "legislative government." South Carolina's chief executive has limited power. He controls the state constabulary.[22] He has power of appointment to state office except many of the really important state agencies. He can grant pardons,[23] send messages to the legislature, and exercise the power of veto; yet he has the narrowest sort of power of direction of state administration. "There's nothing to it except the honor" is the common atti-

---

[22] "The state constables," concludes the Charleston *News and Courier*, "are not always futile. They may be of notable value in lifting any kind of governor into the United States Senate."—November 23, 1946.

[23] It was proposed in 1948 to deprive him of this power.

tude. Of the governor's powers, W. D. Workman, of the Charleston *News and Courier,* writes with a wry humor:

> Discussions of the governor's limited powers in South Carolina generally overlook the authority vested in him by Section 3095 of· the state code. It provides:
> "Full power and authority is given to the governor to make, by proclamation, such regulations as in his opinion may be necessary to prevent the entrance of Asiatic cholera into this state, and the spreading thereof in this state." [24]

The legislature has grasped firm control of the critical sectors of state administration. The chairman of the senate finance committee and the chairman of the house ways and means committee, with the governor as a minority of one, compose the state budget commission. The state highway commission, often a bone of contention in South Carolina politics, consists of fourteen members, one from each judicial circuit elected by the legislative delegation from the circuit. The public service commission, the utility regulatory agency, consists of seven members elected by the legislature. Not only does the legislature choose the chiefs of some of the more important state agencies; now and again individual legislators hold these posts by election of their colleagues. In other instances, the governor or the responsible commission appoints them to such places. Thus, in 1948 a senator was general manager of the South Carolina public service authority, charged with the construction and operation of the Santee-Cooper power project. South Carolinians now and again protest against dual office-holding, and appropriate gestures of mollification are forthcoming. Thus, in 1947 Mr. Sol Blatt, for many years speaker of the house, resigned from the board of trustees of the University of South Carolina. The legislature replaced him with Mr. Sol Blatt, Jr.

The legislature not only controls the strategic points of state administration. County legislative delegations constitute the real governing bodies of their respective counties. County-delegation autonomy in local legislation is, of course, not peculiar to South Carolina, but the scope of local legislation is unusually broad. The legislature, i.e., in fact the local delegations, makes county appropriations and fixes the local tax levy or it enacts the county "supply bill," as the process is called in South Carolina. By its power to appropriate county funds the legislative delegation, of course, controls county government. It goes further usually and becomes associated directly or indirectly with the designation of appointive county officials. County boards of welfare, for example, are appointed by the state department upon the recommendation of a majority of the county legislative delegation. In addition to these extraordinary powers, the legislative delegation puts through the legislature the usual sorts of local bills: "A bill empowering the Folly Island township commissioners to promulgate

[24] *News and Courier,* January 20, 1947.

and enforce zoning regulations"; "A bill to increase the salary of the principal of the Ridgeland grammar school."

The legislative delegation, in effect, makes most of the important local governmental decisions and usually the senator from the county becomes its first-ranking politician. His position is often symbolized in bills authorizing the legislative delegation to take action between legislative sessions. The decision—on such matters as transfers among appropriation items—must be taken by the senator and a majority of the house members. All of which gives the senator the final say on such questions. The power and position of the legislative delegation in local government have reached such a point that a proposal has been made to authorize it to enact county laws between sessions of the legislature.

Such is the formal allocation of governmental powers in South Carolina: a weak executive, a legislature that takes a hand in the management of administrative departments, and a legislature whose county delegations, with the senator as the kingpin, in effect, govern their respective counties. And within the state the position of the legislature is accorded due recognition. To a higher degree than elsewhere in the South, public attention—as measured by newspaper coverage and by observation of the attitudes of politicians over the region—is focused on the legislature, where, as between the two houses, the senate holds primacy. And the senate regards itself as something of a gentleman's club, not without reason, for South Carolina senators are a cut—a broad cut—above the usual run of state legislators.

The formal role of the legislature takes on significance, however, only when viewed in its general position in the game of state politics. It is the legislature, and primarily the senate, that gives direction, coherence, and continuity to the policy of the state. Within the legislature, in recent years it has been the so-called Barnwell Ring that has provided leadership. The dean of the senate, and undoubtedly the most powerful man in the government of South Carolina for many years, has been Edgar Allen Brown, of Barnwell County. Lawyer, banker, businessman, he served in the house, became its speaker, moved on to the senate in 1929, and eventually became its president pro tempore, and chairman of its finance committee. His long service and leadership in the senate plus the presence of several of his associates from Barnwell County in positions of prominence created a conspicuous concentration of power open to attack as the "Barnwell Ring." Mr. Brown, the senior senator, had as a fellow townsman, Sol Blatt, for ten years an able speaker of the house. At one time nearby lived Governor Harley, who had succeeded from the lieutenant-governorship. Winchester Smith, chairman of the house ways and means committee and state chairman of the Democratic party, lived up the road at Williston, also in Barnwell County.

Such a monopolization of office invited attack and the Ring beat a strategic retreat by a reallocation of rewards. In reality, the Barnwell Ring has consisted of a great deal more than Barnwell County. Senator Brown early established himself as the leader of like-minded conservative senators, many of them elected from the less-populous counties of the state. Included in the group are men who, like Mr. Brown, are men of substance in their own right—businessmen, bankers, lawyers, planters, and others with a large stake in the established order and with sympathy for those who have an even larger stake. Although the Barnwell bloc includes senators from all sections of the state, its most reliable members come chiefly from the counties of the Coastal Plain, which are said to re-elect their senators for longer periods than the upland counties. The less-frequent turnover in their representation permits their senators to benefit under the rule of seniority. Moreover, the viewpoint of the ruling groups of such counties is strengthened by their overrepresentation in the senate: one county, one senator.[25]

From their position in the legislature this fairly cohesive group of senators exercises a power based on their very real ability plus the knowledge that comes from long legislative experience. In legislation they adhere generally to a conservative policy, yielding a bit here and there, as may be strategically necessary, to the forces demanding change. They are keenly conscious of their role in defense of the status quo and equally aware that they are fighting a delaying action; appropriations and taxes steadily increase, they ruefully conclude, however steadily they resist the trend.

Senator Brown as chairman of the senate finance committee becomes virtual manager of the state administration. As a member of the state budget commission and as legislative leader, he has over the years made many decisions affecting state agencies. Over the same period he has had a big hand in state patronage. By the patronage channel, he developed sources of information and points of influence on state action. In a sense he came to exert more executive influence than the governor. If all state employees were taken down to the city auditorium, an informed observer concludes, and "told to hold up hands for Brown or the governor, Brown would get the most." His influence permeates the entire state administration; and his allies in the senate have, of course, their own channels of influence.[26]

It is a veritable law of politics that the Barnwell Ring will be at war

[25] Another tactical advantage enjoyed by senators from the small rural counties is that they often cannot be hurt in their constituencies by the groups whose interests they oppose. Thus, an observation about the author of an antilabor bill: "The only workers in his county are the telephone operators, and they're afraid they'll be hit over the head."

[26] For what it is worth, it may be recorded that Senator Brown's daughter married the son of Senator Jeffries who in 1948 was also general manager of the Santee-Cooper project.

with the governor—unless he governs on the Ring's terms. The Ring inevitably comes into conflict with a governor with a program, for such a governor inevitably comes into conflict with the interests for which the Ring speaks. Members of the legislative group philosophically accept the probability that in about every third governor they will come up against a man who wants to appeal to the rag tags, the poor whites, and the lintheads, and that they must be prepared to hold him in check, prevent him from building himself up into a Tillman or a Blease. Thus, Governor Johnston, during his first term, battled the Ring, not over any question of high principle, but over control of the state highway department (of which Senator Brown's brother-in-law was the chief), an important patronage source. The governor took control of the highway department by armed force. The Barnwell Ring reacted by opposing everything the governor proposed, good or bad, and proceeded to strip him of such powers as it could. Johnston, properly chastised, came back as governor in 1942, worked with the legislature, and the Barnwell Ring stood with him in his successful race for the United States Senate in 1944.

The institutional structure almost perforce casts the governor in the role of popular leadership and drives the legislature to a role as defender of the status quo. When the governor is independent, ambitious, and aggressive, he has a head-on collision with the legislature. And, says a senator, governors propose ambitious programs, not out of any sincere regard for the needs of the people, but as a means to higher office. That behavior points to the principle that mass welfare can often, and perhaps only, be advanced by harnessing to it forces seeking private or personal advantage. Governor Thurmond, a senator opined in early 1948, "is one of those who is trying to build himself up for the Senate and he is full of a program of his own and full of things he wants to do, and we just naturally come into conflict." [27]

In the legislature the anti-Barnwell bloc is much more loosely organized than the group it opposes, although at times it has had recognized floor leaders and a semblance of unity. On some measures the upland manufacturing counties and Charleston join in a natural alliance of urban and manufacturing communities. Thus, in 1947, Representative W. Lewis Wallace, of York County, and Senator O. T. Wallace, of Charleston,

---

[27] By a curious reversal of roles in the history of parliaments, representative institutions in the United States have, on the whole, become defenders of vested interests; and chief executives, the tribunes of the people. Apparently the great tides of sentiment moving the masses have freer play in the mechanisms for the choice of chief executives than in elections of legislators from small districts. Even in two-party jurisdictions this phenomenon occurs, but perhaps the distinction between legislator and chief executive is sharpened under the conditions of a one-party system in which legislative candidates stand on their own feet and do not ally themselves with one or the other of the gubernatorial candidates. In a legislative campaign, less conspicuous and far more ambiguous in its issues than gubernatorial campaigns, groups and interests with their eye on the main chance and their hand on the campaign chest enjoy great advantage.

spearheaded opposition to anti-check off and anti-closed shop bills.[28] Legislators from Richland County, the seat of the state capital, also are generally regarded as not unfavorable to labor. Despite the relatively low degree of organization of South Carolina labor and the small membership of labor unions—perhaps 50,000—in the state, antilabor legislation has been stalled off more effectively than in most southern states.

South Carolinians make much to-do about the Barnwell Ring, which is, of course, only a transient grouping. Its members are growing old, and it has had to make strategic retreats. Yet other such groupings will in all probability replace it. The Ring has served as a convenient whipping boy. Candidates for governor have gone into the populous northwestern counties and slugged at Senator Brown and at the Barnwell Ring and thereby garnered votes. The debate seems on the whole to have had the strange emptiness of much American political debate. The attack is in terms of rings, cliques, and monopolization of power rather than of the public-policy positions of the legislative bloc led by Senator Brown.

South Carolinians, like most of us, have a strange hesitancy to reconcile themselves to the proposition that to govern requires power and that the problem of democracy is not to break down power but to grant power adequate to necessities and then to control it. If South Carolinians were a bit more experimental, they could begin anew their earlier contributions to politics by giving responsible cabinet government a trial. In practice, they have developed legislative leadership and hegemony, with Senator Brown functioning as in the manner of a prime minister and the governor little more than a ceremonial chief of state. The transformation would be complete by recognizing the senator for what he is—and making him responsible. No other southern state has a tradition (or a legislative personnel) so fitted for transition into a responsible cabinet government.

[28] In the debate on the closed-shop measure, Representative Wallace conducted a twelve-hour filibuster. In the course of the discussion Representative Roger W. Scott, of Dillon County, ridiculed the Farm Bureau's support of the closed-shop bill. "Mr. Scott said 'nobody has come here truthfully representing the farmers.' He went on to say 'we've got a closed shop in tobacco growing. . . . Why should we come up here and cuss out closed shops for other fellows.' "—Charleston *News and Courier*, March 23, 1947. The remarkable uniformity with which the Farm Bureau has taken an early and aggressive position on antilabor measures in the states of the South suggests the desirability of a full-dress inquiry, empowered to compel testimony and subpoena documents, to determine the nature of the nexus between the Farm Bureau hierarchy and those interested in such legislation.

Chapter Eight | **L O U I S I A N A :**

THE SEAMY SIDE OF DEMOCRACY

EW would contest the proposition that among its professional politicians of the past two decades Louisiana has had more men who have been in jail, or who should have been, than any other American state. Extortion, bribery, peculation, thievery are not rare in the annals of politics, but in the scale, variety, and thoroughness of its operations the Long gang established, after the death of the Kingfish, a record unparalleled in our times. Millions of dollars found their way more or less directly to his political heirs and followers. From the state treasury, from state employees, from gambling concessionaires, from seekers of every conceivable privilege, cash flowed to some members of the inner circle.

Huey P. Long's control of Louisiana more nearly matched the power of a South American dictator than that of any other American state boss. Many American states have had bosses whose power seemed well-nigh complete, but they were weaklings alongside the Kingfish. He dominated the legislature. He ripped out of office mayors, parish officials, and judges who raised a voice against him. Weapons of economic coercion were employed to repress opposition. When they failed the organization did not hesitate to use more direct methods. Huey, at the height of his power, brooked no opposition and those who could not be converted were ruthlessly suppressed.

Why a virtual dictatorship in Louisiana and not elsewhere in the

South? Of course it may not be conceded that virtual dictatorship has been confined to Louisiana. In Tennessee Crump ruled without question only in Memphis; he had to fight for his power in the remainder of the state. And Byrd was representative in Virginia of a ruling class with a tradition of responsibility. Long, as he modestly admitted, was *sui generis*. What inner compulsion of Louisiana politics produced a Huey Long? If there had been no Huey, did conditions in Louisiana make it inevitable that some person would occupy a like position? Or should the whole episode be explained in terms of the "great man theory" of politics?

1. Why a Huey Long?

Early in his career, Huey Long looked like just another southern heir of Populism: an anticorporation man, a politician skilled in identifying himself with the poor farmer, a rabble-rouser in the familiar southern pattern. He gave no reason for worry, in the opinion of those philosophically disposed. Other states had had such men, most of whom had followed a well-worn course. Sooner or later they sold out to the interests they attacked or became moderate, with experience and success. They mouthed a humbuggery to capture the loyalties of the gullible and ignorant. They had no sincerity in their promises; a slush fund would quiet the barking dog.

The apostles of complacency turned out to be wrong. Huey welded to himself a following fanatically loyal. Unlike a Blease or a Ferguson, his program held more than words and sympathy. He kept faith with his people and they with him. He gave them something and the corporations paid for it. He did not permit himself, in an oft-repeated pattern, to be hamstrung by a legislature dominated by old hands experienced in legislation and frequently under corporate retainer. He elected his own legislatures and erected a structure of political power both totalitarian and terrifying. To charges that he came to terms with the interests, the reply of the Long partisan is that the terms were Huey's. He is not to be dismissed as a mere rabble-rouser or as the leader of a gang of boodlers. Nor can he be described by convenient label: fascist, communist. He brought to his career a streak of genius, yet in his program and tactics he was as indigenous to Louisiana as pine trees and petroleum.

Long dramatized himself as the champion of the people against the sinister interests and his production was by no means pure melodrama. For there are sinister interests and there are champions of the people, even though there may always be some good about the sinister and at least a trace of fraud in self-styled champions. One of his first brushes with the interests, Huey related, was at the age of 22 when he sought to advocate before a legislative committee modification of a law that severely

restricted the right of recovery for injury or death incurred in the course
of work. When he requested the right to speak the committee chairman
asked,

"Whom do you represent?"

"Several thousand common laborers," Long replied.

"Are they paying you anything?"

"No," he replied.

"They seem to have good sense." [1]

Such episodes rankled, and early Long proclaimed the basic ideas
that later flowered into his "share-the-wealth" program. In 1918, in a
letter to the New Orleans *Item,* he asserted that two per cent of the people
owned from 65 to 70 per cent of the nation's wealth and that the concentration of wealth was proceeding apace. He saw the greatest cause for
"industrial unrest" in tremendous inequality in educational opportunity.
"This is the condition, north, east, south and west; with wealth concen-
trating, classes becoming defined, there is not the opportunity for Christian uplift and education and cannot be until there is more economic
reform. This is the problem that the good people of this country must
consider." [2]

Huey set out to help the good people of this country consider the
problem. In 1918, at the age of 25, he won election to the state railroad
commission, as the utility regulatory body was then styled. He began a
running fight, to last through most of his career, with Standard Oil. The
major oil producers, through their control of pipelines, threatened to
squeeze out independent producers by denial of access to market, an
ancient form of piracy. Long, himself a stockholder in several independent companies, undertook to bring the majors to task. He injected the
oil issue into the 1920 gubernatorial campaign and was bitterly disappointed in the successful candidate, whom he had backed. He charged
that the governor called in Standard Oil lawyers to help draft laws affecting that corporation. Long also took on the telephone company and compelled rate reductions. His battles against the interests attracted great
attention. The next logical step for him was to run for governor and he
did so in 1924.

The narrowness of his margin of defeat gave hope for the future; in
1928 he ran again and won. The campaign produced florid passages of
oratory, passages that Huey's partisans enshrine among the immortal say-
ings of the saints. In a speech delivered under the Evangeline Oak, Long
said:

And it is here under this oak Evangeline waited for her lover,
Gabriel, who never came. This oak is an immortal spot, made so by

[1] *Every Man A King, The Autobiography of Huey P. Long* (New Orleans: National Book Co., Inc., 1933), p. 27.

[2] Ibid., pp. 38–49.

Longfellow's poem, but Evangeline is not the only one who has waited here in disappointment.

Where are the schools that you have waited for your children to have, that have never come? Where are the roads and highways that you sent your money to build, that are no nearer now than ever before?

Where are the institutions to care for the sick and disabled? Evangeline wept bitter tears in her disappointment, but it lasted through only one lifetime. Your tears in this country, around this oak, have lasted for generations. Give me the chance to dry the eyes of those who still weep here! [3]

And from Huey's speech, campaign oratory though it may have been, one learns, perhaps, why he was able to erect a virtual dictatorship. The tears of the people of Louisiana had in reality lasted for generations. While no measuring rod is handy for the precise calibration of the tightness of oligarchies, a plausible argument can be made that the combination of ruling powers of Louisiana had maintained a tighter grip on the state since Reconstruction than had like groups in other states. That ruling combination included elements not present, at least to the same degree, in other southern states. The New Orleans machine bulked large in state politics and had established itself early. In every respect it was an old-fashioned machine, effective in its control of the vote and, in turn, itself beholden to the business and financial interests.[4] Add to the mercantile, financial, and shipping interests of New Orleans, the power wielded by the sugar growers, an interest peculiar to Louisiana, then add the cotton planters of the Red River and the Mississippi. The lumber industry constituted perhaps a more powerful bloc than in any other southern state and also enacted a spectacular drama in exploitation apparent even to the most unlettered. Later came oil. Like other industries it hoped to minimize taxation, but in Louisiana state ownership of oil-bearing lands gave petroleum a special interest in politics. Add to all these the railroads and gas and electrical utilities, and you have elements susceptible of combination into a powerful political bloc.

The stakes of the game and the relatively greater strength of the upper-bracket interests in Louisiana probably laid the basis for a more complete and unbroken control of public affairs than in any other southern state. As good a supposition as any is that the longer the period of unrestrained exploitation, the more violent will be the reaction when it comes. Louisiana's rulers controlled without check for a long period. Even the Virginia machine suffered setbacks from time to time and had to trim its sails. In other states there arose spokesmen for the masses who gave the people at least hope. Louisiana had no Blease or Watson or

---

[3] Ibid., p. 99.

[4] Orleans parish gave Long only 22.7 per cent of its vote in 1928. The city's opposition gave Huey a convenient whipping boy.

Vardaman to voice the needs and prejudices of ordinary men. It had its rabble-rousers to be sure, but its annals include no outstanding popular hero acclaimed as the leader of the common cause.

Whether such men of other states did anything for their people may be, in a way, irrevelant in comprehending Louisiana politics. They at least functioned as a safety valve for discontent, and the common people felt that they had a champion. Louisiana, on the other hand, was a case of arrested political development. Its Populism was repressed with a violence unparalleled in the South, and its neo-Populism was smothered by a potent ruling oligarchy. It may be that the crosscurrents introduced into Louisiana politics by the presence of a large French Catholic population contributed to the prevention of the social catharsis of expression of discontent. Differences between the Protestant north and the Catholic south furnished a convenient advantage to those who, with their eye on the main chance and unencumbered by ecclesiastical prejudice, would divide and rule. Perhaps, too, the religious, linguistic, cultural division of the people itself made it difficult for a leader to arise who understood both groups, who constituted a common denominator capable of giving full-throated voice to the common unhappinesses and aspirations of both peoples in rip-roaring political campaigns—after which everyone could go back to work.

The explanation of why Louisiana—rather than some other southern state—provided the most fertile soil for a Huey Long, requires demonstration that the ruling oligarchy of Louisiana really pressed down harder than did the governing groups of other states. As sensitive an index as any of the efficacy of financial oligarchy—in the American milieu, at least—is the status of the education of the people. Universal education—with its promise of individual betterment—is the open sesame of American utopianism. And universal education, with its impact on the tax structure, invariably comes into conflict with the oligarchical elements in American society for fiscal if not ideological reasons.

If the status of the people's education is an index to the strength of an economic elite, the Louisiana governing class excelled in exploiting of its position. In Louisiana, as late as 1940, 14.8 per cent of the rural, native white males over 25 years of age had not completed a single year's schooling. About one out of seven rural white men probably had never been to school a day. The proportion of rural white men without a year's schooling more than doubled that of the next ranking state, Virginia, almost tripled that of Texas, and was about five times that of Mississippi. Another 25 per cent of Louisiana rural white males over 25 had not had more than four years' schooling. Thus, in Louisiana in 1940 about four out of ten farm men had not gone beyond the fourth grade. Though Long won the loyal support of many of these people, it does not follow that fanatical loyalty must be based on illiteracy. The status of education is cited only as a probable indicator of the effectiveness of the ruling clique in holding down public services.[5]

TABLE 15

Louisiana's Rank in Rural Illiteracy: Percentages of Rural Native White Males 25 and over Completing No Years, and from 1–4 Years, Schooling, 1940

| STATE | PER CENT RURAL, NATIVE WHITE MALES 25 AND OVER COMPLETING— | |
	NO YEARS OF SCHOOLING	1–4 YEARS OF SCHOOLING
Louisiana	14.8	25.1
Virginia	6.8	21.8
North Carolina	6.0	21.6
South Carolina	5.2	21.4
Georgia	5.1	23.0
Alabama	5.1	20.8
Tennessee	5.0	22.8
Texas	4.5	16.1
Florida	3.7	17.4
Arkansas	3.5	19.9
Mississippi	3.0	13.3

In winning the governorship in 1928 Long scored heavily in the old Populist areas. In state after state in the South an impressive continuity of attitude has existed in the areas in which agrarian radicalism was most marked in the 1890's. Even today a candidate in the Populist tradition can win a relatively heavy vote in the old Populist counties.[6] In 1928 a fairly close relation prevailed between the distribution of Long's popular

[5] The 1930 census data are not comparable with those of 1940, but the 1930 findings on illiteracy ("Whether able to read and write") placed Louisiana first by a wide margin. The chances are that at the time of Long's election in 1928, about one out of five rural white men was unable to read and write.

In explanation of this state of affairs one has a lingering suspicion that perhaps responsibility for illiteracy rested in no small degree on the shoulders of Mother Church, in view of the importance of parochial schools in Louisiana education. This factor, however, may not invalidate the general argument, for one of Huey's strokes of genius was to cut through legalisms and give, through textbook distribution, a measure of aid to children attending parochial schools.

[6] It is apparent that, as in two-party states, there is in the South a striking persistence of local variations in political attitude. Since these differentials are not associated with party labels, they do not reveal themselves by simple analysis, but examination of thousands of county votes brings out local gradations in attitude of great durability. The phenomenon suggests many questions of social and political theory. A political crisis, such as Populism, may amount to a social trauma that leaves an imprint on the attitudes of a community to be transmitted, at least for a generation or so, by social inheritance. The stability of variations in attitude is, of course, attributable in part to the stability of variations in objective conditions, such as the fertility of the soil, with their reactions on economic status. Nevertheless, there appear to be continuities in community attitude not explicable in terms of continuing physical environmental influences on status and attitude.

strength and that of the Populist candidate for governor in 1896. In the northern half of the state the relation was closest, with Long weakest in the Mississippi River counties and in the counties with larger towns and cities, as the Populist candidate had been.

As governor, Long recommended concrete programs of action and did not hestitate to run roughshod over opposition to obtain their adoption. In his free-schoolbook legislation he dealt with the Protestant-Catholic issue by furnishing books to school children rather than to schools, and thereby avoided the constitutional inhibition of state assistance to private institutions. The constitutional dodge did not hurt him with French-Catholic voters. By his program for construction of highways and free bridges he won popular support and, incidentally, took a swing at one group of political antagonists, the owners of toll bridges and ferries. All these programs required money, and another group of Huey's antagonists, oil and other natural resource industries, found justification for their alarm in boosted taxes.

In the maintenance of its power and in the execution of its program, the Long organization used all the techniques of reward and reprisal that political organizations have employed from time immemorial: patronage, in all its forms, deprivation of perquisites, economic pressure, political coercion in one form or another, and now and then outright thuggery. Beyond these short-range tactics, Long commanded the intense loyalties of a substantial proportion of the population. The schoolbooks, roads, bridges, and hospitals were something more than campaign oratory. The people came to believe that here was a man with a genuine concern for their welfare, not one of the gentlemanly do-nothing governors who had ruled the state for many decades.

Long's erection of a structure of power based on mass loyalty was aided by the new channels of communication not available to neo-Populist leaders who came on the scene earlier in other states. Long had the radio and means to reach the people with printed matter quickly. Normally the mails were used, but when speed was essential—as in his campaign to beat the 1929 impeachment move—a system of direct distribution was put in motion. If necessary, Long said, "a document prepared by me in the evening could be printed and placed on the porch of practically every home in the State of Louisiana during the morning of the following day." [7]

Such systems of communication were made necessary by the practically universal opposition of the press, which, incidentally, Long attempted to counter with a special tax on advertising. It is an elementary rule of southern politics that most large newspapers will oppose any candidate who seriously threatens the perquisites of the dominant economic interests. The politician who seeks mass support perforce must

[7] Long, *Every Man A King*, p. 151.

maintain his own channels of communication with the electorate. The press works itself into the position by which its endorsement tends, somewhat like a CIO endorsement, to be a kiss of death. The little people observe that the newspapers oppose all whom they believe would befriend them; to them it follows, not by impeccable logic, that all whom the newspapers support are enemies of the people. Huey Long gave currency to a new word, "lyingnewspapers," and his people would believe him in preference to the newspapers.[8] And in 1948 Huey's son, Russell, running for the Senate, pictured himself as a battler for the people against the press.

The business of politics takes money and thereby hangs the tale of the Long organization. A candidate pledged to policies acceptable to the major economic interests has ample political financing. Politicians not so financed have to find other sources of funds and in so doing they often get into trouble. Long had the support of a few men of wealth. They were mainly mavericks of one sort or another who did not "belong" because of their ancestry, the sources of their money, or their accent. Such a person was Robert S. Maestri, who provided money at critical times early in Long's career, became a power in Long's organization, and, after Long's death, mayor of New Orleans.[9] If a political leader cannot annex the support of a segment of the economic upper crust, once in office he can manufacture a new economic elite attached to the regime. Public purchases provide one means. In Louisiana state control of petroleum production permitted favoritism worth millions. Louisiana's gambling habits make gambling concessions profitable. Frankie Costello, one-time New York slot-machine czar, got the New Orleans slot-machine concession and developed, says Kane, "a million and a quarter annual business." [10]

By these and other methods the Long organization created its own vested interests, which were tied to it by golden bonds and could help pay the cost of politics. Other revenues were not neglected. Assessment of public employees was justified, with the familiar rationalization that this type of financing was far better than reliance on the corporations. The distinctions of Robin Hood morality, however, were hard to maintain and political and personal finances became mixed, with the inevitable results in neglect of politics through the pursuit of private advantage.

After Huey's assassination in 1935 his prediction that his associates would go to the penitentiary if he were not around to hold them in check began to come true. In 1936, Maestri and his New Orleans associates held the whiphand in the formation of the Long organization

[8] Huey had his own newspaper, *The Progress*. Most colorful southern political leaders seem sooner or later to establish a personal journal. Ferguson had *The Ferguson Forum*; Talmadge, *The Statesman*; Folsom, *Folsom's Forum*.

[9] On a visit to New Orleans, Franklin Roosevelt lunched with Mayor Maestri whose single comment to the President was, it is reported: "How do you like them ersters?"

[10] Harnett T. Kane, *Louisiana Hayride* (New York: William Morrow and Company, 1941), p. 401.

ticket, which won in the primary. The Long ticket included Richard W. Leche, for governor, Earl Long, who had often fought his brother, for lieutenant governor, and Allen Ellender, for the United States Senate. During Leche's administration scandals broke, and Leche resigned to be succeeded by Earl Long. In the prosecutions after Huey's death not so many men were sent to the penitentiary as should have been. Now that Huey was dead, the organization saw no point in continuing his battle against the Roosevelt Administration. In turn, the Administration saw no point in carrying out criminal prosecutions on income-tax charges of organization leaders and hangers-on. The arrangement was dubbed the "Second Louisiana Purchase." The Federal authorities, however, pushed their civil cases and collected about $2,000,000.[11] Later, under a new Attorney General, Federal prosecutors returned to the fray and, if they sent but few to prison, they at least ventilated irregularities.

Of Huey Long, most interpretations are too simple. They range from the theory that he and his crowd were ordinary boodlers to the notion that here was a native fascism. Boodling there was, to be sure. Fascism? Huey was innocent of any ideology other than the sort of indigenous indignation against the abuses of wealth current in the epoch of William Jennings Bryan. The Long phenomenon must be explained in terms of the pathological situation in which he arose, in terms of traditional anti-corporationism, plus the genius of the man himself in political manipulation and organization.

2. The Louisiana Voter's Dilemma

Before Long, so the folklore of Louisiana goes, the voters had no choice. They could vote for one of two candidates, neither of whom would do anything for the people. Since Long, the people have the alternative of a venal administration with a dynamic program, or an honest, do-nothing administration belonging to the corporations. Like most popular myths, these notions are sharpened by exaggeration yet, perhaps also as popular myths often do, they contain an element of truth.

Since Long the state has had, with some deviations, a bi-factional fight between, on the one hand, the "good government" or "better-element" crowd and, on the other, the Long faction, or at least a group claiming to be the heirs to the mantle of the martyred Huey. In 1940 Sam H. Jones, the reform candidate, ran to victory in the wake of revelations of corruption, although his victory depended partially on a split in the old Long following.[12] In 1944, the best the "better element" could do by

[11] Ibid., 184.

[12] The first-primary vote was: Sam Jones, 154,936; Earl K. Long, 226,385; J. H. Morrison, 48,243; H. V. Moseley, 7,595; James A. Noe, 116,564. The second-primary vote was: Sam Jones, 284,437; Earl K. Long, 265,403.

way of a candidate was Jimmie ("You Are My Sunshine") Davis, he of the dance band, but Jimmie was enough to defeat Lewis Morgan, the Long candidate. In 1948 the Long faction regained control in the election of Earl K. Long, Huey's brother who quarreled with him in life but has been his zealous political ally in death. Later in the year Huey's twenty-nine-year-old son, Russell, confirmed the return of the Longs by gaining election to the Senate.[13]

The business interests tend to line up with the "good government" faction, although they are ordinarily more concerned about policies affecting business than about good government in the abstract. Taxation is usually a live issue, with the natural resource industries the most nervous about the severance tax.[14] The broad issue, however, is not cast as one of liberal versus conservative. The conservatives label themselves as the champions of good government and the liberals rarely call themselves radicals.[15]

When political disputes are put as battles between good and bad government—as they often have been in southern states—class differences between Populist-agrarian and business tend to be cloaked in moralities. And indeed, real moral issues may be involved—between thieves and relatively honest men—but they are often paralleled by moral issues of a higher order, viz., for whom is a government to be run. The debate between good and evil subtly divides the electorate along class lines, although a substantial proportion of the electorate may be quite unconscious that anything other than honesty and good government are at stake.

The southerner regards himself, if one gives weight to W. J. Cash's perceptive generalizations about *The Mind of the South,* as a hell-of-a-fellow. The hell-of-a-fellow complex has captured the lesser rural peoples

[13] In the run-off for governor the vote was 432,528 to 223,971. The vote for Senator was 264,143 to 253,668.

[14] As well they might be. To finance an expansion of state services and benefits—increased old-age pensions, a veterans bonus, boosts in teacher pay, free school lunches, improved roads, new hospitals, and more—Governor Earl Long pushed through his 1948 legislature measures to triple the oil severance tax, double the severance tax on other natural resources except sulfur, quadruple the gas-gathering tax. He also soaked the poor. He sponsored bills to double the 1 per cent sales tax and to add a tax of two cents to each gallon of gas and five cents to each bottle of beer. Old disciples of Huey conclude that Earl is not the friend of the poor man that Huey was.

[15] Among voter groups usually aligned with liberal candidates in the South are organized labor and the Negro. Though not powerful, organized labor has generally supported the Longs. Long's 1948 legislature repealed the Goff Act of 1946, which, like other recently adopted state acts, outlawed certain types of strikes and certain labor practices. The legislature also prohibited transportation of strikebreakers into the state and increased maximum benefits under workmen's compensation. While Louisiana Negroes do not vote in appreciable numbers, many of them looked with favor on the Kingfish, who is quoted as saying: "I've never been a party to any piece of legislation calculated to hurt the Negro. . . . I've always wanted to help them."—"The Negro in Louisiana Politics," fifth anniversary edition of *The Sepia Socialite* (New Orleans, April, 1942).

more completely than the planter or town class. And, by this fact, the Populist-like candidate, with an earthy, occasionally profane, rip-roaring appeal, colored by disrespect if not ridicule of the nicer people, enjoys great advantage on the hustings in wooing the vote in the uplands, at the forks of the creek, and along the bayous. Contrariwise, the conservative, respectable candidate tends to direct his appeals to citizens not so imbued by the hell-of-a-fellow complex, and in doing so makes all sorts of pretensions of moral superiority. Campaigns become at times great moral dramas in which good battles evil, and evil, being so attractive to a hell-of-a-fellow, almost invariably wins. The morality duel glosses over a blurred class politics, made articulate not in terms of economic policy but in terms that the people best understand, right and wrong. And the poor-white hell-of-a-fellow, a man of native shrewdness, often sees through the gloss and votes for evil and neo-Populism, at least when he has the choice.

Louisiana, like Texas in an earlier day, has campaigns in which competent, conservative candidates identify themselves with good government, honesty, efficiency, and all the related virtues. In 1948 Sam Jones, opposing Earl K. Long for governor, proclaimed at New Orleans: "I have been part and parcel of the fight for good government since 1940." [16] Governor Jimmie H. Davis declared that Sam Jones was "a man who is capable, a God-fearing man and a man who is honest and sincere in purpose." [17] At Alexandria, Jones warned that "a terrible moral issue lies beneath all the surface issues of performance and economic health. These are surface issues compared to the threat of permanent moral blight which in sober truth hangs over the state." The question was "proud progress or depravity." [18]

"It is the age-old struggle," Sam Jones argued in a radio broadcast, "between good and evil. On one side is Maestri and the hot-oil crowd, aided and abetted by Costello and his racketeers. On the other side is the ordinary, everyday God-fearing Christian people." [19] His supporter, Mayor deLesseps Morrison of New Orleans, predicted that the people would "vote for the proposition that government should be honest, fair and above purchase." [20] Jones, on returning to New Orleans from a stumping tour, reported gains: "The people who want to continue good government will vote for one candidate—for one ticket. That is the Sam Jones ticket." [21]

The candidate thrown into the role of the protagonist of evil gen-

---

[16] *Times-Picayune* (New Orleans), January 15, 1948.

[17] Ibid., November 28, 1947.

[18] Ibid., January 30, 1948.

[19] Ibid., January 26, 1948.

[20] Ibid., January 28, 1948.

[21] Ibid., December 22, 1947. Louisiana observers, it should be noted, regard the reform aspect of the conservative faction as tinged with humbuggery.

erally makes electoral capital thereby. Earl Long berated his opponents for calling him names: "They're calling me Earl Kangaroo Slickum Crookum Long. That don't hurt me at all, but believe me, I don't want to rob a man of his good name just to win an election. I don't want to be governor that much." [22] To charges that about $45,000 in "dee ducts" from employees' salaries had gone to Long, his reply was, the *Times-Picayune* said: "Is it worse to take contributions from the little people so we can give them the benefits, or have the big shots put up the money so they can control the government?" [23] Or such a candidate diverts the argument. "A lot of people cuss Huey Long and a lot of people cuss Roosevelt. Do you know why? Well, if you touch some peoples' pocketbooks you strike their heart. Just relieve them of a few dollars to help some poor devil, and you will hear them yell." [24]

Against roughhouse tactics on the stump, the respectable candidate often becomes a reed blown by the hilarious laughter of the hell-of-a-fellow, gusty and lusty man that he is. Thus, one of the most elegant descriptions of Sam Jones in his 1940 race against Earl Long: "He's High Hat Sam, the High Society Kid, the High-Kicking, High and Mighty Snide Sam, the guy that pumps perfume under his arms." [25] What can one say in reply to that sort of thing? Jones, in a 1948 campaign speech, conceded that he had campaign weaknesses "because it has always been hard work for me to cultivate the politician's knack for easy back-slapping, for the convivial bottle, for the obscene joke and the windy, unfillable promise." [26] And better-element candidates often retire from the fray, beaten, with sombre reflections on the unwisdom of getting into a name-calling contest with a polecat and the opinion that politics is no game for gentlemen.

The choice of the Louisiana electorate is not in reality clearly one between black and white, between a do-nothing government and a venal administration with a program, as some observers would have us believe. Long left a lasting imprint on the conservative element in the state by showing the people that government could act. By the defeat of the machine in 1940, the voters did not kill Longism. The conservatives adopted much of Long's program, and Sam Jones, the conservative leader, in his 1940 campaign in strong Long localities did not whisper when he remarked, "My pappy was for Huey." A corporation lawyer of humble origins, his father had indeed been an ardent Long supporter. And Sam, himself, in a way "was for Huey" because the better-element group has had to champion much of the program that Long sold to the people and, like their counterpart, the Republican party in the nation, to promise to

[22] Ibid., December 7, 1947.
[23] Ibid., January 4, 1948.
[24] Ibid., December 22, 1947.
[25] Kane, *Louisiana Hayride*, p. 434.
[26] *Times-Picayune* (New Orleans), January 31, 1948.

administer it better. The people, though, have lingering suspicions that the better-element leaders are not really honest tories and have, in their campaign promises, unexpressed reservations.

If the conservative element has accepted some of Longism, the successors to Long have also made their peace with business—or at least with some segments of the business community. Of a country bank in the 1948 campaign: "Everybody connected with the bank from the chairman of the board to the janitor will vote for Earl Long." And other businesses, sensitive to the necessity of amicable relations with those who win, manage to have a friend in the Long camp. And others, perhaps as one cynical observer tells us, have never been with the "better element." "They got their snoot in the trough before 1940 and wanted to keep it there."

The 1948 victory of Earl Long meant at bottom that a majority of Louisiana voters preferred the promises of a Long, backed by a history of action, if not always pretty action, to the pronouncements of a Jones who posed for goodness and virtue but accomplished little to help humble citizens. They saw through the façade of "good government." (Later on in the year Sam Jones turned out to be a Dixiecrat.) They preferred the hazards of buccaneer government to the conservatism of "reform" rule. Like good citizens everywhere, Louisianans hoped that the democratic process would one day produce a candidate not only devoted to the welfare of the mass of the state's citizens but able to serve them through economical and efficient government. Some thought that Judge Robert Kennon, an independent candidate in both the gubernatorial and Senate races of 1948, offered such a hope. In the Senate race he barely lost to young Russell Long, and in the earlier run-off for governor many were sure that he would have fared better against Earl Long than did Jones. Perhaps the Louisiana voter will find a way out of his dilemma. At least the processes of democracy are in ferment in Louisiana.

3. A Disciplined Factionalism

As southern one-party factions go, Louisiana's factions manifest a high degree of cohesion and continuity. The state's politics tends toward a bi-factionalism organized on pro- and anti-Long lines. Even before Huey's time there had been a relatively well-organized politics—perhaps as a consequence of the pervasiveness of the Old Regular organization of New Orleans—but the Kingfish caused factional lines to be drawn more tightly.

Although local politicians assert that their arrangements are "just the same damn thing" as a two-party system, the state's factionalism fails to approximate a bipartisan scheme. Longism persists powerfully but, as is often true, the "opposition" has failed to consolidate into a cohesive political force. As in earlier analyses, a crude index of the splintering of the Louisiana electorate is provided by the proportion of the first gubernatorial primary vote received by the two leading candidates. The smaller the vote going to lesser candidates, the closer is the approximation of bi-factionalism. As Long gained in power the state moved toward pure dual factionalism. (See Table 16.) With his passing, third and fourth candidates began to grow in importance. Nevertheless, two major camps exist and splinter groups attain less significance than in a state such as South Carolina.

Primary "tickets" or "slates" differentiate Louisiana factionalism from that of other southern states. In states with loose, personal factions, the tendency is for each candidate to run on his own and to avoid identi-

TABLE 16

Bifactionalism and Multifactionalism in Louisiana Gubernatorial Politics: Division of Vote in First Democratic Primaries, 1924–48

YEAR	PER CENT OF TOTAL VOTE TO TWO HIGH CANDIDATES	PER CENT OF TOTAL VOTE TO THREE HIGH CANDIDATES
1924	69.1	100.0
1928	72.2	100.0
1932	85.5	99.6
1936	99.7	100.0
1940	68.9	89.9
1944	62.4	78.3
1948	64.4	84.2

fication with candidates seeking other offices at the same time. In Louisiana, however, factional "tickets" approximate party "tickets" in two-party states. The voter has an opportunity to vote the "Sam Jones Ticket" or some other ticket carrying the name of its head. Each ticket includes, with exceptions to be noted, candidates for offices all the way from governor to police juror.[27] The factions that put up these tickets more closely approach the reality of a party system than do the factions of any other southern state. Virginia's organization ticket is not so extensive in its coverage or so well advertised in the campaign as is the custom in Louisiana. Tennessee coalitions are limited mainly to the top offices. Georgia has seen joint campaigning by candidates for Senator and governor. In Louisiana, however, each faction puts out a slate that includes candidates for most offices elected by a state-wide vote, usually candidates for Senate and House vacancies, and candidates for a large proportion of the state legislative posts. Moreover, many candidates for local office ally themselves with one or the other of the state tickets. An "independent," that is,

[27] The governing body of the Louisiana parish (county) is known as the police jury.

a person not affiliated with one of the "tickets," has little chance of victory.

In making up his ticket, a candidate for the governorship has the same problems that beset the party organization in a two-party state in preparing its primary slate. The head of the ticket must heed the wishes of political allies and the slate for state-wide offices must be "balanced;" that is, it must accord proper recognition to the various sections of the state, to the cities and to the rural areas, to French and non-French, to Catholics and Protestants. Tickets do not always include candidates for all state-wide offices, and sometimes they include candidates with independent followings who are also endorsed by competing tickets. The members of the ticket conduct a joint campaign—and Louisiana campaigns are probably the most intensive in the South—in much the same fashion as members of a party slate in a two-party state. Joint campaigning is coupled with advocacy of a common platform and the plea that election of the entire ticket is necessary to put over the program.

In many southern states such collaboration among candidates would be frowned upon. In Louisiana it is accepted as a matter of course and the voters mark a straight ticket about as consistently as they do at a general election in a two-party state. For instance, in the 1948 run-off primary the total votes for Earl K. Long and the four state-wide candidates who had campaigned with him were as follows:

Earl K. Long, for governor	432,528
William J. Dodd, for lieutenant-governor	421,627
Wade O. Martin, Jr., for secretary of state	433,097
Bolivar E. Kemp, Jr., for attorney general	405,601
W. E. Anderson, for commissioner of agriculture and immigration	405,279 [28]

The discipline among the voters supporting the Long ticket is most vividly revealed by an examination of the vote parish by parish. The relation between the 1948 second primary vote for Long and Dodd, his running mate for lieutenant governor, pictured in Figure 31, was about as close as that resulting from straight-ticket voting in a two-party state.

[28] Only these five campaigned together. The incumbent state treasurer won in the first primary with the endorsement of three of the four tickets. The incumbent register of the state land office ran on the Jimmy Morrison ticket but with extrafactional support won in the first primary. The incumbent state auditor ran on the Morrison ticket and, presumably with Long factional support, won over the candidate on the Jones ticket in the second primary. The Jones ticket candidate for superintendent of public education won in the second primary over the incumbent who had run in the first primary on the Morrison ticket. In his campaign, the winner had had one foot in and the other out of the Jones camp: "Although a member of the Sam Jones ticket, S. M. Jackson, candidate for state superintendent of education, emphasized that he was presenting only his own candidacy as he told the crowd of his qualifications after 23 years in school work, and outlined some of the major projects in his platform."—*Times-Picayune* (New Orleans), September 27, 1947. A full-fledged member of the ticket would have sought support for the ticket from top to bottom.

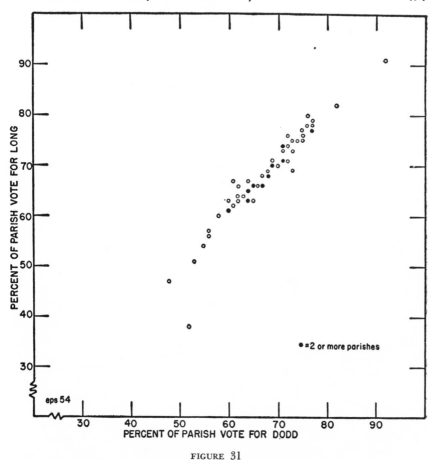

FIGURE 31

Organization Discipline: Relation between Percentage of Parish Votes for Long for Governor and for His Running Mate, Dodd, for Lieutenant-Governor, Second Democratic Primary, 1948

Such a result can occur in a one-party state only through the work of a highly organized factional system and by widespread acceptance of the idea of a factional ticket.[29]

[29] It would require a more intensive analysis than has been feasible to determine the structure of factional organization. The comment of Louisiana politicians is that the parish sheriff is generally the kingpin of local politics and that he is often aligned with one or the other of the state-wide factions. The sheriff, in turn, has a major interest in one of the minor issues of state politics, "home rule." "Home rule" in Louisiana means that the state administration will keep the state police out of gambling and permit "home rule" to the sheriffs in its control. Thus, Sam Jones, the 1940 reform candidate, won the support of sheriffs by promising "home rule." The gossip is that later he lost support of some sheriffs because some of his state police, unbeknownst to him, insisted on a cut of the take from gambling in some of the parishes. In no other southern state does gambling play the role in politics that it does in Louisiana. Those who

Straight-ticket voting is, of course, most marked in the two-man races of the run-off primaries. In the first primary the departures from dualism in the appearance of third and fourth tickets mar the regularity of voting from parish to parish. Candidates for minor state-wide offices also often have independent strength, based on localism or some other factor, that

TABLE 17

Straight-Ticket Voting in Louisiana: Per Cent of Vote Polled in Selected Parishes by Members of Sam Jones Ticket, First Primary, 1948

PARISH	GOVERNOR	LIEUTENANT-GOVERNOR	SECRETARY OF STATE	REGISTER OF STATE LANDS [a]	ATTORNEY GENERAL
Assumption	21.1	29.1	20.1	25.2	28.2
Bossier	10.6	28.7	13.4	28.0	18.1
Cameron	20.8	33.0	18.6	33.7	24.2
De Soto	13.8	35.4	15.5	35.6	23.3
Evangeline	12.3	26.6	11.1	27.4	20.4
Iberville	25.5	39.6	23.8	28.9	31.2
Lafayette	29.6	44.4	27.5	45.6	40.0
Livingston	12.1	28.1	13.7	23.1	12.4
Orleans	34.8	37.6	35.0	38.1	34.2
Rapides	25.5	22.5	28.1	34.1	26.2
St. Bernard	22.2	8.8	17.3	20.8	20.0
St. John	27.3	27.9	24.9	29.3	32.4
St. Tammany	22.8	35.7	22.1	27.2	24.6
Union	9.1	25.2	16.2	34.8	7.7
Webster	6.3	26.0	10.4	28.8	11.1
Winn	12.8	23.1	19.5	36.3	15.3
State	22.9	34.6	22.2	32.7	26.3

[a] Candidate also endorsed by another ticket.

gives them higher votes in some parishes than their ticket. All these deviations from dualism and from factional discipline affect the parish-to-parish regularity in ticket support in the first primary, as may be seen from the sample parish votes in Table 17.

The slates of the principal factions in many instances include candidates for state legislative seats, party posts, and even parish offices. These

---

regard themselves as "in the know" emphasize its role in political finance and its importance as an issue. Mayor deLesseps Morrison, of New Orleans, tried to come to grips with the problem in New Orleans by legalization, but southern parish sheriffs, fearful that legalized gambling might spread to their bailiwicks, joined with Bible Belt sentiment to block passage of licensing legislation.

In the structure of state factionalism New Orleans is, of course, a special situation. Huey Long, through the power of the legislature to pass "ripper" legislation and to take other reprisals, brought the New Orleans organization into his orbit. In the tradition, Earl Long's 1948 legislature took punitive steps against the city whose Mayor Morrison had been anti-Long.

local candidates more often attach themselves to a state ticket in New Orleans and in the southern French-speaking parishes than in the northern and southwestern parts of the state where the more general southern custom of autonomous candidacies prevails. The Louisiana practice is, of course, in marked contrast to that of southern states having a disorganized politics.

Alliance of legislative candidates with the ticket of a gubernatorial candidate is probably of special importance in laying the basis for factional unity within the legislature. A legislative candidate commonly joins the top members of his ticket as they campaign through his county or district. The ticket's state headquarters at times puts money into the races of affiliated legislative candidates not, however, says a campaign manager, so frequently as it is requested. Occasionally legislative candidates who would prefer to run as independents are compelled to identify themselves with a state ticket. To refuse to do so in a county overwhelmingly in favor of one of the gubernatorial candidates would assure defeat. All this collaboration in campaigns and the nature of campaign debate point to a much sharper recognition in Louisiana of the necessity for something approximating a party to achieve a program than exists in any other southern state. Outside Louisiana one rarely hears statements like the following by a state senatorial candidate from Baton Rouge: "Since the first primary, many voters have asked me what position I would take with reference to the governor's race. Knowing the issues involved, I have no desire to duck or sidestep on this question. I recognize the right of every voter to know how each candidate stands on this issue, and I expect to make my position crystal clear now. I will vote for, and support, Sam Jones for governor on Feb. 24." [30]

The factional solidarity demonstrated by straight-ticket voting is paralleled to some extent by deliverability of a factional vote. Outside the two main factions lesser leaders have minor followings and when such a leader runs for governor there is spirited bidding between the majors for his support in the second primary.[31] Most southern politicians scoff at the notion that such a person can deliver his following to another candidate. He may be able to hold his loyal supporters to his own candidacy from primary to primary, but he cannot vote them as a bloc for another person. In Louisiana, however, some leaders have a following that can, at least at times, be voted fairly solidly for another candidate. An illustration comes from the 1940 gubernatorial primary when Sam Jones ran against the remnants of the Long organization. The Long leadership was divided. It had fallen on evil days; grand juries and peni-

---

[30] *Times-Picayune* (New Orleans), February 3, 1948.

[31] Diligent search of the statutes has failed to substantiate the avowal of a Louisiana politician that second-primary hold-ups and sell-outs became such a scandal that the legislature enacted a punitive statute.

tentiaries beckoned. Two candidates had a claim on the Long vote, James A. Noe and Earl Long. The first primary vote was as follows:

Sam H. Jones	154,936
Earl K. Long	226,385
J. H. Morrison	48,243
H. V. Moseley	7,595
J. A. Noe	116,564

Both Jones and Long sought Noe's support in the run-off. "Earl Long charged that Noe . . . asked $150,000 to come out for Long. Noe replied that this was a slight error; that he had been offered $300,000, but had turned it down." [32] All of which Long denied. Noe endorsed Sam Jones on the promise of patronage for his followers.[33] Apparently most of those who had supported Noe voted for Jones. It may be that they would have gone over to Jones without Noe's endorsement, although that is unlikely since Noe held himself out as the true disciple of Long while Jones promised to redeem the state.

The second primary vote was: Jones, 284,437; Long, 265,403. The increase in the Jones vote was 129,501, only slightly more than Noe's first primary vote of 116,564. By excluding those parishes in which Morrison, the fourth candidate, polled more than 10 per cent of the vote in the first primary, one isolates those parishes in which there was essentially a three-way first-primary race. In such parishes Jones' gain in the second primary approximated Noe's first primary vote, as is shown in Figure 32.[34]

Although the degree of factional solidarity in Louisiana is unusual in a southern state, the play in its factional system is considerably higher than that between parties. The capacity of any Louisiana faction to carry its following for all members of its ticket appears considerably less than the ability of the party to deliver its vote to all members of its slate in a two-party state. Moreover, in Louisiana the possibility remains for Senators and Representatives to develop personal followings quite independent of the major factions of the state.

The play in the factional system is also indicated by the influence of localism, which occasionally appears despite the fact that generally in Louisiana factional loyalties cut through attachments to local personages.

[32] Kane, *Louisiana Hayride*, p. 444.

[33] Ibid., p. 444.

[34] Not all Louisiana factional followings are deliverable. In 1948 Sam Jones ran again and the first primary vote was divided among four candidates. Jones and Long again fought it out in the second primary. This time Jimmy Morrison, the fourth-ranking candidate in the first primary, endorsed and campaigned for Jones. Morrison's capacity to deliver his following was far less than that of Noe in 1940. On the other hand, Morrison's 1948 vote consisted in considerable measure, not of his own following, but of support from the New Orleans "Old Regular" organization which further analysis would probably show was able in the second primary to deliver its vote against Jones, the ally of deLesseps Morrison, mayor of New Orleans and foe of the "Old Regulars."

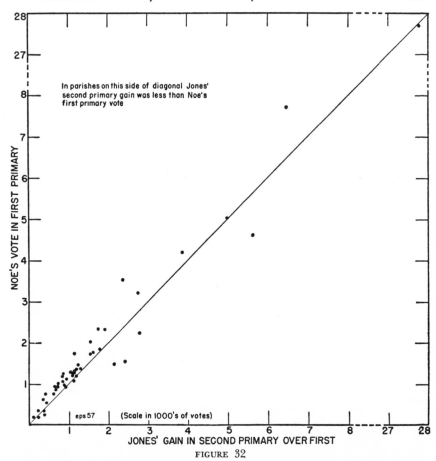

In parishes on this side of diagonal Jones'
second primary gain was less than Noe's
first primary vote

NOE'S VOTE IN FIRST PRIMARY

eps 57   (Scale in 1000's of votes)

JONES' GAIN IN SECOND PRIMARY OVER FIRST

FIGURE 32

Deliverability of Factional Followings in Louisiana: Relation between Parish
Vote for Noe for Governor in First Primary, 1940, and Increase in Second Primary
over First of Vote for Jones, Endorsed by Noe [a]

[a] Excluding parishes in which Morrison polled more than 10 per cent of the vote
in the first primary.

Thus, Representative Jimmy Morrison, of the sixth congressional district,
partially through his success in coping with the problems of the straw-
berry farmers, has built up a following localized mainly in his district
that will support him in his periodic forays into gubernatorial primaries.
Even within his own district, however, he does not receive the lopsided
vote that the local candidate pulls in some other states. (See Figure 33.)

Another aspect of the nature of factionalism relates to the durability
from election to election of voter loyalty. Some persons loyal to Huey but
disillusioned by the shenanigans of his lieutenants and successors ridicule
the notion that there is a "Long faction" and say that the present Long
group is a different crowd from that put together by the Kingfish. The

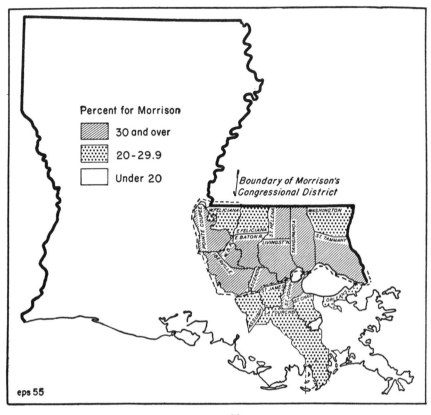

Percent for Morrison

30 and over

20-29.9

Under 20

Boundary of Morrison's
Congressional District

eps 55

FIGURE 33

Subdued Localism: Distribution of Vote for Jimmy Morrison for Governor in
First Democratic Primary, 1948

fact seems to be that the Long following has held together fairly well, as
factional cohesion goes in the South. The parish-to-parish vote for Richard W. Leche, Long candidate for the governorship in 1936, and for Earl
K. Long in 1948 shows some correlation. Generally Long was weak in the
parishes in which Leche had been weak twelve years earlier and strong
where Leche had been strong. Continuity of factional affiliation does not
match that of party loyalty in a two-party state, although in comparison
with the fluid factional systems of other states the Long support shows
considerable continuity.

The question naturally arises from what classes of people comes the
loyal following of the opposing factions. Without a more refined analysis
than has been feasible, no satisfactory solution to this problem can be
presented, although a few aspects of the factional cleavage are fairly obvious. By ranking the parishes according to the percentage of their total
vote for the antiorganization candidate in four gubernatorial primaries—

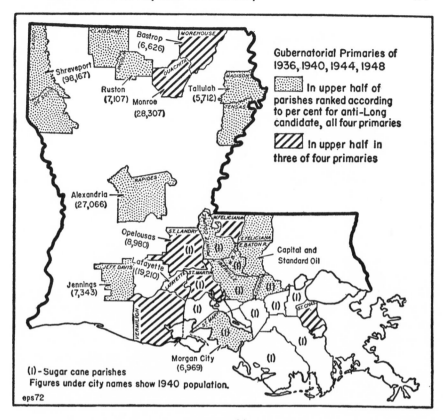

Gubernatorial Primaries of
1936, 1940, 1944, 1948

▦ In upper half of
parishes ranked according
to per cent for anti-Long
candidate, all four primaries

▨ In upper half in
three of four primaries

Capital and
Standard Oil

Bastrop
(6,626)

Shreveport
(98,167)

Ruston
(7,107) Monroe
(28,307)

Tallulah
(5,712)

Alexandria
(27,066)

Opelousas
(8,980)

Lafayette
(19,210)

Jennings
(7,343)

Morgan City
(6,969)

(I) - Sugar cane parishes
Figures under city names show 1940 population.
eps72

FIGURE 34

Centers of Anti-Long Strength: Parishes in Upper Half of All Parishes Ranked According to Percentage of Popular Vote for Antiorganization Candidate in Gubernatorial Primaries of 1936, 1940, 1944, 1948

1936, 1940, 1944, 1948—those parishes may be identified that have consistently ranked high in antiorganization strength. Those parishes that were in the upper half of parishes in percentage of antiorganization vote in all four primaries are shown on the map in Figure 34, as are those that so ranked in three of the four primaries. One fact that protrudes from the map is that most parishes including cities and considerable towns—7,000 or 8,000 up—rank high in antiorganization strength.[35] Shreveport, Alexandria, Baton Rouge, Monroe, Lafayette are all in counties giving a

[35] Said Russell Long, after his Senate victory in 1948: "I want to thank all my friends and supporters, especially those good boys who laid down their cotton sacks, plows and hoes and went to the polls to elect Russell Long U. S. Senator. I never would have made it without a heavy country vote. But I am most thankful also for my faithful city workers who kept me from being badly snowed under in the cities."—*Birmingham Post*, September 3, 1948.

relatively high percentage of their vote to antiorganization candidates for governor.[36] High antiorganization strength seems to be associated even with small-scale urbanism. While the merchant, lawyer, doctor, and the white-collar class generally may provide a center of conservatism, it would require more detailed analysis than has been made to pin down such a finding.[37] An embarrassing feature of the theory that urbanism has anything to do with opposition to Longism is that the two are not everywhere related. Thus, Calcasieu parish, containing Lake Charles, a city of 21,000 in 1940, does not turn up on our list of parishes consistently high in antiorganization strength, although it was the home of Governor Sam Jones. The local explanation is a relatively high degree of labor alertness in Lake Charles. Nor is New Orleans consistently anti-Long, but that city is explicable in terms of the relations of its organization to the state organization. Several, but not all, sugar-cane parishes rank high in antiorganization voting.

To locate the peak Long strength it is necessary only to repeat the process and identify those parishes that most consistently ranked high in the percentage of their popular vote for the Long-faction candidates. The large section of northwestern Louisiana included in the area of persistent Longism is conspicuous on the map in Figure 35. This Long stronghold is spotted with national forests established on poor agricultural and cutover lands, all of which provides a crude index of the region's economic status. Similar in characteristics is another parish in the Long ranks, Washington parish, one of the "Florida parishes," likewise a cutover parish. A few sugar-cane parishes also break into the inner circle of parishes ranking consistently high in their support of Long candidates. Two parishes in the deep delta—St. Bernard and Plaquemines—report extremely high votes for Long candidates. Plaquemines went 91.4 per cent for Earl Long in 1948. Plaquemines has been an autonomous principality under its local boss. When Governor Sam Jones appointed a sheriff to fill a vacancy in Plaquemines, his sheriff had to be re-enforced by a National Guard detachment for several months lest the local crowd chase him and his deputies out of the parish.[38] St. Bernard, the adjoining parish, is less consistent in its loyalties. In 1936 it went 98.2 per cent for Leche; in 1940, 80.7 per cent for Earl Long. In 1944 it shifted across the line and gave 68.2 per cent of its vote to Jimmie Davis, the so-called reform candidate. In 1948 it got back into line and went 92.6 per cent for

[36] Emphasis must be given to the phrase "relatively high." A parish vote may be absolutely quite low, but it is high in relation to that of other parishes. Thus, in 1948 Caddo parish turned in 45.8 per cent of its vote for Sam Jones, but only two parishes gave him a higher percentage.

[37] Compare Talmadge, of Georgia, and the townspeople. See above, chap. 6.

[38] Harnett T. Kane, *Deep Delta Country* (New York: Duell, Sloan and Pearce, 1944), chap. 16, "La Politique. . . . She Stink, She Stink!"

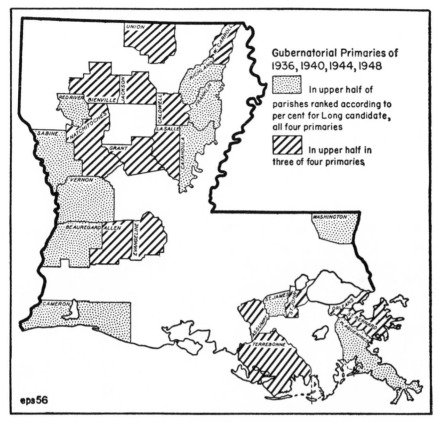

Gubernatorial Primaries of
1936,1940,1944,1948

In upper half of
parishes ranked according to
per cent for Long candidate,
all four primaries

In upper half in
three of four primaries

eps56

FIGURE 35

Centers of Long Strength: Parishes in Upper Half of All Parishes Ranked According to Percentage of Popular Vote for Long Candidates in Gubernatorial Primaries of 1936, 1940, 1944, 1948

Earl Long. The charitable explanation for such oscillation of affection is to attribute it to the mercurial French temperament.[39]

[39] The analysis of votes by their territorial distribution to obtain a rough idea of who votes for whom requires a sharper territorial segregation of different kinds of voters than exists in Louisiana. When politics takes on the form of a class division, with the different classes interspersed throughout the territory under analysis, gradations in political attitude from place to place are not so sharp as under a sectional politics. For these and other reasons, conclusions have to be drawn cautiously from Louisiana election statistics. Harold Gosnell concludes that nothing can be learned about the economic status of the Long supporters by correlation of the vote with census data. (See his *Grass Roots Politics*, Washington, D. C.: American Council on Public Affairs, 1942, chap. 8.) Casting discretion to the winds, we can go beyond the analysis produced by the map and rely on something of an intuitive interpretation of many maps and analyses of Louisiana elections to make some supplementary observations about the Long strength. The heavy vote in the so-called northwestern hill parishes evidently parallels that for progressive candidates in other southern states in the highland counties, with

4. The Better Element, Democratic Leadership, and the One-Party System

Louisiana is not unique as a case in the pathology of democracy. Louisiana's afflictions have been only more acute than those of other states of the South. To mention the tribulations of the states to the north would be indelicate. At any rate, the problems of Louisiana have not been simply corruption. Venality occurs in many contexts and the context of Louisiana irregularities must be kept in mind to identify a crucial problem in Louisiana politics, and, perhaps in lesser degree, of some other southern states.

That problem, if it may be exaggerated for emphasis, is that the common people have to rely for leadership on spectacular personages who, even if their own characters are spotless, are often aided by lieutenants, with no clear realization of what belongs to them and what belongs to the state. Not all so-called southern demagogues are in the Populist tradition; leaders of all doctrinal hues adapt their stump appeal to the inclinations of their constituency. Yet many, if not all, southern political leaders who have won the loyalties of the lesser people have been crude in their appeals, and their administrations have been accused, rightly sometimes, of extensive irregularities.

These observations raise the problem of democratic leadership. A democratic regime is not a perpetual motion machine. The great mass of citizens cannot make laws and administer the affairs of state; they can choose from among competing leaders. From where are these leaders to come who offer themselves to the people? From what sources are they to get the huge funds that are necessary for political campaigns?

The operation of democracy may depend on competition among conflicting sections of the "better element" for the support of the masses of voters. Hence, the workings of democracy require a considerable degree of disagreement within the upper classes. If true, it follows that as the upper classes become less rent by dissension among themselves, the less likely it is that they will contribute leaders who compete for mass support; or the competition will become sham in nature, with appeal based on

---

relatively few Negroes, many small farmers, a Populist background, and, further back, restrained enthusiasm for the Civil War. In the bottom-land parishes, although the Long strength is erratic, it is generally weaker than elsewhere and presumably this situation parallels the conservative position of counties in the black belts of other states.

Of the parishes ranking high in Long strength on the map in Figure 35 only one, Red River, had more than 50 per cent Negro in 1940 (50.3 per cent). On the other hand, nine of the fifteen parishes with more than 50 per cent Negro population were included in those ranking high in anti-Long strength in the map in Figure 34. In Louisiana the typical southern pattern of politics is undoubtedly thrown out of balance by the peculiar political behavior of the French parishes.

irrelevancies rather than on the promise of measures of genuine import to the people.

In the absence of popular leadership from the "better element," the breach may be filled by persons and groups with few scruples and often with little ability. It is impressive to note, for example, the frequency over the South with which candidates concerned with more than the few must depend for their campaign finance on such sources as road contractors, i.e., persons who can be rewarded from the public treasury in case of victory without, paradoxically, selling out to the "interests." Further, those leaders with a mass appeal quite often have pitifully little understanding of the technical problems of government and administration. About all they have is an ability to speak the language of the people and —they should be given the benefit of the doubt—a sincerity of purpose. Men of greater natural talents are drawn off into the opposite camp by its greater regards.

There may be within the economic and social structure of the South special obstructions to the development of an adequate competition in leadership.[40] The South may have a relatively small economic elite that possesses high cohesion and the corollary power of discipline of dissenters. Similarly the South may have less in the way of inherited wealth that might serve as a base for the development of political leaders. Further— with the destruction of the landed aristocracy by The War—the economic elite over the years perhaps came to consist in unusually high degree of persons whose wealth came quickly from undertakings dependent on grant of public privilege or public inaction in the face of ruthless exploitation of resources. The outcome has been a social and economic structure in which the gulf between rich and poor has been extraordinarily wide.

Whether the one-party system aggravates the problem of development of popular leadership is a question of another sort. The chances are that it does, although perhaps not to so great a degree as might be thought. Obviously the two-party system provides alternative lines of career. Minority leaders within the state have open to them the patronage, perquisites, and posts of honor of the Federal service when their party is in power nationally. And if a close party competition exists within the state, two channels to local eminence are open. If close party competition exists, persons of status will be attracted to both parties, and one might plausibly expect a different kind of person to be attracted to politics than under one-party conditions.

Yet the chances are that the problem goes deeper than the one-party system—to the social and economic structure of the region. One does not

---

[40] The problem is by no means limited to the South and that the situation there is any worse than the rest of the country is a conclusion that must be offered with diffidence.

create a two-party system by concluding that it would be desirable. A two-party system must have two strongly based interests to maintain itself, each of which can recruit, train, and support leaders who periodically reach out and attempt to win control of the state as a whole. Given the social and economic structure of most southern states—the comparatively small working class, the absence of organization and political sophistication among the lesser agricultural peoples—it would be rash to suppose that a two-party system would change radically in short order the nature of southern political leadership.

Chapter Nine | # ARKANSAS:
PURE ONE-PARTY POLITICS

Most southern states exhibit in their politics some salient feature that gives each a distinctive character. Alabama's sectionalism, Virginia's Byrd machine, Georgia's Talmadge and anti-Talmadge groupings, Tennessee's Shelby-East Tennessee coalition give the politics of those states a recognizable quality and color. Arkansas politics manifests no such singular trait. Its press speaks of a "state machine," yet Arkansas has no state-wide factional organization with either cohesion or continuity. True, in the days of Jeff Davis it had a bitter conflict between the hills and Little Rock and the lowlands, but the cleavage has long since dissolved. Not for many years has Arkansas had a spectacular leader capable of arousing such deep loyalties and hatreds that a factional politics, pro and anti, came to be organized around him.

Arkansas' multiplicity of transient and personal factions reminds us immediately of South Carolina and Florida. Yet Arkansas—a state with comparatively few Negroes, about one person in four—has no inexorable law that drives many of its political leaders to cap their careers by hysteria on the race question, as there seems to be in South Carolina. Nor is Arkansas politics complicated either by the localism of scattered urban concentrations or by a vague division between old and new parts of the state as in Florida.

Perhaps in Arkansas we have the one-party system in its most undefiled and undiluted form. Without means for the injection of persistent divisive factors into the electorate a politics results that is almost devoid of issue other than that of the moment. Perhaps because of the low level of voter participation, Arkansas' active electorate possesses a high degree of homogeneity. If true, that homogeneity may contribute to a politics in which genuinely important issues are not raised. They are already settled, at least for those who vote, by common consent. The result is a politics in which the debate is over the means of accomplishing what everyone assumes ought to be done and over the choice of personnel to carry out such commonly accepted, and often unarticulated, programs.

A number of Arkansawyers, who have more than passing acquaintance with other states and hence standards by which to judge, regard plain, simple, clean government as their state's most pressing need. It is indicative of the content of the state's politics that they feel this battle must be fought out before any item of real importance can be put on the political agenda. They conceive Arkansas's first problem to be the establishment of the essential mechanisms of democratic government. Since World War II it has been precisely that problem that has generated the principal controversy in the state. It would seem that in Arkansas, more than in almost any other southern state, social and economic issues of significance to the people have lain ignored in the confusion and paralysis of disorganized factional politics.

1. Policy Consensus and Factional Fluidity

An Arkansas publisher says that his paper does not take sides in gubernatorial primaries except when a matter of significant "public policy" is involved. The paper took a position in 1916 when one candidate tried to align the rest of the state against the cities as did Jeff Davis, neo-Populist governor of Arkansas in the early years of the century. Since 1916 no question of public policy of sufficient importance has been at stake to require his paper to take a stand.

The militant agrarianism of Jeff Davis died out without leaving the residue that similar movements left in some other southern states. Occasionally candidates hark back to old Jeff, but only in reminiscence and not imitation. Elected attorney general in 1898, Davis brought a series of prosecutions of corporations under a statute that prohibited any concern having any agreement to control prices anywhere from doing business in Arkansas. "The high-collared roosters" and the "silk-stocking crowd" of Little Rock, Davis reported to the people, ganged up against him. So he ran for governor in 1900 and won re-election twice, a feat that has not since been repeated.[1] His war against the corporations, like those of his

---

[1] Old Jeff's qualities are suggested by the contemporary characterization of him by the *Helena World*, a conservative journal of the lowlands: "a carrot-headed, red-faced,

contemporaries in other states, ended in futility. The great upthrust of organized business killed off the loud but feeble agrarian protest.[2] For a few years the political groupings that he had organized persisted but they soon disappeared. And since Jeff Davis' day the financial and business interests have managed better. The state has had an unbroken succession of conservative governors. The only recent governor who distinguished himself by suspecting that anything was wrong with Arkansas and that something could be done about it was the late Carl Bailey (1937–1941), for whose intellectual capacity and grasp of public problems even cynical newspapermen and practicing politicians express admiration.

When for 30 years no issue is raised of sufficient importance that a leading newspaper takes a stand in the election of a governor, an extraordinary consensus on public issues prevails. In Arkansas, former governors, unsuccessful gubernatorial candidates, newspaper reporters deny the existence of even the vaguest sort of grouping of voters and political leaders along conservative-progressive lines. This does not mean that there are no politicians of liberal leanings (such as Brooks Hays and Bill Fulbright) or of conservative inclinations (such as Ben Laney and John McClellan), or that occasions do not occur when individuals of like policy-disposition act in concert. But, much as in Florida, there have not developed in Arkansas alignments of political leaders organized to give effective expression to differences in political viewpoint. Nor have there developed continuing groupings of voters along liberal-conservative lines. To a greater or lesser degree these conditions exist over the entire South, but from conversations with scores of politicians over the region, the impression builds up that Arkansas exhibits a case of political consensus in exaggerated form. And that consensus comes fundamentally from the fact that conservatives control without serious challenge. There is not discernible in Arkansas state politics convincing evidence of an emerging durable division over broad economic policy, as we shall examine later in the treatment of Texas politics.[3]

---

loud-mouthed, strong-limbed, ox-driving mountaineer lawyer, and a friend of the fellow who brews forty-rod bug-juice back in the mountains."—Quoted by J. G. Fletcher, *Arkansas* (Chapel Hill: University of North Carolina Press, 1947), p. 292.

[2] The growth of farm tenancy since 1900 may have had something to do with the death of agrarian radicalism in Arkansas (and in other parts of the South as well). In 1900, 35.1 per cent of Arkansas white farm operators were tenants; by 1935, the percentage had grown to 50.5 per cent. That this change should be reflected in political behavior rests on the assumption that generally when an owner becomes a tenant he loses his spunk and his concern about public affairs. The reduction of a free and independent (though mortgaged) yeomanry to the status of sharecroppers, too poor to pay a poll tax and too depressed to have hope, may underlie the disappearance of most of the fire from southern politics. The idea has plausibility but it would require further investigation to test its validity. Parallel changes, of course, have played a role. The development of commercial, rather than subsistence, farming has converted the larger and more prosperous farmers into allies of their erstwhile business and financial enemies in the cities and towns.

[3] See below, chap. 12.

Arkansas leaders see no issues in their politics other than who is the "best-qualified" candidate, or what is the best way to do what everyone, i.e., everyone who has a hand in the state's politics, agrees ought to be done. For example, a principal politician of reflective bent says that he has thought at length about the one-party system, and has concluded that election contests and factional divisions are "rivalries" that turn around "personalities and emotions" of the moment. "We have," he said, "a natural situation" in which the assumption is that all persons are loyal to the state and from that common point of departure, you go ahead to have a free selection of individuals presumably on the basis of competence. He went on to say that in Arkansas there has been no attachment of political factions to philosophies or issues. The alignments are entirely in terms of a person's "connections," and of what may be found "distasteful" about other politicians, and so on. Of the groups that had surrounded him and his political opponents, "Did they represent different viewpoints?" "Absolutely not." The competition between himself and his principal opponent had been entirely personal rivalry. He considered his rival as personally unreliable and an opportunist of the first order. And he had seized on any failings of his opponent that he could detect and magnified them.

Another person, a one-time candidate for governor with long experience in state politics, concluded that there are no opposing groups that stick together with any consistency. Campaigns are "dog fights" and nothing more, and in the absence of real issues he saw no basis for expecting consistent groupings of voters. He recalled that about 1913 the governor had said to him, "There are no friendships in politics; there are only alliances." In this, our would-have-been-governor found the key to Arkansas politics—a system of alliances built up in each campaign around particular candidates.[4]

Another one-time gubernatorial candidate—who came within a shade of winning—had difficulty grasping the import of inquiries about issues that would attract a specific group of voters. He put the problem of campaigning for governor as one of convincing local political leaders—who control a substantial vote—that you are the "best-qualified" candidate. Some of these leaders can be bought. Others are not for sale, and they have to be convinced that you are the "best qualified."[5] Competence is un-

[4] This observer's conclusions are underpinned by the story of the Arkansas Representative who ran for the United States Senate. The Representative had supported the Farm Security Administration, an action that should have won him votes in a state whose white farmers were more than 50 per cent tenants—if they voted. Yet his defeat, the Farm Bureau bureaucracy could claim, came from the publicity they gave to his farm security votes. It may need to be repeated, to make the point, that the Farm Bureau is run mainly for the benefit of farmers who hire tenants—not farmers generally.

[5] In the 1948 gubernatorial primary "Uncle Mac" MacKrell, radio evangelist and flour salesman, was running like a prairie fire, and the opposition felt obliged to counter his threat by clerical authority. From a statement by a Baptist minister critical

doubtedly important, but the placing of great, almost sole, emphasis on "qualifications" carries with it the tacit assumption that all issues are either settled or quiescent.

In recent years the political battles of the state have been, in the opinion of local observers, largely between the Bailey faction and the Adkins faction. The late Carl Bailey (governor, 1937–1941) and Homer Adkins (governor, 1941–1945) were the leaders of the two groups. Adkins, who has a reputation as a superb campaign manager, organized a campaign in support of Miller for the Senate as an independent in 1937 and succeeded in defeating Bailey, who had accepted a nomination from the state Democratic committee as a candidate in a special election. In 1940 Adkins, who had been collector of internal revenue, defeated Bailey in his try for a third term as governor; opportune investigations of the income-tax affairs of Bailey leaders influenced the outcome. In 1944 Bailey had his turn when his candidate for the Senate, J. W. Fulbright, defeated Adkins. Governor Adkins' board of trustees had earlier removed Fulbright from the presidency of the University of Arkansas.

When the popular votes are subjected to close examination, it is plain that neither the Bailey nor the Adkins faction has had a state-wide political organization of any consequence or a following of voters with any impressive loyalty. And, indeed, the differences of views between the two men are not wide enough to draw a sharp cleavage among voters. The factions consisted, not of clear-cut groupings of voters, but of rather sharply defined groups of first-, second-, and third-string lieutenants loyal to the leader for personal reasons—mainly the desire for office—and, like all such groupings, their life expectancy was short.

The looseness of the bonds that bind Arkansas factions can be deduced from the scatter-diagram in Figure 36. In 1944 Homer Adkins, whose second term as governor was coming to an end, ran for the Senate against J. W. Fulbright, of Fayetteville. In most counties Adkins was weaker in 1944 than in 1940 but the decline in his strength had none of the regularity from county to county that would be found in a crystallized factional system. The shifts varied markedly from county to county and the correlation between his vote in the two primaries was quite low. The counties with the most-marked losses in Adkins' strength were mainly northwestern counties whose voters presumably responded to the regional friends-and-neighbors appeal of Fulbright, a native of that area.[6] This kind of localism, of course, appears in only a weak form in cohesive factional systems.

---

of "Uncle Mac," which was read at a huge mass meeting, the press felt obliged to quote only the "one big reason" why "Uncle Mac" should not be elected governor: "He simply is not qualified."—*Arkansas Gazette* (Little Rock), July 27, 1948.

[6] It may be that in the response of the hill counties to the Fulbright candidacy there was a glimmer of the general tendency of the upland people over the South to be more enthusiastic over candidates who can be pictured as progressive.

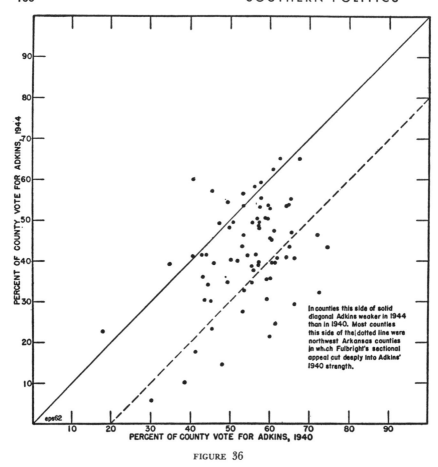

In counties this side of solid diagonal Adkins weaker in 1944 than in 1940. Most counties this side of the dotted line were northwest Arkansas counties in which Fulbright's sectional appeal cut deeply into Adkins' 1940 strength.

FIGURE 36

Fluid Factionalism: Relation between County Percentages of 1940 Arkansas Primary Vote for Adkins for Governor and His 1944 Primary Vote for Senator

As would be expected, the looseness of voter attachment to faction is accompanied by a multiplicity of candidacies. The factions, such as they are, do not have sufficient potency to freeze out third and fourth candidates, as can be seen from the fractionalization of the vote in recent gubernatorial primaries appearing in Table 18. The table omits those races in which a sitting governor was seeking a second term because Arkansas governors by custom receive a renomination without serious contest.[7]

[7] The concentration of the total vote on two candidates in 1940 (see table) again suggests the possible significance of the limited gubernatorial term in obstructing the creation of meaningful factions. In 1940 Governor Bailey sought a third term in violation of Arkansas tradition. The threat that a single individual would stay on the scene six years was enough to concentrate practically all opposition strength on a single candidate, Homer Adkins. Factions thus tend to be limited to what can be built around and in opposition to an individual during four years.

Loose and changing groupings of voters may be the cause, or the result, of a politics devoid of issues and dedicated to the choice of the "best-qualified" candidate. Probably there is an interaction between the nature of issues and the nature of factionalism. If real issues are raised, voters may be expected to divide along lines of their fundamental interests. On the other hand, if a well-organized faction is in power, those in opposition must raise issues of a sort simply to have weapons of political

TABLE 18

Percentage of Vote Polled by Leading Candidates in Arkansas
Gubernatorial Primaries

YEAR	CANDIDATE	PER CENT OF TOTAL VOTE	YEAR	CANDIDATE	PER CENT OF TOTAL VOTE
1932	Futrell	44.8	1940	Adkins	55.7
	Terral	21.3		Bailey	43.7
	Priddy	13.4		Two others	0.6
	Four others	20.5			
1936	Bailey	32.0	1944	Laney	38.5
	McDonald	30.3		Sims	34.5
	Cook	25.6		Terry	27.0
	Two others	12.1			
			1948	McMath	34.1
				Holt	23.4
				MacKrell	22.1
				Thompson	18.9
				Five others	1.5

warfare. Whether Arkansas' fluid factionalism or its issueless politics came first, or whether each feeds on the other, the upshot is a politics singularly free of anything save the petty argument and personal loyalty of the moment. A brief look at the 1948 gubernatorial primary will underpin these general remarks about the political battle in Arkansas.

The 1948 campaign brought out four principal candidates for governor—McMath, Holt, MacKrell, and Thompson. Five others had their names on the ballot and together polled 1.5 per cent of the total vote in the first primary.

James ("Uncle Mac") MacKrell threw his hat into the race first when he began his 1948 campaign in December, 1946. Uncle Mac, a Baptist minister with a folksy manner, had meddled in politics for years and had become widely known through his radio Bible Lovers Revival. In 1946 he fought a proposal to consolidate small school districts into larger districts, and dramatized himself as the friend of the people at the "crossroads and in the fencecorners." [8] When the 1948 campaign got under way he hit the hustings with his quartet, which opened his rallies with religious songs, and Uncle Mac usually took the opportunity to do a little advertising—

[8] *Arkansas Gazette* (Little Rock), November 17, 1946.

like his Texas contemporary, W. Lee O'Daniel, Uncle Mac mixed flour-selling, the old-time religion, and politics. One of his appeals was: "You know what Governor Laney has done. You know what his two predecessors did. I know I can't be any worse than any of them." [9] Uncle Mac had all the attributes of the demagogue thought to be typical of the South: that is, an appeal based mainly on irrelevancies, a fantastic ignorance of governmental problems, a spectacular platform manner, and a capacity to stir the rustic.[10]

As the campaign moved on it turned out that the principal issue would be highways. Everyone was in favor of highways, but the debate, insofar as it had a focus, was about how construction should be financed. Sid McMath, leader of an aggressive group of Garland County veterans, had been boomed for the governorship ever since he had ousted the long-entrenched McLaughlin machine in Hot Springs. McMath advocated the issuance of bonds to finance road construction. The white knight crusading against corruption and special privilege had somehow by the time he got into the governor's race been transmuted into the champion of a fiscal policy too recondite to have much dramatic value. He also urged more generous provision for education and hammered at the issue of honest elections. Over and above the debate, his personality and his record gave him political appeal. He looked like a winner.[11]

Another candidate, recently resigned as collector of internal revenue and formerly associate director of the state extension service, Horace E.

[9] Ibid., June 4, 1948. "Spider" Rowland, self-styled greatest columnist on earth (a characterization that his devotees take more seriously than does the "Spider"), observed: "As most of you know, Mr. James ('Uncle Mac') MacKrell is a most unusual character, for which many people are grateful."—Ibid., August 15, 1948. Uncle Mac had to cope with rumors circulated by his opponents. The "Spider" reported: "The other day in his speech at Star City, Uncle Mac told the audience his political enemies had been scattering rumors about him that were no more true than a two buck cornet. 'But,' he went on to say, 'if every man who ever took a drink of liquor or the second look at a woman voted for me I'd be elected governor in the first primary.' "—Ibid., June 2, 1948.

[10] "Spider" Rowland: "The question of how many votes Uncle Mac has any earthly out of winding up with is a fraction harder to figure out than tieing your shoes. Of course, in such places as Little Rock he will get washed out completely. In the cities, Uncle Mac won't get enough votes to wad a BB gun. On the other hand, in the rural districts the woods are full of folks who are sold solid on the idea that Uncle Mac hung the moon, single-handed. There isn't an earthly out to pull them up, either. Putting the hammer in against Uncle Mac makes no more impression on some of them than a mild dew does on Hoover dam."—Ibid., June 2, 1948.

[11] The Young Democrats, as "Spider" Rowland reported, "pitched a feed for eight gubernatorial candidates that came within an inch of being turned into a Sid McMath rally. Applause was the usual sort of thing, customary at such gatherings, but when McMath appeared the roof fell in. This, of course, was less welcome to his opponents than water in their shoes. The Gazette said the other seven candidates appeared 'dumfounded over the demonstration,' but there was no occasion for it. It was as natural as hair in biscuits and shouldn't have been any more of a surprise than the discovery of water in a lake."—Ibid., June 4, 1948. McMath was a former president of the Young Democrats.

Thompson, like all the others, favored better roads, higher payments to the needy aged, and better schools. On the matter of finance he opposed the issuance of bonds. He faced the issue of road finance in a forthright manner and told the voters exactly how he would get the money: "With the assistance of the Legislative Council, and members of the legislature, I will appoint a committee to develop a plan to solve this problem." [12] Earlier Mr. Thompson had said: "You are going to hear the candidates talk a lot about what they will do. So far, there has been little difference in what they say they will do—except who will do it." [13]

Jack Holt, a former attorney general, who had made an unsuccessful race for the Senate in 1942, came out flat-footedly in favor of more roads. He opposed the issuance of bonds and suggested that state invested surpluses be borrowed to finance construction. Holt tried to get someone to argue with him about President Truman's civil rights program: "I am convinced that a victory for the civil rights bill would be a defeat for the Bill of Rights." [14]

How did the so-called factions of the state line up in the campaign? The answer, as "Spider" Rowland, the *Arkansas Gazette's* famed editorial paragrapher, might say, is not so easy as tieing your shoes. The two leaders of the supposedly antagonistic factions, former governors Carl Bailey and Homer Adkins, wound up together in the McMath ranks. About the only explanation the voters had of the alliance of antagonists was that by "Spider" Rowland. Bailey was an ardent supporter of Senator Bill Fulbright. "Bill is up for re-election in 1950 and there is," the "Spider" reported, "quite a bit of jabber to the effect Governor Laney will be his opponent." If Bailey could help elect McMath governor, he would remove him as a possible candidate against Fulbright in 1950. "Another thing," the "Spider" opined, "that probably appeals to Carl Bailey is that the possibility of McMath and Laney patching up their political differences is very remote. So, it is what is generally called the Brazilian nuts that McMath wouldn't do anything to elect Laney to the Senate." [15] "Mr. Ad-

[12] Ibid., June 19, 1948.

[13] Ibid., June 4, 1948.

[14] Ibid., June 4, 1948. Arkansas has on the whole tranquil race relations. The University of Arkansas in 1948, to the accompaniment of only moderate mutterings, admitted a Negro to its law school at Fayetteville and another to its Little Rock medical school.

[15] "The first time I heard that old chesnut about 'Politics making strange bedfellows' I bit a hunk out of the dice cup I was cutting my teeth on. I have seen political expediency bring about some amazing mergers but all the other strange bedfellows look perfectly normal compared to Holy Homer and King Carl.

"I would have bet the nubbin that Carl and Homer would never be caught going through the cut for the same candidate and felt safer than a glass of milk at a reporters' convention. You can now move the seven wonders of the world up to eight.

"You might say the Bailey-Adkins amalgamation was simply a shotgun wedding or a case of any old port in a storm. Neither Homer nor Carl are responsible for the situation; it just slipped up on them like long handle underwear."—Ibid., June 10, 1948.

kins," the front page reported, "is offering moral support to Mr. McMath in return for past political assistance." [16] The "Spider," on the inside pages of the *Gazette,* intimated that the secret of it all was that Mr. Adkins had a deep dislike for Mr. McMath's mortal enemy, ex-Mayor Leo McLaughlin, of Hot Springs. "It is pretty generally circulated around that Homer goes for ex-Mayor Leo McLaughlin with the same enthusiasm that a cat does mustard." [17]

The lesser political figures who had been regarded as Bailey men and Adkins men divided in the campaign. Most of Bailey's top lieutenants supported Horace Thompson. Adkins' men lined up mainly with McMath, but some of his followers took spots in the Thompson and Holt campaign organizations. Just where outgoing Governor Laney stood in the whole affair was obscure, at least in the public discussion. He announced that he would not be a candidate for a third term and admonished state employees to keep out of the primary. He was beating the bushes for his anticivil-rights movement and expressed belief that Holt's highway financing plan was the "soundest" offered. Holt thought civil rights was a "burning issue," but he could not work up much of an argument with anyone about the proposition.[18]

And how did the voters respond? They gave McMath 34.1 per cent of the first primary vote and Holt, 23.4 per cent. MacKrell and Thompson trailed with 22.1 and 18.9 per cent, respectively. When the vote is plotted on a map, its main explanation appears to be a modified "friends-and-neighbors" pattern. Thompson ran best in several east Arkansas counties with plantation economies and many Negroes. He had worked in that area and his wife came from there. His "local boy" appeal coincided with sentiment favorable to his opposition to civil rights. On the other hand,

[16] Ibid., June 10, 1948.
[17] Ibid., June 10, 1948.
[18] The looseness and discontinuity of state-wide factions probably results in a special emphasis on legislative politics, i.e., the election of legislators and lobbying. The Farm Bureau is regarded by observers as a powerful lobbying group. It engages more or less quietly in elective campaigns and gives publicity to the records of legislators on bills in which it is concerned. As in other states of the South, the Farm Bureau has shown a keen interest in labor legislation. The usual close tie exists between the Farm Bureau and the Agricultural Extension Service, in effect a governmental subsidization of the organizing efforts of a private organization. The Arkansas Education Association is powerful enough at times to bring the governor to terms, in part because of its influence with the legislature. The public utilities, led by the Arkansas Power and Light Company, have a keen interest in the legislature and in the state government generally; the extent of their activity in gubernatorial politics has probably been exaggerated. The liquor interests are active. One of their recent objectives has been to narrow the discretion of state authorities in the granting and revocation of licenses. There is dark gossip that this discretionary authority generates at least fear of shakedowns. The governor in 1947 vetoed a bill to reduce this discretionary power. The Arkansas Free Enterprise Association, a group of businessmen and planters, has been prominent in legislative politics in support of legislation restrictive of labor. The County Judges Association, composed of the chief administrative officers of the counties, makes the usual representations to the legislature on behalf of counties.

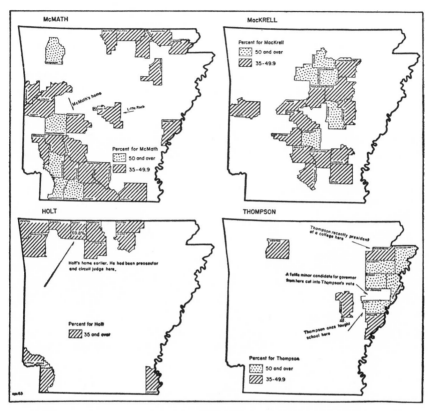

FIGURE 37

FIGURE 37

Distribution of Vote for Leading Candidates in Arkansas First Gubernatorial
Primary, 1948

Holt, who got into the run-off, drew his strongest support from northwestern Arkansas, where he had once lived. In these predominantly white
counties voters are usually not much concerned with the race issue. They
voted for a local boy who could not make much headway in the counties
with heavy Negro populations despite his position on civil rights. Mc-
Math, on the other hand, ran well in southwestern Arkansas, counties in
the vicinity of his home, and won pluralities in other counties scattered
over the state. He did no Negro-baiting. Nevertheless, he did well in
some counties where it might have been supposed that Holt's racial appeals would have been more soothing. "Uncle Mac" apparently took what
was left. His areas of greatest strength lay in the center of the state, surrounded by the local strongholds of the other candidates.[19] (See Figure
37.)

[19] The distribution of Uncle Mac's strength coincides roughly with the primary
coverage of Little Rock's KLRA, a station that had carried his Bible Lovers Revival
for several years.

In the run-off McMath defeated Holt by a bare majority. "Uncle Mac" managed Holt's run-off campaign.[20] Thompson endorsed McMath. Holt injected the race issue more insistently than he had in the first campaign. McMath deplored the resurrection of social hatred "through the processes of desperate demagoguery," but he, too, opposed President Truman's civil rights program. McMath called Holt's road-financing plan a "rose colored, misleading delusion." To build roads, you had to have money. There remained in the McMath campaign youthful crusading spirit despite the old-time politicians who had been picked up as allies. And the voters? The black counties, which by normal expectations would

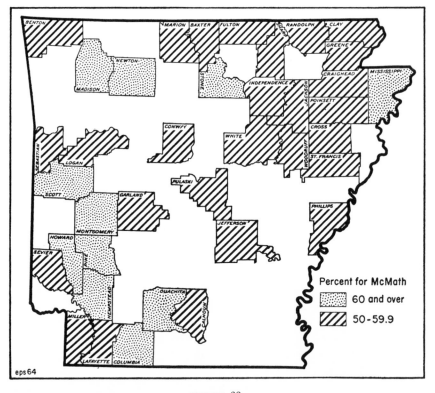

FIGURE 38

Vote for McMath in Arkansas Second Gubernatorial Primary, 1948

[20] "Uncle Mac" stated: "After the primary Sid McMath took my hand and said he would give me $15,000 cash and $10,000 after the election to remain neutral and stay out of the run-off campaign." "Absurd and ridiculous," replied McMath. "James MacKrell sent an emissary to me and offered his support for $15,000 down, and $10,000 when the election was over on the further contention that he be permitted to name both the revenue commissioner and the commissioner of education."—*Arkansas Gazette* (Little Rock), August 5, 1948.

have gone for Holt, in large part did so. Some delta county machines, however, were either realistic enough not to let a spurious issue keep them off the band wagon or were beaten on their home grounds. (See Figure 38.) On the other hand, McMath failed to carry many predominantly white rural counties which he would have been expected to carry if Arkansas highlanders followed the general southern pattern of relative indifference to the race question. The chances are that these departures from expectation were produced in part by Holt's old-home following and by the power of Uncle Mac to sway the rustic. In any case, the distribution of the vote, as shown by the map, suggests the existence of a relatively uncrystallized political system among the voters in which irrelevant and diversionary appeals may exert great influence.

2. A Politics of Personal Organization and Maneuver

In the absence of broad and continuing issues and of dominating personalities around which factions might coalesce, the formation of statewide factions becomes in no small degree a matter of winning the support of local leaders, often at sub-county levels, who can deliver votes. The would-be leader of a state faction appeals to such local personages both directly and through other state leaders who can carry with them local leaders and their immediate followings. The neighborhood rural bellwether plays a part all over the South (and elsewhere as well), but extensive interviews give the impression that these local potentates loom larger in Arkansas than in most southern states. Arkansas has, it may be noted, next to Mississippi, the highest percentage of rural farm population in the South. Like urban precinct captains, rural leaders seem to exert most influence when issues are blurred and it is immaterial to the voters how they mark their ballots.[21] When the issues—or their personification in the candidates—can be made plain to the voters, the webwork of political workers has less influence.

To give concreteness to these general observations would lead into a maze of political maneuver and management. Arkansas politicians, like those elsewhere, are not much given to generalization about their trade. They think in terms of particular and concrete situations. A candidate explains that he was strong in this county because old so-and-so was for him and weak in that county because he has never gotten along with another so-and-so. One politician with considerable state-wide experience

---

[21] These observations are in accord with inferences that can be drawn from the Arkansas election returns. For example, extremely sharp shifts in attitude from campaign to campaign in one county, while the surrounding counties remain fairly stable, suggest either management of voters or manipulation of the count. Or, when the peak strength of a candidate occurs in widely separated places quite unlike geographically, one may infer, subject to check, a concert of local leaders.

classified the vote into three categories. One group of voters is controlled by local leaders who will agree to swing the votes they influence for fifty or a hundred or five hundred dollars depending on the number involved. These leaders say they pass the money on to their voters but probably seldom do.

A second category of voters consists of those controlled by local leaders (in sub-county areas usually) who will not sell their influence. There are many such leaders, our practical politician assures us. They would be insulted if you offered them money.[22] It would be "like waving a red flag." They throw their support to the candidate they believe to be the "best man" for the office. Much of a candidate's task is to reach and sell these leaders the idea that he is the "best man." Such a local leader, of more than average statue, several politicians say, is Dr. T. E. Rhine, of Thornton in south Arkansas. The good doctor is a beloved and respected local practitioner in whose honor the community declared a holiday and conducted festivities on the forty-ninth anniversary of the beginning of his medical career in the community.[23] In a third category are the voters who are influenced by speeches, campaign literature, and newspapers.

Generally the locus of political influence is with leaders in small communities and rural neighborhoods rather than in county-wide bosses, although a few counties are thoroughly controlled by county organizations.[24] Most machine counties are delta counties along the Mississippi,

[22] A northwest Arkansas judge relates that there are a few old men on the mountain who control the votes in their districts. Although some of them will take money for "expenses," many won't let you give them anything and are genuinely offended if they are offered it. Many of these persons who control votes in their districts by virtue of their positions of prominence and prestige take pride in doing their political friends a favor and in demonstrating their influence.

[23] *Arkansas Gazette* (Little Rock), June 18, 1948. The doctor, one politician says, backs a candidate on the basis of merit and his people vote as he votes. "He won't trade out; you wouldn't dare suggest it to him." An explanation of "trading out" as it is practiced in some, but by no means all, Arkansas counties, can be illustrated by an example: All the key men in one faction and a few fence straddlers got together the night before election in a store downtown. One man was extremely interested in the race for county treasurer and controlled one or two precincts. He would find another man particularly interested in a different county race. He would then agree to swing his one or two boxes in favor of that man's candidate in return for the other fellow's swinging his boxes for his candidate for treasurer. This kind of trading went on for several hours, with the participants trying to work out combinations to produce a result most satisfactory to all concerned. When the negotiations were completed one of the candidates for county judge had been "traded out." They called him down to the store and he was told by the boys that they liked him, and so on, but that they just happened to be more interested in the other races and they thought he should withdraw to avoid the embarrassment of a sound defeat. The candidate agreed and the election judges were informed of that fact the next morning when the ballot boxes were delivered to them, many of the judges being the same persons in attendance at the negotiations.

[24] Arkansas politicians make a recondite differentiation between machine counties and crooked counties. A machine county is not necessarily crooked nor is a crooked county necessarily a machine county. Yell County, for example, one politician assures us, is a machine county but not crooked. With considerable regularity it returns an overwhelming majority (75 to 90 per cent) of its vote for its favorite for governor. The

counties with a plantation economy, with high percentages of Negro population, and with a ruling class which, on the whole, justifies the lurid descriptions applied without discrimination to all southern plantation operators. Some directors of large-scale plantation and lumbering operations in the Arkansas delta counties really deserve to be called hard-boiled. It is here that are to be found the headquarters and the moving spirits of the Arkansas Free Enterprise Association, which backed a "right-to-work" amendment to the state constitution, urged the adoption of the Taft-Hartley Act, and gave enthusiastic support to Governor Laney's crusade against the Truman civil rights program. The machines of the delta counties depend fundamentally on the relation of dependence between the landlord and tenant. "Plantation owners in the delta counties," the newspapers can write in a matter-of-fact tone as if merely recording common knowledge, "usually control the votes of their many tenants, who cast their ballots in boxes set up in the owners' commissaries." [25] Lack of secrecy of the ballot and control of election machinery by plantation operators assure, at least in many boxes, predictable election results. "The people co-operate very well," one operator remarks. The election results do not reveal, however, that delta county leaders invariably work together in gubernatorial campaigns. In the legislature, on the other hand, delta counties collaborate against the hills on such matters as school equalization issues. "We pay all the taxes and they want to spend the money," delta leaders aver, with some exaggeration.

Outside the delta, so-called "machine" counties are scattered more or less at random over the state. Yell County, a hill county northwest of Little Rock, has a reputation as a machine county. Garland County for many years was controlled by the organization of former Mayor McLaughlin of Hot Springs. A few far northwestern counties, in some of which the Republicans are in the majority locally, have a voting behavior somewhat like that of East Tennessee counties; that is, in the Democratic primaries they deliver huge majorities to whatever candidate it appears will be able to do something for them. But even in this pursuit of self-interest the northwestern counties are not consistent.[26]

The influence of local leaders and of machines makes for erratic distributions of the popular vote among candidates, and only the most mi-

---

boys in Yell merely get together and decide how the county is to go and that's all there is to it. The leaders of a crooked county, on the other hand, manipulate the count or the returns for a consideration.

[25] *Arkansas Gazette* (Little Rock), June 10, 1948.

[26] A former state legislator describes the conservative faction of Arkansas politics as being a combination of the delta counties, the scattered mountain machine counties, and the financial and business interests of Little Rock. In gubernatorial politics the delta and upland machine counties are not always allied in their popular vote although at times this combination occurs. The combination may have existed frequently enough to give rise to the notion that it is more persistent than it is in fact. And the combination may appear in the politics of the legislature and the lobby.

nute inquiry yields a satisfactory interpretation of the vote in a particular primary. Two maps of relatively simple votes, however, are presented in Figure 39. One map shows the counties with the highest popular percentages for Ben Laney for governor in the 1944 primary. In a three-way race Laney polled 38.5 per cent of the vote; the next ranking candidate, J. Bryan Sims, declined to make the run-off and Laney became something of an accidental governor.[27] Laney, a resident of Ouachita County in South Arkansas, ran on his record as a businessman: oil had been discovered on the family holdings.[28]

His peak counties in 1944 appear in part as a "friends-and-neighbors" pattern typical of states with loose factional systems. A few other counties removed from his local sphere show up on the map. One of these —Lee County in the delta—was the home of the political leader "who put him in the race for governor." Compare the companion map showing the counties of Laney's peak strength in 1946 when he ran for the routine nomination for a second term. The areas of highest strength shifted markedly between the two primaries. Since Laney would be renominated as a matter of course, the machine counties came through with huge majorities, presumably on the theory that such enthusiasm would not injure them in their dealings with the statehouse during his second term. The delta counties delivered an overwhelming vote for "Business Ben" —97.3 per cent in Crittenden County was the record. The Democrats in the northwestern counties with strong Republican votes moved up high in the rank of enthusiasts for Laney. Yell County, a machine county, came through with a heavy vote, as did Prairie, not highly regarded in the state as a machine county but thoroughly enough controlled to stimulate a GI independent slate to oppose the "ins" in the 1946 general election.

Explanations by candidates of why they were weak here and strong there provide significant insight into the character of Arkansas politics. They almost invariably explain their strength in particular areas in terms of their relations with local leaders rather than from the fact that their policy positions conflicted or agreed with local interests. Thus, why was a candidate weak in one county and strong in surrounding counties? The leaders in the northern part of the county had always been "at outs" with

[27] One of the great mysteries of Arkansas politics is why the late Mr. Sims did not choose to make the run-off campaign. About as plausible an interpretation as we could find was that his financial backers ran out on him in the second primary, and the large contributions available to him from alternative sources for the run-off would have placed him under commitments which he did not care to undertake. Such an interpretation is entirely consistent with Mr. Sims' high reputation for honor and probity.

[28] A person connected with Laney's campaign recalls that the campaign finances were different from any he had ever seen. Usually during a campaign you "die a thousand deaths" because of the shortage of money. When a bill came in all you had to do was to take it over to the campaign treasurer and he would write out a check. "Boy, that is the way to run a campaign."

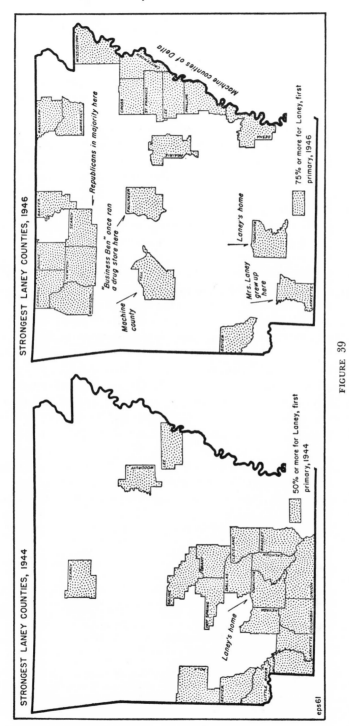

FIGURE 39

Vote for Laney in Arkansas Gubernatorial Primaries, 1944, 1946

him. Or why was he generally weak in a group of northwestern counties? A bitter enemy in the area disliked him so intensely that he was in the habit of setting out in his car and "buying" those counties away from our candidate. Or why did he lose strength in this southern county from one campaign to another? Some of the people who put an opponent in the race against him had lived in that county. Why was he weak in this delta county? Well, there was a fellow in the sheriff's office who was always against him, and a state police official who had always been unsympathetic toward him, and another man who was a disappointed office-seeker. The great emphasis by candidates on their alliances with local leaders (and their local enmities) in explanation of their electoral strength underpins our general interpretation of Arkansas politics.[29]

The independence of candidacies, which we have come to expect in a loose factionalism, prevails in Arkansas. Each candidate avoids public alliance with others running simultaneously. The people, it is said, regard such tactics as an effort to build up a machine and it is thought that if candidates team up all will suffer. There is, however, considerable undercover meddling by candidates and leaders in other races. This usually takes the form of A arranging with his local followers over the state to throw their influence to B or perhaps merely to oppose C. State legislators, of course, run without identification with state factions; there are simply no factions of sufficient definiteness with which they might identify themselves if they desired to do so.

In all these relations between state leaders and county and sub-county potentates electoral irregularities creep in from time to time. Candidates for governor at times find it advisable, for example, to arrange for early and reliable reports to Little Rock on election night from counties in which they know they are strong. If these early returns show a candidate to be in the lead, counties with flexibility in the count may be encouraged to get on the band wagon. Independent collection of figures from the precincts serves also to check shenanigans in reporting from the county seat.[30]

[29] Practical politicians in other states are wont to explain their local strengths and weaknesses in terms of their relations with local leaders. They are often unaware of social and economic factors associated with voting behavior. When a candidate is consistently weak in a few counties for a perfectly valid reason of unlikeness of views between himself and the people of the area, he is disposed to explain it on grounds of the personal enmity or coldness of local political leaders. The voters are probably much smarter than they are supposed to be; they may sense the policy inclinations of a candidate through all the confusion a little more clearly than the candidate himself, who is engrossed in the process of political organization and maneuver.

[30] In Arkansas, as in Tennessee, one hears extraordinary tales of electoral manipulation. It is impossible to check the authenticity of these stories but their repetition from many sources probably means that they have at least some foundation in fact. Thus, in a congressional race the principal county leaders are said to have gotten together and agreed to count and report the ballots as cast. On election night county A held up its returns and the rumor began to circulate on the long distance wires that

3. The GI's and Common Honesty

If it were possible to get to the truth of the business, one might conclude that a one-party system runs a better chance of corruption at the
polls than a two-party system. Two-party election machinery is built on
the principle that if two would-be thieves watch each other, an honest
count will result. The general purity of elections, of course, does not by
any means depend entirely on the wholesome surveillance of competitors
at the count. In one-party states the poorly organized factions that spring
up for a campaign are rarely well-enough manned or managed to get
election officials appointed and watchers to the polls. In fact, in a politics
in which it is every man for himself, precinct watchers to look out for
each primary candidate would at times make a small mass meeting.

Arkansas does not hold the record for electoral irregularity. The
palm perhaps goes to Tennessee, although that award could not be defended to the last ditch.[31] Arkansas' local machines and habits of electoral
fraud merely happen to have been ventilated in several localities by
movements led by GI's in 1946. The established holders of power have
tried to pin a pink ribbon onto the GI's, yet when the GI leaders are
pushed back to their basic political doctrines their program adds up to
little more than an advocacy of common honesty in elections. In a number
of Arkansas communities this is, of course, the fundamental issue, for
without free and honest elections the entire democratic process falls. In
these communities free and honest elections would be radical, or revolutionary, for an honest count would overthrow the established order.

All the trouble started in Garland County, the seat of Hot Springs,
spa and gambling center long dominated by the political machine of
Leo P. McLaughlin. In Hot Springs, Sid McMath, a lieutenant colonel
of the Marines, returned from the wars and gathered about him a group
of GI's to throw out the long-entrenched rascals. Held together by the
qualities of personality and leadership of McMath—"you can't talk to
Sid for ten minutes without knowing that he is honest"—this group of
young field officers planned, as if it were a military operation, the capture
of Hot Springs and executed the operation with skill and courage. Cold
courage and determination were essential, for their antagonists consisted
of some of the nation's leading professional gamblers and many of the
town's principal businessmen who prospered under an "open"-town
policy. While the GI's did not actually wear weapons during their campaign, they carried them in their automobiles.

---

its leaders were backing down on the agreement. County B checked the process by
threatening to start meddling with its returns on another district race, prosecuting
attorney, still unreported, which concerned the leaders of county A much more than
the congressional race.

[31] See below, chap. 21.

The GI's attacked first in the Democratic primary of the summer of 1946. Sid McMath captured the nomination as prosecuting attorney for his district, composed of Garland and Montgomery counties; his running mates for Garland County offices did not fare so well. The GI ticket, unrestrained by the custom that the verdict of the Democratic primary should be final, carried the battle into the general election. The high crime of bolting the party was to plague them later, but they won the offices of sheriff, tax assessor, county judge, and several others. Three days before the GI's took office in January, 1947, gambling houses in Hot Springs closed.

In the spring of 1947 the GI campaign committee took another objective by putting over its candidate for mayor of Hot Springs, Earl T. Ricks, who had piloted the first plane into Nagasaki after the atom bomb. In March, 1947, a special grand jury convened to investigate McLaughlin's activities. It returned a spate of indictments, whose chief consequence was publicity rather than convictions. The organization fought prosecution with all the customary delaying tactics, cried persecution, and a few of the smaller fry were convicted. A jury declined to accept the defense plea that monthly payments by gamblers to the city attorney, Jay Rowland, were "retainers" to him to look out for their interests.[32] Ed Spear, special deputy assessor under McLaughlin, pleaded guilty to a charge that he robbed two GI campaign workers of a brief case containing affidavits by citizens who denied that they had authorized the McLaughlin organization to obtain their poll-tax receipts.[33] The big fish often get away, and McLaughlin won an acquittal when tried on a change of venue in a rural court on a charge that gamblers had been permitted to operate in return for their obtaining poll-tax receipts that could be voted for his organization.[34] In the fall of 1948, after winning the governorship, McMath announced that he would bring McLaughlin to trial on other indictments.

The political thinking of the Garland County GI's, as they consoli-

[32] Aside from the "retainers," most of the witnesses "said they had also paid Mr. Rowland about 50 per cent of house bank rolls which he recovered after the money had been confiscated by State Police."—*Arkansas Gazette*, October 11, 1947. During his trial Rowland admitted he had received $50,000, which he split with five others, from buyers of a $2,000,000 city bond issue.—Ibid., October 16, 1947. The state supreme court affirmed lower court action; in September, 1948, Rowland petitioned the supreme court to reconsider.

[33] Ibid., October 15, 1947.

[34] The "licensing" of gambling through periodic fines provided considerable revenue. In the course of the McLaughlin trial, "City Clerk Emmett Jackson disclosed that gamblers paid $60,757.25 in monthly fines during 1945–46. Gamblers operated under this unofficial licensing system. They paid $131.30 a month, of which $100 went to the city and $25 to the prosecuting attorney as a fee. 'Did anyone else get any of this money?' asked Mr. Donham. 'No, not any of THAT money,' he replied, with emphasis on the 'that.' Judge Cummings had to rap for order to halt the laughing."—Ibid., November 22, 1947.

dated their victories in the county and contemplated moving in on the state, limited itself to the sort of ideas that prevailed in the muckraking era of decades earlier. They had exposed in Hot Springs one segment of a process involving special privilege, graft, corrupt elections which existed in many counties. They could demonstrate to the people of Arkansas what had been going on all over the state. The conviction was that the preliminary step to any real progress in Arkansas—in social legislation, in public works, in policy to the left or to the right or middle of the road —was the establishment of the basic essentials of honest and representative government.

McMath's campaign in Garland County stimulated like movements in a half dozen or so other counties where in the 1946 general elections GI candidates opposed the regular party nominees. In Crittenden County, across the Mississippi from Memphis, a GI slate headed by Royce Upshaw, dealer in oil products and well known as a former basketball coach, lost in the general election to Judge C. H. ("Sly Cy") Bond's machine. A river-bottom plantation county, Crittenden had long been noted for electoral irregularities. In the plantation precincts the custom has been to offer a voter a ballot already marked with request that he sign it.[35] And obliging election officials have marked the ballot for citizens too busy to turn up at the polls. Pressure on employers brought the discharge of workers who had voted wrong.

All the beneficiaries of the organization naturally opposed the veterans. The big planters, at the mercy of the county organization because of its control of road and drainage work, lined up with the county machine. The GI's, they agreed later, had not been able to get well-known men of substance to run against the machine. Such men had too much at stake. The GI's just back from the wars had much to gain and little to lose. They got the vote, as one of them says, of the "peckerheads" around the county with nerve enough to vote against the big planters, and a considerable vote in the towns. "Lots of people," he continued, "came to him more or less on the sly and wished him luck and said they were sorry they couldn't vote for him."

The Crittenden leaders, like those of Garland, move toward the most restricted political objectives. One of them says he has no complaint about anything except elections and election laws. You must get honesty in elections, he argues, to the end that the people can "vote freely." If then, in a free election, they select the wrong man, that is all right. Another, when pressed pointedly for what the GI's stood for, talked a long time but it all boiled down to honest elections "through which the will of the people can be expressed." And perhaps a step further. All kinds of improvements

[35] In Arkansas the voter signs a duplicate ballot which is preserved in a separate box which is not supposed to be opened except in case of contest. The common rumor is that in some counties officials regularly inspect the duplicates.

would naturally follow from honest elections and accurate representation of the people.

As the 1946 general election approached there was some fear among the old-line politicians lest the boys trained in violence apply their training at home. In Cleveland County the GI's demanded a fair count or else. They promised to seize the ballot boxes and conduct a recount on the spot if they did not receive a fair deal. "Fraud is difficult to prove after an election. The proper way to halt such practices is to act when and if they happen," one of them said.[36] The GI's made a clean sweep of the offices they sought in Cleveland County. They elected their candidates for county judge in Montgomery County and in Pope County; and in other counties they gave the regular Democratic nominees a stiff battle. In Pine Bluff, the veterans swept out the city administration by a landslide. One of the outgoing mayor's supporters voiced the sentiment of many Arkansas politicians: "You may say for me that Pine Bluff politics is getting rough." [37]

Sid McMath and his Hot Springs boys provided inspiration for the local GI "revolts" around the state, but each local group proceeded independently. All local GI groups developed a common cause, however, in 1947 when it appeared that Democratic party rules would be invoked to exclude from the 1948 Democratic primaries as candidates all the GI's who had run as independents in 1946 and to exclude, as well, those who had supported GI's in the general elections. In Crittenden County, Judge Cy Bond, the organization leader and Democratic county chairman, announced that the 1946 GI's would be excluded from the 1948 primary. Officials of the state Democratic committee remarked that, under the rules, such action was left up to the county committees.[38] The prospect that county machines could thus exclude their opponents from the primaries stirred up a commotion. The state committee met, discovered that it had the power to adopt a state-wide rule on the matter, and resolved that no person should be barred from participation as voter or as candidate in the 1948 primaries because of past violations of the anti-bolting rules.

Not all GI leaders were white knights leading crusades against wicked local machines. The revolts picked up the usual quota of opportunists whose chief sincerity was in their wish to ride the GI band wagon into office. Nevertheless, the movement, if it could be called that, included a number of men of extraordinary idealism coupled with skilled and coolness in the hard-boiled tactics of politics. That the GI's knew what they were about was shown by McMath's election as governor in 1948.

[36] *Arkansas Gazette* (Little Rock), September 29, 1946.
[37] Ibid., November 13, 1946.
[38] *The Democrat* (Little Rock) , October 2, 1947.

Chapter Ten | # NORTH CAROLINA:
PROGRESSIVE PLUTOCRACY

DESPITE common inheritances of war and reconstruction each southern state possesses characteristics that combine into a unique personality. Though their differences are known to anyone who has looked beneath the surface, they are often ignored in general comments about the region. There are deeply rooted dissimilarities in the economic and social fabric. There are differentiations in the tone and nuance of politics. There are distinguishing attributes that can be measured and others that can only be felt. The prevailing mood in North Carolina is not hard to sense: it is energetic and ambitious. The citizens are determined and confident; they are on the move. The mood is at odds with much of the rest of the South—a tenor of attitude and of action that has set the state apart from its neighbors. Many see in North Carolina a closer approximation to national norms, or national expectations of performance, than they find elsewhere in the South. In any competition for national judgment they deem the state far more "presentable" than its southern neighbors. It enjoys a reputation for progressive outlook and action in many phases of life, especially industrial development, education, and race relations.

North Carolina's position of respectability in the nation rests on more than popular imagination. Its governmental processes have been scrupulously orderly. For half a century no scandals have marred the state administration. No band of highwaymen posing as public officials has raided the public treasury. No clowns have held important office—save the erratic and irrelevant Bob Reynolds—and there have been no violent outbursts by citizens repressed beyond endurance. The state university has pioneered in regional self-examination; it has become famed for academic freedom and for tolerance.[1]

The state has a reputation for fair dealings with its Negro citizens. Its racial relations have been a two-sided picture, but nowhere has co-operation between white and Negro leadership been more effective. Nowhere, except perhaps in Virginia, have over-all relations, year in and year out, been more harmonious. In 1947 a northern Negro reporter, hearing of the harmony that prevailed, visited North Carolina. He looked with critical eye and concluded that it bid fair to be a model community in its race relations, "something of a living answer to the riddle of race." [2]

North Carolina has outstripped other southern states in the development of a virile and balanced economy. In 1940 a larger proportion of its labor force was employed in manufacturing,[3] and the total value added by manufacture was larger than that of any other state in the South.[4]

The comfortable picture of the Tar Heel state as an area of progress, tolerance, and enlightenment is scotched most forcefully by North Carolinians themselves. They are aware of the rough and hard struggles within their state. They know the bitter conflicts that surround the Negro and organized labor. They know the fights over state appropriations and tax sources. They know that every liberation from ancient taboo is bought or buttressed by shrewdness and hard work and endless patience. Yet they take pride in what they accomplish and seldom indulge in complacency that ignores work yet undone.

1. A Modern Renaissance

North Carolina's chroniclers trace the distinctive character of their state [5] to its atypical origins in the Old South and to a political and educational renaissance that took place at the turn of the century.

[1] The University's president has been Frank Graham, by all odds the South's most prominent educator and versatile public servant. In the forefront of American progressiveism, it is significant that Dr. Graham is indigenous to North Carolina and himself a product of the University. In 1949 he was appointed to the United States Senate.

[2] *News and Observer* (Raleigh), July 17, 1947.

[3] By rank: North Carolina, 26.9; South Carolina, 22.8; Virginia, 20.1; Georgia, 18.5; Tennessee, 18.3; Alabama, 17.4; Louisiana, 12.9; Florida, 11.7; Texas, 9.9; Arkansas, 9.9; Mississippi, 9.2.

[4] By rank: North Carolina, $545,952,289; Texas, $453,105,423; Virginia, $379,488,-055; Tennessee, $320,341,902; Georgia, $283,316,138; Alabama, $247,383,611; Louisiana, $200,085,837; South Carolina, $169,846,619; Florida, $118,015,863; Mississippi, $73,462,-419; Arkansas, $67,390,149.

[5] Illustrative of North Carolina's individuality was its action in the 1948 controversy over President Truman's civil rights recommendations. Most members of its congres-

Much of the distinctiveness of modern North Carolina stems from differences between it and the rest of the South that existed at the time of The War. It refused by popular vote in 1861 to call a secession convention. It refused to leave the Union until Lincoln issued his call for troops and Virginia and South Carolina made it a lonely island of loyalty between them. Its fundamental difference from the Deep South was the smaller relative importance of its plantation economy. North Carolina had large numbers of slaves, to be sure, but large land- and slave-holdings played a less-important part than in other states. North Carolina had fewer slaves than any of the seven principal slave states and a much smaller number of large slaveholders. It had fewer manorial plantations to support violent states' rights politicians. It had less of a ruling class to impress its fixations of economics and of race on the state. It was less

TABLE 19

Slaves and Slaveholdings in Principal Slave States, 1860

STATE	NUMBER OF SLAVES	NUMBER OF SLAVE-HOLDINGS OF 50 OR MORE SLAVES
North Carolina	331,059	744
Virginia	490,865	860
Georgia	462,198	1314
Louisiana	331,726	1576
South Carolina	402,406	1646
Mississippi	436,631	1675
Alabama	435,080	1687

dependent on plantation production and less imbued with the associated attitudes.

With its relatively few baronial slaveholders, North Carolina became in the nineteenth century conscious of its lowly position. The arrogant glare of the gentry in neighboring Virginia and South Carolina gave it a sense of inferiority, or at least so say some North Carolinians. A poor-relations complex put the state on the defensive. But if there was a sentiment of inferiority, it was belligerent. And if the elegant accomplishments of others gave it an awareness of mediocrity, the mediocrity was militant.[6] After The War this odd child bestirred itself sooner and more productively than its prouder neighbors. It seemed less shackled than

---

sional delegation were cool in the hysteria that beset the region. Its governor failed to applaud Senator Tom Connally of Texas when that gentleman called the program a "lynching of the Constitution" at a Jefferson-Jackson day dinner in Raleigh.—*Atlanta Journal,* March 1, 1948. In the Democratic national convention of 1948 North Carolina split its vote but gave the President his only support in the South.

[6] See Robert W. Winston, "North Carolina: A Militant Mediocrity," *The Nation,* 116 (February 21, 1923), pp. 209–12; and Jonathan Daniels, *Tar Heels* (New York: Dodd, Mead & Company, 1941), pp. 1–16.

they by the ghosts of lost grandeur; it had had less grandeur to lose. Perhaps its inner spirit was pricked by the ill-concealed condescension that it often received. In any event, at the turn of the century a revival in the life of the state launched it upon a new and vigorous era.

The causal influences in any social gestation are elusive. What moves a people to action, what gets the ball of social inertia rolling one direction instead of another, or rolling at all, is a pretty question. Yet once a trend starts, it is strongly disposed to persist, difficult to reverse. A sequence of historical events often stimulates a social organism to a particular line of action. Those events are sometimes manifestations of deep evolutionary processes and may give the impression that they are the prime movers themselves.

North Carolina's spirit reveals itself in the purposeful direction of its social action commencing about 1900. Philosophers and historians find the origin, if not the explanation, of this spirit in the political struggles at the end of the past century, which propelled the state into its modern era of liberalized Democratic government. These struggles centered around Republican and Populist forces which captured control of the state legislature in 1894 and elected a Republican governor in 1896. Fusion successes, in addition to removing the state's affairs from Democratic hands, increased the prominence of Negroes in public life. Their number in elective and appointive places expanded to the acute irritation of Democratic whites. And, as had occurred elsewhere, when the competition became intense, Democrats maintained that Negroes were moved by every base incentive and that, in fact, their presence in the electorate was responsible for the shameless corruption that prevailed. In bitter white-supremacy campaigns the Democrats recovered control of the legislature in 1898 and the governorship in 1900.

The modern era dates from the administration of the newly elected governor, Charles Brantley Aycock. Aycock has come down as "the educational governor." His energies in office and out were consumed with the advancement of public education. The key to his fame, which in North Carolina is great, lies in the success with which he recruited the support of Carolinians, including those who would have to pay the tax bill, to the cause of universal instruction. A great schism split the state for years over private versus public institutions of higher learning. Supporters of denominational colleges fought appropriations for the state university. There was great concern not only over secular instruction but over the tax money that would have to be spent on it. Aycock, in company with others, fought and won the battle for the general principle that the best investment a state can make is in the education of its children.

Aycock spoke for universal education, and he and North Carolina did not exclude the black man from the universe. The campaigns of 1898 and 1900 had been fought on a pledge to remove the Negro from politics.

The legislature proposed and in 1900 the people approved a reading and writing qualification for voting. (A temporary grandfather clause accommodated illiterate whites.) And then having disfranchised the Negro on the grounds of illiteracy, North Carolina set about to make him literate. Aycock spoke in 1904: "When the (suffrage) fight had been won, I felt that the time had come when the negro should be taught to realize that while he would not be permitted to govern the State, his rights should be held more sacred by reason of his weakness." [7] His rights included the right to education along with the white citizenry. While North Carolina has been no picnic ground for its Negro citizens, the spirit of Aycock has persisted in a consistently sensitive appreciation of Negro rights.[8]

TABLE 20

Value of Farm Products by States, 1899 and 1939

STATE	1899	1939	PER CENT INCREASE
Florida	$ 18,309,104	$ 88,904,396	385.6
North Carolina	89,309,638	262,437,677	193.9
Texas	239,823,244	509,736,065	112.5
Arkansas	79,649,490	159,098,085	99.7
Virginia	86,548,545	150,912,239	74.4
South Carolina	68,266,912	110,748,841	62.2
Georgia	104,304,476	165,956,195	59.1
Louisiana	72,667,302	114,046,616	56.9
Mississippi	102,492,283	158,940,942	55.1
Tennessee	106,166,440	156,491,597	47.4
Alabama	91,387,409	119,740,527	31.0

From this educational revival springs in large measure the spirit of self-examination that still sets North Carolina apart in the South. As the state struggled to educate its people it made great strides, too, in the fundamental base of a healthy society, productivity. Perhaps fortuitous economic circumstances impelled tobacco and textile production. Perhaps

[7] Address before Democratic state convention, June 23, 1904.—Hugh Talmadge Lefler, North Carolina History told by Contemporaries (Chapel Hill: University of North Carolina Press, 1934), p. 410.

[8] The Negro Year Book (Tuskegee: Tuskegee Institute, 1947), p. 76, has measured the relative status of Negro and white education by the percentage that the cost per white pupil exceeds the cost per Negro pupil. Using the "value of school property and current expense per child in average daily attendance," the cost per white pupil was greater than the cost per Negro pupil in 1943–44 by the following percentages: North Carolina, 43; Texas, 47; Florida, 102; Arkansas, 136; Alabama, 174; Louisiana, 201; South Carolina, 207; Georgia, 212; Mississippi, 499. Not only did North Carolina hold a favorable "per pupil" position, but the proportion of Negroes in school was closer to that of whites in school than in most southern states.

it was something as simple as the conflux of energies of able men of good will. Whatever the causes, as North Carolina began to educate it also began to produce, and there were set in motion the progressive, productive forces that today distinguish the state. Not that it has achieved a material welfare greater than other southern states but, rather, it has been on the way. Once started, it has demonstrated a relentless forward determination. By many economic indices the state ranks far down the ladder, even among southern states, none of which, however, has shown more sustained progress.

TABLE 21

Value of Manufactured Products by States, 1900 and 1939

STATE	1900	1939	PER CENT INCREASE
North Carolina	$ 94,919,663	$1,421,329,578	1397.4
Texas	119,414,982	1,530,220,676	1181.4
Virginia	132,172,910	988,813,246	648.1
Alabama	80,741,449	574,670,690	611.7
South Carolina	58,748,731	397,512,863	576.6
Tennessee	108,144,565	728,087,825	573.3
Florida	36,810,243	241,538,534	556.2
Georgia	106,654,527	677,402,657	535.1
Louisiana	121,181,683	565,265,273	366.5
Mississippi	40,431,386	174,937,294	332.7
Arkansas	45,197,731	160,166,984	254.4

Increases in the value of farm products between 1899 and 1939 are shown for each southern state in Table 20. North Carolina's percentage increase exceeded that of every other southern state except Florida. Florida's farm production was so low in 1899 that even a small increase resulted in a high rate of growth. Over the same period North Carolina's advance in the value of manufactured products was even more marked, as is made clear by Table 21.

It has been the vogue to be progressive. Willingness to accept new ideas, sense of community responsibility toward the Negro, feeling of common purpose, and relative prosperity have given North Carolina a more sophisticated politics than exists in most southern states. The spirit of the state has not tolerated strident demagoguery. The spirit that has not feared to face community needs, and to levy taxes to meet them, has had no place for a Huey Long. The spirit that recognizes a responsibility to citizens who long were unable to participate in their government does not tolerate a Talmadge. The spirit that is unchained to a social and economic hierarchy of great tradition and authority has no place for a Byrd machine.

2. Rule of an Economic Oligarchy

Industrialization has created a financial and business elite whose influence prevails in the state's political and economic life. An aggressive aristocracy of manufacturing and banking, centered around Greensboro, Winston-Salem, Charlotte, and Durham, has had a tremendous stake in state policy and has not been remiss in protecting and advancing what it visualizes as its interests. Consequently a sympathetic respect for the problems of corporate capital and of large employers permeates the state's politics and government. For half a century an economic oligarchy has held sway.

North Carolina's economic-political combination has exhibited a sense of responsibility in community matters. It has not been blind to broad community needs. It might impose a sales tax during the depression and at the same time reduce ad valorem taxes. Yet it had the courage and foresight to embark in the 'twenties on a huge highway construction program financed by borrowed money. The traditional, organization governor in 1947 recommended to his legislature increased salaries for teachers and state employees, expanded highway construction, an enormous and costly good health program, substantial capital outlay for institutions of higher learning. The kind of economic-political system favored by the oligarchy was described by a former governor as the "capitalistic system liberally and fairly interpreted." [9] And that pretty well sums up the view of the prevailing forces in North Carolina.

The state has been run largely by lawyers.[10] While many of its governors may have been stodgy and conservative they have never been scoundrels or nincompoops. It would be inaccurate to portray a direct line of authority, or even of communication, from the skyscraper offices of industrial magnates to the state capitol. It would be inaccurate to suggest that North Carolina's top politicians and policy makers have been other than generally independent, conscientious citizens in the execution of their charges. The effectiveness of the oligarchy's control has been achieved through the elevation to office of persons fundamentally in harmony with its viewpoint. Its interests, which are often the interests of the state, are served without prompting.

The pre-eminence of these politicians has been accomplished through two "machines" or organizations. Even if North Carolinians did not constantly talk about them, their existence would be suggested by the voting behavior of the state. On the basis of our observations in Tennessee, Georgia, and Virginia, Table 22 clearly indicates the presence of a political organization. Instead of a dispersion of the vote among many candi-

[9] O. Max Gardner, quoted in *Atlanta Journal,* December 23, 1946.
[10] Kerr Scott, elected in 1948, was the first governor not a lawyer in fifty years. Of 170 members of the 1947 legislature, only one could be called a "labor man."

dates, as occurs in a loose and anarchic factional system, the North Carolina primary vote clusters mainly around two major candidates. In every contested primary since 1916, save one, about three-fourths of the vote has gone to the two leading candidates.

In fact, the organizations indicated by the figures have existed. First, the "Simmons machine" and, then, the "Shelby Dynasty" dominated the state's politics so thoroughly that the people generally felt that their candidates were picked for them long in advance by a small inner circle of politicians. Furnifold M. Simmons organized the Democratic campaign of 1898, which wrested control of the legislature from the fusion forces. While primarily created to fight the Republicans and Populists, the powerful Democratic organization inevitably possessed a personal loyalty to

TABLE 22

Percentage of Total Vote Received by the Two and Three Highest Candidates in the First Democratic Primaries for Governor of North Carolina, 1916–48

| | PERCENTAGE OF TOTAL VOTE RECEIVED BY | |
YEAR	TWO HIGHEST CANDIDATES	THREE HIGHEST CANDIDATES
1916	100.0	——
1920	76.5	100.0
1924	100.0	——
1928	100.0 [a]	——
1932	73.1	100.0
1936	74.2	98.7
1940	54.0	75.8
1944	99.3	100.0
1948	78.3	96.3

[a] Unopposed.

Mr. Simmons. It extended to every county and into many precincts. Mr. Simmons employed it to assure his dominance within the Democratic party. It put him in the United States Senate in 1900 and kept him there until 1930. For thirty years he determined who should be his Senate colleague and, with one exception, supported the winning candidate for governor. In 1908 he lost control of the organization, and his candidate for governor, Locke Craig, was defeated by William W. Kitchen. By 1912, however, he regained mastery. Craig was unopposed for the governorship and Simmons was renominated for the Senate against Kitchen and a third candidate.

In 1928 North Carolina cast its electoral votes for Herbert Hoover, who was supported actively by Simmons. Senator Simmons was not a candidate that year. When he ran in 1930 resentment against his 1928 bolt assured his defeat by Josiah W. Bailey, a former follower.

After 1908, the machine's severest test occurred in 1920. Its candidate, Cameron Morrison, fought a bitter race against an extremely popular maverick, Max Gardner of Shelby in Cleveland County, who lost by the narrowest of margins. By the time Gardner ran again in 1928 he had so strengthened his position that Simmons supported him and he went unopposed for the Democratic nomination. He won over the Republican candidate in the election in which Hoover carried the state.

In 1928, with Gardner's unopposed nomination and Simmons' bolt of the party, transition of party control commenced; it was completed in 1930 with Simmons' defeat. Even with the depression Gardner's influence remained sufficient for his personally selected candidate, J. C. B. Ehringhaus, to win in 1932. In 1936 Gardner's brother-in-law, Clyde R. Hoey, also of Shelby, was elected. The Shelby Dynasty became a byword.

Whereas the Simmons strength had rested primarily on a personal network of followers extending from county to county over the state, the Gardner-Ehringhaus-Hoey power rested chiefly on the elective and appointive offices of the state administration.[11] Particularly important, by common repute, have been the highway and revenue departments in their political activity and significance. This loose confederation, the "state administration," found strength in unity. It split in 1940, but in 1944, with a resident of Gaston County, next-door-neighbor to Shelby, in the race, it held together to assure his election. The 1948 contest found state officials split, although most of them were on the side of Charles Johnson, the state treasurer, identified long before the primary as the administration's favorite. To the astonishment of most observers he went down before a surprise entrant, Kerr Scott, the commissioner of agriculture.

Unlike Senator Simmons, who kept taut his reins on the state's politics, former Governor Gardner made no attempt after leaving office to maintain detailed leadership of the "Shelby Dynasty" or of the administration that supported it. On leaving office in 1933 he moved to Washington, D. C., to practice law. His position of leadership thereafter undoubtedly grew from legendary embellishment, which found root in his tremendous personal prestige, the succession of his friends in office, and the helping hand he could lend to candidates through the raising of campaign funds.

In the long life of the Simmons and Gardner organizations it has never been doubted that the ultimate political power of the state repre-

---

[11] The relatively high degree of centralization of North Carolina's state government may aid in the formation of state-wide political organization, although the administrative structure does not have all the features that contribute to machine discipline in Virginia.

sented large business and financial interests. Simmons was hotly accused of favoritism toward corporations and his voting record in the Senate suffered sustained criticism from the state's more liberal Democratic leadership. His conservative leanings became so pronounced that in 1912 his long-time political friend, former Governor Aycock, and two liberals announced against him for the Senate. Aycock died before the primary and Simmons won easily over the other opponents. He became marked as the leader of conservative Democratic sentiment in the state.[12]

The only threatening electoral challenges to the economic oligarchy were repelled by the Gardner followings in 1936 and 1944. In both races Dr. Ralph McDonald, a professor of government who had seen brief service in the legislature, waged strong campaigns against the administration. He had fought the sales tax, attacked the incumbent administration on many scores, and had been labeled a radical. In 1936 a third man, A. H. Graham, participated in the first primary, but in the run-off threw his support to Hoey. In 1944 the lines were clearly drawn between the allegedly dangerous and unreliable McDonald and Cherry, the only two consequential candidates. The full resources of the administration enabled Cherry to win.

It is no accident that North Carolina has not produced a spokesman of the downtrodden like Folsom or Ferguson or Florida's Catts. In the time of Simmons and since, ambitious, young politicians have seen the way to advancement through the favor of those already in power. It is as old a story as politics itself. Campaign money is there for those whose views harmonize with the predilections of the suppliers of the funds. Encouragement to aspiring contestants is thus on a selective basis. Perhaps some incipient mavericks have thought better of their daring and gradually, or suddenly, conformed to the mold. Sometimes they have persevered as Mayne Albright did in 1948. Young, able, energetic, Albright based his campaign on opposition to machine government. He ran third, with 18 per cent of the vote in the first primary. And when a full-fledged opposition candidacy has developed as it did in the person of McDonald, the weight of the whole financial community has been thrown against him. In North Carolina, as everywhere else, money talks in politics.

It has not been necessary for politicians in North Carolina to be, or to pretend to be, poor men. It has not been necessary for them to cultivate a rusticity to get votes. They have been unblushingly and unapologetically in favor of sound, conservative government. Progressive, forward-looking, yes, but always sound, always the kind of government liked by the big investor, the big employer. While investors and employers have been willing to be reasonable, they have aimed to keep control. As a venerable North Carolinian put it: The big interests have known when

[12] A. L. Brooks, *Walter Clark, Fighting Judge* (Chapel Hill: University of North Carolina Press, 1944), pp. 177–79.

to give way and when to play ball. They have been willing to be fair but not at the expense of their power.[13]

3. Black Belt in the Minority

A center of consistent resistance to North Carolina's political machines shows up in a patch of northeastern counties, south of the Virginia border and west of Albemarle Sound, which resemble the Deep South more than any others in the state. The heart of the North Carolina black belt, this area has been the foundation of opposition in a long series of elections. The maps in Figure 40 show the points of highest strength of the leading opposition candidate in four races beginning with 1932. In the three gubernatorial contests represented, antiorganization strength clearly focused in the blotch of black counties.[14] This focus was especially noticeable in Fountain's race in 1932 because he himself came from the heart of the section, Edgecombe County. The same localization of support shows up, however, in races in which the candidates do not live in the black belt. In 1936 the pattern appeared clearly in the second primary in which liberal conservative lines were drawn drum tight between Hoey and McDonald. The latter, "radical" and opposed to the sales tax, received his greatest proportionate support in the black belt. Similarly, in 1948 Mayne Albright, running on a platform that stressed his opposition to machine government and actively supported by organized labor, found his greatest appeal there. In the 1932 Senate race the poor man's candidate, Bob Reynolds, who made fun at the expense of Gardner-backed Cam Morrison, drew heavy support not only around his home in the western highlands, Buncombe County, but also in the plantation crescent.

Why this area should be the bed of revolt against the ruling clique in the Democratic party can be understood only in terms of its minority position in North Carolina's new prosperity. It is not strange that the black belt should exhibit an antipathy to the rest of the state. We have seen such sectional temperament displayed in Alabama and will see it again in Mississippi. What is odd is that the black-belt counties should champion candidates of insurgence rather than candidates of the status quo.

We saw the occasional emergence in Alabama of an alignment of black-belt counties with "big mules" of the cities in opposition to the

---

[13] Illuminating articles on North Carolina politics by Robert E. Williams appeared in the *News and Observer* (Raleigh, N. C.), February 16, 1947, and July 4, 1948. The inauguration of Governor Kerr Scott in 1949 may have marked the beginning of a new phase in the state's politics. Governor Scott showed signs of a more aggressive liberalism than the state has been accustomed to in the past.

[14] The maps in Figures 40 and 42 on pages 216 and 225 identify these counties as an area of relative organization weakness.

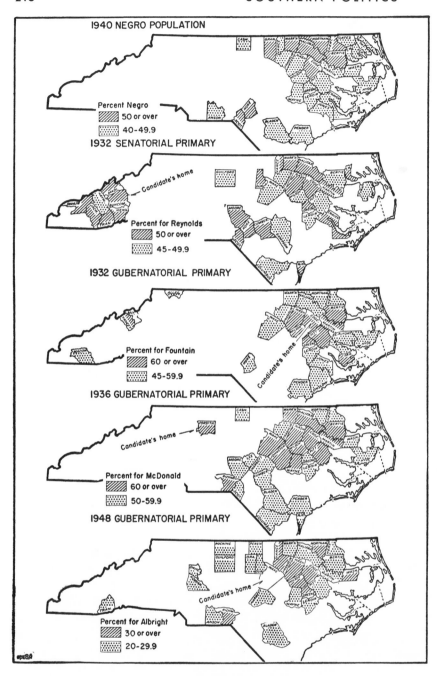

FIGURE 40

North Carolina's Black Belt: A Center of Resistance to the State Machine

Northern and wiregrass sections of the state. The coalition there was essentially a combination of large planters and large businessmen who had a common concern over the tax rate and a desire for conservative government. Their opponents were the poorer farmers, with smaller holdings in sections of the state with few Negroes, and organized labor.

The odd aspect of North Carolina sectionalism is that protest arises in the black belt instead of the Piedmont. Agrarian radicalism, reminiscent of the Populists and centered in the same areas as the strength of the People's party, is found in the Alabama counties with fewest Negroes. In North Carolina opposition to the political machine, to the economic oligarchy of manufacturing and financial interests, comes from the counties with the most Negroes. These counties as a group did not constitute the area of greatest Populist sentiment in the 'nineties. Some of them, however, such as Nash, Pitt, and Warren, had strong Populist leanings in the elections of 1892 and 1894 despite the presence of large numbers of Negroes.[15]

The most meaningful explanation of the contrast between the Alabama and North Carolina black belts is found in their sharp disparities. Table 23 contrasts selected characteristics of each state's counties that had 40 per cent or more Negro population in 1940. Three important differences exist between the two states. First, a greater degree of urbanization in the North Carolina black belt presumably contributes to its liberation from traditionalism. Second, the number of large land operations is much greater in the Alabama counties. The 1945 census of agriculture records the number of multiple-unit operations of 500 acres or more in most black-belt counties of each state. The number of such operations in the median Alabama county was 83 as compared with 33 for North Carolina. Proportionately more North Carolina farm units were in multiple units in the black-belt counties, but there were fewer multiple-unit operations of great size. These conditions no doubt disperse economic influence in the area, lessen the political significance of large landholders, and narrow the distance between the top and bottom rungs of the economic and social ladder. A third difference lies in the character of tenancy. The ratio of tenancy in Alabama tended to be higher but the proportion of tenants white much lower. In North Carolina's black counties there is a comparatively large number of white tenants, a factor perhaps contributory to the difference in political flavor of the two areas.

The political insurgency of the North Carolina black belt helps free the state political leadership of racial attitudes of areas of high Negro population. Though the North Carolina black belt exhibits tendencies

[15] S. A. Delap, "The Populist Party in North Carolina," *Historical Papers* (Durham: The Trinity College Historical Society, XIV, 1922), p. 57; William Alexander Mabry, "Negro Suffrage and Fusion Rule in North Carolina," *North Carolina Historical Review*, XII (April 1935), p. 84.

toward insurgency in economic matters [16] there is no suggestion of a radically atypical attitude on race relations. In Alabama, black-belt whites are often among the political big shots who set the style of state policy and politics. The lesser role of plantation princes in North Carolina's executive and legislative affairs contributes not only to a de-emphasis of harsh, racial attitudes but also to less effective assertion of the extremely conservative viewpoints of all kinds that are usually associated with a plantation economy.

TABLE 23

Comparison of North Carolina and Alabama Black Belts

	ALABAMA	NORTH CAROLINA
Number of counties 40% or more Negro, 1940	24	31
The following data pertain to these counties:		
Percentage of counties 20% or more urban, 1940	20.8	35.4
Median County in		
Percentage of farm units in multiple-unit operations, 1945	12.2 [a]	23.8 [b]
Number of multiple units of 500 acres or more, 1945	83 [a]	33 [b]
Percentage of farmers who were tenants, 1940	71.9	60.8
Percentage of tenants who were white, 1940	31.6	52.6

[a] Based on 21 counties.
[b] Based on 28 counties.

4. Sectionalism and the Republicans

"The political questions in North Carolina have always been questions of east and west, or the upcountry against the lowlands, of crystalline schists and granites against unconsolidated clays, sands, and gravels." These remarks of a university professor [17] are oft quoted in explanation of North Carolina's political disputes. They have much foundation in fact as can be inferred from the behavior of the black belt.

[16] The lack of enthusiasm of these counties for Ehringhaus in 1932 has been attributed to the severe privations suffered by the farmers during the depression, responsibility for which they fixed on the Gardner administration which supported Ehringhaus.

[17] Collier Cobb of the University of North Carolina, quoted in S. H. Hobbs, *North Carolina Economic and Social* (Chapel Hill: University of North Carolina Press, 1930), p. 69.

The Democratic organizations that ruled the state for almost fifty years possessed a decidedly sectional character. With regularity far from coincidental the area of their greatest strength has been in the west, and most frequently in the far-western counties of the Blue Ridge. And the sectionalism within the Democratic party has gone hand in hand with a sectional division of strength between Republicans and Democrats.

North Carolina has more-tender sectional sensibilities than any other state in the South, including even tripartite Tennessee. Invariably one Senator must come from the east and one from the west. The rule has been, too, that the governorship rotates between the east and the west.[18] The line between east and west is not precisely drawn and mid-state politicians sometimes find their ambigious position advantageous and sometimes not.[19]

Sectional consciousness appears in many phases of state life, political and nonpolitical, and extends back to the early days of North Carolina. Many a crucial vote in North Carolina's history has divided along the fall line, which separates the Piedmont from the coastal plain, a diagonal running northeastward from Anson County to Northampton. In 1835 the eastern planters wrangled with the western small farmers over the apportionment of legislative seats, a question of which should rule the state. In 1861 the heaviest opposition to the calling of a secession convention came from the western section of smaller land- and slave-holdings. In alliance with the west were the counties in the Northeast around Albermarle Sound, also an area not dependent on the plantation system, and this alliance repeats itself almost ninety years later in Democratic primaries.[20] In 1900 the west showed far less enthusiasm than the east for Negro disfranchisement. Even the prohibition vote in 1908 reflected the east-west division in the superior inclination of the mountain counties to vote dry.

[18] Some observers hold that this practice, which halves contests for which candidates are eligible, imposes an undesirable limitation on the use of the state's leadership. There is no assurance that talent for public office will be equally distributed between the east and the west.

[19] The continuous awareness of this sectionalism was demonstrated in 1948. Kerr Scott of Alamance county, in mid-state, ran in the year reserved for eastern candidates. It was contended that Alamance had always been considered a western county and that Scott was violating the rotation tradition. At a rally for candidate Johnson, principal Scott opponent, leaflets were distributed that proclaimed: "Preserve Party Harmony—Give the East its Governor . . . By the terms of the [rotation] agreement, the County of Alamance has always been considered in the West. Now is the time for the Governorship to come from the East! Uphold the argument! Vote solidly to nominate a man from the East—Charles M. Johnson of Pender County . . . Failure to elect an EASTERNER will mean the rotation agreement is broken."—*News and Observer* (Raleigh), March 31, 1948. When Scott was elected one of his opponents, Mayne Albright, commented that the victory meant the end of the "east-west selection system."—Ibid., June 30, 1948.

[20] See maps in Figure 42, p. 225.

The bulk of population, money, and productive activity now rests west of the fall line and gives that section the pre-eminence long ago held by the agricultural counties of the coastal plain and tidewater. Sectionalism lives on, however, with perhaps the most sensitive issue being that of taxation. The wealthy Piedmont laments its large share of taxes, which are spent over the state without regard to source. The Mayor of Greensboro, a prosperous west Carolina city, complained in 1948 that the Piedmont paid the state's bills but the eastern section received most of the benefits.[21]

By far the most significant residue of a long history of sectional antagonism is the Republican party. In the familiar pattern of all southern states, those North Carolina counties that had had fewest slaves emerged from The War with the strongest Republican leanings. North Carolina had many such counties, most of which were located in the Blue Ridge —the great spine of Republicanism which runs down the back of the South.

The Republican party in North Carolina today is a sectional party, as is apparent from the maps in Figure 41. Most votes for Republican presidential and gubernatorial candidates are cast west of the fall line in counties that are more rural than urban. In 1944, 81 per cent of the state's Republican presidential vote came from the 52 counties west of the fall line. There are, however, spots of Republican strength in eastern North Carolina, the most conspicuous being Sampson County. Eastern Republicanism is found in coastal counties with relatively small numbers of Negroes and in counties like Sampson where Populist forces were so bitter toward the Democratic party that they refused to support it when their own party expired, early in the century. An eastern county, Tyrrell, has sent three Republican representatives to the state legislature in the past fifty years. Others have shown sympathy to the Republicans, but the sectional outlook of the party is reflected by the fact that in 1948 an eastern Republican campaign headquarters was set up for the first time. The west, however, elects virtually all the Republican legislators and local officials. There Democrats must gerrymander to keep Republican victories to a minimum. There, too, the hottest congressional races take place.

Lily-whiteism has had sectional overtones in that western Republicanism does not have to contend with an eastern Negro wing. Negroes, who are concentrated below the fall line, once formed an important element in the party, but today Republican leadership offers little or no

[21] The Raleigh News and Observer thought the Mayor's statement undoubtedly correct and that the situation was as it should be. So long as North Carolina is a "state," the editor wrote, those best able would and should aid those most in need.—May 10, 1948.

encouragement to them.[22] In some areas, the Democrats facilitate participation in their primaries by Negroes, who might otherwise strengthen the Republicans. On the other hand, Negro concentration in the east has traditionally induced white attachment to the Democracy and strengthened its control in that area. No such incitement to white soli-

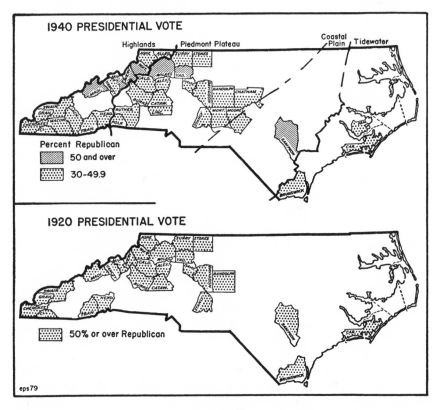

FIGURE 41

Sectional Character of North Carolina Republicanism: Republican Presidential Vote, 1920, 1940

darity prevails in the west. The geographical distribution of the races thus aids in molding the state's politics.

The Republican party in North Carolina is a major electoral force of relatively constant strength, as Table 24 testifies. The median of its

[22] When a Negro physician was appointed in 1947 as "director of finance, Republican national committee, Negro division for North Carolina," the appointment was announced by the national committee rather than by the state Republican organization. The Republican candidate for the Senate in 1948 campaigned on his opposition to the Democratic civil rights plank; he likened it to the "force bill" of 1868.

proportion of the total gubernatorial and presidential vote in eight recent elections is approximately one-third. Moreover, the total turnout at the general election is always materially higher than at the Democratic primary, an indication of the importance that voters attach to it. The Republican party is strong enough to give North Carolina many earmarks of a two-party state yet not strong enough to threaten Democratic supremacy.[23]

Unable to make a serious bid for the governorship, the Republican leadership focuses its interest on local and district offices, where it has a chance for victory, and attends to the selection of delegates to the national convention. Campaigns are made for national and gubernatorial candidates, with no hope for victory but with an eye to the support that these campaigns give to candidates for local offices.[24] Republican leaders

TABLE 24

North Carolina Republicanism, 1920–48

YEAR	TOTAL VOTE IN FIRST DEMOCRATIC PRIMARY FOR GOVERNOR	TOTAL VOTE IN GENERAL ELECTION FOR GOVERNOR	REPUBLICAN PERCENTAGE OF TOTAL VOTE	
			GOVERNOR	PRESIDENT
1920	128,233	538,326	42.8	43.3
1924	234,771	480,068	38.7	39.6
1928	Unopposed	651,424	44.4	54.9
1932	379,657	710,218	29.9	29.3
1936	516,864	812,982	33.1	26.6
1940	469,396	804,146	24.3	26.0
1944	321,757	759,993	30.4	33.3
1948	423,125	780,525	26.4	32.7

complain of the difficulty of getting candidates to run in localities where the party is in the minority. One of the highest party officials concludes that there is little chance of genuine two-party competition state-wide because of the satisfaction with which Republicans regard Democratic performance. The Democratic party, he concluded, through its able leaders had kept in touch with the people and with their needs, had expanded state services, and in general given satisfactory government. He even went on to say that in the administration of the state government he had detected no discrimination against Republicans. The end result is that Republicans have not carried the state for any offices since 1900 except President in 1928. In that year, in which two congressional seats were

[23] In Maine the Democratic gubernatorial candidate polled in 1938, 47.1 per cent of the two-party vote; in 1940, 36.2; in 1942, 33.2; in 1944, 29.8. In Vermont the same figures were: 1938, 33.3; 1940, 36.0; 1942, 22.1; 1944, 34.2.

[24] In 1946, 13 of North Carolina's 100 counties elected a Republican to the state House of Representatives. Twenty-three Republicans offered for the 50 state senate seats and 62 for the 120 house seats.—*News and Observer* (Raleigh), Sept. 23, 1946.

also won, Hoover's victory came from Democratic and not Republican efforts.

5. Republicanism and the Character of the Democratic Party

Although the Republicans do not endanger Democratic control of the state, they profoundly influence the nature of the Democratic party. The dominant faction of the Democratic party, thanks to the Republicans, possesses a relatively high degree of discipline, and the party as a whole has a consciousness of being and of responsibility. In consequence, North Carolina has an organization that can be called a Democratic party, a condition that does not exist in such states as Florida, South Carolina, or Arkansas. And, a corollary of Republican infusion of discipline into the Democratic group is that a bi-factional battle, rather than a multifactional melee, is waged within the party for its control.

The Republican contribution to Democratic discipline is plain. In those counties in which Democrats are in a minority, or must fight desperately to win local offices, leaders look to the state for aid and succor. Faced by a common threat they appreciate the necessity for concerted action under strong state leadership, and the result is a relatively cohesive state organization. It is in the counties with greatest Republican strength that the Simmons machine and its successor, the Shelby organization, found their most intense support.

Simmons was strong in some sure Democratic counties in the southeast around his home, but the counties most intense in their loyalty to him and to his organization were in the west. Candidates of the Shelby Dynasty had essentially the same pattern of support, although by their time the geographical base of the organization had taken a sharper sectional form. The series of maps in Figure 42, showing the vote in one of Simmons' races and in several races by Shelby candidates makes plain the intensity of organization support in the western counties of high Republican strength.

The organization, discipline, and state-wide viewpoint that both organization and antiorganization Democratic factions are compelled to accept largely override influences of localism in voting. In states with fluid factional systems, as we have observed, candidates exert a powerful pull on their friends and neighbors. The same influence makes itself felt in North Carolina but not nearly to the same degree. In the maps in Figures 40 and 42, the homes of candidates have been shown and inspection indicates that their local followings distort the normal voting pattern only slightly. Even in those occasional primaries in which the organization is split, the friends-and-neighbors influence is of little import. In such races a candidate may or may not be strong in his home county. In any case he will make a showing in widely scattered counties, a pattern of voting indicative of factional struggles for control of the organization rather than of the attempts of purely local potentates to expand a group of local admirers into a state-wide following.

Cohesion of the organization faction of the Democratic party and the relative unimportance of localism must be credited to the existence of the Republican party. Comparison of the various maps showing the distribution of organization strength in Democratic primaries and of Republican strength in the general elections roughly shows the relation between the two. By compelling the Democratic party to fight, the Republicans give it a backbone composed of those counties in which it has to fight. The organization is not, of course, completely without support in counties with few or no Republicans. Nor does the popular strength of organization candidates increase from county to county precisely with Republicanism. Nevertheless, the organization is likely to carry in the Democratic primary most if not all counties with Republican majorities, while it can count on no such uniform support in the sure Democratic counties.[25]

The alignment of western counties with the state organization resembles the alliance that prevailed between Tennessee's eastern Republican counties and the Crump machine when it controlled the state government. The same incentives move Democratic leaders in North Carolina's highly competitive counties to establish close ties with the state administration. Frequently denied local patronage, they seek other ways to support and reward the faithful and the state government is the logical source. In competition with local Republicans they desire a sympathetic central authority to whom recourse can be had. They rely on the big guns of the party to come out from Raleigh to help in their campaigns, and the state committee sends some money to the county committees for general election campaigns. By no means the least significant advantage of fidelity to the state organization is that the local Democratic leaders obtain control of the election machinery, even in Republican counties.[26]

Western Democrats also are able to share in the fruits of victory in some races because of the sympathetic collaboration of their eastern allies in drawing district lines. It has been possible to maintain a solidly Democratic House delegation only by the artifices of political geography. In the 1944 presidential election 14 counties gave the Republican candidate a majority and in 27 others he polled over 35 per cent of the vote.

---

[25] In 1936 Hoey, the organization candidate, carried in the second primary all save one of those counties that gave the Republican gubernatorial candidate more than 45 per cent of its vote in the following general election. Of the 52 counties less than 30 per cent Republican, he had a primary majority in only 26. Of the 48 counties more than 30 per cent Republican, he polled more than 50 per cent of the Democratic primary vote in 42.

[26] See the discussion of this point below, pp. 450–52.

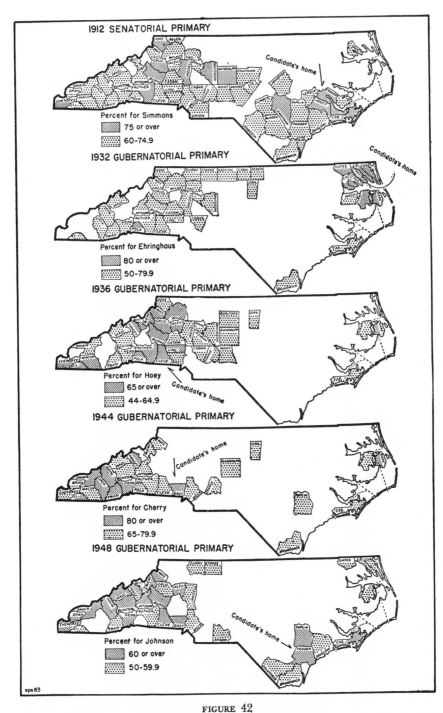

FIGURE 42

Points of Highest Strength of "Organization" Candidates in North Carolina
Democratic Primaries

Despite the concentration of these counties in the west, the Republicans won not a single Representative. "Bacon strip" congressional districts cut across the highlands and Piedmont to smother the Republicans by linking Republican counties in the west with even heavier Democratic counties in the east and south.[27] The odd shapes of the districts that result may be seen in the map in Figure 43.[28]

Democrats in the uncertain counties, thus, are dependent in many ways on the party's state leadership. Out of their adversities is created a branch of the party wedded to the party's state leadership regardless of the geographical origins of that leadership. In turn, the leadership depends on the faithful support of those who understand the wisdom of

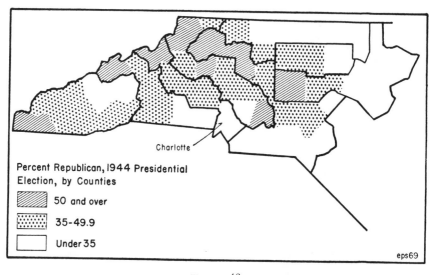

Percent Republican, 1944 Presidential Election, by Counties

50 and over

35-49.9

Under 35

eps69

FIGURE 43

Congressional District Gerrymandering in North Carolina

unity. And those who must fight the Republicans to win have little sympathy with the view that it is quite all right to harbor within the Democratic party a fifth column which at propitious times lines up with the

[27] Western Democrats are grateful also for such fortuities of North Carolina politics as the election of circuit judges by the state at large. Democratic nominees, selected in primaries held by districts, some of which unavoidably contain large numbers of Republicans, are elected by the party's majority in the state as a whole.

[28] The map gives no notion of the size of the vote in the counties included in each district. The extreme situation is illustrated by the tenth district, which stretches from the western border to include Mecklenburg County which contains Charlotte, the largest city of the state. The city's Democratic majority overcomes the Republican lead in the west. In 1946 the Democratic candidate won with a majority of 3,518 votes in a total vote cast of 45,710. In two counties the Republican candidate led by 2,604 votes and in the other four, the Democrat led by a total of 6,122, of which 3,649 came from Mecklenburg. The net Democratic majority was thus 3,518, or about the same as the Democratic lead in Mecklenburg.

GOP. Organization devotion to party regularity demonstrated itself dramatically in the shift of attitude of many western counties toward Senator Furnifold M. Simmons in 1930 after his heresy in supporting Hoover in 1928. The story is told in the two maps in Figure 44. In 1924 Simmons' candidate for governor, Angus McLean, handily defeated Josiah W. Bailey whose most intense support came from the traditionally, anti-

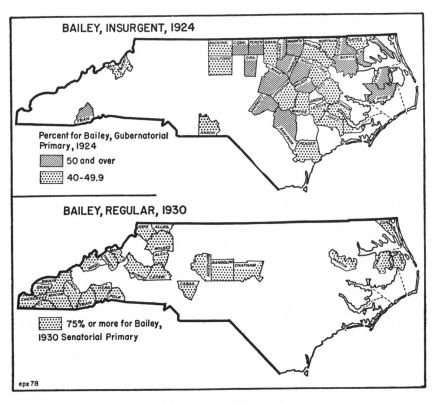

FIGURE 44

Shift in Location of Simmons' Machine Support between Democratic Gubernatorial Primary of 1924 and Senatorial Primary of 1930

organization eastern counties. The close western counties, as is the custom, contributed heavy majorities to the machine candidate. In 1930 Bailey ran for the Senate against Simmons, thirty years a Senator and chief of the state Democratic organization. The close counties, the loyal organization counties, could not afford to tolerate party treason. They joined to dethrone the old boss and to elect Bailey, to whom they had shown little sympathy six years before.

By whatever test, the conclusion emerges that North Carolina's Republicans contribute mightily to the unity of the dominant faction within the Democratic party. And the creation of a single cohesive faction almost inevitably unites the opposition elements into a minority faction, with the result that the battle within the Democratic party resembles a two-party conflict. Party discipline is not simply a matter of neat maps of academic interest only: its consequences for the government of the commonwealth are far-reaching. Fundamentally those consequences come down to the fact that a disciplined faction provides the power to govern. Governments derive their power not from constitutions and charters alone but from the support of organized citizenry. North Carolina's Democratic party, by virtue of its discipline, can suppress the mountebank and clown, can deal with him who would incite the citizenry by inflammatory racial appeals, and can develop some sense of direction and responsibility.

Awareness among North Carolina Democrats of their role and their responsibility should be emphasized. High political leaders and sophisticated political observers constantly refer in private discussions to the quality of government the Democratic party has brought to the state. It has been over fifty years since the Republicans won a state election, but memories of their last regime burn brightly in the minds of the older leaders who warn the younger generation in horrendous terms of what might be expected of the Republicans. A definite consciousness of party provides the base for a sense of group responsibility transcending any one governor or individual. The event of the moment must be regarded from the standpoint of its bearing on the fortunes of the party as a whole in the long pull.[29] Such observations, as good North Carolinians would be the first to say, exaggerate the realities. Nevertheless, partly from the nature of its political organization North Carolina does not suffer the erraticism, the instability, and the incapacity to act that characterize most southern states with an unorganized politics.

[29] In testifying before a legislative committee in 1947 on a proposed state "good health" program, Josephus Daniels based his plea for the program not on its merits, as most advocates had done, but on party loyalty. He cited the platform pledge of such a program and recalled the great advances of the state under Democratic administrations. He cited earlier party platforms and the record of party fulfillment of its responsibilities. Incidentally, a factor of no mean importance in explanation of the general tenor of North Carolina politics was Josephus Daniels. A newspaper editor who can call his soul his own, who is usually right, and who has the courage to express his views can exert a powerful and lasting influence.

Chapter Eleven | MISSISSIPPI:
THE DELTA AND THE HILLS

Mississippi adds another variant to the politics of
the South. Northerners, provincials that they are, regard the South as
one large Mississippi. Southerners, with their eye for distinction, place
Mississippi in a class by itself. North Carolinians, with their faith that
the future holds hope, consider Mississippi to be the last vestige of a
dead and despairing civilization. Virginia, with its comparatively digni-
fied politics, would, if it deigned to notice, rank Mississippi as a backward
culture, with a ruling class both unskilled and neglectful of its duties.
And every other southern state finds some reason to fall back on the soul-
satisfying exclamation, "Thank God for Mississippi!" Yet Mississippi only
manifests in accentuated form the darker political strains that run
throughout the South.

On the surface at least, the beginning and the end of Mississippi
politics is the Negro. He has no hand in the voting, no part in factional
maneuvers, no seats in the legislature; nevertheless, he fixes the tone—
so far as the outside world is concerned—of Mississippi politics. The
state has a higher proportion of Negro population than any other: 49.2
per cent in 1940. Nor is the influence of color mitigated by any considerable area with few Negroes. Sixty of the state's 82 counties were in 1940
more than 30 per cent Negro; 35, more than 50 per cent; 17, more than 70
per cent.

The Negro determines the policy of Mississippi in the nation: resistance to external intervention. Yet within the state, issues other than the Negro—everyone is agreed on the Negro—give its politics a distinctive character. Within its predominantly agricultural economy, tremendous distances separate the planter and the tenant to form the base for a lively political conflict. Mississippi politics in the end reduces itself to a politics of frustration. As in South Carolina, when it faces the ultimate consequences of its logic, the politics of the have-nots is quenched by contemplation of its bearing on race. Nor is the race problem moderated by a considerable urban population that need not be preoccupied with that question to the same extent as a rural people. Mississippi is the most rural of southern states. The population of only 12 towns exceeded 10,000 in 1940; the largest of these, Jackson, the capital, had a population of only 62,000. The small urban centers—supply-points for the surrounding agricultural regions—do not bulk large enough to temper the robust tone of a rural politics.

Mississippi politics is a politics of frustration not only because of the race question; its politics distills down to oratory also because the state is miserably poor. The gap between rich and poor is wide, but as a whole the state is so poor that a welfare politics can only become a politics of fulmination and little more. Louisiana's neo-Populism could tap the state's resources and take action. Mississippi's neo-Populism under the leadership of Vardaman, Russell, Bilbo sooner or later ran against the limitations imposed by poverty.[1]

1. Rednecks and Delta Planters

Mississippi politics may be regarded, if one keeps alert to the risks of oversimplification, as a battle between the delta planters and the rednecks. It is a battle of diminishing intensity, but the cleavage between the planters of the delta and the rednecks of the hills has persisted for half a century and even yet appears from time to time, as it did in the guberna-

[1] Mississippi's poverty may not be permanent. Recent discoveries of oil may be a forerunner of further development. Local boosters have faith in their "balance agriculture with industry" program, and it may hold promise as it goes beyond the period of subsidization of industry and of invitation to exploit cheap labor. Mechanization of cotton production will eventually increase individual output. Poverty, however, is in no small measure associated with race. An economy prevented by racial taboos from developing the potential skills of its mass of black labor is doomed to relatively low productivity. All this is no news to Mississippi leaders. Thus, Ransom Aldrich, president of the State Farm Bureau, asserts: "Just so long as we keep the negroes an economic liability, just so long do we retard Mississippi's progress. We talk about 'Damnyankees.' We'd better do something to show the 'Damnyankees.' Too long have we misused education funds in Mississippi. This thing has got to be solved by ourselves or somebody is going to come in and solve it for us—and it won't be solved the way we want it solved."—*Commercial Appeal* (Memphis), October 29, 1948.

torial primary of 1947. Planters and rednecks do not face each other armed to the teeth along the line that divides the delta from the hills. The attitudes of the delta are shared by many in the hills and the spirit of the redneck has invaded the delta. "Delta planter" and "redneck" come to be symbols something like "capitalist" and "worker" in an industrial society. Nevertheless, insofar as any geographical division remains within the politics of the state it falls along the line that separates the delta from the hills.

Along the River, from Memphis to the Yazoo at Vicksburg, stretches a flat shelf of fertile alluvial soil about two counties wide. This plain is the domain of the delta planters, masters of huge plantations cultivated chiefly by Negro sharecroppers. Behind the towering levees that restrain the River, the delta produces a million bales of cotton a year—in some years a tenth of the American crop—and ranks as one of the great cotton-producing regions of the world. Their common battle against the River is in itself enough to unite the planters; but like men of property every-where they are bound together in the promotion and protection of their interests.

The "redneck," "peckerwood," or "peckerhead" inhabits another world. His "hills"—the highest altitude is around 700 feet—run from the northern end of the state and occupy roughly its eastern half, broaden-ing out almost to the River in the south and petering out in the pine forests of the coastal region. A rich prairie, an extension of Alabama's black belt, breaks into the hills at about the center of the state's eastern border and provides the base for a small, rich agricultural region, whose sympathies run generally with the delta. The "hills" are supposed to be the habitat of the redneck, the white tenant farmer, the lesser white farm-owner. Here the soil is not so fertile; the hardest labor produces only the most miserable livelihood. (Mississippi ranks lowest in the South in per-capita income.) Excluded from the rich lands by the delta planter and the Negro, the white must eke out a livelihood on the farms of the hills. In 1945 white full-owners in Mississippi farmed land worth an average of $29.00 an acre; white croppers cultivated soil that averaged out at $37.26 per acre. All white tenants (including croppers) farmed land valued at $31.00 per acre. Negro croppers worked land worth $58.07 an acre.

Mississippians (like South Carolinians) observe that old-time sec-tional animosities have softened, if indeed they ever existed as sharply as legend has it. Peckerwoods, planters say, have moved down into the delta, especially into the towns, and diluted its purity. In the hills the growth of towns, the development of transport and communication, the extension of education have reduced rural isolation. At one time, however, the preachers in the hills could inveigh against all the sin that was supposed to go on in the big houses of the delta, and the politicians could rally the rednecks against the rich planters who were supposed to regard "niggers" more highly than white men. And the delta planter and the redneck stride on, not as sharply defined geographic groups, but as states of mind formed long ago.

The delta and redneck states of mind owe much for their existence to James K. Vardaman, former governor and Senator. Mississippi Populism never amounted to much, but the neo-Populist governor, Vardaman, gave the politics of the state a spirit and a form that Theodore Bilbo carried on through the decades. Elected governor in 1902 with some support from the delta, Vardaman's center of strength soon shifted to the hills where the Populists earlier had been strongest.[2] A picturesque demagogue, Vardaman became a popular idol. He bundled up all the Populist doctrines—anti-corporationism, the cause of the common man—with the advocacy of white supremacy. He urged more adequate educational opportunity for rural whites—at the expense of the delta. As for the Negro, "why squander money on his education when the only effect is to spoil a good field hand and make an insolent cook."[3] Vardaman, as governor, took progressive steps in education and in the management of state institutions and, like Jeff Davis in Arkansas, tilted with the corporations. He obtained legislation to limit to $2,000,000 the amount of property that a corporation might hold. "Millionaires produce paupers —the concentration of riches in the hands of the few breeds poverty and squalor among the many," the governor argued.

Vardaman gave a beautiful demonstration of the uses to which the race issue can be put—by persons without scruple. His contribution to statesmanship was advocacy of repeal of the Fifteenth Amendment, an utterly hopeless proposal and for that reason an ideal campaign issue. It would last forever. The rednecks—and some delta planters—did not know that they were being humbugged and they loved it. He managed to push the delta planters into a position of defense of the Negro whom he called a "veneered savage."[4] "The negro problem," Vardaman's conservative opponent, Critz, said, "is being agitated for sinister motives of gain by those who have not the interest of their state at heart."[5] After his defeat, Critz said that the "cry of 'white supremacy' carried the day for the victor in the extreme excitement that prevailed at the election, but there was no such issue between me and my opponent and could not have been; there was no such issue between democrats in Mississippi and could not have been."[6]

It is a puzzling characteristic of southern politics that candidates can

[2] Heber Ladner, "James Kimble Vardaman, Governor of Mississippi, 1904–1908," *Journal of Mississippi History*, 2 (1940), pp. 175–205; W. D. McCain, "The Populist Party in Mississippi" (Master's thesis, University of Mississippi, 1931).
[3] Ladner, *Vardaman*, p. 177.
[4] Ibid., p. 199.
[5] Ibid., p. 178.
[6] Ibid., p. 183.

at times get themselves elected by their skill in advocacy of something on which everyone is agreed. Honorable and decent men—who agree with the demagogues on the race issue—are branded by the Negro-baiters as less-devout communicants in the common faith.[7] Vardaman, of course, had an appeal broader than the race issue; his neo-Populism alone might have carried the day.[8]

The line dividing the delta and the hills is more than economic. The mores, morals, and ways of life of the two groups differ—perhaps not so much as their preachers would have them believe but enough to have political significance. State-wide prohibition, for example, receives least support in the delta. The preachers of the hills fight demon rum and their followers vote for prohibition, while the sinful delta votes for liquor. The planters find allies on this question in Biloxi and Gulfport and in all the wicked gulf coast counties as well as in the larger cities, as may be seen from Figure 45.

Prohibition, like Vardaman's repeal of the Fifteenth Amendment, represents an unattainable objective and has a special appeal to the hill people, while the delta planters, less disposed to pursue will-of-the-wisps, take a more realistic view. The state's lawmakers, with prohibition a reality, reconciled themselves to the situation by adopting a black-market tax, i.e., a tax on illegal sales. The state maintains agents in adjoining states who spot shipments of whiskey into Mississippi. They report to Jackson on consignments to the principal liquor distributors and the state tax authorities "bluff" these "tough thugs" into paying the tax.

The governor, at a special legislative session early in 1947, recommended repeal of the black-market tax, but a bloc of legislators, chiefly from the delta, was able to check repeal. The delta, perhaps because it was both wet and would probably have to make up a substantial part of the loss of revenue, was willing to worry along with the black-market tax.[9]

[7] The explanation of the significance of the issue about which there is no disagreement may be simple. Systems with rigid doctrines probably insist on most unquestioning acceptance and have the least toleration of deviation, e.g., white supremacy, and the weak believer cannot be tolerated. The competition may become one in intensity of dedication to common doctrine.

[8] The frequency and intensity with which the race issue is raised varies roughly from state to state with the proportions of Negro population. Mississippi undoubtedly has harbored the most unrestrained and most continuous advocates of white supremacy. A case can be made for the hypothesis that a candidate generally has to have more than an attachment to white supremacy to win.

[9] Vicksburg in 1947 levied a municipal black-market tax on top of the state tax. Liquor retailers were assessed $100 a month, wholesalers $150, and punchboard operators $100 a month.—*Commercial Appeal* (Memphis), July 9, 1947. Natchez passed a similar ordinance in 1948.—*Times-Picayune* (New Orleans), April 7, 1948. Another town, up the delta, dealt with the problem informally through a group of prominent citizens who told one of the principal bootleggers that if he would open a package store he would have no trouble with the local law enforcement officers. The bootlegger agreed and pays $100 a month to a local hospital as an informal license fee. Later a second store was opened under a similar arrangement. Leading citizens report that they have eliminated bootlegging and have cut out corruption.

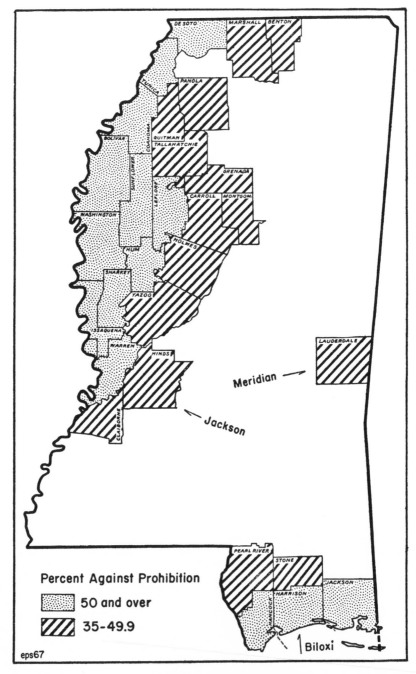

The Hills and the Delta: Vote on State-Wide Prohibition in 1934 Special Election

The prohibitionists and preachers, failing in their effort to repeal the tax, organized Christian citizens leagues to press for prohibition enforcement under the leadership of a minister aided by a subvention from the Mississippi Baptist Convention. Most of the local leagues were outside the delta.

The liquor issue is not, of course, solely a matter of the delta versus the hills. All kinds of subsidiary groups become involved. An observant capital correspondent concludes that the sheriffs are "probably the most powerful lobby" before the legislature. They seek the preservation of local self-government. They have managed to keep the state patrol out of prohibition enforcement; thereby arrangements between sheriff and bootleggers remain purely local, with no means by which the state police can demand a cut, as they have in some other states. The temperance lobby has powerful but unacknowledged allies in the bootleggers whose enterprises depend on the continuation of prohibition.[10]

Apart from prohibition, the chief bone of contention between the delta and the hills in the legislature is that of taxation and public expenditure. Delta counties ordinarily draft able citizens to represent them in the legislature, a practice said to have been established in an earlier day when the state played a more important role in public improvements of interest to the delta. Delta spokesmen, by force of ability rather than of numbers, try to protect and promote their position, but, says one of them, the hills "pour it at us" on taxation. While the wealthy delta in the normal course of events would pay heavily in taxes, its share is increased by a homestead exemption of $5,000, advantageous to the hill country of many small farms. Even yet the delta encounters resistance from the hills to its proposals on the ground that the planters promote the cause of the blacks.[11] And for self-interest, if for no other, the planters must speak for their Negroes in such programs as health and education.

[10] The allocation of authority for prohibition enforcement makes the sheriff's post extremely important and the campaign for this office one of the hardest fought in county politics. In some counties the legitimate fees of the office mount up, and outside the genuinely dry counties supplementary revenues are available. Prohibition, Jesse M. Byrd, a candidate for governor in 1947, averred had "created conditions in some communities where the sheriff's office is more lucrative than that of the supreme court justices of the United States."—*Delta Democrat-Times* (Greenville), July 23, 1947. Common gossip makes Mr. Byrd's estimate overly modest. In some counties local bootleggers back a candidate for sheriff. If there are competing factions of bootleggers, each may back a different candidate. The bootlegger candidate does not always win. Thus, a local Negro leader in a delta county expressed high approval of a candidate who in an earlier term had cleaned out the bootleggers, closed up the night joints, and broken up the practice of Negro women staying with white men. "He put thirteen Negro women in jail."

[11] The most significant source of legislative proposals of interest to the delta is the Delta Council, something of a combination of a farm bureau and a chamber of commerce and representative of the large planter and business interests of the delta. The Council looks out for its own immediate interests, such as flood control, and becomes concerned, like the rednecks, about will-of-the-wisps, such as the Taft-Hartley Act, but

The animosity of the hills toward the delta may have cooled over the years, as Mississippi politicians aver, yet when divisive alternatives are presented the voters split as of yore. Perhaps not so large a proportion of each group is on opposite sides of the political fence as earlier and campaign oratory is less bitter. In the 1947 gubernatorial primary the delta-hill division was still perceptible. The candidate certain to win was Fielding Wright, who was running for a full term after moving up from the lieutenant-governorship on the death of Governor Thomas L. Bailey. By accident Wright had become the first delta governor in decades. His chief opponent was Paul B. Johnson, Jr., who was making the race to get acquainted around the state and to lay the foundations for a political future.

Early in the campaign Johnson visited Bilbo leaders over the state and sold them on the idea that Bilbo would support him because Bilbo and his father, the late Governor Johnson, had supported each other. Many local leaders got out on a limb in support of Johnson before Fielding Wright worked a squeeze play on the ailing Bilbo whose Senate seat was in question. Wright, who would be governor until early in 1948 whatever the outcome of the primary, announced that he would reappoint Bilbo if the Senate declined to seat him on the race question. It ill-behooved the Bilbo people to oppose Wright, and A. B. Friend, Bilbo's manager, set to work to undo the commitments that Johnson had obtained. In the northeastern part of the state many local Bilbo people were too far out in support of Johnson to back down and work for a candidate of their old enemy, the delta.[12] Wright thus had the support of politicians whom he and his friends had been fighting all their lives.

Wright, from Rolling Fork in the delta, so busily disassociated himself from the delta that some of his delta friends feared that he might actually do something for the people of the hills. Johnson, in turn, made a campaign pleasing to the hills. He promised to veto any bill legalizing liquor, and claimed that Wright had voted for liquor seven times while

---

it also has broader concerns. For example, in 1946 its educational policy committee recommended a Negro school program, which included state funds to encourage the building of "negro school buildings where needed throughout the state," appropriation for a "negro teachers college to be located in the Delta area to train teachers for negro schools of the Delta," a program of vocational education for returned veterans, and a salary schedule to "permit teachers to be paid according to training and successful experience." It required some trading with the hills to get the teachers college, and the legislature appropriated $3,000,000 for "negro or white" schools, whereupon the Delta Council recommended to the administrative authorities that at least one-half of the $3,000,000 be spent on Negro schools. See Delta Council, *Annual Report*, 1945–1946, p. 9, and ibid., 1946–1947, p. 10.

[12] The chairman of the Carroll County Democratic executive committee, a long-time supporter of Bilbo, published an indignant reply to Mr. Friend's request for support of Wright. Another Bilbo leader of the same county published a reply in which he recalled that the late Governor Johnson had supported Bilbo. "This I have never known Fielding Wright to do."—*Clarion-Ledger* (Jackson), June 20, 1947.

in the legislature. He charged that a major oil corporation had "put a bale of money" into Wright's campaign. He advocated a generally progressive program, all in a magnificent oratory—and the hill man is a great connoisseur of political declamation.[18]

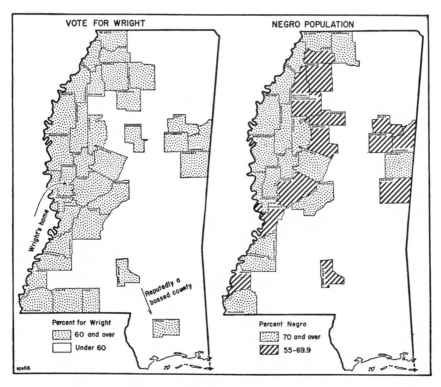

FIGURE 46

Plantation Solidarity: Mississippi Counties Casting 60 Per Cent or More of their Vote for Wright for Governor, Democratic Primary, 1947; Counties with 55 Per Cent or More Negro Population, 1940

When the votes were in Wright had won, as everyone had known he would, but his popular strength was greatest in the delta and in the other plantation counties. The people along the River below Vicksburg and in the block of rich farming counties on the eastern border saw in Wright, the delta candidate, a sound man, as did his neighbors. Johnson,

[18] Johnson's speeches ended with a beautiful piece of flamboyance that had been used by his father in three campaigns: "I want to so live that when my summons come to cross the Great Divide and enter my Father's house, a house not made with hands, eternal in the heavens, that I shall be able to look back upon the long stretching sands of time that flow down across this country and see where my earthly feet have trod, find footsteps of service to the people of Mississippi. That when I go down to the silent tomb of the dreamless dead, that I shall be able to hold in the hollow of my right hand a record of service to my fellow man."—*Memphis Press-Scimitar,* July 28, 1947.

the young veteran a little on the radical side, drew his highest vote in the hill counties. Note the maps in Figure 46. Wright's vote generally was highest in the counties with extremely high proportions of Negro population, whose distribution coincides fairly closely with the plantation economy.[14]

2. Rout of the Aristocracy: The Percys and the Bilbos

The hills are dry; the delta is wet. The hills are radical; the delta is conservative. The delta and the eastern prairie often vote together against the hills. The hills and the delta—as states of mind—have their roots in the past. Their interpretation requires a backward look, as well as a description of attitudes too subtle to fit readily within the angular conformations of the English language. The delta mind, at its best, possesses a high sense of duty, a compelling sense of honor, and a rigid code of right and wrong. Withal it is characterized by a remarkable isolation from the mind of the hills. And it must be remembered that not all delta dwellers share in the delta mind. Nor are all hill people rednecks.

The careers of LeRoy Percy and Theodore Bilbo personify, even caricature, the chasm between the delta and the hills. The Percys, of Washington County, in the heart of the delta are one of the great families of the South. By no means do all delta planters share in the virtues of the Percys, but this family has embodied all the qualities thought desirable by aristocrats and would-be aristocrats. Bound by a tradition of honor, of dignity, of fair-dealing, the family has typified the best of the old southern aristocracy.

The Percys, and those like them, were engulfed by a tidal wave which they fought but probably never really understood. It all began with James K. Vardaman, and the story has been best told by LeRoy's son, William Alexander Percy.[15] Vardaman, William Alexander relates, was "a kindly, vain demagogue unable to think, and given to emotions he considered noble. . . . For political platform he advertised his love of the common people and advocated the repeal of the Fifteenth and the modification of the Fourteenth Amendments to the Federal Constitution." [16] In 1910 the legislature sat to elect a United States Senator, and it was Vardaman against the field. "Father rather liked Vardaman—he was such a splendid ham actor, his inability to reason was so contagious, it was so impossible to determine where his idealism ended and his demagoguery began. Besides he had charm and a gift for the vivid reck-

---

[14] Compare also Wright's vote with the 1934 prohibition vote in Figure 45.

[15] William Alexander Percy, *Lanterns on the Levee* (New York: Alfred A. Knopf, 1941), chap. 13, "The Bottom Rail on Top."

[16] Ibid., p. 143.

less phrase. A likable man, as a poolroom wit is likable, but surely not one to set in the councils of the nation." [17] Several anti-Vardaman candidates entered the lists, with the plan eventually to combine on the strongest man. "With this strategy in mind and confident that no Delta man and no gentleman could possibly be elected, Father consented to be one of five prominent citizens to enter the race against Vardaman." [18] On the fifty-seventh ballot four other candidates withdrew, and Percy became United States Senator from Mississippi. "While the overt issue in Father's race before the legislature had been Vardaman's stand on the Negro question, the undeclared issue had been the unanswerable charge against Father that he was a prosperous plantation-owner, a corporation lawyer, and unmistakably a gentleman." [19]

Enter Theodore Bilbo. About two months after the election, Bilbo, a member of the legislature and a lieutenant of Vardaman, waved before the grand jury currency that he said he had accepted as a bribe to vote for Percy. He had not carried out his part of the bargain, but had stood by Vardaman. (No gentleman would accept a bribe; but if he did he would keep his word.) It turned out that many of Bilbo's bills had been issued after the day on which he said he had accepted them. "His story was a palpable and a proved lie." [20] By one vote Bilbo escaped expulsion by his fellow legislators, who contented themselves with an expression of their opinion of the man:

> Resolved, in view of the unexplained inconsistencies and inherent improbabilities in the testimony of Senator Bilbo, his established bad character and lack of credibility, that the Senate of Mississippi does hereby condemn his entire bribery charge, and the statement of the role he played as detective and decoy, as a trumped-up falsehood, utterly unworthy of belief; resolved further, that as a result of the conduct of Theodore G. Bilbo in this matter, and the testimony produced in this investigation, the Senate pronounces Bilbo as unfit to sit with honest, upright men in a respectable legislative body, and he is hereby asked to resign. [21]

Bilbo did not resign; he began to build a political career on the old plea of persecution. Soon in a campaign between Percy and Vardaman, "All over the state roved the self-accused bribe-taker vomiting his own infamy and cheered to the echo. . . . A man of honor was hounded by men without honor—not unusual perhaps, but the man was my Father," wrote William Alexander Percy. [22] Of one crowd that listened to his father, he recalled:

[17] Ibid., p. 144.
[18] Ibid., pp. 144–145.
[19] Ibid., pp. 146–147.
[20] Ibid., p. 147.
[21] Quoted by Allan A. Michie and Frank Ryhlick, *Dixie Demagogues* (New York: Vanguard Press, 1939), p. 94.
[22] Percy, *Lanterns on the Levee*, pp. 147–48.

I looked over the ill-dressed, surly audience, unintelligent and slinking, and heard him appeal to them for fair treatment of the Negro and explain to them the tariff and the Panama tolls situation. I studied them as they milled about. They were the sort of people that lynch Negroes, that mistake hoodlumism for wit, and cunning for intelligence, that attend revivals and fight and fornicate in the bushes afterwards. They were undiluted Anglo-Saxons. They were the sovereign voter. It was so horrible it seemed unreal.[23]

The sovereign voter chose Vardaman, and Bilbo took a broad stride forward in his political career. "It was my first sight of the rise of the masses, but not my last," the younger Percy wrote in 1941. "Now we have Russia and Germany, we have the insolence of organized labor and the insolence of capital, examples both of the insolence of the parvenu; we have the rise of the masses from Mississippi east, and back again west to Mississippi. The herd is on the march, and when it stampedes, there's blood galore and beauty is china under its hoofs."[24] The Mississippi Senate had long since expunged from its records its denunciation of Bilbo.

While the presence of the Negro in great numbers explains much of the puzzle of Mississippi politics, the chances are that one has to go further to understand why the people of Mississippi chose Bilbo over the Percys and their kind. Great landed ruling classes may be far less adaptable even than urban, financial, industrial, and managerial classes when faced by the compelling demands of a democratic ferment of the masses. The line that separates the great lord of the land and the tenant is drawn far more sharply than that between industrial employer and worker; at least, in the agrarian economy of the Mississippi sort no great middle class—not even an agrarian middle class—dulls the abruptness of the line between lord and serf. The big houses and the tenant shacks stand as symbols of nether worlds.[25] And bitterness is compounded by the fact that often Negroes have the best tenant shacks. Class envy is intensified by the difficulty of crossing the line: resistance to interclass mobility, the sociologists call it. The opportunity for advancement, exaggerated though it may be, up the industrial hierarchy through the acquisition of skills and the exercise of initiative and native wit probably exists to a much lesser degree in a semifeudal agrarian economy. The tenant and the share-cropper are regarded as lazy, degenerate, shiftless fellows who get what

[23] Ibid., p. 149.

[24] Ibid., p. 153.

[25] Lest all this language seem melodramatic it ought to be pointed out that Mississippi is in high degree an area of large-scale, multiple-unit agriculture. In 1945, 19.5 per cent of its farm "units" were in multiple-unit operations; the only state with a higher percentage was South Carolina, 20.4 per cent. A larger-scale operation, however, characterized Mississippi which had 1151 multiple-unit operations with 20 or more sub-units and 1623 with from 10–19 sub-units. South Carolina had only 136 operations with 20 or more sub-units and 435 with from 10 to 19. Contrast with Mississippi Alabama where only 8.3 per cent of the farming units were in multiple-unit operations.

they deserve, the sort of people "that attend revivals and fight and fornicate in the bushes afterwards." The responsibility of the lord is to his tenant—who will always be a tenant, and whose son will probably be a tenant.

Within the intellectual world of the honorable aristocrat there is no place for advancement of the masses by political means. It is dishonorable to pander to the people, for the politician who does is humbugging them. Given the resources and administrative skills of a state as poor as Mississippi, the substantial truth of the position ought to be conceded.[26]

And, so, the people turned to Bilbo. What sort of a man was he? Though William Alexander Percy does not deign to mention his name, he characterizes Bilbo in a paragraph of great insight:

> The man responsible for tearing Father's reputation to tatters and saddening three lives was a pert little monster, glib and shameless, with that sort of cunning common to criminals which passes for intelligence. The people loved him. They loved him not because they were deceived in him, but because they understood him thoroughly; they said of him proudly, "He's a slick little bastard." He was one of them and he had risen from obscurity to the fame of glittering infamy—it was as if they themselves had crashed the headlines.[27]

The people understood Bilbo; and Bilbo understood the people, at least better than did the men of honor and of the delta mind. For three decades he was the most powerful personality in the politics of the state. Building on the Vardaman faction in 1911, the self-confessed bribe-taker persuaded the people of the hills that he was the victim of persecution and they chose him as their lieutenant-governor. In 1915, by a majority of 1,072 he became governor. His term was marked by constructive actions in aid of education and eleemosynary institutions. In 1919, unable to succeed himself, he threw his strength to Lee M. Russell, another old Vardaman man, and during Russell's term violent "resentments against all 'enemies of the people'—deep jealousies and hatreds, inhibited for years—sprang savagely to the surface. . . . In the minds of the newly powerful hill people of Mississippi, the large corporations and 'trusts' became confused with their old masters, the delta folk." [28] Mississippians did not have much in the way of trusts to attack, but they took it out against Ford dealers and insurance companies.

Bilbo, defeated for Congress in 1920, returned to the fray in 1923 in an unsuccessful race for governor. He announced his candidacy from the

[26] Poverty or no, on some matters Mississippi could have moved more rapidly. In 1948, for example, its legislature adopted a workmen's compensation act, the forty-eighth state to adopt such legislation. Even at this late date a policy considered elsewhere to be only the most elementary justice aroused extended and bitter debate.

[27] Percy, *Lanterns on the Levee*, p. 148.

[28] C. E. Cason, "The Mississippi Imbroglio," *Virginia Quarterly Review*, 7 (1931), pp. 235–36.

jail, where he served a ten-day sentence for contempt of court. He had evaded process-servers who sought his testimony in a seduction suit brought by a statehouse stenographer, described by the chroniclers as lissome, against Governor Russell. The governor won his case, and Bilbo ran to succeed him. Again, he capitalized on his "persecution" but to no avail. Henry Whitfield defeated him. And thereby hangs another tale.

Whitfield had been for many years president of the Mississippi State College for Women and had been ousted, along with other educators, during Russell's term of office. Bilbo and Russell had treated colleges as a part of the patronage pool. They underestimated Whitfield, who had consciously set about to moderate social conflict by assuring representation in the student body from every county of the state in contrast with "Ole Miss," the fraternity school, catering to the delta, and the A. & M. College, the hill school. Whitfield's girls dressed alike, belonged to no sororities, lived alike, and lived together, whether they were from the delta or the hills. They rallied to his cause and helped carry the day against The Man Bilbo.

Bilbo spent the years from 1923 to 1927 preparing to run for governor in 1927, a campaign in which he recalled again his persecutions and won by a narrow margin. By the end of his term early in 1932 the State— in common with many others at the time—was practically bankrupt; Bilbo had been stymied in his dealings with the legislature; and he had been, his delta enemies thought, completely discredited. But Bilbo was not easily downed. A Washington sinecure took care of him until the 1934 senatorial campaign.

In 1934, Bilbo brought into play his genius for rough-and-tumble campaigning. He wore, from an earlier campaign, a scar won in his oratorical battles for the people. He had been rapped over the head with a pistol butt by an opponent whom he had described as "a cross between a hyena and a mongrel . . . begotten in a nigger graveyard at midnight, suckled by a sow, and educated by a fool." [29] In the 1934 campaign as in others Bilbo—who had earlier done a little Baptist preaching—salted his oratory with bastard King Jamesian orotundities, long familiar to his audiences from the sermons of their evangelical preachers: "Friends, fellow citizens, brothers and sisters—hallelujah.—My opponent—yea, this opponent of mine who has the dastardly, dewlapped, brazen, sneering, insulting and sinful effrontery to ask you for your votes without telling you the people of Mississippi what he is a-going to do with them if he gets them—this opponent of mine says he don't need a platform. . . . He asks, my dear brethren and sisters, that you vote for him because he is standing by the President. . . . I shall be the servant and Senator of all the people. . . . The appeal and petition of the humblest citizen, yea,

---

[29] R. J. Zorn, "Theodore G. Bilbo" in Salter's *Public Men in and out of Office* (Chapel Hill: University of North Carolina Press, 1946), p. 284.

whether he comes from the black prairie lands of the east or the alluvial lands of the fertile delta; . . . yea, he will be heard by my heart and my feet shall be swift, . . . your Senator whose thoughts will not wander from the humble, God-fearing cabins of Vinegar Bend . . . , your champion who will not lay his head upon his pillow at night before he has asked his Maker for more strength to do more for you on the morrow. . . . Brethren and sisters, I pledge . . ." [30]

The communicants in the faith of Bilbo shouted, "Amen, Hallelujah!" They roared at his little obscenities.[31] And, again by a narrow margin, he won and became a Senator of the United States from Mississippi. It was a far cry—and a revolution—from another and earlier Senator, John Sharp Williams, Episcopalian, gentleman, lawyer, planter, of Yazoo City, to Theodore Bilbo, Baptist, lawyer, farmer, of Poplarville in Pearl River County.

Between the delta planter and Bilbo there was no issue on the place of the Negro. The delta thought it unsporting and vulgar of him to demagogue about the poor devils, but beyond this they were in fundamental agreement on that issue. As governor of an incredibly poor state he could do little for the rednecks but as a Senator he could vote for measures for their benefit. He went down the line for the New Deal; all of its works were anathema to the delta. He was for farm-tenancy legislation; the plantation economy depended on tenancy. He was for old-age pensions which did not have to be matched by the states; to the delta this was an invasion of states' rights. He was for generous relief; to the delta this was destructive of moral fiber. And Bilbo, the people of the delta firmly believed, had no interest in the people of Mississippi but was concerned solely with number one. He got his support from the uneducated and improvident and from those who wanted something from their government, which they had no right to have, and were willing to provide campaign funds.

In 1940 he returned to the Senate by defeating Hugh White, wealthy former governor, by the ample margin of 91,000 to 62,000. In Washington he continued to make political capital at home by filibustering against antipoll-tax measures, but he was a New Dealer on other issues. In 1944 he had a hand in blocking an effort by the delta-minded people to put the state's presidential electors on record against Roosevelt. By spending a few thousand dollars, working quietly, and taking the Roosevelt forces off guard, they had captured the state convention and nominated a slate

[30] Quoted ibid., p. 285.

[31] See the discussion of Louisiana, above, pp. 165–67. A dispatch from Leland, Mississippi, during a later campaign, reported: "Senator Theo. G. Bilbo, defending himself against charges of racial and religious intolerance said here last night that he was for 'every damn Jew from Jesus Christ on down.' "—Senate, Special Committee Investigating the National Defense Program, 79th Cong., 2d sess., Hearings, Transactions between Senator Theodore G. Bilbo and Various War Contractors, Part 2, Exhibit No. 112.

of electors pledged to vote in the electoral college against Roosevelt.[32]
Later the legislature—mainly through Governor Bailey's influence—
nominated another slate pledged to vote for Roosevelt. And the anti-
Roosevelt electors were soundly defeated. "Roosevelt," it is said in the
delta, "had much more in common with Bilbo than with Pat Harrison."

In 1946, Bilbo ran for re-election. It may be a surprise to many persons that he had to rebut the canard that he was not really for white
supremacy. At some time in his career he had argued against the poll tax,
a step that would appeal to the hills. This was twisted into the charge
that he favored repealing the tax to make it possible for Negroes to vote.
"In this fight for White Supremacy in the South we must have men in
Washington who believe in the poll tax, and as Bilbo says he is against
the tax, it must be assumed that he is against it. We must retain the poll
tax and only men who believe in it will really wholeheartedly fight for it."
The same campaign broadside that contained this charge carried a photograph of "Bilbo's Black Peckerwood, the Nigger in the Wood Pile." The
caption read: "Bilbo slipped this negro into the gravy." Bilbo's District
of Columbia Committee had cleared the nomination of a Negro to the
position of Recorder of the District of Columbia, a patronage post traditionally reserved for Negroes.[33]

By 1946 the turn of events had brought to Bilbo allies in the delta
and among the delta-minded elsewhere. The FEPC, antipoll-tax proposals, communism, bureaucracy, socialism, threats to the American way
of life, and antilynching bills were bad enough. But insult was added.
Life and other such journals ran big spreads ridiculing the state and advising Mississippians to defeat Bilbo. The drama played itself out in a
scene of high and ironic tragedy. Many a delta planter held his nose and
voted for Bilbo. "I guess we all did," they relate in a low and apologetic
voice, and add that much of Bilbo's vote in the delta came from peckerwoods who had moved down from the hills.[34]

After Bilbo's 1946 victory the story is not long. Before the voting he
had issued statements to discourage Negro voting in the exercise of rights
newly asserted by the Supreme Court. Manifesting its ignorance of history, the Republican minority of a Senate committee reported: "Never
to the knowledge of the undersigned has such vile, contemptible, inflammatory, and dangerous language been uttered in a campaign for the purpose of procuring nomination and election by an incumbent and Member

[32] Bob Hannegan, the Democratic national chairman, charged that $50,000 has been
sent into Mississippi to corrupt the state convention. A Mississippian who had a hand
in spending around $5,000 on the project observed, with some unhappiness, that if
$50,000 was sent into the state whoever got it kept it.

[33] Senate, Special Committee Investigating the National Defense Program, 79th
Cong., 2d sess., Hearings, Transactions between Senator Theodore G. Bilbo and Various
War Contractors, Part 2, Exhibit No. 112.

[34] Hodding Carter's novel *Flood Crest* (New York: Rinehart and Company, Inc.,
1947) builds on the theme of the reconciliation of Bilbo and the delta.

of the United States Senate, sworn to uphold the Constitution." [35] Then, another Senate committee looked into his dealings with war contractors, a matter that had been discussed in detail in his campaign. In an opponent's campaign circular containing about the same charges as those before the Senate committee, Bilbo declared that he found "at least 25 separate, distinct, contemptible, pusillanimous and limicolous lies." The committee, however, found that "Senator Bilbo improperly used his high office as United States Senator for his personal gain in his dealings with war contractors." [36] His days were numbered and the Senate, rather than debate for weeks on whether to seat a dying man, let him go off to Poplarville to die.

And what of the delta? Driven from its position of leadership, many of its people took refuge in the romantic notion that the ancient code of noblesse oblige continues to govern all. In the delta, the presence of LeRoy Percy is as powerful as it was the day he went to the Senate.[37] And there are men of the Percy sort who live on as men of honor, fulfilling their obligations to their Negroes, the inheritors of a noble tradition. Their fellow planters, a little envious, nevertheless are quick to point to them in rebuttal of all falsehoods from the outside world.[38] And there are those of the delta-mind who fancy themselves to be LeRoy Percys when they are not.

As the principal source of intelligent leadership for the state the delta is curiously handicapped. Its older generation of leaders remains

[35] Special Committee to Investigate Senatorial Campaign Expenditures, Senate Report No. 1, 80th Cong., 1st. sess. (1947), p. 23.

[36] Special Committee Investigating the National Defense Program, Senate Report No. 110, part 8, 79th Cong., 2d sess. (1947), p. 4.

[37] In discussing a local political campaign an editorial columnist wrote in the *Delta Democrat-Times* (Greenville), on June 18, 1947: "A banker-friend met us on the street today. 'I think you've got something,' he said, 'but I'm afraid you won't get anywhere, because the liquor crowd are too well-organized.' We are not prepared to admit that, for that is the same thing as saying that the good in Washington County is outweighed by the bad. But even if Mr. Carnahan was correct in thinking that the cards were stacked, we should still be inclined to play out the hand. That would have been the way LeRoy Percy and his friend Will Crump would have wanted us to do it. The Senator was a man whose judgments of men were infallible, and those who were close to him knew that he knew that he didn't have a Chinaman's chance in his campaign for the Senate against Jim Vardaman in 1911. But he knew the fight should be made so he made it. He was no campaigner. He couldn't remember faces or names, nor could he tickle babies under their chins and mutter inanities at their mothers. . . . All he could do was talk sense to his audiences all over the state of Mississippi and that wasn't what they came to hear.

"So he made the fight and failed. But he could and did keep his home county, and his home town clean, and you who live here today are the direct beneficiaries of his vigilance. . . .

"So, we must make the good fight, must register and vote. . . ."

[38] The delta is sympathetically pictured by David L. Cohn in his *God Shakes Creation* (New York: Harper and Brothers, 1935) and other writings. Hodding Carter's *Lower Mississippi* (New York: Farrar & Rinehart, 1942) includes valuable material on the delta.

in intellectual isolation, untouched by the progressive movements of thought of this century. Long before the 1948 states' rights revolt, they discussed the project solemnly. "We in Mississippi are all agreed," one heard in the delta, oblivious of the lessons of 30 years of Bilbo. Mississippians are all alike; the South is all like Mississippi. We should simply stand up against the world and demand our rights. So odd an estimate of the South could come only from men whose horizon was circumscribed by the limits of the delta. Within the younger generation there is ferment; change will come. Yet even men of good will are perplexed. Self-interest alone dictates that they grasp control and assure their people education, health, safety. Yet in so doing they fear that they might unleash forces that they could not control, and to do so they must somehow command the support of the rednecks, men who distrust the delta and hate the Negro. Blocked in all directions by obstacles not of their own making, many of the younger generation ally themselves with the old in despair of a way out of the dilemma.

3. Structure of Factionalism

While Mississippi politics may be fundamentally a conflict between the delta mind and the hill mind, its factionalism is poorly organized for effective expression of these or other competing viewpoints. Neither group has a political organization approaching a party machine in character. Nor are candidates clearly identified with either viewpoint in many races. From campaign to campaign divisions among voters change—a consequence of confusion, localism, and other factors associated with a fluid factionalism. The principal element of continuity in voter division has been the personal following of Bilbo, but even this was an incohesive grouping. When Bilbo was a candidate the delta-hill division appeared in more or less clear form. In other races there often appeared a confusing criss-crossing of lines between delta and hills. The advantage in such a politics almost invariably goes to the delta. Even without formal political organization the lawyer-planter-merchant group can act in concert; about the only means for the expression of the hill viewpoint is through a personality such as Bilbo.

The political life-cycle of a southern Senator may follow an oft-repeated sequence. He manages to get himself elected, perhaps by a rabble-rousing appeal, and then builds his fences so well with the moneyed interests that no opponent can raise a campaign fund large enough to make much of a fight against him. Re-election succeeds re-election without serious contest. That Bilbo always had a fight on his hands when he ran for re-election may be indicative of the intensity of the factional dispute in Mississippi and may mean that his dealings with war contractors and corporations never went so far that he could be considered a "sound" man by the delta-minded.

The votes in the primaries in which Bilbo ran reflect the operation of a personal organization far less disciplined and loyal than a political party. On the other hand, at least in Bilbo's campaigns, the voting behavior of Mississippians makes much more sense in terms of the conflict of the haves and have-nots than that of Arkansas, if it be granted that Bilbo

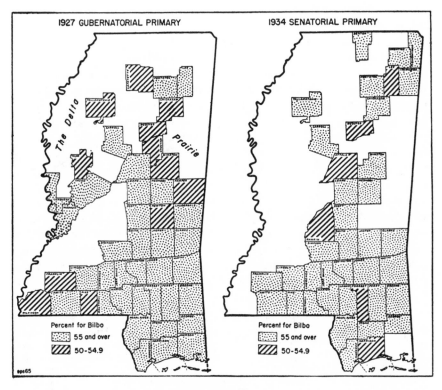

FIGURE 47

Delta and the Hills: Vote for Bilbo, Second Gubernatorial Primary, 1927, and Second Senatorial Primary, 1934

spoke for the have-nots. Despite his appeal, his following could be wooed away in particular regions by candidates with a friends-and-neighbors attraction and in particular counties by local leaders moved by grudge, caprice, or the cash bid of the opposition.

The pattern of the Bilbo vote appears in the two maps in Figure 47. One shows his strength in the 1927 race for the governorship against Dennis Murphree, in which he polled 52.8 per cent of the vote. The other shows his 1934 vote for the Senate when he attracted 51.8 per cent of the vote to defeat Senator Hubert Stephens. The maps indicate that in 1927 and in 1934 Bilbo had about the same following. In both campaigns he was weak in the delta, although in 1927 he made inroads in Warren County (Vicksburg) and in the adjoining county of Issaquena, which polled a total of only 215 votes. In both campaigns he was also weak in the prairie counties, the seat, it will be recalled, of a rich agriculture sympathetic toward the delta. In the hill counties he was strong, although he was weaker in the northern than in the southern hills. Perhaps his strength in the south was in part a regional friends-and-neighbors following, and his strength in the north may have been cut into in 1934 by a friends-and-neighbors loyalty to Stephens.[39]

Bilbo's two campaigns for re-election to the Senate illustrate the shifting bases of his support. His greatest popular strength remained generally in the hills, yet his strength in individual counties varied from campaign to campaign. In 1940 he easily defeated Hugh White, a former governor so wealthy that he could finance his own campaigns. Bilbo polled 59.3 per cent of the vote. In 1946 he polled 51.0 in the first primary against two principal opponents, Tom Q. Ellis, clerk of the state supreme court, and Ross Collins, a former Congressman. Between 1940 and 1946 the peaks of Bilbo's strength shifted as may be seen from the maps in Figure 48. White, in his home county and in the adjacent territory in southeast Mississippi, was able in 1940 to cut into Bilbo's traditional strength. In 1946 Bilbo picked up strength in that area but lost relatively in counties in Collins' old congressional district and in some of the north-eastern counties in which Ellis was strong. The shifts in strength and the potency of the friends-and-neighbors attraction reveal the looseness of a following even as strong as Bilbo's.[40]

[39] Compare the distribution of Bilbo's strength with the map in Figure 46 showing the location of counties with highest proportions of Negro population. Incidentally, one should hesitate before drawing conclusions from Mississippi election statistics, particularly about isolated or individual counties. Internal inconsistencies in figures led to a comparison between the figures for the 1943 first gubernatorial primary published by the secretary of state and those in his office. Twenty-nine of the 328 county figures (four candidates; 82 counties) in the *Blue Book* differed from those in the office records. The margin of error was usually small but large enough to bounce percentages in the smaller counties. The published figure for at least one candidate was in error for 23 of the 82 counties.

[40] Discussions with Bilbo managers concerning some of the detailed differences between his popular strength in 1940 and 1946 are of interest as indicative of the beliefs of Mississippi politicians about the nature of the political process, if not indicative of causal forces. Thus, Itawamba County was strong for Bilbo in 1940 (71.3 per cent) and weak in 1946 (42.5 per cent). The explanation: A man of great local influence had a grudge because Bilbo had not supported him for lieutenant-governor in 1940. Bilbo was weak in Jackson County in 1940 (46.6 per cent) and stronger in 1946 (56.8 per cent). The explanation: In 1940 Bilbo's local manager in introducing him had taken the occasion to "tell off" all the local politicians against whom he had a grudge and the county was lost before Bilbo began to speak. In 1946 this local personage was kept in the background. Warren County (Vicksburg) gave increased support to Bilbo in 1946 (58.3 per cent as against 45.7). Bilbo was always weak in the cities but by 1946 his

When Bilbo was a candidate factional lines held to some extent, and the line-up of delta versus the hills was usually perceptible. When he was not a candidate, however, divisions among the voters were apt to take other forms. And in this difference, of course, is to be found one of the most significant departures of the one-party system from a two-party arrangement. Absence of continuing factional groupings with which indi-

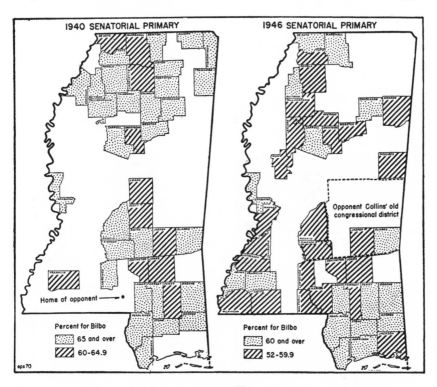

FIGURE 48

Shifting Bases of Popular Support: Popular Vote for Bilbo in Senatorial Primaries, 1940, 1946

vidual candidates are routinely identified confuses the voter, makes choice difficult, and aggrandizes irrelevant considerations such as localism. The gubernatorial campaigns of 1939 and 1943 are illustrative. Bilbo is commonly credited with "electing" Paul B. Johnson as governor in 1939. He

opposition to Yankee interference had won him some business support as, for example, a leading businessman of Vicksburg who had opposed Bilbo for years became a convert and contributed to the campaign. Why was X county strong for Bilbo in 1946, weak in 1940? It is a miserably corrupt county. It goes to the man who gets there fustest with the mostest the night before election. Why was Bilbo weak in Tunica County in both elections and strong in adjoining Quitman County? Tunica County has a strong betterelement machine which had consistently opposed Bilbo; his chief manager had an office in Quitman County and many friends over the county.

rallied the "Bilbo people" to the support of Johnson who won with 54.7 per cent of the vote, over the bitter anti-New Deal candidate, former governor Mike Conner. Johnson's vote, shown in Figure 49, bears a vague resemblance to the Bilbo vote shown in earlier maps. On the other hand, Johnson was strong in some counties—as in the eastern prairie and delta —in which Bilbo was consistently weak, and weak in some counties in

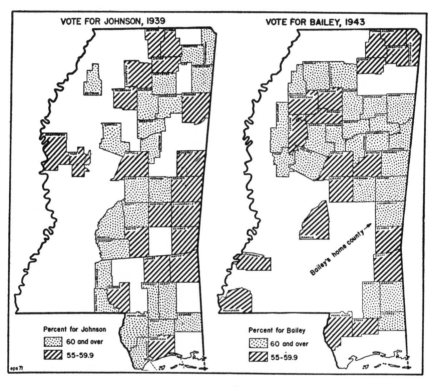

FIGURE 49

Instability of Faction: Popular Vote for Johnson for Governor, 1939, and for Bailey for Governor, 1943

which Bilbo had been consistently strong. Bilbo's capacity to deliver his own vote to another candidate varied greatly from county to county. And Johnson, opponent of an unreconstructed conservative, could win strength in areas that might be expected to go against him under a rational politics.[41]

In 1943 Bilbo again threw his influence against Mike Conner for governor. Conner had led Thomas L. Bailey in the first primary by 111,028 to 68,893, and, as precedent went in Mississippi, was expected to win the

[41] A scatter-diagram reveals only a slight positive relation between the county-by-county vote for Johnson in 1939 and that for Bilbo in 1940.

run-off. Although Bailey had in the legislature opposed Bilbo's programs, Bilbo preferred him over Conner as did Dennis Murphree, a perennial candidate who had run third in the first primary. The elder Johnson also backed Bailey. The Bilbo people over the state were activated in support of Bailey, who polled 53.2 per cent of the vote to lead Conner by 143,153 to 125,882. If the Bilbo faction had been as cohesive as a party, Bailey's vote would have resembled that of Bilbo in earlier campaigns. Bailey, however, had great strength in regions where Bilbo was consistently weak, as in the eastern prairie counties. Nor was Bailey especially strong in many of the southeastern Bilbo counties. Those delta counties adjacent to the River were less enthusiastic for Bailey than were the hill counties. Although he carried some delta counties, in the delta were counties that ranked low among the counties of the state in their support of him as they had ranked in their zeal for Bilbo. (See Figure 49.) In the sources of the popular strength of Bilbo, Bailey, and Johnson there were marked differences, at least partially indicative of the looseness of the Bilbo faction.[42]

From careful inspection of the series of maps, it is apparent that some Mississippi counties are extremely erratic in their voting behavior; they move this way and that for no immediately apparent reason. Some of this erraticism comes from the friends-and-neighbors factor.[43] Some of it is accounted for by the behavior of what Mississippi politicians refer to as "money counties." The consensus among the practitioners seems to be that 12 or 15 non-delta counties can be rallied to a candidate for state office by payments to a local leader or leaders. Not all counties into which a candidate has to put money are "money counties." Some counties are poor but honest and a candidate's local supporters cannot finance local campaign activities. Nor are all counties with fairly cohesive local machines money counties. In Mississippi, as elsewhere in the South, extremely wide differences exist in custom and tradition even in adjacent

[42] Although Mississippi Senators often become involved in gubernatorial races and governors in senatorial races, the state otherwise follows the practice of autonomy of candidacy usually characteristic of states with fluid factional systems. Candidates for minor state offices usually attempt to build their own following. Sometimes they attach themselves to a gubernatorial candidate and are permitted to make an announcement at each "speaking" but they will have a representative in the entourage of other gubernatorial candidates. Candidates for the House of Representatives also usually keep clear of other candidacies.

[43] A Mississippi commentator suggests that a desirable independence of action may also contribute to erraticism in the returns of particular counties. It should be said that the art of inference from electoral behavior is in a primitive stage. The assumption made throughout is that when most counties behave alike from primary to primary, a fairly tightly knit factional organization exists with a persistently loyal voter following. On the other hand, when counties vote erratically the inference is that localized rather than state-wide factors are influential. The further inference is that "independence" is apt to be distributed fairly evenly over a state; when an individual county by statistical analysis diverges one suspects the existence of a local machine, the impact of a friends-and-neighbors influence, or some factor other than a localized voter independence.

counties about the use of money in elections. Variations in local customs put into a strategic position those professional campaign managers who "know the situation" in the counties.[44]

It is evident that in the absence of a unifying personality around whom a faction may form, and against whom the anti's can unite, Mississippi politics tends to disintegrate into a multifactionalism. In 1947

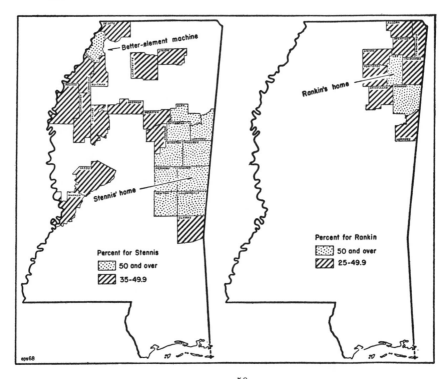

FIGURE 50

Localism: Vote for Stennis and for Rankin, Special Mississippi Senatorial
Election, 1947

several candidates ran in a special election to fill the Senate vacancy created by Bilbo's death. John C. Stennis, of Kemper County on the east-

[44] Mississippi apparently has a fairly high degree of separation of state and local campaigns, at least on the surface. Managers of state campaigns explain the situation by the fact that the county officials are running at the same time as state candidates and have their hands full in their own races. Nor is there a principal county functionary, such as Alabama's probate judge, around which county politics tends to revolve. Mississippi local government is highly decentralized; in many counties each of the five county supervisors, in effect, constitutes a sort of county government for his "beat." Whenever a chief factotum of county government develops, he tends to be the chancery clerk who serves as secretary of the board of supervisors. Insofar as state factions have organizations, the machinery seems in the main to be built around persons other than local officials.

ern border of the state, won with 26.9 per cent of the total vote. A digni-
fied, conservative candidate, not given to ranting about the race question
although in fundamental agreement with the Biblo viewpoint, his strongest support came from the counties composing the circuit he had served
as judge. In the prairie counties of the east his friends-and-neighbors
vote was heavy: he polled 93.5 of the vote in his home county. Reflecting
the community of attitude between the prairie and the delta, the counties
ranking next—but much lower—in enthusiasm for him were mainly
delta counties. W. M. Colmer, conservative Congressman of Pascagoula
on the coast, drew his heaviest support in the counties composing his
district. John E. Rankin, similarly, drew heavy support only from counties in his congressional district in the northeast.[45] Forrest Jackson, former
aid to Bilbo, who claimed to be the political heir, drew support in southwestern Mississippi. The Bilbo faction did not follow him. The vote in
the special election—in which only a plurality was required to elect—
resembled the fractionalization of the electorate that occurs in first primaries. Nevertheless, absence of a strong personality, such as Bilbo,
brought a higher degree of atomization of the electorate than would have
prevailed with a strong candidate in the race.

[45] Mr. Rankin polled only 12.6 per cent of the vote. His weakness suggests the observation, perhaps shocking to outlanders insensitive to the nuances of southern politics,
that it takes more than Negro-baiting to win an election in Mississippi. Mr. Rankin had
undoubtedly established himself, in the eyes of the world at least, as a close second to
the late Senator in extremeness of declamation on the black, but he drew only about
25,000 votes in the state. It would also follow that Mr. Bilbo's support had bases other
than his race policies.

Chapter Twelve | # TEXAS:
A POLITICS OF ECONOMICS

WE have sought to identify the basic conflicts of the internal politics of each state. In some states the issues involved a clash of disparate geographic sections. In some the fight has been between a state machine and those who would depose it. In others, personal factions led by colorful figures have given form to the political battle. In a few, campaigns have been confused free-for-alls in which no consistent or meaningful pattern of voting has been detected. In all, the presence of large numbers of Negroes has been influential in determining the lines of political division and often in diverting the attention of the electorate from nonracial issues.

Texas conforms to none of these patterns. Yet, like other southern states, it is a one-party state because in 1860 a substantial part of its population consisted of Negro slaves. Most of its people then lived in East Texas, and the land to the west was largely undeveloped. The changes of nine decades have weakened the heritage of southern traditionalism, revolutionized the economy, and made Texas more western than southern. Democratic supremacy persists, although its original basis has shrunk to minor significance. In 1940 only one Texan in seven was a Negro. White Texans, unlike white Mississippians, have little cause to be obsessed about the Negro. The Lone Star State is concerned about money and how to make it, about oil and sulfur and gas, about cattle and dust storms and irrigation, about cotton and banking and Mexicans.

And Texans are coming to be concerned broadly about what government ought and ought not to do. In our times the grand issues of politics almost invariably turn on the economic policies of government. To what extent shall wealth and power, corporate or personal, be restrained for the protection of the defenseless? What services shall the government perform? Who shall pay for them? Such are the great questions that divide people and that politicians must solve provisionally from day to day to keep the wheels of our system turning. While the issues are always present, in the confusions and distractions of one-party politics broad issues of economic philosophy are often obscured or smothered by irrelevant appeals, sectional loyalties, local patriotism, personal candidacies, and, above all, by the specter of the black man.

In Texas the vague outlines of a politics are emerging in which irrelevancies are pushed into the background and people divide broadly along liberal and conservative lines. A modified class politics seems to be evolving, not primarily because of an upthrust of the masses that compels men of substance to unite in self-defense, but because of the personal insecurity of men suddenly made rich who are fearful lest they lose their wealth. In 40 years a new-rich class has arisen from the exploitation of natural resources in a gold rush atmosphere. By their wits (and, sometimes, by the chance deposit in eons past of an oil pool under the family ranch) men have built huge fortunes from scratch. Imbued with faith in individual self-reliance and unschooled in social responsibilities of wealth, many of these men have been more sensitive than a Pennsylvania manufacturer to the policies of the Roosevelt and Truman Administrations.

The confluence of the anxieties of the newly rich and the repercussions of the New Deal in Texas pushed politics into a battle of conservatives versus liberals, terms of common usage in political discourse in the state. By no means has the pattern appeared consistently, yet after 1940 this alignment emerged in about as sharp a form as is possible under a one-party system. In the process the ties that bind the state to the Democratic party were strained, possibly in portent of the rise of a bipartisan system.

1. Emergence of Economic Alignments

The terms "liberal" and "conservative" have real meaning in the Democratic politics of Texas. Tight and clear ideological lines appeared in the state Democratic convention of September, 1948, on the issues of the nomination of a senatorial candidate, the instruction of presidential electors, and control of party machinery. The convention sustained disputed election returns that gave the senatorial nomination to Lyndon

Johnson instead of his conservative opponent, Coke Stevenson. The convention backed Harry Truman when it voted to oust several presidential electors whose loyalty to the national nominees was in question and when it named a new state executive committee purged of all suspected Dixiecrats. When the convention ejected "conservative" representatives from Dallas, Fort Worth, and Houston and replaced them with delegations predominantly favorable to Lyndon Johnson and Harry Truman, the press reported a victory for the "liberals."

The dramatic 1948 conflict reflected a division between the right and left wings of the Texas Democracy that unmistakably had been emerging over a series of elections. Clear evidence of a sharpened alignment came in the 1944 battle over control of the state's delegation to the national conventions. In presidential years Texas has two state conventions. The first, which meets in May, names delegates to the national convention and nominates presidential electors. The second, which meets in September and is called the "governor's convention," has traditionally been concerned mainly with the declaration of the results of the summer primaries and adoption of a platform. At the May, 1944, convention it became apparent that forces unsympathetic to Roosevelt's renomination had control and would send anti-Roosevelt delegates to the national convention and attempt to divert the state's electoral vote from the Democratic nominees. A third of the convention marched out (singing "The Eyes of Texas Are Upon You"), reconvened as a rump convention at the other end of the capitol, and named a competing slate of delegates. The national convention seated both delegations and split the state's vote between them.

Roosevelt was renominated, and Texas was left with an anti-Roosevelt slate of Democratic electors named by the May state convention. Pro-Roosevelt Texans won control of the September convention by a narrow margin and named a Roosevelt slate, an action unanimously upheld by the Texas Supreme Court. The electors of the party's conservative wing, uninstructed but committed against Roosevelt, appeared on the general election ballot as "Texas Regulars." [1] The party fission isolated the extreme right-wing Democrats who had enough conviction and independence to take their fight outside the party if they could not win within it. The issue of the split was crystal clear: the New Deal. Texans endorsed the Democratic candidate: Roosevelt 821,605; Dewey 191,425; the Texas Regulars, 135,439.

In the 1944 split state offices were not involved and the lines of controversy were defined by differences over policies of the national govern-

---

[1] Their campaign manager was Merritt H. Gibson, who four years later served as national campaign director for the Dixiecrats. The Texas Regulars were more concerned about economics than race, but they adopted a resolution condemning Supreme Court decisions in the white-primary cases and alleged efforts to break down segregation.

ment. No United States Senate seat was at stake, and Governor Coke Stevenson received the customary second term over slight opposition. Two years later, however, in a wide-open race for the governorship, Texans lined up for and against two viewpoints, one purportedly looking left and the other right.

By 1946 the party breach had been formally healed. The Texas Regulars were readmitted to party councils and participated in the convention of that year. The line-up in the gubernatorial primary, however, revealed the same broad difference in general philosophy of government that had appeared two years earlier. Beauford Jester, successful in the second primary, was acclaimed by the Texas Regulars, although he was nearer to the middle of the road than several reactionary candidates who were eliminated in the first primary. He also had the support of Roosevelt Democrats who shied away from the alleged radicalism of his opponent, Homer P. Rainey. Dr. Rainey had been fired as president of the University of Texas in 1944 after a fight with the Board of Regents [2] in which he and academic freedom lost. His race for governor was the race of a martyr. The first primary was a trial heat in which his four chief opponents levelled most of their fire at him. It served to select the anti-Rainey candidate for the second race. Dr. Rainey was no radical, yet he was portrayed as a threat to all American virtue. In fact, he held conventional New Deal views and did not hestitate to discuss concretely what he felt were the issues of the campaign. He received sympathetic support among CIO members and Negroes, as well as liberals generally. The election was fought around his supposed super-liberalism.[3] Politically inexperienced and sometimes inept, he was roundly defeated, receiving a third of the votes cast in the run-off.

The onslaught against the liberal gubernatorial candidate extended its influence to other candidates who were labeled liberal. In Dallas, for instance, Judge Sarah Hughes, six times a winner in county-wide races, was defeated for Congress. She ran against a "fighting conservative," who had previously been beaten three times. She was friendly to labor and the OPA; her opponent was openly hostile. She lost even in her own precinct, which she usually carried by large majorities.

The alignments in the 1944, 1946, and 1948 contests were by no means identical, as is evidenced by the difference in outcome. There was, however, a general consistency, in that those who had been most ardent

---

[2] Headlined the *Austin American*: "Multimillionaire Regents Fire Rainey."—quoted by John Gunther, *Inside U. S. A.* (New York: Harper and Brothers, 1947), p. 857.

[3] A fabulous collection of campaign tales grew out of the campaign, not a few of which concerned the opposition's successful efforts to identify Rainey personally with certain passages appearing in John Dos Passos's *U. S. A.* Dr. Rainey had defended the right of a faculty member to recommend the book to his classes. One candidate held "for men only" meetings at which, holding the book in gloved hands, he read some of the juiciest passages.

Texas Regulars were the most fearful of Rainey: those who supported Rainey had in the main been sympathetic to Roosevelt.[4] And many liberal leaders in the 1948 convention had been Rainey supporters in 1946.[5]

A less-clear but nevertheless definite split between liberals and conservatives occurred in the 1948 fight to succeed Senator W. Lee O'Daniel. Most observers thought New Dealish Congressman Lyndon Johnson a bit brash to challenge Coke Stevenson's bid for the Senate. Coke had served longer than any other governor. He had been the wartime chief executive and was admired by Democrats of property and affairs who regarded him as safe. Congressman Johnson had received Roosevelt's blessings in the special senatorial election of 1941, which he lost to Governor O'Daniel by an eyelash. Earlier rather vigorous in his liberalism, Johnson had conformed to the necessities of building a state-wide following and in later years had lost much of his crusading sheen. Nevertheless, in 1948 he was to the left of Governor Stevenson.

Of the differences between Johnson and Stevenson, political sophisticates were aware, although the rank-and-file voter may have been a bit perplexed. Stevenson gained the endorsement of the conservative state federation of labor, which had also supported Jester in 1946. He made straddling statements about the Taft-Hartley Act, while Johnson made no bones about his vote for it in the House. Johnson's effectiveness as a Washington expediter had earned some business support for him. Nevertheless, most of the conservative leaders of 1944 and 1946 turned up in the Stevenson camp in 1948, while most of the Roosevelt-Truman men backed Johnson who emerged from the primary with an 87 vote margin.[6] Stevenson in the state convention unsuccessfully challenged the vote of some of the South Texas counties that had reported overwhelming majorities for Johnson. His dissatisfaction with the outcome led him to support Republican candidate Jack Porter in the general election.

The 1948 fight over presidential electors was the reverse of 1944. Most of the electors selected in the May convention were willing to vote for Truman. The conservatives set out to gain control of the second convention and to replace them with electors pledged to Thurmond and Wright. They failed. The alignments in the contests over the senatorial vote and over the naming of electors were the same.

[4] In general those counties that turned in the highest anti-Roosevelt vote in 1944 were also strongest for Jester in 1946. Beyond these intensely conservative counties, however, no close correlation exists between the two votes.

[5] Governor Jester took the lead in holding Texas for Truman. In effect, he changed camps, an act that did not go without comment from some of his 1946 friends whom he now opposed. In the 1948 reorganization of the state executive committee 46 of its 64 members were replaced. Jester named the chairman but 25 of the new members had been active Rainey supporters in 1946.

[6] With approximately a million votes cast, this was surely one of the closest elections in American history.

All in all Texas has developed the most bitter intra-Democratic fight along New Deal and anti-New Deal lines in the South. To be sure, such cleavages exist in other states, though elsewhere the controversy does not seem so sharp, and divisions along lines of economic philosophy are blurred by crosscurrents of various sorts. One-party political behavior in Texas has many features in common with other states. It also has significant differences, which are probably partly attributable to the state's extremely fluid social structure. Rapid population growth, partially by immigration, extensive migration within the state, large-scale urbanization, and the wholesale manufacture of new members of the upper economic orders are among the forms of flux in a fluid social structure. Add to these factors the absence of powerful traditional factional, sectional, or other political loyalties that might lend political stability. The result is a population somewhat like a loose pile of iron filings. There was little obstruction to bi-polarization when the two poles of the political magnet—New Deal and anti-New Deal—came on the scene. The general situation resembles that of Florida, although Texans detect a strident tone of irreconcilability in their politics that seems to be missing in the bland politics of Florida.

Most types of analysis applied in earlier chapters to the politics of other states yield little when used on the Texas voting statistics. The friends-and-neighbors pattern, for example, turns up, especially in the vote of weak candidates. In so large a state, however, a few friends and neighbors make little difference in the outcome. Nor do local followings seem to grow into sectional or regional groupings as happens in other states.

Although Texans have a keen consciousness of sectionalism, their regional loyalties seem to have little bearing on divisions in gubernatorial politics. West Texans have in the past talked of secession, but in the popular voting there appears no persistent cleavage such as the tri-sectionalism of Tennessee or the upcountry-lowland antagonism of South Carolina. Absence of a habit of sectional division can be credited in part to the absence of major geographical divisions with clearly antagonistic interests. Thus, there is no lowland-big-farmer group against which demagogues can rally an upland-poor-farmer area. While tremendous variations in types of economic activity exist in different areas of the state, a comparatively high level of prosperity prevails. Moreover, the state has no inherited sectional antagonisms, such as those growing in some states out of The War and the Populist rebellion. Or at least, if it has, they play no controlling role in the divisions among voters nowadays.

It might be supposed that East Texas, the home of most Texas Negroes, would be an area in which common concern about race would produce a regional political bloc comparable in its solidarity to the black belts of other states.[7] As the oldest-settled section of the state, East Texas profits from advantages in apportionment of legislative representation, and perhaps its political leaders have enjoyed the special status that goes to those first on the ground. Yet the region scarcely constitutes a sectional bloc as do some black belts. Several factors offer plausible explanations. East Texas is no solid bloc of counties with high proportions of Negroes. The area of Negro residence is broken by numerous counties in which blacks are outnumbered by whites more than three to one. Moreover, the usual black-belt economy of multiple-unit plantation agriculture has been diluted by other forms of economic activity. The odor from oil refineries settles over the cotton fields and makes scarcely perceptible the magnolia scent of the Old South.[8] Further, the settlement of West Texas, largely since 1900, created a huge territory with few Negroes and thereby reduced the significance in the state as a whole of those counties immediately and intensely concerned with the race question. In addition, the urbanization of the state, which by 1940 had made it the second most urban southern state, has had its effects on attitudes towards the Negro. By 1940, too, the state's population was only 14.4 per cent Negro (compared with 11.7 per cent Mexican-American in 1930), and the black belt, such as it was, had come to be overshadowed politically.

In explanation of the relatively amorphous character of Texas politics weight should be assigned to the great size of the state. Though it may not be so gargantuan as Texans assert, the political import of its great distances cannot be ignored. The personal followings of James E. Ferguson and W. Lee O'Daniel by no means constituted the sort of organization that exists in Virginia, Tennessee, Louisiana, or North Carolina. In any one-party state the erection of an institutionalized machine that almost amounts to a party is difficult enough; the effect of great distances in handicapping the consultation and negotiation necessary to develop and maintain well-knit organizations may increase that difficulty. Even the formation of state-wide personal followings is not easy; O'Daniel depended on the radio, and in 1948 Lyndon Johnson campaigned over the state in a helicopter. Some Texans contend, also, that the great expanse of Texas, by increasing the cost of campaigning, make large contributors both more essential and more importunate.

The upshot of the introduction of conservative-liberal debate into Texas politics in recent elections has been the formation of divisions of voters, at least superficially, unlike those elsewhere in the South. A loose, unorganized factionalism exists, somewhat on the order of that of Arkansas or Florida, yet the division of voters takes a form peculiar to Texas.

---

[7] In 1940 all counties with 15 per cent or more Negro population were north of Victoria and east of San Antonio.

[8] In 1946, 158 of Texas' 254 counties produced petroleum commercially.

SENATOR TOM CONNALLY OF TEXAS

Not all southern politicians are rabble-rousers.

HOUSTON SCENE

Southern urban Congressmen often vote with northern Democrats.

Instead of geographical cleavages that recur in other states, in recent elections competing candidates have shown an astonishing uniformity in popular strength from county to county over the entire state.[9] This sort of division of the popular vote suggests the hypothesis that voters divide along class lines in accord with their class interests as related to liberal and conservative candidates. Apparently, however, sharp divisions along class lines do not consistently occur in the balloting. That result may flow from the fact that even with the ideological clashes between Texas candidates, the one-party system does not assure that the electorate becomes keenly conscious of those differences. Or, of course, the conclusion could be that a liberal-conservative split between candidates need not be paralleled, in consonance with the doctrine of economic determinism, by a like division within the electorate.

2. Rural Demagogues

Political controversy in Texas since 1944 has been pitched on the broad level of progressive versus conservative government. While no such simple cleavage consistently appeared in earlier primaries and elections, it may be that the underlying conflict all along has been economic. It has not been clearly visible because the waters have been muddied by the high jinks of such leaders as James E. Ferguson and W. Lee O'Daniel.

As in other southern states, the years from about 1890 to World War I saw a continuous political dispute over regulation of corporations, taxation of business, public control of public utilities, and general governmental policy toward industry and industralization. Liberal sentiment of the time found its ultimate success on the national scene in the New Freedom of Woodrow Wilson; and in state governments, in the establishment of utility regulatory commissions, enactment of antitrust laws, prosecutions of foreign corporations for alleged violations of state laws, and the like.

During the Populist era and briefly thereafter the conflict was essentially of the same kind as Texans were campaigning about in 1944,

[9] Random comparison of widely separated elections suggests that variations in popular strength from county to county may have declined as politics took the form of a liberal-conservative debate. The percentages of the county votes for Dan Moody for governor in the run-off primary of 1926, for example, dispersed more widely from his percentage of the state total than did the county votes for Jester in 1946. Or, conversely, Jester's percentages of county votes clustered more closely around his percentage of the state total. The number of counties, in each case, within 5, 10, 15, and over 15 per cent of the state percentage were as follows:

	5%	10%	15%	OVER 15%
Jester	121	188	226	27
Moody	88	155	177	72

1946, and 1948. For the first two decades following The War the prevailing attitude in Texas toward business was friendly. While the majority of the people were farmers, agricultural distress did not become sufficiently acute until the late 'eighties to stir agrarians to political action. Then the Farmers' Alliance and the People's party focused attention on reforms to cure the farmer's ills and to call to account those held responsible for his plight: the railroads, which transported his crops; the financial houses, which held his mortgages; the trusts, which fixed prices on his supplies; businesses and creditors of any description that benefited from depressed farm values.

In 1890 James Stephen Hogg, attorney general and a Democrat, was elected governor on a platform vigorously attacking business abuses. He served four years and was succeeded by his attorney general,[10] Charles A. Culbertson, whose administration continued the policies and philosophy of Hogg, the great governor of modern Texas history. Hogg's influence extended over more than a decade. When Joseph D. Sayers took office in 1899, to be succeeded in 1903 by S. W. T. Lanham, a much more moderate and conservative government prevailed. Both gentlemen were ex-Confederates, the last to serve Texas in the governor's chair, and little disposed to wage the progressive battle commenced by Hogg. In 1906, however, Thomas M. Campbell, endorsed by Hogg, took up the fight. His administration strengthened antitrust legislation, instituted control over lobbies, provided for regulation of public utilities by municipalities, enacted a maximum hour law for railroad labor, adopted a pure food act, pushed measures permitting increased taxation, effected tax reform, and strived generally to make government better serve the mass of citizens. In 1910 reaction set in against Campbell's attitude toward organized wealth, and a government more friendly to business came to power under Oscar Branch Colquitt. Colquitt's successor in 1915 was James E. Ferguson, who posed as a "businessman's candidate" but who turned out to be quite different, or at least so thought the businessmen.[11]

Before the time of Ferguson, elections were contested on issues that held deep meaning for the people of Texas. How the state was to protect its citizens from organizations of wealth, what the state was to undertake by way of public services for its citizens, for what citizens these services were intended, and who should pay the tax bill—these are ultimately the

[10] In Texas, apparently more often than in other southern states, holders of minor, state elective positions become contenders for the governorship. Dan Moody in 1926 and James Allred in 1934 also graduated from attorney general. Lieutenant-governors and members of the railroad commission have been strong and sometimes successful contenders in recent campaigns for the highest office. The significance of various pools of talent from which states customarily draw their governors is a subject worthy of inquiry by students of political leadership.

[11] See Rupert Norval Richardson, *Texas: The Lone Star State* (New York: Prentice-Hall, Inc., 1943), pp. 325–419.

great concerns of democratic government, second only to the maintenance of the democratic processes themselves in their importance to the citizenry.

The Ferguson administration introduced a period of over two decades during which emphasis on economic matters diminished and other, often more dramatic, questions monopolized the voters' attention. The World War itself disturbed the normal pattern of political controversy, and the comparative prosperity of the 1920's reached enough people to assuage latent concerns about state economic policy. When the great depression struck, business and plain people alike found themselves in so desperate a plight that the effort to survive was not posed sensitively in terms of state policy toward business. The emergency actions of the New Deal absorbed the full attention and attracted the general support of the state and its politics. The dynamic program of the Roosevelt Administration, however, laid the groundwork for the conflict over broad philosophy of government, which appeared in the 1940's and which in its essence comprised the same fundamental issue that had predominated in the pre-Ferguson era: for whom is government to be run.

Just as the New Deal projected national issues into the internal politics of the state, likewise earlier Populism and Bryanism were potent influences in the formation of election alignments and in propelling critical questions to the fore in state politics. In the earlier period, Democratic factionalism, as reflected in the primaries for governor, had strongly tended toward a dual division, which gave the voters a simple choice between two alternatives. After 1918 there was a rapid increase in candidacies. This trend paralleled the political disintegration that took place in Florida, Arkansas, South Carolina, and other southern states. It produced the same difficulty in distinguishing between policy attitudes of candidates and gave them the same opportunity to evade issues. In Texas, perhaps more clearly than elsewhere, can be detected the re-emergence of alignments directly related to the broad governmental issues of the time.[12]

The period dominated by Ferguson and O'Daniel is subject to no simple characterization. While both men were rural demagogues, neither employed the cry of race as did their counterparts in other states. Skilled in the arts of swaying the multitude, their electoral successes often de-

---

[12] The character of one-party politics may differ markedly from time to time with the nature of the issues of national politics. Scattered evidence suggests that in periods of little national interest in issues, as in the 1920's, one-party factionalism becomes most chaotic and least organized. When political tension on the national level increases, the conflicts eventually percolate down into a one-party state and reflect themselves in a more tightly organized system of factions and in campaigns with issues more readily discernible. In the intervals of national political disinterest and one-party state disorganization, the electorate may be more susceptible to the depredations of demagogues with an irrelevant appeal. And, when issues become important, one-party states may exhibit considerable lag in adjusting their politics to the new realities.

pended on factors totally irrelevant to the welfare of the state or of even their own supporters. Yet their victories had a veneer of logic in that they posed as champions of the rustics, vaguely in the manner of Talmadge in Georgia.[13]

"Fergusonism" became an issue in itself. "Farmer Jim" was an enigma; a stem-winder on the stump, his methods and manners outraged many respectable Texans. He preached for the poor farmer, was impeached and convicted by the state legislature during his second term, and barred from again holding office "under the state of Texas." [14] Yet on more than one occasion he turned up on the side of liberal and democratic government. Ferguson was elected in 1914. His first important act was to have legislation adopted putting a ceiling on farm-tenancy rentals.[15] The law was held unconstitutional but it branded Ferguson as the farmer's friend. His most notable accomplishment was to increase state support for rural education. Though his 1917 impeachment made him ineligible, he ran in 1918 for governor and lost. He ran unsuccessfully for President in 1920 (on the ticket of his own American party, receiving 9.9 per cent of the Texas presidential vote) and for the Democratic nomination for Senator in 1922. Then he conceived the stratagem of running his wife for governor. ("Two governors for the price of one.") Mrs. Miriam Amanda ("Ma") Ferguson ran for the state's highest office in 1924, 1926, 1930, 1932, and 1940. She was elected in 1924 and 1932; "Pa" set up his office next to hers and was the actual governor.

The Fergusons were the liberals of the 'twenties, at least in Texas. The standards of liberalism change as public attention shifts from one public question to another. When prohibition was a subject of controversy, the liberal was wet. When the Klan rides, those who oppose it are liberal. Though personally dry the Fergusons were politically wet. In the 1922 senatorial campaign "Pa" scared the Klu Klux Klan. In the 1924 gubernatorial campaign the issue was the Klan. To their everlasting credit, the Fergusons were against it. Their stand attracted the support of many people who had regarded them with distaste before and would do so again. The narrow moralism of the prohibition and Klan doctrines assumed the right of some men, through the law or outside it, to regulate the private lives of other men. Ferguson shunned such pious presumption,

[13] They did not pit the "country" against the cities as did Talmadge, who enjoyed the inequities of the county-unit system. See above, pp. 117–124.

[14] Among the gravest charges against him were that he had appropriated to his own use certain state funds, that he was guilty of irregularities in the deposit of public funds in a bank in which he owned stock, and that he had accepted a "loan" of $156,000 from brewery interests which had never been repaid. Public opinion was organized against Ferguson because of actions prejudicial to the University of Texas.

[15] The proportion of Texas farms operated by tenants had been steadily rising and reached 52.6 per cent in 1910. Of 155 speeches in the 1914 campaign, only 10 were before audiences not comprised mostly of farmers.—Richardson, *Texas*, p. 407.

for whatever reason, and in addition was for a free-spending government to meet the needs, or so he claimed, of folks plain and poor.[16]

In the rollicking prosperity of the 'twenties, in a state enjoying a boom, politics was not characterized by the clear-cut issues of economic policy that dominated the Hogg-Sayers-Campbell-Colquitt era. Nor were there posed broad issues of governmental philosophy that have been prominent in more recent years.

Jim Ferguson, farmer, lawyer, and banker by trade, directed his campaign appeal (and that of his wife) to the rural voter. The Fergusons were elected by rustics. As has often been true of southern governors with vivid personal appeal, they produced little in the way of governmental action to justify the support. The Ferguson personality, dominating Texas political life for over two decades, distracted the voter's attention from other matters and caused him to think of politics in terms of his like or dislike for "Farmer Jim." "Ferguson men" swore by Old Jim. Yet he developed only a loose personal following, by no means comparable in discipline or consistency of attachment with the factions of Virginia or the parties of a two-party state. Popular belief that his most loyal adherents were the farmers at the forks of the creek tends to be borne out by statistical analysis. The counties that consistently gave the Fergusons their highest majorities were rural counties mainly in eastern Texas. (See Figure 51.) Moreover, few counties with cities of more than 5,000 ranked high among the state's counties in the proportion of their vote for Ferguson. He (or "Ma") did not always run well in rural counties, though they usually fared better there than in cities. (See Table 25.)

Jim Ferguson was perhaps the most important leader in the state's politics for two decades. Other governors there were, who, for the most part, were conscientious, able public servants. None, though, will be remembered in history for embracing a great cause or for any accomplishment that touched the hearts and minds of men. Nor did they develop an organized politics capable of ruling the state with decency and decorum. Perhaps they could not under one-party conditions. At any rate, they left no organizational obstacle to the rise of a mountebank alongside whom Old Jim looked like a statesman—and was.

Wilbert Lee O'Daniel, grandson of a Union veteran, born in Ohio, reared in Kansas, moved to Texas in 1925 as sales manager for a large flour mill. In 1935 he organized his own firm. He became widely known in Texas for his hillbilly band, which he directed on the air in a daily radio program advertising "Hillbilly" flour. His announcing, the poems and songs [17] he wrote, the folksy and religious character of the programs built

[16] "Ma" failed of re-election in 1926, in part because of the issuance of over 2000 pardons in 20 months and charges of irregularities in the maintenance and construction of highways.

[17] The most favored: *Beautiful, Beautiful Texas*.

up a wide popular following. He began to hold programs commemorating
the Constitution, honoring Texas heroes, and counseling on personal
problems. "Erring husbands were advised to correct their behavior,
school children were given good advice on thrift and conduct, traffic
safety was emphasized, childless couples were advised to adopt babies,

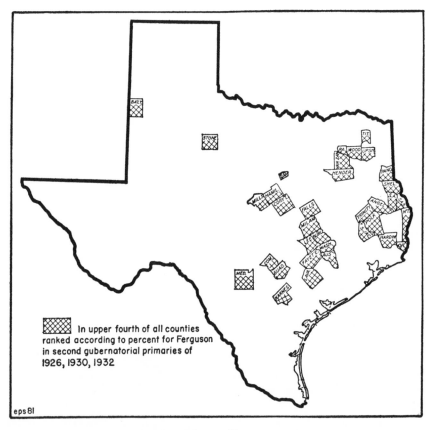

FIGURE 51

Areas of Consistently Heavy Majorities for Ferguson: Counties in Upper Quartile
in Percentage of Popular Vote for Ferguson in Texas Gubernatorial Primaries
of 1926, 1930, 1932

and religious and humanitarian movements and organizations were
supported." [18]

That by his skill in selling flour over the radio a man could become
governor and United States Senator is in itself an eloquent commentary
on the one-party system. No political organizations existed to obstruct the
rise of a political "outsider"; moreover, no factional cliques existed with

[18] Seth Shepard McKay, *W. Lee O'Daniel and Texas Politics, 1938–1942* (Lubbock:
Texas Tech Press, 1944), pp. 22–23.

power enough to name their own candidates. Attention-getting antics substituted for an organized politics. O'Daniel explains that he became interested in the governorship as a result of letters from his radio audience. On Palm Sunday 1938 he asked his listeners whether he should make the race. Messages, he said, from 54,499 urged him to run and only four advised to the contrary. With the backing of a number of wealthy businessmen—including Carr P. Collins, chairman of the board of the Fidelity Union Life Insurance Company, who had an aversion to one of the other principal candidates—"Pappy" O'Daniel was elected in the first primary over three major and nine minor opponents. His victory was

TABLE 25

Ferguson and the Rural Vote: Relation between Urbanization of Counties and their Ranking in Percentage of Vote for Ferguson in Second Democratic Primaries 1926, 1930, 1932 [a]

COUNTIES WITH TOWNS IN 1930 OF—	NUMBER OF COUNTIES IN CLASS	NUMBER TIMES COUNTIES IN EACH CLASS VOTED—	TIMES COUNTIES IN EACH CLASS WERE, IN ANY OF THREE RACES, IN—	
			TOP QUARTILE OF COUNTIES	LOWEST QUARTILE OF COUNTIES
25,000 or more	14	42	1	25
10,000 and none over 25,000	18	54	2	14
5,000 and none over 10,000	41	123	29	22
Counties wholly rural	126	378	117	85

[a] For each primary all counties were listed in the order of the proportion of the county vote received by Ferguson. The top quartile consists of the upper fourth of all counties in the order of the percentage of their vote for Ferguson and the lowest quartile consists of the one-fourth of the counties at the other end of the scale.

an upset. He had campaigned for the Ten Commandments, abolition of the poll tax, pensions of 30 dollars per month for all persons over 65, and he had opposed a sales tax. "Less Johnson grass and politicians; more smokestacks and businessmen." Though the pensions were not forthcoming and he urged a sales tax which he insisted on designating a "transaction tax," his popularity rose and he was re-elected in 1940 in the first primary.

In April 1941 Morris Sheppard died, leaving vacant a seat in the United States Senate. A special election (with no Democratic primary) was scheduled. Twenty-six candidates announced. The race resolved itself into a contest between O'Daniel [19] and Congressman Lyndon John-

[19] Like many a governor before, O'Daniel was faced with the problem of appointing an interim Senator who would not oppose him in the special election and whose ap-

son, who ran with the blessing of Roosevelt. The third candidate was Attorney General Gerald Mann and a poor fourth was Congressman Martin Dies. O'Daniel won with 30.7 per cent of the vote, leading Johnson by 1311 votes out of well over half a million cast, in an outcome that seesawed for days before the final results were known.

In the 1942 primary to select a nominee for the full six-year term O'Daniel was opposed by two former governors, both respected and liked, Dan Moody and James Allred. Allred, who had been the state's most constructive recent governor, was the first candidate to force O'Daniel into a run-off. He was narrowly edged out of the second race by O'Daniel. The victor was vigorously attacked for his isolationist sentiments, especially his vote against extension of the draft just before Pearl Harbor. As always, he found most of the press against him.

Like Ferguson, O'Daniel appealed most strongly to the rural voter. Most of the counties of his greatest consistent strength, however, are scattered over western and southern Texas, rather than East Texas, and like those of Ferguson they possess no identifiable pattern of common characteristics. (See the map in Figure 52.) Table 26 demonstrates that O'Daniel's popularity was lowest in counties with large cities and greatest in rural areas.

Emphasis on O'Daniel's appeal to the rural voters does not mean that he had no following in the cities: farmers were merely more nearly unanimous for him than were city folks. In October, 1940, Joe Belden's "Texas Surveys of Public Opinion" found O'Daniel's popularity at a peak. Yet on a poll to determine whether people "approved him as a governor," the degree of approbation varied among different social classes. The percentages of approval by contrasting groups were as follows: [20]

Farmers	77.6
Cities of 100,000 or more	69.2
Poorer voters	68.7
Above average income voters	57.9

O'Daniel's amazing political career came at least to a temporary end in 1948 when he declined to run for re-election. Opinion surveys early in 1948 indicated that he had lost favor with the public. Many of his financial backers began to look around for another favorite. Various factors

---

pointment would be accepted in public favor. He resolved the dilemma by probably the most ingenious appointment in senatorial history. On the one hundred and fifth anniversary of the battle of San Jacinto he named to the post General Andrew Jackson Houston, eighty-seven-year-old son of Sam Houston, hero of the battle. The General had been a Republican candidate for governor in 1892. The old gentleman was not in robust health. He managed to make the trip to Washington in the care of a nurse, took the oath of office, fell ill, and died in a Baltimore hospital while the campaign to determine his successor was at its height.

[20] Quoted by McKay, *O'Daniel*, p. 345.

entered into his decline, his lack of enthusiasm for war legislation sponsored by the Administration undoubtedly being important. Too, he seemed to lose touch with the people by his long absences from the state. Out of favor with the national Administration and possessing no independent standing, he could not "get things done" in Washington for his

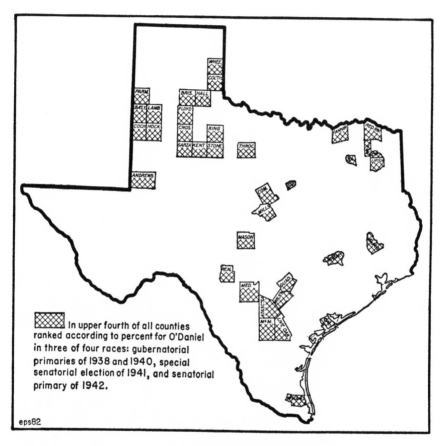

FIGURE 52

Areas of Consistently Heavy Majorities for O'Daniel: Counties in Upper Quartile of Counties in Percentage of Popular Vote for O'Daniel in Three of His Four State-Wide Races: 1938, 1940, 1941, 1942

constituents. The key to his fall, however, rests in the inherent contradiction of his career. He had drawn his chief support from the old folks, the poor, the farmers. As governor he had been ostensibly concerned with old-age pensions and taxes to finance them. In the Senate, however, his attitude on a wide variety of matters was consistently contrary to the interests of the people whose votes elected him. His voting record was more Republican than that of most Republicans,[21] which no doubt pleased many of the Texas "blue chip boys," among whom O'Daniel could always count ardent supporters. In 1944 he had campaigned for the Texas Regulars. By the curious processes of politics, which at times startle us with their directness, the people seem to have found they were being duped. One group, however, knew what it was getting in "Pappy" O'Daniel. In August, 1948, the state Republican convention nominated a candidate for United States Senator, but with the nomination went the

TABLE 26

O'Daniel and the Rural Vote: Relation between Urbanization of Counties and their Ranking in the Percentage of their Vote for O'Daniel in Democratic Gubernatorial Primaries of 1938, and 1940, Special Senatorial Election of 1941, and Second Democratic Senatorial Primary of 1942 [a]

| | | | TIMES COUNTIES IN EACH CLASS WERE, IN ANY OF FOUR RACES, IN— | |
COUNTIES WITH TOWNS IN 1940 OF—	NUMBER OF COUNTIES IN CLASS	NUMBER TIMES COUNTIES IN EACH CLASS VOTED	TOP QUARTILE OF COUNTIES	LOWEST QUARTILE OF COUNTIES
25,000 or more	17	68	1	53
10,000 and none over 25,000	22	88	6	31
5,000 and none over 10,000	43	172	27	23
Counties wholly rural	100	400	148	78

[a] For each of the primaries and for the special election all counties were listed in the order of the proportion of the county vote received by O'Daniel. The top quartile consists of the upper fourth of all counties in the order of the percentage of their vote for O'Daniel and the lowest quartile consists of the one-fourth of the counties at the other end of the scale.

stipulation that should Mr. O'Daniel ultimately prove willing to run the nominee would step aside for him.[22]

O'Daniel's races might be interpreted as an expression of the underlying division of the electorate along lines of economic self-interest. Had he been clearly a champion of the measures best understood as conducive to the welfare of the people who gave him most votes, emergence of a liberal-conservative split might have been discernible in Texas before the 1944 anti-Roosevelt uprising. As it was, O'Daniel's showmanship, like the

[21] O'Daniel ranks as the most Republican of southern Democrats. See Table 39 and the discussion below, pp. 360–62.

[22] Dallas Morning News, August 10, 1948. Of the 27 counties in which Republicans received 31 per cent or more of the 1940 presidential vote, 13 were in O'Daniel's highest quartile (66 counties) in 1941 and 15 were in his highest quartile in the second 1942 primary.

colorful antics of Ferguson, formed voters' attitudes largely by irrelevant appeals.

All in all, O'Daniel's career presents a puzzling phenomenon. Backed by a few wealthy men, he won the votes of many poor men. He talked the language of the lesser people, but on the whole he acted and voted about as a *Chicago Tribune* Republican. The people of two-party states have been duped on more than one occasion. For those who would speculate about the one-party system, the significant question is whether the irresponsibility and anarchy of a one-party system make it easier for a hillbilly band leader to get himself elected governor than do conventional arrangements.

3. The "Mexicans" and the "Germans"

The absence of national minority groups contributes to the fluidity that usually prevails in southern one-party systems. In the North and East national minorities with a persistent cultural and group identity have served as the basis of political organization. The South, however, has received relatively few immigrants, and the essentially Anglo-Saxon homogeneity of the white population has been perpetuated. There are some isolated exceptions.

The French preceded the English and Spanish to Louisiana and remain a culturally conscious and politically important minority. Latin Americans in Florida stamp the political climate in restricted parts of that state. Texas has two groups of distinctive national origin that arouse special curiosity. The Mexican-American, located chiefly above the border in the valley of the Rio Grande (see Figure 53), comprised 11.7 per cent of the population in 1930, the last year in which the census enumerated them separately. The "Germans" are numerous in a group of counties, roughly a circular configuration with its center southeast of Austin. The "German counties" get their name from settlers who fled Europe during and subsequent to the revolution of 1848.

The presence of large numbers of persons of Spanish and Mexican descent [23] along the Mexican border introduces special problems of political organization and produces special characteristics of electoral behavior.[24] The Mexican-American voters have been managed in the same way as national minority groups in major urban centers. For the most part they remain unassimilated into the cultural pattern of Texas. Many of

[23] The popular designation for these people is "Mexican." Many of them prefer to be called "Latin American." The term "Mexican-American" is used in this study as being most accurately descriptive.

[24] For a treatment of voter organization and the political environment in the lower Rio Grande Valley, see O. Douglas Weeks, "The Texas-Mexican and the Politics of South Texas," *American Political Science Review*, 24 (1930), pp. 606–27.

them do not speak English, have meager schooling, and have only the most remote conception of Anglo-Saxon governmental institutions. Often of low economic status, they are subject to the coercive influences usually brought to bear on depressed groups. Their social status lies somewhere between the "whites" and the Negroes. Their group pride contributes to

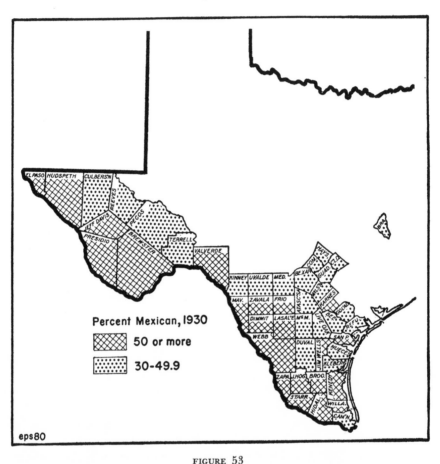

FIGURE 53

Distribution of Mexican-American Population in Texas by Counties, 1930

political cohesiveness and makes easier the task of the politician who would manage them. Mexican-Americans suffer unmistakable discrimination and some forms of segregation, though not to the same extent as Negroes. As might be expected, there occurs among the Mexican-Americans a high incidence of political indifference, ignorance, timidity, and sometimes venality.

There is a markedly lower voter participation in the counties with large numbers of Mexican-Americans than in other comparable counties.[25] It is explainable not alone by political indifference but also by voting requirements. Though disfranchisement measures have not been directed specifically at Mexican-Americans, their effective enfranchisement has often been brought about by individuals primarily interested in utilizing their votes. In many counties, unsponsored individual Mexican-Americans meet a barrier to the ballot similar in character if not in degree to that which discourages Negro voting in most of the South.

Several large and small political machines, famous for their success in delivering lopsided majorities, are built on the Mexican-American vote; they are confined mainly to the personal holdings of from 25 to 1000 votes of small-time bosses, or *jefes*. These political organizers have relied on the traditional techniques of ward leaders in dealing with immigrant groups everywhere: counsel in solving personal problems, aid in economic distress, patronage, assistance before governing authorities. The individual usually becomes qualified to vote at the behest of his *jefe*, who may pay his poll taxes and who often holds the tax receipts until election day to insure discipline and orderly procedure. Economic dependency often makes the control easier, and in south Texas there are large landholdings with whole communities employed on a single ranch. A corollary of such employer-employee relationships is political amenability, which simplifies the role of the political leader, sometimes a Mexican-American himself but often not. Where the Mexican-Americans are in a numerical minority their leader is often the politician who will serve as their spokesman in a community dominated by persons of other national origins. The larger the relative number of Mexican-Americans the greater is the chance that the boss will be one of their own number.

To a large extent the politics of the Mexican-American counties is necessarily a matter of negotiation with major and petty bosses. There is greater emphasis on the trade, the swap out, the *quid pro quo* than elsewhere in the state. The politician attempting to appeal over the heads of the local bosses encounters a remarkable degree of personal attachment that he cannot break through with funds or oratory. In negotiating with some *jefes* an ample supply of campaign funds is no handicap. It also appears that some bosses are fickle, and the candidate who gets there last with the cash or promise of favor sometimes cuts out an opponent who thinks he has already sewed up the vote.

The success of a machine can be measured best, perhaps, by the de-

[25] In the first Democratic primary for governor in 1940 there were 36 counties with cities of less than 45,000 population in which 32 per cent or less of the adult white population voted. Twenty-six of them had 30 per cent or more population Mexican-American in 1930. Of the 47 counties with 30 per cent or more Mexican-American population in 1930, 33 appeared in the lowest quartile of 1940 participation among Texas' 254 counties and 43 in the lower half.

gree of unanimity with which a vote is delivered and the flexibility with which it can be delivered to different candidates under different conditions. The most famous of all Texas machines is that of the Parr family in Duval County. It gained national prominence in 1948 along with neighboring Jim Wells County when Lyndon Johnson won the second senatorial primary by a state-wide margin of 87 votes. The vote in Duval was 4,622 for Johnson and 40 for Coke Stevenson. The boss of Duval and the leader in the 18-county twenty-seventh state senatorial district, is George Parr, rancher and oil operator, who inherited his domain from his father, Archie, the "Duke of Duval." Following the 1948 election George Parr took offense at complaints by Stevenson about bloc voting in Duval and surrounding counties. He pointed out that in four previous elections Stevenson had solicited his support and his counties had gone for Stevenson with about the same enthusiasm then as they voted for Johnson this time. "And I never heard a complaint from him then about the bloc vote in Duval County." [26]

Duval County's performance in a series of state races over a twenty-year period is shown in Table 27. Almost invariably the leading candidate received over 90 per cent of the vote. The voters showed a remarkable fickleness in attachment to particular candidates, the clearest indicator of a managed, or manipulated, vote. It can be seen from the table that insofar as picking the state winner is concerned Duval may not have always been right, but it was never in doubt. Duval County went wholeheartedly for "Ma" Ferguson in some elections and equally wholeheartedly against her in others. Similar vacillation affected Allred, O'Daniel, Stevenson, and others. Like the machine counties of Arkansas, Duval usually goes almost unanimously for a sitting governor seeking his second term although it may have been against him at his first election. Among other Mexican-American counties only Starr and Webb have a record of thus swinging back and forth as a unit. Their arcs, however, are not so wide as that of Duval, whose performance is indicative of the way election results can be obtained in such counties, although usually in much smaller blocs. Often within a single county the blocs will split so that the effect is to cancel each other out.

The so-called German counties of Texas, although they do not bulk large in the politics of the state, constitute an item of southern political curiosa that attracts attention because of the rarity of minority politics in the South. Somewhat like the mountain Republican counties of Tennessee and North Carolina, the German counties illustrate the remarkable persistence of partisan loyalties. Furthermore, they complicate the statisti-

---

[26] Mr. Parr also said he would welcome an investigation of the integrity of the vote.—*Dallas Morning News*, September 8, 1948. There are charges that in some counties the deliverable votes depend on manipulation of results as well as on an amenable electorate.

cal analysis of Texas voting, for they seem to vote differently than do other counties like them save for the heritage of national origin.

The German counties of today are not readily identifiable, for there is no way to determine the exact proportions of the population of German origin. A rough indication of their location is provided by the census of 1890, although, of course, shifts in population have altered the proportions of persons of German origin in each county since that time. This

TABLE 27

Manageability of Vote in Duval County, Texas, in Selected Elections, 1924–48

YEAR	DEMOCRATIC PRIMARY	FIRST CANDIDATE IN COUNTY	PER CENT	SECOND CANDIDATE IN COUNTY	PER CENT	STATE LEADER	PER CENT IN STATE
1924	1st Gov.	L. Davidson	98.2	W. Davidson	0.8	Robertson	27.5
1924	2nd Gov.	Ferguson	99.6	Robertson	0.4	Ferguson	56.7
1926	1st Gov.	Ferguson	97.9	Moody	1.5	Moody	49.9
1926	2nd Gov.	Ferguson	98.0	Moody	2.0	Moody	64.7
1930	1st Gov.	Miller	93.8	Sterling	3.8	Ferguson	29.2
1930	2nd Gov.	Ferguson	93.8	Sterling	6.3	Sterling	55.2
1932	1st Gov.	Sterling	92.4	Ferguson	6.0	Ferguson	41.6
1932	2nd Gov.	Sterling	92.0	Ferguson	8.0	Ferguson	50.2
1934	1st Gov.	McDonald	72.0	Small	16.2	Allred	37.5
1934	2nd Gov.	Hunter	96.8	Allred	3.2	Allred	52.1
1936	1st Gov.	Allred	96.7	Hunter	1.3	Allred	52.5
1938	1st Gov.	McCraw	84.0	O'Daniel	7.9	O'Daniel	51.4
1940	1st Gov.	O'Daniel	95.4	Thompson	2.6	O'Daniel	54.3
1941 [a]		Johnson	93.1	O'Daniel	4.0	O'Daniel	30.7
1942	1st Gov.	Stevenson	97.3	Collins	2.5	Stevenson	68.5
1942	1st USS	Allred	94.0	O'Daniel	5.0	O'Daniel	48.3
1944	1st Gov.	Stevenson	99.5	Porter	0.2	Stevenson	84.6
1946	1st Gov.	Sellers	95.8	Jester	2.0	Jester	38.2
1946	2nd Gov.	Jester	98.5	Rainey	1.5	Jester	66.3
1948	1st USS	Johnson	87.9	Stevenson	14.1	Stevenson	39.7
1948	2nd USS	Johnson	99.1	Stevenson	0.9	Johnson	50.0

[a] Special general election for U. S. Senate.

indicator, however, turns up a blotch of counties on the map in south-central Texas.

Historically, the German counties have inclined toward Republicanism. During The War they found themselves out of sympathy with their neighbors who would destroy the union to preserve slavery. The Germans were not slaveholders; they were liberals and revolutionists who took their American democracy literally. Their coolness toward the Confederacy brought reprisals in some areas, with the result that they were driven into a binding wedlock with Republicanism, as were recalcitrant groups elsewhere in the South. Their Republicanism persists and some of these counties had a hand in the election of Texas' lone Republican Congressman of recent decades. In the 'nineties, however, they shied away, unlike most southern Republicans, from coalition with the Populists, whom they considered prohibitionists and illiberals, though much in the People's party program had an appeal for them.

The clearest differentiation between the German counties and the remainder of the state occurs in their Republicanism and their wetness, as may be seen from the data in Table 28. An odd trick of fate placed the old 'forty-eighters in the dry and conservative Republican party of

TABLE 28

Voting Behavior of the "German Counties" of Texas: Selected
Primaries and Elections, 1926–46

PRIMARY OR ELECTION	STATE-WIDE	SEVENTEEN GERMAN COUNTIES		
		MEDIAN COUNTY	HIGHEST COUNTY	LOWEST COUNTY
Per Cent for Prohibition Repeal, 1935	54.2	83.0	95.7	38.2
Per Cent Republican, 1936	12.4	21.4	63.1	8.1
Per Cent Republican, 1940	19.1	46.0	86.0	15.0
Per Cent anti-Roosevelt, 1944 [a]	28.4	54.9	90.6	31.1
Per Cent for Ferguson, 1926	35.4	59.7	73.0	30.6
Per Cent for O'Daniel, 1942	51.0	64.3	80.0	49.6
Per Cent for Jester, 1946	66.3	75.8	85.5	44.9

[a] The anti-Roosevelt vote consists of the Republican vote plus the Texas Regular vote.

the 1920's. Party loyalties forged by The War held firmly, although when the issue of prohibition per se came along the German counties voted wet. In 1935 all but one of the counties favored repeal more heavily than did the state as whole.[27] The Fergusons usually ran more strongly in the German counties than elsewhere, a compound perhaps of their stand against prohibition and the Klan and their appeal to the farm vote. Consistently with their Republicanism, these counties usually gave more enthusiastic support to the more conservative Democrats, such as O'Daniel and Jester.

[27] The table omits the 1890 German counties of Bexar (San Antonio) and Travis (Austin), on the assumption that the influx of population has probably changed their population composition radically. The same change may have occurred in some of the other counties also, a factor that may account for the wide dispersion of the German counties on some votes.

Chapter Thirteen   # A NOTE ON
THE REPUBLICAN PARTY

AN Arkansas Negro leader of some note regularly votes, without challenge, in the Democratic primaries, yet he refuses to affiliate with the Arkansas Negro Democratic Association. Such a connection, he feels, would prove embarrassing to him when he turns up at the Republican state convention as a delegate and, even more embarrassing, when that great day comes, if it does, for the Republicans to distribute Federal patronage. In the Texas Democratic convention in 1946, by great effort a resolution was put through to exclude two delegates who had recently served also as delegates to the Republican state convention.

These cases are illustrative of the problem of talking about Republicanism in the South. One never knows who is and who is not a Republican. The party places no imperative obligation of constancy on its communicants. It scarcely deserves the name of party. It wavers somewhat between an esoteric cult on the order of a lodge and a conspiracy for plunder in accord with the accepted customs of our politics. Its exact position on the cult-conspiracy scale varies from place to place and from time to time. Only in North Carolina, Virginia, and Tennessee do the Republicans approximate the reality of a political party. Party or not, they are elements of the political landscape and some account has to be taken of them. There are, however, Republicans and Republicans. Perhaps the best approach to an understanding of southern Republicanism is to identify the different kinds of Republicans.

1. Presidential Republicans

Indigenous to the South is a strange political schizophrenic, the presidential Republican. He votes in Democratic primaries to have a voice in state and local matters, but when the presidential election rolls around he casts a ballot for the Republican presidential nominee. Locally he is a Democrat; nationally, a Republican. Some presidential Re-

TABLE 29

Presidential Vote in the South by States, 1944

STATE	DEMOCRATIC	REPUBLICAN	PER CENT OF 2-PARTY VOTE REPUBLICAN
Tennessee	308,707	200,311	39.4
Virginia	242,276	145,243	37.5
North Carolina	527,399	263,155	33.3
Arkansas	148,965	63,551	29.9
Florida	339,377	143,215	29.7
Texas	821,605	326,864 [a]	28.5
Louisiana	281,564	67,750	19.4
Alabama	198,918	44,540	18.3
Georgia	268,187	56,507	17.4
Mississippi	158,515	11,601 [b]	7.3
South Carolina	90,601	4,547	4.8

[a] Includes a vote of 135,439 for Texas Regular slate of electors, an anti-New Deal uninstructed slate.

[b] Total for both regular and Independent Republican slates.

publicans are genuine Republicans, who apologetically enter the Democratic primaries to fulfill a local civic duty.[1] Others are genuine Democrats who vote Republican nationally, with a touch of pride in their independence and a glance of condescension toward the benighted fellow who supports the Democratic ticket from top to bottom. In a few states the Democratic party has granted more or less official recognition to the presidential Republican by excepting the presidential candidates from the list of party nominees that the voter pledges himself to support in the general election when he participates in the Democratic primary.[2]

The extent of the infiltration of presidential Republicans into the

[1] This type of Republican is often an immigrant from the North. Many of them are gradually assimilated into the Democratic party. Other newcomers from Republican areas retain their Republicanism and would provide a substantial contingent of voters if the Republican organizations had anything to offer in the way of candidates. The immigrant Republican is most numerous in Florida, Arkansas, and Texas.

[2] See the treatment of this matter, below, pp. 429–30.

Democratic party is usually exaggerated, although no certain method exists for the estimation of their number. The excess of the vote for Republican presidential candidates over that for Republican candidates for governor or Senator may provide a rough estimate, if not of the absolute number of presidential Republicans, of their relative significance in the total Republican presidential vote from state to state. The data for the states electing a Senator or a governor in 1944 are presented in Table 30.[3]

Presidential Republicans probably constitute the largest proportion of the total Republican presidential vote in Texas, Arkansas, and Florida. In both Texas and Arkansas there are about as many presidential Republicans as there are full-fledged Republicans. In Texas, if one classifies the 1944 Texas Regular vote as Republican, the presidential Republicans

TABLE 30

Presidential Republicans: Excess of Republican Presidential Vote over Vote for Republican Candidates for Governor or Senator, 1944

STATE	PRESIDENTIAL VOTE	GUBERNATORIAL OR SENATORIAL VOTE	EXCESS	EXCESS AS PER CENT OF GUBERNATORIAL
Texas	326,824 [a]	100,547	221,394	220.2
	191,425		90,878	86.2
Arkansas	63,551	30,442	33,109	108.8
Florida	143,215	96,321	46,894	48.7
South Carolina	4,547	3,214 [b]	1,333	41.5
Tennessee	200,311	158,742	41,569	26.2
North Carolina	263,155	230,998	32,157	13.9
Alabama	44,540	41,983 [b]	3,557	6.1

[a] This figure is the total for both the Republican and Texas Regular slates.

[b] Senatorial votes.

outnumbered those of the true faith by about two to one. The Texas Regular, it may be said parenthetically, is a political species to be differentiated from Democrat, Republican, and presidential Republican. The Texas Regular slate of electors in 1944 was an anti-New Deal slate, uninstructed, put out to appeal to disgruntled Democrats unwilling to move over to the status of presidential Republicans.

The relatively large number of presidential Republicans in Texas and Florida reflects the comparative weakness of Democratic loyalties in

[3] Votes on Republican senatorial and gubernatorial candidates in nonpresidential years drop sharply and cannot well be compared with votes in presidential years by the method used in the table. Thus, the Republican candidate for governor in Alabama in 1942 polled 8,167 votes; the Republican candidate for Senator in 1944 polled 41,983 votes. An effective way to weaken a minority party is to schedule gubernatorial elections in nonpresidential years, a practice that exists in Virginia, Alabama, Mississippi, and South Carolina. In Louisiana gubernatorial elections are held in the spring of presidential years. Local minority candidates are thus deprived of the presidential coat-tail support.

these states. Both have large areas which, in contrast with other southern states, have only vague recollections of The War. In Texas Democratic solidarity is not re-enforced by the presence of large numbers of Negroes. Florida has a large immigrant Republican population which has not been well activated by the Republican organization.

The figures suggest that the presidential Republican is of least importance in North Carolina, Tennessee, and Virginia. In each of these states there is a continuing Republican party and the habitual Republican vote is sufficient to compel the Democrats to make a campaign of sorts for their ticket before the general election. The Republican threat—weak though it may be—probably serves to keep the Democrats in line for most posts on the ticket. In substantial areas the Republicans either control county governments or constitute a genuine threat to the Democrats. The traditional GOP partisans make up a large part of the Republican presidential vote.

In Louisiana, Mississippi, Alabama, Georgia, and South Carolina presidential Republicans are few indeed. They may bulk large in the total Republican presidential vote, whose small size, however, makes clear that Republicans of all kinds, dyed-in-the-wool as well as presidential, are few. In these Deep South states, with high proportions of Negro population and sharp recollections of The War, it still requires fortitude to vote Republican. Democratic candidates for governor and Senator do not always meet even pro forma Republican opposition.

Prevalence of the presidential Republican in considerable numbers in Texas, Florida, and Arkansas makes it relevant to point again to the significance of the Presidency as an organizing influence in state and local politics. The issues of the Presidency are dramatic enough to reach down into traditional one-party states and divide the voters. If Republican leaders of Texas and Florida had either incentive or ability, they might over the long run build a Republican party of the midwestern variety by using the pulling power of the presidential campaign.

2. Mountain Republicans

Unlike presidential Republicans, southern mountain Republicans regularly win elections or consistently threaten the Democrats. In the highlands from southwestern Virginia to northern Alabama and in the Ozarks of Arkansas they control local governments, elect a few state legislators and an occasional Congressman, and sometimes even make the Democrats fearful lest they lose control of their states. Unlike presidential Republicans, mountain Republicans are not hyphenated Republicans. They vote a straight Republican ticket election after election. Nor are the mountaineers Republicans by choice; they are Republicans by inheritance.

The principal concentrations of mountain Republicans are in southwestern Virginia, western North Carolina, and eastern Tennessee. In these states Republicans control a considerable number of county and municipal governments and send Republicans to the state legislature. Two eastern Tennessee congressional districts usually elect Republicans. Western North Carolina Republicans have on a few occasions elected their congressional candidates. In Virginia's southwestern congressional district Republicans and Democrats regularly fight over the congressional

TABLE 31

Proportion of Counties with High Republican Percentages of Popular
Vote in Presidential Election of 1944, by States [a]

STATE	COUNTIES 50 PER CENT AND OVER REPUBLICAN	COUNTIES 40–49.9 PER CENT REPUBLICAN	TOTAL NUMBER OF COUNTIES	PER CENT OF COUNTIES 40 PER CENT REPUBLICAN
Tennessee	34	9	95	45.3
Virginia	16	21	100	37.0
Virginia (independent cities)	2	4	24	25.0
North Carolina	15	17	100	32.0
Arkansas	4	9	75	17.3
Florida	0	7	67	10.4
Alabama	1	3	67	6.0
Texas	6	6	254	4.7
Georgia	2	5	159	4.4
Louisiana	0	0	64	0.0
Mississippi	0	0	82	0.0
South Carolina	0	0	46	0.0

[a] Based on Republican percentages of total vote as shown in Bureau of the Census, *Vote Cast in Presidential and Congressional Elections, 1928–1944* (1946).

seat; and national landslides have carried the Republicans at times to victory here as well as in the Shenandoah valley and in the district south of Norfolk.

Outside North Carolina, Tennessee, and Virginia, highland Republicanism is relatively weak. In northern Georgia, the Republican vote is heavy in several counties, but Fannin is the only county that regularly elects Republican officials. Similarly, several upland counties in northern Alabama poll a fairly good Republican vote, but only Winston County elects Republican local officials. In Arkansas, the Republican vote is heaviest in the Ozarks, but only two counties—Searcy and Newton—are controlled by the Republicans and one or two other counties occasionally elect local Republicans.

Mountain Republicans in all the southern states have a common origin. Before The War the small, upland farmer constituted a class apart from the lowland planters. The yeoman of the hills was reluctant to abandon the Union for the cause of the planter and his slaves. When the people voted on secession or related issues, the upland farmers, showed hostility toward secession or at least far less enthusiasm than the lowlands. When secession conventions were called delegates from the hills usually formed the bulk of Union strength. Even the planters were by no means unanimous: among them were strong Union men.

The legends of Winston County, Alabama, illustrate the relation of The War to mountain Republicanism. In this hill county there were in 1860 only 14 slaveowners who held among themselves 121 slaves. Most of the farmers tilled their own soil. Winston chose as its delegate to the secession convention, "Chris" Sheats, a Jeffersonian-Jacksonian candidate, who promised to "vote against secession, first, last and all of the time." "Chris" was in the minority down at Montgomery, and soon after he returned to Winston County six riders were dispatched in six different directions to summon the citizens to a mass meeting at Looney's Tavern on July 4, 1861, to decide what action should be taken. The mass meeting adopted resolutions, according to the Honorable John B. Weaver, local Republican patriarch, in substance as follows:

> We agree with Jackson that no state can legally get out of the Union; but if we are mistaken in this, and a state can lawfully and legally secede or withdraw, being only a part of the Union, then a county, any county, being a part of the state, by the process of reasoning, could cease to be a part of the state.
>
> We think our neighbors in the South made a mistake when they bolted, resulting in the election of Mr. Lincoln, and that they made a greater mistake when they attempted to secede and set up a new government. However, we do not desire to see our neighbors in the South mistreated, and, therefore, we are not going to take up arms against them; but on the other hand, we are not going to shoot at the flag of our fathers, "Old Glory," the Flag of Washington, Jefferson and Jackson. Therefore, we ask the Confederacy on the one hand, and the Union on the other, to leave us alone, unmolested, that we may work out our political and financial destiny here in the hills and mountains of Northwest Alabama.

Mr. Weaver reports in his two-column, "A Brief History of Winston County," that on the reading of the resolution, Uncle Dick Payne, one of the few Confederate sympathizers present, remarked: "Oh, oh, Winston secedes! The Free State of Winston!" And, in Alabama, the "Free State of Winston" it has been ever since. Mr. Weaver, reflecting the still-prevalent local sentiment, writes in anger that the Confederates would not let the Free State live in peaceful neutrality as it wished. Instead, the Confederate cavalry invaded the county, arrested those subject to the conscription act, and "gave them only five days to make up their minds to go and fight for the Confederacy, or to be shot in the back." It did not take long "for our people to change from an attitude of neutrality to one of indignation and hostility." And Mr. Weaver becomes as indignant to-day in recounting Confederate encroachments on Winston County during The War as Georgians do in recollection of Sherman's march.

The story of mountain Republicanism, in from 100 to 200 counties strung along the Appalachian highlands, is in essence the story of Winston County. The highland yeomanry did not want to fight a rich man's war; the Democratic party was, or at least became, the planters' party and the war party. The Democratic party forced the hills into The War, and for this it has never been forgiven. There is, of course, more than the recollection of war underlying the Republicanism of the hills. The natural political cleavage between lowlands and hills had found expression before The War.

In the states having substantial numbers of mountain counties controlled by the GOP, the Republican state party organizations have about as much vitality as the Democrats in some northern states in which they are a permanent minority. The strongest Republican state organization in the South is that of North Carolina. Governor R. Gregg Cherry in 1946, a whimsical reporter wrote, was "stunned by the subversive suggestion that North Carolina should have a two-party system." "What do you mean?" the Governor asked. "We've got one. Why, there are 300,000 Republicans in North Carolina. . . . There are some counties where we have ding-dong fights every year, and the Republicans are really tough in Presidential election years. Why, you know how strong they are west of Asheville; I'll have to go up there a couple of times before November 5." The Governor was referring to the necessity under which North Carolina Democrats labor of having to campaign against the Republicans, an indignity to which no other southern Democrats have had to submit with the same regularity since 1920.[4]

In turn, an official of the North Carolina Republican organization marvels at the way the Republicans can scare the Democrats in about 75 per cent of the counties. He sees no reason for it, but when Republicans show the slightest activity in the precincts, the Democratic party will sound off as though a major threat to its dominance had arisen and will campaign forcefully and actively. He spoke as though the Democrats bring out a meat ax to kill a mosquito. Although they constitute no imminent threat to Democratic control of the state government, North Carolina Republicans are enough of a danger to cause the Democrats to

[4] Burke Davis, "Gov. Cherry Thinks We've Enough Republicans," *Charlotte News*, October 11, 1946.

tighten their organization, to talk about the party as an entity that amounts to something, and to compel a much higher sense of party responsibility among Democrats than in any other southern state.[5]

Tennessee and Virginia are the other states with substantial numbers of local governments controlled by mountain Republicans, yet in neither does the party put the fear in the hearts of the Democrats that it does in North Carolina. Tennessee Republicans ought by all the rules of political arithmetic to be as influential as North Carolina Republicans, but they are not. The explanation seems to rest in a lower level of integrity of leadership. The Republican party, it may be startling to recall, was New Dealish in its early crusading days, and in the mountains it attracted the support of the lesser yeomanry, who disliked slavery but who also resented the control of government by and for the benefit of the people who lived in the big houses in the lowlands. The Republican fusion with the Populists in the 1890's was not solely a marriage of political convenience; the highlanders, Republicans though they were, were also democrats in the true Republican tradition and the heady Populist doctrines were good Republicanism.

Among top Republican leaders in North Carolina even today one senses an attachment to the ancient Republican traditions. In Tennessee, on the other hand, the Republican machinery was captured years ago by Carroll Reece, a Taft Republican, who is in political belief more of a Crump Democrat than a mountain Republican. In the minority factions of the organization leadership there are mountain Republicans, such as John W. Kilgo, 1944 Republican candidate for governor, but the Reece leadership has usually managed not to put forward candidates who might appeal to the old-time rebelliousness of the mountain Republicans. And in Tennessee, political gossip is common of deals between Republicans and Democrats; the Democrats concede a couple of congressional seats in return for which they meet only half-hearted opposition in gubernatorial and senatorial campaigns.[6] Whether these arrangements are explicit conspiracies or simply a tacit live-and-let-live understanding, the results are the same.

Virginia Republicans, although they are strong in a number of counties, make less of a show in state politics than either the North Carolina or Tennessee Republican organizations. Although there are occa-

[5] For a full discussion of North Carolina Republicanism, see above, pp. 218–223.

[6] In 1948 Mr. Reece guessed wrong before the national convention and supported Taft, while Republican Representative John Jennings, Jr., of Knoxville, guessed right and came out for Dewey before Philadelphia. Mr. Jennings had high hopes that Dewey as president would "recognize" those who so valiantly led the fight for him before Philadelphia. He announced that in this new era, "The present corrupt alliance between certain Republican Party leaders in Tennessee and Crumpism in Memphis will end."—*Memphis Press-Scimitar*, June 25, 1948.

sional reports of bipartisan deals between local Republican and Democratic leaders, Virginia Republicans are not in so strong a bargaining position as are those of Tennessee. The consensus of Democratic politicians consulted is that in the mountain counties of southwestern Virginia the Republicans are fighters, but that in most of the remainder of the state they are a faction of the Byrd organization. They and their "sound" leadership, as one Democratic politician put it, enter the Democratic primaries and support Byrd candidates.

In the three states with considerable areas of mountain Republicanism—North Carolina, Virginia, and Tennessee—the Republican party has the strongest foundation on which to build a competing party. The existence of a two-party system virtually requires a sectionalism or an urban-rural division of sentiment. Without territorial unevenness in distribution of strength the majority party must inevitably win all offices. Territorial divisions, however, assure to the minority seats in the legislature and control of some local governments. Areas in which the state-wide minority is the local majority provide a base for the maintenance of the party and for the recruitment and training of party leaders and candidates.[7]

The Republican party's embarrassment in these states is that expansion of its mountain vote into a majority would require the state organizations to adopt lines of policy contrary to those of the national party. To win, the Republicans would usually have to become the radical party, both to build up the enthusiasm of their traditional adherents and to recruit disgruntled Democrats. Traditional Republicanism in the hills has little in common with the manufacturing-financial orientation of the party nationally. To reflect faithfully its mountain constituencies the party would have to be more Populist than Republican in doctrine.

Mountain Republicanism should give pause to those who speak enthusiastically about imminent party realignments, who spin theories about the rational character of party attachments, and who talk about setting up a two-party system as though it could be made to order like a suit of clothes. Although the great issues of national politics are potent instruments for the formation of divisions among the voters, they meet their match in the inertia of traditional partisan attachments formed generations ago. Present partisan affiliations tend to be as much the fortuitous result of events long past as the product of cool calculation of interest in party policies of today.

[7] In all three states the Democratic majority in the legislature uses its control over local legislation to demoralize the Republican minority, small though it may be. The North Carolina Republican legislators, for example, regularly caucus and announce a general program at the beginning of the session. They soon cease talking about their general program when the majority bottles their local bills up in committee. In Tennessee the Crump majority indulged in the same tactics.

3. Negro Republicans

From Reconstruction until Franklin D. Roosevelt, most southern Negroes, insofar as they had partisan inclinations, were habitually Republican in the tradition fixed when they had a taste of political power. Eventually Negroes became about the only Republicans. They won control of the Republican machinery in several states, and in the process became valuable to the Republicans in the North as a symbol of the party's concern for the colored man. The Republican party in the South came to be branded as a Negro party and therefore unattractive to most whites. When whites moved into it, the issue of white versus Negro control of the party arose, and every state was plagued by the question of black-and-tan versus lily-white.

The intricacies of Mississippi Republican politics illustrate the uses of the southern Negro for the national Republicans and a type of Negro Republicanism that was earlier more prevalent in the South. Since about 1924 the chief officers of the Mississippi regular Republican organization have usually been Negroes; before that time a few white party officials led a predominantly colored group. Perry Howard, a Mississippi-born Negro lawyer resident in Washington, D. C., has been for many years the national committeeman. Dr. S. D. Redmond, wealthy Negro lawyer of Jackson, was, until his death in 1948,[8] chairman of the state executive committee, and Mary Booze, daughter of Isaiah T. Montgomery, amanuensis to Jefferson Davis and the founder of the all-Negro community, Mound Bayou, has served as national committeewoman. Always the organization has included a handful of whites, but Dr. Redmond in 1947 estimated that 85 per cent of the regular Republican voters were Negroes, an estimate that would put Negro Republican strength at considerably less than 5,000.

Perry Howard's black-and-tan party has been challenged over a couple of decades by a lily-white group led by George L. Sheldon, onetime Republican governor of Nebraska. When Sheldon moved to Mississippi in 1909, he called on the Republican chairman and told him that he wanted to join up. The newcomer was told that the Republican party in Mississippi was mainly Negro and that the Governor ought to line up with the Democrats. Since no good Nebraska Republican could backslide to the party of William Jennings Bryan, Sheldon stayed with the regular Republican organization until the old white leadership died off and Perry Howard took over.

Sheldon and a few other whites sought a way out of their predica-

[8] "The late Dr. S. D. Redmond, believed to have been the wealthiest Negro in Mississippi history, left an estate of $604,801.09."—*Birmingham Age-Herald,* August 13, 1948.

ment in 1927 and 1928. State Republican conventions had been conducted without meticulous regard for the laws governing party conventions. The postmaster would round up a fellow Republican or so, they would designate themselves as delegates, and go to Jackson to the convention. Sheldon obtained an injunction to restrain the Howard forces from holding a convention in violation of state law. He and his associates held their convention, with due regard for all the technicalities, which elected a delegation to the national convention including two Negroes as a gesture toward the sentiments of the national party. Howard, nevertheless, turned up at the national convention accompanied by a slate of delegates which was seated.

In the 1928 presidential election the Sheldon group put a slate of independent Republican electors on the ballot. The independent slate, profiting from the anti-Smith sentiment, polled 26,202 votes while the Howard-Redmond slate polled only 524 votes.[9] Sheldon's group persuaded itself that the Republicans of Mississippi had spoken and in 1932 set out to the national convention with a delegation; again Howard was seated. From 1928 to 1948, the independent Republicans regularly were rebuffed by the national convention in favor of the regular slate.[10]

Howard's operations as patronage referee for the Republicans in the 1920's brought down on the GOP a great deal of criticism and a resurgence of the belief that the southern Republican organization existed to sell patronage. Good Mississippi Democrats, to whom by official count 93 per cent of the patronage had gone, rallied to Howard's cause and kept him out of the penitentiary—in their opinion at least.[11] Further, Howard's own testimony about the sums—small though they were—that he had been "allowed" for political expenses by Hoover managers in the 1928 pre-convention dickerings kept alive the old story that southern Republican delegations were for sale, a characterization that must now be applied to southern delegates most selectively.[12]

Despite all Howard's troubles, the Republican national convention

[9] In the presidential elections of 1928, 1932, 1940, and 1944, the vote for the independent slate exceeded that for the regular slate.

[10] After the credentials committee in 1948 voted to seat Howard, Sheldon filed suit against convention officials, without success.

[11] A Mississippi Democratic politician relates that the government made certain that a conviction would not be obtained against Howard when it announced that 93 per cent of the patronage distributed under Howard went to Democrats. His acquital was made doubly certain when the government sent a lawyer from Washington to prosecute him. Another Mississippi politician relates that a Negro in his part of the state sold one post office that "stuck," i.e., was delivered, and then sold another that "did not stick." Whether the local Negro was duly authorized to sell post offices or was just running a racket, our informant could not say. At any rate, after the sale that did not "stick" the local people found it necessary to take a buggy whip to him one Saturday afternoon and he left the community.

[12] U. S. Senate, Hearings Before a Special Committee Investigating Presidential Campaign Expenditures, 1928, 70th Cong., 1st sess., Pt. III, pp. 718–35.

continued to seat his delegation and to recognize him as Republican national committeeman from Mississippi. The reason for all this is simple. Sheldon's independent Republicans espouse the cause of white supremacy quite as "steadfastly"—an adjective from their 1947 platform—as do the Democrats of Mississippi. To seat a Mississippi Republican delegation committed to Negro disfranchisement and to white supremacy would, so the reasoning goes, damage the Republican cause in the northern states. For decades the Republican party operated on the theory that all it had to do to retain Negro support in the North was to give a few seats in the national convention to southern Negroes.

Mississippi's Republican party is an anachronism and, now that the Democrats have most of the northern Negro vote, the GOP has little to gain by bearing the odium of such organizations. The recent shift in South Carolina Republican leadership illustrates a type of change that has been taking place over the South. For forty or fifty years the chief figure in South Carolina Republicanism was the late Joseph W. Tolbert. From 1900 to 1944 he was either a delegate or a contestant for a seat at every Republican national convention. Known as "Tieless Joe" ("I don't bother with nothing I can do without."), he was the son of a Confederate army captain, who, although bitterly opposed to secession, saw his duty and did it. He returned from The War to become a staunch Republican, and his son, a resident of the upcountry community of Ninety-Six, carried on the family tradition. His organization consisted of himself, a few other whites, and handpicked Negroes over the state, and its functions were to choose delegates to the national convention and to distribute patronage.

"Tieless Joe" made the South Carolina Republican party a national joke, and in 1938 J. Bates Gerald, a wealthy lumberman, formed another Republican group whose slate of delegates won recognition from the 1940 national convention. His organization remains the regular Republican party of the state. Its top leadership is white, but the organization is not lily-white in the manner of the Mississippi independent Republicans. "The South Carolina Republican party is not a private club," Mr. Gerald says. "It is a recognized organization composed of the best citizens of both races." [13] Negroes hold posts in its local units, and a Negro or so is usually included in the delegation to the national convention. Mr. Gerald's faction early won the support of important figures in the South Carolina Negro community. They had little esteem for Tolbert. "I didn't want," says a Negro woman, "a dirty old man for my leader." If they were to have a white leadership, they preferred a more respectable type. (Negroes are sharp judges of quality.) So the Negro college presidents, lawyers, doctors, and many of the businessmen went over to the new Republican party, and, amusingly enough, the white leaders have a defensive pride in the quality of their Negro membership: He has a couple of hundred thousand

[13] Press Release, February 16, 1947.

dollars and, "as one southerner to another, you know that is quite a bit of money for a Negro in the South."

The official Republican party does not go unchallenged. Remnants of the old Tolbert faction contest the official slate at the national convention and attempt to maintain an organization in the state. The chief leaders of the so-called Tolbert-Leevy-Hendrix faction are B. L. Hendrix, white, another lumberman, of Estill, but not a native South Carolinian, and I. S. Leevy, Negro undertaker of Columbia. This group in 1947 and 1948 set to work organizing "Lincoln Emancipation Clubs" over the state in an attempt to supplant the regular organization. All this activity was in anticipation of a 1948 Republican victory which would have made control of the organization worth while. The national convention seated the regular delegation.[14]

Apart from Mississippi, whites have taken control of the Republican organizations. White supremacy in the Republican party came in part as a result of the recognition by the Hoover Administration of white factions as patronage referees, a policy flowing from southern support of Hoover in the 1928 election and from the hope that under white leadership a Republican party might be built up in the South. There are, however, degrees of lily-whiteism among southern Republican organizations. The Mississippi independent Republicans stand four-square with their Democratic brethren on the race question. Some other southern Republican organizations are equally white but indulge in no flamboyant denials of Negro rights. Others have a few Negro party officials and customarily take along a few Negro delegates or alternates to the national convention as a gesture in memory of Abraham Lincoln. As a Florida Republican leader observes, "We have resolved the racial difficulty by 'taking in' the right kind of Negroes. By giving them representation the issue has been kept down." Others, such as Alabama, Virginia, and North Carolina, usually do not make the gesture.[15]

Several southern Republican organizations in 1948 put themselves on record against at least parts of President Truman's civil rights program. In 1948 the Tennessee convention expressed a belief in "the unobstructed exercise by every citizen of all the civil rights guaranteed by the Constitution" but looked "with apprehension upon the efforts of misguided theorists and political opportunists to have the federal government take over the ballot boxes, election laws and public schools of the state." [16]

[14] At the 1944 presidential election the regular Republican slate of electors drew 4,547 votes; the Tolbert slate, 63.

[15] In 1936 Alabama, Florida, North Carolina, Texas, and Virginia had no Negroes in the national convention delegation. Arkansas, Georgia, Louisiana, Mississippi, South Carolina, and Tennessee had a total of 43 Negro delegates and alternates. In 1940 Alabama, North Carolina, and Virginia had completely white delegations, and the other states had a total of 27 Negro delegates and alternates, 11 of whom came from Mississippi.

[16] *Memphis Press-Scimitar*, April 30, 1948.

Arkansas Republicans denounced the proposed FEPC as a "glaring example of invasion of the rights of the states and of curtailment of the freedom of individual citizens—all in violation of the constitution of the United States." [17] The Texas Republican state executive committee adopted a resolution condemning the entire civil rights program.

Lily-white and black-and-tan factional politics, of course, has no particular interest for most Negroes; [18] it concerns only those who would like to be convention delegates, party functionaries, or patronage farmers. Many Negro votes have since 1932 moved over into the Democratic party and, more important numerically, those Negroes who have just begun to vote have started voting as Democrats. Most of the remaining Republican Negroes are older persons who, as an Alabama Negro says, consider it heresy for the younger and newer voters to go Democratic. In North Carolina, Republican officials complain, Democratic registrars in some localities decline to register Negroes as Republicans and the Negroes, sensitive to realities, calculate that they had better string along with the dominant Democratic organization. From place to place, however, one finds Negroes of prominence who manage to keep a foot in both party camps. [19]

A columnist for a Florida Negro newspaper explains the drift of Negroes to the Democratic party:

> In the good old days of our fathers, all southern Negroes were Republicans. It was a crime bordering on treason for a Negro to talk about being a Democrat. . . .
>
> The southern Democrats were very happy to let us love our Republican gospel, and they encouraged us in the worship of Abraham Lincoln in the hope that we would become so doped with this doctrine of the "Republican party is the ship, all else is the sea," that they could forever keep on running the city and the county and the state governments.
>
> But some Negro woke up and saw through things and began to shout to our white friends to come over and share the wealth and take half of our Republican gospel and give us half of the city and the county and the state monies for sanitation and pavement and school facilities and the like.
>
> Why, brethren, we were having a good time yelling about Father Abraham, but catching hell with our slum districts, because the men who issued out the money were elected in the Democratic primaries. We Lincoln children had nothing to do with the primaries, so we got no money and when we got our petitions together and worded them with our favorite "whereas" and concluded with our delightful "Therefore, be it resolved," our white friends in the political job just tossed them in the waste baskets and kept on their merry ways of ignoring the Republican children.

[17] *Arkansas Gazette* (Little Rock), May 15, 1948.

[18] An inquiry of a Florida NAACP leader about Negro Republicans brought the straight-faced response that he was not interested in patronage and therefore was not acquainted with Republican politics.

[19] For a discussion of Negro Democratic organizations, see below, pp. 647–50.

Then, there came along some rebellious young Negroes who had read some history and found out that our fathers didn't know exactly what they were saying about Father Abraham and his great humanitarian love for Negroes, and so, they said we ought to look at the present moment.

The old folks kept shouting about the past and what had been done for us, so the young upstarts quoted the Bible from Paul who told them to forget the things behind them and reach toward the things before. That stumped the fathers because they never did learn how to defeat a Bible argument. . . .

Then they started talking common sense about the men we live with every day. They said, "why Mr. Jones, the county commissioner is my boss-man. He is a fine man but he is a Democrat. He is in a little fight and if we could help him, he would help us." That argument started to making sense, until after while, some smarter fellows said we ought to crash the Democratic primary because that's where all the issues have been settled since the days of Henry Grady.

Now, if anybody thinks we ought to leave this Democratic ship and jump back into the Southern Republican skeleton and help put some meat on its bones, they have got some more thought coming. Brethren, we had too hard a time getting on this ship and we are going to stay, sink or swim.[20]

The loss of the Negro vote is of no real concern to the Republican organizations since they are not vote-getting organizations, but some southern Republicans toy with the idea of bringing the Negroes back to the GOP. One Republican state chairman says that the party is now open to them, "We have nothing against the niggers," but he expects few of them to take advantage of the open door. His familiarity with the Negro community was illustrated by his supposition that the editor of the leading Negro newspaper of the state, a red-hot New Dealer, was a Republican. In other states one encounters white Republican leaders with about the same degree of political skill who express some interest in regaining the Negro vote.

National Democratic policy since 1932 has definitely ended the Republican monopoly of Negro support even in the South. It is, of course, doubtful whether the Republican party has ever been helped materially in the North by its recognition and maintenance of Negro organizations in the South. Battles in the national convention to seat southern Negro delegations have been pictured to the Negro as a fight by his white Republican friends on his behalf. Southern Republican leaders, however, indicate that the Negro's great friends in such contests have been motivated more by the way the delegation proposed to vote on the presidential nomination than by abstract concern over Negro rights. Nevertheless, an incidental by-product over the years has been a Negro national committeeman or two for display to the colored voters of doubtful states.

[20] C. Blythe Andrews in *Florida Sentinel* (Tampa), November 29, 1947.

4. Republican Leadership

Southern Republican leaders—save those who get themselves elected to local offices—are not politicians in the usual sense of the word. They might be called palace or bureaucratic politicians, since their chief preoccupation is not with voters but with maneuvers to gain and keep control of the state party machinery, an endeavor that requires convention manipulation at home and intrigue with national party leaders up North. So complex is Republican factional politics in some states that only those with a high order of skill in palace politics can stay on top for long. Staying on top is fundamentally the result of playing one's cards right with the national leadership, for the "official" state Republican leadership is so by virtue of its recognition by the party's national convention and by Republican presidents. Primacy within the state has little to do with winning support of the Republican rank and file.

The stakes in control of southern Republican organizations nearly all turn on their relations with the national party; no southern Republican leader entertains seriously the notion that his party will during his lifetime gain control of his state government. Presidential aspirants, invariably nonsouthern, are interested in control of state organizations only because of the votes they can deliver in national conventions.[21] Those inside the states are interested in control of the organizations because of the local Federal patronage that they control when their party wins the Presidency. Southern Republican leaders are usually pictured as vultures awaiting the day when the party wins the nation and they can distribute patronage in the South. Meantime, they exert themselves only to keep the party weak in the South in order that there will be fewer faithful to reward. Thus an old-line Virginia Republican leader some years ago quenched the enthusiasm of a young upstart who wanted to build up the party by the observation that already they had more deserving Republicans than jobs. Such an attitude is thought to be characteristic of southern Republican leaders, but they are not all patronage farmers or would-be patronage farmers. The old-time patronage referee has pretty generally died off; since 1932 there have been no jobs to distribute.[22]

Although the character of top-drawer Republicans differs from state to state, southern state-wide GOP leadership since 1932 has become more

[21] The attractiveness of southern organizations to outsiders has been lessened by a series of steps beginning in 1916 which reduced the South's representation in Republican national conventions. A move in the rules committee of the 1948 convention to reduce still further representation from states polling few Republican votes failed of adoption.

[22] "It's a wonder we have a skeleton force left after being pushed away from the trough for 15 years," B. L. Noojin, Alabama Republican national committeeman, concluded at a southern Republican conference held at Cobbstead, the Lake Hamilton country showplace of Osro Cobb, Arkansas Republican state chairman.—*Arkansas Gazette* (Little Rock), March 15, 1947.

THE SOUTHERN DEMOCRATIC-REPUBLICAN COALITION

Senator Harry F. Byrd, of Virginia, with Earl Bunting, president of the National Association of Manufacturers, 1947.

ATLANTA NEGROES PETITION FOR NEGRO POLICE

The urban Negro meets less obstruction to political action.

typically a business leadership, quite as ineffective as the old-time patron-age type but nevertheless different. The Republican chairman or national committeeman is apt now to be a businessman, of considerable wealth, who frankly regards his Republicanism as a hobby, an expensive hobby. He derives great satisfaction from the quadrennial overtures of the presidential candidates for his support; he cherishes memories of visits from their emissaries and is particularly elated when he can tell of his conversations with Tom Dewey, Harold Stassen, Bob Taft, or some other Republican big shot. In his office there is likely to be prominently displayed autographed photographs of such party bigwigs. In conversation he is apt to make occasion to refer with quiet pride to letters he has just received from Herbert Hoover or Joe Martin. If the conversation proceeds long enough, he will refer to the high quality of persons in party positions in the state and to the respectable character of recent candidates: This man has a million dollars; that man is a big operator; another has a string of eight banks.[23] These party officials often have only the foggiest notion where the Republican voters in the state live and who they are. Most of them are overwhelmed by the futility of it all, but they keep the faith in a quiet spirit of dedication not unlike that of the Britisher who, although living in the jungle surrounded by heathen, dresses for dinner.

Not all southern Republican leaders are of the new business type. Most state organizations have their share of the old-time patronage seekers, but it is quite wrong to speak of most top-level southern Republican leaders as persons who sell their national convention votes. Most of them are prominent, respected, solvent citizens; they may do a little bargaining but they do not need to sell their votes.[24] The usual state organization has

[23] The anxiety of Republican party officials to give the financial rating of their inner circle appears with such frequency in conversation to warrant special note. Whether this is a defensive reaction against the long-standing reputation, well deserved, of nonrespectability of southern Republican politicians or simply political naivete, we cannot say. It is reported for what it is worth. Thus one state chairman mentioned numerous people prominent in the party and with considerable pride pointed out each man's wealth. One state chairman mentioned, for example, that their last gubernatorial candidate had been a man of great respectability and a man of means. Another candidate had made a huge amount of money in coal; another, a substantial profit in oil. They had, he said, a few farmers but they owned many thousands of acres. In another state a Republican leader pointed to the party treasurer, "a man with half a million dollars." In another state the chairman spoke with deep admiration for men who had served in party posts. One was "terribly capable"; he had made more money in one year as a salesman than any other man in American history. Another had been a partner in a respected private banking house. When Louisiana's former state chairman, J. Paulin Duhe, announced for Congress in 1948 he made his status clear: president of the New Iberia National Bank, head of the Duhe, Bourgeois Sugar Company, president of the Edmundson-Duhe rice mill, third vice-president of the American Sugar Cane League, and president of the St. Martin-Iberia-St. Mary Flood Control Association.— *Times-Picayune* (New Orleans), August 1, 1948.

[24] An Arkansas Republican leader volunteered the information, for example, that Arkansas has never in his day accepted money from the candidates for the Republican presidential nomination, "not even expense money."

its quota of lesser leaders who fit the old-style conception. Usually, for example, a few Republican lawyers around the state occupy posts as county chairmen and as members of the state executive committee. The lawyer periodically assembles the local Republican party in his office and it elects him as the delegate to the state convention. He gets some free advertising, lives in hope of a district attorneyship, perhaps a judgeship, and has the chance of professional advantage as a Washington fixer during Republican administrations. A Georgia Republican patriarch observes that except for a small group of wealthy men at the top the party is riff-raff interested only in patronage.[25]

The infiltration of business leadership into the top levels of Republican organizations has given them a more respectable façade but often has not changed the basic character of the party hierarchy. In Georgia, for example, Wilson Williams, textile machinery manufacturer, served as national committeeman from 1940 to 1948. Mr. Williams, a man of vigor with high hopes for the development of a two-party system, considers himself a fish apart from many other southern Republican leaders. Many of them dislike him intensely because he adheres to the notion that the party in the South should exist for something other than delivery of convention votes and allocation of patronage. In 1946 he proposed, as a means of reducing the deliverability of southern convention votes, the holding of Republican presidential primaries in the South. The reaction from many leaders in other southern states was "something fierce." The primary, they feared, would replace the closed-club arrangement whereby a little clique manages state conventions and delivers the delegates. It would strike at the roots of their power, and perhaps attract more Republican voters; hence the howl. Even within his own state, Mr. Williams failed to carry his organization along with him in his desire to make a real campaign in a mountain district where the GOP seemed to have a fighting chance to win a House seat.

Texas is one of the few states that retain the old-style, patronage-minded top leadership, and there business Republicans have challenged the power of R. B. Creager, state Republican boss. Early in 1947 a group of Dallas Republicans, led by Capt. J. F. Lucey, oil man, set up the Republican Club of Texas and announced a plan to organize "cells" of "aggressive Republican sentiment in every precinct of every county of the

[25] The formal organization of most Southern Republican parties is a paper affair. State leaders will brandish a list of county chairmen and state committee members but then readily concede that only a few of them are "active." A notable exception to the rule that Republican leaders carry around the party headquarters in their hats is found in Miami, Florida. There a permanent clubhouse with a full-time secretary was established in 1948 ("a $35–40,000 development, and at a good address"). Miami Republicans could well afford to finance the undertaking, which seemed to operate independently of the state headquarters.

state." [26] Creager issued a statement suggesting that he did not believe the base rumor that the Republican Club leaders sought to gain control of the state organization to enable its promoters to hand-pick delegates to the 1948 convention. "Full faith and credit," he said, should be given to their announced purpose of strengthening the party and making Texas a two-party state.[27]

The Republican old guard considered the Texas Republican Club a threat to its position. The insurgent leaders regarded the regular Texas Republican organization as similar to the handiwork of a Japanese gardener whose greatest accomplishment is the growth of a stunted plant. Creager's forces, experienced in the control of the party machinery, outmaneuvered the "Dallas millionaires." The Republican Club, for example, unsuccessfully promoted legislation to check the abuse of proxies in the control of state conventions. A leader in the Creager faction advised all county chairman that "a millionaire element in our party is sponsoring this legislation." [28] In June, 1947, Creager's state chairman, George C. Hopkins, removed Ralph W. Currie, as Dallas County Republican chairman, and replaced him with an appointee favorable to the Creager leadership. In July, 1947, the state executive committee further purged the regular organization by ousting its general counsel and state finance chairman.[29] In 1948 Creager firmly controlled the state convention, which declined to seat county delegations unfavorable to Creager who desired to send a Taft delegation to the national convention. Nothing in the operations of the Creager organization dispels the Texas belief that it desires no electoral victories. A Republican representative or so might be elected by vigorous campaigning. In 1946 in the congressional district at the northern end of the Texas Panhandle, a Republican candidate polled a respectable vote in a campaign in which the regular organization was conspicuously inactive.

Those who picture southern Republican leaders as engaged in a conspiracy to keep down the Republican vote, of course, misrepresent the situation. In few places do they have to try hard to keep from winning elections. On the other hand, Republican organizations in the South—save perhaps those of Virginia and North Carolina—make little effort to get people into the habit of voting Republican. The way is long and hard.

[26] Gerald Cullinan, "Republican Activity in Texas," *Southern Weekly,* January 18, 1947, p. 3.

[27] *Southern Weekly,* January 25, 1947.

[28] The *Two-Party News,* organ of the Republican Club, June, 1947, replied: "It is perhaps wise to point out also that the millionaires Mr. Hopkins so bluntly accuses are members of the board of directors of the Republican Club of Texas. Those few members of the board who are millionaires are products of the American way of life. They were born in humble circumstances and made their way to the top through industry and perseverance."

[29] *Dallas Morning News,* July 31, 1947.

"There's no use fooling ourselves about" winning any seats in South Carolina in the congressional elections, J. Bates Gerald, the Republican state chairman announced in 1946. "So we're offering no candidates in the general election, in order that every cent of money contributed in the state can be sent into doubtful states to finance campaigns there." [30] In 1947 John E. Jackson, Louisiana Republican national committeeman, urged Republicans to refrain from running for state and local offices in order that they might contribute funds and work to elect a Republican President and Congress in 1948.[31] The elder statesmen of southern Republicanism consider it good sense to spend their money in doubtful states rather than waste it in hopeless campaigns. The execution of this policy requires some restraint on the youthful enthusiasm of those who would make gallant but losing races at home.

Concern of state Republican organizations with raising money for campaigns up North results partly from the pressure of the national headquarters, which assigns to each state a quota to be raised for the congressional and presidential campaigns. The national organization has been no more concerned than the patronage-minded state leader in building up the party in the South. It encourages the state leaders to devote their energies to raising funds to be spent in doubtful states.[32] It does not treat the South as a foreign mission which, of necessity, must be subsidized if converts are to be made. Instead it milks the missionaries to help maintain the mother church. National leaders come down occasionally and make speeches about the great advantages of the two-party system. They hesitate, however, to finance a campaign, even when the Republican candidate has a fighting chance to win or when the Republican organization could gain strength by sustained effort over a period of years. The Republican national committee is so parsimonious that it does not always provide southern organizations with as much literature as they could use during a presidential campaign. One party official, denied an adequate supply from headquarters in 1944, even went so far as to have campaign literature reprinted locally.

This Republican leader possessed exceptional initiative. More common is the type described by an Arkansas GOP bigwig who commented that the Republicans of Arkansas are proud of their leaders, most of whom are successful businessmen. They are not politicians and are not desirous of office. They are sound, reputable people—and undoubtedly

[30] *News and Courier* (Charleston, S. C.), October 2, 1946.

[31] *Times-Picayune* (New Orleans), September 8, 1947.

[32] The aggregate of reported contributions in sums of $500 or more from Texas to the 1944 anti-Roosevelt campaign was $220,915. Contributions in smaller sums and unreported gifts undoubtedly brought the total flowing out of Texas to aid the Republican national campaign to well over a quarter of a million dollars. Southern Republican leaders indicate that it is far easier to raise money for the presidential campaign than for state campaigns. "They are practical businessmen who do not want to see their money wasted by being spent locally," explains one Republican leader.

they are. They are honest, and, again, undoubtedly they are. The people, however, who build political parties are politicians. They are keenly desirous of public office, an honorable ambition, perhaps the most honorable of all ambitions. Only through the clash of such ambitions can the ideals of democracy be approached.

Chapter Fourteen | NATURE AND CONSEQUENCES
OF ONE-PARTY FACTIONALISM

DㅤㅤㅤIFFERENCES in the factional systems of southern states are far more arresting than their similarities. Only in a limited sense is it possible to speak of "the" one-party system. Commonly, of course, discussion of the one-party system has concerned the attachment of southern states to Democratic presidential candidates rather than the internal factional competition within the Democratic party of the South. From the former aspect southern states could be dismissed with the observation that they are all alike politically. From the standpoint of the character of their factional systems, however, southern states differ widely. Although for groups of two or three states fundamental similarities are identifiable, each state has marked peculiarities of political organization and structure.

In the running of state governments—in the determination of what is done, for whom it is done, when it is done, and who pays for it—factions of the Democratic party play the role assigned elsewhere to political parties. Usually democracies rely principally on the political party as an instrument to provide leadership. Parties put forward candidates for office, advocate particular courses of governmental action, and, if their candidates win, create enough of a sense of joint responsibility among various officials to aid them in the fulfillment of a group responsibility for the direction of government.

The South really has no parties. Its factions differ radically in their organization and operation from political parties. The critical question is whether the substitution of factions for parties alters the outcome of the game of politics. The stakes of the game are high. Who wins when no parties exist to furnish popular leadership?

1. Types of One-Party Politics

To appraise one-party factions as instruments of popular leadership requires a comparison of the results of one-party and two-party systems. Differences in governmental action under the two systems might be attributed to dissimilarities in political organization. The problem thus phrased presupposes that one-party systems are alike, but they are not; that two-party systems are alike, but they are not. Moreover, two-party states have not been subjected to intensive analysis and the essential facts for the comparison are lacking.[1] One-party states, however, vary in the degree to which their factional systems approach the nature of a two-party system. North Carolina, for example, is in reality quite as much a two-party state as some nonsouthern states, while Arkansas and South Carolina present examples of one-party factionalism in almost pure form. Hence, comparisons of the workings of different types of southern factional systems along with casual allusions to commonly understood features of two-party politics ought to yield some sort of estimate of the significance of the southern one- or non-party system.

To make such a comparative analysis requires a recapitulation that differentiates the salient features of the factional systems of the eleven southern states. At one extreme of southern factional organization lie the states of Virginia, North Carolina, and Tennessee. Even these states fit no single pattern exactly, but all have been characterized by a relatively tightly organized majority faction within the Democratic party. In all three the majority faction has had a long life and something of a corporate or collective spirit. In each the majority has been opposed by a minority Democratic faction far less cohesive than the majority faction. Of the three, Virginia perhaps has had the weakest opposition faction. In Virginia and North Carolina the majority faction has been representative of the upper half of the economic scale, an upper half inclusive of more industry and finance than commonly exists in southern states. Crump's Tennessee machine, on the other hand, reflected a less-stable political combination than the majority factions of North Carolina or of Virginia. Although it had the support of business generally, it rested

---

[1] We express, out of scientific curiosity rather than agreement with the "you-are-another" school of southern thought, concurrence with the defensive remark of a southern judge, "Why don't you study the politics of northern states?"

in large measure on the tenuous coalition of a bossed Memphis and patronage-fed machines of eastern mountain counties.

The cohesiveness of the majority faction in these states points to the extraordinary influence of even a small opposition party. In both North Carolina and Tennessee the majority Democratic factions derive unity from the opposition of Republicans; in both states the Democrats of the counties with substantial Republican votes accept state leadership and discipline in the battle against a common foe. Virginia's extremely low voter participation makes it difficult to determine much about the nature of its politics, but the chances are that the Virginia Republican minority has a significant bearing on the unity of the majority faction of Democrats in Virginia. In all three states Republican opposition contributes to the creation of one tightly organized Democratic faction. By the same token existence of one relatively cohesive faction generates within the Democratic party an opposition group, producing something of a bi-factionalism within the dominant party.

The remaining eight states possess no outstanding features that suggest obvious classifications into sub-groups. Each of the eight differs from the others, yet from time to time similar characteristics emerge, at least for short periods, in all of them. The eight states vary widely in the degree to which their factional organization approximates a bi-factional division, as measured by the tendency of voters to divide into two camps in the first gubernatorial primary.[2] Georgia tends toward a dual division while at the other extreme the electorates of Mississippi and Florida fractionalize into many groups. While the tendency towards multifactionalism represents a significant aspect of the political structures of the eight states, other characteristics of factional organization and disorganization contribute to differences in their political structure.[3]

In North Carolina and Tennessee a cohesive minority party vote contributes to the development of disciplined and continuous Democratic factions. Other explanations must be sought for cohesive factions that arise in the absence of a substantial minority party. Georgia and Louisiana represent instances in which relatively cohesive majority factions have been built around personalities. Eugene Talmadge was a powerful organizing force in Georgia politics and his influence has continued in his son. Huey Long in Louisiana likewise was a potent influence in the division of the electorate into two opposing camps. In both Georgia and Louisiana factors other than personalities have contributed to the organization of political factions. Georgia's county-unit system created conditions favorable to a leader such as Talmadge who could rally the

[2] An analysis of this point was presented above at pp. 15–18.

[3] An institutional factor that may stimulate multifactionalism is the requirement of majority, rather than plurality, nominations. The run-off or second primary, in which a majority is required to nominate, may encourage a multiplication of factions and candidacies in the first primary. See below, pp. 416–23.

whites of rural counties, many of them in the black belt, and at the same time garner the support of urban finance and industry. A minority could be converted into a continuing faction around a spectacular leader. In Louisiana, on the contrary, a leader such as Long could build around a group of poorer rural whites a radical faction with a relatively high degree of cohesion and continuity. In some respects—such as the "ticket" system symbolizing the combination of candidates for all state posts and many legislative offices—Louisiana factionalism more nearly approaches the organizational realities of a two-party system than that of any other southern state. In all probability the long-standing machine of New Orleans—in whose operations the "ticket" system had to be an integral part just as are "organization slates" in the work of urban machines elsewhere—had an important influence in habituating voters to factional unity in campaigning and in the operation of state government.[4] Similarly, Memphis may have influenced Tennessee's factional form.

The remaining states—South Carolina, Alabama, Mississippi, Arkansas, Texas, and Florida—enjoy a far more chaotic factional politics than the states that have been mentioned. These six states cannot, of course, be differentiated sharply from those with tighter political organization, nor are they themselves uniform. Nevertheless, certain patterns of behavior recur in them and provide clues to the nature of their politics.

In marked contrast with two-party politics, these states manifest varying degrees of multifactionalism. The tendency toward a dualism—often acclaimed as a great virtue of American politics—is at times replaced in these states by a veritable melee of splinter factions, each contending for control of the state somewhat after the fashion of a multiparty system.[5]

Those states with loose factional systems usually also have factional groupings of the most transient nature. Cleavages among voters form and reform from campaign to campaign depending on the issues and candidates involved. In extreme situations only the most shadowy continuity of faction prevails, either in voter grouping or in composition of leadership. This discontinuous and kaleidoscopic quality of faction contrasts markedly with the stability of electoral loyalty and the continuity of

---

[4] In a sense the New Orleans machine, with a large proportion of the state vote in its constituency, may have had an effect on Louisiana factional structure similar to that of the Republicans of western North Carolina in that state. The New Orleans machine, out of the necessities of urban politics, backed candidates for all state offices; whatever group was in opposition had to do the same. Hence, a force may have existed productive of competition between more or less unified factions involving the collaboration of many candidates instead of the more usual southern custom of autonomous candidacies.

[5] Of course, within each party of a two-party state factions exist. They are, however, usually less numerous than are those of a one-party state, and they ordinarily possess a degree of continuity and a discernible policy orientation that differentiate them from the fluid and discontinuous factions of a highly disorganized one-party state.

leadership of true political parties. It also differs, of course, from the factionalism of such states as Virginia and North Carolina.

Among the influences determining factional alignments in particular campaigns an important place must be assigned to localism. A local potentate or a leading citizen of a county who takes a notion that he wants to be governor polls an extremely heavy vote in his own bailiwick. In two-party states the force of party tradition and the strength of party cohesion minimize, although they do not entirely erase, localism. A faction built around a local following perhaps differs little in principle from a personal faction. In one instance the personal following happens to be geographically localized; in the other it may be scattered over the entire state.

Beyond localism—whose potency may be an indicator of the absence of a class politics or at least the disfranchisement of one class—economic and social groupings at times express themselves despite the confused factionalism. The projection of these economic differences into factional politics becomes most apparent at times of crisis—crises generated by economic depression or created by the appeal of a candidate. They disappear with a decline in social tension only to be replaced by confused alignments explicable on no rational grounds.

The alignment that most often forces its way into southern factional politics is the old Populist battle of the poor, white farmer against the plantation regions. In South Carolina, occasionally the Piedmont and plain battle it out; in Mississippi at times the lines form between the delta and the hills; in Alabama the black belt unites against the predominantly white counties of the northern and southern parts of the state. In Louisiana, Huey Long rallied the farmers of the northwestern hills as the most loyal element of his coalition, which included urban workers but few plantation operators. In Georgia, the lines have been confused but most of the diehard Talmadge counties have been in the black belt. In all these situations the counties with many blacks and many multi-unit farming operations tend to ally themselves with big-city finance and industry as well as with the top-drawer people of the smaller cities and towns. By no means, however, are such meaningful lines always drawn in these states.

2. Limitations of Factional Leadership

When one-party factionalism is reduced to a few adjectives descriptive of its form—multifaceted, discontinuous, kaleidoscopic, fluid, transient—it becomes in appearance a matter of no particular import. Nevertheless, these characteristics point to weaknesses of profound significance in one-party factions as instruments of popular leadership and, by contrast, point to the extraordinary importance in the workings of popular government of political parties, imperfect though they may be. Although it is the custom to belittle the contributions of American parties, their performance seems heroic alongside that of a pulverized factionalism.

Consider the element of discontinuity in factionalism. Although conditions differ from state to state and from time to time, in many instances the battle for control of a state is fought between groups newly formed for the particular campaign. The groups lack continuity in name—as exists under a party system—and they also lack continuity in the make-up of their inner core of professional politicians or leaders. Naturally, they also lack continuity in voter support which, under two-party conditions, provides a relatively stable following of voters for each party's candidates whoever they may be.

Discontinuity of faction both confuses the electorate and reflects a failure to organize the voters into groups of more or less like-minded citizens with somewhat similar attitudes toward public policy. In political discussion a high value is placed on the independent voter who claims to be free of party loyalty in casting his vote, but the fact is that the consistent party supporter may be acting quite as rationally in the promotion of his political interests as the independent. Under a system of fluid factions, however, the voters' task is not simplified by the existence of continuing competing parties with fairly well-recognized, general-policy orientations. That is, this party proposes to run the government generally in one way; the opposition, another. Factions that form and reform cannot become so identified in the mind of the electorate, and the conditions of public choice become far different from those under two-party conditions. The voter is confronted with new faces, new choices, and must function in a sort of state of nature.

American politics is often cynically described as a politics without issue and as a battle between the "ins" and the "outs." In a system of transient factions—in its most extreme form—it is impossible to have even a fight between the "ins" and the "outs." The candidates are new and, in fact, deny any identification with any preceding administration. Without continuing groups, there can be no debate between the "ins" and "outs" on the record. Party responsibility is a concept that is greatly overworked, but in a fluid factional system not a semblance of factional responsibility exists. A governor serves his tenure—fixed either by constitution or custom—and the race begins anew. The candidates are, as completely as they can manage it, disassociated from the outgoing administration. The "outs" cannot attack the record of the "ins" because the "ins" do not exist as a group with any collective spirit or any continuity of existence. Moreover, the independence or autonomy of candidacies means that legislative candidates are disassociated from the gubernatorial races, and if the electorate wants to reward the "ins" by another term or to throw the rascals out—if electorates behave that way—it has no way of identifying the "ins." All of it may come down to the proposition that if one considers some southern state governments as a whole, there is really no feasible way of throwing the rascals out.

The lack of continuing groups of "ins" and "outs" profoundly influences the nature of political leadership. Free and easy movement from loose faction to loose faction results in there being in reality no group of "outs" with any sort of corporate spirit to serve as critic of the "ins" or as a rallying point around which can be organized all those discontented with the current conduct of public affairs. Enemies of today may be allies of tomorrow; for the professional and semiprofessional politician no such barrier as party affiliation and identification exists to separate the "ins" from the "outs." No clique, given cohesion by their common identification as "outs," exists to scheme and contrive for control of the government. Under two-party conditions when Republicans control, leaders carrying the Democratic label are definitely out and have in common at least a desire to oust the Republicans.

When two distinct groups with some identity and continuity exist, they must raise issues and appeal to the masses if for no other reason than the desire for office. Whether the existence of issues causes the formation of continuing groups of politicians or whether the existence of competing groups causes the issues to be raised is a moot point. Probably the two factors interact. Nevertheless, in those states with loose and short-lived factions campaigns often are the emptiest sorts of debates over personalities, over means for the achievement of what everybody agrees on.

Not only does a disorganized politics make impossible a competition between recognizable groups for power. It probably has a far-reaching influence on the kinds of individual leaders thrown into power and also on the manner in which they utilize their authority once they are in office. Loose factional organizations are poor contrivances for recruiting and sifting out leaders of public affairs. Social structures that develop leadership and bring together like-minded citizens lay the basis for the effectuation of the majority will. Loose factions lack the collective spirit of party organization, which at its best imposes a sense of duty and imparts a spirit of responsibility to the inner core of leaders of the organization. While the extent to which two-party systems accomplish these ends are easily exaggerated, politicans working under such systems must, even if for no other reason than a yearning for office, have regard not only for the present campaign but also for the next. In an atomized and individualistic politics it becomes a matter of each leader for himself and often for himself only for the current campaign.

Individualistic or disorganized politics places a high premium on demagogic qualities of personality that attract voter-attention. Party machinery, in the advancement of leaders, is apt to reject those with rough edges and angular qualities out of preference for more conformist personalities. Perhaps the necessities of an unorganized politics—lacking in continuing divisions of the electorate and in continuing collaboration of partyworkers—provide a partial explanation for the rise to power of some of the spectacular southern leaders.[6] No group with any sort of internal cohesion or capacity to act exists to put forward leaders and to fight for their election. The candidate for state-wide office must win by his own exertions, his own qualities. On occasion the essentially personal power of political leaders may have consequences far more serious than the production of picturesque governors and Senators. A state leader whose fortunes have been cast over the years with a fairly compact political group which he is bound to consult on decisions of major import is apt to be a different kind of governor from one whose power rests more completely on his own qualities, demagogic or otherwise. Organization both elevates and restrains leaders; disorganization provides no institutional brake on capriciousness when the will in that direction is present. The frequency with which some southern governors have brought the National Guard into play on matters involving no question of public order suggest the possibilities. Individual factional leaders, unrestrained by organizational ties or obligations to political colleagues, may have all the erraticism of Mexican generals of an earlier day.

Factional fluidity and discontinuity probably make a government especially susceptible to individual pressures and especially disposed toward favoritism. Or to put the obverse of the proposition, the strength of organization reflecting something of a group or class solidarity creates conditions favorable to government according to rule or general principle, although it is readily conceded that such a result does not flow invariably. In a loose, catch-as-catch-can politics highly unstable coalitions must be held together by whatever means is available. This contract goes to that contractor, this distributor is dealt with by the state liquor board, that group of attorneys have an "in" at the statehouse, this bond house is favored. Such practices occur in an organized politics, to be sure, but an organized politics is also better able to establish general standards, to resist individual claims for preference, and to consider individual actions in the light of general policy. Organized groups—with a life beyond that of the particular leader—must perforce worry about the future if they are to survive. Individualistic leaders of amorphous groups are subjected to considerations of a different order.

Weak and kaleidoscopic coalitions built around individual leaders produce in the operations of government itself a high degree of instability. In the work of state institutions and in the programs of state gov-

---

[6] Personality is everywhere significant in political leadership, but the chances are that in the American milieu, spectacular demagogues flourish most luxuriantly under local conditions of social disorganization or flux, and these localities are not confined to the South.

ernments uncertainty and insecurity rise as a gubernatorial campaign approaches. The erratic changes in personnel and policy associated with control by a succession of unrelated and irresponsible factional groups make the consideration, much less the execution, of long-term governmental programs difficult. Consequently groups concerned with particular governmental agencies indulge in all sorts of constitutional and statutory dodges to insulate the agency that concerns them from "politics," with the result that most southern state governments become disintegrated mechanisms incapable of moving forward on a broad front.[7]

All these propositions do not apply to all southern states all the time. Their general validity, however, can be indicated by contrast with the politics of those states to which they are least applicable. North Carolina and Virginia have tightly organized factional systems as southern politics goes.[8] In each the dominant faction has a relatively high degree of continuity. A genuine battle between recognizable groups of "ins" and "outs" occurs. The strength that comes from factional cohesion enables the governments of these states to avoid much of the favoritism and graft that often—but not always—occur in loose, personal factionalisms. Adventitious observation of the two states gives the impression of a fundamentally more responsible official attitude, one that seems to be connected with the sense of corporate responsibility of the controlling organization for the management of public affairs.

Even on the question of race, both states have a far different atmosphere from most southern states. This difference comes in part from other factors, but the relevance of the nature of political organization should not be underestimated. A cohesive faction has the power to discipline wild-eyed men. A chaotic factionalism provides no block to unscrupulous and spectacular personalities. The kinds of individuals thrown into positions of state-wide leadership in North Carolina and Virginia over the

[7] Comparative analysis of some southern and some northern states suggests the inference that theorists of the state reorganization movement have by and large failed to see the relation of political organization to the problem of state administrative organization. A state such as New York adapts itself to an integrated state administration under the direction of a governor who is the leader of a relatively cohesive and responsible party. A governor in a loose factional system does not have organized about him social elements necessary to produce enough power to control the entire state administration. Nor does he occupy a position as party leader that makes him appear sufficiently accountable to warrant vesting him with broad authority for the direction of administration. On the other hand, in such states as Virginia and North Carolina, a comparatively well-disciplined factional system provides a political base for a fairly well-integrated state administration. It should not, however, be forgotten that an integrated administration may, in turn, contribute to factional discipline because of its concentration of the power to reward.

[8] Both states also have a relatively high degree of centralization of functions in the state governments which may contribute to factional discipline. On the other hand, the existence of organized, state-wide factions with a state-wide point of view may be an essential prerequisite to the centralization of functions in state government.

past thirty years contrast markedly with many of those who have risen to power in states with more loosely organized politics.[9]

The significant question is, who benefits from political disorganization? Its significance is equalled only by the difficulty of arriving at an answer. There probably are several answers, depending on the peculiar circumstances in each case. Politics generally comes down, over the long run, to a conflict between those who have and those who have less. In state politics the crucial issues tend to turn around taxation and expenditure. What level of public education and what levels of other public services shall be maintained? How shall the burden of taxation for their support be distributed? Issues of public regulation and control have, of course, varying importance from time to time and place to place, and occasionally the issue of democracy itself arises, but if there is a single grand issue it is that of public expenditure.

It follows that the grand objective of the haves is obstruction, at least of the haves who take only a short-term view. Organization is not always necessary to obstruct; it is essential, however, for the promotion of a sustained program in behalf of the have-nots, although not all party or factional organization is dedicated to that purpose. It follows, if these propositions are correct, that over the long run the have-nots lose in a disorganized politics. They have no mechanism through which to act and their wishes find expression in fitful rebellions led by transient demagogues who gain their confidence but often have neither the technical competence nor the necessary stable base of political power to effectuate a program.

In speculation about the broad theme of political conflict it has to be kept in mind that the scales in the have-have-not conflict have been tipped by the exclusion of a substantial sector of the have-not population —the Negroes—from effective participation in politics. Similarly substantial numbers of whites of the have-not group do not vote but the extent to which suffrage limitations are responsible for their nonvoting is debatable.[10] The have-have-not match is settled in part by the fact that

[9] A loosely organized politics with no stable centers of power or leadership for an entire state is in one sense admirably suited for dealing with the Negro question. A pulverized politics decentralizes power to county leaders and county officials and in some areas devolution is carried even further in that public officials do not cross the plantation boundary without invitation and government is left to the plantation operator in his domain. In a granulated political structure of this kind with thousands of points of authority there is no point at which accountability can be enforced. Private and semi-private acts of violence can be subjected to no real check. By the same token, a disorganized politics makes it impossible for a state really to meet the obligations that its leaders assert it undertakes with respect to a dependent people. Loud protestations that "we are doing something about the Negro"—which contain more truth than is commonly supposed—have no buttress of political power to support a systematic program for dealing state-wide with the race question.

[10] The suffrage question is explored at length below, chaps. 25–30.

substantial numbers of the have-nots never get into the ring. For that reason professional politicians often have no incentive to appeal to the have-nots.

Within this framework of a limited suffrage, at times state-wide campaigns are but personal rivalries uncomplicated by substantial social and economic issues. The issue becomes one of who is the "best man" or the "most competent" man to carry out what everyone is agreed upon. In a broader sense, the politics of such a situation amounts to control, whatever governor is in office, by the conservative groups of the state who squabble among themselves for the perquisites of office, which are, after all, relatively minor in the total flow of income and in the total status system of a society. In a sense the absence of issues comes from the fact that these groups are unchallenged; when someone stirs the masses issues become sharper. Under such a chaotic factionalism, it is impossible to make any rational explanation of how the people of a state vote in terms of interest. They are whipped from position to position by appeals irrelevant to any fundamental interest.

A loose factional system lacks the power to carry out sustained programs of action, which almost always are thought by the better element to be contrary to its immediate interests. This negative weakness thus redounds to the benefit of the upper brackets. All of which is not to say that the upper brackets stand idly by and leave to chance the protection of their interests. A loose factionalism gives great negative power to those with a few dollars to invest in legislative candidates. A party system provides at least a semblance of joint responsibility between governor and legislature. The independence of candidacies in an atomized politics makes it possible to elect a fire-eating governor who promises great accomplishments and simultaneously to elect a legislature a majority of whose members are committed to inaction. The significance of an organized politics appears starkly when Louisiana, for example, is contrasted with Texas or Florida. The Long faction in 1948 came into power with a legislative majority (under the "ticket system") committed to a program of increased public expenditure—old-age assistance, school outlays, and so forth. The legislature convened and through factional discipline promptly put through a program of legislation. In a state with looser factional organization the powers of obstruction in a legislature elected quite independently of the governor are enormous.[11] In the whole scenario of southern politics the legislature undoubtedly plays an important obstructive role that warrants more investigation than it has received.[12]

[11] In Florida, a state with an extremely disorganized politics, one hears, for example, stories of a man in the background of state politics who is the representative of an important eastern financial group with local interests and who functions as a collector and distributor of campaign funds for legislative candidates.

[12] One matter of great significance peculiar to the South is the effect of malapportionment. Everywhere discrimination against cities in legislative representation inflates

Although individual corporations, individual industries, and particular groups, if they are skillful manipulators, can gain great immediate advantage in the chaos of a loose one-party factionalism, it is by no means clear that the upper brackets generally can depend on a disorganized politics to look out for their interests. They can expect no sustained attack from the lesser peoples, who lack organization, but they cannot rely on a disorganized politics to dispense its favors among all those of the upper brackets impartially. The upper brackets can look forward themselves with greater confidence to equitable treatment—as among themselves—in the security of an organized politics. The great risk is that when they are organized, they become targets for attack and they become in a sense accountable—because they have a means to act—for their governance of the state. Furthermore, organization begets counterorganization and business runs the risk that the organization with which it is affiliated may be superseded by another with power to act. Even a dominant conservative organization must from time to time accede to discontent to remain in power.[18]

All in all the striking feature of the one-party system, the absence of organized and continuing factions with a lower-bracket orientation, is but one facet of an issueless politics. This is not to say that a stream of rebelliousness does not run through southern politics. The factional system simply provides no institutionalized mechanism for the expression of lower-bracket viewpoints. By chance and by exertions of temporary leaders and connivers, candidates are brought into the field, but no continuing, competitive groups carry on the battle. The great virtue of the

---

the strength of the coalition of urban financial interests and rural conservatism. In the South, however, this inflation is magnified by the fact that malapportionment is compounded by the inclusion of nonvoting Negroes in the population of legislative districts. Consequently an extremely small number of whites of the large-farming class in the black counties control an extremely large number of legislators. It is these large agricultural operators—not white farmers generally—who are most disposed to ally themselves with finance, utilities, and such industry as the South has. Thus, a few whites in the Mississippi delta, along the South Carolina coastal plain, and in the Alabama black belt exercise a greatly disproportionate power in state legislatures.

[18] A study by Clarence Heer of taxation of manufacturing corporations in North Carolina, Virginia, Tennessee, South Carolina, Georgia, and Alabama wound up with the conclusion that in the median city of each state "a corporation earning 2 per cent on its investment would have a lower tax bill in North Carolina than in any of the other five states except Virginia. At a 10 per cent rate of earnings, its tax bill in North Carolina would be lower than in any neighboring state except Virginia and Tennessee. At a 20 per cent rate of earnings, three states, Virginia, Tennessee, and South Carolina would offer more favorable tax treatment." In another study, James W. Martin and Glenn D. Morrow call attention to the relatively low level of taxation in the South in relation to taxable capacity, perhaps an index of the effect of a disorganized politics on the level of public services. They also point to the relatively large share of southern state revenues derived from consumer taxes, an indicator perhaps of the effect of a disorganized politics in the allocation among classes of the burden of tax action.— *Taxation of Manufacturing in the South* (University, Alabama: Bureau of Public Administration, University of Alabama, 1948).

two-party system is, not that there are two groups with conflicting policy tendencies from which the voters can choose, but that there are two groups of politicians. The fluidity of the factional system handicaps the formation of two such groups within the southern Democratic party, and the inevitable result is that there is no continuing group of "outs" which of necessity must pick up whatever issue is at hand to belabor the "ins." Even in such states as Virginia, North Carolina, and Tennessee the "outs" tend to be far less cohesive than do the "outs" of a two-party state.

Students of politics tend to express impatience with an issueless politics. They impute virtue to the conflict inherent in a politics of issues and fail to emphasize that the practicing politician—one-party or two-party—spends an extremely large portion of his time in ignoring, repressing, postponing, or composing differences. The raising of issues, the exploitation of differences, always starts a battle. It stirs up opposition and may bring an untimely end to a career in office. The chances are that the one-party or nonparty system facilitates the combination of those satisfied with current arrangements and encourages as well the inclination of the politician to let sleeping dogs lie.

While much political conflict may not be a "good thing," the danger point has not been approached in the South. A modicum of political conflict probably aids in the maintenance of the health of a capitalistic order. Within the capitalistic society, the tendencies in negation of competition, toward the maximization of short-run returns to the immediate holders of power, constitute a powerful drive toward self-strangulation. Economic competition alone may not serve to maintain a healthy ruling class; a continuing political challenge compels a defense and a strengthening of a ruling class. The upper bracket that goes unchallenged develops privileges and repressions destructive of mass morale and often restrictive of the potentialities of the productive system. And ruling groups have so inveterate a habit of being wrong that the health of a democratic order demands that they be challenged and constantly compelled to prove their case.

3. Effects of Isolation from National Politics

It seems clear that the factional organization within the Democratic party of the southern states fails to provide the political leadership necessary to cope reasonably well with the governmental problems of the South. In their weakness of political leadership the southern states may merely have in exaggerated form a weakness common to many American states. It is difficult to build a well-organized politics solely around the issues of state government. Isolation of state politics from national politics inherent in the one-party system removes the opportunity for the easy projection into the state arena of national issues and national political organization. It would be agreed on every hand that over the past half century fairly significant differences in tempo, if not in direction, have characterized the national parties. These debates seep down into the battles between their state subsidiaries, and perhaps become blurred in the process, but even the chance for this sort of issue does not exist in one-party jurisdictions.

Transfer of the great issues to the Federal sphere deprives state politics of many questions that form voters into antagonistic groups and compel the organization of politics. And perhaps one reason why some issues of peculiar interest to the South have been transferred to the Federal sphere is the default of initiative attributable to the one-party system.[14] Even without the growth in importance of Federal action, it is doubtful that an autonomous politics can be maintained in a state of a federal system. State political organizations must be to a considerable extent hitchhikers on national politics. Without that connection, the political battle is apt to become either a chaos of personal factionalism or no battle at all in which an oligarchy rules without genuine challenge.

If state politics must be organized fundamentally along the same lines of division as national politics, the maintenance of a disorganized state politics depends fundamentally on a continuation of those conditions that induce southern unity in national politics. The race question and the heritage of The War have been more powerful drives toward unity—or at least toward the dominance of the top-drawer group—than the counter-divisive influences of national politics. In recent years, however, the sharpening of the issues of national politics and the parallel diversification of interests—such as the growth of industry within the South—have put a severe strain on the one-party system. The issues of national politics come to outweigh the forces of unity. One-party dominance, and a disorganized politics, may be expected to erode—gradually to be sure—first in those states in which the race issue is of least importance. In Texas, in Florida, in Arkansas, the days of a fluid factionalism are numbered. In Virginia, in North Carolina, in Tennessee the odds are against the survival of the one-party arrangement. While change will not come quickly, it is inevitable as the issues of national politics become more important than the peculiar regional interest.

[14] To illustrate: An official of an organization concerned with the status of tenant farmers when asked whether his organization lobbied before state legislatures and state departments explained that they did not bother with state governments. Everything of any importance to his organization was handled by the Federal Government. No more eloquent testimonial of the failings of the one-party system could be cited. One of the grand problems of the region goes without action and almost without discussion in a sterile politics.

PART | TWO

Political Leadership:

The One-Party System in the Nation

THE one-party system of the South is an institution with an odd dual personality. In state politics the Democratic party is no party at all but a multiplicity of factions struggling for office. In national politics, on the contrary, the party is the Solid South; it is, or at least has been, the instrument for the conduct of the "foreign relations" of the South with the rest of the nation. Yet the two facets of the one-party system are mutually dependent. If the South were contested territory in presidential elections, it could not long remain without active party competition for the control of state government. In nonsouthern states the forces organized by the contest for the Presidency furnish much of the motive power for the maintenance of the bipartisan system locally.

We ought to be both specific and candid about the regional interest that the Democratic party of the South has represented in national affairs. It must be conceded that there is one, and only one, real basis for southern unity: the Negro. While the South is a poor region, some southerners are poorer than others, far poorer. And southern Democrats on the national scene rarely gain renown as champions of the poor South against rich Yankee land. The South is predominantly agricultural, yet it has its cities and growing industries. And there are farmers and farmers, peanuts and cotton, cattle and citrus, big and little, rich and poor. Agriculture is not the foundation of southern solidarity. In an earlier day perhaps a common interest in the tariff cemented southern states together in national affairs; nowadays—apart from the indubitably potent habit of voting Democratic—about all that remains to promote southern solidarity is the Negro.

We need to be even more exact. As has been contended earlier, it is not the Negro in general that provides the base for white Democratic unity in national affairs: it is fundamentally the rural Negro in areas of high concentrations of colored population. It is here that whites are relatively fewest, that the plantation system of agriculture is most highly developed, that the economic system is most dependent upon black workers, and that the white-black socio-economic system, commonly thought to be characteristic of the entire South, is most highly developed. Here we find the persistent strain of southern unity.

The maintenance of southern Democratic solidarity has depended fundamentally on a willingness to subordinate to the race question all great social and economic issues that tend to divide people into opposing parties. Contrariwise, solidarity is threatened as these other questions come to outweigh in the public mind the race issue. Analysis of southern voting in presidential elections and by southerners in the House and Senate reveal clearly the foundation of southern unity in national politics. The same analysis points with equal clarity to elements of diversity within the changing South that are driving wedges into its unity.

Chapter Fifteen | # HOOVERCRATS AND DIXIECRATS

HOWEVER one regards the peculiar institutions that southern politicians have sought to defend, southerners are justifiably proud of the technical virtuosity of their politicians. The South lost the crucial battles but its politicians won The War—at least for three-quarters of a century. Within the Democratic party they maintained the right to veto prospective presidential nominees, and by united action in the Senate they filibustered to death hostile legislative proposals. All in all their strategy of obstruction provides an instructive illustration of the great power—at least negative power—of cohesive and determined minorities.[1]

In order that a minority may retain power, it must maintain cohesiveness. On two occasions since 1876 major splits have occurred in the Solid South in presidential politics: in 1928 when Tennessee, Florida, North Carolina, Texas, and Virginia went for Herbert Hoover and in 1948

[1] In presidential politics other minorities also exercise a veto on nominees; the South, however, is the only minority that has elevated the right of veto to the level of principle. It is ordinarily supposed that the former rule requiring two-thirds to nominate in the national convention furnished the foundation for the southern veto, but the veto has rested on the more fundamental power of any cohesive and determined minority in our politics. In fact, even under the two-thirds rule, a united South would have to recruit outside allies to block a nomination. In 1944 the eleven southern states had 276, or 23.5 per cent, of the 1176 convention votes. With Kentucky and Oklahoma added to the southern bloc, its proportion of the total vote rose to 27.4 per cent. In 1948 the southern percentage of the total convention vote was 24.1; with Kentucky and Oklahoma annexed, the figure was 28.2 per cent.

when Louisiana, Mississippi, Alabama, and South Carolina voted for J. Strom Thurmond, states' rights candidate. If it is true that the sources of inner strength as well as the points of inner weakness of a social group are revealed in moments of stress, analysis of these two crises ought to identify the fundamental elements of unity in the South.

1. The Bolt of 1928

The split of the South in the 1928 presidential election outlined starkly the fundamental basis of southern solidarity. In that year the ties that held the South to its traditional stand were strained by the Catholicism of Alfred E. Smith, the Democratic presidential candidate, as well as by his opposition to prohibition. Further, as a New Yorker he symbolized the aspects of urbanism most likely to arouse rural animosities. In Herbert Hoover, a dry and a Protestant, the Republicans offered a candidate whose qualities appealed to southerners for the very reasons that they found Smith repugnant. If we can identify those southerners who went over to the Republicans and those who resisted the Hooverian lure, perhaps we can get close to the essence of the southern Democracy.

What the election figures show is that generally the whites of the black belts remained most steadfast in their loyalty to the Democratic party, while in the areas of few Negroes the shift to Hoover was most marked. Hoover polled his lowest vote—and, contrariwise, defections from the Democracy were least—in the two states with the highest proportions of Negroes in their population: Mississippi and South Carolina. Only 4.6 per cent of the votes of South Carolina were Republican; in Mississippi, 17.4 per cent. All the states that cast Republican majorities had relatively low percentages of Negro population. The Republican percentages of the total presidential vote were as follows: [2]

Florida	56.8	Alabama	48.5
North Carolina	54.9	Arkansas	39.3
Virginia	53.9	Georgia	27.7
Tennessee	53.8	Louisiana	23.7
Texas	51.8	Mississippi	17.4
		South Carolina	4.6

Supplementation of this state-by-state picture by more minute analysis defines more sharply the areas of unwavering Democratic loyalty. Within each state the counties with high percentages of Negro population generally cast Democratic majorities, whereas counties with comparatively few Negroes yielded most readily to Republican blandishments. A south-wide view of voting by counties at opposite ends of the

[2] Bureau of the Census, *Vote Cast in Presidential and Congressional Elections, 1928–1944*, p. 11.

racial spectrum appears in Table 32. Of the 191 counties over 50 per cent Negro, 184 cast a majority for Smith. Usually these counties gave few votes indeed to the Republicans, historically the party of emancipation, reconstruction, and civil rights for Negroes. Of the 266 counties with less than 5 per cent Negro population, only 79 returned a majority for Smith. Only in Arkansas did most of such counties resist the Republican appeal, and there probably the vice-presidential candidacy of Arkansas' Senator Joseph Robinson helped to hold the state in the Democratic camp.

The vote distribution places the center of gravity of the southern

TABLE 32

Loyalists and Bolters in 1928: Most Counties with Many Negroes Remained Democratic; Counties with Few Negroes Tended to Bolt

	COUNTIES 50 PER CENT NEGRO AND OVER, 1930		COUNTIES UNDER 5 PER CENT NEGRO	
STATE	NUMBER	NUMBER WITH SMITH MAJORITY	NUMBER	NUMBER WITH SMITH MAJORITY
Alabama	18	18	6	1
Arkansas	9	9	29	21
Florida	4	4	1	0
Georgia	48	46	11	3
Louisiana	16	16	0	0
Mississippi	35	35	0	0
North Carolina	9	9	14	1
South Carolina	25	25	0	0
Tennessee	2	2	37	11
Texas	4	4	150	37
Virginia	21	16	18	5
Total	191	184	266	79

Democracy in the black belt. The whites of the black-belt counties were bound in loyalty to the Democracy by a common tradition and anxiety about the Negro. Whites elsewhere could afford the luxury of voting their convictions on the religious and prohibition issues.[3]

A sketch in broad strokes of the division between white and black counties conceals many gradations of correlation, as well as exceptions to the general proposition that the black counties were most strongly Democratic. A closer inspection of each state suggests, however, only limited qualification of the general proposition.

In Florida, the southern state with the highest popular-vote percentage for Hoover, immigrant Republicans contributed to the result, but

[3] As has been shown in several instances earlier the black belts tend to be wet. They had, in addition to their Democratic tradition, an antiprohibition leaning to hold them to the Democratic nominee.

fundamentally the diehard Democratic vote had the same characteristics as elsewhere in the South. When a county's population was more than 35 per cent Negro, the chances were two to one that it would go Democratic. When its Negro percentage fell below 35, the chances were three to one that it would go Republican. The exact figures were as follows:

	NUMBER OF COUNTIES	NUMBER FOR HOOVER	NUMBER FOR SMITH
Over 35% Negro	21	7	14
Under 35% Negro	46	34	12

The relation between Negro population and Democratic strength appears vividly in a contrast of counties with less than 15 per cent and those with over 50 per cent Negro population. For these counties, at the opposite extremes of Negro concentration, the presidential vote was as follows:

	PER CENT NEGRO 1930	PER CENT FOR HOOVER
Holmes	3.5	75.5
Hardee	9.0	71.6
Okaloosa	10.3	73.4
Madison	52.5	25.7
Gadsden	56.8	22.6
Leon	58.7	25.0
Jefferson	68.0	20.4

In the counties between these two extremes, the relation between racial composition and voting was not uniform. Some counties with high Negro percentages turned in Republican majorities. Others with low Negro percentages turned in surprisingly low Republican percentages.[4]

In Texas, defections to Hoover were principally in the white counties. Eastern Texas, which contained most of the Negro population of the state, polled the heaviest vote for Smith. Western Texas, settled mostly since The War and where Negroes are few, could vote for Hoover unembarrassed by recollections of Reconstruction or by fears of the consequences of party apostasy for the socio-economic system. The relation between the Negro population of a county and the probability of its reporting a majority for Hoover is shown in Table 33. Only one of 22 counties with more than 35 per cent Negro population went Republican, while 113 of 150 counties with less than 5 per cent Negro population turned Republican. Of those counties predominantly white that remained

[4] Some counties with low Negro and low Republican percentages were older settled counties that once had a much higher Negro percentage of population. The inference may be that a diehard Democratic tradition, once established in such a county, could withstand greater strain than the Democratic tendencies of a county that had never had such a population.

Democratic, many had substantial numbers of Mexicans. The metropolitan counties also diverged from the general pattern. Thus, Harris (Houston), Dallas, and Tarrant (Fort Worth) counties returned Republican majorities, while rural counties with similar Negro percentages usually gave a lower proportion of their popular vote to Hoover.

In North Carolina, which also went Republican, a slightly different pattern of voting behavior prevailed. The state normally has a warm Republican-Democratic competition. Party loyalties have been built up which in general follow the black-Democratic correlation. The traditionally strong Republican vote in the white counties was merely swollen by the events of 1928. Some of the 1928 departures from the white-Republican correlation reflected traditional voting patterns. A few counties regularly turn in a fairly high Republican vote despite their relatively heavy Negro population. Sampson County, for example, was 34.1 per

TABLE 33

Relationship between Percentage of Negro Population in Texas Counties and Presidential Vote by Counties in 1928

PER CENT NEGRO AT 1930 CENSUS	NO. OF COUNTIES	NUMBER OF COUNTIES IN CLASS THAT WENT—		PER CENT OF COUNTIES GOING REPUBLICAN
		DEMOCRATIC	REPUBLICAN	
0.0–4.9	150	37	113	75.3
5.0–14.9	33	16	17	51.5
15.0–24.9	26	19	7	26.9
25.0–34.9	23	19	4	17.3
35.0 and over	22	21	1	4.5

cent Negro, and on the basis of the behavior of counties of comparable hue, it would have been expected to return a high vote for Smith, but 70.9 per cent of its electors marked their ballots for Hoover. The results were a continuation of a deviate political behavior in the county dating back to the Populist revolt. On the other hand, in some white counties the strength of party attachment was powerful enough to stem the tide to Hoover. Cleveland County, with only 23.2 per cent Negro, "should" have gone Republican along with other counties of about the same Negro percentage. It remained in the Democratic column by a margin of less than one per cent. Its county seat, Shelby, base of the "Shelby Dynasty" that was to lead the Democracy of the State for many years, was the home of O. Max Gardner, Democratic candidate for governor. Maps showing in detail the relation between Negro population and Democratic strength appear in Figure 54.

These exceptions indicate that under certain circumstances a party tradition existed powerful enough to offset the pull of the campaign issues, but in general the higher the proportion of Negroes in a county, the greater was the probability that it would return a majority for the Democratic candidate. The odds were almost seven to one that a county with less than 35 per cent Negro population would turn in a majority for Hoover. The distribution of the counties was as follows:

	NUMBER OF COUNTIES	NUMBER FOR HOOVER	NUMBER FOR SMITH
Less than 35% Negro	61	53	8
Over 35% Negro	39	10	29

These figures suggest, of course, that factors other than the presence of a given percentage of Negroes in the population influenced the popular vote. One was party loyalty; another, urbanization. Thus, in the category of counties with 30.0–34.9 per cent Negro population, the median Democratic percentage was 44.5, but Durham and Forsyth (Winston-Salem) counties gave the Happy Warrior only 33.9 and 33.4 per cent of their vote, respectively.

In Tennessee, as in North Carolina, the addition of dry Protestant Democratic support to the customary Republican vote gave the state's electoral vote to Hoover. The peculiar partisan loyalties of Tennessee, described at length in an earlier chapter,[5] projected themselves into the presidential voting. Counties with large Negro populations are usually Democratic but there are also, mainly in Middle and West Tennessee, counties with few Negroes and traditional Democratic majorities. White counties dominated by Republicans are chiefly in East Tennessee. In the 1928 voting the Negro counties went for Smith by huge majorities and the white counties that had been habitually Democratic resisted Republican blandishments with greater resolution than did white counties in other southern states. The white Republican counties followed their usual inclinations but their Republicanism was fortified by desertions from the Democrats. All this comes down to saying that the Democratic party of Tennessee is a different sort of animal from the party in most other southern states. It approaches more closely the reality of party than it does in the Deep South states. In 1928 the loyalty of its adherents in the white counties tended to outweigh the diversionary appeals about rum and Romanism.

The validity of these general remarks can be supported by a few specific facts. Of the counties with more than 20 per cent Negro population only two went for Hoover. One of these, Davidson, includes within its boundaries Nashville, and the element of urbanism plus a substantial customary Republican vote resulted in an outcome different from that in rural counties with similar colored population percentages. The other was Hamilton, which normally had a heavy Republican vote and of which Chattanooga was the county seat. In considering the influence of urbanism, it ought to be noted also that Shelby (Memphis) County re-

[5] See above, chap. 4.

turned a far smaller plurality for Smith than did nearby rural counties with like Negro percentages.

Although Tennessee counties with heavy Negro populations usually went Democratic as in other states, traditionally Democratic counties with low Negro percentages often remained Democratic, albeit by narrower margins than ordinarily. The point is illustrated by the following sample of counties with less than 5 per cent Negro population:

COUNTY	PER CENT NEGRO	PER CENT FOR SMITH
Anderson	2.3	18.9 *
Benton	2.2	56.7
Campbell	2.3	16.3 *
Cannon	3.5	51.4
Carter	1.8	9.4 *
Claiborne	2.4	32.3 *
Clay	3.0	50.9
Cocke	3.3	19.9 *
Cumberland	0.6	29.9 *
DeKalb	3.6	42.8
Fentress	0.5	21.1 *
Grainger	2.4	24.1 *
Grundy	1.6	61.5

* Republican in 1924 presidential election.

In Virginia, as in Tennessee, the 1928 voting reflected the state's traditional voting patterns in which there are exceptions to the Negro-Democratic and white-Republican correlation. Nevertheless, most counties with high proportions of Negro population reported high percentages of their vote for Smith. On the other hand, nearly all the counties with extremely low Democratic votes were predominantly white. But not all counties predominantly white went for Hoover. Of the 21 counties with more than 50 per cent colored population, only five went for Hoover and three of these went Republican by a very narrow margin. Counties with less than 35 per cent Negro population manifested a greater tendency to remain within the Democratic fold than like counties in most other southern states. The figures, with 35 per cent as the dividing line, are as follows:

	NUMBER OF COUNTIES	NUMBER FOR HOOVER	NUMBER FOR SMITH
Over 35% Negro	42	14	28
Under 35% Negro	58	35	23

In the states that stood by the Democratic candidate—Alabama, Arkansas, Georgia, Louisiana, Mississippi, South Carolina—the Democratic proportion of the vote was smaller than usual, although in South Carolina the dip in Democratic strength was scarcely perceptible. In these states the heaviest Democratic losses occurred in the white counties. The

Republican shift did not go far enough to carry these states into the Hoover camp, in part because the predominantly white areas were relatively smaller and less populous than in those states that moved over to the Republicans.

In Alabama a shift of 7100 votes would have given the state to Hoover.[6] Twenty-six of the 67 counties turned in pluralities for Hoover.

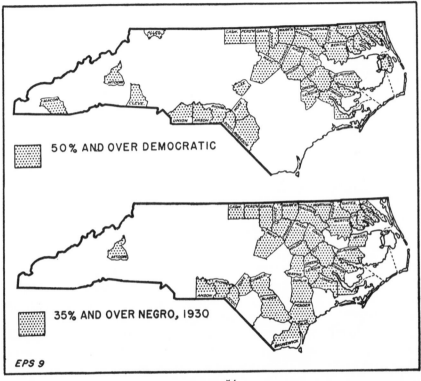

FIGURE 54

The Black-Belt and the Diehard Democratic Vote: North Carolina Counties over 50 Per Cent Democratic in 1928 Presidential Election and Counties with 35 Per Cent or More Negro Population, 1930

Of these 26 counties, only five had more than 30 per cent Negro population.[7] One of the five, Chambers County, with 45.6 per cent Negro population, was the home of Senator J. Thomas Heflin, who bolted the Democratic party to lead the fight for Hoover. Jefferson County, dominated by

[6] Of Alabama, William Allen White, an ardent Hooverite, opined: "I think we were counted out there." White saw the relation of the race question to the Republican vote: "We mustn't forget that our victories this year have had some relation to the decreasing proportion of colored voters in the states we won."—Walter Johnson (ed.) *Selected Letters of William Allen White, 1899–1943* (New York: Henry Holt and Company, 1947), pp. 288–89.

[7] Thirty-five counties were more than 30 per cent Negro.

Birmingham, gave Hoover a majority despite its 38.9 per cent Negro population.[8] Detailed examination of sub-areas within two Alabama counties reveals a cleavage between the voters of very small areas similar to that shown within the state as a whole by the county analysis. In these counties the beats (or precincts) in the prosperous valleys (which also contained a high concentration of Negroes) returned the largest majorities for Al Smith, while the poorer whites of the hill beats, where Negroes were fewer, voted for Hoover.[9]

Arkansas' county-by-county voting behavior in 1928 was erratic. Perhaps the vice-presidential candidacy of Senator Robinson kept the state in the Democratic ranks and also brought about some of the oddities of the returns. These curious features consisted principally in a heavier Democratic vote than might be expected in many white counties. Eight counties of peak Democratic strength gave more than 75 per cent of their popular vote to the Democratic candidates in contrast with the state percentage of 60.7. All these counties, in accord with hypothesis, were in the eastern part of the state and most of them were delta counties with high proportions of Negro population. On the other hand, counties that gave Hoover pluralities had low Negro population percentages, although by no means all the white counties went Republican. The 10 Hoover counties were, with the exception of Cleburne, in the western part of the state and several of them were Ozark counties that, like highland counties of other southern states, even in normal times have a high Republican vote.

The Republican candidate made inroads in Georgia but not sufficient to carry the state. Hoover's proportion of the vote tended to be

[8] Some of the high-Negro-percentage rural counties that gave Hoover pluralities had long manifested odd political characteristics. Thus, Chambers County, although the home of Heflin and presumably Hoovercratic for that reason, had in 1892 given the Populite, Kolb, 55.7 per cent of its vote in contrast with the prevailing Democratic standpattism of counties with large Negro populations. Similarly, Elmore, with 41.4 per cent Negro population in 1930, gave Hoover a plurality as it had Kolb in 1892. Coosa, another Hoover county, had gone Populist in 1892 despite its 33.7 per cent Negro population. Escambia's plurality for Hoover is not surprising since it had only 30.6 per cent Negro, yet in 1892 it had given Kolb 48.1 per cent of its ballots. The long persistence of deviate political attitudes in such counties, of course, points to factors influencing voting behavior not brought to light by the extensive sort of analysis here employed.

[9] Karl Bosworth, *Tennessee Valley County* (University, Ala.: Bureau of Public Administration, University of Alabama, 1941), pp. 14–15 and *Black Belt County* (University, Ala.: Bureau of Public Administration, University of Alabama, 1941), pp. 12–13. The conclusion regarding the Tennessee Valley county is: "The range for all ballot boxes was from 94 per cent for Hoover to 89 per cent for Smith, with the mountain-toppers all over the county registering 62 per cent of their votes for Hoover while the remainder of the county cast 72 per cent of their votes for Smith." In the black-belt county Smith's vote was highest in those beats with highest Negro population percentages. Bosworth interprets this "broadly to mean that the areas of regular party strength are the areas where the plantation system has operated; that is, that party regularity is a characteristic of the local aristocracy and upper middle class, while partisan independence is concentrated in the areas characterized by white tenancy and small, poor, agricultural holdings."

highest where Negroes were fewest. On the contrary, Smith's vote tended to be heaviest in the black counties. When the Negro percentage of population fell below 35, a county's attachment to the Democracy perceptibly weakened. The pair of maps in Figure 55 contrasts the territorial distribution of Republican strength and Negro population. From Atlanta north, Smith was weakest. In the far-northern counties the Republicans in normal elections poll a higher vote than elsewhere in the state.

In a few counties along and near the coast Hoover drew much heavier support than in the black-belt interior, despite the relatively heavy Negro population in some of these counties. The coastal counties have a long record of deviation from the political line established by the interior black-belt counties. In a few instances, urbanism apparently outweighed racial restraints. Thus, in the counties in which Augusta, Savannah, and Brunswick are located, the Republican percentage of the vote was higher than for rural counties with like proportions of Negro population. In Augusta and in a few nearby counties the chances are that the anti-Catholicism of the late Senator Tom Watson lived on in the voting.[10] In other counties, peculiar local factors had a bearing. Thus, in Effingham County, the local explanation of the Hoover majority is that the substantial Lutheran population was less willing to swallow its Protestantism than were Methodists and Baptists in other counties with similar proportions of Negroes.

Mississippi, with its huge Negro population and no considerable areas predominantly white, operates under conditions that tend to stifle cleavages between white and Negro regions. A Negrophobia spreads out and engulfs the small areas where Negroes are few. Nevertheless, such variations as occurred in the 1928 Mississippi vote coincided with the general pattern. The state gave only 17.4 per cent of its popular vote to Hoover. In 19 counties, however, he polled more than 25 per cent of the popular vote and in three of the 19 he won a majority. The Republican vote was heaviest in the extreme northeastern corner of the state and along the coast. In the northeast, in Itawamba and Tishomingo, Hoover polled 27.9 and 37.0 per cent, respectively, of the popular vote. This bettered his record in adjacent counties with higher proportions of black population. Itawamba was 5.7 per cent black; Tishomingo, 6.3.

The other counties with high Hoover votes formed a block along the coast. Coastal counties in all the southern states often exhibit a political divergence from the inland areas. The Mississippi coastal counties, however, in which the Republicans made most headway also had comparatively small percentages of Negroes. Such counties more than 40 per cent Republican were:

10 Fredeva Ogletree, "The 1928 Presidential Campaign in Georgia" (M. A. Thesis, University of Georgia, 1942), pp. 109–10.

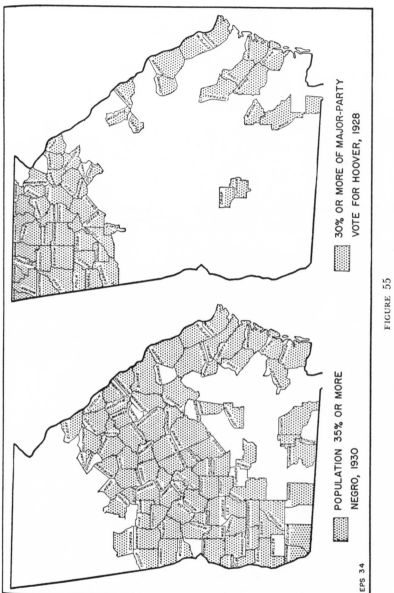

FIGURE 55

Hill-Country Republicanism: Georgia Counties with 30 Per Cent or More of
Major-Party Vote for Hoover in 1928 and Counties with 35 Per Cent or over
Negro Population in 1930

	PER CENT REPUBLICAN	PER CENT NEGRO
Forest	44.7	32.0
George	52.3	16.8
Jones [11]	43.2	26.9
Pearl River	50.6	26.5
Perry	49.3	33.5
Stone	62.7	25.0

Minute examination of the relation between the distribution of the Al Smith vote and the Negro population amply sustains the major thesis: that the diehard Democratic strength in 1928 centered in counties with high proportions of Negroes. The same examination, however, indicates that refinements of the broad thesis are in order.

Counties with large urban centers tended generally to be more Republican than were rural counties with comparable proportions of Negro population. In part, this was probably a continuation of a past tendency, but the circumstances of the campaign may have emboldened the considerable urban population with Republican leanings (on grounds other than prohibition and Protestantism) to vote that way. Further, the conditions of city life free whites from the urge toward political solidarity that prevails in the rural-agricultural-Negro county.

Other departures from the general pattern point to another type of local differential in political behavior. While it may sound queer to speak of variations in intensity of party tradition in the Democratic South, party traditions quite like those in nonsouthern states have developed in North Carolina, Tennessee, and Virginia. In the growth of this interparty competition there arose local departures from the Negro-Democratic correlation, and some predominantly white counties have quite as strong a Democratic tradition as the black-belt counties. On the contrary, in these

[11] Some of these counties evidently had a history like that of upland counties in other states. A *Times-Picayune* (New Orleans) reporter (November 24, 1946) recalls an interview in 1920 with Cap'n Newt Knight of the "Free State of Jones." Cap'n Newt, after a few drinks of bourbon chased with a gourd of branch-water from a bucket, related the history: "Confederacy drafted a lot of us Jones county men back in 1861. Sent around a sergeant with a couple of squads of riflemen; told us to come along. Marched us over near Montgomery, Alabama. Found out we was supposed to fight the Nawth to keep ouah nigrah slaves. We Jones county men didn't own no nigrah slaves. Then we hear the Confederacy passed a law any man owned five nigrah slaves, they wouldn't draft him. He was supposed to stay home and raise vittles for fighting men. We Jones county men talked it oveh. I told 'em: 'This is a rich man's war and a poor man's fight. Let's go home.' One night we took our guns and ammynition, slipped out of camp one at a time, different directions, met where we said we'd meet, and we started home. Got home. Went about ouah business. Three times they sent Confederate soldiers afteh us. We warned 'em to keep outa Jones county. They came on. We ambushed 'em and shot the hell outa 'em. They let us alone afteh that. That's all they was to it. Union army came along afteh awhile; said they heard we was surrounded by Johnny Rebs and fightin' for the Union. We said: 'Hell, no. We ain't Union. We're Jones Free State. We ain't fightin' 'less'n we got a real reason to fight. Yo'-all want nigrah slaves, help you'selves. We don't own none.'"

states a few counties with many Negroes habitually have a heavy Republican vote. These particular deviations, often traceable to the Populist crisis, persisted in the 1928 voting.

After all the exceptions and gradations are accounted for, we are still left with the conclusion that the irreducable core of the southern Democracy had its center of gravity in 1928 in the rural, agricultural counties with high proportions of Negro population. Moreover, they tended to be cotton counties and "the historical pattern of the cotton plantation county has been one of large ownership and small operating units; of a small white planter group controlling a large Negro and, in some cases, white tenant group; of educational opportunities for Negroes rigidly limited by the economic interests and social ideology of the planter group." [12] Thus, not only high Negro population ratios were associated with Democratic steadfastness. A complex of factors—ruralism, cotton-growing, plantation organization, intense Reconstruction memories—as well as anxieties about the racial equilibrium characterized the Democratic areas.

2. The Revolt of 1948

If the backbone of the Solid South is the black belt, the loyalists of 1928 would be expected to be the rebels of 1948. Although some old Hoovercrat leaders were in the states' rights camp in 1948, the most intense support for the 1948 southern revolt came from the areas with most Negroes. The foundations of the revolt were symbolized in its presidential and vice-presidential candidates, J. Strom Thurmond, of South Carolina, and Fielding Wright, of Mississippi, chief executives of the two states with the highest proportions of Negro population.

A new ingredient, however, had been added since 1928. The New Deal had sharpened issues and had stimulated a closer alliance of the black-belt counties with industry. Both had reason to oppose national Democratic policies. Ostensibly the bases for opposition were different. Fundamentally, however, the black-belt counties shared with industry and finance a conservative viewpoint; it was not the race question alone that drove black-belt leaders into tighter alliance with business reactionaries.[13]

[12] C. S. Johnson, *Statistical Atlas of Southern Counties* (Chapel Hill: University of North Carolina Press, 1941), p. 15.

[13] *The Hale County* (Alabama) *News* (quoted in *Birmingham News*, September 29, 1948) observed that the states' righters had "taken up the battle cry of 'states' rights' and claim to be the defenders of the individual's liberty and freedom. Actually the real issues are entirely different. Their protestations against civil rights and for states' rights are merely a camouflage to cover their real purposes. The bolt has been led by a coalition of entrenched reactionaries who are primarily interested in maintaining their privileged stations. Their stranglehold upon the politics of their respective states has

Actually the southern revolt began in the campaign of 1944. In that year the Mississippi Democratic convention put a slate of uninstructed electors on the ballot. The strategy reflected the fantasy that life might be breathed into the electoral college and that unpledged southern electors could grasp a balance of power.[14] Even in Mississippi the strategy failed in 1944.[15] In Texas, where anti-New Deal sentiment arose more from opposition to economic policies than from concern about racial policies, the "Texas Regulars," the corporation wing of the party, put a slate of uninstructed electors on the ballot. About the only satisfaction southerners got out of their 1944 maneuvers was the defeat of Henry Wallace as vice-presidential nominee in the national convention.[16]

By 1948 a lot of water had gone over the dam. Roosevelt had died. The 1946 congressional elections seemed to indicate that the country was moving to the right and the conservative wing of the southern Democracy took heart, along with the Republicans. In October, 1947, the President's Committee on Civil Rights recommended a program for the protection of the civil rights of minorities, including Negroes, and the report fueled the embers that southern Negro-baiters had been trying to fan into flames.

Even before President Truman requested congressional action on civil rights, Governor Fielding L. Wright, of Mississippi, sounded the call for revolt in his inaugural message of January 20, 1948.[17] He attacked the proposals of the Committee on Civil Rights and called for a break with the Democratic party if its leaders continued to support legislation "aimed to wreck the South and our institutions." He regretted the prospect of a break with the Democratic party, "But vital principles and eternal truths transcend party lines, and the day is now at hand when determined action must be taken." [18]

Undeterred by Governor Wright's oratory, President Truman on February 2 recommended to Congress the enactment of legislation to effectuate some, but not all, of the proposals of his Committee on Civil Rights. A few days later Governor Wright carried his crusade to the Southern Governors Conference meeting at Wakulla Springs, Florida. He proposed that the conference serve notice on the leaders of the Demo-

been challenged and seriously endangered by the sweep of a liberal movement across the South that is interested in progress and the development of our resources. The reactionaries have seized upon the strategy of stirring up prejudice and fomenting racial strife as a blind to their real purposes."

[14] Cynics observed also that the fantasy reflected a deficiency in training in simple arithmetic. In all four Roosevelt elections all 11 southern states could have gone Republican without affecting the outcome.

[15] See above, pp. 243–44.

[16] See J. B. Shannon, "Presidential Politics in the South," *Journal of Politics,* 10 (1948), pp. 464–89.

[17] It will be remembered that Governor Wright had received heaviest popular support in his election in the counties with most Negroes and that he was regarded as a spokesman of the delta rather than of the hills of Mississippi. See above, pp. 236–37.

[18] *Times-Picayune* (New Orleans), January 21, 1948.

cratic party that "we no longer will tolerate the repeated campaigns for the enactment" of civil rights legislation and call a "Southern Conference of true Democrats" to meet at Jackson, Mississippi, March 1, to "formulate plans for activity and adopt a course of action." [19] The governors preferred "calm and deliberate" action. They decided to appoint a committee to confer with the Democratic national chairman and to meet again within 40 days to hear its report.

In due course the conference committee called on J. Howard McGrath, Democratic national chairman. The committee asked whether he would use his influence "to have the highly controversial civil rights legislation, which tends to divide our people, withdrawn from consideration by the Congress." Mr. McGrath's reply was "No." The committee inquired whether he would support a return to the two-thirds rule for nominations in the national convention. McGrath considered the proposal "a backward step." Governor R. Gregg Cherry, of North Carolina, who seemed to regard the whole commotion with restrained enthusiasm, remarked that the governors who met McGrath "with blood in their eyes didn't get exactly what they were after." [20]

On March 13, the Southern Governors Conference met in Washington to receive the report of its committee. With the governors of Florida, Tennessee, Louisiana, and North Carolina not in attendance, the conference recommended that the forthcoming state Democratic conventions resolve that their presidential electors would not vote in November for any candidate favoring civil rights and that delegates be sent to the national convention instructed to oppose Mr. Truman's nomination.

Meanwhile Governor Wright had kept the pot boiling in Mississippi. After his failure to move the southern governors at Wakulla Springs to quick action, he called a mass meeting of Mississippians. On Lincoln's birthday four thousand persons assembled at Jackson, Mississippi, sang Dixie, waved Confederate flags, and adopted resolutions. The session resolved that the Mississippi state Democratic executive committee should call a conference of "all true white Jeffersonian Democrats" to assemble later at Jackson. It resolved that Mississippi and the South could best solve their own problems and that "those on the outside merely handicap us and . . . hinder progress being done." It condemned efforts of the Federal Government "to confiscate the tidelands as manifesting a strong tendency towards the destruction of state rights . . ." and thus early gave ground for the charge that perhaps the petroleum industry, rather than the Negro, was at the bottom of the movement.[21]

The Mississippi Democratic executive committee met March 1 to plan the next steps in the revolt and to lay the groundwork for the nation-

[19] *Arkansas Gazette* (Little Rock), February 8, 1948.
[20] Ibid., February 24, 1948.
[21] *Times-Picayune* (New Orleans), February 13, 1948.

wide conference of true white Jeffersonian Democrats. The committee resolved to conduct a campaign in Mississippi to assure that its delegates to the national convention and its presidential electors would "stand firmly for states' rights and therefore against any nominee for president or vice-president of the United States who refuses to take an open and positive stand against the 'civil rights' recommendations." The committee proposed that national convention delegates be instructed to withdraw from the convention if the civil rights program should be placed in the platform and if the party nominees did not give proper assurances.[22]

While Mississippi was preparing for the nation-wide conclave of white Jeffersonian Democrats, Alabama was debating its course of action. The primary to choose Democratic presidential electors and delegates to the national convention was scheduled for May 4. Gessner T. McCorvey, Democratic state chairman and a leader of the conservative, black-belt, big-mule wing of the party, late in February called on candidates for presidential elector to pledge themselves to support only a "real Democrat of the states' rights type." [23] Horace Wilkinson, Birmingham attorney, 1928 Hoovercrat, outspoken opponent of Negro voting, and a candidate for presidential elector, requested signed pledges from elector candidates that they would vote against Truman or any other Democratic nominee unless the convention and its nominees disavowed the President's civil rights program. The Democratic state executive committee, in an unusual display of partisanship, went on record in support of those candidates for elector pledged to vote against any national nominee favoring a civil rights program. The committee also asked delegate candidates to pledge themselves to walk out of the convention if a civil rights plank were included in the platform. The campaign for delegates shaped up as a fight between those pledged to bolt the convention and those who declined to commit themselves to bolt and contended that differences ought to be fought out within the Democratic party. Prominent among the anti-bolting candidates were Senator Lister Hill, the principal progressive leader of the state, Governor James E. Folsom, former Governor Chauncey Sparks, and Attorney General Albert Carmichael.

After the first primary and the run-off on June 1, the delegation to the national convention was split almost half and half between those pledged to walk out and those pledged to remain in the convention even

[22] Ibid., March 2, 1948.

[23] *Birmingham News*, February 26, 1948. Alabama conservatives engaged in some sharp maneuvers. Thus, the possibility was suggested that Democratic electors might not vote for the Democratic national nominee shortly before March 1, the closing date for filing as candidate for elector. After the closing date, the issue became sharpened and the national Democrats found themselves not well prepared for the fight. By their success in committing the electors at the time of the presidential primaries, the conservatives succeeded in preventing an expression of the views of the voters after the nominations by both parties and after the debate of the national campaign.

though a civil rights plank were adopted. Of the presidential electors, all were pledged to vote against any nominee unsatisfactory on the civil rights question. What the voting proved was uncertain. Although all delegates were opposed to Federal legislation on civil rights, the voting suggested that at least half the Alabama voters were disposed to work out their destiny within the Democratic party. In the run-off primary, for example, Attorney General Albert Carmichael, a Folsom progressive, nosed out Gessner McCorvey, who had started all the trouble, by a vote of 111,731 to 111,548.[24]

While Alabama was waging its campaign between the walk-out and anti-walk-out delegate candidates, steps were being taken to convene the true white Jeffersonian Democrats of the nation. In March Herbert Holmes and Arthur L. Adams, chairmen, respectively, of the Democratic executive committees of Mississippi and Arkansas called the conference to meet May 10 at Jackson, Mississippi. By March it was apparent that the clefts in southern solidarity would be too apparent if the convention was limited to delegates officially representing the Democratic party organizations of the various states. The "conference" would be composed of "volunteer citizens" who sincerely believed in states' rights and opposed civil rights. That is to say, anyone who wished could attend the conference and participate in its deliberations.[25]

By the time of the Jackson conference it became clear that the rebellion had its deepest roots in Mississippi and South Carolina. Governor Wright was temporary chairman; Governor Thurmond keynoted the convention. Governor Laney of Arkansas—who mysteriously vacillated in and out of the rebellion—served as permanent chairman. Governor Thurmond defied the Federal government: "All the laws of Washington, and all the bayonets of the Army cannot force the negroes into their (southerners) homes, their schools, their churches and their places of recreation and amusement." That Truman's program had no such objectives seemed irrelevant.[26] The President had said nothing about social equality or en-

[24] The vote in the McCorvey-Carmichael race in general followed the historic Alabama pattern in conservative-progressive contests. Carmichael was strongest in the hill counties of northern Alabama, the home territory of Jim Folsom and John Sparkman, while McCorvey ran best in the black belt.

[25] Registrants signed a card to indicate their approval of the conference, to formulate "the basic American principles of states' rights, and for the purpose of taking such other and further action as may be deemed proper and necessary for the preservation of constitutional government."—*Times-Picayune* (New Orleans), May 10, 1948.

[26] Throughout, states' rights leaders grossly misrepresented the President's program. Whether this arose from deliberate misrepresentation, ignorance of the President's program, or judgments of its long-run possibilities is difficult to say. The President did not go so far as his Committee on Civil Rights. He recommended (1) a Joint Congressional Committee on Civil Rights, (2) a Division of Civil Rights in the Department of Justice, (3) strengthening of statutes protecting citizens in the enjoyment of rights secured by the Federal Constitution, (4) an anti-lynching statute, (5) protection of the

try to homes, schools, churches, or places of recreation and amusement.[27]

Lest all their high jinks brand them as bolters from the party, the Democrats at Jackson attempted to make it seem that the northern Democrats were the ones who were bolting. Horace Wilkinson, of Alabama, one of the "volunteer citizens" at Jackson, explained: "There is no idea here of organization of a separate party. We've already got a party. We are going to work within the party. The idea is to coordinate activities of the Democratic party in each of the southern states and in other states that will go along with us."[28] Governor Thurmond called for the conference to give notice to the Democratic national committee before the convention that the southern delegates would not support civil rights nominees. "If we do this," he said, "no one will be able to say that we are bolting or breaking faith with the party if our people shall subsequently cast their electoral votes for other such nominees."[29] Just how this legerdemain accomplished the purpose the governor did not explain. The conference called on the Democratic party in each state to select national convention delegates and presidential electors "who will publicly repudiate the President's so-called but misnamed civil rights program, and will vote in the convention and in the electoral college only for individuals who firmly support States' rights." The conference also called a meeting at Birmingham after the Democratic national convention to "take all necessary and appropriate actions" if the national convention failed to abandon the President's civil rights program.

As the Democratic national convention approached, southerners opposed both Mr. Truman's nomination and his civil rights program, but they differed among themselves about what they would do if they lost at Philadelphia, as they were sure to do. Governor Wright's Mississippi delegation even had to put up a fight to be seated. Southern irreconcilables refused to accept the platform committee's middle-of-the-road plank on civil rights. They proposed that the convention accept the southern view; the convention voted down their amendments. Northern leaders, perhaps moved by southern irreconciliability, then induced the convention to

right to vote including prohibition of poll taxes as a condition of voting in Federal elections, (6) a Fair Employment Practice Commission, and (7) prohibition of the enforcement of segregation in interstate carriers by the carriers themselves. State laws requiring segregation had been held void.—*Cong. Record*, vol. 94, pt. 1, pp. 928–29.

[27] In a radio address directed primarily to Negroes on the eve of the Jackson conference, Governor Wright defended the policy of segregation. He spoke of the harmony possible under segregation and of the lack of kindness in some northern states. "With all this in mind, and with all frankness, as governor of your state, I must tell you that regardless of any recommendation of President Truman, despite any law passed by Congress, and no matter what is said to you by the many associations claiming to represent you, there will continue to be segregation in Mississippi. If any of you have become so deluded as to want to enter our hotels and cafes, enjoy social equality with the whites, then kindness and true sympathy requires me to advise you to make your home in some state other than Mississippi."—*Birmingham News*, May 9, 1948.

[28] *Birmingham News*, May 10, 1948.

[29] *Richmond Times-Dispatch*, May 11, 1948.

adopt a firmer civil rights position than that proposed by the platform committee.[30] With the adoption of the platform the Mississippi delegation and half of the Alabama delegation walked out.[31] In the voting on the nomination the southern delegations finally united on Senator Richard B. Russell, of Georgia.[32] Russell drew all the votes of all the Confederate states save North Carolina, 13 of whose 32 votes were recorded for Truman.

According to schedule the states' righters convened at Birmingham on July 17. The gathering consisted of the big brass of the Democratic party of Mississippi, of conservative leaders of Alabama, of Governor Thurmond of South Carolina and his entourage, and a miscellaneous assortment of persons of no particular political importance from other states.[33] It could scarcely be called a convention; it was, in fact, officially a "conference," although speakers often stuttered over the word. There was a good deal of oratory about the threat of admission of Negroes to "our homes, our theaters, and our swimming pools." The conference endorsed J. Strom Thurmond for President and Fielding Wright for Vice-President and adopted a mendacious "declaration of principles." [34]

The maneuvers within each state in preparation for the Democratic national convention and the actions of leaders during the presidential

[30] The civil rights plank finally read as follows: "The Democratic party is responsible for the great civil rights gains made in recent years in eliminating unfair and illegal discrimination based on race, creed or color. The Democratic party commits itself to continuing efforts to eradicate all racial, religious and economic discrimination. We again state our belief that racial and religious minorities must have the right to live, the right to work, the right to vote, the full and equal protection of the laws, on a basis of equality with all citizens as guaranteed by the Constitution. We highly commend President Harry Truman for his courageous stand on the issue of civil rights. We call upon the Congress to support our President in guaranteeing these basic and fundamental rights: (1) the right of full and equal political participation, (2) the right of equal opportunity of employment, (3) the right of security of person, (4) and the right of equal treatment in the service and defense of our nation."

[31] The Florence (Ala.) *Times* editorialized: "The surprising thing is that the delegation was not thrown out. Never have the Democrats of Alabama been burdened with such an overstuffed bunch of obsolete and repudiated leadership."—Quoted in *Birmingham News*, July 18, 1948.

[32] The vote was Truman 947½, Russell 263, McNutt ½. It suggested that the crv for restoration of the two-thirds rule might be ill-founded. Russell's vote was 21.3 per cent of the total vote of the convention. Mississippi was not represented at the time of the roll call. Had its vote been added to that polled by Russell, his percentage of the total would have been 23.1.

[33] Thus, in the conference demonstrations an Alabamian carried the North Carolina standard. "Somebody's got to carry it," he explained.

[34] The declaration included the following reference to the Democratic national convention: "This alleged Democratic assembly called for a civil-rights law that would eliminate segregation of every kind from all American life, prohibit all forms of discrimination in private employment, in public and private instruction and administration and treatment of students; in the operation of public and private health facilities; in all transportation, and require equal access to all places of public accommodation for persons of all races, colors, creeds and national origin." Compare with this the phraseology of the Democratic platform quoted earlier.

campaign permit a sharper identification of the groups supporting the rebellion. Although fringe considerations were of influence in each state, repeatedly the progressive wings of the Democratic party stood by Truman or at least kept quiet while the conservative and reactionary factions usually beat the bushes for Thurmond and Wright.

In North Carolina, Virginia, and Tennessee—states with the rudiments of a two-party system—the Republican threat influenced Democratic action. In May the North Carolina Democratic convention refused to toy with the proposal of a bolt. It called on all Democrats "to join their forces and to submerge their differences in the face of a common enemy." Cameron Morrison, former governor, did not "want any of this revolting business." If Truman is not beaten at the convention, he said, "let's step under the Democratic flag and help elect him. Then, we'll let our Congressmen and Senators beat him down when he needs beating." The platform committee summarily rejected a proposal by the delegation from Granville County (51 per cent Negro, 1940) to instruct the national convention delegates not to vote for Truman or any other civil rights advocate.[35] Democrats to whom Republicans were live, mountain voters and not just people up North, could not afford the luxury of bolting.

Virginians are less troubled by Republicans than are North Carolinians, but the threat was enough to keep the Byrd organization from openly supporting either Thurmond or Dewey. Late in February, Governor Tuck and the high command of the Byrd faction set out to railroad through the legislature a plan to permit the state party convention or a party committee to determine, after the national convention, for whom Virginia's Democratic electors would be instructed. Senator Byrd and other organization stalwarts endorsed the proposal but the normally docile legislature rebelled and gave the Byrd leadership its most serious setback in years. Leaders of the progressive faction quickly attacked. Representative John W. Flannagan, who had had to fight Republicans in the "Fighting Ninth," and Martin Hutchinson, opposition liberal leader, made themselves heard. Governor Tuck had to back down and accept a modification of his proposal. In the summer primary campaigns opposition candidates challenged organization candidates for House and Senate nominations to say where they stood on the question of bolting. After the national convention Senator A. Willis Robertson, organization candidate for re-election, announced his support of the Truman-Barkley ticket. The state Democratic executive committee, incredible as it may seem, announced through its chairman a policy of neutrality between Thurmond and Truman in the presidential race but urged all good Democrats to support the nominees for other offices.[36] It was left mainly to the opposition-progressive wing of the party to make the campaign for the national

[35] *News and Observer* (Raleigh), May 21, 1948.
[36] Robert Whitehead and Martin Hutchinson, of the Truman-Barkley Straight

ticket, although individual organization men here and there endorsed the national ticket, most enthusiastically, it seemed, when they were running for re-election against a strong Republican.

The imperatives towards party regularity were stronger in Tennessee than in Virginia, but the Democratic factional attitude toward the national ticket resembled that of Virginia. Crump, boss of the conservative faction, early announced that he would not vote for Truman in November. Crump, however, could not even keep his own organization in line. Governor McCord, who faced a primary contest that he was to lose, played a moderating role in the Southern Governors Conference. He would not pledge himself to bolt and thereby help elect a Republican in Tennessee. Crump's man, Roane Waring, who had been hobnobbing with the Dixiecrats down at Jackson, Mississippi, met defeat when the state convention rejected his anti-Truman resolution and sent an uninstructed delegation to Philadelphia. Crump's candidates lost in the gubernatorial and senatorial primaries, and the progressive faction, led by Kefauver and Browning, took over the party leadership. They had reservations about the civil rights program, but were in harmony with the national Administration on its policies generally. Even Senator McKellar broke with Crump and came out for Truman. Democrats faced by the most serious Republican threat since 1920 had little disposition, as well as little reason, to join up with Mississippi's crusade to preserve segregation at the cost of losing an election themselves. The states' righters tried to smuggle a fifth column into the Democratic electoral slate, but the state Democratic committee took steps to eliminate them from the slate. To put their own slate on the ballot and to carry on the campaign the states' righters formed a state organization at a mass meeting at Somerville in Fayette County, one of the two counties of the state more than half Negro (72.5 per cent, 1940).

In another group of states—Florida, Texas, and Arkansas—the Democratic party had no tradition of discipline generated by opposition from Republicans in state and local races, although recollections of the fate of Democratic bolters of 1928 had a chastening influence on practical politicians in all three states. More fundamentally, the fact that the three states had relatively few Negroes made for a weaker white-supremacy faction than in such states as Mississippi and South Carolina. In all three states the national campaign boiled down to maneuvers by the black-belt, conservative coalition for control of the party machinery and

Democratic Ticket Committee, commented on the statement of Chairman Alvin Massenburg: "The so-called leaders of the Democratic party in Virginia present to Virginia and the nation a sad spectacle. Lacking the courage to do the thing they set out to do last winter, they now take refuge in a cowardly act of negation called neutrality as between Harry S. Truman, the regular party nominee for President, and the 'Dixiecrat' rump convention nominee, Thurmond. It is a new low in political cowardice and a distinct disservice to Virginia and the Democratic party."—*Richmond Times-Dispatch*, October 15, 1948.

electors against the progressives and others who opposed a break with the national leadership.

Florida's revolt began in February when Frank D. Upchurch, an old antagonist of Senator Pepper and a member of the state Democratic executive committee from St. Johns County (35.3 per cent Negro, 1940), proposed that the state committee join with other state committees of the South to fight the renomination of President Truman. The Associated Industries of Florida, early in March, condemned the President's civil rights program "as an iniquitous, insidious and malicious scheme, promulgated for selfish political expediency, at the expense of creating racial and sectional prejudice and hatred." [37] At about the same time the Putnam County (42.2 per cent Negro, 1940) Democratic executive committee resolved that the Truman program would "destroy cherished customs and traditions"; the Madison County (47.7 per cent Negro, 1940) executive committee took similar action as did a mass meeting of Democrats of Dixie County (43.4 per cent Negro, 1940).

In the primary campaign for convention delegates and electors, two of 112 delegate candidates announced for Truman. The battle was between those who wanted to go all the way with Mississippi and those who opposed Truman's nomination but had no intention of bolting. The extremists, led by Frank Upchurch, won 11½ of the delegation of 20 and, under the unit rule, thereby won control of the delegation. At the same primary the Democrats designated their presidential electors: four of the eight pledged not to vote for the Democratic nominee in November. Upchurch and other opponents of Senator Pepper, however, failed to gain control of the state Democratic executive committee which remained in the hands of the progressive wing. Before the election, a special session of the legislature provided for separate lists of electors for all candidates. By the elimination of the Thurmond-Wright fellow travelers from the Truman slate, the voter was given a clear-cut choice. The liberals and anti-bolters, aided perhaps by the threat of a growing Republican vote, were able to hold the party together and to carry the state for Truman.

Insofar as the tangles of Arkansas politics can be unraveled, the same pattern prevailed there as in Florida. The center of agitation against Truman's renomination and for commitment of the Democratic electors for Thurmond and Wright was in plantation counties of eastern Arkansas. The Arkansas Free Enterprise Association, with headquarters in that area, was prominent in all the Dixiecrat maneuvers. Its executive director, John L. Daggett (his home: Lee County, 63.3 per cent Negro, 1940), and his associates attended Governor Wright's Jackson conference in full force. The same association, consisting of big planters and industrialists, had earlier sponsored a "right-to-work" amendment to the state constitution, and it had been hostile to all the New Deal foolishness. Governor

[37] *Florida Times-Union* (Jacksonville), March 5, 1948.

Laney's exact position was unpredictable from day to day, but he finally wound up as chairman of the states' righters of Arkansas. On the other hand, the late Carl Bailey, former governor with progressive inclinations, announced early that he would support Truman for renomination. Sid McMath, the winner of the gubernatorial nomination over rivals with pronounced civil rights views, gave no comfort to the Dixiecrats.[38] Senator William Fulbright, a northwestern Arkansawyer, preached party regularity, perhaps prudently because it was thought that Governor Laney might run against him in 1950. Representative Brooks Hays, liberal Arkansas leader, had no enthusiasm for the civil rights program but he saw nothing to be gained by bolting the party. When the showdown came, the Free Enterprise Association simply did not have the votes in the state convention to instruct the Democratic electors for Thurmond and Wright. It capitulated without a roll call. The combination of traditional Democratic loyalties, the threat offered by the Republicans in a few areas of the state, and a strain of liberalism overcame the coalition of conservatives and black belters.

In Texas, as in Florida and Arkansas, Negroes were too few in number to govern white political action and the pro- and anti-Truman fight became by and large a progressive-conservative struggle for control of the party machinery and the party's presidential electors. The Texas Regulars, 1944 predecessors of the Dixiecrats, were in the forefront of the anti-civil-rights movement. In the Democratic state convention in May the liberal, pro-Truman group was unable to obtain a delegation to the national convention instructed for Truman; on the other hand, the Texas Regulars failed to win approval of a plan for the delegation to walk out if the two-thirds rule were not restored. Governor Jester, who opposed bolting, controlled the convention. In later party actions Jester, no left-winger himself, had as allies the labor and liberal sections of the party which had opposed his election as governor, while his erstwhile associates of the extreme right went for Thurmond and Wright or supported the Republican candidates.

The foregoing paragraphs account for two groups of states—those with a rudimentary two-party competition and those with no Republican party of consequence but also with comparatively few Negroes. A third group consists of the Deep South states, South Carolina, Georgia, Alabama, Mississippi, Louisiana, all of which have comparatively high proportions of Negroes in their population. In these states, as elsewhere, the objective of the states' righters was to instruct the regular Democratic

---

[38] The *Arkansas Gazette* (Little Rock), (February 21, 1948), described the line-up as follows: "Yet it should be recognized that the race issue is by no means the sole cause of the great division in Democratic ranks. It is no accident that those who are loudest now in denouncing Mr. Truman are the same Southern Democrats who have also taken issue with him and with his predecessor on many other matters—labor legislation, price controls, public power, federal spending, etc."

electors to vote for Thurmond and Wright. (The states' rights candidates, significantly, won only in those states in which they succeeded in appropriating the regular Democratic label.) And the contest over this question seemed to be generally a fight between the New Deal and anti-New Deal factions of the party.

Dixiecrats completely controlled the situation in Mississippi. Thurmond and Wright appeared on the ballot as the Democratic nominees, and a group of "loyal Democrats" put Truman and Barkley on the ballot. At their organization session the loyalists characterized the states' rights movement as "an unrealistic, negative, backward looking program suggested by demagogic, bolting politicians and front men for grasping corporations." [39] Among the leaders were former associates of the late Senator Bilbo, labor union officials, Federal employees, and Mississippi liberals. They set up headquarters for their hopeless campaign in the hotel suite that had been Bilbo headquarters in earlier days.[40]

In Alabama the Democratic electors were early committed through the primary to vote against Truman. Under the state law no method existed to put the names of the national nominees on the ballot. About the only voices raised in favor of legislative action to permit Trumanites to record their vote were those of labor and liberal leaders. Governor Folsom, as the election approached, campaigned for the national ticket. "A handful of slickers have tried to take the vote away from 3,000,000 people in the state," he asserted and promised legal action to compel the state's Democratic electors to vote for Truman.[41]

The commitment of South Carolina's Democratic electors to Thurmond and Wright was accompanied by considerably more debate than occurred in Mississippi. The movement to bolt got off to an early start in the low country. Early in February the Jasper County (64.1 per cent Negro, 1940) Democratic committee called a county convention to "consider withdrawing from the national Democratic party." [42] The county convention acted according to plan later in the month and at about the same time the Dorchester County (57.4 per cent Negro, 1940) Democratic executive committee recommended, unless Truman backed down, that southern electoral votes be withheld from the national Democratic nominees. The Greenwood County (37.1 per cent Negro, 1940) committee, on the other hand, proposed that the fight be kept within

[39] *Commercial Appeal* (Memphis), October 5, 1948.

[40] John W. Scott, secretary-treasurer of the loyalists and a Telephone Workers Union official, said: "It is certainly not inappropriate that the Mississippi Democratic Committee's headquarters should be in the old headquarters of the late Senator Bilbo, for he certainly was a party man, a Roosevelt Democrat and a close political and personal friend of Senator Barkley."—Ibid., October 11, 1948.

[41] A state statue requiring party electors to vote for the national nominees had been held void in an advisory opinion by the state supreme court.

[42] *News and Courier* (Charleston), February 10, 1948.

the party.[43] In the May state convention, opposition to instruction of the party's electors to vote against any Democratic candidate favorable to civil rights came mainly from the Piedmont. The upcountry was also the source of most of the opposition in the state executive committee in September to the successful proposal to commit the state's electors to Thurmond and Wright.

In Louisiana also the Dixiecrats succeeded in designating Thurmond and Wright as the official Democratic nominees. Louisiana seemed destined to go for Truman until late in the campaign when the Dixiecrats pulled a coup in the state committee. In the early stages Governor Earl Long expressed no sympathy for the revolt; in March W. H. Talbot, the national committeeman, opposed revolt in the party ranks. The agitators for revolt were the conservatives, such as Sam Jones and John U. Barr. The states' rights group apparently gave up in its attempt to capture the Democratic electors and circulated petitions to place a slate of Thurmond-Wright electors on the ballot. As the campaign moved on, however, Talbot turned up in the states' rights ranks and on September 10, the Democratic state executive committee (with Long absent) without warning made Thurmond and Wright the official nominees of the state party. It seemed that Truman and Barkley might be excluded from the ballot, but Governor Long convened the legislature which permitted the names of Truman and Barkley to appear on the ballot though not "under the rooster" in the regular Democratic column. The behind-the-scenes story of the Louisiana larceny has not been told, but rumors float around about tidelands oil. A factor in the timing of the Louisiana action may have been the desire not to muddy the waters until after the senatorial primary of August 31. Robert F. Kennon, who opposed Russell Long, tried in the primary campaign to make political capital of Earl Long's silence on the civil rights controversy. Governor Thurmond at least explained the delay in Louisiana's action in these terms: "They have had a hot local political fight on down there in Louisiana. . . ."[44]

The sequence of events in Georgia somewhat resembled that of Louisiana, though the outcome was different. Early leaders of both the Talmadge and anti-Talmadge factions proclaimed an intention to fight out the civil rights question within the party. James S. Peters, state Democratic chairman and Talmadgite, attended Governor Wright's Jackson conference but declined to participate when the resolutions committee proposed a bolt. The gubernatorial primary campaign was in progress during the summer and apparently neither faction wanted to be accused of bolting. After the Talmadge victory early in September, however, uncertainty arose about what the Talmadge controlled state

[43] *Columbia Record*, February 23, 1948.
[44] *Times-Picayune* (New Orleans), September 11, 1948.

committee would do. The rumor got abroad that the Talmadgites, the conservative faction, had been merely keeping quiet until after the primary before delivering the electors to Thurmond and Wright. Gessner T. McCorvey, Alabama state chairman, said: "Jim Peters told us in Atlanta not to worry about Georgia going for States Rights. After the Talmadge victory . . . I talked with Peters again and he said the regular electors, when they are named, will be for Thurmond and Wright." [45] Perhaps the fear that a bolt on the presidential candidate would bring a contest in the general election for governor restrained the Talmadge organization. Whatever the reason, the Talmadge-dominated state committee designated as Democratic electors persons pledged to support the ticket. The states' righters had to take a place on the ballot outside the Democratic column. The chairman of the states' rights Democrats claimed "the Talmadge organization is behind us 100 per cent," although young Talmadge carefully avoided personal involvement in the movement. Several states' rights electors were strong Talmadge men. Governor M. E. Thompson and other anti-Talmadge leaders were most insistent on party loyalty, and the congressional delegation, save for Eugene Cox, an extremely conservative representative (from Mitchell County, 52.7 per cent Negro, 1940) stood by the national ticket.

Thus, even in the states of the Deep South, states with the highest proportions of Negroes, the will to bolt the national party was by no means universal. In these states it was not tradition alone that gave strength to the regular ticket; substantial groups of citizens regarded the general economic program of the Democratic party as of greater importance than the prospect of action on civil rights. The chances are that Thurmond carried Alabama and Louisiana only because of the maneuvers that made him the "Democratic" nominee in those states.

The foregoing discussion of the divisions among Democratic leaders in the 1948 campaign, if read in conjunction with the earlier treatments of state factional systems, throws considerable light on the character of the cleavages within each state. When the battle moves to the level of national politics, the policy tendencies of Democratic groups become more perceptible. The more liberal faction usually went down the line for the national Administration, although the picture was sometimes complicated by party loyalties arising from Republican competition rather than ideological compatibility with the national administration. As for the voters, in 1948 their behavior was generally the reverse of that in 1928. Thurmond usually polled his heaviest vote in those counties with the highest proportions of Negroes while the white counties remained most loyal to the national ticket. Departures from this correlation, as in 1928, were often associated with traditional party loyalties

[45] *Atlanta Journal,* September 13, 1948.

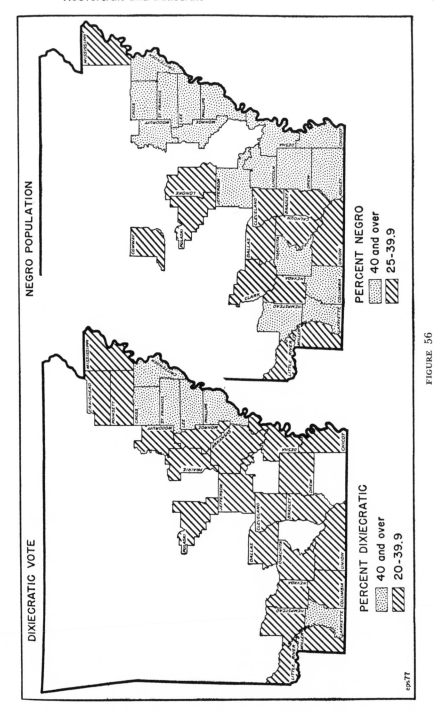

FIGURE 56

The Black Belt and the Thurmond Vote in 1948: The Case of Arkansas

arising out of intrastate Republican-Democratic competition. Space is not available for a comprehensive analysis of the county-by-county Thurmond vote, but the distribution of his Arkansas vote, shown in Figure 56, illustrates the generally prevalent pattern of relationship between Negro population concentrations and intensity of sentiment on civil rights.

Chapter Sixteen | **SOLIDARITY IN THE SENATE**

Aɴᴀʟʏꜱɪꜱ of two critical presidential campaigns, in the preceding chapter, pointed to the fundamental basis for the Democratic allegiance of the South. By consistent support of Democratic presidential candidates, the South has sought to defend its peculiar regional interest. Southern solidarity also finds expression in consistent representation by Democrats in the Senate and the House. Examination of the way in which southern legislators vote in Congress ought to throw more light on the nature and effects of the one-party system than does the study of presidential voting. Legislators must stand up and be counted on every conceivable sort of issue while a presidential campaign usually raises only one or two major questions. Perhaps, for example, the legislative record would show that southern solidarity contains elements other than a dominant attitude toward the Negro.

The voting records of southern members of Congress do not, of course, tell the whole story of the uses of regional Democratic loyalty in the promotion and protection of southern interests. The re-election of individual Senators and Representatives over long periods wins a special advantage for the South through the workings of the seniority principle. Southern voters have a keen awareness of the benefit accruing from long congressional service and the challenger of an elder statesman cannot easily persuade the electorate that young blood is preferable to seniority on committees and in congressional leadership.

The tactical advantage that the South enjoys through the capacity of its committee chairman to bottle up measures does not reflect itself in congressional roll calls, but the voting records do provide the data to show what one-party loyalty amounts to on the national political scene. For example, we have the legend of southern solidarity. Is the South actually united in Congress? If so, on what issues? We have the popular characterization of the South as "reactionary" and as "conservative." Does the record support such epithets? On the other hand, earlier analyses of Democratic party structure have demonstrated that in each state the party is no party at all but a holding company for competing factions. Do these cleavages within the party project themselves into the voting of southern Senators and Representatives? If so, what are the points of unity of the South as a whole? What are the lines along which southerners divide in Congress?

Only by a detailed analysis of how southerners actually vote in congress can satisfactory answers be obtained to such questions. To that end an examination has been made of Senate roll calls for seven sessions— those of 1933, 1935, 1937, 1939, 1941, 1943, and 1945. This analysis provides—at least for these sessions—a more comprehensive measurement of the attitudes of southerners in Congress than has ever been made.[1]

1. Degree of Southern Cohesiveness

Just how "solid" is the "Solid South" in the voting of its Senators? To speak of solidarity in absolute terms ignores the realities of the behavior of American legislative bodies. Party discipline can rarely compel unanimous acceptance of the party line by its members. Nor does any sub-group of a legislative body—except the smallest handful of members —vote consistently together. Hence, solidarity is a relative matter. One group may be more or less cohesive or "solid" than another. To answer the question one must apply a measure of the degree of cohesiveness or solidarity of southern Senators in comparison with other senatorial groups.

The upshot of analysis by such a method is that on the 598 roll calls of the seven sessions the average cohesiveness or solidarity of southern Senators exceeded that of Republicans, that of nonsouthern Democrats, and that of all Democrats. Yet the margin of superiority in cohesion of southern Senators was so slight that one can speak of the "Solid South" only in the most restricted sense.

[1] Different results might have been obtained by the analysis of different sessions. Hence, the conclusions in this chapter must be limited to these sessions, during which the Democratic party was in the majority and in control of the Presidency, factors that exert no inconsiderable influence on congressional voting. Further, all these sessions were in years immediately after elections. The record of pre-election years might be different.

These conclusions come from the use of an index of cohesion in an analysis of 598 roll calls.[2] This index is a measure of group solidarity.[3] The nontechnical reader need only remember that it is somewhat like a thermometer or a cost-of-living index. When the index moves toward 100 group cohesion increases. When it declines toward zero, the likeness of voting behavior among members of the group declines. When it reaches zero, the group is split 50–50. When it climbs to 100, the group is completely united.

By the use of this index on the 598 roll calls the following averages are obtained:

Southern Democrats	55.4
Republicans	51.8
Nonsouthern Democrats	46.9
Democrats	46.0

Although southern Democrats, on the average, voted together in greater degree than did the other groups with which they are compared, the differences were by no means large.

The extent of differences in cohesion among the groups analyzed may be more comprehensible if the indices are converted into equivalent percentages. The average index of cohesion of the southern Democratic group, 55.4, amounts to an average of 77.7 per cent of the group voting on the same side of all issues. Or contrariwise, almost one-fourth of the members, on the average, diverged from the view of the majority of the group. The equivalent percentages for each of the groups whose index is listed above is as follows:

Southern Democrats	77.7
Republicans	75.9
Nonsouthern Democrats	73.4
Democrats	73.0

Such are the overall averages for the seven sessions examined. It is well to be wary of averages, for they may conceal the meat of the problem. Do the indices on roll calls cluster closely around the grand average or are they widely scattered? Or, to translate the statistical problem into everyday language, it is safe for a boy to dive into a pool averaging 10

[2] The 598 roll calls include all recorded votes of the seven sessions except: (a) votes on the election of president pro tempore of the Senate; (b) votes on which the dissenters numbered less than 10 per cent of the majority. The rationale for the exclusion of these almost unanimous votes is, of course, that no issue existed of sufficient importance to compel significant cleavages within the Senate.

[3] Stuart A. Rice, the inventor of the index, describes it in his *Quantitative Methods in Politics* (New York: Alfred A. Knopf, 1928), pp. 208–9. A group's cohesion is at zero when its members divide 50–50 on a roll call. Cohesion moves to 100 when all members of the group vote together, either affirmatively or negatively. At intermediate points the index shows the degree of departure from a 50–50 split toward unanimity. Thus, a 75–25 division is half way between the two extremes and is represented by an index of 50.

feet in depth if it is 11 feet deep here and 9 there, but the venture requires more calculation if 18 feet of water covers the bottom at one point and two at another.

The wide scatter of the indices of cohesion on individual roll calls, shown in Table 34, makes it clear that the grand average for each group

TABLE 34

Distribution of Senate Roll Calls of Southern Democrats, Nonsouthern Democrats, and Republicans by Degree of Group Cohesion

RANGE OF	SOUTHERN DEMOCRATS		NONSOUTHERN DEMOCRATS		REPUBLICANS	
INDEX OF COHESION ON ROLL CALLS	NUMBER	PER CENT	NUMBER	PER CENT	NUMBER	PER CENT
0–9	48	8.0	56	9.5	58	9.7
10–19	54	9.0	52	8.7	47	7.8
20–29	55	9.2	72	12.0	69	11.5
30–39	43	7.2	77	12.9	53	8.8
40–49	48	8.0	68	11.4	59	9.9
50–59	55	9.2	69	11.5	56	9.5
60–69	65	10.9	71	11.9	62	10.4
70–79	66	11.0	51	8.5	50	8.3
80–89	74	12.4	35	5.8	65	10.9
90–100	90	15.1	47	7.8	79	13.2
Total	598	100.0	598	100.0	598	100.0

of Senators does not mean much in description of differences among groups of Senators. Nevertheless, from the table one fact of significance emerges. Southern Democrats find occasion to cohere in high degree on a considerably larger proportion of roll calls than do the groups with which their voting behavior is compared. The percentage of roll calls on which each group had an index of cohesion of 70 or more (the equivalent of an affirmative or negative vote of 85 per cent or more) for the seven sessions lumped together was as follows:

Southern Democrats	38.5
Nonsouthern Democrats	22.1
Republicans	32.4

From these figures the inference may well be that on the average southern Senators have little more cohesiveness than other groups but on certain types of issues they tend more toward unity than do other groups of Senators. If we can identify those issues clothed with a compulsion toward solidarity, we may isolate the essence of southern unity, such as it is.

2. Southern Solidarity: How Much and on What Issues?

Southern Democrats in the Senate, it becomes evident, on the average stick together in slightly higher degree than do Republicans or non-southern Democrats. However, the high southern average is produced by the fact that southern Democratic cohesion reaches a high level on a larger proportion of all roll calls than is the case with other groups. These roll calls of high southern cohesiveness may contain the key to southern solidarity. To get down to the essence of the question of solidarity the examination of the record must be carried several steps further.

Cohesiveness in voting by a group of legislators takes on significance only in relation to the behavior of other groups. Southern Democrats and Republicans may, for example, line up unanimously in support of the same proposition. Both groups have high cohesiveness, but they may be registering routine agreement to a noncontroversial proposal. On the other hand, when southern Democrats all vote one way and Republicans all vote the other, a more significant question is apt to be involved.

On more than half the roll calls in each of the seven sessions examined, a majority of southern Democratic Senators disagreed with a majority of Republican Senators. The facts are arrayed in Table 35. A majority of the southerners opposed a majority of the Republicans on 60.0 per cent of all the roll calls of the seven sessions. The proportion of roll calls on which a majority of southern Democrats disagreed with a majority of Republicans fluctuated from session to session. The peak came in

TABLE 35

Senate Roll Calls with Majority of Southern Democrats Opposing
Majority of Republicans, by Sessions, 1933–45 [a]

CONGRESS, SESSION, YEAR	TOTAL ROLL CALLS	ROLL CALLS WITH MAJORITIES IN DISAGREEMENT	
		NUMBER	PER CENT OF TOTAL
73:1(1933)	82	54	65.8
74:1(1935)	108	59	54.6
75:1(1937)	58	35	60.3
76:1(1939)	79	50	63.3
77:1(1941)	84	59	70.2
78:1(1943)	105	58	55.2
79:1(1945)	82	45	54.9
Total	598	360	60.0

[a] Although the caption so states, it may be well to specify that roll calls on which either group split exactly 50–50 are not tabulated as roll calls with majorities in disagreement.

1941 when southern Democrats united against Republicans on a large number of roll calls in connection with the lend-lease act.

It should be kept in mind that this matter of majorities in disagreement is relative. On one issue southern Democrats may vote 49 per cent affirmatively and Republicans 51 per cent affirmatively. Their majorities disagree. At the other extreme, 100 per cent of southern Democrats may oppose 100 per cent of the Republicans. Between these two ends of the scale there may occur an infinite number of combinations of divisions of group sentiment, each constituting an instance of opposing majorities.

While these warnings must be heeded in interpreting the data in Table 35, certain conclusions seep out of the figures. The canard about southern Democrats being allies of Republicans demands at least modification in the light of the facts. On a large proportion of roll calls, a majority of southern Democrats stands up against a majority of the Republicans. Yet a majority of southerners allied themselves with a majority of Republicans on 40 per cent of the roll calls. This fact in itself comes principally from congressional practice of making many decisions on other than partisan lines. On only some issues of southern Democratic and Republican majority alliance is their concurrence an indicator of a fundamental community of political interest.[4]

The identification of those issues on which southern Democrats maintain an extremely high degree of solidarity in opposition to Republican majorities will perhaps isolate the bases of southern solidarity. Such issues—those on which less than 10 per cent of southern Democratic Senators deviated from the majority view within their group—are tabulated in Table 36. The hypothesis underlying the selection of these roll calls for analysis is that such roll calls must be on issues on which some compelling interest peculiar to the South drives southern Senators toward unanimity.

On only 85 of 598 roll calls did at least 90 per cent of southern Senators vote together in opposition to Republican majorities. The occurrence of roll calls with a high level of southern cohesion, as may be seen in Table 36, varied somewhat from session to session, with a peak 23.8 per cent for the session of 1941 when southern Senators voted solidly time and again against proposals to weaken the lend-lease bill.

On 85 of the 598 roll calls at least 90 per cent of the voting southerners opposed varying majorities of Republicans. To get down to the basis of southern solidarity we need to distill off another fraction of our statistical brew. How did the nonsouthern Democrats stand on these 85 votes? On 76 of the 85 roll calls, a majority of nonsouthern Democrats agreed with their southern colleagues. The issues impelled southerners toward unanimity and presumably had a high rating in the southern scale

---

[4] On about three-fourths of the roll calls of southern Democratic-Republican majority agreement, a majority of nonsouthern Democrats concurred.

of political values, but they had as allies a majority of their fellow Democrats from outside the South.

With 76 of the 85 roll calls disposed of, nine are left on which at least 90 per cent of southern Senators opposed majorities of both Republicans and nonsouthern Democrats. At least 90 per cent of the southern contin-

TABLE 36

Senate Roll Calls of High Southern Democratic Cohesion [a] in Opposition to Republican Majorities, by Sessions, 1933–45

CONGRESS, SESSION, YEAR	TOTAL NUMBER OF ROLL CALLS [b]	ROLL CALLS OF HIGH SOUTHERN COHESION		NUMBER OF SUCH ROLL CALLS ON WHICH SOUTHERN DEMOCRATIC MAJORITY—	
		NUMBER	PER CENT OF TOTAL	AGREED WITH NONSOUTHERN DEMOCRATIC MAJORITY	DISAGREED WITH NONSOUTHERN DEMOCRATIC MAJORITY
73:1(1933)	82	4	4.9	4	0
74:1(1935)	108	16	14.8	13	3
75:1(1937)	58	8	13.8	6	2
76:1(1939)	79	12	15.2	10	2
77:1(1941)	84	20	23.8	20	0
78:1(1943)	105	12	11.4	11	1
79:1(1945)	82	13	15.9	12	1
Totals	598	85	14.2	76	9

[a] That is, those roll calls on which less than 10 per cent of the southern Democratic Senators deviated from the views of a majority of their brethren.

[b] These totals, it will be remembered, exclude those roll calls on which less than 10 per cent of the Senators voting dissented from the prevailing view, as well as votes on the selection of president pro tempore.

gent lined up against the rest of the country. These nine roll calls ought to represent southern solidarity in its most extreme form; they require detailed examination.

Seven of the nine roll calls raised the race issue in one form or another. Three were in 1935 on motions relating to an antilynching bill. Two more occurred in 1937 on the same subject. One was in connection with a parliamentary maneuver on an antilynching bill and another came on a motion to tack an antilynching rider onto a bill to limit the length of freight trains. In 1943 the race issue arose in connection with a proposal for Federal aid to state educational systems. An amendment to prohibit discrimination along lines of race or color in the administration of the funds drew unanimous southern opposition. In 1945 the race question reared its head in yet another guise in a proposed appropriation for the Committee on Fair Employment Practice; southern Senators unanimously opposed.

In two of the nine roll calls race, at least in form, was not involved. Both occurred in August, 1939, on motions by Senator Pat McCarran, of Nevada, to suspend the rules to permit amendments in the nature of legislation to a WPA appropriation bill. He proposed to restore the prevailing wage rate for WPA work, to reduce urban-rural differentials in pay, and to eliminate a regional wage differential discriminatory against Arkansas, Kentucky, Louisiana, Oklahoma, Texas, and Virginia.[5] Apparently his proposal, without an increase in total appropriation, would have reduced the number of WPA workers. It is conceivable that in their opposition southern Senators were moved by race considerations: Negroes on the WPA were thought to be receiving too much money. Yet the Senate debate contains no reference to the relation of the proposal, if any, to the Negro.[6]

By a process of elimination we have identified those few issues on which the South stands solidly against both Republicans and nonsouthern Democrats and those issues reflect a common determination to oppose external intervention in matters of race relations. The common element in the critical votes is objection to Federal intervention. The southern Senators voted against Federal investigators who would look into lynchings, against Federal inspectors who would inquire whether Negroes were discriminated against in the expenditure of educational funds, and against Federal officials who would seek to prevent discrimination against Negroes in employment.

The question may well be raised whether southern solidarity amounts to anything more than a prevailing attitude toward the Negro. That is clearly the bedrock of southern unity, but perhaps other factors contribute to it. The analysis began with 85 roll calls on which at least 90 per cent of southern Senators voted together against a majority of the Republicans. On the critical nine, southerners opposed both Republican and nonsouthern Democratic majorities. What of the other 76 roll calls of high southern cohesion on which southerners agreed with a majority of nonsouthern Democrats?

On these 76 roll calls southern Senators, while in agreement with a majority of nonsouthern Democrats, demonstrated a higher degree of unity than did their fellow partisans from outside the South. Solidarity is a relative matter and on some types of issues the South apparently is different in degree. The 76 roll calls covered an extremely wide range of issues; many of them reflected no special regional interest but merely recorded the routine views of a majority party with responsibility for the management of the Senate.

Thirty-four of the 76 roll calls dealt with questions of foreign policy

---

[5] A still lower scale applicable to other states of the South would not have been affected by his proposal.

[6] *Congressional Record*, vol. 84, pt. 10, pp. 11,009–17.

and, although both southern Democrats and nonsouthern Democrats had majorities opposed to the majority of Republicans, southerners cohered in higher degree than did their fellow Democrats. The foreign policy roll calls can be best examined by grouping them into smaller blocks of more or less related questions. The reciprocal trade program accounted for nine of the foreign policy roll calls. The averages of the indices of cohesion on these issues by several groups were as follows:

Southern Democrats	89.8
Nonsouthern Democrats	68.2
Republicans	73.3

To translate these indices into percentages: southern Democrats, on the average, voted 94.8 per cent for trade agreements, while on the average only 84.1 per cent of nonsouthern Democrats supported the program. On the other hand, on the average 86.6 per cent of the Republicans opposed. The conclusion has to be that the free trade tradition in the South has not vanished. When issues of specific tariffs—peanuts or sugar, for example—arise, southerners, like northerners and westerners, desert their principles with alacrity, but the facts suggest that the South remains the area with the most intense attachment to free trade.[7]

Another nine of the 34 foreign policy roll calls dealt with a variety of issues that can be lumped together as measures concerned with preparation for or anticipation of war.[8] On these issues again southern Democrats maintained higher cohesion than did nonsouthern Democrats. The average indices of cohesion for the several groups on these measures were:

Southern Democrats	95.3
Nonsouthern Democrats	62.1
Republicans	63.0

Or, to translate these indices into equivalent percentages, the southerners on the average voted 97.6 per cent in support of preparatory measures and nonsouthern Democrats 81.0 per cent, while the Republicans averaged 81.5 per cent in opposition.

A closely related group of roll calls came on the lend-lease bill in 1941. Here again the southerners were more nearly unanimous in their support of the bill and in their opposition to amendments calculated to emasculate or to weaken it. The averages of the indices of cohesion on 12 roll calls for the several groups were as follows:

[7] The technical reader will know, and the nontechnician may be reminded, that contrasts between southern Democrats and other groups need to be interpreted strictly within their limits. For example, in these comparisons Republicans are treated as a single group. A different picture might develop if separate analyses were made for northeastern Republicans or midwestern Republicans.

[8] Included in the nine were two 1937 roll calls on the Neutrality Act, two 1939 roll calls on the purchase of strategic materials, a 1941 roll call on passage of the Priorities Act, three others in the same session on the Selective Service Act, and another on an act relating to the requisition and purchase of foreign merchant vessels.

Southern Democrats	91.7
Nonsouthern Democrats	53.7
Republicans	57.9

The equivalent average affirmative percentages of southern and nonsouthern groups would have been 95.8 and 76.8, respectively, while the equivalent Republican negative percentage averaged 78.9.

In the 1945 session four other foreign policy roll calls fell into the category of high southern Democratic cohesion. Three related to the United Nations and were on hampering amendments while the fourth concerned the international bank agreement. Again the southerners demonstrated higher cohesion in support of international collaboration and against hampering amendments than did their nonsouthern party colleagues. The averages of the indices were:

Southern Democrats	99.3
Nonsouthern Democrats	72.8
Republicans	40.0

The average percentages, again translating the indices, were for the southern Democrats, 99.1, for the nonsouthern Democrats, 86.4, while, on the average, 70 per cent of the Republicans recorded themselves in opposition.

Evidently the South, as represented by its Senators, differed from nonsouthern Democrats to some degree and radically from Republicans on matters of foreign policy involved in the 34 roll calls analyzed. These attitudes, however, did not set the South against the rest of the country as did the race question. Southerners simply had less dissent within their own ranks than did the nonsouthern Democrats, although majorities of both groups opposed a majority of the Republicans. In these matters partisan considerations played a part. The Democrats, in power, tended to rally together to support the Administration and the Republicans, perforce, had to oppose. Yet Republican opposition on the foreign policy questions, one must conclude from common knowledge, reflected more than the registration of pro forma disagreement with Administration proposals.

The analysis of foreign policy roll calls accounts for only 34 of the 76 roll calls on which 90 per cent or more of southern Senators joined a majority of nonsouthern Democrats in opposition to the majority of Republicans. The other 42 roll calls cover a wide range of subject matter, and apparently playing an important part in the extremely high southern Democratic cohesion were partisan considerations, in the sense of solidarity in support of Administration measures in opposition to Republican pro forma obstruction. Thus, on the vote on the final passage of the Economy Act of 1933 the Democrats lined up against the Republicans.

Strategy and habit of party warfare are perhaps more significant in such roll calls than are fundamental cleavages of attitude. Further, many of the 42 roll calls were votes on final passage—after all the controversy is taken out of a bill by amendment—and the Democratic-Republican opposition distilled down to the routine registration of partisan sentiment.

3. The Southern Democratic-Republican Coalition

Commonly a southern Senator is caricatured as a frock-coated, long-maned, and long-winded statesman of the old school, who conspires in the cloakroom with Republicans to grind down the common man. He is supposed in return to receive generous campaign contributions from Wall Street as well as kudos from the conservative columnists who praise him as a constitutional scholar, a man of statesmanlike vision, and an embodiment of the virtues of the Founding Fathers. While there is in all this enough truth to embarrass good southern Democrats, the report of the Southern Democratic-Republican congressional coalition has been not a little exaggerated.

Earlier it was shown that on about 6 out of 10 roll calls in the 7 Senate sessions examined a majority of southern Democrats opposed a majority of Republicans. We are left with about 35 per cent of the roll calls on which a majority of southern Democrats agreed with a majority of Republicans, after allowing for those instances in which one or the other of the groups split 50–50. Under any circumstance, of course, it is at least a misdemeanor for a southern Democrat to agree with a Republican, but the gravity of the crime varies with circumstance. When majorities of both southern and nonsouthern Democrats agree with the Republicans, either no substantial issue is at stake or the southern Democrats are in no more grievous error than their nonsouthern colleagues and ought not to be singled out as the sole enemies of progress.

On about three-fourths of the roll calls on which Republican and southern Democratic majorities agreed, a majority of nonsouthern Democrats went along with the prevailing view. There are left 54 roll calls on which southern Democratic and Republican majorities joined in opposition to a majority of the nonsouthern Democrats. Here we have, on less than 10 per cent of all roll calls, the classic southern Democratic-Republican coalition. On many of these roll calls the southern Democrats were badly split. In the identification of common denominators between the South and Republicans perhaps most significance should be assigned to those roll calls of relatively high southern Democratic cohesion in coalition with a Republican majority against the nonsouthern Democrats. On 26 of the 54 roll calls more than 70 per cent of the southern Democrats united with the Republican majority against a majority of nonsouthern Democrats. Presumably issues were at stake on which the South had in the highest degree a common interest with the Republicans.

Although the 26 roll calls dealt with a variety of topics, their isolation sharply defines those aspects of southern regionalism that nurture coalition with Republicans against nonsouthern Democrats. The list enlightens because of the type of question it does not include, as well as the type it does. Consider the Fair Labor Standards Act. Proposed amendments to the wage and hour provisions of the bill provoked the three

TABLE 37

Southern Democratic-Republican Coalition: Senate Roll Calls with Majorities of Southern Democrats and Republicans in Agreement in Opposition to Nonsouthern Democratic Majorities

CONGRESS, SESSION, YEAR	TOTAL ROLL CALLS	NUMBER OF ROLL CALLS WITH MAJORITIES OF SOUTHERN DEMOCRATS AND REPUBLICANS IN AGREEMENT			
		TOTAL	NSD MAJORITY CONCURRED	NSD MAJORITY OPPOSED	IN OPPOSITION TO NSD MAJORITY WITH HIGH SD COHESIONS [a]
73:1 (1933)	82	25	17	8	2
74:1 (1935)	108	44	37	7	1
75:1 (1937)	58	19	9	10	3
76:1 (1939)	79	24	19	5	2
77:1 (1941)	84	20	16	4	3
78:1 (1943)	105	44	28 [b]	15	12
79:1 (1945)	82	31	25 [b]	5	3
Totals	598	207	151	54	26

[a] Roll calls on which no more than 29.9 per cent of southern Democrats deviated from the prevailing view.

[b] On one roll call the nonsouthern Democrats split exactly 50–50. Hence, this figure and the one in the next column do not equal the total column.

1937 roll calls of high southern cohesion in coalition with the Republicans. One was to exempt from the act seasonal workers in tobacco warehouses, cotton compresses, cotton warehouses, and cotton gins. Another proposed to exempt workers packing or processing perishable agricultural products during the harvesting season, while a third was to exclude seasonal employees engaged in cotton ginning and baling. All three proposals had a concrete regional application and affected workers closely connected with agriculture. Only these three wage and hour issues evoked a high degree of southern cohesion in coalition with the Republicans. On other roll calls on issues relating to workers generally, the southern Senators either maintained low cohesion in collaboration with Republicans or a majority of them joined with nonsoutherners against the Republicans.[9]

[9] For example, on a motion by Senator Connally to recommit the wage-hour bill, 55 per cent of the southern democrats voted yea; 25 per cent of the nonsouthern Democrats; 93 per cent of the Republicans.

High southern Democratic cohesion in alliance with a Republican majority against the nonsouthern Democrats sometimes appears on agricultural issues. In such coalitions a common concern about agriculture outweighs partisan enmities, although at times the coalition has a flavor of log-rolling. Two roll calls on a 1941 proposal, by Senator Butler, to tax imports of oils, starches, and jute fall in the log-rolling category. The proposed taxation of oil imports pleased producers of cottonseed oil; corn growers liked the idea of taxing starches while the jute tax had an appeal to cotton farmers. Senator Butler could say: "This amendment is not a sectional bill. It is intended to improve the prices and markets of crops in every section of the country." [10] The Senator's amendment was, of course, a double-pronged vote-catcher designed to ally different but nonconflicting interests. An example of common agricultural concern rather than a log-rolling coalition appeared in the vote on a 1943 proposal by Senator O'Mahoney to tighten up agricultural deferments from the draft. Southern Democrats and Republicans joined to maintain a special position for agriculture, while nonsouthern Democrats lacked enthusiasm for generous agricultural exemptions.[11]

On some agricultural coalitions, the bonds are strengthened by a shared antipathy. Five 1943 roll calls of high southern Democratic cohesion in company with majorities of Republicans were on the wartime food subsidy program. Farmers, as farmers, preferred that their income accrue from higher prices rather than from fixed prices plus a government subsidy. Coupled with this and other objections to the subsidy program was a rural opposition to the subsidization of urban workers who supposedly were waxing fat on high wages and on both economic and moral grounds ought to be required to pay for their own groceries. A majority of nonsouthern Democrats, on the other hand, out of both partisan loyalty and urban interest, supported the Administration's subsidy proposal as an element of the price control program.[12]

Another group of the 26 critical votes related to the position of labor in war and reconversion. In 1941 southern Democrats and Republicans allied in support of an amendment to the Selective Service Act condemning strikes in defense industries. The amendment merely expressed an opinion and had no effect except to aggravate friction. In 1943 the same coalition appeared again on three roll calls on the War Labor Disputes Act, popularly known as the Smith-Connally Act. Southern Democrats joined with Republicans to vote down a motion to recommit the

[10] *Congressional Record*, vol. 87, pt. 7, p. 7351.

[11] The yea percentages on the motion were: southern Democrats, 11; nonsouthern Democrats, 65; Republicans, 33.

[12] Another coalition on an agricultural vote occurred in 1933 to defeat a proposal by Senator Frazier to write the principle of a guarantee of the cost of production into the AAA program. Southern Democrats, perhaps a bit more conservative than Senator Frazier, supported the Administration proposal as did a majority of the Republicans.

bill, to agree to the conference report, and to override the presidential veto of the bill. In 1945, in the congressional battle over reconversion policy in which the relations between the agrarian and labor wings of the Democratic party were strained, southern Democrats and Republicans got together in support of a measure to require transfer of the employment offices from Federal to state administration and against a measure to supplement state employment compensation payments with Federal funds during the reconversion period.[13]

On only two votes on work relief did southern Democrats and Republicans ally themselves in a manner to qualify for inclusion in the list of 26 roll calls. In 1939 Senator Pepper proposed to increase the work relief appropriation by $150 million, in accordance with a presidential request. Senator Barkley said that $100 million additional was all that could be put through and more than 70 per cent of the southerners agreed with him as did a majority of the Republicans. Later in the same session Senator Murray proposed, with support of the WPA administrator, to give administrative leeway by modifying a rule requiring those who had been on the WPA rolls 18 months to be discharged. Southern Democrats and Republicans voted the amendment down.

Two race issues, oddly, are included in the 26 roll calls. In 1943 Republicans joined with southern Democrats, with a majority of non-southern Democrats in opposition, to recommit a bill for Federal aid to education. Just before the recommittal, an amendment had been adopted to prohibit discrimination on account of race or color in the expenditure of Federal funds by state schools. Southern disagreement with the anti-discrimination clause coincided with Republican dissent from the principle of Federal aid. At the same session a vote on the soldier voting bill brought southern Democrats and Republicans together. The Republicans did not want the soldiers to vote Democratic. The southern Democrats did not want colored soldiers to vote.

Three of the 26 votes remain to be accounted for. In 1933 a coalition voted down Senator LaFollette's amendment to the Economy Act to provide that the compensation of no Federal employee would be reduced below $1000 by the general terms of the act. In 1935 an amendment by LaFollette to the banking act was rejected. The amendment, the Senator stated, would prevent weakening of earlier legislation to keep commercial and investment banking separate. In 1943 the southern Democratic-Republican team clicked in support of an appropriation rider to prohibit payment of salaries of Goodwin B. Watson, William E. Dodd, Jr., and

---

[13] In the same session the southern Democratic-Republican coalition appeared on an amendment to exempt the civil functions, i.e., rivers and harbors activities, of the Corps of Engineers from the presidential power of administrative reorganization. Non-southern Democrats, more dependent on the national administration, were less susceptible to the lobbying efforts of the corps than were Democrats from safe states.

Robert Morss Lovett unless their appointments were confirmed by the Senate, a provision later held void.

What do the facts about the southern Democratic-Republican coalition mean? From the standpoint of quantity alone, on less than 10 per cent of the roll calls does a majority of southern Democrats join with a majority of Republicans against a majority of nonsouthern Democrats. On less than five per cent of the roll calls were more than 70 per cent of the southern Senators in alliance with the Republicans. All of which means, of course, that while individual southern Senators may frequently vote with the Republicans, a majority rarely does; and when it does, the group as a whole is badly split more than half the time.

From a qualitative point of view the roll calls evoking coalition suggest several observations about the nature of the southern Democratic-Republican alliance. The listing suggests that a peculiar combination or cumulation of circumstances is necessary to force more than 70 per cent of the southerners into coalition with the Republicans against nonsouthern Democrats. The wage and hour votes in which labor locally, not labor generally, brought the southern Democrats and Republicans together illustrate the compounding of regional interest plus agrarian antipathy toward labor. It is entirely probable that more extensive analysis might lead to the conclusion that the most potent factor leading to the kinds of coalitions under analysis is that of a common interest, attitude, and philosophy of the agrarian elements of the two parties rather than a community of interest between southern planter and northern financier, as is so often asserted. The votes on work relief measures suggest this basis for coalition. In conservative agrarian coalitions there may, of course, be a big business concurrence, but only one of the 26 roll calls on its face showed a planter-financier coalition. Perhaps over the long pull urban Democrats have more reliable allies in southern agrarians than in Republican agrarians.[14]

4. Departures from Solidarity: The Southern Political Spectrum

The preceding analysis indicates that on the race question, and on that question alone, does a genuine southern solidarity exist. On other questions southern Democrats split and southern solidarity becomes a

[14] A reader of the manuscript observed that the attempt to take into account degrees of party loyalty reminded him of the woman who claimed to be 85 per cent virtuous. When the southern bloc kicks over the traces on a single critical roll call, it may wreck party responsibility. The only answer that can be made is that in a land where there are no virgins, virtue must be a relative matter. American parties, loose coalitions that they are, cannot claim the adherence of their members on 100 per cent of the roll calls. Under these circumstances party loyalty must be measured in shades of gray rather than in black and white.

matter of degree. Some southern Senators tend to vote with their northern, urban, fellow Democrats; others have Republican leanings. This diversity of view is, indeed, only what would be expected from a southern Democratic party that encompasses all shades of political attitude. If the theory that legislators reflect attitudes of their supporters has validity, southern Senators, in their voting records, would shade from the extreme right towards left of center in consistency with the differences in their factional affiliations at home. That is, this would be the result unless the regional compulsion toward solidarity spreads out from the race question and induces a higher degree of solidarity on other matters than would otherwise prevail.

The measurement of gradations in attitude of southern Senators and the relation of these differences to the factional systems of the several states present no easy problem. The usual procedure in analyzing the voting behavior of southern Democrats is to classify votes as "right" or "wrong;" this process involves some pretense of infallibility. Earlier claims to a monopoly of that quality have a precedence that we do not care to contest. Further, the technique has a more serious limitation. It reveals nothing about southern Senators as a group and, the relativity of politics being what it is, the voting behavior of one group assumes significance only in contrast with that of other groups.

To spot the peaks, so to speak, of conservatism in the South the following method was devised: Those roll calls were segregated on which a majority of southern Democrats opposed a majority of Republicans. From these roll calls were isolated those on which only from 0.0 to 29.9 per cent of southern Democrats deserted their fellow southerners and voted with the Republicans. It was assumed that on these roll calls of fairly high southern cohesion the compulsion toward solidarity made itself felt most strongly. It was supposed that those southern Democrats who voted most frequently with the Republicans on these roll calls were the most "Republican" Democratic Senators. The results of sifting out those roll calls with relatively high southern Democratic cohesion in opposition to the majority of Republicans appear in Table 38. On 360 of 598 roll calls, at least a majority of southern Democrats opposed a majority of Republicans.[15] On 245 of the 360 roll calls, no more than 29.9 per cent of the southern Democrats deserted their sectional brethren and voted with the Republicans. Or, to put the matter in reciprocal form, on these 245 roll calls at least 70 per cent of the southern Democratic Senators recorded themselves in opposition to a Republican majority.

Which Senators deserted the southern Democrats most frequently and joined the majority of Republicans on these 245 roll calls? The answer should identify the extreme rightist elements in the southern

[15] As in the earlier tables those roll calls on which either group split precisely 50–50 are not included in the majority-in-opposition category.

Democracy, if it is assumed that the Republican majority consistently adheres to a rightist position. The 11 southern Senators who yielded most frequently to the urge to vote Republican on our 245 roll calls are listed in Table 39, which includes only those Senators who voted Republican more than 14 per cent of the time.

TABLE 38

Senate Roll Calls on which Majorities of Southern Democrats and Republicans were Opposed and Only 0–29.9 Per Cent of Southern Democrats Voted with Majority of Republicans

CONGRESS, SESSION, YEAR	(1) TOTAL ROLL CALLS	(2) ROLL CALLS WITH OPPOSING SD AND R MAJORITIES	(3) ROLL CALLS WITH 0–29.9% SD'S VOTING WITH R'S	PER CENT (3) OF (1)
73:1 (1933)	82	54	31	37.8
74:1 (1935)	108	59	41	38.0
75:1 (1937)	58	35	23	39.6
76:1 (1939)	79	50	36	45.7
77:1 (1941)	84	59	47	55.9
78:1 (1943)	105	58	35	33.3
79:1 (1945)	82	45	32	39.0
Totals	598	360	245	41.0

The listing of Senators most disposed to desert their southern Democratic colleagues and vote with the majority of Republicans does not sift out cleanly Senators of like political hue, but the rankings shown in the table are not purely fortuitous. The wide differences in the tendency of Senators to vote with the Republicans provides support for the proposition that the Democratic party of the South consists of factions ranging across the political spectrum, although it would be absurd to suppose that the rankings of the Senators in the table measure exactly the degrees of "Republicanism" in the different states.

W. Lee O'Daniel, of Texas, by our method, earns the ranking as the most Republican of southern Democrats. Pappy O'Daniel got into the Senate by his political adroitness in organizing a coalition of the rich and the credulous in Texas at a time when the reaction against the New Deal had set in. He went to the Senate first in 1941 by winning a special election, rather than a Democratic primary, in which he nosed out a New Deal candidate in a multicornered race. He won with only 30.7 per cent of the popular vote and had less than fourteen hundred votes to spare. In 1942 he won the primary for the regular term. In view of the sharpened political struggle along progressive-conservative lines in Texas since 1940, O'Daniel's 1942 victory, although within the confines of the Democratic party, approached the equivalent, for example, of a Republican triumph over the Democrats in Ohio.

The high rank of Virginia Senators on the list of Democratic Republicans also conforms to the known facts about Virginia politics. The Byrd organization has stood out as the most thoroughly disciplined state

TABLE 39

The Most Republican Southern Democrats: Those who Voted Most Frequently with the Majority of Republicans on Roll Calls on which at Least 70 Per Cent of Southern Democrats Opposed a Majority of Republicans [a]

	VOTES IN SEVEN SESSIONS			VOTES EXCEPT IN 1941		
	NUMBER OF VOTES		PER CENT WITH R'S	NUMBER OF VOTES		PER CENT WITH R'S
SENATOR	TOTAL	WITH R'S		TOTAL	WITH R'S	
O'Daniel	69	44	63.8	54	39	72.2
Glass	98	35	35.7	61	30	49.2
Byrd	202	91	45.0	158	72	45.6
Long	45	19	42.2	45	19	42.2
Bailey	169	55	32.5	136	49	36.0
Smith	144	40	27.8	114	27	23.7
Trammell	64	14	21.9	64	14	21.9
Overton	164	24	14.6	129	24	18.6
Reynolds	135	36	26.7	106	19	17.9
George	202	29	14.3	160	27	16.9
McClellan	55	9	16.4	55	9	16.4

[a] Two southern Senators who saw short service during the years under study and had high ratios of agreement with Republicans are not listed. Stephens, of Mississippi, in the 1933 session voted 28 times, 17.7 per cent of the time with the Republicans. Berry, of Tennessee, in 1937, voted on 8 roll calls, 50 per cent of the time with the Republican majority.

political machine in the South, and it prides itself on its conservatism. The table makes it clear why a high Byrd organization leader could smile about the activities of a few Republicans to energize their organization in 1947: "The Republicans are delighted with the government the Senator is giving Virginia; they are putting on a little show to get in on the Federal patronage after 1948."

Parenthetically, an explanation can be made at this point about the table. Separate computations were made on the records with the exclusion of the 1941 session. In 1941 a large number of roll calls occurred on lend-lease issues; some southern Democrats adhered more consistently to the Democratic foreign policy than to its domestic policies. Hence, as in the case of the late Senator Glass, with the exclusion of the 1941 votes, a considerably higher degree of agreement is shown with the majority of Republicans on our 245 roll calls.

Senators from North Carolina ranked high in their degree of Republicanism but considerably lower than Virginia Senators. The late Senator Bailey, who won his Senate seat first in 1930, had a marked inclination to desert his fellow southern Democrats and vote with the Republicans, but he agreed with the Republicans less frequently than did Senator Byrd. This difference paralleled a difference in the tone of the dominant organizations in Virginia and North Carolina. Antiorganization leaders in Virginia look with some envy on North Carolinians who enjoy the leadership of a conservative Democratic faction that is in their opinion, in comparison with the Byrd machine, progressive and forward-looking.

The appearance of former Senator Reynolds on the list suggests one of the odd results of our method of separating the sheep from the goats. Reynolds, a western North Carolinian, won in 1932 in a rip-roaring campaign against Cam Morrison, a politician of a more conservative and sedate school. Reynolds presumably won by riding the general wave of depression resentment and, in effect, represented a different voter-grouping than Senator Bailey. Reynolds won his way to our list of Democratic Republicans for two curious reasons: he was, on some issues, more "radical" than the majority of his southern colleagues and voted with the Republicans who, pro forma, opposed the Democratic majority. On international issues, he was more isolationist than his southern colleagues and found congenial company among the Republicans. Out of tune with the sentiment of his constituency, Senator Reynolds found it inexpedient to seek re-election in 1944.

Long and Overton of Louisiana were among the southern Senators who utilized more than 14 per cent of their opportunities to vote with the Republicans. Overton won a place on the list by his position on the reciprocal trade act and related tariff questions. Without the influence of the politics of sugar, his ratio of Republicanism would have fallen below the 15 per cent mark. Long's record of dissent resembled somewhat that of Reynolds of North Carolina. On some questions Long was more of a New Dealer than the southern majority and, for a time, he was at war with the Administration.

The record of Bailey and Reynolds, Senators from the same state, suggests a hypothesis about one of the consequences of the one-party system in congressional politics. Here we have from the same state two Senators, one an arch conservative yet internationalist, the other something of a hybrid of Huey Long and Robert Taft. Can there be any rational sort of explanation why a state can be represented simultaneously by two Senators so different? [16] This North Carolina situation is, of course, not peculiar. On our table of Republican Democrats we have Smith of South

[16] Of the roll calls analyzed in Table 39, both Bailey and Reynolds voted on 99; they voted together on 44 and disagreed on 55.

Carolina, but not Byrnes; George of Georgia, but not Russell; McClellan of Arkansas, but not Caraway; O'Daniel of Texas, but not Sheppard or Connally.

The divergence in the records of Senators is explained in part by the varying extent to which individual Senators vote. If Senator A had turned up at the roll call as frequently as Senator B, his ranking might have been at least slightly different. Another element is the period of service of the Senator. Some were in the Senate for all seven sessions. Others served only in later sessions where the differences among Democrats were sharper.

The long-continued divergences in attitude of Senators from the same state, however, require additional explanation. A plausible theory is that in the factional structure of one-party system the electorate lacks a party label as a guide to aid it in choosing candidates. In a two-party state, when the electorate becomes aroused, it can boot out the Republicans and put in the Democrats or vice versa. In the South the electorate can only choose from among Democrats, and the differences among them are not always readily apparent. The extremist, who is markedly out of tune with his constituency, may be spotted, but differences are more apt to be only of degree. The incumbent Senator can build up a following and an organization and, in the never-never land of one-party politics where everyone is alike but different, he can get himself re-elected without regard to his policies, unless they are extremely far out of line.

Our short-cut method of identification of peaks of conservatism has its limitations. Nevertheless, the same method may be applied to the other end of the political scale in an attempt to identify those southern Democrats most disposed to break away from the majority of their fellow southerners and join with a majority of nonsouthern Democrats. It was presumed that the most significant roll calls for this purpose would be those on which a majority of nonsouthern Democrats opposed majorities of both southern Democrats and Republicans. A southerner who voted with nonsouthern Democrats on such roll calls would presumably be a genuine New Dealer. Only 54 of the 598 roll calls meet our conditions. Their incidence by sessions is shown in Table 40.[17]

Southerners who voted with nonsoutherners on our 54 roll calls would be New Dealers, of course, only if the nonsouthern group maintained a consistent policy, as it does not. Nevertheless, the analysis of the voting records of individual Senators (Table 41) produces a ranking of southern dissenters that appears to be by no means fortuituous or a reflection of the personal predilections of the individuals concerned. The

[17] It ought perhaps to be said twice that in the selection of these roll calls majority disagreement is the criterion. In the preceding analysis of Republican Democrats only those roll calls were used on which at least 70 per cent of southern Democrats opposed a varying majority of Republicans.

rating of the various Senators in the table is connected with the factional systems of their respective states.

Black and Hill, of Alabama, rank high in the list of southern Democrats who crossed the line to vote with their nonsouthern Democratic colleagues. In the curious politics of Alabama factional groups with fairly cohesive inner circles of leaders do not appear in as clear-cut fashion as in

TABLE 40

Senate: Roll Calls in Seven Sessions on which Majorities of Nonsouthern Democrats Opposed both Southern Democratic and Republican Majorities

CONGRESS, SESSION, YEAR	(1) NUMBER OF ROLL CALLS	ROLL CALLS WITH SD AND R MAJORITIES IN AGREEMENT [a]		ROLL CALLS WITH NSD MAJORITIES OPPOSING SD AND R MAJORITIES [b]	
		NUMBER	PER CENT OF (1)	NUMBER	PER CENT OF (1)
73:1 (1933)	82	25	30.5	8	9.7
74:1 (1935)	108	44	40.7	7	6.5
75:1 (1937)	58	19	32.7	10	17.2
76:1 (1939)	79	24	30.4	5	6.3
77:1 (1941)	84	20	23.8	4	4.7
78:1 (1943)	105	44	41.9	15	14.2
79:1 (1945)	82	31	37.8	5	6.1
Totals	598	207	34.6	54	9.0

[a] The sharp-eyed reader may discover that the number of roll calls with SD and R majorities in agreement, plus the number of majorities in disagreement, shown in Table 38, does not equal the total number of roll calls. The explanation is that those roll calls with either group divided precisely 50–50 do not fall in either classification.

[b] On most roll calls on which the SD and R majorities were in agreement, so was the NSD majority. But the exact number of roll calls on which majorities of all three groups were in agreement cannot be obtained by subtracting the number of this column from the numbers of roll calls on which R and SD majorities were in agreement. In some instances the NSD group split 50–50.

North Carolina, for example. Rather, over an extremely long period of time the most persistent factional groupings have centered in sectional dispute between the black belt of the state and predominantly white northern Alabama, with some aid from the southern coastal plain. The consequence has been the recurrence of political debate of some substance, with the center of conservatism in the black belt, which did not provide the main strength of either Black or Hill.[18]

[18] Senator Bankhead's record fits the general estimate of Alabama politics. In the earlier analysis he joined with the Republicans against the southern majority on only 4.1 per cent of his votes; in this series, he joined with the nonsouthern Democrats on 22.6 per cent of his votes.

The appearance of Louisiana Senators high on the list of solons crossing the line to vote with nonsouthern Democrats is also explicable in the light of the general tendencies of the Long faction in Louisiana. The doctrine of "Every Man a King," free textbooks, and free bridges emanated from a political group diverging radically from, for example,

TABLE 41

Southern Dissenters: Southern Democrats Voting More than 30 Per Cent of the Time with Nonsouthern Democratic Majority on Roll Calls with Nonsouthern Democratic Majority Arrayed Against Majorities of both Republicans and Southern Democrats [a]

	NUMBER OF RECORDED VOTES		PER CENT OF
SENATOR	TOTAL	WITH NSD'S	TOTAL WITH NSD'S
Black	19	15	78.9
Long	9	6	66.6
Sheppard	23	15	65.2
Ellender	26	15	57.7
Robinson	16	9	56.2
Pepper	25	14	56.0
Hill	28	15	53.6
Bachman	13	6	46.1
Caraway	33	13	39.4
Reynolds	36	13	36.1
Bilbo	25	9	36.0
Byrnes	30	10	33.3
Harrison	28	9	32.1

[a] Several Senators with brief tenures are excluded from the list because of the extremely small number of roll calls in the category examined on which they voted. They were: Johnston, of South Carolina; Berry, of Tennessee; Hoey, of North Carolina; Spencer, of Arkansas. All cast more than 30 per cent of their votes on these roll calls with the nonsouthern Democrats, but the most extensive voting record was that of Berry, with 8 votes, all cast with the nonsouthern Democratic majority.

the Democratic machine of Virginia.[19] The record of Sheppard, of Texas, provides another illustration of the point made earlier that the personal-factional politics by which Senators and Representatives get themselves re-elected probably assures a lag in adjusting the attitude of constituency and representative. An old Wilsonian, Sheppard could go down the line for the Administration with no real anxiety about the consequences on election day.

The fact that Mississippi Senators appear on the list may cause astonishment, given the popular impression about Mississippi. The indi-

[19] Overton of Louisiana voted with the nonsouthern Democrats on 27.5 per cent of the roll calls on which he voted. He appears also, it may be remembered, on the list of Democratic-Republicans chiefly because of his sugar-tariff votes.

vidual roll calls on which Harrison deserted his southern brethren present no consistent pattern, but Bilbo's record shows a relatively consistent attachment to the New Deal. Because of Bilbo's race views, it is often overlooked that he depended on the loyalties of the "rednecks" and to a high degree he kept faith with them.[20]

In general, after 1940 there was a marked decline in the tendency of southern Democrats to join with a majority of nonsouthern Democrats against a majority combination of Republicans and southerners. This shift may have been associated with a change in the kinds of questions considered and with changes in personnel; though probably more fundamentally it reflected the general heightening of tension between the southern and northern wings of the party.[21]

No sharply etched gradation of states emerges from our analysis; the southern political spectrum is blurred. Yet some gross differences in senatorial behavior appear and they can be connected with the nature and structure of the intraparty factional system in each state. On the conservative end of the spectrum, the records of the Virginia Senators mirror the character of the dominant Democratic machine which would in Ohio, for example, be Republican. The record of O'Daniel, of Texas, rests on a different sort of system. Although he possessed no organization comparable to that of Virginia, his election came concurrently with the beginnings of a bi-polarization of Texas voters into progressive and conservative camps, a grouping stimulated by the New Deal. At the other end of the spectrum, the Senators from Alabama speak for a progressivism long manifest in the factional struggles within the state. And Senators from other states distribute themselves between these extremes, and in each instance their position finds partial explanation in the balance of factional power within their states.[22]

Although Senators differ widely in their voting records the question may well be raised—but not necessarily answered—whether the compul-

[20] Included in the record that placed him on the list in the table was a vote against a motion to recommit, i.e., to kill, the Fair Labor Standards bill, a vote for a motion to reconsider an amendment by Byrd to limit the cost of publicly financed housing projects, a vote for an increased work relief appropriation, a vote against a Byrd amendment to reduce expenditures for highway purposes. See the discussion of Bilbo's electoral support, above, pp. 246–53.

[21] A rough measure of the change is provided by the percentage of votes by all southern Democratic Senators (on measures with SD and R coalitions against NSD majorities) which were cast with the NSD majority. The percentages were: 1933, 36.1; 1935, 39.2; 1937, 36.0; 1939, 43.1; 1941, 23.7; 1943, 13.0; 1945, 20.5. The character of the shift is indicated by the fact of 32 southern votes with the NSD majority in 1943, 19 were furnished by Caraway, Hill, and Pepper.

[22] Those with a speculative disposition may reflect on the positions of the individual Senators in the right and left tabulations in the light of earlier treatments of the factional systems of each state. It should be remembered, however, that there tends to be, in varying degrees, a separation of state and federal factions. The correspondence between state and federal policy tendencies seems to be closest when a single faction concerns itself with both state and federal office.

sion toward unanimity on the race question does not carry over into other fields and produce a higher degree of solidarity than would exist under two-party conditions. The chances are that progressive Senators, lacking a real party system to back them up at home, may be under special pressure to trim their sails.

Chapter Seventeen | **THE SOUTH IN THE HOUSE**

Tʜᴇ story of the South in the House of Repre-
sentatives can be told quickly, for in the preceding chapter our method of
analysis has been explained. While the voting behavior of southern Representatives shows fundamentally the same characteristics as that of the
Senators, the fact that Representatives speak for smaller constituencies
than Senators permits identification of features of the South not revealed
in senatorial voting. The principal additional finding sifted out of the
House analysis is that Representatives from urban districts tend to diverge
in their voting from the line fixed by their rural colleagues, a fact potentially of great future significance as urbanization proceeds.

The voting records of only four House sessions have been studied—
those of 1933, 1937, 1941, 1945. The labor of tabulating House roll calls—
in which one must deal with 435 members—far exceeds that in dealing
with Senate roll calls. Hence, conclusions about the behavior of House
members are based on a shorter period of legislative operation. The 275
votes analyzed include all roll calls of the four sessions save those on
which dissenters amounted to less than 10 per cent of the prevailing vote
and those on House organization.

1. Degrees of Solidarity

Of the groups examined in the House, the southern Democratic
group turns out, as in the Senate, to have the highest average level of

cohesion. Furthermore, the averages of the indices of cohesion for southern Democrats, Republicans, nonsouthern Democrats, and all Democrats rank in the same order as in the Senate. Yet group cohesion in the House is generally at a higher level. The averages of the indices of cohesion on 275 House calls for each of the four groups and the comparable figures for the Senate were as follows:

	HOUSE	SENATE
Southern Democrats	70.4	55.4
Republicans	66.0	51.8
Nonsouthern Democrats	61.7	46.9
Democrats	58.5	46.0

Thus, on the average 85.2 per cent of the southern Democratic Representatives voted together. The average percentage equivalents for the other House groups were: Republicans, 82.9; nonsouthern Democrats, 80.8; Democrats, 79.2.

As in the Senate, the indices of cohesion are scattered over the entire range from zero to 100. In the House, however, a tighter party discipline places a far larger proportion of the roll calls in the higher brackets of cohesion. For all House groups almost twice as large a percentage of roll calls as in the Senate shows an index of cohesion of 70 or more (the equivalent of an affirmative or negative vote of 85 per cent or more of the group). The proportions of roll calls on which each group registered an index of cohesion of 70 or more for the four House sessions and the seven Senate sessions were as follows:

	PER CENT OF ALL ROLL CALLS	
	HOUSE	SENATE
Southern Democrats	60.4	38.5
Nonsouthern Democrats	48.4	22.1
Democrats	43.6	21.6
Republicans	53.8	32.4

In this comparison, southerners cohere in markedly higher degree than do other groups. On six out of ten roll calls at least 85 per cent of southern Democratic Representatives voted together.

2. Solidarity: The South Against the Nation

The hard core of southern solidarity manifests itself on those issues on which the South tends towards unanimity and is opposed by majorities both of nonsouthern Democrats and of Republicans. As in the Senate analysis, it is presumed that by isolation of those issues on which southern Representatives cohered in extremely high degree one can identify policies associated with southern attitudes of the highest intensity. The underlying assumption is in effect akin to the idea that one can obtain some rough notion of the general contours of a mountain range by locating the peaks. Examination of roll calls showing lesser degrees of group cohesion and antagonism would give a profile of the mountain sides.

On 7 of 10 roll calls in the four House sessions examined a majority of southern Democrats disagreed with a majority of Republicans. This ratio, as may be seen in Table 42, fluctuated from session to session, with the most consistent party antagonism being maintained in the 1933 session. Of the 275 roll calls, majorities of southern Democrats and Republicans disagreed on 194. On 112 of these 194 roll calls at least 90 per cent

TABLE 42

House Roll Calls with Majority of Southern Democrats Opposing
Majority of Republicans, by Sessions

CONGRESS, SESSION, YEAR	TOTAL ROLL CALLS	ROLL CALLS WITH MAJORITIES IN DISAGREEMENT	
		NUMBER	PER CENT OF TOTAL
73:1 (1933)	56	47	83.9
75:1 (1937)	77	50	64.9
77:1 (1941)	67	50	74.6
79:1 (1945)	75	47	62.7
Total	275	194	70.5

of southern Democrats voting opposed the Republicans. These figures reflect the striking differences in party discipline in the House and Senate. On 40.7 per cent of the House votes, at least 90 per cent of southern Democrats opposed a majority of Republicans; the corresponding figure for the Senate was only 14.2 per cent. (See Table 43.)

Southern Democratic-Republican opposition alone does not make a roll call significant. When southern Democrats oppose both Republicans and nonsouthern Democrats, a genuine sectional issue is involved. On 101 of the 112 roll calls with high southern Democratic cohesion in opposition to the majority of Republicans, southern Democrats were in agreement with a majority of nonsouthern Democrats. These 101 questions involved matters on which southern and nonsouthern Democrats could make common cause against the Republican foe. After skimming off these 101 issues, only 11 roll calls remain on which over 90 per cent of southern Democrats opposed majorities of both Republicans and nonsouthern Democrats.

Of the 11 critical roll calls, four dealt immediately and three at least tangentially, with the race question. In 1937, more than 90 per cent of southern Democrats opposed Republican and nonsouthern Democratic majorities on four roll calls on an antilynching bill. A similar alignment of House forces appeared on three roll calls in 1945 on a bill to abolish the poll tax. This measure, of course, was not in form or in reality a race question, but southerners often associate the poll tax with the limitation of Negro voting. Hence, the conclusion is justifiable that 7 of the 11 critical roll calls dealt with the race issue. Thus the inference to be drawn from House behavior is similar to that deducible from Senate voting:

TABLE 43

House: Issues of High Southern Democratic Cohesion [a] in Opposition to Republican Majorities, by Sessions

CONGRESS, SESSION, YEAR	TOTAL NUMBER OF ROLL CALLS	ROLL CALLS OF HIGH SOUTHERN COHESION		NUMBER OF SUCH ROLL CALLS ON WHICH SOUTHERN DEMOCRATIC MAJORITY	
				AGREED WITH NON-SOUTHERN DEMOCRATIC MAJORITY	DISAGREED WITH NON-SOUTHERN DEMOCRATIC MAJORITY—
		NUMBER	PER CENT OF TOTAL		
73:1 (1933)	56	28	50.0	28	0
75:1 (1937)	77	25	32.5	20	5
77:1 (1941)	67	35	52.2	32	3
79:1 (1945)	75	24	32.0	21	3
Total	275	112	40.7	101	11

[a] That is, those roll calls on which less than 10 per cent of southern Democratic Representatives deviated from the views of the majority of their brethren.

southern attitude toward the Negro provides the bedrock of southern sectionalism.

The higher general level of discipline within the House than the Senate pulls into the category of roll calls of high sectional cohesion issues other than that of race. The other four of the 11 critical roll calls identify other cohesive factors high in the ranking of the ties that bind the South together. In 1941 southern Representatives solidly backed a provision of the Selective Service and Training Act broadening the power of the President to seize defense plants when production was interrupted. While the provision looked primarily toward the seizure of struck plants, it authorized seizure when production was impeded by any cause. Republican leaders attacked the bill as a property conscription measure. Representative Harness thus vowed: "I do not believe that we should permit the seize-property exponents to strike at labor and our free enterprise in this indirect manner. . . . While this legislation was designed primarily to break strikes, it goes far beyond that and endangers our entire economic system." The AFL and CIO opposed while the Administration supported the measure. Southern Democrats, unmoved by the threat to free enterprise, had the satisfaction of supporting the Administration, backing the defense program, and perhaps taking a crack at labor.[1] It required the compounding of a triple motive to produce this high cohesion.[2]

Cotton, under some parliamentary situations, can put the South in opposition to the rest of the nation. Such a situation arose in 1941 in a vote on a conference report on an agricultural marketing quota bill. The portion of the bill attracting most attention in effect froze stocks of cotton and wheat held by the Commodity Credit Corporation. Stocks would be disposed of solely for lend-lease and export purposes and only when such disposition would not reduce the market price. Such a measure would find favor with cotton growers who at this time (August, 1941) were anxious lest sale of CCC controlled cotton depress the price of the new crop. Another part of the bill relieved wheat farmers of penalties for chiseling on their wheat production quotas if they had fed the excess wheat to poultry and livestock, used it for seed, or converted it into flour for consumption on the farm. This amnesty to those not in compliance was attacked as a threat to the crop-control system. "The non-compliers," said Representative Cannon, "like the poor, we have with us always." The Secretary of Agriculture opposed the bill in its entirety. The threat to the price of cotton held the South together, but nonsouthern Democrats supported the Administration. The Republicans were badly split, although a majority opposed the southern Democrats.[3]

A third nonrace issue that set the South against the rest of the country was a 1941 motion to kill a bill proposed by Representative Hobbs, of Alabama, for the "detention" of aliens ordered deported who could not be sent abroad because of conditions in their home country. Opponents of the bill called it a "Concentration Camp Bill." Representative Hobbs defended detention until deportation should become feasible or other "departure arranged." [4] The native-white South almost solidly lacked sympathy for the alien ordered deported, while the nonsouthern Democrats and the Republicans, hailing from constituencies with many foreign born, stood for a looser policy.[5] A similar issue and a similar alignment appeared on the fourth nonrace issue. In 1937 on a private bill for the relief of one Lazer Limonsky, southern Representatives voted against a proposal to cancel a deportation order based on illegal entry, while majorities of Republicans and nonsouthern Democrats supported the legislation.

[1] *Cong. Record*, vol. 87, pt. 6, pp. 6417–25.

[2] Four per cent of the southern Democrats supported the motion to recommit the conference report; 69 per cent of the Republicans and 80 per cent of the nonsouthern Democrats supported recommittal, i.e., were against the measure.

[3] The affirmative percentages on the bill were: southern Democrats, 91.6; non-southern Democrats, 35.3; Republicans 42.2.

[4] *Cong. Record*, vol. 87, pt. 8, pp. 8967–93.

[5] The percentage of each group for the motion to strike out the enacting clause was: southern Democrats, 5.2; nonsouthern Democrats, 67.2; Republicans, 72.0.

3. The Southern Democratic-Republican Coalition

Just as the extent of southern solidarity against the nation is commonly exaggerated, so is the degree to which the South fuses with Republicans. The usual pattern of legislative behavior in the House, as we have seen, is that a majority of southern Democrats opposes a majority of the Republicans. On a few roll calls southern Democrats and Republicans unite against nonsouthern Democrats, but this sort of split between southern and northern Democrats occurs far less frequently than all the talk about it might lead one to suppose. In the four House sessions analyzed this type of coalition existed on 28, or 10.2 per cent, of the 275 roll calls. On only 17 of the 28 roll calls were 70 per cent or more of the southern Democrats joined with the Republicans against a majority of nonsouthern Democrats. The importance of these roll calls is not, of course, to be judged by the relative insignificance of their number. Nevertheless, identification of the issues they dealt with isolates matters provocative of strain within the Democratic ranks and productive of a communal feeling between southern Democrats and Republicans.

Of the 17 measures, seven dealing with labor in one way or another constituted the largest category. In 1941 the coalition appeared on: a roll call to authorize draft deferment of men over 28 to which was attached an antilabor rider; two roll calls on a proposal by Representative Smith, of Virginia, to regulate labor disputes in defense industries.[6] In 1945 the coalition reappeared on four labor measures: two votes on which the chief question was the return of the United States Employment Service to the states, a labor issue with overtones of states' rights; a measure originated by the Committee on Military Affairs to regulate labor; an antiracketeering proposal by Representative Hobbs, of Alabama.[7]

In 1937 on two roll calls on an omnibus measure for the relief of specified aliens illegally in the country southern Democrats and Republicans got together.[8] The southern attitude was expressed by Representative Rankin: "Let them go to the countries whence they came, and if they come to America at all, let them come with clean records and clean hands." [9] A similar question brought a southern Democratic-Republican coalition in 1945. They united against an amendment to the Nationality

6 *Cong. Record,* vol. 87, pt. 6, p. 5893, 9396, 9397.

7 Ibid., vol. 91, pt. 7, p. 9818; pt. 9, p. 11,939, p. 11,846.

8 These roll calls and those in the preceding section of this chapter on which Republican majorities united with nonsouthern Democratic majorities against the South reveal more about the South than about the Republicans. In the roll calls on alien questions in both this section and the preceding the Republican position was fixed by a small margin.

9 Ibid., vol. 81, pt. 4, p. 4741.

Act of 1940 to permit Americans who had acquired foreign nationality through the naturalization of their parents to return to the United States and take up permanent residence and be considered as American citizens.[10] On these roll calls Republicans manifested a much lower degree of cohesion than did southern Democrats. From suspicion toward labor organizers and aliens it is but a short step to hostility toward alleged radicals, especially those with odd names. The coalition appeared again in 1941 in favor of an amendment by Representative Dirksen to a relief and work relief appropriation: ". . . no part of the appropriation shall be used to pay the compensation of David Lasser." [11] Lasser had won attention as

TABLE 44

Southern Democratic-Republican Coalition: House Roll Calls with Majorities of Southern Democrats and Republicans in Opposition to Majorities of Nonsouthern Democrats

CONGRESS, SESSION, YEAR	(1) NUMBER OF ROLL CALLS	ROLL CALLS WITH MAJORITIES OF SD'S AND R'S IN OPPOSITION TO MAJORITIES OF NSD'S		
		TOTAL	PER CENT OF (1)	WITH HIGH SD COHESION [a]
73:1 (1933)	56	0	0.0	0
75:1 (1937)	77	7	9.1	3
77:1 (1941)	67	9	13.4	7
79:1 (1945)	75	12	16.0	7
Total	275	28	10.2	17

[a] That is, not more than 29.9 per cent of the southern Democrats voted against the Republicans.

president of the Workers' Alliance, an organization of WPA workers. An agrarian culture may be innately hostile toward the labor unionist— he who would have a greater share of the fruits of the earth in return for less sweat—and the alien—the stranger who perhaps claims our soil as his own. However that may be, an agrarian culture undoubtedly reacts to protect its own economic status. Two of the 17 roll calls reflect a coalition based largely on a community of economic interest between southern Democratic farmers and Republicans. In 1941 Representative Sabath, of Chicago, proposed the creation of a committee to study prices "paid for the necessities of life." Southern Democrats and Republicans opposed nonsouthern Democrats. "There are lots of us," Representative Cox, of Georgia, declared, "who have a suspicion that this is something of a drive against the people who stir the soil and make it produce the food

[10] Ibid., vol. 91, pt. 4, p. 4649.
[11] Ibid., vol. 87, pt. 5, p. 5151.

that feeds the people." [12] In 1945, a similar coalition occurred on a proposal to keep the War Labor Board out of farm labor matters, including workers packing and processing agricultural commodities.[13]

The remaining four of the 17 critical measures dealt with a variety of matters. In 1937 southern Democrats and Republicans lined up against a private bill appropriating $165,000 to pay the Union Iron Works for costs incurred beyond contract prices on boats built for the Navy at the time of the Spanish-American War. Nonsouthern Democrats were badly split on the bill; only 52.2 per cent favored payment. In 1941 a proposal to create a committee to investigate the feasibility of moving government agencies from crowded Washington won a bare majority (55.5 per cent) of nonsouthern Democrats (who probably wanted government agencies moved into empty office space in their cities) and was opposed by southern Democratic and Republican majorities. At the same session 50.8 per cent of nonsouthern Democrats voted against overriding the President's veto of a bill to supplement the Federal Aid Road Act, while southern Democratic and Republican majorities voted to override. The President grounded his veto on the argument that funds should be expendable at points of most serious need for roads for defense purposes rather than be allocated among the states according to population and other elements in the traditional Federal aid formula. The pattern reappeared in southern Democratic and Republican support of the Tax Adjustment Bill of 1945, a bill that in effect reduced excess profits tax rates on the theory that industry needed cash to reconvert.

It may be objected that the mere fact that southern Democratic majorities align themselves with Republican majorities is not the whole story. Perhaps on those roll calls on which majorities of southern and nonsouthern Democrats hold together, the southerners cross the aisle and vote with the Republicans in higher degree than do the nonsoutherners. The conclusion from looking at the facts is that the southerners oppose the Republicans more consistently than do the nonsoutherners. In the four House sessions majorities of southern and nonsouthern Democrats opposed Republican majorities on 164 roll calls. On 125 of the 164 votes southerners approached unanimity more closely in their opposition than did the nonsoutherners. On the remaining 39 votes the nonsoutherners showed higher indices of cohesion, i.e., held together better, in opposition to Republicans than the southern Democrats. The details by session are set out in Table 45.

A few of the 39 roll calls may be mentioned to suggest the kinds of questions that stimulated more southerners than nonsoutherners to cross the line and vote with the majority of the Republicans. The nonsoutherners demonstrated much higher cohesiveness on final passage of the price

[12] Ibid., vol. 87, pt. 5, p. 5634.
[13] Ibid., vol. 91, pt. 6, p. 7534.

control act by the House in November, 1941, than did the southerners.[14] Price policy on cottonseed oil in particular had raised southern temperatures. Similarly, in 1945, one vote on an amendment to the bill to extend the price control act evoked much higher cohesion among the nonsoutherners than the southerners.[15] Other roll calls that brought much higher cohesion among nonsoutherners than southerners included roll calls in 1937 on relief and work relief and on the final passage of the housing program.

TABLE 45

Relative Solidarity of Southern and Nonsouthern House Democrats when Majorities of Each Group Oppose Majorities of Republicans

CONGRESS, SESSION, YEAR	TOTAL ROLL CALLS	SOUTHERN AND NONSOUTHERN DEMOCRATIC MAJORITIES AGAINST REPUBLICAN MAJORITIES		
		NUMBER	WITH HIGHER SD COHESION	WITH HIGHER NSD COHESION
73:1 (1933)	56	44	38	6
75:1 (1937)	77	41	27	14
77:1 (1941)	67	39	36	3
79:1 (1945)	75	40	24	16
Total	275	164	125	39

These roll calls again point to the significance of ruralism or agrarianism in the internal difficulties of the Democratic party and in creating ties between the southern wing of the Democratic party and the solid, conservative, rural Republican who is apt to be especially prominent in the affairs of his party when it is in the minority. Individualistic farm people—and their representatives—have an inbred hostility toward relief. The idea of government subsidy for housing—primarily urban housing—arouses little enthusiasm among rural people. Price control, especially of farm products sold to city people, is likely to be opposed by farmers. These and other such issues split the southern Democrats. Yet, and this must be remembered, a majority of the southern Democrats went along with the nonsoutherners. On all these roll calls at least a majority and usually more of the Republicans opposed the nonsouthern Democratic viewpoint. The Republican position came in part from the fact that the opposition party is compelled by parliamentary ritual to vote no, but the exigencies of the parliamentary role may have happily coincided with conviction. While southern Democrats do not vote always as nonsouthern Democrats would like, they do in larger proportion than

[14] The affirmative percentages were, SD's, 55.9; NSD's, 83.3; R's, 37.6.
[15] The affirmative percentages were: SD's, 46.9; NSD's, 9.9; R's, 93.7.

do Republicans. Nonsouthern Democrats in their quest for allies can win the support of a larger proportion of southern Democrats than of Republicans. Between the extreme of urban industrialism and of prosperous, rural Republicanism, the poor, southern Democracy occupies a position in the political center. It throws its weight now to the right and now to the left, but in the long run nonsouthern Democrats can expect a higher degree of support from the South than from rural, northern Republicans.[16]

4. Clefts in Solidarity: Southern Urbanism

That urbanization dilutes an agrarian regionalism is the most arresting fact emerging from analysis of the voting records of southern Democratic Representatives. The finding springs from an examination of the 28 roll calls, discussed in the preceding section, on which majorities of southern Democrats joined with majorities of Republicans against majorities of nonsouthern Democrats. The supposition was that those southerners who voted with nonsoutherners most frequently on such roll calls could be regarded as having the closest community of interest with the party outside the South.

The results of the analysis, presented in Table 46, on the whole, support the theory that it is from the southern urban centers that the northern Democrats are most likely to win allies when a majority of southerners votes with the Republicans. Ramspeck, of Atlanta, Patrick, of Birmingham, Kefauver, of Chattanooga, Thomas, of Houston, stand out in the list. Not every Representative from a district dominated by a metropolitan center has a voting record that ranks him high enough for inclusion in the table. Thus, Sumners, of Dallas, and Lanham, of the Fort Worth district, are not on the list. Yet it is chiefly such districts, rather than rural and small-town districts, whose Representatives string along most regularly with their nonsouthern colleagues on issues of critical importance to the northern wing of the party.

Examination of the records of Representatives voting with nonsoutherners less frequently than those listed on the table will strengthen the general proposition. In Tennessee, only the Representatives of the Chattanooga district voted with nonsoutherners on these critical roll calls more than 45 per cent of the time, the cut-off point for listing in the

---

[16] Far-western Republicans are a horse of another color. In weighing the significance of our factual findings it ought to be kept clearly in mind that both the Republican and Democratic groups change ideological coloration with changes in the size of their congressional representation. An increase in the Republican contingent, by adding representatives from doubtful districts tones down the reaction of northeastern rural Republicanism. On the Democratic side, the group takes on a different tone by the addition of members from urban and semi-urban close districts to the permanent southern representation.

TABLE 46

Southern New Dealers: Southern Democratic Representatives Voting Most Frequently with Nonsouthern Democrats on Roll Calls with Southern Democratic and Republican Majorities in Coalition against Nonsouthern Democrats in House Sessions of 1937, 1941, 1945

STATE AND DISTRICT	PRINCIPAL CITY OF DISTRICT	REPRESENTATIVE	TIMES VOTING	PER CENT OF VOTES WITH NSD'S
Tennessee, 3	Chattanooga	McReynolds, Kefauver	21	61.9
Alabama, 9	Birmingham	Patrick	26	61.5
Georgia, 5	Atlanta	Ramspeck	25	56.0
Texas, 8	Houston	Thomas	26	57.7
Virginia, 2	Norfolk	Hamilton, Daughton	14	50.0
Virginia, 9		Flannagan	21	52.4
Florida, 4	Miami	Cannon, Wilcox	15	46.7
North Carolina, 5	Winston-Salem	Hancock, Folger	24	45.8

table. The combined records of the Nashville Representatives, Atkinson and Priest, came to 40.9 per cent and those of the Memphis Representatives, Chandler and Davis, 30.0 per cent. In Georgia, the figure for Vinson, whose district includes Macon, was 40 per cent, while the rates for the other Representatives ranged from 4.3 to 16.7 per cent. In Texas, Maverick, from San Antonio, who served in only one of the three sessions examined, voted with the nonsoutherners on all the roll calls; when his record is combined with his successor, Kilday, the resulting percentage is 39.8. The appearance of the Norfolk Representatives on the high-ranking list may appear inconsistent with the position of the Byrd machine, but it will be remembered that Tidewater Virginia is a center of opposition to the organization.

Four states have no Representative on the list. It is not mere coincidence that three of them—Mississippi, South Carolina, and Arkansas—rank lowest in the South in proportion of urban population. In Arkansas and South Carolina differentials in the records of Representatives, however, are closely associated with urbanism. The highest South Carolina rate of collaboration with nonsoutherners, 32.0, came from the Spartanburg-Greenville district. The rates of the other five districts ranged from zero to 15.8 per cent. Similarly, in Arkansas, the highest rate, 29.2, came from the combined records of Terry and Hays, who represented the district including Little Rock, the largest city of the state.[17]

[17] The rates for the Mississippi districts were: 1 (Rankin), 3.6; 2, 7.1; 3, 12.5; 4, 8.0; 5, 17.6; 6, 8.3; 7, 14.3. The highest rates thus came from the fifth district in which Meridian is located, and the seventh which includes Jackson and Vicksburg. Yet no

Louisiana, also, produced no Representative with a record high enough to win a place in the table. Moreover, the variations within the state do not parallel urban-rural differences and the state voting record constitutes one of the inevitable exceptions to a generalization. The two New Orleans districts had rates of only 28.6 and 31.2, both of which may have been influenced by the fact that the Representatives of both districts voted on only about half (14 and 16) of the 28 roll calls under analysis. The Representatives of the Baton Rouge district chalked up a rate on their combined records of 41.7 and they were slightly bettered by Representative Mills, of the fifth district, a predominantly rural district in the northeastern corner of the state.

One name on the table—Flannagan, of the "Fighting Ninth" of Virginia—points to another element in the politics of the South that makes itself felt in the voting records of Representatives. The highlands, areas of few Negroes, often with a Populist tradition, and perhaps with an independence of spirit, tend to be, as earlier analyses have shown, regions of insurgency. Mr. Flannagan's voting record placed him among the metropolitan Representatives. It is not without significance that his constituents included many miners. In other states the upland complex projected itself less forcefully into the House, but in some instances its influence is apparent. In Arkansas the rates for the second and third districts in the northern highlands exceeded those of the lowland districts.[18] In Tennessee, the rate for Representative Gore's district which edges into the eastern highlands exceeds that of the other rural districts of the state.[19]

If metropolitan Representatives vote with nonsouthern Democrats most frequently, it follows that, at least on the type of roll call under examination, Republicans find their most reliable southern allies among Representatives from rural districts. This points again to the rural, agrarian basis for occasional southern Democratic coalitions with Republicans. This community of interest, from the nature of the issues involved, does not seem to rest chiefly on common economic interest. The economic interests of northern and southern agrarians as often as not conflict. The bond of unity rather, it may be suspected, wells from a shared antipathy toward urban people and perhaps a common lack of sympathetic understanding of the problems of an urban, industrial society.[20]

---

particular significance ought to be attached to the narrow differences between the rates for these and the other districts of the state. It is of significance, however, that all Mississippi districts are predominantly rural and all have a much lower rate than most metropolitan districts.

[18] The rates for each district were: 1, 9.1; 2, 16.7; 3, 19.2; 4, 11.1; 5 (Little Rock), 29.2; 6, 9.1.

[19] It is of significance that Joe Starnes, of Dies committee fame, came from a district that edged up into northern Alabama. He was defeated and replaced by Rains, whose record in the 1945 session departed from the precedents set by Starnes.

[20] Interpretation of the entire analysis in this section must be restrained because of the hazards of dealing with small numbers. A roll call or two missed may seriously

The showing of Representatives from the uplands constitutes an important negative finding. From the earlier analyses of factional divisions within the states, it might be expected that Representatives of the predominantly white, rural regions would diverge markedly from other rural

TABLE 47

Contested and Uncontested Democratic Nominations for House
Seats, by States [a]

STATE	NUMBER OF PRIMARIES COVERED	NUMBER OF NOMINATIONS	NUMBER CONTESTED	NUMBER UNCONTESTED	PER CENT CONTESTED
Alabama	14	132	60	72	45.0
Georgia	10	106	51	55	48.1
North Carolina	5	57	30	27	52.6
Mississippi	10	73	45	28	61.6
Arkansas	12	84	53	31	63.1
Texas	5	102	66	36	64.7
Louisiana	10	80	52	28	65.0
South Carolina	8	48	32	16	66.6
Florida	11	55	39	16	70.9
Total		737	428	309	58.1

[a] The years for which information was available for each state were as follows:
Alabama: 1920–46.
Arkansas: 1920–42.
Florida: 1924 and 1928–46.
Georgia: 1920, 1928, 1930, and 1934–46.
Louisiana: 1920, 1926, 1928 and 1932–44.
Mississippi: 1920, 1928–36, and 1942–46.
North Carolina: 1934–38 and 1942–44.
South Carolina: 1932–46.
Texas: 1926 and 1940–46.

Representatives. It is along such lines that battles for state office are frequently drawn. That expectation, however, is not confirmed by the facts. The correct inference may be that the one-party system creates a peculiar situation with respect to the dependence of House members on their constituencies. The frequent independence of House races from state factional politics and the absence of party machinery to assure a contest for House seats may permit relatively easy control of these races by the upper orders.

A clue to the situation may be provided by the record of uncontested nominations, i.e., in reality uncontested elections, for House seats. Observe, in Table 47, that of 737 nominations for House seats in nine states,

affect the percentage record of a member. Nevertheless, consistencies within the figures lend a strong presumption of validity in general.

309 or 41.9 per cent were uncontested. The rate of nomination (or election) by default varies considerably from state to state. More than half the nominations in Georgia and Alabama during the period covered were made without contest while in Florida 70.9 per cent of the nominees had opposition. The variations among the states must be interpreted with reserve since the periods covered by the state data differ.

Representatives who do not meet opposition in their campaigns for re-election presumably work in a different context than do those who know that the opposition party will put up a candidate whatever the chances for success may be. The difference is suggested by instances in which southern factions do take the trouble to put up opposition candidates. Thus, a Representative identified with the Long faction in Louisiana said that he had had opposition at the last primary: "The Sam Jones crowd didn't want me to get renominated without having to go to some trouble and to spend some money." The situation in the House may differ from that in the Senate since the importance of a Senator stimulates contests supported by opposing interests in the state. As for the House, a South Carolina politician says, "We get the best man we can and keep supporting him. The job is, you know, about as desirable as a county night policeman's." An individual's yearning for an office, which would play havoc with a good law practice, present or prospective, furnishes weak stimulus for the conduct of a campaign against the sitting Representative. And in the absence of an organized competitive politics, as prevails often with respect to House seats, the individual yearning for office tends to be about the only basis for opposition campaigns. Under these circumstances it is probable that the wide range of actual differences of political attitude within the South are not accurately reflected in the records of Representatives.

PART | THREE

The One-Party System:

Mechanisms and Procedures

A THEME of the preceding chapters has been that the term "political party," in its standard connotation, has only limited applicability in description of the politics of the South. In state politics factional groupings with more or less resemblance to conventional parties perform the function of political leadership. On the national scene, the spokesmen for the region are almost all labeled Democrats. Yet their power is based on a political organization radically different from that which prevails under bipartisan competition. In national affairs the Democratic party of the southern states becomes at bottom a spokesman for a single peculiar regional interest. On nonrace matters southern spokesmen on the national scene, popular impression to the contrary notwithstanding, often disagree among themselves. These differences are often traceable to the fact that the party contains within itself groups of citizens who would, under other circumstances, be divided among two parties.

The conclusion could well be that there is in reality no party in the South. Nevertheless, there is in each state some sort of institution called the "Democratic party" that has an existence and performs political functions of importance. In name and form the "party" in the South looks on paper—in the statutes, in the rules and regulations—precisely like a party in a two-party situation. It possesses an organization; it is the mechanism for making nominations; it has a hand in the conduct of voting. Yet in the performance of these functions the party operates in a different context than does a party in a dual-party system, and party organization or party nominations are usually quite different in reality though in name they may be the same. The chapters that immediately follow are devoted to an exploration of some of the more important aspects of political mechanics and procedures under one-party conditions.

Chapter Eighteen | **PARTY ORGANIZATION**

"Cᴴᴬᴵᴿᴹᴬɴsʜɪᴘ of Democrats Goes Begging"[1]

"County Democratic Jobs A-Begging in 59 Areas"[2]

"Thirty Qualify for 40 Posts on Committee—Election Assured to Democratic Body"[3]

"Lone Contest for Post in Party Slated—Democratic Committeemen Unopposed Except in Precinct 16-B"[4]

These headlines spell the spirit of Democratic party organization from Virginia to Texas. Few southerners really care much about "the party." In North Carolina the governor expressed confidence that some "patriot" could be found to take the vacant Democratic state chairmanship. A Texas county chairman, over 40 per cent of whose precinct posts were unfilled, implored good citizens to file as candidates for precinct committeemen. The dollar an hour they could earn as election judges would, he said, offset the dollar filing fee. He appealed also to higher motives: "Our precinct committeemen are the very grass roots of our system of government and the party machinery. Unless our citizens offer themselves for these positions, neither our government nor party can operate very well."[5]

[1] *Richmond Times-Dispatch*, June 19, 1948.
[2] *Dallas Morning News*, June 16, 1948.
[3] *Richmond Times-Dispatch*, June 12, 1947.
[4] *Florida Times-Union* (Jacksonville), March 18, 1947.
[5] *Dallas Morning News*, June 16, 1948.

The bald fact is that in most of the South most of the time party machinery is an impotent mechanism dedicated largely to the performance of routine duties. It has few functions that lend it prestige or power. Its officers in many states exert little influence in politics. They are often, as one Democratic county chairman put it, "a bunch of do-nothings." It is not literally true that southern party officials do nothing at all. Nor are their duties always limited to administrative routine. And it is manifestly untrue that the governing bodies of the parties—conventions and committees—have no significance whatever. They appear devoid of significance only in contrast to party organizations of states with dual party competition.

In two-party states party machinery is often moribund, but at times it takes on vitality. Party organizations may be ladders to political power, channels for the distribution of patronage, agencies of partisan discipline, campaign mechanisms. Each "organization"—those who control the party posts—may occupy an important position in the operations of its own party. It frequently sponsors a slate of candidates for party offices and for party nominations. Those who control the party organization often control access to the general election ballot and hence the access to public office.

None of these characteristics can be ascribed to party organizations where parties have nothing to do with the election of public officials. Within the South the Democratic party becomes a framework, presumably and usually nonpartisan, for the settlement of factional contests. Its organization can scarcely be considered partisan machinery. The more secure the Democratic party is in its dominance, the more applicable is this observation. Prestige and influence rest with personal and factional leaders rather than party functionaries. Party jobs are routine and frequently obscure. No wonder many of them go begging.

1. Party Machinery: Neutral, Not Partisan

Conventional ideas about party organization have little relevance in one-party states. Our common notions about it spring from the workings of party functionaries in two-party states. Supposedly in such states disciplined armies of party workers, ranging from precinct captains, through ward committeemen, district leaders, county chairmen, to the state chairman spring to life during campaigns to fight the party's battles and to elect its candidates. Once the election is won, a common cause—the desire for future re-election—holds together its elected officials in all branches of the government. Furthermore, patronage and perquisites contribute to party unity.

When the party does not have to fight campaigns—i.e., when it is not a vote-getting institution—party organization departs radically from the usual conception of it. Democratic nominees in the South win with only the most feeble electioneering in the general elections. Lacking opposition, no external pressure drives the party toward internal unity and discipline. Patronage does not function as a cohesive force; it remains beyond the reach of party functionaries as such: the party has little to do with putting into office those who control patronage. The party organization, therefore, becomes merely a framework for intraparty factional and personal competition. It has the usual complement of conventions, committees, and officials, but the resemblance to genuine party organization is purely formal.

Although the absence of the necessity for intensive general election campaigning influences the character of southern party machinery, in some states some of the time some campaign effort precedes the general election. It is in those states that party organization most closely approximates the usual concept of a party. The Democratic party conducts the most elaborate campaigns in North Carolina, Virginia, and Tennessee; the biggest show is usually put on in presidential years and in counties of sharpest local competition. State headquarters are opened, speakers sent on circuit, and campaign funds raised. Radio broadcasts, newspaper advertising, and even some transportation of voters to the polls reflect a concern over the outcome uncommon in other southern states. Usually the regular party machinery handles general election campaigns. The more active the local Republicans are, the more alert the local Democratic organization is likely to be. When party officials fail, other Democrats may fill the breach.[6]

In the more predominantly Democratic states the party sometimes goes through the motions of a general election campaign, especially in presidential years in such states as Texas and Florida where the margin of Democratic supremacy is not so wide. In Deep South states such as South Carolina, Georgia, and Mississippi there is hardly any campaign. When a show of activity is needed, the regular organization is sometimes so untrained in the campaign arts that it is incapable of performing the chore. Mr. Wilkie in 1940 aroused some fears among Florida Democrats. The state committee tried to run a campaign through the county committees. "They got into the damndest mess yet," one politician recalls, and it was necessary to call in an old campaigner of broad experience in the primaries to run the show.

[6] Thus, in 1946 in a North Carolina county with few Republicans the Democratic county chairman showed no signs of activity before the general election. A local supporter of the Democratic congressional nominee rustled around a few days before the election, rounded up funds from loyal Democratic officeholders, had some radio announcements made urging a large vote, and hired a few cars to carry voters to the polls. Supporters of the congressional candidate were interested in the race because other counties in the district had Republican majorities and it was important to get out a large vote in the Democratic counties.

Aside from its responsibility for campaigns, such as it is, the party's duties vary from state to state. The most onerous task, assigned to the party in several states, is the conduct of the primaries.[7] The party sometimes makes and enforces party loyalty standards which have a peculiar significance in the southern milieu. Earlier the party had an important role in the fixing of suffrage requirements.[8] Occasionally party committees or conventions make an unaccustomed splash when it falls their lot to make nominations for special elections or to replace nominees removed from the ballot between the primary and the general election. In most states the selection of national convention delegates and presidential electors falls to party organs, and, as will be shown later, the party organization assumes its greatest significance in its relation to national affairs.

The role of party organization in the South can best be understood by contrast with party hierarchies elsewhere. When parties are parties, the inner core of workers and officials who make up the "organization" exert considerable influence in party nominations. As a disciplined minority they often can put over, in convention or primary, their favored candidates. Often contests for nominations are between the regular or organization slate and others who aspire to control of the party. Battles are waged for control of the party machinery also because of its power in intraparty affairs, such as the channeling of patronage. The southern contrast is marked. Usually the party machinery is impartial toward personalities and factions competing in the primaries. There is considerable variety, however, in the types of individuals who hold party posts and in the nature of their political interests. As individuals, they often have preferences among contests for nominations, but they usually do not employ the party organization as weapons of favoritism—and often they could not, if they wished. Sometimes patriarchs with no real power serve the party dutifully and take little personal interest in primary squabbles.

In states with powerful factional machines the line between party organization and faction is sometimes thin, but in reality the faction has independent foundations and takes over party posts as an incident to its general dominance. In Virginia, for instance, where the local units of the Byrd organization are usually the most active political forces in their communities, Byrd supporters control most conventions and party posts. Similarly, in Tennessee the Crump faction has in past years dominated much of the party machinery, especially the state committee. As the most cohesive political force in the state, its local candidates for state committee places were often unopposed in the primaries. When opponents offered, they seldom could overcome the organization bloc of votes. Yet Crump's use of the state committee was not, even in Tennessee, in accord

---

[7] For a treatment of the party and the primary, see below, pp. 444–50.
[8] For a discussion of these matters, see below, pp. 619–24.

with the locally orthodox doctrine of the party's role. That doctrine was expounded in editorial discussion in 1948 of the naming of a successor to J. Frank Hobbs, Crump state chairman:

> . . . The chairman is a very important man in Democratic primary elections. The committee, among other things, sits as judge over primary election contests.
>
> The chairman, because of his position, should remain impartial in primary elections. He should represent both sides. Mr. Hobbs never did. Altho technically not McCord's manager while chairman of the committee, Hobbs always acted more or less—more rather than less—as director of the McCord campaigns.
>
> This certainly did not make for impartiality in any matters which came before him. It was bad for the Democratic Party—and it was bad for Tennessee.[9]

In Louisiana Huey Long lost little time in taking over control of the Democratic party. In later years slates of candidates identified with the important contenders for the governorship have sometimes included candidates for state or parish Democratic committees.

The advantages accruing from capture of party machinery vary with the functions assigned to the party. Tennessee gives the state executive committee supervision over the primary, and the county committees play a major part in naming county primary boards. Contests are decided by party authorities. Leaders of the opposition to Crump complain that he ruthlessly employed his control over party functionaries when issues of concern to him fell within their purview. In Virginia, however, appointment of primary officials and settlement of primary contests lie outside the party organization. At times in Louisiana Democratic committees have used party funds raised by assessments on all candidates to advance the campaigns of some of them.[10] Though favoritism in the use of party machinery on a state-wide basis is not customary, state committees occasionally must settle controversies bearing on the fortunes of factions or candidates. Thus, the Georgia committee, which is dominated by the newly nominated governor, in 1946, at the behest of Governor Arnall, agreed in response to court decisions to admit Negroes to the gubernatorial primary of that year.[11]

At lower party levels Democratic committees display the widest variance in favoritism toward candidates. From one end of the South to the

[9] *Memphis Press-Scimitar,* August 27, 1948.

[10] Alden L. Powell, *Party Organization and Nominations in Louisiana* (University, Louisiana: Bureau of Government Research of Louisiana State University, 1940), pp. 19–20.

[11] The partisanship of the Georgia committee can be inferred from the action of the chairman of the state Democratic committee in 1948. He introduced candidate Herman Talmadge as "the next governor of Georgia" to a meeting of his committee called to make arrangements for the primary.—*Atlanta Journal,* June 4, 1948.

other, however, one is told that county committees, with rare exceptions, remain aloof from factional and personal primary fights. Individual committee members and party officers have their preferences among contestants, but there is seldom unanimity of viewpoint or concerted partisan action. In states such as Florida the paucity of duties entrusted to the party makes it immaterial who controls the county committee. One veteran politician remarked that when he was county chairman the competition for county committee posts was so slight that he had to name 90 per cent of the candidates, who ran, unopposed, in the primary.

North Carolina county chairmen formerly had de facto authority to appoint county boards of elections, and thus to control the designation of registrars and other polling officials. One chairman testified that naturally he employed his power to enhance his own political security; he received no instructions of a partisan nature from state Democratic officials and his activities within his own county were entirely self-directed. In such local situations there may be genuine competition for committee posts. In a north Mississippi county we were told of a bitter family feud in one precinct that extends back a hundred years. The feud includes an intense rivalry in all political races including the "beat" [12] mass meetings that select county committeemen. By custom the three committeemen select the primary polling officials, a prerogative considered advantageous to the faction holding the posts. Where favoritism results from such local rivalry it is spot manipulation and not large-scale warfare built around control over party machinery.

In some instances party organs that are neutral on candidacies use their position to advocate a policy about which there may be the deepest controversy among party members. Alabama's state Democratic chairman has been particularly energetic in this wise. In 1946, for example, the state committee, under his leadership, went on record in favor of the Boswell amendment—a scheme to limit voting by Negroes and perhaps others— and spent party funds in support of the proposition, which won the approval of only 53.7 per cent of the voters. The state committee sought to rally county Democratic committees to its line; some followed and others did not. In 1948 an extraordinary use of committee prestige for factional advantage occurred. The state committee spent party funds, collected as fees from all primary candidates, to advocate the election of anti-Truman candidates, including its chairman, as delegates to the Democratic national convention and as presidential electors.

Party authorities sometimes express themselves officially on issues about which there appears to be general agreement among members. In 1948, for instance, the Texas Democratic state committee (and the Republican state committee) went on record in support of Federal legislation to grant the states title to tidelands oil. By and large, however, party

[12] As precincts are called in Mississippi and in some parts of Alabama.

officials are confined to an impartial administration of their offices free
from political controversy, at least in intrastate politics.

2. Federation or Confederacy?

The dual nature of the Democratic party in the South has been
earlier noted. In state and local affairs it is no party at all, while in
national affairs it has functioned as a party, or at least as an expression
of the solid front of the South on issues of peculiar regional concern.
These two facets project themselves into the workings of party organization. Generally on state and local matters, with exceptions of degree, party
organization as such plays no significant role and the locus of its control
may be of no great moment. In national affairs, on the contrary, party
machinery takes actions, such as the selection of delegates to national
conventions and the nomination of presidential electors, that elevate it
at times to a position of significance and stimulate infrequent but bitter
battles for its control.

In their relations to the national party, southern state Democratic
organizations are subjected to internal strains because of their anomalous
position as spokesmen in national party councils for states that have contradictory political yearnings: they want to be united and they also want
to divide. The race issue and the heritages of history drive toward unity
and provide the bases of one-partyism. On the other hand, the issues of
national politics threaten unity—and one-partyism—by the drive toward
division inherent in questions that in two-party states would be fought
out not so much within as between parties. Moreover, those forces that
drive toward Democratic unity within the South tend to disunite the
Democratic party of the nation as a whole. When racism triumphs within
the South—and extreme conservatives often ally themselves with racism—
the state party organizations are apt to assert their independence because
they are at odds with the national majority. Both those concerned with
large economic affairs and those concerned with the status of the Negro
must be states' righters. The stronger they are within a southern state the
more apt the local party is to stand against the national majority of the
party.

All these forces—of local unity and disunity, of national unity and
disunity—play on the state party organization in its role as a part, federal
or confederate, of the national party machinery. But the heat of the battle
should not be overrated, for it is not usually one that deeply stirs the
populace. It is rather a battle of law offices, corporate headquarters, labor
temples, county courthouses, and state capitols. In most southern states
delegates to national conventions are chosen by conventions or committees, and where the presidential primary prevails circumstances have not

conspired to mold it into an effective instrument of popular expression. The South's position on great national issues, since it lacks party competition, must be settled mainly through Democratic party conventions and committees, institutions that yield readily to control by numerically insignificant minorities. Since these party mechanisms are most of the time moribund, their normal susceptibility to manipulation is accentuated and of special significance in those occasional southern crises when their control becomes critical.

The inappropriateness of the party machinery for the expression of popular stands on national issues reaches an extreme in three states whose state executive committees name delegates to the national convention. The Arkansas state committee by law has authority to name delegates. The committee relies on recommendations of caucuses of its members from congressional districts which, in turn, are frequently guided by the wishes of the governor.[13] Georgia's governor, in effect, names the delegates through his domination of the state executive committee in which formal authority is vested.[14] Louisiana practice has varied. Selection was by convention in 1940 and by state committee in 1944 and 1948.

Somewhat greater opportunity for popular participation prevails in those states whose state conventions choose delegates to the national convention. Conventions, however, are usually susceptible to manipulation, and southern state conventions ordinarily are not even under a compulsion to worry about whether the presidential candidate ultimately chosen can carry their state. Convention states are Texas, Mississippi, Tennessee, Virginia, North Carolina, and South Carolina.[15]

Two states—Alabama and Florida—choose national convention delegates by party primaries. Florida practice rests on statutory prescription, while the Alabama state Democratic executive committee determines the method and by custom uses the primary.

Several states provide opportunity for expression of popular opinion on presidential candidacies, but the procedures are either defective or unused. Alabama's primary election of delegates, for example, includes no indication on the ballot of the presidential preferences of candidates

[13] The state committee, elected by the state convention, consists of 35 members (two from each of seven congressional districts, one member from each of 18 judicial districts, and three members from the state at large).

[14] The state convention, which consists of persons chosen in each county by the county committee from among supporters of the gubernatorial candidate with a plurality in the county in the immediately preceding primary, names about half of the committee. The delegates from each of 10 congressional districts select six committee members; the convention chairman names an additional 60 members. The governor formerly exercised this power of the convention chairman. In addition, the officers of the convention are ex officio committee members. Governor M. E. Thompson was unable to name national convention delegates in 1948 because the executive committee had been set up by the late Eugene Talmadge, the gubernatorial nominee of 1946 who died before he took office.

[15] In Virginia congressional district conventions choose district delegates.

for delegate posts, a procedure that handicaps popular decision. Florida's laws provide for a presidential preference vote in the same primary at which delegates are chosen; preferential votes were taken in 1924, 1932, and 1936. Candidates for delegate may indicate their presidential preference on the ballot, but such is not the custom and the electorate has no workable way to make its delegate preferences coincide with its presidential preferences.[16] The use of Arkansas' presidential preference is discouraged by the heavy assessment that candidates would have to pay to meet its heavy cost.[17] Georgia's Democratic State committee has discretion to call a presidential preference primary, but it does so infrequently.

In form the mechanisms of party action in national affairs differ little from those of other states. In control, perhaps they differ little also. Compact minorities control party mechanisms everywhere. Yet for lack of the chastening influence of an opposition, compact cliques in a one-party environment may have special significance at critical junctures. That special significance was also based in 1948 on the fact that several state party organizations asserted independence from the national party organization and claimed the right to instruct Democratic electors to vote for candidates other than those of the national convention.

A basic doctrine of the Dixiecrat rebellion was that the Democratic party of each state was an independent entity not bound by actions of the national convention. As units of a confederate rather than a federal system they retained their independence of action and through their control of Democratic presidential electors could vote for or against the presidential nominee of the national convention. In the instruction of Democratic electors for Thurmond and Wright, state party organizations were not bolting. Governor Ben Laney, of Arkansas, argued: "The national party organization is merely an association of the various state party organizations." [18] In their acceptance speeches, Thurmond and Wright did not regard themselves as nominees of a new states' rights party; they accepted nominations tendered "by the Democratic parties of South Carolina, Alabama, and Mississippi." [19]

The exact procedure by which the doctrine of confederation was expressed differed somewhat from state to state. The Mississippi state

[16] Primary returns from 1920 to 1948 show no delegate candidates identified with presidential aspirants. In 1948 three Democratic delegate slates were in the field, but they were not identified as such on the ballot.

[17] Harold Stassen requested the Republican state committee in 1948 to call a primary but none was held after the committee established an aggregate ballot fee of $40,000 to be met by Stassen and such other candidates as might choose to run.—*Arkansas Gazette* (Little Rock), January 21, 1948.

[18] Ibid., June 13, 1948.

[19] In all this folderol the states' righters were, of course, trying to ride two horses. They wished to bolt without being charged with bolting. The South Carolina executive committee put itself in the ludicrous position of instructing electors for Thurmond and Wright yet refusing to raise funds for the Thurmond-Wright ticket on the ground that such action would constitute a severance of ties with the national party.

Democratic convention was called into session after the "conference" at Birmingham had "recommended" Thurmond and Wright, and the state's Democratic electors were instructed to cast their ballots for the states' rights ticket. The state committees of South Carolina and Louisiana took it upon themselves to designate Thurmond and Wright as the official Democratic nominees.

The Alabama party took the same position of independence from the national party by a different route. Its electors were chosen in May, prior to the national convention, by primary and were pledged not to vote for Mr. Truman. After the convention these electors, whose names would appear on the ballot in the Democratic column, announced their support of Thurmond and Wright. In the primary, voters had pledged themselves to support the primary nominees, including electors. Thus in November the individual voters were faced with the question of confederacy versus federalism. Did they owe loyalty to the state party or to the national party? Since no procedure existed for putting the Truman-Barkley electoral slate on the ballot, the only way voters could express loyalty to the national party was by refraining from voting for the nominees of the state party.

The 1948 southern revolt provided another episode indicative of the weaknesses of our national party organizations. Yet variations in attitude among even the southern states pointed to a source of strength of the national organization. The doctrine of local autonomy was asserted least vigorously where Republicans were most numerous. The Tennessee convention, for example, rejected proposals for anti-Truman action before the national convention. The Virginia revolt died down when local Democratic candidates who would face Republican opposition reflected on the possibilities. The North Carolina organization from the first would have nothing of the whole business, while such "border" states as Arkansas, Texas, and Florida showed no boiling enthusiasm for a repetition of 1860.

3. Government of the Party

The party machinery, which sometimes conducts primaries, chooses national convention delegates, and performs other duties, differs little in form from party organization in two-party states. The supreme governing authority in each state is either a state convention or a state committee which is chosen by election in the primary. Alabama, Florida, and Louisiana do not regularly hold conventions; they rely on state committees to handle party affairs.[20]

[20] Arkansas, North Carolina, South Carolina, Tennessee, and Virginia hold conventions every two years; Georgia and Mississippi, every four years. The Mississippi convention meets in presidential years (rather than the years of gubernatorial pri-

As the supreme governing authority of the party, the convention, save in South Carolina, Virginia, Georgia, and Arkansas, has little power to determine the party's mode of operation. In the four states mentioned the party has relatively broad authority to formulate procedures, such as those for the operation of the primary, and this authority is exercised in the final analysis by the party convention. Party autonomy, of course, is broadest in South Carolina which in 1944 repealed all laws regulatory of party activity. Apart from these four states, however, party activity is closely regulated by statute. So detailed is this regulation that no party rules have been adopted in Florida, Alabama, Mississippi, Tennessee, Texas, and Louisiana.[21]

The state convention consists of delegates chosen by county conventions,[22] except in Georgia, and presents no peculiar feature. Georgia county committees name convention delegates from among the supporters of the gubernatorial candidate with a plurality in the county in the immediately preceding primary. The gubernatorial nominee is assured of a predominant influence in the convention, a condition that does not always prevail when processes of nomination of candidates and selection of convention personnel are separated.

The state convention, as the governing body of the party, assumes significance only when an issue arises that divides the party sharply and is within the purview of the convention. Its routine duties, such as the declaration of the party nominees selected in the primary and the adoption of a party platform, customarily receive only pro forma attention. In all the convention states in 1948 convention action was highly important in the decision whether to instruct presidential electors for the states' rights candidates, although only two convention states refused to go along with the national nominees, Mississippi and South Carolina. In 1944 the same sort of question arose in the Texas and Mississippi conventions. Forces opposed to the renomination of President Roosevelt captured the 1944 Mississippi convention by careful maneuvering in the precinct mass meetings and county conventions. The ease of their success, according to one of the leaders, demonstrated the facility with which a little concerted action can overcome the will of the people untranslated into organized effort.

Generally, however, party conventions do not settle major contro-

---

maries) and thus functions chiefly to choose national convention delegates. The Texas convention meets in the spring of presidential years to select delegates to the national convention and after the state primary in even years to declare the results of the primary, adopt a platform, name a state committee, and transact other party business.

[21] The party in Louisiana has a printed sheet of resolutions adopted by the state committee in 1934, which, with other resolutions subsequently passed but not printed for distribution, constitute the party's regulations supplementary to the statutes.

[22] And, in Virginia, by city conventions.

versies.[23] They are more often sounding boards for a few of the state's politicos, a time for formal organizing of the party, a day of whoop and holler. In some states any qualified voters willing to pay their own transportation are permitted to go as delegates from their county. From the precinct up, the process is largely in the hands of the professionals—so much so that there is cynical reference to the "office mass meetings" which some political leaders have been known to call in their places of business when a few cronies drop around. By design or by default, in most southern states the general electorate plays small part in the convention.

Conventions themselves, their composition and conduct, are largely unregulated by statute except in Texas and Mississippi. Elsewhere the party is free to run its conventions as it sees fit, with the exceptions of some provisions governing nominations.[24]

Between conventions, and in states that do not have conventions, party affairs are conducted by a hierarchy of committees similar in general contour to party structures outside the South. In all states of the South there are at least two levels, a committee for each county and a committee for the state as a whole. States other than Alabama, Arkansas, and South Carolina have an intermediate layer of district committees. Where the latter exist a separate committee is usually set up for each district office: a congressional district committee, a state senatorial district committee, a state representative district committee, and so on. Where they do not exist the state committee exercises jurisdiction over offices for which nominations are made by the electorate of more than one county. County committees, in most of the states, follow the usual pattern in that their members are chosen from precincts or whatever the local title of sub-county electoral units is.

The thorough ward and precinct organization usually associated with urban machines in the North and East appears only rarely in the South. The famed Choctaw Club of New Orleans, a factional organization like Tammany Hall, has off and on for a great many years been indistinguishable from the Democratic organization of Orleans parish. The Old Regulars, as its members are called, have secured their votes and offices by the time-honored techniques of machine politics. In recent years the rival Crescent City Democratic Association has contested with it for control of the parish and the city of New Orleans. Outside New Orleans the nearest

[23] The infrequent use of the convention by the Democratic party for nominating purposes is treated below, pp. 438–40.

[24] The lack of statutory rules for the convention permits manipulation. Thus the Arlington County, Virginia, executive committee in 1948 called a county "convention" to choose delegates to the state convention. It prescribed that any Democrat might be a "delegate" by paying a $5 fee. The rule happened to exclude Federal civil servants, numerous in the county, from participation in the selection of state convention delegates. Federal rules prohibited their participation in party conventions.

approach to the traditional urban party structure is found in the few
southern cities with well-organized machines. Crump's in Memphis is
most famous and most thorough. Charleston has sported one of the most
effective machines for one of the longest periods of time. Other cities have
had them, including Savannah, Augusta, Jacksonville, Chattanooga,
Montgomery, and San Antonio. In all these instances the organizations
have been private affairs designed to maintain the power of a boss or
series of bosses and have not been extensions of the organization of the
Democratic party. They have operated within the party, not as the party.

Except in Georgia, party committees are selected by convention or
primary or a combination of the two, some for two years and some for
four years. In Alabama, Florida, and Louisiana they are elected. County
committees in Arkansas and Texas are elected and the state committees
are selected through convention. In Tennessee, county committees are
selected by county conventions and the state committee is elected. In Virginia the county and city committees are elected (unless the sitting committee determines otherwise) and the state committee is named by the
state convention.

The Democratic county committees in Mississippi are selected by
county conventions. The state committee is selected by the congressional
district delegations to the state convention. (Most state committees are
based on geographical representation. In many instances membership is
formally or informally determined by district delegations to the state
convention.) In North Carolina the chairmen of the precinct committees
comprise the county committee. County conventions elect delegates to
the state convention. The delegations from the counties in a congressional
district join to name representatives on the state committee. In South
Carolina the members of each "club" elect a member of the county committee. The state committee is composed of one member from each county
elected by the county convention.

Georgia places exclusive control over district and state committees in
the hands of the successful primary candidates. The state committee is
named in part by the congressional district delegations to the state convention and in part by the convention chairman. Congressional and state
senatorial district committees are named by the nominee in each instance
and hence are his personal agencies. County committees are popularly
elected.

The chairmen and secretaries of county and state committees constitute the continuing party machinery between primaries and conventions. Since there is little concern among serious politicians with party
machinery, especially outside the conventions, the county or state party
office becomes a one-man show. The office of chairman or secretary can be
to a large extent what the individual wishes to make it. The chairman of
the Democratic state executive committee in Alabama, for instance, has

exerted marked personal leadership of his committee. On the contrary in Arkansas, where the successful gubernatorial candidate customarily names his campaign manager as the state chairman, the office when occupied by one recent chairman was hardly more than titular. In South Carolina the state chairman is vested with great responsibilities because of the party's discretion in the conduct of its affairs, including the primaries. A recent chairman, however, was generally regarded as an errand boy for a more potent state leader who was credited with his selection. In one state the secretary of the state committee was a veteran home from the wars put in office by his seniors as window dressing. He had only the faintest notion of party affairs and referred inquiries about the party to the secretary of state. In Virginia and North Carolina persons of genuine political potency are likely to hold the top party position. Thus in Virginia the mayor of Richmond (subsequently a major candidate for governor) was state chairman. Recent chairmen of the party in North Carolina have included a major contender for the United States Senate and a former lieutenant-governor, both individuals of considerable political importance. In many other states, of course, average citizens, even some politicians, do not know the name of the state party officials.[25]

Indicative of the low regard for party organization is the haphazard way in which most party records are kept. Fortunately many party officials turn over their tabulations of primary results to some public office, such as the secretary of state or department of archives and history, but in some instances even this precaution is not observed. Otherwise, party records—minutes of meetings, copies of resolutions and regulations, certifications of returns—usually lie in disorder until the office of secretary changes hands and then are destroyed or stored in some inaccessible attic. The general attitude is that the conduct of the party's business, like the secretaryship of a dancing club, is a chore to be performed with as little effort as possible. Hence, persons drafted to fill the office are sometimes of lesser caliber who can be counted upon to do faithfully but incompetently an onerous job.

County chairmen frequently go unnoticed. Occasionally a local patriarch will be repeatedly selected for the post because of the confidence in which he is held by his compatriots. Thus in one Mississippi delta county "a paragon of southern virtue" has been county chairman for more than two decades. He is known for his unequivocal views, but his integrity and determination to administer the party's affairs impartially are respected.

The plight of party dignitaries in one-party states has been most

[25] The general position can be sensed from the testimony of one state chairman who said it was the nominal rule that he should be consulted on matters of major Federal patronage. He observed philosophically that if he should ever express disapproval, "I'd be shown the error of my ways."

heart-rendingly dramatized in Texas. In that state the chairmen of the county committees have formed the Texas Association of Democratic Chairmen. They sounded the lament: "they are tired of being the forgotten men of party politics." [26] In 1947 the secretary-treasurer, apparently with a completely straight face, solemnly announced the three purposes of the organization:

> That each county chairman head the delegation from his county to the state convention to exercise his prerogative as titular leader in his county.
> That the county chairman of the county executive committee be the presiding officer and permanent chairman of all county conventions. That all county chairmen, regardless of the size of the county, be recognized as the key man of the party in the county and that credit be given where credit is due.[27]

4. Campaign Organization

When the formal party organization fights no general campaigns and is virtually precluded by its position from taking a hand in primary campaigns, other organizational mechanisms must be created to perform the electioneering function usually assigned to the party machine. In a sense campaign organization in the South is the counterpart of party organization outside the South, though campaign organization is unlike the usual party machinery in many respects.

Party machinery has continuity. It survives campaign after campaign no matter how overwhelming the victory or how crushing the defeat. It functions—with varying degrees of enthusiasm—for whatever candidates the party puts up. It can campaign for a relative newcomer or for an old warhorse. Its institutional nature provides established channels of communication, a ready reserve of personnel, and a body of "technical knowhow" which can be marshalled with a minimum of lost motion. The call to arms is dependent mainly on party patriotism, nourished partly by an orderly allocation of favors in which party officialdom often plays a commanding part.

A candidate's problems of organization in a primary campaign depend largely on his experience in state politics, the character of his opposition, and the nature of his appeal to the voters. One type of southern politician is singularly independent of normal campaign machinery. Notable men of this sort have been the brothers Blease of South Carolina, Cole, who served as governor and United States Senator, and Eugene, a former chief justice of South Carolina, who ran for the Senate in 1942. Even their enemies admitted that they did astonishingly well without the

[26] *Dallas Morning News*, November 15, 1947.
[27] Ibid., September 19, 1947.

normal campaign funds and mechanics. They relied on stump appeal and on the host of followers built up over Cole's long career, persons who spontaneously volunteered their electioneering efforts and who did not require the prodding or incentives offered by an alert and energetic hierarchy beginning with a state headquarters and extending down to county and precinct chairmen.

Most candidates, however, face at the outset of each race the necessity of creating an entire campaign engine de novo. The machinery employed and the manner of recruitment of personnel to man it vary from race to race and from state to state. Conversations with experienced managers of state, district, and county primary campaigns reveal numerous individualities. They indicate, too, certain practices and necessities that recur.

Managers generally point to four important phases of a full-scale, adequately financed state-wide campaign for governor or United States Senator: central direction, provided by a strategy committee composed of three or four of the candidate's highest counselors; the raising of funds, assigned to a single individual, usually not prominently identified with the campaign although he may be a prominent citizen, who may have a small committee working with him; the conduct of the open campaign, involving publicity in its many forms and the work of the state headquarters, all of which is often directed by a small committee; and the organization of support in the counties, the most delicate and most critical phase of campaigning.

State headquarters performs the publicity routine—preparation and distribution of literature, posters, press releases, radio addresses—in a manner much like that of a party-conducted campaign. Key technical personnel in the process are frequently on salary but most workers volunteer. Occasionally an advertising firm handles publicity for a fee.[28] More frequently newspapermen sympathetic to the campaign direct publicity work, sometimes at a salary when on leave rather than loan from their employers. Decisions on major policy matters, such as the line the candidate is to take on a hot campaign issue, are sometimes made by the publicity committee if there is one, or more often by the strategy committee. The publicity staff is usually confined to the technical implementation of such decisions through their professional skills.

The finance director of the campaign is ordinarily a man of standing in the community whose knowledge of the responsive sources of funds has been acquired from long observation or experience. It is usually part of his job to keep the candidate and the campaign manager (and most other people) in ignorance of the exact channels through which the sums flow, how much is given by "X" and how much is given to "Y."[29]

[28] In Texas public relations firms play a more significance role in campaign management than in other southern states. The huge population and area of the state accentuate the importance of publicity as a campaign technique.

[29] For a discussion of campaign finance, see below, chap. 22.

A factional or personal candidate has no established party hierarchy —state chairman, county chairmen, precinct committeemen—to carry the message to the voters. Substitute mechanisms have to be constructed. Factions with continuity, such as the Byrd machine, or leaders long on the scene, such as Gene Talmadge or Olin Johnston, develop a set of followers on whom the candidate depends in campaign after campaign. When their usefulness and devotion have been tested they come to occupy positions in the grand scheme of factional affection and loyalty, a hierarchy that resembles vaguely a formal party organization.

The need for experienced counsel and skillful aid in the conduct of a state-wide campaign is met by individuals whose services are frequently for sale to the highest bidder, or to the most persuasive talker, or to the most likely winner. Often campaign managers are purely decorative. In 1946 many veterans were put in front positions for the sake of appearances. The real management, however, remained in the hands of experienced practitioners, some of whom are irrevocably wed to one candidate—as A. B. Friend was to Senator Bilbo in Mississippi—and may, at the behest of their principal, put in a helping hand in other campaigns. Some managers acquire independent stature of their own, such as Homer Adkins of Arkansas, who made himself governor after establishing a reputation as the state's best organizer by managing several successful campaigns for others. Some are frankly technicians, as Boyce Williams in Florida or Ed Reid in Alabama, who may be in one camp one year and another the next.[30] Occasionally one of these persons develops so much influence of his own that he tends to dominate the candidate for whom he works, as many have thought to be the relationship between Roy Harris and Herman Talmadge of Georgia.

The special asset of these men is not their organizing ability or their political acumen alone; it is their intimate acquaintance with county politics and politicians. The entire machinery for distributing publicity, arranging rallies, beating the partisan drums, advising on local issues and local reactions to campaign efforts, punching doorbells or contacting farmers, the whole business of preparing for election day, arranging for transportation, designating watchers or officials, the complete procedure for appealing to voters where the voters are, in the counties and in the precincts, must be set up anew for each primary. To launch a successful operation in a county requires knowledge of local points of sensitivity and familiarity with politicos of potency, those to be solicited and those

---

[30] Mr. Williams, an orange-grower of Lake County, is a former tax collector who for twelve years headed the state association of tax collectors. He worked in the gubernatorial campaigns of Spessard Holland in 1940, Ernest Graham in 1944, William Shands in 1948, and Holland's senatorial race of 1946. Mr. Reid, who is secretary of the Alabama League of Municipalities, was associated with Lister Hill's 1944 senatorial campaign and Handy Ellis' 1946 gubernatorial race.

to be avoided, those who are buddies and those who are mutually incompatible.

It is such specialized local information that is of utmost value to a candidate, especially if he is new to state-wide campaigning. The ability to "organize a campaign over the telephone" by calling on old friends, knowing the predilections of local potentates, being able to pair one local faction off against another is a precious skill in any race. An individual with such information knows from experience (often painful) how to raise charges on which the opponents are most vulnerable and how to avoid those that might harm his candidate. He wields influence in all aspects of campaign operations and sees service in the highest councils. In setting up county machinery the candidate who is an old campaigner has advantage, for over the years he has won followers in almost every county who will handle his affairs. The problem of central headquarters under those circumstances is to activate the local leaders and to keep tab on their efforts. The new candidate may have personal friends of varying political usefulness around the state but his major task is to get competent county managers and allied helpers. Failing to get satisfactory volunteers, he may have to hire local managers.

When a county or portion thereof is "deliverable," negotiations with county, or more often sub-county, bosses can be conducted in an atmosphere of reality only by a politician of sufficient experience to treat with them as equals. He must not be duped by a pretender to influence over votes. He must not accept support that will alienate more important influences. He must know the vital interests at stake in intracounty politics—from family feuds to the location of the needed highway. The experienced campaigner will know, too, how the greatest support can be extracted from groups like labor unions, business associations, and Negro clubs.

A candidate in his first state-wide race particularly needs the aid of professionals who can recruit county leaders. The candidate himself can impress some local big-wigs into his service. A veteran organizer, however, can by his personal influence gather to the fold political cronies that he has used and who have used him in previous years.

The relationship between the state command and county managers must be direct if the local boys are to feel that they are really part of the show. Some campaigns, most often in Virginia it would seem, have used district managers, an intermediate layer of administrators between the top and the counties and precincts. They are most useful, however, in informal roles as traveling emissaries who keep an ear to the ground and are enough at home in their section not to arouse antagonism or suspicion. Seldom will a county's "patriotism" permit a neighbor to come in and "tell it what to do." State headquarters always has an important set of employees rarely in the public eye: a corps of trouble-shooters who spend most of the campaign going from one hot spot to another, sometimes on the call of local managers, co-ordinating campaign efforts, negotiating about money needed from above, advising on strategy.

A significant adjunct to many campaigns is an instrument for checking campaign progress in local areas. State managers must determine the effectiveness and faithfulness of local adherents. One leader sends out periodically during the campaign a questionnaire tailored specifically for each stage of the contest. The persons reporting do so in strictest confidence and are not known to be informants by the political workers in their counties. Another manager has used the facilities of a retail credit firm to get confidential reports. In one state an old hack, whose political influence is so meager "he couldn't carry his wife," has an unerring instinct for political evaluation. He is for hire in any campaign, and when he hits the road everyone knows what he is up to, yet the valuable reports he brings in after nosing around the precincts assure him ready employment in every race. Other managers use anonymous individuals who have a similar intuitive judgment, who can spend half a day in a county and come out with a fair appraisal of what the score is, what will improve it, and who has been falling down on the job.

Only rarely are primary campaigns in the South outside of Tennessee, Virginia, and Louisiana [31] jointly conducted for more than one office. Joint campaigns are not feasible in an atomistic, individual politics. Campaigns for governor steer scrupulously clear of formal connections with other state races and races for Federal and local offices. Campaign organizations for each office are entirely separate, in sharp contrast with party campaigning in a general election in a two-party state. But the sub-rosa operations of professional politicos, especially in the counties and precincts, breed criss-crossing of lines and complexities of alliances which the politicians themselves seldom can identify and which may often be contradictory.

Although the organization set up for the primary campaign in a one-party state serves the same purpose as party organization in two-party states, it is almost invariably less tenacious, less cohesive, less continuous. Hence, as an instrument of popular leadership, it is less responsible or accountable. Primary campaign organizations, even when successful, hold together only loosely after the campaign. Local leaders closely identified with a particular candidate are called upon by their fellow citizens when communication must be had with the throne on matters of grievance or patronage. Similarly, the officeholder calls for counsel from his trusted local lieutenants. In some cases, therefore, a person gets to be known as "a big Folsom man" or "the Laney leader" in the county. A network of such persons over the state might be called a factional machine. It can

[31] For a description of the Louisiana ticket system, see above, pp. 169–74.

be kept together to some extent by the judicious distribution of benefits. Such a development is infrequent, however, except in the states with formal factional organizations, primarily Virginia and Tennessee. A candidate's ultimate ascent to power (or its retention) is less certain than a party's and there is little adhesive influence within the factional organization other than personal loyalty to the candidate.

Chapter Nineteen | THE NOMINATING PROCESS

WRITERS on political institutions often confuse their readers—and themselves—by the use of words that have different meanings at different times and places. "Governor" in South Carolina, as earlier discussions have shown, has connotations far different from "governor" in Virginia. "Political party" in Illinois designates an institution with some form, discipline, and durability; "political party" in Arkansas has virtually no institutional reference in the Illinois sense. Even among southern states "Democratic party" carries diverse connotations. It has real meaning to North Carolinians; no meaning at all to Floridians, at least for state politics. To carry the idea into another realm and to an extreme, what is regarded in one culture as a solemn ritual surcharged with pious emotion may in another be considered simply as cruelty to animals.

So it is with the terms "nominations" and "direct primaries." Writers who theorize about American political parties attribute to them great importance because of their function of "nomination" of candidates for office. If the people are to choose their rulers wisely, so the reasoning goes, competing groups must put forward a limited number of candidates from among whom the voters may select their governing officials. The principal method of making nominations in the American states, so the story goes, is the "direct primary," an election in which only the members of a party may participate. In a few states and in the nation the "party" nominates through a representative body called the "convention."

In the South, with no "political parties" in the ordinary sense of the word, nominations are made by other means. It seems that in some states the business of putting forward candidates is left almost entirely to the chance urges of individuals to run for office. In states with amorphous factions little sustained attention is given by anyone to the recruitment of candidates. On the other hand, in states with relatively tightly organized factions within the Democratic party the inner circle of the faction performs a role in settling on a candidate similar to that of the party organization in two-party states.

Nominally in the South "candidates" are chosen in the Democratic "primary." Such is the formal language. In fact, the Democratic primary is no nominating method at all. The primary is the election and in the South the primary takes on peculiar forms in recognition of its peculiar function. In two-party states the person receiving a plurality in the direct primary, i.e., the largest number of votes, which need not be a majority, becomes the party's candidate for the election. In most southern states a double primary system is used. In the "first primary" all those candidates run who have "nominated" themselves or been "nominated" by factional organizations or other groups. In this "first primary" often no person receives a majority. The two leading candidates then go before the electorate again in a "second" or "run-off" primary, and the winner becomes the party's candidate. He is in reality elected, for the Democratic "nominees" almost invariably win in the "general election."

1. The Primary as the Election

The Democratic primary in the South is in reality the election. The Democratic "nominees" not only usually win the general election but in an overwhelming majority of instances, if one includes local officials in the calculations, are unopposed. Not uncommonly Democratic nominees for the governorship, the United States Senate, and the national House of Representatives meet no opposition in the general election.

In 114 gubernatorial elections in the eleven southern states during the period 1919–48, the Democratic nominee won 113 times. A Tennessee Republican in 1920 rode into office in the Harding landslide. In 131 of 132 elections of United States Senators the Democratic nominee won. In 1937 a nominee designated by the Arkansas Democratic state committee, rather than by a primary, was defeated by a Democratic Congressman running as an independent in a special election to fill a vacancy. The controlling issue was that the nomination had been made by the party committee rather than by primary.

In only two congressional districts of the South—East Tennessee's first and second—do Republicans consistently win general elections. Over the remainder of the South during the period from 1920 to 1948 Republican encroachments on Democratic hegemony were principally incidents of the 1920 national Republican landslide and of the 1928 revolt against Al Smith. In 1920 Democratic nominees lost to Republicans in three Tennessee districts (the third, fourth, and eighth) in addition to the two consistently Republican districts. In Virginia the Republicans carried the southwestern "Fighting Ninth." In 1928 Democratic nominees lost in two North Carolina districts (the ninth and tenth) and in three Virginia districts (the second, seventh, and ninth). The Republicans managed to carry one Virginia district again in 1930 (the second). Apart from these instances the only other place in the South in which a Republican congressional nomination has had a chance was Texas' San Antonio district, which was represented from 1920 to 1932 by a Republican, Harry Wurzbach, who had support among Democratic professional politicians.[1]

In the Republican strongholds in the mountains, Democrats encounter serious opposition and are often in the minority. In these areas the Democratic primary is not the election. (In fact, in these areas the convention—rather than the primary—is often used as a method of nomination.) No southern state collects data on the party affiliations of its local government officials, but a rough idea, probably an underestimate, of the extent of Republicanism in local government is provided by figures on the party connections of state legislators. Here again, as may be

TABLE 48

Republican Members of Southern State Legislatures[a]

STATE	LOWER HOUSE		UPPER HOUSE	
	TOTAL MEMBERSHIP	REPUBLI-CANS	TOTAL MEMBERSHIP	REPUBLI-CANS
Alabama	106	1	35	0
Arkansas	100	3	35	0
Florida	95	1	38	0
Georgia	205	1	54	1
North Carolina	120	13	50	2
Tennessee	99	18	33	4
Virginia	100	6	40	3

[a] *The Book of the States, 1948–1949* (Chicago: Council of State Governments, 1948), p. 107. At the time of the compilation of this table no Republicans sat in the legislatures of Louisiana, Mississippi, South Carolina, and Texas.

[1] In 1940 Percy Priest, running as an independent, defeated the Democratic nominee in Tennessee's Nashville district. Priest, a Democrat, subsequently was nominated in the Democratic primaries and elected several times.

seen in Table 48, the upshot is that the primary is the election except in a few legislative districts.

Since the primary determines the outcome, voters have no occasion to become excited about the general election. General election turnout varies with Republican strength. With the total general election vote for governor as a percentage of the total Democratic primary vote for governor, the states rank in general election interest as follows: [2]

North Carolina	209	Alabama	62
Tennessee	127	Georgia	47
Virginia	114	Louisiana	28
Florida	91	Mississippi	18
Arkansas	72	South Carolina	13
Texas	69		

The three high states in this list are those with greatest Republican strength. In North Carolina's western counties warmly fought bi-party contests over local offices bring out the electors, who incidentally vote for governor and swell the general election total.[3] The same factor operates to some extent in Virginia, but in Tennessee general elections for local officials are held at different times than for state officials.

The foregoing average ratios of general election vote to Democratic primary vote exaggerate voter-interest in general elections of state officials. Interest in the presidential campaign inflates the averages for some states. North Carolina, the first-ranking state, elects its governor only in presidential years and owes its rank in part to the power of the presidential race to pull the voter to the polls. The same is true of Florida. Calculation of separate averages of the ratios of general election vote to primary vote for presidential and nonpresidential years for those states electing governors biennially provides a rough measure of the effect of the national campaign. Those averages, for the same period as the grand averages above, are as follows:

	PRESIDENTIAL YEARS	OFF YEARS
Tennessee	172	89
Texas	99	43
Arkansas	84	63
Georgia	78	24

These differentials between presidential and nonpresidential years help explain the low general election vote of Louisiana, Mississippi, Alabama, Virginia and South Carolina where gubernatorial elections are not held at the same time as the presidential balloting.

[2] The figures shown are the averages of the percentages that general election votes were of Democratic primary votes over the period 1921–47.

[3] See above, pp. 218–22.

2. Pre-Primary Nominations

In reality no formal nominating procedure exists in one-party states; hence the inquirer must look beyond the formal procedures to determine how nominees are chosen.[4] By informal processes of negotiation, group designation, and individual initiative before the Democratic primary, candidates make their way to the ballot. In most local governments the chances are that "nomination" is the decision by an individual that he wants the job. Our inquiries have been directed chiefly toward nominations for state-wide office.[5] In many two-party states the "regular" party organization advances a slate of candidates for nomination in the primary, and often their ratification by the party rank and file occurs routinely. In southern states party organizations are officially neutral in the primaries and nearly always so in fact.

The process by which a person becomes a "serious" contender for the governorship depends on the character of the factional system within a state's Democratic party. When there are cohesive, continuing factions, each, by its more or less informal internal processes, reaches a decision on whom it will support in the primary. In states with factions of an amorphous and transient character, the personal initiative of would-be candidates may be more important than group decision. The would-be candidate, in effect, nominates himself and rallies a faction to support him in the campaign. Then there is the perennial candidate with a large and loyal state-wide following who can run at his own pleasure. And there are all sorts of conferences in smoke-filled rooms to agree upon candidates, to raise a kitty on which to make the campaign, and to draft a candidate.

The outcome of these pre-primary procedures is that by the time of the voting the "serious" contenders for the governorship have been narrowed to a handful of candidates. Instead of confronting the voter with a choice between two major candidates, the pre-primary nominating proc-

[4] Another interpretation would be to consider the Democratic first and second primaries equivalent to a nonpartisan primary and election. The first primary is in essence a nonpartisan primary. If no person receives a majority, in those states using the run-off, the two high candidates run in the nonpartisan election, i.e., the second Democratic primary. Fervent advocates of nonpartisan primaries and elections should ponder well the consequences of nonpartisanism in southern states.

[5] From time to time in scattered localities more or less formal pre-primary arrangements have existed. In Arkansas Ku Klux Klan "preference primaries" were privately held in several counties in order that the Kluxers might agree on persons to support in the primary. The Democratic party outlawed these "primaries" and their nominees were barred from the primary ballot.—H. M. Alexander, "The Double Primary," *Arkansas Historical Quarterly*, 3 (1944), p. 225. In a few east Texas counties white primaries have, even recently, been held privately before the official primary to agree upon candidates whom the whites would support in the official primary. See J. A. R. Moseley, "The Citizens White Primary of Marion County," *Southwestern Historical Quarterly*, 49 (1946), pp. 524–31.

ess in the South commonly gives him a choice of from three to five principal contenders. The result more nearly resembles that of a three- or four-
party system than of a two-party system.

The number of candidates receiving 5 per cent or more of the total
vote cast perhaps provides a measure of the number of "serious" candidates and of the results of the pre-primary sifting and marshalling of support. The median number of such candidates in the southern states ranges
from two to six, as may be seen in detail in Table 49. In the character of

TABLE 49

Number of Candidates Receiving 5 Per Cent or More of Total Vote Cast
in First or Only Gubernatorial Primary, 1919–48 [a]

STATE	MEDIAN NUMBER	LOW NUMBER	HIGH NUMBER
Virginia	2	2	3
Tennessee	2.5	2	4
North Carolina	3	1	5
Georgia	3	2	4
Louisiana	3	2	5
Alabama [b]	3	3	5
Mississippi	4	3	5
Arkansas	4	3	6
South Carolina	4	2	6
Texas	4	2	7
Florida [c]	6	5	9

[a] The median, high, and low numbers of candidates receiving 5 per cent
or more of the vote were determined by the exclusion of those primaries in
which the incumbent sought re-election in Arkansas, Georgia, South Carolina, Tennessee, and Texas.
[b] For the period since 1931 when the preferential primary was abandoned.
[c] For the period since 1929 when the preferential primary was abandoned.

the factional system is to be found the key to the nature of the pre-
primary "nominating" process. The ranking of the states in the table
roughly parallels the earlier general characterizations of the factional
systems of the states, ranging from Virginia's rigid machine and antimachine factional competition to the chaos of Florida factionalism. The
pre-primary nominating process in the former reaches the highest degree
of formality and in the latter the highest degree of informality.

In Virginia the Byrd machine has had a fairly regularized procedure
for determining whom it would support in the primary. The machine, it
will be recalled, is the avenue for political advancement in Virginia; a
young man going into politics affiliates with the organization and begins
his apprenticeship as a state legislator or in some other lesser capacity.
If he plays ball and impresses the machine leaders with his soundness and
ability, he advances over the years to positions of higher responsibility.

Eventually he may become a gubernatorial possibility, and, under the rules of the organization, he has been free to drum up support for himself, not so much with the public generally as with the organization leaders in the counties and cities around the state. Gradually over a period of more than a year before the primary, sentiment of the organization rank and file crystallizes. Some aspirants see that they cannot win the favor of the organization stalwarts and drop out of the running. The high command of the organization—Senator Byrd and his close associates—listens to the expressions of approval and disapproval flowing up the hierarchy and eventually reaches a decision. "The nod" is Virginia terminology for the decision of the high command. Once the "nod" is given, the newspapers begin to carry announcements by lesser leaders in support of the organization designee and the ranks close for the primary. Rival contenders fight it out for the favor of the organization. Once the "nod" is given etiquette has demanded that all hands fall in line. Occasionally, for lesser offices, the high command has permitted a public battle, i.e., something of a free primary, between equally loyal candidates. The wiser heads regard the tolerance of this sort of spectacle as a mistake.[6]

Existence of a dominant, well-organized faction, such as the Byrd machine, probably unifies all elements in opposition. At any rate, Virginia's primary battles tend to be two-sided. The opposition consists of labor groups, parts of the Negro population, reform groups, those favoring expanded public services, disaffected Byrd followers, and liberals generally. Three or four persons have won recognition as antiorganization leaders, and the pre-primary nominating procedure has been simply a question of obtaining agreement among them on a candidate whom they will support against the man who has the organization "nod." In the face of the powerful common enemy the antiorganization faction remains amenable to a comparatively small and cohesive leadership. Theirs has been a unity of desperation.

Virginia's Democratic party has two wings, each of which decides within itself what candidates it will offer for state offices. One wing is strong and well feathered; the other flutters limply. Each performs a highly important function in designating the major candidates to go on the primary ballot. In their modes of operation they resemble quite closely the operations of party factions and parties in two-party states.

At the opposite extreme is Florida. Virginia's pre-primary sifting usually puts before the electorate two major candidates in the first primary. Florida's amorphous politics precludes the existence of an effective pre-primary sifting and "nominating" procedure. In the absence of such arrangements, candidacies in large measure come to be self-inspired rather than the consequence of group deliberation and consultation.[7] To illus-

[6] See above, pp. 23–26.
[7] On Florida's multifactional system, see above, pp. 87–96.

trate the process, consider the case of William A. Shands, an unsuccessful candidate in 1948. Before his formal announcement of candidacy, he toured the state to rally to his support as many individuals or groups as possible. A prominent cattleman, advertising executive, banker, and supplier of road-building materials, he had acquaintances in these activities over the state. As a state senator he had built up friendships here and there and as the sponsor of a sales tax he had made friends and enemies. The expectation was that he would be labeled as the "cattlemen's candidate," but he sought commitments of support from persons in all sorts of endeavor. Often would-be candidates, after making a tour of the state and weighing their prospects, decide not to make the race.

As Florida campaigns shape up, the gossip often identifies particular candidates with important economic and vocational groups, but these groups, as organizations, play no formal public role in putting forward candidates. A group's members, or some of them, however, may encourage aspiring individuals in pre-primary negotiations for support. This passive role is true of labor unions as well as of other economic groups. The history of Florida labor in politics is one of division and confusion. Not only have the major unions differed among themselves on candidates, but there have been embarrassing disagreements within individual unions. A peer among the champions of labor's rights, such as Senator Claude Pepper, will attract wholehearted support; otherwise the unions, like other groups, pick and choose from among self-advanced candidates. The array of candidates finally lined up for the primary race usually includes representatives of the principal geographic sections, although they are not sponsored by sectional machines. The candidate's strength in his home area reflects friendship and local prominence.

Florida's pre-primary nominating practices thus come down in large measure to the personal volition of the would-be candidate. No formidable coalitions or personalities perennially compete for control of the government. No organized alliances squeeze out certain aspirants and center like-minded strength on a single candidate before the first primary. Individuals put themselves forward and if it looks as though they have a remote chance they can attract enough financial support to make a campaign. The sifting of candidates is performed by the voters in the first primary. The voter chooses from a long list of self-nominated individuals, and in the multiplicity of candidacies and general confusion the primary becomes something of a lottery. At times candidates of the extreme right, and less frequently, of the extreme left, turn up on the ballot and make their views well-enough known for the electorate, with its usual good sense, to bat them down. More often, the voter must choose from among indeterminate shades of gray.

While each state factional system has its own individuality, the pre-primary sifting process in Tennessee and North Carolina resembles in general that of Virginia. Through pre-primary designation by competing groups, organization and antiorganization candidates are usually put forward. At the other end of the scale, Mississippi, Arkansas, South Carolina, and Texas have more in common with Florida than with Virginia. Occupying an intermediate position are Louisiana, Georgia, and Alabama, although Louisiana and Georgia veer toward the Virginia end of the scale and Alabama in the opposite direction.

Tennessee's "Crump machine" differs in many respects from the "Byrd machine," yet the essential features of pre-primary nominations in both states are the same.[8] In Tennessee Crump personally selects the organization candidates for the three state-wide offices, governor, Senator, and railroad and public utilities commissioner. Those candidates who run with his endorsement usually, though not always, conduct a coalition campaign from joint headquarters. Within the Crump organization there is much less "democracy" on candidacies than within the Byrd organization. Crump goes into executive session with himself, perhaps after consulting only a few persons, decides on the organization candidate, and the announcement comes down from on high.

Presence of a strong machine in Tennessee, as in Virginia, has produced a degree of unity among the outs. To some extent opposition candidacies are self initiated. More generally before 1948 a handful of opposition leaders agreed among themselves and then induced their designee to make the race. Once a likely candidate was persuaded, he received such support as the loose and often demoralized opposition faction could muster.

North Carolina has an organization, less well-knit than those of Virginia and Tennessee, which usually puts forward candidates for the gubernatorial nomination. Legend has it that the "Shelby Dynasty" has ruled North Carolina for almost a generation. The legend is not entirely true, though there can be no doubt of the dynasty's role in pre-primary nominations. The late O. Max Gardner, a native of Shelby County, and a man of great personal popularity, won the Democratic nomination for governor in 1928 without opposition. When 1932 rolled around his personal choice as a successor was J. C. B. Ehringhaus, who defeated two strong candidates in the primary. In 1936 the Gardner-Ehringhaus influence was thrown to Clyde Hoey, brother-in-law of Gardner and also from Shelby. He, too, won the primary after a stout fight. In both races candidates of the same general policy inclinations as the Shelby nominees also entered the fray, indicating a machine with less power to exclude from the list of serious contenders than that of Virginia or Tennessee.

The North Carolina machine has not had the rigid hierarchy of Virginia. Rather it has been a coalition of high state officials who are sometimes able to see a common interest and to plug together to put over

[8] See above, pp. 62–69.

a candidate. In 1936 and 1944 these state officials were solidly behind the same candidate. Their unanimity was strengthened, if not caused, by the candidacy of Dr. Ralph McDonald, a personal candidate representing no clique. He opposed the sales tax and was favorably known to organized labor.[9] He made a strong though unsuccessful race in 1936. Under North Carolina's custom of rotation of the governorship between the east and the west sections he was not eligible to run again until 1944. When he did, the "machine" was ready for him with a single candidate, which it elected, although in the intervening race in 1940 the state officials were split, as they were in 1948. The candidate's need for support from weathered department heads and lesser state officials long accustomed to working together gives these politicians important influence in determining who decides to get on the primary ballot.

Louisiana's Long and anti-Long factions have considerable resemblance to the duality of faction prevalent in Virginia and Tennessee. For the principal elective state offices the small clique of Long leaders agrees upon a slate of candidates who campaign together.[10] The Louisiana situation, however, bears a resemblance to another type of situation that recurs in the South. Outside the three states with something of a continuing factional organization, from time to time independent leaders arise who command a substantial popular following. These persons—the Fergusons of Texas, the Talmadges of Georgia, Bilbo of Mississippi— have been in a sense messiahs, around whom voters flocked, rather than organization heads in the Virginia or North Carolina sense. When such leaders are candidates themselves they are of course self-nominated. Their presence may compel all opposition elements to unite on a single candidate in advance of the primary, but more commonly the opposition becomes divided, if not pulverized. Thus in Georgia prior to the 1946 Democratic primary, anti-Talmadge leaders maneuvered and conferred in an attempt to unite on a candidate to oppose Talmadge. Arnall followers, "good government" people, Talmadge enemies, many labor and civic groups, and certain newspapers cast around for a common candidate and finally centered on James V. Carmichael. Not all elements of opposition, however, could be united. Former Governor Ed Rivers wanted the nomination himself, and he made an independent, and weak, race. Yet he divided the opposition to Talmadge.[11] Not uncommonly candidates are put into the race for the purpose of dividing the enemy, and in states such as Georgia the factional organization is not always strong enough to discourage independent and divisive candidacies.

Generalization about the pre-primary nominating process in states without real factional organizations is dangerous. In reality, little or no

9 See above, p. 214.
10 See above, pp. 169–74.
11 See above, pp. 127–28.

sifting of candidates occurs. Individuals who have gained prominence by political exploits of one sort or another become gubernatorial possibilities. Perhaps, too, the absence of any real organization to select and advance candidates in such states places a premium on the more spectacular individual. Of the many individuals who are "possibilities" a goodly number usually remove themselves before the primary. It becomes evident that they have little popular support or they are unable to attract enough financial backing to make a campaign. The operations of the people with the "big money" are veiled with secrecy. Scattered bits of evidence suggest that on the whole the candidate attracts the money rather than that the money stirs up the candidate.[12] Often a year or so before the primary several persons become likely possibilities, and enough money moves in behind them to finance speaking tours, publicity, and other endeavors to keep their name before the public and to build them up.[13]

In multifactional states the first primary assumes great importance as a sifting device. No factional groups with any particular cohesiveness operate to narrow down the alternatives. A handful of people here back one man; a second little group backs another.[14] Three, four, five, six, or even more candidates battle it out in a free-for-all in the first Democratic primary, and the voters "nominate" a couple of candidates to make the run-off campaign.

3. The Run-Off Primary

The direct primary method of nomination, rather than the convention, was an inevitable consequence of the one-party system in the South.

[12] The free-for-all in the first primary and the preliminary maneuvers provide opportunity for campaign financiers to size up the prospects, and under some circumstances they unite on a single candidate in the first primary. Thus, in one primary the process of uniting the blue chips on a candidate in the pre-primary trial heats was about as follows: One aspirant had an unimpressive war record; he had become a farmer at a time that enabled him to take advantage of the agricultural draft exemption. Another had a bit of embezzlement in his past, not publicly known but which might be raked up. Another had had a connection with a concern that had dabbled in "hot oil," and he was vulnerable to the espionage service of a rival candidate. Among the others one with a relatively clean record turned up and around him the blue chips united against a so-so liberal.

[13] Bits of information fortuitously collected suggest the probability that vocational groups—insurance, real estate, railroads, labor groups—frequently take the initiative in a discreet manner in putting candidates into primaries for legislative posts. It is, of course, not always necessary for such interests to put a few candidates into races in order that they may have spokesmen in the legislature.

[14] The following news dispatch probably describes an often-recurrent situation: "Little Rock, Ark., March 23.—Between 25 and 30 prominent Arkansans met in Little Rock today 'trying our best' to get Gov. Ben Laney to reconsider his Jan. 19 decision not to seek re-election. Meeting behind closed doors at a hotel, the group admitted that the entire morning session was taken up with a discussion of ways and means of convincing Laney he should seek a third term. 'All I can say is we're trying our best to get the governor to run,' said Highway Commissioner Dan Felton of Mariana, in whose room the meeting was held.' "—Memphis Press-Scimitar, March 23, 1948.

When single-party action determines the results of elections in advance, the logic of democracy requires a direct vote on nominees rather than nomination through the convention system. When two parties compete, the question of convention versus direct primary nominations assumes a different significance than when the nominee of the same party invariably wins. The repression of competition between Democrats and Republican-Populist fusions in the southern states in the 1890's accelerated the demise of the convention as a nominating method.[15] The direct primary, through statute or party rule, replaced the convention for most nominations, and it became, in reality, the election.

Under one-party conditions, the logic of majority decision makes the run-off primary a concomitant of the direct primary. Although plurality elections are the general American rule, they are probably so because usually the two-party system limits the major candidates to two, one of whom inevitably wins a majority of the popular vote. As an auxiliary to the direct primary, southern states have developed the second or run-off primary which is held when no candidate receives a majority in the first polling. The two high candidates compete in the run-off.[16] Within the South, only two states, Tennessee and Virginia,[17] nominate by a plurality. Their dual factional organization ordinarily limits the principal contestants to two, one of whom naturally receives a majority. The other nine states use the run-off system. In multifactional states the odds are about even that no candidates will receive a majority in the first primary. It may be that multifactional states are multifactional because of the existence of the run-off—a question to which we will revert later. It is sufficient to note here that, save for North Carolina, the states with relatively coherent dual factional organizations do not use the second primary.[18]

The extent of its application and the form of the run-off differ among the states. Save in Mississippi, no run-off is held if the second-ranking candidate in the first primary does not choose to make the contest. In Mississippi, the third-ranking candidate may demand a run-off if the

[15] In the South, as elsewhere, one encounters persons of great prominence who firmly believe that all the troubles of this country can be charged to the direct primary and that the convention system of nomination should be reestablished. Their views are accorded no respect in the South. On the remnants of the convention system in the South, see below, pp. 438–42.

[16] Outside the eleven southern states only Kentucky, Oklahoma, and Utah have used the run-off system, and all these states have abandoned it.

[17] In Tennessee a run-off is held only in the unlikely event of a tie in a race for state-wide office.—*1932 Code*, secs, 2227.15a, 2227.35. Virginia authorizes city and county party committees to hold primaries in which a majority is required to nominate.—*1942 Code*, sec. 225.

[18] The dates of adoption of the present run-off statutes were as follows: Alabama, 1931; Arkansas, 1939; Florida, 1929; Georgia, 1917; Louisiana, 1922; Mississippi, 1902; North Carolina, 1915; South Carolina, 1915; Texas, 1918. Alabama used the run-off in gubernatorial primaries of 1902 and 1914 under party rule. Arkansas adopted the run-off in 1933 and abandoned it in 1935 only to re-establish it in 1939. Louisiana also used the run-off for a time prior to 1916.

second declines, the fourth if both the second and third decline, and so on.[19] Except in North Carolina, a second primary is held automatically unless the runner-up declines to run. In that state the second-ranking man must request within five days after the first primary that a second be held.

The interval between the two pollings varies from two to five weeks. In Alabama, Florida, North Carolina, and Texas the interval is four weeks; [20] in Mississippi and South Carolina, three; in Georgia and Arkansas, two; and in Louisiana, five. Louisiana's prudent lawmakers, however, provide for a six-week lapse if necessary to avoid conflict with Mardi Gras.

With exceptions in Georgia, Louisiana, and Mississippi, the run-off applies to all offices. Georgia uses the run-off only for nominations for governor and United States Senator.[21] In Louisiana contestants for minor state offices must make a run-off only if there is a second gubernatorial primary. In certain Mississippi counties and cities no run-off is held in nominations for certain special elections.[22] Until 1947 county party committees in Texas had discretion on whether to hold a run-off for local nominations, but now the run-off is mandatory for all nominations.[23]

Two states—Arkansas and Georgia—have systems that depart in major respects from the general pattern. Arkansas has a peculiar "preferential" primary which is followed in two weeks by a "regular" primary. In the preferential primary, only those offices are voted upon for which there are three or more candidates. Lacking a majority decision, the two ranking candidates appear on the regular primary ballot which also carries, for the first time, the names of the candidates for those nominations for which there are only two contestants. The explanations for this weird arrangement are that it provides less opportunity for the winner of a conventional first primary race to interfere or meddle in second primaries for other offices and that interest is maintained in both primaries.[24] The rationalization that the system maintains voter-interest is

[19] In 1947 the fifth ranking candidate for lieutenant-governor opposed the first-primary leader in the run-off. The Florida law provides that if several candidates tie for second place, all of them may run against the first-primary leader. In the absence of a majority in such a run-off, the nomination is made by the cognizant party committee.—*Florida Statutes 1941*, Title IX, sec. 102.48.

[20] Texas holds its first primary on the fourth Saturday in July and the second, on the fourth Saturday in August.—*Texas Election Laws*, 1946, art. 3102.

[21] The run-off rule also applies to municipal nominations in certain classes of cities.

[22] *1930 Code*, sec. 5910.

[23] *1947 Laws*, p. 258.

[24] H. M. Alexander, *op. cit.*, p. 243. At times, to avoid postponing the voting until the "regular" primary, one of the two contenders induces a third person to enter the "preferential" primary. Once the machinery is set in motion, such a "dummy" candidate may even withdraw before the voting after having served his purpose.

without merit unless Arkansas voters differ materially from those of other states.[25]

Georgia's county-unit system provides the second major variant of the ordinary run-off. In that state an odd arrangement prevails for the defeat of popular majorities.[26] Each county is allotted a number of "unit votes" equal to twice the number of its representatives in the lower house of the state legislature. The candidate receiving a *plurality* of the county's popular votes receives all its unit votes. In effect, there are 159 plurality nominations, that is, one for each county. A majority of unit votes is necessary to nominate. In the absence of a majority, a "run-over," as Georgians say, is held. The Georgia system is scarcely a run-off in the true sense, for it is possible to obtain a majority of the unit votes without a popular majority. In two of sixteen gubernatorial races from 1915 through 1948, the nomination was made without a popular majority and in one instance the winner did not have a plurality of the popular vote. In only three of the sixteen races was a run-off necessary.[27]

The fact that in Virginia and Tennessee—states without the run-off —a dual kind of factionalism has developed and that in most states with the run-off a looser multifactional arrangement has grown up leads to the query whether the nomination procedure itself may affect the form of factional organization. The hypothesis runs generally to the effect that

[25] For 38 southern gubernatorial run-offs between 1919 and 1948, turnout declined in 30. In 16 of the 30 instances the drop in the run-off vote was under 5 per cent of the first primary vote. In only four instances was the decrease more than 10 per cent. In three Georgia run-offs the decline was 34, 27, and 29 per cent (1920, 1926, and 1930, respectively). The sharp drop in Georgia second primary turnout is probably attributable to the fact that the mandatory run-off rule does not apply to state legislative races or to such county government primaries as are held concurrently with the state primaries. The second primary thus lacks the drawing power of contests for county offices, a magnet that drew voters to the first.

[26] See above, pp. 117–28.

[27] The extent to which the plurality rule for the award of county-unit votes inflates a candidate's strength when his popular vote is translated into unit votes depends on the territorial distribution of his popular pluralities. The under-representation of urban counties in the legislature makes it possible for a candidate strong in such counties to win a popular plurality, even a popular majority, and still have less than a majority of unit votes. In practice no uniform relation seems to exist between proportion of popular votes polled by candidates and their proportion of the unit vote. The relation between the two porportions, for those candidates polling more than 25 per cent of the popular vote, 1932–1948, have been as follows:

PER CENT POPULAR	UNIT	PER CENT POPULAR	UNIT	PER CENT POPULAR	UNIT
28.4	22.9	42.4	36.3	51.6	77.6
31.6	7.3	42.4	30.7	51.7	76.1
32.2	3.9	*43.0*	*59.0*	57.7	63.7
36.0	19.5	45.2	23.9	60.0	90.7
42.0	*64.4*	45.3	35.6	65.9	96.1
		50.7	68.8		

with one office to be filled by a plurality vote—that of governor, for example—the organizers of political effort would form alliances in order to maximize their chance of belonging to a combination with a single chance to win. If the man with the largest number of votes takes all, no matter how small a proportion of the total vote they may be, the incentive of political leaders and sub-leaders is to try to maneuver into a winning combination in the first primary. On the other hand, if there is a second voting a candidate can take a chance that his support—no matter how weak it may be—will be enough to place him first or second, with an opportunity to run in the final sweepstakes. This kind of reasoning—applied to our general practice of electing legislators and executives —has been advanced as an explanation of the dual nature of our party division.[28]

The general argument, if carried further in application to the southern scene, would be that in the formation of bi-factional combinations and coalitions to win pluralities, groups of politicians would develop habits of working together and more or less continuing factional organizations would grow up. In the absence of such incentive to work together, numerous clusters of political leadership maintain their independence, work up their temperatures in the first primary campaign, and develop only an arms-length and transient alliance in the second primary.

Like many beautiful theories, the truth of the general idea is hard to determine. One could compare Virginia and Tennessee—states without the run-off—with the other southern states and attribute the differences in factional structure to the run-off.[29] Obviously, the conclusion would ignore other variables. The presence of a goodly number of Republicans in Tennessee, Virginia, and North Carolina compels a higher degree of Democratic unity. For reasons stated earlier, the existence of opposition appears to be associated with a duality of contest for control of the Democratic party.[30]

Another test of the effects of the run-off on factional structure is a

[28] See F. A. Hermens, *Democracy or Anarchy?* (Notre Dame: The Review of Politics, 1941); E. E. Schattschneider, *Party Government* (New York: Rinehart and Company, 1942). W. R. Sharp points to the influence on party division and coalition in the double system of elections—equivalent in form to southern first and second primaries—in use in France.—*The Government of the French Republic* (New York: Van Nostrand, 1938), chap. 3.

[29] The exception of Arkansas to this correlation between nominating procedure and factional structure is to be accounted for. Its factionalism seems to have more closely approximated a dual form since the 1939 adoption of the run-off than before. In this connection consider the suggestions on the effect of the New Deal on state factional structures, above, p. 310.

[30] Although North Carolina, Virginia, and Tennessee all have fairly coherently organized factional systems, North Carolina leaders, who operate under the run-off, have not organized the voters into two groups to the same degree as those of Virginia and Tennessee. The median percentage of the total first-primary vote going to the two leading candidates in Virginia is 98.3 and in Tennessee (for the years in which no incumbent sought reelection), 98.7; in North Carolina, 77.4.

Huey Long, "The Kingfish"

"Just call me sui generis." *And he was.*

GRAND DRAGON SAMUEL GREEN OF THE GEORGIA KU KLUX KLAN

A dying movement in which southerners take no pride.

before-and-after adoption analysis. If the run-off stimulates division of leadership and fractionalization within the electorate, there should be a larger number of "serious" candidates in the first primary and a wider dispersion of the popular vote after the adoption of the second primary system than before. The empirical findings by this method are mixed, al-

TABLE 50

Texas Factionalism Before and After Adoption of Run-Off Primary

YEAR	NUMBER OF GUBERNATORIAL CANDIDATES	NUMBER RECEIVING 5% OR MORE OF VOTE	PER CENT OF VOTE TO TWO HIGH CANDIDATES WHEN	
			INCUMBENT A CANDIDATE	INCUMBENT NOT A CANDIDATE
1908	2	2	100.0	
1910	4	4		63.3
1912	2	2	100.0	
1914	2	2		100.0
1916	3	2	98.4	
Run-off adopted				
1918	2	2		100.0
1920	4	4		67.2
1922	4	3	87.1	
1924	9	4		48.3
1926	6	3	84.4	
1928	4	2	93.2	
1930	11	7		49.6
1932	9	3	72.2	
1934	7	6		54.2
1936	5	4	75.3	
1938	13	4		72.2
1940	7	5	75.9	
1942	6	2		97.1
1944	10	2	90.4	
1946	14	5		63.2
1948	8	3	75.9	

though they give some support to the hypothesis that the run-off encourages a multiplicity of faction. The before-and-after situation in Texas appears in Table 50. The rule of nomination by simple plurality prevailed only a short time before the adoption of the run-off—perhaps too short a time to give a thorough test to the idea that a plurality rule induces a dual grouping. Only two primaries were held before the run-off in which the incumbent governor—who receives a courtesy second term— was not a candidate. In one of them, a high degree of fractionalization of the electorate occurred, but in the second a dual division formed. After the adoption of the run-off, as the table shows in detail, Texas politics became consistently multifactional. One cannot know whether strong forces toward a dual factionalism would have been generated if the run-off had not been put into effect. At any rate, with the run-off in existence, the incentive for coalition in advance of the first primary disappears.

The before-and-after analysis of Florida yields about the same result as in Texas. In other states for which data are available over an adequate period—Georgia and Alabama—the differences in fractionalization of leadership before and after adoption of the run-off were not marked. These states, it will be recalled, occupy a middle position in the degree of multiplicity of factions, as measured by the analysis on page 17. Those inclined to quarrel with our theory may inquire why Georgia and Alabama have not fractionalized to the same extent as Texas and Florida. The explanation seems to rest in the fact that in Georgia and Alabama during the period covered by the analysis individual leaders with personal followings arose who were regarded by their political competitors as having a chance to win the gubernatorial nomination in the first primary by garnering a majority of the popular votes. Eugene Talmadge and Bibb Graves had followings of that size; the opposition, if it were to have a show at all, realized that all hands had better get together in the first-primary campaign. On the other hand, the Ferguson "vest pocket" vote in Texas was never large enough to create that expectation by the various elements in opposition. In Georgia, it must also be remembered that the county-unit system makes even the first primary approach in nature a system of nomination by popular plurality. Louisiana also occupies a middle position in the multiplicity of factions, and here the influence of Huey Long in organizing the politics of the state is patent.

The runner-up in the first primary often wins the nomination in the second primary (see Table 51), a fact often advanced to support the contention that the popular will would be defeated by awarding nomination to the winner of a plurality in a single primary. The chances are, however, that the result would be the same over the long pull. In the absence of a second primary, the forces that unite behind a single man for that race would join in the first or only primary and produce the same results. Short-run considerations, however, are important in politics, and legislatures in adopting the run-off system have been moved by no desire to alter the nature of political organization. Insofar as the data are available, prime considerations in the adoption of the run-off have been attachment to the abstract idea of majority nomination, without much thought of the consequences for factional organization, and expectations of the effect on the fortunes of an individual candidate. Unable quickly to form a coalition against a strong leader, his divided opposition calculates that it can, in effect, fight out its own differences in the first primary and then unite on the runner-up to such a strong personality in the second pri-

TABLE 51

Extent of Use and Results of Run-Off Primary in Gubernatorial
Nominations, 1919–48

STATE	NUMBER OF NOMINATIONS	NUMBER RUN-OFFS	RUNNER-UP IN FIRST WON SECOND	RUNNER-UP DECLINED RUN-OFF
Alabama	4	2	0	1
Arkansas	6	1	0	1
Florida	5	5	2	0
Georgia	14	3	1 [a]	0
Louisiana	7	4	2	1
Mississippi	8	7	3	0
North Carolina	8	4	1	1
South Carolina	9	6	2	0
Texas	15	7	3	0
Total	76	39	14	4

[a] Candidate with second highest number of popular votes in the first primary won the run-off. Georgia races are determined by unit votes.

mary. In the process of operation, some minor political leaders gain a vested interest in the system. They run in the first primary and then, for a consideration, usually described as a reimbursement of expenses, announce for one of the two leaders in the second primary. The custom seems to be most prevalent in Mississippi.

The significance of inquiry into the effects of the run-off system turns on the question whether the nature of factional organization influences the kind of political leadership and the kind of government that a state has. A prima facie case at least can be made for the proposition that the competition of fairly coherent factional groups produces results different from those of the transient, fluid groupings characteristic of multifactional systems. A coherent faction, with something of a corporate spirit, with a degree of continuity should, in the long run, recruit a different type of leadership from that thrown up by ad hoc groupings gathered together by an individual who looks only to the end of one term. A two-party type of political organization and leadership can develop within the Democratic party only when a durable dual-factional organization exists. Plurality nominations would not immediately and automatically assure that type of factional system, but they would create incentive for movement in that direction.

Chapter Twenty | # ENSURING FINALITY
OF THE PRIMARY

IT is fundamental to Democratic supremacy in the South that the party's nominees shall go without effective challenge in the general election. In all probability the rock-bottom basis for the authority of Democratic primary decisions has been southern attachment to Democratic presidential nominees. That attachment insulated southern politics from the divisive issues of national campaigns. If those issues had been raised more effectively and more consistently in the South, they would have spread by infection to state politics and would have provided powerful coat-tail support for Republican state and local candidates. The potent unifying force of the threat of external intervention on the race issue, however, caused the South to close its ranks in national politics and thereby removed the possibility of a dual party system in state and local affairs.

Patterns of behavior established in crisis situations have an extraordinary tenacity. Loyalty to party labels, Republican, Democratic, or Socialist, survives intense strains. These loyalties, once they come into existence, tend to re-enforce themselves, for many individuals gain a vested interest in the status that they possess because people have these loyalties. Powerful taboos against voting Republican grew up. A Republican came to be considered by definition as either a postmaster, a "nigger lover," or a Federal district judge. Voting a Republican ticket in the

general election came to be regarded, not as the erraticism of a mug-
wump, but as a desecration of the memory of Robert E. Lee, disrespect
for one's gallant forebears who fought at Gettysburg, and an open invitation to boycott one's grocery business.[1]

All such social compulsions have underlain the finality of choice of
the Democratic primary. In most states the commonly accepted obligation
of party loyalty has been formalized either in statute or party rules,
which have two chief objectives: to create an obligation for the voter to
support the nominee in the general election, and to establish bars against
defeated primary candidates who might challenge the party nominee in
the general election. Of these, the second is the more significant; its grand
effect is to re-enforce the rule that the sole channel to political advancement is the Democratic party.

1. The Voter and Party Loyalty

Political institutions and procedures may be the same in form from
place to place yet differ in their import. While the direct primary is
similar in form and name in Florida and Illinois, its realities diverge
markedly. So it is with some of the more technical features of the primary.
In two-party states party managers try to limit participation in the primary to persons who are "real" Republicans or "real" Democrats. Those
controlling the party organization fear that outsiders will "raid" its primary. In some instances a deliberate raid led by the Democrats, for
example, may be calculated to nominate a weak Republican to make the
going easier for the Democratic nominee in the general election. In spon-
taneous primary raids, voters may move into a party primary and nominate an appealing candidate not of the true party faith, e. g., a progressive Republican. This tactic worries not only the old-guard party leaders;
those concerned about maintaining the integrity of the two-party system
fret lest in the looseness of the primary system the parties become even
less capable of presenting the electorate with candidates who represent
alternative viewpoints.

To cope with raids, many states have closed primaries, in which
some test of party loyalty may be applied to exclude those not of the
true faith from a hand in making the party nominations. In the South
the closed primary and the accompanying tests of party loyalty are not
designed to keep out Republicans: a corporal's guard of Republicans
cannot conduct much of a raid. The southern closed primary is designed
to assure the finality of the primary, i.e., to keep the voters loyal to the
party nominee rather than to prevent raids. Yet in the formal language

---

[1] It scarcely need be said that similar considerations influenced Republican loyalties on the other side of the Mason and Dixon line.

of the statutes and rules a southern closed primary looks very much like a nonsouthern closed primary.[2]

Although the most general test for participation in Democratic primaries in the South is a promise—in language of varying degrees of awesomeness—to support the nominee in the general election, other more or less formal tests exist. Except in South Carolina participation in the primary is limited to persons qualified to vote in the general election. Thus primary voters must meet requirements of poll-tax payment, literacy, understanding, good character, and age as specified in the statutes of each state.[3]

In addition to the ordinary qualifications for voting in general elections, several states require party membership or "affiliation" to participate in the primary. South Carolina's Democratic party sets up such a qualification; elsewhere the requirement is statutory. In Florida, Louisiana, and North Carolina an elector indicates his party affiliation at the time of registration; he is eligible to participate only in the primary of the party with which he so affiliates. In these three states the Republican party is required to make its nominations by direct primaries which are conducted by public, rather than party, authority. Hence, determination of party affiliation in advance of the primary becomes especially important.[4] Tennessee, Alabama, Texas, Georgia, and Virginia also set up the requirement of party membership or affiliation, although in these states the requirement has no perceptible significance. Arkansas party rules specifically—in violation of state statutes [5]—declare that party membership is not a requirement for participation in the primary. Only whites may be party members; only party members may be party officials or candidates.[6]

Another test for primary participation, sometimes associated with the membership test, is adherence to party principles. In Arkansas, Mississippi, and South Carolina this test is chiefly calculated to discourage

[2] The most thorough study of the problem is by Clarence A. Berdahl, "Party Membership in the United States," *American Political Science Review*, 36 (1942), pp. 16–50, 241–62.

[3] South Carolina's Democratic party makes its own rules for participation in the primary, and they require qualifications resembling those for voting in the general election except that poll-tax payment is not demanded. Rules adopted in 1948 required that Negroes to vote in the primary had to present certificates of qualification to vote in the general election. Federal District Judge Waring, of Charleston, struck down the distinction between black and white. For a treatment of the matter, see below, pp. 627–32.

[4] In the mountain Republican areas of Tennessee and Virginia crossing party lines in the primaries is open and notorious. If there were any disposition to check this practice, the introduction of registration systems requiring enrollment with indication of party affiliation some time in advance of the primary would reduce raids and trades organized just before primary day.

[5] *Pope's Digest 1937*, sec. 4749; Party Rules, 1948, sec. 2(b) – 2(d).

[6] The exclusion of Negroes from party office and party candidacy would probably be held void if challenged.

Negro participation.[7] The party principles in these states, to be sure, contain specific declarations which, if applied strictly, would exclude many whites from the primaries. But they are meaningless in application, as is the requirement of adherence to party principle in Alabama and Virginia. Thus, the state Democratic executive committee of Alabama is empowered to determine qualifications to participate in the party primaries, and the call of the primary usually stipulates that primary voters must "believe in the principles of the Democratic party." The chairman of the committee in 1947 explained that the principles are nowhere set down except in the platform and in their "general acceptance" by the people. The 1922 state platform, a document not in wide circulation in 1947, contained the most recent official enunciation of "principles." Virginia also requires belief in "principles," but party officials of the state profess to know of no statement of such principles.

The principal instruments for binding the voter to party are tests of previous party loyalty and of intent to remain loyal, i.e., to support the primary nominees in the general election. Arkansas, Florida, Mississippi, and Virginia make past support of party nominees a condition for voting in the primaries. All southern states except Florida and Tennessee require, as a condition of voting in primaries an intention to support the primary nominees in the general election.

The exact verbiage of the loyalty requirement differs from state to state. Arkansas disqualifies any person who "at the last preceding general election voted against any state, county, district, township, or municipal Democratic nominee, or, who, at the last preceding general election voted for, or espoused the cause of, any candidate for any office in this State who was not a Democratic nominee. . . ."[8] Florida's exclusion makes no reference to espousal of treasonable candidates. The statute merely declares that any voter who "voted, at the next preceding general election for any nominee of any political party for any office for which nomination" is made under the state primary law "shall not be entitled to receive or vote the ballot of a different political party" at the primary election.[9] Mississippi simply states that no person shall be eligible to vote in the primary "unless he . . . has been in accord with the party holding such primary within the two preceding years. . . ."[10] Presumably this language requires support of past nominees. Virginia permits no person to vote "unless . . . in the last preceding general election, in which such person participated, he or she voted for the nominees" of the party conducting the primary.[11] Texas statutes contain a test of past support of

[7] See below, pp. 629–43.
[8] Party Rules, 1948, sec. 3 (a).
[9] *Florida Statutes 1941*, Title IX, sec. 102.40.
[10] *1930 Code*, sec. 5887.
[11] *1942 Code*, sec. 228. The "Primary Plan" (1932) of the Virginia Democratic Party phrases the requirement differently. The party rules limit participation to persons

party nominees, which is ignored because of a later legislative declaration that "no person shall ever be denied the right to participate in a primary in this state because of former political views or affiliations. . . ." [12]

Nine states require an intention to support the primary nominees as a condition of voting in the primary. In summary, the essential features of these arrangements are:

> *Alabama*: Only those persons may vote "who agree and bind themselves by participating in said Primary, to abide by the result of said Primary Elections and to support the nominees of the Democratic Party therein. . . ." Resolutions of State Democratic Executive Committee of Alabama, adopted January 12, 1946, and June 22, 1946. The primary ballot carries the following language: "By casting this ballot I do pledge myself to abide by the result of this primary election and to aid and support all the nominees thereof in the ensuing general election."—*1940 Code*, Title 17, sec. 350.
>
> *Arkansas*: No person is permitted to vote "who will not pledge himself to vote for and support at the ensuing general election the candidate of the Democratic Party for State offices nominated in the Democratic primary election in which he is voting."—Party Rules, 1948, sec. 3 (a) (5).
>
> *Georgia*: The Primary ". . . voter must pledge himself or herself to support in the general election . . . all candidates nominated by the Democratic Party of Georgia in this primary, or any run off or special primary held in Georgia by said Party, for the nomination of county, district or state officers, preceding the general election. . . ."—Resolutions, 1948 state convention.
>
> *Louisiana*: The primary ballot carries the following pledge: "By casting this ballot I do pledge myself to abide by the results of this primary election and to aid and support all the nominees thereof in the ensuing general election."—Act 46 of 1940, sec. 38. "No one who participates in the primary election of any political party shall have the right to participate in any primary election of any other political party, with a view of nominating opposing candidates, nor shall he be permitted to sign any nomination papers for any opposing candidate or candidates. . . ."—Act 46 of 1940, sec. 87.
>
> *Mississippi*: "No person shall be eligible . . . unless he . . . intends to support the nominations in which he participates. . . ."—*1930 Code*, sec. 5887.
>
> *North Carolina*: The obligation to support the nominee is ambiguous: ". . . anyone may at any time any elector proposes to vote challenge his right to vote in the primary of any party upon the ground that he . . . does not in good faith intend to support the candidates nominated in the primary of such party. . . ." The election judges decide the challenge. But: ". . . nothing herein contained shall be construed to prevent any elector from casting at the

---

"who voted for all the nominees of that party at the next preceding general election in which they voted and in which the Democratic nominee or nominees had opposition. . . ."

[12] See O. D. Weeks, "The Texas Direct Primary System," *Southwestern Social Science Quarterly*, 13 (1932), pp. 95–120.

general election a free and untrammelled ballot for the candidate or candidates of his choice." *General Statues of 1943*, chap. 163, sec. 126.

South Carolina: The primary managers at each box must require every voter to sign and deliver to them a "Voter's Oath" which includes the following: "I further solemnly swear that I will support the election of the nominees of this primary in the ensuing general election, and that I am not a member of any other political party." —*Party Rules*, 1948, sec. 36.

Texas: The primary ballot carries the following pledge: "I am a Democrat and pledge myself to support the nominee of this primary."—*Texas Election Laws*, 1946, art. 3110.

Virginia: "All . . . persons . . . who will support all of the nominees of that party at the ensuing general election" may vote in the Democratic primary.—"Primary Plan," 1932.

The phraseology of voter-loyalty tests often relieves Democratic voters of even the moral obligation to vote for the party's presidential nominee. Thus are assuaged the feelings of guilt by Republicans and presidential Republicans for their participation in the Democratic primary. The Alabama pledge applies to nominees of the primary, including presidential electors. In 1948 presidential electors chosen at the primary had pledged themselves to vote against Truman in the electoral college. Out of this situation could come the ingenious charge that those voters who supported the nominees of the national convention at the general election were party bolters. "It is ludicrous," said the chairman of the state Democratic executive committee, a leader of the anti-Truman faction, "for anyone to refer to those of us who are voting the straight ticket of the Democratic Party of Alabama as 'bolters.'" [13] Those who would support Truman were the bolters.[14]

Applicability of the loyalty test to support of the presidential nominees turns on the meaning of the phrase "nominees of the party" or "nominees" of the primary. "Nominee of the party" may apply only to nominees of the party of the state; the pledge to support "nominees of the primary" may exclude presidential electors. Virginia's attorney general, following the defection of Democrats to Hoover in 1928, held that "nominees of said party" did not include presidential electors, who were not named in the primary. Therefore, persons who had voted for the Republican electors were eligible to participate in the succeeding Democratic primary. In 1948, in the midst of the southern revolt against the Truman civil rights program, the attorney general by the same reasoning held that the pledge did not bind either voters or candidates

[13] Letter in reply to an editorial entitled, "Booby-Trapped," *Tuscaloosa News*, July 26, 1948.

[14] Although Florida requires of voters no pledge to support the nominee, in 1948 the legislature ruled that for the election of that year no voter should "be considered as having violated any pledge imputed to him by reason of his registration as a member of such party by reason of the fact that he may vote" at the 1948 election for candidates for presidential elector of another party.

in the primary to support any particular set of presidential electors at the forthcoming general election.

In practice, of course, no serious effort is made to determine whether a person who presents himself at the polls has actually supported the party nominees at preceding elections. Nor is the pledge to support the nominees administered with impressive solemnity, if at all. In Alabama, Louisiana, and Texas the pledge appears on the ballot, the marking of which constitutes, in effect, a written promise to support the nominees. In all states with pledges of support to the nominee a would-be voter may be challenged on the firmness of his intent of loyalty. Few election officials can recall an instance of challenge.

The off-hand nature of the loyalty pledge may be inferred from the uproar that greeted a change in party rules in South Carolina in 1948. Until that time the party rules imposed on the polling officials the duty of requiring that each voter take the following oath and pledge: "I do solemnly swear that I am a resident of this club district and am duly qualified to vote at this primary according to the rules of the Democratic party, and that I have not voted before at this election, and pledge myself to support the nominees of this primary." [15] The 1948 convention adopted rules requiring that, before casting his ballot, every voter should sign a "Voter's Oath" which included the following: "I further solemnly swear that I will support the election of the nominees of this primary in the ensuing general election, and that I am not a member of any other political party." [16] Although other portions of the oath drew most of the criticism, the idea that an oath should be required of all voters was not received with universal acclaim. The provision had been on the rule books all along, yet it had occurred to few election managers to require voters to take the pledge.[17]

Search of court reports dredges up no decisions that breathe life into the party pledge. In two Texas decisions in the 1920's efforts of party committees to exclude persons who had violated the pledge led to decisions that it was only a matter of "moral restraint" and not otherwise binding. The pledge was only an expression of intention, and if a voter had not carried out his past intention to support the party's nominee that was a question between him and his conscience.[18]

[15] Party Rules, 1946, sec. 32.

[16] Party Rules, 1948, sec. 36.

[17] In Texas' July, 1948 primary the Dallas county chairman instructed election officials to quiz voters suspected of not taking the pledge in good faith and to exclude from the primary those voters they judged not to be a Democrat or not pledging themselves in good faith to support the nominee. Dixiecrats were alarmed lest their followers be excluded, and the courts enjoined the party officials from questioning voters.

[18] *Briscoe* v. *Boyle*, 266 S. W. 275 (1926); *Cunningham Party Membership* v. *McDermott*, 277 S. W. 218 (1925). For discussion of these cases, see Berdahl, p. 32, and Weeks, "The Texas Direct Primary System," pp. 108–10.

In fact, of course, the matter of voter loyalty to Democratic nominees assumes practical importance in only two or three types of situations. The party pledge has generally been interpreted to exclude the national nominees from its terms; therefore the considerable number of Democratic primary voters who support Republican presidential nominees do not violate the letter of the party gospel and often not the spirit.[19] Apart from political hybrids who vote Democratic locally and Republican nationally, the bolting voter rarely takes on significance in state and local elections. The usual concept of "crossing party lines" and "raiding" primaries has no meaning, for there are usually no organized Republicans to raid Democratic primaries and often there is no Republican primary that Democrats could raid if they had the inclination. The question of the exclusion of non-Democrats from Democratic primaries seems to have aroused attention chiefly in county primaries in areas in which Republicans are numerous, though not numerous enough to win elections, and in isolated state-wide primaries. Thus, Republican party officials observe that many Republicans register as Democrats in North Carolina and participate in Democratic primaries. Crossing party lines is common in eastern Tennessee, a state with no party pledge. In Alabama's northern counties, which have a sizeable Republican vote, Republicans usually participate in Democratic primaries. The chairman of the state Democratic executive committee in 1947 described the practice as a "perfect headache" and the committee discussed, without solution, ways and means of dealing with the problem.

Simply because the party pledge has, and can have, no legally binding effect, it should not be dismissed as a completely meaningless ritual. On those rare occasions when the Democratic nominees are threatened at the general election, the party faithful beat the drums to remind the voters of the high moral obligation to which they have subscribed. In 1924 in Texas, for example, when Mrs. Miriam A. ("Ma") Ferguson won the Democratic gubernatorial nomination, droves of those who had pledged themselves to support the nominee threatened to vote Republican in the general election. Ferguson supporters argued that no "good Democrat's pledge should be a scrap of paper only. His moral obligation should be as binding as his legal obligation." The Democratic state committee denounced as "undemocratic" those who would violate their pledge; the Republican candidate pointed to the inconsistency in the law which at one point "extorted" a pledge and at another prescribed the manner by which a voter might vote a split ticket at the general election.[20] In each of two general elections at which Mrs. Ferguson was the Democratic

[19] See earlier estimates of the numbers of presidential Republicans, above, p. 278. In 1944 Florida had 46,448 registered Republicans who could participate only in the Republican primary; 143,215 Floridians voted for Dewey. Louisiana had 2,077 registered Republicans and Dewey received 67,750 votes in Louisiana.

[20] Weeks, "The Texas Direct Primary System," pp. 108–9.

nominee, 1924 and 1932, probably no less than 200,000 voters violated their primary pledge by supporting the Republican candidate for governor.[21]

Even under two-party conditions tests of party loyalty are futile as a means of limiting primary participation to those of the true party faith. The logic of the one-party system demands that they be ineffective. The continuation of the one-party system depends on a primary admission policy flexible enough to permit participants in the South's occasional insurgent movements to find their way more or less happily back to the local Democracy. An exclusion rule that worked would create a body of voters ripe for activation by Republican leadership.[22]

2. The Candidate and Party Loyalty

The elaborate formal rules and tests to limit primary voting to loyal Democrats have little to do with ensuring the finality of the primaries. Inconstant voters are welcomed, even lured, back into the party. The inconstant candidate, however, presents a greater danger to Democratic supremacy. By means of his leadership and influence the party might be rent or even destroyed. Against him sterner measures must be adopted. To protect the party, statutes and party rules bar from the primary ballot candidates who have been disloyal to the party or who will not pledge their future allegiance. Once its dominance was established, practically all persons skilled in political leadership became affiliated with the Democratic party. So long as most of them remain Democrats, voters with insurgent inclinations have no place to go since there are no leaders to follow outside the party. Under these conditions limitation of candidacies in the primary to tried and tested Democrats takes on a significance different from like rules in two-party states. The main effect in two-party states is that a politician usually has to work out his political career in the party in which he started; the effect under one-party conditions is to retard the development of a competing party.

The usual rule that defeated primary candidates may not run in the

[21] 1924: Democratic second primary vote, M. A. Ferguson 413,751; F. D. Robertson, 316,019; general election, M. A. Ferguson, 422,558; George C. Butte (Rep.), 294,970. 1932: Democratic second primary, M. A. Ferguson, 477,644; R. S. Sterling, 473,846; general election, M. A. Ferguson, 528,986; Orville Bullington (Rep.), 317,807.

[22] It may be correct to forecast, however, that those southern Democratic leaders who acquiesce in, even encourage, voters to bolt the party's national nominees are opening the way for a threat to Democratic supremacy in state and local affairs in the long run. Voters get into the habit of voting Republican nationally. The taboo against Republicanism gradually wears down. Eventually the potency of the obligation to support state and local Democratic nominees erodes. And, more important, the powerful divisive issues of national politics are projected into state affairs and create a condition conducive to the development of an opposition party.

general election as independents prevails in all southern states except Tennessee. Beyond this conventional preventive measure, candidates must in some states meet tests of previous loyalty to the party and, in a larger number, pledge themselves to future loyalty to party candidates. These tests are applied in a more solemn manner to candidates than to voters. Usually a candidate must actually take an oath. Voters usually have to take no such affirmative action; their accord with loyalty obligations is generally more or less assumed by all concerned. More important, the candidate may be subjected to sanctions—such as denial of the right to run in future primaries—while in practice the voter is immune from penalty for party disloyalty.

Standards of previous party loyalty generally are limited to an oath that the candidate voted for the party nominees at the preceding general election. A treacherous candidate thus may purge himself of disloyalty with the passage of time, which, however, may be long enough to kill him politically. The previous-loyalty tests are as follows:

Alabama: The candidate must take oath to the following: "I hereby certify that I did not vote, in the [last] general election held . . . a Republican ticket or any independent ticket of any party or group, other than the Democratic Party, or for anyone other than the nominees of the Democratic Party, or any ticket other than the Democratic ticket, or openly and publicly in said election oppose the election of the nominees of the Democratic Party or any of them."— Resolutions of the state Democratic executive committee, adopted January 12, 1946, sec. 7.

Arkansas: "No one shall be eligible as a candidate . . . who shall have participated in any run-off or primary other than a run-off or primary held under the authority of the Democratic Party. . . ." —Party Rules, 1948, sec. 55.

Florida: Candidate must take oath ". . . that he did not vote for any nominee of any other party, national, state or county, at the last general election; that he did not register as a member of any other political party during the two years immediately last past. . . ."—*Florida Statutes 1941*, Title IX, sec. 102.29.

Texas: Candidate for United States Senator must state in application "That if he voted at the preceding election he voted for the nominees of said party."—*Texas Election Laws*, 1946, Art. 3093.

Virginia: Candidate must take oath: "I . . . do state on my sacred honor . . . that I voted for all of the nominees of said party at the next preceding general election in which I voted and in which the Democratic nominee or nominees had opposition. . . ."—Primary Plan 1932.

Most of these requirements are in conventional form; the Arkansas test, however, is unusual. It seems to have originated in 1924 after the Ku Klux Klan had held preference votes among its members in several counties to agree upon candidates to back in the regular primary. The

Democratic state committee condemned the practice and barred nominees thus chosen from the Democratic primary ballot.[23]

Six states require of candidates pledges of future loyalty to the nominees of the primary, i.e., pledge themselves to accept the results of the primary. The details of the pledge are as follows:

Alabama: The candidate's statement must include the following: "I further agree to abide by the result of the Primary Elections in which I am a candidate and to support the Democratic nominees in said elections."—Resolutions of state Democratic executive committee, adopted January 12, 1946, sec. 7.

Arkansas: "I pledge myself to abide by the results of said Primary election and to support all the nominees thereof. I declare that I am not now and will not become the candidate of any factions, independent or otherwise, either privately or publicly suggested in opposition to a regular Democratic nominee."—Party Rules, 1948, sec. 57.

Florida: The candidate takes oath ". . . that he pledges himself to vote for all nominees of such party—national, state or county, whose names shall appear upon the ballot at the next succeeding general election. . . ."—*Florida Statutes, 1941,* Title IX, sec. 102.29. After the 1948 primaries the Florida legislature adopted an act declaring that no candidate who failed to support his party's presidential electors in November, 1948 should "be considered as having violated the oath" taken in accord with the general law.

North Carolina: "I hereby pledge myself to abide by the results of said primary, and to support in the next General Election all candidates nominated by the Party."—*General Statutes of 1943,* chap. 160, sec. 119.

South Carolina: "I hereby pledge myself to abide by the results of such primary, and support the nominees of this primary . . . and I declare that . . . I am not nor will I become the candidate of any faction, either privately or publicly suggested, other than the regular Democratic Party of South Carolina."—Party Rules, 1948, sec. 29.

Virginia: Candidate's declaration: "If I am defeated in the primary I hereby direct and irrevocably authorize the election officials charged with the duty of preparing the ballots to be used in the succeeding election not to print my name on said ballots."—*1942 Code,* sec. 229. Candidate's oath: "I . . . do state on my sacred honor . . . that I shall support and vote for all the nominees of said party in the next ensuing general election. . . ."—Primary Plan, 1932.

The standards of loyalty applicable to candidates have loopholes with respect to national nominees. The Virginia language, as noted earlier, places on Senator Byrd no obligation to support the presidential nominee. Arkansas and South Carolina party rules specifically limit the pledge to nominees of the primary and thereby exclude the presidential nominee. Florida has specifically required support of the national nomi-

[23] H. M. Alexander, "The Double Primary," *Arkansas Historical Quarterly,* 3 (1944), pp. 225–26.

nees, although an exception, limited to the 1948 election, was made for Dixiecrats. Where presidential electors are primary nominees, as in Alabama, the pledge to support such nominees may mean support of electors opposed to the national convention's nominee, as 1948 demonstrated.[24]

The infrequent application of sanctions for violation of the party pledge is in itself a measure of its effectiveness. Yet penalties for party disloyalty are invoked in the South more often than they are elsewhere in the country. Although conservative Democratic lawyers try to rationalize a separation of state and national party, most of the litigation and sound and fury over bolting by candidates has originated in bolts of the national ticket. In 1928 Senator J. Thomas Heflin and others supported Hoover, and the Alabama Democratic state executive committee won court approval of its exclusion of Heflin and others from the 1930 primaries.[25] Heflin, nevertheless, ran as an independent in the general election and lost. The potency of the Alabama sanction against candidates was illustrated again in 1948 when presidential electors pledged against the Democratic presidential candidate were nominated in the state primary. Many state political leaders had been candidates at the same primary and had taken the pledge to support the nominees of the primary; other leaders would be candidates in future primaries. Any politician who advocated support of the national nominee endangered his political future. The chairman of the state Democratic executive committee announced:

> I think it would be well for any Alabamian who has political ambitions to stop, look and listen before fighting the nominees of our Democratic Primaries, because I am confident that when our State Committee calls the 1950 Primaries of the Democratic Party of Alabama it will require of each prospective candidate that before his name will be permitted to go on the ballot in our Primary Elections he shall make an oath to the effect that in the General Election in November, 1948, he not only did not vote a Republican or Independent ticket, or the ticket of any party or group other than the ticket containing the names of the nominees of our Democratic Primaries, but furthermore that he did not openly and publicly, in the General Election in November, oppose the nominees of our Democratic Primaries. This has been the usual custom and practice and it is sound.[26]

In Texas, as in Alabama, the 1928 bolt had its aftermath. In 1928 Tom Love openly avowed his opposition to Alfred E. Smith and sought at the same time to run for the Democratic nomination for lieutenant-governor. The courts upheld a county executive committee's exclusion

[24] As can best be determined from statutes and party rules, Tennessee, Mississippi, Georgia, and Louisiana make no loyalty requirements of candidates over and above those applicable to them as party members.

[25] *Wilkinson* v. *Henry*, 128 So. 362 (1930).

[26] *Tuscaloosa News*, July 26, 1948.

of Love from the ballot.[27] In 1930 the Democratic state executive committee unsuccessfully tried to exclude Love from the Democratic primary as
a candidate for governor. It attempted to bar from the primary any person
who had violated his 1928 pledge by opposing Democratic nominees; it
also tried to require a pledge in writing that primary candidates would
support the nominees, such pledge to be taken "in good faith without
any reservations." The Texas Supreme Court held that the committee
action exceeded the powers granted to the party by statute.[28] Love's
judicial victory was an empty one, for he ran fourth in the primary.[29]

Outside Texas and Alabama few, if any, efforts were made to exclude
the 1928 Hoovercrats as candidates in the 1930 primaries. In North Carolina, F. M. Simmons, thirty years a Democratic Senator and a 1928 Hoovercrat, was defeated in the 1930 primary; perhaps the voters administered
sanctions of their own against a man disloyal to the party. In truth,
of course, the efficacy of the sanctions against bolting depends ultimately
on public support; consequently, tests of party loyalty may mean more
or less than they say. Thus, in Virginia in 1948 Senator Byrd and Governor Tuck attempted to take their machine out of the Democratic party
nationally,[30] a step all in due accord with the language of the party
pledge as interpreted. Machine men seeking nomination in the primaries
of that year, however, were presently challenged by opponents to state
their intention toward the national nominees. Were these primary candidates true Democrats or did they rely on convenient interpretations of
the pledge to weasel out of an obligation that every good Democrat, regardless of what the lawyers said, understood to mean support of the
ticket from top to bottom? Fearful of the consequences of bolting, organization men, from Senator Willis Robertson on down, presently announced that they would support the nominees of the national convention. All of which left Senator Byrd and Governor Tuck perched out on
a limb.

Further illustrations of the proposition that the potency of sanctions
against bolting ultimately depends on public sentiment come from Arkansas. In that state, under earlier rules, party committees have occasionally
made nominations, particularly for special elections. The committee
nominees sometimes have been opposed in the election by Democrats

---

[27] *Love v. Taylor*, 8 S. W. (2d) 795 (1928).

[28] *Love v. Wilcox*, 28 S. W. (2d) 515 (1930).

[29] In Texas the state Democratic committee has had its troubles with J. E.
McDonald, who was nominated for the tenth time as commissioner of agriculture in
1948. He supported Willkie in 1940, Dewey in 1944, and in the 1948 pre-convention
campaign came out for MacArthur. In 1946 the committee failed to find a legal way
to exclude McDonald from the ballot and it campaigned against his renomination
without success. After McDonald began to support Republican presidential candidates,
the Texas Republicans declined to put up candidates against him in the general election.

[30] See above, pp. 336–37.

running as independents, who were, of course, technically subject to exclusion from later primaries. In 1937 Governor Carl Bailey, who had been loud in his denunciation of committee nominations, accepted such a nomination for the Senate to fill the vacancy left by the death of Joseph T. Robinson. A Democrat, John E. Miller, resigned from the House of Representatives, ran as an independent, and defeated Bailey. Reprisals against the "bolters" were not in order.

In 1946 in scattered counties over Arkansas GI slates lost in the primaries and ran again in the general election. In others the GI slates were formed after the primaries to enter the general election. In either type of case the candidates committed treason to the Democratic party and the question arose whether they would be admitted as candidates in the 1948 primary. The feeling of the state committee at first seemed to be to exclude them; veterans, however, drummed up sentiment in support of their position.[31] The state Democratic committee forgave the 1946 insurgents. No "person shall be barred," it resolved, "from participating in any primary election as a voter or as a candidate due to a violation of Sections 2 and 3 which occurred prior to October 1, 1947." [32] And, Sidney McMath, who had been the top-ranking GI rebel, was elected governor on the Democratic ticket in 1948.[33]

In addition to tests of past loyalty and future intent, in some states candidates must pledge themselves to support the "principles" of the party. In others, as party members, they are presumably bound by party principles, which are most specific on matters relating to race.[34] If a Congressman, pledged by his adherence to party principles to oppose poll-tax repeal, should support a Federal antipoll-tax act, presumably he would be subject to exclusion from the next party primary. No such situation has come to our attention. It is only in theory that statements of party principles subject party nominees, when elected, to the rigid discipline characteristic of the Communistic party.[35]

[31] "Spider" Rowland, the noted editorial paragrapher of Little Rock, reported an Amvet meeting: "Neither Senator McClellan nor Congressman Mills ran over anyone to take a definite stand on the Democratic party proposal to rule Independent GIs off the track in 1948. However, the rank and file of the Amvets present were not the least bit backward in expressing their opinions. All agreed that the State Democratic Committee is stirring up trouble with a big spoon and that if the members possessed sense enough to peel bananas they would start backing down like a paperhanger at 12 o'clock."—*Arkansas Gazette* (Little Rock), September 19, 1947.

[32] Party Rules, 1948, sec. 4.

[33] McMath defeated Jack Holt in the second primary and serious consideration was given by Holt and his supporters to carrying the fight into the general election. Mass meetings were held to "draft Holt" and temperatures ran high for several weeks. Holt finally declined to run as an independent in the general election.

[34] See below, pp. 629–41.

[35] When adherence to party principle is required of candidates, party committees, when properly authorized, may exclude dissenters from primary candidacy. The only instance of this sort coming to our attention was that of a would-be candidate for justice of the peace in the Washington County, Mississippi, Democratic primary of

The various squabbles over the loyalty of candidates and would-be candidates are, of course, not matters of high principle. Those who insist on party loyalty are moved by no attachment to abstract principle. They are moved by the desire to gain advantage in a particular situation by disqualifying or hamstringing opposing candidates. The potency of this sanction in the short run helps preserve the finality of primary action, for those with political ambition, if they dare bolt, run the risk of cutting short their political careers. Yet in the final analysis the Democratic party is helpless against bolting. If the party wants to keep the fight within the family and to avoid giving the Republicans an entering wedge, it has to take back into the fold those candidates and groups of candidates who could seriously threaten Democratic candidates in the general election. The sanctions, however, may be an effective restraint on timorous individuals to whom the idea of bolting occurs.[36]

3. Remnants of the Convention System

While most southern nominations are made by direct primary, the convention system of nomination is still used in certain areas. In Florida, Louisiana, Texas, and Mississippi the primary is the mandatory mode of nomination for all offices. In Tennessee and North Carolina the primary is mandatory only for certain offices. In North Carolina about five counties are exempt from the mandatory provision and may use the convention to make nominations for county and township office.[37] The primary is prescribed in Tennessee for offices elected by the state as a whole, United States Representatives, and members of the state legislature. For other offices, the cognizant party authority may determine whether to use convention or primary. In all the states with mandatory primary laws, save Mississippi, the statutory definition of political parties to which the man-

---

1947. The county committee ruled one Patrick off the ballot on the ground that he was not a qualified party member subscribing to the party principles. He had been listed as a Republican candidate for Congress in 1944 while, he said, he was out of the state and without his knowledge.—*Delta Democrat-Times* (Greenville, Miss.), July 9, 1947. The same county, however, earlier had sent to the legislature, by way of the Democratic primary, a former Republican Governor of Nebraska, George L. Sheldon, who later became the leader of the Independent Republican party of Mississippi.

[36] Tennessee has no formal rules to prevent candidates from bolting the primaries. In 1932 and 1934 Lewis Pope was defeated in the Democratic primary for governor and each time he made a strong second try in the November election. In 1934 he and his successful primary opponent were the only two candidates in both races. Pope and his supporters suffered no ill consequences for their bolt.

[37] These counties are all that remain of a larger number formerly exempt. By local act, county after county has been brought under the mandatory primary law. In some counties the exemption affects only one political party and in some the county executive committee has power to decide the method of nomination.

datory primary law applies sometimes permits Republicans to nominate by convention.[38]

In the remaining states—Alabama, Arkansas, Georgia, South Carolina and Virginia—the use of the primary is optional with the political party. South Carolina leaves entirely to the political party the method and manner of making nominations. While the other four states have statutory regulation of primaries, the party may determine whether to nominate by primary. In Alabama the option of the state executive committee of a party is negative; the primary must be used unless the committee declines to do so.[39] In Arkansas nominations may be by primary, convention, or petition as the party authority determines. A Virginia party may take advantage of the privilege of conducting a primary at public expense only if it polled at least 25 per cent of the total vote at the last presidential election. It is left to the cognizant executive committee—state, district, county, or city—to determine the method of nomination for any office chosen within its jurisdiction.

Democratic Use of Conventions. Discussion of the extent to which the convention is used may best be handled by separate treatment of the two parties. In all the optional primary states the primary is the normal method of Democratic nomination of candidates for governor, United States Senator, and other state-wide offices. The party's legal "option" is in fact purely fictional; a move to nominate by convention would result only in a quick deposition of the party officials proposing it. For local and district offices the option is almost equally illusory in South Carolina, Georgia, Arkansas, and Alabama.[40]

[38] The relevant statutory definitions of political party are as follows:

Florida: Political parties which within four years preceding the date of a primary had registered as members more than 5 per cent of the total registered electors must nominate by primary.—*Florida Statutes 1941*, Title IX, sec. 102.02.

Louisiana: The primary act defines party as one that cast at least 5 per cent of the total vote in the last gubernatorial or presidential election. Act. No. 46, 1940, sec. 3.

North Carolina: The statute makes the primary mandatory for a party which polled 3 per cent of the total vote for governor or for president at the last general election or any group of voters "who shall have filed with the State Board of Elections . . . a petition signed by ten thousand qualified voters, declaring their intention of organizing a State political party. . . ." *General Statutes of 1943*, chap. 163, sec. 1; see also sec. 144.

Tennessee: Excluded from the primary act are parties polling less than 10 per cent of the total vote for governor at the last general election.—*1932 Code*, sec. 2227.1. See also sec. 2227.28.

Texas: Primaries are mandatory for parties "that cast two hundred thousand (200,000) votes or more at the last general election" for governor.—*Texas Election Laws*, 1946, arts. 3101, 3154.

[39] Parties to which the primary procedure applies are only those that cast more than 20 per cent of the vote at the preceding general election.

[40] In Arkansas the Democratic party makes nominations for local offices by convention in a single county.—H. M. Alexander, *Organization and Function of State and Local Government in Arkansas* (Fayetteville: University of Arkansas, Bureau of Research, 1947), p. 9. In North Carolina about five counties use the convention.

Tennessee and Virginia are strongholds of the convention system. The Tennessee option extends only to local and district officials other than state legislators and United States Representatives. Although complete information on local practice is not available, Tennessee politicians conclude that in general Democrats make local nominations by convention in those counties in which they are in the minority, principally East Tennessee counties. Minority nominations are not much sought after and the generalization, if not true in all particulars, has a timbre of plausibility. Even for legislative posts, the Democratic nomination in reality may be by informal convention; by agreement of party leaders an unopposed candidate enters the primary to fulfill the legal necessities.

The convention assumes greatest importance in Virginia. The Byrd machine normally nominates for state-wide office through the direct primary, but district and county party authorities often exercise their option to use the convention. Traditionally the Democrats in the "Fighting Ninth," a congressional district in which Democrats meet stout opposition, nominate their candidate for the House of Representatives by convention. Until 1948 it was also used in the seventh district, "the Valley" and home of Senator Byrd, to nominate congressional candidates.

As in Tennessee, no census of local nominating customs is available for Virginia. The state Democratic chairman in 1947 indicated that for local nominations the convention is almost universally used in the ninth congressional district and that in local jurisdictions in the sixth and seventh districts the practice is generally "mixed." These are areas in which mountain Republicans have been fairly strong or even a majority. Presumably in areas of interparty competition the bossism inherent in the convention technique arouses no fatal antagonism.

Republicans and the Convention. Republican nominating customs are almost exactly the obverse of those of the Democrats. Only in areas in which Republicans have local majorities are there apt to be Republican primaries; elsewhere the nomination, if any, is likely to be by convention. These arrangements can be, and frequently are, made even when the mandatory primary law applies to the Republican party. When in a weak minority, party leaders in caucus or convention, formal or informal, can designate a person to enter the primary whose candidacy it is understood on all sides will not be opposed.

Under the statutory definitions of parties to which mandatory primary laws apply, the Republicans must, at least in form, nominate by primary in Florida, North Carolina, Louisiana, Mississippi, and, for the offices to which the law applies, in Tennessee. In Texas the primary used to be mandatory for parties polling 100,000 votes for governor at the preceding general election, and the Republicans, much against their wishes, held primaries in 1926 and 1934. After polling 100,287 votes in 1944, they were saved the trouble and expense of a 1946 primary when the

Democratic legislature obligingly raised the minimum vote making primaries mandatory from 100,000 to 200,000.

Of course, in states with mandatory primaries often there are no Republican primaries; for most offices there are no Republican candidates, nominated by primary or otherwise. When there are Republican nominees in such states they are often selected informally and declared nominated without opposition or, if legally necessary, placed on the primary ballot as a matter of form. This practice is common not only in Florida and North Carolina but also in those sections of Tennessee where the party is weak and in Mississippi where the party has extremely little strength. Occasionally a contested state-wide Republican primary is held in Tennessee and North Carolina, and even in Florida.

In the optional primary states the convention predominates, although in a few counties the Republicans use the primary. In Alabama's Republican "Free State" of Winston nominations for local office usually are made by primary; in 1948 several other north Alabama counties held Republican primaries. In Searcy County, Arkansas, in the Ozarks, and occasionally, in nearby Madison County, Republicans conduct primaries for county offices. Fannin County, a Georgia county of mountain Republicans, once used the primary, but abandoned it in 1932.[41]

Virginia's Republican party in 1946 altered its rules to permit the use of the primary, and in the eighth congressional district, after considerable controversy, it was arranged in 1948 to nominate a congressional candidate by primary. Republicans from the Washington suburbs of Alexandria, Fairfax, and Arlington urged the change. Committee members from old, rural Virginia resisted with all their might. "Southern district Republicans," an Albemarle County spokesman urged, "would not turn out to vote in the traditionally Democratic area. A man would rather stick his hand in a furnace than ask for a Republican ballot." [42] Once arrangements for the primary were made, party leaders could not "recall whether a similar Republican primary ever had been held in Virginia. They knew of none in recent decades." [43] Virginia Republicans have differed among themselves on nominating methods. One faction argues that lively primary contests would attract more voters to the party; others contend that the question is academic since it is hard enough for a convention to high pressure a single man into accepting a candidacy. Where would you get two to fight for a nomination in a primary? In Tennessee, it will be recalled, the primary is mandatory only for state, congressional, and state legislative nominations. For other offices, the general rule, Republican leaders say, is that they nominate by primary

[41] L. M. Holland, *The Direct Primary in Georgia* (mss., Ph.D. dissertation, University of Illinois, 1945), pp. 143–45.
[42] *Washington Post*, March 7, 1948.
[43] *Richmond Times-Dispatch*, May 4, 1948.

when in the majority and by convention when in the minority locally. In South Carolina, on the rare occasions when Republican nominees offer themselves at the general election, they are put forward by informal agreement of party leaders. The importance of the matter is suggested by the absence of any mention of nominating procedures in the 1946 rules of the South Carolina party.

Over most of the South it makes no difference how Republicans make their nominations. In states such as Texas, however, where there is some possibility of building up a Republican party, use of the primary over a period of years might stimulate party growth. The party's top leadership in that state, of course, views the primary with horror; the parties have to finance their own primaries in Texas. A complacent leadership, skilled and secure in convention management, could be challenged in the primaries. A political show in the Republican primary would attract the attention of politically alert citizens at a time when they are politically alerted, the period of the Democratic primary. A primary contest now and then might get Republican politicians into the habit of regarding politics as a calling concerned with the solicitation of votes.

Chapter Twenty-one | # CONDUCT OF ELECTIONS

I F a democratic regime is to work successfully it must be generally agreed that contestants for power will not shoot each other and that ballots will be counted as cast. Consensus on these propositions has been reached pretty well over the entire South except in some counties of East Tennessee, which have a high incidence of electoral irregularity and a high mortality from gunshot during political campaigns. The southern disposition to accept the outcome of balloting, however, may be more apparent than real. The Democratic party met the last real threat to its hegemony—the Populist-Republican fusions of the 'nineties —with widespread election fraud. It would be foolhardy to predict what would happen if the Democratic party, unaccustomed to the risk of losing state elections, were faced by a real threat of a redistribution of perquisites such as accompanies the loss of a general election.

Over most of the United States, the conduct of elections is the most neglected and primitive branch of our public administration, and the South is no exception to this general rule. Incidence of electoral fraud and irregularity varies enormously over the South; the exact degree of variation is in the nature of things difficult of determination. From extensive conversations with practicing politicians a conclusion, and probably a defensible one, emerges that Tennessee has the most consistent and widespread habit of fraud, with Arkansas a close second. While North Carolina has localized irregularities, the state as a whole has a record of progress in election administration to match that of any state outside the South. The impression develops that, with local exceptions, Texas and Florida have relatively clean elections. The other states rank somewhere between these extremes. Everywhere habits of fraud and of rectitude in election management seem to have great powers of persistence. One county will year after year conduct its elections honestly and fairly and an adjoining county will with equal regularity operate irregularly.

The South's peculiar problems of election administration arise from the fact that the chief elections are the Democratic primaries. Special difficulties in election administration are also present in primaries in two-party states, where, however, at least in the general elections the whole apparatus of party competition is brought into play as a check on the conduct of elections. Republican and Democratic election officials and watchers, in theory, check on each other to assure honesty in election management. The efficacy of such bipartisan arrangements in assuring electoral honesty is vastly overrated, but under unipartisanism even that type of obstruction to electoral irregularity usually does not exist.

1. Party vs. Public Responsibility for Primary Management

In the early development of the primary, party organizations conducted the balloting without legal limitation or regulation. While in most states the primary is now publicly financed and publicly managed, six southern states still leave the management of Democratic primaries—in effect, the management of elections—to party officials. In the four states, Virginia, Florida, North Carolina, and Louisiana, where party primaries are conducted by public authority, the weakness of the Republican party means that in fact primaries are conducted almost exclusively by Democrats. Alabama has a hybrid system which amounts to party conduct of the primary. Thus, everywhere the problem is posed of maintaining probity in elections without benefit of whatever incentive to regularity is provided by the surveillance of an opposition party.

With the exception of South Carolina, those states that leave to the party organization the conduct of primaries subject them to varying degrees of regulation. Usually the party official, in his conduct of an election, is subject to as detailed statutory guidance as is the election official of a state that reserves to itself the conduct of primaries. The reality may be that the party official acting as election administrator is as much a public official as is a conventional election official. He follows substantially the same procedures and is subject to the same penalties for his misdoings as the general election official.[1]

[1] All such general remarks are subject to the reservation that at times election officials, party and public, pay little heed to the niceties of election law. Thus, a

To these general observations, South Carolina became an exception in 1944 when its state legislature, in an abortive effort to preserve the white primary, repealed its direct primary laws and left entirely to the party the determination of the forms and procedures of primaries and their administration. The state convention adopts rules to govern the holding of primaries. These rules assign responsibility for management of the voting to the county Democratic committees which designate the precinct election managers. In fact, the member of the executive committee from a precinct, in keeping with the customary practice of such bodies, designates the election officials for his precinct. Primary administration is thus highly decentralized. The only supervision by state party authorities arises from the power of the state committee to hear contests of state nominations and appeals from contests for local nominations decided in the first instance by county committees. In turn, county committees exercise little or no supervision over the work of precinct election officials. Nevertheless, the use of the election machinery for the advantage of incumbent officials is said to be limited chiefly to the "feudal" counties of the coastal plain. Charleston has had a reputation for electoral irregularities; the opinion of local observers seems to be, however, that the introduction of voting machines there has been accompanied by a striking reduction in electoral fraud.

Fraud increased after the repeal of state laws regulating primaries, if shop talk of working politicians constitutes any sort of index to events. In fact, there can be no real penalties for fraud when the party conducts the primary without state regulation. When the state conducts or regulates the primary, penalties are imposed infrequently enough, but not even the remote threat of a fine or imprisonment confronts the South Carolina election manager. Apart from fraud in elections, relegation of the primary to the party places in the hands of party committees powers that may be abused without judicial recourse. Thus, in one South Carolina town the city Democratic committee refused to place a would-be candidate on the ballot on a question of residence. The candidate took the matter to court; the judge observed that while it looked as though the candidate was right, he had no jurisdiction. Action by his court would be similar to interference in a church election.

Those states that considered the adoption of the South Carolina plan in each instance hesitated, in part because of the fear that elimination of public control of primaries would increase fraud. In Florida, in Alabama, and in Mississippi the rebuttal to proposals to follow the footsteps of South Carolina was that fraud would flourish with the removal of the threat of penalties. In Georgia, the bill sponsored by the Talmadge fac-

---

Georgia justice of the peace, active in elections for over 50 years, said: "We never pay any attention to election laws. There is practically nothing with as little regulation as a primary here."—*Atlanta Journal*, April 11, 1948.

tion in 1947 to repeal statutes regulating primaries carefully excluded from repeal those sections that penalized frauds.

In five states—Arkansas, Georgia, Mississippi, Tennessee, and Texas —the party organization performs in general the same functions in the conduct of the primary as does the South Carolina party. Party action, however, is controlled in varying degree by statute. In all these states appointment of election judges, managers, or officials is a duty of the party. While ordinarily the chief county party authority—chairman, executive committee, central committee—has the appointing power, often the precinct committeeman in fact makes the choice. Party authorities also prepare ballots, provide election supplies, and canvass the returns. Only three states—Mississippi, South Carolina, and Tennessee—permit the party authorities to hear and decide contests, and in Mississippi their decision can be appealed to the courts. Four states—Arkansas, Georgia, South Carolina, and Texas—leave to the party the financing of the primary, the only American states that still follow this practice.[2]

Although Alabama's primary is not in form conducted by the party, it approaches closely in fact management by the party organization. The county "appointing board"—an ex officio board with the function of appointing general election officials—receives nominations for primary election officials from the county committee. It must appoint these nominees if they are legally qualified. The party committees also receive and canvass returns, and hear and decide contests, and the county chairman retains custody of the ballot boxes for thirty days after the primary.[3]

If southern party organizations were really party organizations, it would probably not be feasible to delegate to them the conduct of primaries. In two-party states, the party organization itself often has a slate of candidates that it seeks to nominate in the primaries. In most southern states the organization as such is officially, and usually in fact, neutral. As an agency occupying a more or less neutral position among the factions, the party organization may be entrusted with the conduct of the primaries.[4]

In some states about all the party organization amounts to is an

[2] In some states with publicly financed primaries, the statutory conditions are such that only a Democratic primary may be so financed. For a Mississippi party's primary to be publicly financed, it must have polled one-third of the state's vote in the last presidential election. To be eligible for public financing, an Alabama party must have cast more than 20 per cent of the vote in the last general election for state and county offices.

[3] The state committee's duty to receive, canvass, and tabulate returns from the counties does not enable it to go behind the certificates of county committees, but Gessner McCorvey, the Democratic state chairman, has for years deemed it his duty to let go with a blast in the newspapers when returns come in that are patently doctored. While his reprimands in specific cases lead to few prosecutions they may have a preventive effect.

[4] In several states with publicly conducted primaries the party organization tends to be less neutral than in most of the states with party-administered primaries.

agency to administer elections, since it has to fight no campaigns. In its operation as an election-administering agency, moreover, the party is extremely decentralized, save in Tennessee, and this fact alone makes it impracticable for a loose, state-wide faction to use, or to be charged with using unfairly the party election machinery as a whole. The county committee or chairman runs the primary, and in county primary races, too, if our random soundings are a fair sample, the party committee as such, in consonance with its role as election administrator, is ordinarily neutral in local races. The chances are that in a large number of southern counties party conduct of the primary approximates the disinterested type of election management sought by election reformers, whatever it may lack in clerical nicety. The Democratic county chairman often is a local elder statesman who commands the respect of all; he is not a party chairman in the northern two-party meaning of the phrase.

In Tennessee one hears charges that the dominant party faction has utilized its control of the primary machinery to its advantage. Among the states that delegate responsibility for the conduct of the primary to the party, Tennessee's arrangements are peculiar in that the county primary boards are designated by the state party authorities. The primary statute makes the state executive committee of each party a state board of primary election commissioners for that party, with authority to appoint for each county a five-member county board of primary election commissioners.

The county board appoints the personnel to man the polls and also canvasses the county results, a procedural point at which it is said fraud and "error" frequently occur.[5] In designating the county boards the state commissioners are supposed to be bound by the recommendations of the county executive committees, which in turn are supposed to divide their lists "fairly" among nominees suggested by the candidates seeking nomination in the next primary election. Nominees of the candidates are supposed to be from the members of the county executive committees. The statutory injunction of candidate representation is in reality unworkable. If there are five places to be filled and fifteen candidates, how are the county board seats to be allocated "fairly"? Furthermore, insofar as state-wide candidates are concerned, conduct of inquiries and the lodging of protests of local recommendations with the state board would require a more effective state-wide organization than the weaker factions, Democratic and Republican, have had. The complaint has been that the Crump organization has used its control of the state executive committee to pack county primary election boards with its supporters, and even within the Republican party complaint of factional favoritism is heard. Likewise, it

[5] In several states managers of state-wide campaigns place great importance on getting returns directly from the precincts quickly. At times they make special arrangements for their own people to obtain the results from each precinct and wire them to state headquarters. The procedure checks manipulation of the returns by the county canvassing board.

is charged that the Democratic state board of election commissioners in years past has been a factional instrument in its determination of contests rather than an unbiased semi-judicial body.[6]

Whether the primary is conducted directly by the party organization or by public officials, the result is the same when there is only one party. It is difficult to apply to primary election administration the check-and-balance notion common in the conduct of general elections in two-party states. That notion is that both parties should be represented in the group of precinct officials in charge of the polling; the underlying assumption, not always borne out, is that this representation tends to assure honesty. In some one-party states, fundamentally the same idea is involved in statutory requirements for the representation of candidates on the precinct board, a principle difficult of application when candidates are numerous.[7] Louisiana, in its continental tradition, designates its five precinct election commissioners by lottery from lists of names submitted to the parish election authorities by the primary candidates. The election laws prescribe in detail the lottery procedure.[8]

Generally, there is no systematic application of the "check-and-balance" system in the composition of Democratic primary election boards. A condition precedent to its application would be, of course, the existence of well-defined factions with continuity and with clearly delineated factional organization. Further, if factions were represented in primary election machinery, there would have to be statutory regulation of factional organization simply for the purpose of determining who would

[6]Tennessee also has a bipartisan state board of supervisors of elections which designates county boards of elections to conduct general elections. The upshot is that Tennessee has a strange and wondrous system of election administration, calculated to operate at the highest possible cost. Three parallel systems operate: a Republican primary election system; a Democratic primary election system; and a system for the conduct of the general elections. The election calendar is also such that all three systems may be in operation simultaneously. In one room of the schoolhouse the Democratic primary for the nomination of state offices will be under way; in another, the Republican primary to nominate candidates for the same offices; and in a third, the general election for county officials will be in motion. Primaries for the nomination of candidates for local office are optional and local party committees schedule these primaries at their discretion. The Davidson County (Nashville) Democratic primary for the nomination of magistrates, for example, was held in August, 1947, one year in advance of the general election to fill these offices.

[7] Nor is there always acceptance of the proposition that the opposition should be represented on the precinct polling staff. In the August, 1948, primary in Memphis opposition candidates were represented by two officials of their nomination at each polling place. This action, the *Memphis Press-Scimitar* characterized as "a radical departure from the representation granted opposition candidates in past elections."—July 16, 1948.

[8] In some instances the conduct of the lottery becomes an appalling ceremony. In Orleans parish in 1947 the drawing to choose 1310 election officials lasted from 11 a.m. to 5 p.m. A pair of youngsters, one aged nine, the other ten, drew numbered balls in the presence of about a hundred spectators. At times the statutory direction of a lottery is disregarded. In 1947 in St. Bernard parish the candidates "agreed to allot commissioners automatically."—*Times-Picayune* (New Orleans), December 24, 1947.

have the authority to designate or nominate precinct election officials. Alden L. Powell has made the suggestion that in Louisiana factions of the Democratic party be given legal recognition and treated in primary election administration as parties are treated in two-party states.[9] Such a suggestion evolves logically out of a situation in which state factions have been fairly coherent and in which the "factional" slate often includes candidates for virtually all offices, much like a two-party contest.

As an alternative or supplement to representation of candidates on election boards, the statutes usually provide for the designation of "watchers" or "challengers" by candidates. If the numerous candidates at most primaries exercised their right, the polling places would have to be quite large halls. In practice the widest variety prevails in the designation of precinct officials and in the use of watchers. Thus in one Alabama county the probate judge remarked that he had never suggested names of election officials and that he thought most of the local candidates did not fool with that sort of thing. He trusted his fellow citizens. In one Mississippi county appointment of precinct election officials by the members of the county committee is regarded as a "worrisome" job because all the candidates are "after you" to have their people named.

At particular times and places under peculiar local factional situations highly formalized systems for representation on the precinct board develop. Thus, in Savannah, Georgia, in 1946 the two managers and three clerks for each "box" were appointed as follows: The Citizens Progressive League, a local reform group, designated one manager; the "administration," the old local machine, appointed the other; the three clerks were allocated among the forces of the three gubernatorial candidates, Talmadge, Carmichael, and Rivers. All sorts of such practices undoubtedly develop beyond the statutes and rules, and only the most extensive field investigations would reveal the steps taken in practice to assure probity in elections. It can only be pointed out that conduct of primaries under one-party conditions presents special difficulties that do not yield to any uniform formula.

When the party conducts the primary, the question of finance arises. In those states with publicly conducted primaries, the cost is paid from the public treasury. Party responsibility for the management of the primary, however, is not in practice incompatible with public assumption of costs. In Tennessee and Mississippi, states with party responsibility for the primary, the cost is defrayed from the public treasury, as it is for Alabama's primary. On the other hand, the party bears the entire cost in Arkansas, Georgia, South Carolina, and Texas. The usual method of party financing is by assessment of primary candidates. Generally, candidates for county office bear most of the financial burden; state-wide candidates

[9] *Party Organization and Nominations in Louisiana* (Baton Rouge: Bureau of Government Research, Louisiana State University, 1940).

are usually protected against excessive (or perhaps equitable) assessment by the county party authorities who have to raise funds to print ballots and pay election clerks.[10]

In the more populous centers the fees collected from candidates to finance the primary become quite burdensome. In lamenting an assessment of $550 on candidates for nomination for constable of precinct 7, the *Dallas Morning News* concluded that the "whole system is wrong, and it makes the burdens of seeking office far, far greater than they ought to be." [11] The assessment on each candidate was large because the Dallas county committee had to raise $50,000 to finance the two Democratic primaries in 1948. A majority of southern states agree with the *Dallas News* and have made the cost of the primary a public charge. Public assumption of primary costs, however, does not make impossible the levy of a fee on candidates for the purpose of discouraging frivolous candidatures and for the incidental purpose of raising revenue to defray, in part at least, the costs of conducting the primary. Tennessee is the only state that has no formal requirement of a fee for inclusion of a name on the primary ballot.[12]

It would probably be wrong to conclude that delegation of power to conduct primaries to party organizations has in itself resulted in more irregularity than occurs when the voting is under public authority. Nevertheless, systems for party conduct of primaries probably have to be regarded as transitional arrangements which will, in due course, be replaced by election machinery publicly operated and publicly financed. The longstanding justification of assignment of such functions to the party organization—a better legal footing for the white primary—has disappeared, and probably in the long run better results will be obtained from election officials who are in every respect public officials, completely accountable for their acts.

2. Democratic Control of General Elections

A Mississippi Democratic county chairman refers to the "mock election" that "they" hold down at the courthouse in November. He does not trouble to exercise his prerogative as Democratic chairman to make nominations to the state authorities, who appoint the county officials in charge

[10] Illustrative of the assessments are those fixed by the Georgia state executive committee in 1948: governor, $500; United States Senator, $500; justices of the supreme court, judges of the courts of appeals, and other statehouse officers, $350; United States Representative, $500; judges and solicitors of the superior courts, $250. For legislative and county office, each county committee fixed the fee.

[11] April 22, 1948.

[12] In the states with publicly conducted and publicly financed primaries—Florida, North Carolina, Virginia, Louisiana—candidates must pay a fee; a part of this fee goes to the party coffers in Florida and Louisiana. Alabama and Mississippi pay the cost of the primary from the public treasury; the filing fee goes entirely to the party treasury.

of the "mock election." [13] Over most of the South the general election is a formality, and election management is mainly a matter of the conduct of the direct primaries. Each state, of course, provides general election machinery. The chief difference between this machinery and that of most American states is the extent to which appointment of county election officials is vested in a state authority.[14]

State appointment results in Democratic control of local election boards even in counties with Republican majorities. For most southern counties Democratic control of the county election board makes no difference; Mississippi law reflects reality when it directs that the board of election commissioners shall consist of three discreet persons who are freeholders and electors in the county and not of the same political party "if such men of different political parties can be conveniently had in the county." Although such is the general situation, in a few states central Democratic control of local election machinery provides a weapon of partisan advantage.

The advantage that control of the election machinery gives to the Democratic party is of importance—that is, it is talked about—chiefly in Virginia, North Carolina, Tennessee, and Arkansas. Virginia's Democratic control of all county electoral boards is accomplished, not through appointment by a state authority, but through designation by the circuit and corporation judges. These judges, in turn, are chosen by the legislature in which the Democrats always have a majority. The judge, of course, is invariably a Democrat and usually a cog in the Byrd organization. In Republican counties he gives the Democrats a majority of the county electoral board; nor does he always appoint the Republican recommended by the county Republican committee. Republicans complain that the arrangement is unjust. They maintain that they ought at least to have one of the precinct clerks but that the county board usually appoints only Democrats. Yet potential disadvantage to Republicans is limited to those areas in which county and district races are close, for the Republican threat to Democratic control of the state has not been formidable.[15] To

[13] Illustrative of the fact that statutes are no satisfactory guide to electoral practice, a circuit clerk of a Mississippi county indicates that his office performs most of the duties of the election commissioners who have legal responsibility for the "mock election," as well as most of the duties of the Democratic county committee which has responsibility for the primary.

[14] Tennessee, North Carolina, Mississippi, Louisiana, South Carolina, and Arkansas vest appointment of county election boards in a state authority. South Carolina has an unusual system of dual elections. The governor appoints for each county two sets of three election commissioners: one for Federal officers, the other for state and local officers. Each board of county election commissioners, in turn, appoints a set of precinct election officials. In practice, the two elections are often held at different places. A person votes for president, Senators, and Representatives at one place and goes across the street to another polling place to vote for state and local officers.

[15] The same electoral boards also conduct primaries. Control of the electoral machinery gives the dominant Democratic faction advantage in the primaries, a matter

determine the actual extent to which Democrats utilize their advantage would require the closest local investigation; nevertheless, it can be supposed that in such areas the Virginia Democrats, like parties everywhere, highly prize control of the election machinery.

North Carolina's bipartisan board of elections appoints a bipartisan board of elections for each of the state's one hundred counties; it relies on recommendations of county party authorities.[16] Save for abuses of the absentee ballot in a few counties, a matter to be dealt with later, the Republicans of North Carolina seem to feel that, on the whole, the Democrats give them pretty fair and honest election administration. The evidence easily accessible seems to bear them out, for the inquiring traveler over the South comes without hesitation to the conclusion that North Carolina is the state best equipped administratively to assure honest elections and that in no other state is there so widespread a determination to keep elections clean.

Democratic control of local election authorities in Tennessee hinges on legislative election of the state board of supervisors of elections. The board in turn designates for each county a board of commissioners of elections which includes minority party representation. The county commissioners in turn designate officials to man the polls, and minority representation is also required. Ordinarily the state board merely appoints the nominees of the county party authorities.[17] Everyone in Tennessee seems to be agreed that election administration is thoroughly corrupt, but oddly enough there is not much specific complaint that the Democratic organization has used its control of election machinery to discriminate against Republicans. It may be that the Democratic-Republican armistice, involving a division of the offices in the general elections, relegated the practical necessity of fraud to the primary elections.

---

that may be of more immediate practical importance than the disadvantage that the Republicans endure.

[16] The county boards also conduct party primaries. The election machinery may be used for party factional advantage as well as for party advantage. The state board has attempted to reduce the possibility by insisting that the recommendations come not from the county chairman individually but that they be approved by a majority of the county executive committee. The county executive committee is composed of the chairmen of each precinct committee and the procedure reduces the chances that one Democratic or one Republican faction will have unlimited license to nominate for appointment to the county election board.

[17] The significance of the control of the county election machinery at critical junctures is suggested by the fact that in 1947 the state board had before it a delegation of twenty persons from Knox County to speak in behalf of party factions competing for the appointment. At the same time "independents" from Polk County, the bailiwick of famed Burch Biggs, sought an appointment on the county commission. Pointing to his opponent, Biggs said: "His crowd ain't Democrats. They even voted agin' Jim McCord and Kenneth McKellar. They want just one new commission member so he'll vote with Henry Crock (Republican county commission member) against our man." —Memphis Press-Scimitar, April 7, 1947.

THE DYING GASP OF THE OLD SOUTH?

J. Strom Thurmond and Fielding Wright, 1948 Dixiecrat presidential and vice-presidential nominees.

The Long Arm of the Supreme Court

Negroes line up for primary ballots at Columbia, South Carolina, after Federal courts outlawed the white primary.

Prior to 1949 Arkansas Republicans argued that a reform in general election administration was an absolute prerequisite for the growth of Republican strength. An ex officio state board of elections, consisting of seven state elective officials, always Democratic, appointed for each county three election commissioners, two Democrats and one Republican. While the state board heeded the recommendations of local Democratic chairmen and Democratic candidates in its choice of Democratic members, charges were made that it often ignored the wishes of local Republicans, even in counties with Republican majorities. It tended to follow Republican recommendations in those counties with few Republicans. In counties with a real general election fight a Republican acceptable to the local Democratic organization was likely to be appointed. To Republican complaints about such practices were added in 1946 the lusty howls of GI groups backing independent candidates in the general election in several counties. Before the state board named the county commissioners in that year the GI's organized a cavalcade, wended their way to Little Rock, held a rally on the statehouse lawn, and made representations to the state board. The general purport of their plea was that unless their nominees were appointed to the county boards they would be robbed. They got little satisfaction from the state board, which in most instances followed the recommendations of established local leaders. After the election the GI's cried that they had been robbed, and perhaps they had been in some instances.[18]

Arkansas Republicans played an important part in the submission of an election reform to the voters in 1948 through the initiative procedure, a means by which several significant changes in election administration have been adopted over the years. The voters approved an initiated act to establish a new state board of elections to consist of the governor, the attorney general, the secretary of state, and the state chairman of each of the two leading parties. Under the new act each county board is to consist of the county chairman of each of the two parties and a third member designated by the state board. In naming precinct judges and clerks, the majority members of the county board appoint five officials and the minority member, three. The new arrangement will thus assure to Republicans the right of representation in county and precinct election administration.

[18] Thus, the chairman of one of the "better government" groups explained the defeat of their candidate for sheriff, Harry ("Fuzzy") Price. "Mr. Price actually was defeated when the state board of election commissioners named our White County three-man election board. In the sections of White County where Mr. M. P. Jones, Jr. named the judges and clerks, the election was honest and the voters got a square deal. However, in some sections the other two board members teamed up against Mr. Jones and there was nothing he could do. The most glaring array of irregularities took place in Bald Knob."—*Arkansas Gazette* (Little Rock), November 13, 1946.

3. Absentee Voting

Over most of the South absentee voting creates no particular diffi-culty.[19] In North Carolina and Virginia, however, the common under-standing is that absentee voting produces Democratic majorities in close counties. By general report abuses of the absentee ballot prevail in some western counties of North Carolina and in some southwestern Virginia counties. In these areas Republicans and Democrats compete on more nearly equal terms than elsewhere, and control of election machinery gives both means and opportunity for the Democrats to maximize their strength by use of the absentee ballot. It might be expected that the same condition would prevail in eastern Tennessee, an area with a high in-cidence of electoral irregularity. Squawks about abuses of absentee voting in East Tennessee are mingled with complaint about other kinds of fraud. The particular procedure does not stand out as it does in western North Carolina and southwestern Virginia.

Over the rest of the South the absentee ballot arouses only sporadic charges of abuse in scattered localities; hence abuses may be less prevalent or, at least, not geographically concentrated. The chances are, of course, that the fact of party competition in Virginia and North Carolina merely through the volume of complaint it generates exaggerates the extent of abuse in these states. Nevertheless, in both states Republicans loudly and regularly complain of election larceny. Apart from these eruptions, the only south-wide issue about the absentee ballot—and it is now a dead issue—was that concerning soldier voting, which was thought to be an opening wedge for Negro voting and for Federal interference with local voting requirements, such as the poll tax.[20]

The absentee-ballot question came to a head in North Carolina in the election of 1938 and the State Board of Elections recommended drastic revisions of the absent-voting law. It found that persons not entitled to vote absentee were using the privilege, a practice which, incidentally, threw the door open to intimidation and to vote selling. Many absentee ballots were cast by persons not entitled to vote and by the forgery of names on voting lists. At times political workers managed to get a supply of absentee ballots and "in 'market basket' fashion go out in quest of votes." Notaries, justices of the peace, and other oath-administering of-

[19] South Carolina's Democratic convention in 1948 removed from its rules provi-sion permitting absentee voting at primaries. In 1946 the state committee had before it charges of irregularities in absentee voting in Chester County.

[20] In southern states absentee voting follows conventional forms but a Georgia curiosity may be noted. There, in addition to the usual absentee voting, a countryman who happens to be at the county seat on election day may vote there instead of at the box in his home beat. He must make oath that he has not voted elsewhere. The pro-cedure creates an opportunity for dual voting, which is said to be exercised occasionally.

ficials certified absentee-ballot documents "without ever seeing the voter" whose name had "been signed to the affidavit" accompanying the ballot.[21] The legislature abandoned absent voting in primaries but retained it for general elections. The explanation was that in the western counties the Democrats were hard pressed by the Republicans and "needed a little leeway out there." The Democrats decided to quit cheating each other in the primary by absentee ballot and to make it strictly an anti-Republican weapon.

Even after it was limited to the general elections, absentee voting continued to provide most of the complaints that came to the state board

TABLE 52

Closely Fought Contests and the Absentee Ballot: Relation between Republican Percentage of Vote for Governor and Proportion of Ballots Cast Civilian Absentee in North Carolina Counties, 1944

PER CENT OF COUNTY VOTE REPUBLICAN	PER CENT OF COUNTY VOTE CAST CIVILIAN ABSENTEE, NUMBER OF COUNTIES			
	0–2.9	3–4.9	5–9.9	10 AND OVER
0–39.9	61	7	0	0
40–49.9	2	3	10	3
50–59.9	3	0	4	1
60–79.9	6	0	0	0

of elections. In 1947, despairing of its efforts to bring about administration of absent voting that would command confidence on all sides, the board reluctantly recommended "repeal of the civilian absentee ballot law in its entirety." It based its recommendation on the belief that such abuses of the absent-voting law as occurred brought the entire electoral process into disrepute rather than on a finding that abuses were widespread. In the heat of a close campaign the county election board chairman "is tempted to let a trusted friend have a few absentee ballots to go hunting with, is tempted to relax his vigilance in inspecting applications and limit his inquiry as to the existence or eligibility of absentee voters." [22]

Those North Carolina counties with close Republican-Democratic contests for local office cast the highest proportions of their ballots through the absentee procedure, as may be seen from Table 52. Not all close counties have a heavy absentee vote but all counties with a heavy absentee vote are close counties. Through the normal process of voter solicitation a sharp contest should produce greater use of the absentee ballot than a virtually uncontested general election. By the same token a

[21] *Recommendations of the State Board of Elections to the Governor of North Carolina and the General Assembly of 1939*, pp. 6–9.

[22] *Recommendations of the State Board of Elections to the Governor of North Carolina and the General Assembly of 1947*, pp. 4–6.

sharp contest is apt to create greater temptation to use the absent-voting procedure for illegal voting. And, once the practice gets started, the names of absent persons on the voting lists, living or dead, may be voted.[23] Even with election administration of the utmost rectitude considerable variation in the use of the absentee ballot would be expected, but the range of variation among North Carolina counties can be accounted for only by the hypothesis that some shenanigans occur. In the 1944 general election, for example, in 53 of the 100 counties, less than 2 per cent of the ballots were cast civilian absentee. In the peak county, 17.4 per cent of the ballots were so cast. In one county, 25.7 per cent of the ballots were absentee, counting both civilian and military absentee.[24]

The "mail ballot," as the absentee ballot is often called in Virginia, appears to be subject to about the same abuses and under about the same circumstances as in North Carolina. Newspapers and Republican politicians make frequent reference to its abuse. Republicans in southwest Virginia counties claim that at the beginning of the polling the absentee procedure has put several hundred ballots in the boxes against them. Democratic workers, by their connections with election officials, have greater freedom to hustle absentee votes. And it seems to be commonly agreed that Democratic control in some counties is maintained through the absentee ballot. The North Carolina practice of permitting party workers to carry absentee ballots to the homes and places of business to solicit the vote of persons who could just as well go to the polls seems to prevail. It is said that vulnerable persons, such as public employees, sometimes are encouraged to vote absentee in order that the organization may make certain that they vote right. Though Republicans complain of their disadvantage, they failed in 1948 to induce the legislature to adopt even so mild a reform as a bill to make public lists of absentee voters. The extent of absentee voting in Virginia is unknown. Scattered figures come to light such as the charge that in 1947 Wise County, with one-fourth as large a population as Richmond, cast 46 times as many mail ballots. The Virginia state board of elections has collected no information on the extent of the use of the absentee ballot, nor has it made aggressive effort, as has the North Carolina board, to correct abuses.

---

[23] In one Alabama county, the story goes, the principal abuse of the absentee ballot is to vote the names of those persons on the voting lists who have departed this earth. It is not recorded whether their old friends, the election managers, do the fair thing and vote them as they would vote, were they able to make oath to their absentee ballot before some heavenly notary public.

[24] Counties with high percentages of their ballots cast civilian absentee in 1944 were: Alexander, 6.6; Alleghany, 10.6; Clay, 17.4; Graham, 8.4; Henderson, 10.9; Jackson, 8.9; Polk, 9.5; Swain, 11.9; Watauga, 10.2; Yancey, 6.9. The percentage for the state as a whole was 2.8. For the same counties the military and civilian absentee vote made up the following percentages of the total vote: Alexander, 13.1; Alleghany, 15.8; Clay, 25.7; Graham, 14.8; Henderson, 16.4; Jackson, 16.0; Polk, 17.1; Swain, 18.7; Watauga, 16.9; Yancey, 11.4. The figure for the state as a whole was 6.7.

Outside Virginia and North Carolina, abuses in the absentee ballot do not seem to be regionalized but rather occur sporadically here and there. The Alabama Legislative Council in 1947 recommended repeal of the state's absent-voting law. "Corruption incidental to absent voting in the State," the Council concluded, "long has been a disgrace which no amount of remedial legislation has been able to prevent." That corruption, however, seems to have been mainly the scattered use of the absentee ballot by one Democrat against another rather than systematic anti-Republicanism. Railroad workers successfully opposed repeal of the Alabama law.

4. Secrecy of the Ballot

Ballot secrecy is essential to democracy. The issue of secret versus nonsecret ballot, at one time warmly debated, has long since been a closed question. The opportunity that a nonsecret ballot creates for intimidation, for bribery, for reprisal make it a procedure intolerable to a free people. Even now, important departures from secrecy of the ballot remain in the South.

South Carolina is always pointed to as the only state with the old-fashioned nonsecret ballot; actually more serious breaches of ballot secrecy prevail in several other southern states. South Carolina's primary ballot is in form secret, while for its general elections the state retains the system of privately printed ballots, which was once used everywhere. Each party prints a ballot containing the names of all its candidates to be voted upon in the general election. It supplies its ballots to each polling place and, in fact, if a voter wishes, he can write out his own ballot before coming to the polling place. Stacks of ballots of each party are usually placed on a table with the ballot box and the voter picks up the ticket of the party he wishes to support, folds it, and drops it in the box.[25] The election managers and all the onlookers can see which party ticket the voter picks up.

The nonsecret ballot accounts in part for the extremely low vote polled by the Republican party in South Carolina. While it would win no elections with the adoption of a secret ballot, its proportion of the total vote would probably double or triple. The Republican party of the state has unsuccessfully sued to enforce the apparent state constitutional guarantee of ballot secrecy,[26] agitated for legislation, and even offered in 1944

[25] A split ticket is made possible by the statutory requirement of three separate ballots (and three ballot boxes), one for Senator, Representative, and presidential electors; a second for state and county officers; a third for constitutional amendments and special questions.

[26] *Gardner* v. *Blackwell*, 167 S. C. 313, 166 S. E. 338 (1932); *Smith* v. *Blackwell*, 115 F. (2d) 186, *Smith* v. *Blackwell*, 34 F. Supp. 989.

to pay for ballots for the entire state, if a secret form were used. Democratic leaders have since 1944 opposed a secret ballot because a publicly financed ballot would create a legal link between the state and the party, a divorce that they maintained in the desperate hope that it would make the white primary legal. In 1948, however, the state Democratic convention resolved in favor of the secret ballot.

Although South Carolina's general election ballot is a political curiosity and probably keeps a few people who participate in the state's Democratic primaries from voting Republican in the presidential election, its practical consequences are less serious than violations of ballot secrecy in Texas, Alabama, Georgia, and Arkansas, where, except in some Georgia counties, the individual voter's ballot is identifiable.[27] In Texas the number alongside the voter's name on the voting list is written on the ballot. In Georgia a similar arrangement prevails, although individual counties, by action of their grand jury, may decide to operate under an optional secret ballot law.[28] A most extraordinary system exists in Arkansas by which the voter makes a carbon duplicate of his ballot; he signs the duplicate which also carries a number to make the possibility of identification doubly sure. The duplicate ballots are deposited in a separate duplicate box, to be opened only in case of contest. Alabama once had a system of ballot-numbering somewhat like that of Texas, but in 1939 modified its practice to require that the number be covered with a black seal which is to be removed only by properly authorized investigators.

The nonsecret ballot is justified on the ground that it must be possible to identify the ballots of persons who have voted illegally as determined by election contests, and in all states whose ballots carry identifying marks penalties are prescribed for those who peep at the numbers except when there is a contest. Nevertheless, everywhere that the ballot is nonsecret one hears frequent expressions of lack of confidence in the actual secrecy of the ballot. The extent to which election officials and custodians of ballot boxes take advantage of the opportunity to find out how their neighbors voted could be discovered only by assiduous labor by a grand jury in every county; that these practices occur in some communities seems to be a matter of common knowledge.[29] Intense agitation of the

---

[27] There are, of course, local exceptions where voting machines are in use in these states.

[28] The number of counties using the secret ballot law is unknown; perhaps half the counties in the state do so. For the results of an incomplete check on this point, see Citizens' Fact-Finding Movement of Georgia, *Georgia Facts in Figures* (Athens: University of Georgia Press, 1946), p. 150. See note 43 on p. 462.

[29] George Stoney's conversations with many local politicians in his travels for the Myrdal survey suggested a fairly widespread violation of the secrecy of the ballot in Alabama and Georgia in 1940.—R. J. Bunche, *The Political Status of the Negro* (mss.), pp. 304–07. Stoney, incidentally, cites the case of a rebellion by the people of one Alabama beat who demanded that the numbers be left off the ballot and they were, state law to the contrary notwithstanding.

issue in Arkansas in recent years suggests the applicability of the adage that smoke is produced by fire. In some rural Texas counties election officials keep tab on the voting habits of their neighbors, a practice regarded as on about the same ethical plane as listening in on party-line telephone conversations.[30] In the states using the nonsecret ballot the visitor picks up stories about violations of ballot secrecy, of reprisals against individuals because of their vote, and of the utility of the opportunity to snoop into the boxes in lining up the votes of vulnerable groups, such as city employees and school teachers. How extensive these practices actually are may not be so significant as is the fact that many individuals believe them to exist and let that belief influence their votes.[31]

In 1947 the lower house of the Texas legislature passed a bill to make the ballot secret, but it did not become law. The chairman of the state Democratic executive committee issued a statement in opposition. He declared that secrecy of the ballot would work a great evil in that it would destroy the "present means of detecting fraud in elections." [32] A considerable proportion of the democratic world manages to get along without violating the secrecy of the ballot and at the same time maintains relatively pure elections. In any case, alternative methods are available to identify questioned ballots without breaching the secrecy of all ballots. In Louisiana, for example, a ballot cast over the protest of a watcher must have attached to it the voter's name and the challenger's name. Such ballots, and only such ballots, may be identified if a contest arises.[33] In North Carolina the voter of a challenged ballot must write his name on the ballot. South Carolina's Democratic party rules outline a procedure similar in its effect under which a challenged ballot is sealed in an envelope, and the question of the voter's eligibility later determined by the county committee.[34] Many states manage without even this sort of breach of ballot secrecy.

The removal of identifying marks from the ballot does not, of course, ensure secrecy. The physical conditions of balloting, such as the absence

[30] It may be that local practice in the states with secret-ballot laws are at times in violation of the statute. Thus, one hears stories in East Tennessee of ballots printed on tissue paper which permits the election judge to see how they have been marked.

[31] C. E. Gregory in the *Atlanta Journal* (March 4, 1948) puts the matter as follows: "The numbered ballot has been the club used by so-called court house rings in Georgia to beat down opposition for many, many years. It is not known how many county officials made a practice of going into the ballot boxes and checking on the ballots deposited by John Doe and Richard Roe, but the possibility of such a check was alarming to many voters. . . . There are a great many ways in which county officials have the power to punish their political enemies. They can increase tax assessments. They can eliminate names from the jury boxes. They can raise or lower the salaries of county employes. They can hire or fire school teachers in many instances. They can work the roads in front of the farms of their political friends and leave their foes in the mud."

[32] *Dallas Morning News,* March 14, 1947.

[33] Act 46 of 1940, sec. 73.

[34] Party Rules, 1948, sec. 38.

of polling booths, may make marking a ballot a rather public affair.[35] In many parts of the South elections are conducted without polling booths. In Arkansas in 1946, for example, it was a matter worthy of attention by the press when Crittenden County bought polling booths, as an incident of a "GI revolt" against the local machine. "We've had a great number of people tell us they'd vote our way—if we could definitely promise them their ballot would really be a secret one," one of the GI leaders stated.[36] How polling booths could assure secrecy, given Arkansas' duplicate ballot, is not clear, but the booths were provided. The *Arkansas Gazette* remarked that it would "be glad to hear about it" if any other county in the state had ever followed the state election law requiring the provision of booths.[37]

5. Directions of Reform

Earlier the impressionistic judgment was expressed that Tennessee ranked first in election irregularities, with Arkansas trailing not far behind. These ratings could not be defended to the death. Many good Georgians would contend that their state deserves a place above either Tennessee or Arkansas.[38] Both Tennessee and Arkansas in 1946 and 1948 saw challenges to established groups and these challenges brought to light practices that may exist without publicity in other states. And, perhaps the heat of the conflict in both states resulted in exaggeration of the actual state of affairs. It should not be supposed that the people of these states are content to leave conditions as they are. A committee of the Tennessee Bar Association in 1948 reported that "it is common knowledge that election irregularities and flagrant violations of the election laws are oc-

[35] Secrecy of the ballot may also be breached by free and easy assistance to voters; and the same practice facilitates bribery and intimidation. From random discussions over the South, provision of assistance to voters appears to be most abused in French-speaking parishes of Louisiana.

[36] *Arkansas Gazette* (Little Rock), October 10, 1946.

[37] November 4, 1946. The state law had required for years that election officers provide one booth for "each 100 electors, or fraction thereof." Election laws in Arkansas, as elsewhere, often have little relation to the actual conduct of elections.

[38] Herman Talmadge's claim to the Georgia governorship, after the death of his father, was based on write-in votes for him in the general election. The *Atlanta Journal's* exposure of fraud in the general election won for its reporter, George Goodwin, a Pulitzer prize. In one precinct Herman received 48 write-in votes; in that precinct 34 persons, as shown by the list of voters, deposited their ballots in the order their names appeared on the registration list, a remarkable chance distribution of voting sequence marred somewhat by the fact that some of the persons on the registration list were dead.—*Atlanta Journal*, March 5, 1947. The impression emerges that over the South electoral frauds are on a lower level of technical virtuosity than in northern urban centers. Southern frauds are often patent on the face of the record; the expert northern machine operator claims that the records on their face are straight.

curring" and the association advocated revision of the election laws.[39] The American Legion has formulated a program for revision of the election laws; the Tennessee Press Association has another program; the League of Women Voters has been active; and in 1948 the governor appointed a commission to investigate and make recommendations. Antedating all these efforts, however, is a lone fight for clean elections by Ben W. Hooper, Republican governor of Tennessee, 1911–15, who set out some years ago to make certain that elections were clean at least in his home county.[40]

After the commotions in Arkansas at the general elections of 1946 the governor named a seventeen-man commission to recommend legislative revisions. Its work was hurried, it was difficult to get the members together for meetings, and the commission functioned without adequate staff assistance. The state senate killed the revision bill; some senators thought the bill to be a "jumble" and that more study was needed, and they were probably right.

Arkansas' experience with an ad hoc commission that worked under pressure to no end points to North Carolina which has set an example worthy of emulation. Usually election administration, not only in the South but everywhere, provides a telling illustration of the maxim that what is everyone's business is really no one's. The election laws by piecemeal alteration finally became a muddle, and the system as a whole develops more and more imperfections because no one has the responsibility to give it continuous attention.[41] Then someone appoints a commission

---

[39] *Memphis Press-Scimitar*, June 18, 1948.

[40] Governor Hooper also published for general distribution, a booklet of practical advice to election officials, *Tennessee Elections* (Knoxville: Chandler-Warters, 1946). The Governor's views about Tennessee conditions are suggested by the following sample of his comments: "The election laws of the State of Tennessee are, in many respects, unfair, unjust and unequal in their application. They are often administered to promote fraud, break down local self-government and destroy the efficacy of our vaunted two-party system. They discourage and intimidate the weak, exalt the unscrupulous and set a premium on dishonesty. Designed, and originally enacted, in part, to curtail Negro participation in politics, they have been used to defraud and disfranchise thousands of white men and women descended from the pioneer stock of our state. Intended to perpetuate in power the Democratic party, they have often been used to defraud Democrats of their civil rights. To a very considerable extent, they have made Democratic primaries a farce, particularly in East Tennessee."—Ibid., pp. 2–3.

[41] Often if election officials tried to follow the letter of the complex election laws, it would be virtually impossible to hold an election. The secretary of the Virginia board of elections in 1946 called attention, for example, to a provision of law requiring the electoral board to print ballots at least 30 days prior to an election and another provision which gave candidates until 30 days before the election to file their candidacy. In another connection the law directed the electoral board to print a number of ballots equal to one and one-fourth the number of registered electors and another provision directed the board to deliver to the precincts ballots equal to twice the number of registered voters.—*Richmond Times-Dispatch*, November 1, 1946. In 1947 the Alabama Legislative Council called attention to one provision of law requiring the probate judges to print absentee ballots at least 60 days before the election, while the names of all candidates were not certified to them until 30 days before the voting.

which makes some recommendations, the legislature passes some laws, and everyone leaves the system to take care of itself. North Carolina makes it the business of its board of elections to give continuous attention to election administration. For many years the board was virtually dormant but Governor J. C. B. Ehringhaus gave it a boost to start it on a career of usefulness. The board observes the workings of the election laws; it comes up with recommendations to the legislature. Sometimes its proposals are accepted, sometimes not. It has powers of investigation and of review of the actions of county election boards, and the relatively easy access to the state board for the airing of complaints creates a wholesome influence.[42]

A continuing state elections authority, properly led, ought to produce far better administrative results than occasional temporary commissions set up when conditions come to a boiling point. However that may be, several lines of development in elections policy will probably come sooner or later. Assurance of ballot secrecy has been too long delayed in several southern states.[43] Public assumption of responsibility for the conduct of primaries will arrive in due course. The Republicans will even get a fairer break and thereby grow stronger. A stronger Republican party, not necessarily strong enough to win elections, would improve Democratic well-being enormously.[44]

[42] The state election authorities in most other southern states, unlike the North Carolina board, fit the general pattern of the American states, i.e., they amount to nothing in practice and their members in conversation often manifest the most incredible ignorance of the elements of their state election laws. The Virginia state board of elections, created in 1946, gives promise of development. In several states the office of the secretary of state has some responsibilities in connection with election administration, but most of these offices, with the notable exception of Florida, seem to manage their functions, routine though they are, without impressive efficiency. In Florida the county supervisors of registration play an important role in handling election routines, and through the stimulation of the state association of these supervisors there is an interesting development of professionalism in their work.

[43] In 1949, while this book was in press, the Georgia legislature made the secret ballot mandatory in all counties. Theretofore the secret ballot could be used at the option of the county.

[44] In the past the election management at the polls has not been of great significance in Negro disfranchisement. Discrimination has usually occurred at the earlier administrative step of registration. With increased Negro registration discrimination at the polls seems to have increased. In the 1946 Georgia gubernatorial primary, for example, election officials in some instances staged a deliberate slowdown at boxes predominantly Negro by insistence on meticulous regard for the niceties of the election laws. The slowdown had as its objective not so much Negro disfranchisement as the reduction of the number of votes against Talmadge. In some Georgia localities separate polling places were provided for Negroes and in the normal course of events some boxes are mostly Negro, others mostly white. Such segregation facilitates discriminatory administration but also has the virtue of minimizing friction.

Chapter Twenty-two | # CAMPAIGN FINANCE

IN a one-party region things are not always what
they seem. Party organizations are not party organizations: they tend to
be impartial holding-companies for loose but competing factions. Nominations are not nominations; they are elections. The Republican party
is not a vote-seeking organization but a club that sends emissaries to
national conventions. Political machines are not machines but usually
figments of frustrated imaginations.

Money, at least, might be thought to be the same in both two-party
and one-party regions. Money talks in both North and South, but even
in the realm of campaign finance the one-party system has its peculiarities.
Those peculiarities differ from state to state, but they stem uniformly
from the absence of the organizational paraphernalia of political parties
to serve as the foundation for a campaign army. In some one-party states,
the changing leaders of transient personal factions have little or nothing
to begin with; they must raise the cold, hard cash to build a campaign
organization from the ground up. They cannot, as can a party candidate
in a two-party state, start with an existing organization, weak though it
may be.[1] They must put the cash on the barrel head. The political financ-

---

[1] It is doubtful that in campaign financing southern states differ materially from
those so-called two-party states in which the real state and local battle is fought out in
the Republican primary. Both groups of states probably differ materially from close
states in which nominations are made in reality by the party organization (whether in
form by primary or convention) and the battle occurs in the general election campaign.

ing of personal factions sometimes creates different relations between donor and donee than does the financing of an institutionalized political party. Of this and other things, we shall speak after looking at the evidence, such as it is, on campaign finance in one-party states.

1. What It Costs to Become Governor

Exceptional is the southern governor whose primary campaign costs less than $100,000. Outlays of twice this size on behalf of individual candidates are not uncommon when the issues are sharply drawn, the stakes are thought to be high, and the battle is hard fought. On the other hand, not infrequently losing candidates make a respectable showing in the popular vote with a war chest of $25,000 or less. Few candidates with such picayune sums at their command expect victory. Yet those with prospects of victory can usually attract a hundred thousand dollars.

Of campaign costs it is impossible to speak with precision. Campaign treasurers do not operate in goldfish bowls. Candidates, campaign managers, and other politicians discuss finance with remarkable candor but promise to deny anything said in print. Even when they tell all, it is not the whole story. Often the local etiquette prescribes that the candidate shall not be informed of the details of campaign finance; [2] they can then with a clear conscience sign and file a report in accordance with the law limiting expenditure. Even managers often do not know what a campaign has cost. Funds may be sluiced through several committees, and state headquarters has no trustworthy information on sums raised and spent by county and city campaign committees. Groups of enthusiastic admirers make up a pot to buy a page advertisement and the outlay never gets on the records. At times even the state headquarters keeps no records of its own finances, and the manager does not in all honesty know how much he has spent.[3]

Under these circumstances speculation about the problem of money and politics must be based on thin evidence. If one accepts the remarks of those of our interviewees closest to the facts and rejects the exaggerations of the poor losers about the extravagances of the victors, a scale of

[2] Thus, in a recent campaign by a young political amateur against a Representative with a pro-labor voting record the common knowledge among the professional politicians was that between $15,000 and $20,000 northern business money had been shipped into the district to aid the cause. The name of the local dispenser of the fund, the general nature of the ultimate source, and what was done with the money were matters of common gossip, which, we are persuaded, never reached the ears of the candidate.

[3] Thus, the manager of a successful gubernatorial campaign of some years ago in Alabama reminisced that he had accepted contributions only in cash, had deposited contributions as received in a safety-deposit box, and had taken from the box such sums as he needed when he needed them. No records were kept either of intake or outgo. He guessed that the outlay at the state level was $40,000.

total costs emerges that has a color of internal consistency. The size of the electorate, the temperature of the campaign, the nature of the issues, the character of a state's political organization, the following with which a candidate starts in a campaign, and, sometimes, how much money a candidate has at his command, all have a bearing on the total expenditure in primary campaigns. In compact South Carolina, with less than 300,000 primary votes, it is possible to make a decent race for the governorship or for the United States Senate under favorable circumstances with as little as $50,000 to spend from state headquarters, although this level is often exceeded.[4] In huge Texas, with more than a million primary votes, a candidate must have in the neighborhood of $75,000 to have a fighting chance of getting into the run-off primary and another $75,000 if he expects to make a respectable showing in that primary. With $200,000 available for both races, he stands a chance of victory, unless the opposition has one of the state's occasional elephantine campaign funds.

A state's political customs and organization may influence campaign costs. Virginia's Byrd organization, with its extensive network of loyal county organizations and its weak opposition, ought to be able to nominate a governor or Senator for less than it costs to build an organization from the ground up in a fluid factionalism such as Florida. With the average weak opposition of the past two decades, the Virginia organization, not the best sources conclude, has spent at the state level for outlays by the headquarters and the candidate as little as $50,000 to $75,000 for the single primary of gubernatorial and senatorial campaigns.[5] Apparently, however, it takes little opposition to make the organization jittery and in those circumstances the outlay goes up. In a state such as Florida, no candidate has much of an organization to start with, and the cost reputedly goes higher in consequence. The Florida candidate must both create an organization and look forward to campaigning in both the first primary and the run-off, in contrast with Virginia's single primary. Each of the half dozen serious contenders in Florida's free for all first primary campaign, a long-time observer of Florida politics concludes, must spend $40,000 to $50,000 to make a respectable showing. If a candidate wins his way into the run-off, his outlays at the state level normally are expected at least to equal the first primary costs and his total two-primary range scales from $100,000 to $200,000.[6] Arkansas' loose factionalism also brings high expenditures. State level expenditures on behalf of a recent guberna-

[4] Joint campaign tours and speakings by South Carolina candidates for state-wide office may reduce the cost of campaigning in that state.

[5] Machine opponents usually make astronomical estimates of machine expenditures, but a leading Virginia antiorganization man fixed outlays for a gubernatorial or a senatorial campaign at no more than $100,000 *including* local expenditures. Such a figure is little more than a guess but it indicates the relative modesty of Virginia expenditures at the state level.

[6] The range of estimate in Florida as elsewhere is wide. A one-time candidate fixes the "absolute basic minimum" at $120,000.

torial candidate in the first and run-off primary are reliably fixed at $200,000.

An unexpected consequence of a highly organized politics seems to be that antiorganization candidates can make a good showing with a picayune expenditure. They cannot hope to win, though the availability to them of the support of all those who oppose the organization for whatever reason gives them a considerable bloc of votes without the necessity of heavy expenditure. Recent campaigns by Virginia antiorganization gubernatorial and senatorial candidates have attracted around a third of the total vote, and these campaigns individually have cost in the neighborhood of $15,000 expended at the state level. Similarly, in Tennessee, until the great overturn of 1948 which probably had substantial sums behind it, anti-Crump senatorial and gubernatorial candidates could rally in the neighborhood of 40 per cent of the total vote, with a state level expenditure little greater than $10,000. Local committees and newspapers, of course, spent in cash and contributed in kind to swell the total outlay, but in a dual factionalism the dominant organization makes its own enemies and they more or less automatically rally around the antiorganization candidate. A factionalism such as North Carolina—in which the dominant faction has not been so dominant as in Virginia and opposition not so hopeless—outlays for both organization and opposition candidates are reported to go higher. Total expenditures at the state level on behalf of either an organization or an antiorganization candidate for governor or Senator with serious expectations seem to be generally set at minimum of around $100,000.

In those few states that finance campaigns for factional tickets as a unit, total costs are not comparable with expenditures in states in which it is every man for himself. Thus, in Louisiana the state headquarters handles the campaign for the governor and all the half dozen or more candidates on his ticket for state-wide elective office. The unification of campaigns and the consolidation of costs results in the report that state level expenditures of the magnitude of $300,000 are not uncommon and, in fact, may be regarded as the minimum in a warmly fought campaign. Such totals sometimes include subventions to legislative candidates aligned with the governor's ticket.[7] Similarly, in Tennessee the Crump organization sometimes conducted coalition campaigns, with a joint headquarters and a consolidated fund, for its candidates for governor, state railroad commission, and the Senate. The organization, never so strongly

[7] The chances are that the depth and reality of the issues in Louisiana campaigns stimulate relatively high expenditures. A more generous estimate of Louisiana outlays is made by a capital correspondent of the *Times-Picayune* (New Orleans), June 1, 1947, in the following statement: "At this point, the only thing certain is that there will be an enormous amount of money spent on the campaign between now and the primary next January, what with three candidates openly admitting campaign war bags exceeding $500,000 each."

entrenched as the Byrd machine, competent observers estimated, ordinarily spent before 1948 from $200,000 to $250,000 on a coalition campaign.

Sometimes a candidate enters a race with some vote-getting asset that makes it possible to keep outlays down. Sitting Senators, strongly entrenched in their states, often have only pro forma opposition, and their campaign for re-election requires only a nominal outlay. Or a person may have a name or a following that can be brought to the polls without great expense. Thus, in 1942, Judge Gene Blease, brother of the late South Carolina Governor and Senator and himself a former chief justice of the state supreme court, announced that he would accept no contributions in his Senate race. He polled 48 per cent of the vote after a campaign involving state level expenditures of less than $10,000, but this performance is highly exceptional. Not all personalities with a name and a following can get by on nominal expenditures. In Georgia, for example, Gene Talmadge has almost always met well-organized opposition, and a modest estimate of state-level expenditures on behalf of him and his principal opposition candidate in a stout race would be around $100,000 each. As a one-time candidate put it, "a man who runs for governor of Georgia with less than $100,000 is crazy."

A type of race that brings out high expenditures is the rich man's campaign. When a man of great wealth or a man with a wealthy friend or so wants to be governor money flows. Such campaigns are illustrated by those of Ben Laney, for governor of Arkansas in 1944, and Francis Whitehair, for governor of Florida in 1940. Laney had struck it rich in oil and also had a wealthy supporter or so, and estimates of the state-level outlays on his behalf run as high as $250,000. Florida politicians recall with awe the unsuccessful 1940 campaign of Whitehair against Spessard Holland as perhaps the costliest in the state's history. The more conservative estimates of the combined expenditures for the two candidates run from $400,000 to $500,000, with Holland, the victor, the beneficiary of much less than half the total. Experienced campaign managers sadly regard the waste in a rich man's race. Money is spent recklessly and often a little graft is involved. The most hilarious instance that gossip records is the case of each of two rival county campaign managers putting the other on his payroll.

Another type of campaign that stimulates huge expenditures is one in which a mildly progressive candidate frightens the moneyed interests by threatening to rouse the rabble enough to win. Conversations with politicians who ought to know about such campaigns brings out figures that seem to belong more to astronomy than to campaign accounting. State-level expenditures on behalf of Handy Ellis, who in 1946 stood as a conservative against Alabama's "radical" Big Jim Folsom, are said to have been around $400,000. In Texas, estimates of outlays on behalf of

Jester, who staved off the threat offered by Rainey, run from $500,000 on up to figures which may be true but their repetition would only strain credulity even more. The 1938 campaign in support of Senator George, of Georgia, against the New Deal purge is another in which the forces of righteousness, inside and outside the state,[8] are said to have shelled out a sum approaching half a million dollars to resist the New Deal.

Citation of sums of $100,000 on up should not be taken to mean that candidates set out to corrupt the electorate or even necessarily that they violate the statutes limiting expenditures. Even the most frugally managed campaign requires large legitimate expenditures and the statutes have loopholes. "Suppose you have $50,000, what could you do with it?" said a seasoned Mississippi manager. After a moment or so of mental arithmetic he answered his question: "You could have complete state newspaper coverage with one political advertisement. You could afford three state-wide radio broadcasts. You could set up your state headquarters, write a lot of letters, and pay for your printing. You could keep about twelve field men going, and that's about all you could do." Obviously $50,000 would not finance a respectable campaign in Mississippi.[9]

Estimates of the total outlays for state-wide campaigns gain validity from the costs of individual items of legitimate expenditure. Radio has, during the past 20 or 30 years, boosted the cost of politics. A recent serious, but unsuccessful, contender for the Georgia governorship fixes radio costs for an adequate campaign at $50,000. The basic radio schedule of one of the 1948 Louisiana candidates—30 minutes per week for 17 weeks —is said to have cost $25,000, but the radio oratory of the head of the ticket is supplemented by speeches by lesser candidates and by friendly leading citizens. A Louisiana politician's estimate that a real campaign budget must allow from $60,000 to $70,000 for radio may not be overly generous. In Texas dual network time sells for $2100 per 15 minutes. The bedrock allowance, says a publicity man with political experience, should be 15 minutes a week for 10 weeks plus an additional half hour in the closing week or a total outlay of $25,200.[10] In a smaller state, Arkansas,

[8] The cumulative impression from many conversations is that senatorial candidates attract much more financial support from outside the state than do candidates for governor, all for obvious reasons. Thus, there is the case, on good authority, of a now deceased Senator of conservative hue who sought re-election and was offered far more outside money than he could use. He was particular about whose money he accepted and he took only what he needed.

[9] The *Arkansas Gazette* (Little Rock), April 18, 1948, estimated that the "average candidate for governor" of Arkansas should have a fund of $107,500. It presented the following itemization which, it said, "a former candidate for governor will recognize:" Headquarters rent, $1,000; Salaries, $5,000; Postage, $4,000; Automobile and loud speaker rent, $2,000; Printing, $10,000; Traveling expenses, $2,500; Signs and banners, $2,500; Radio advertising, $10,000; Newspaper advertising, $40,000; Telephone and telegraph, $2,500; Run-off campaign, $25,000.

[10] The plausibility of the estimate may be judged by a sample of the radio schedule, taken from the radio pages, of George Peddy, 1948 senatorial candidate. His 18 broad-

a candidate reports an expenditure of $12,000 for radio time in a campaign costing around $65,000, far less than the typical total cost for that state.[11]

Extensive newspaper advertising quickly runs into money. In a recent Arkansas campaign, well-financed, the management bought full-page, state-wide coverage about ten times. At $7,000 apiece, the total bill came to around $70,000. The frequency with which Mr. Crump has expressed his views in quarter-page, half-page, and full-page spreads in the principal papers of Tennessee gives a color of truth to estimates of campaign costs in that state. Other types of publicity likewise bring huge bills for even thin coverage. Texas campaigners make extensive use of direct-mail advertising. To get a piece of second-class mail into the hands of each of the state's potential electors is said to cost around $50,000. And some campaign managers use first-class mail on the assumption that it may be read. To prepare and deliver a first-class letter to each voter would entail a minimum aggregate cost of from $80,000 to $90,000.

If one adds to the large items for publicity, such obviously necessary outlays as travel for the candidates and his entourage, the cost of maintaining a staff at headquarters, bills for extensive use of long-distance telephone, the cost of posters, postage, printing, and so forth, the minimum sum of $100,000 soon melts away. Certain other categories of expenditure, which sometimes verge on bribery, must be made in the best-regulated campaigns. Payments to local leaders may be subventions in aid of local campaign efforts or they may be payments for influence. Save in a few valley counties, such practice seems not to be widespread in Texas. Elsewhere over the South managers of state campaigns indicate, in varying degrees, that budgetary allowance must be made for payments to local potentates. Georgia's county-unit system creates a powerful incentive to purchase support in close counties, but the practice is by no means limited to that state. And it ranges in coloration all the way from outright bribery to more or less systematic precinct organization work, but everywhere managers must know with whom they are dealing and be wary of self-styled local bosses who assert that they carry the county in their pocket.[12] In some areas the hiring of automobiles to transport voters

---

casts from Dallas stations alone over a thirty-day period would have cost over $3,000 at commercial rates, which are usually lower than political rates. Multiplying by five to estimate state-wide network coverage, one could spend $15,000 a month. Doubling this to get the cost of a short campaign, one comes out with $30,000, a modest estimate of radio costs.

[11] Radio rates reported by campaign managers almost invariably exceed the published commercial rates. In the ratebooks radio stations often indicate that religious and political rates will be furnished "on request." As in newspaper advertising, the radio political rate is probably fixed somewhere between the commercial level and a rate in excess of what the traffic will bear.

[12] A. L. Henson, a Talmadge associate, in a book deserving of more critical acclaim than it has received, tells of the "turner-downer" at state headquarters whose job it is

to the polls has become customary, particularly in some rural areas where car owners are few and the polling place is not in streetcar reach. References to the hiring of cars seem to crop up with special frequency in conversations with south Louisiana politicians. At a minimum of $10 a precinct the item can run to $2500 for a 250-precinct congressional district. And, in scattered localities, one must report that campaign budgets earmark items for the buying of votes.

2. Sources of Campaign Funds

Only a few candidates can finance campaigns for major office from their own pockets.[13] Yet huge sums must be raised for even a modest campaign, and such war chests are not made up of gifts of five or ten dollars each. The bulk of the costs of a major campaign must come from a handful of contributors, 25, 50, or 100 at the most. And even the smallest of these figures is sometimes too high.

A few men fuel the engines of democracy, and the question on every lip is, what do they expect in return? The ready reply is that A gives to B in return for a promise of C. Most speculation in this vein has been

---

to deal with people who want a new roof for the tabernacle and that sort of thing. The "turner-downer" also takes "care of the excited fellow (and his tribe is legion) who turns up in everybody's campaign headquarters with stories about how the other side is making inroads down in his district. He never wants a cent for himself—No! But, he confides, the other side is putting up a wad of dough with so-and-so down there, and if something is not done immediately things are sure to go to the 'dimnition bowwows.' He can, of course, take so much (about the price of the new suit he needs) and tie up that district so tight the good apostle Paul could not come down there and blast one precinct from the proper column. It is surprising how often this resolute outsmarts the most cautious 'turner-downer,' particularly during the last stages of the campaign. I have seen his type many times walk out of these hotels late in the afternoon with moochings equal to the returns from a one-horse cotton crop, and his roll contained bills from every candidate in every race." *Red Galluses* (Boston: House of Edinboro Publishers, 1945), pp. 81–82. Amateurs are especially susceptible to the promises held out by chiselers. See Bernarr Macfadden's account of his $75 weekly outlay to a pair who purported to have great influence with the isolated fishermen of the Everglades, *Confessions of an Amateur Politician* (New York: Bernarr Macfadden Foundation, 1948), pp. 33–35.

[13] For many local offices and legislative posts in small communities outlays are small and candidates finance their own races. In most southern states expenditures in races for minor statehouse offices are often only a few thousand dollars and it is not uncommon for candidates to provide much of the cash for these campaigns. Occasionally one finds a Congressman who pays his own way as in the case of a South Carolina Representative who recalled that he had never spent more than $2,000 on a campaign and had accepted only one contribution and that for $5.00. Some Georgia Congressmen told him that he was crazy for not accepting contributions; they told him, he says, that they took all they could get. At times men of unusual wealth can finance all or part of a state-wide race. Ross Sterling, winner of the Texas governorship in 1930, J. William Fulbright, Arkansas Senator, Elbert Boozer, unsuccessful candidate for governor of Alabama in 1946, Cameron Morrison, one-time North Carolina senator, and a few other major candidates have not been dependent entirely on contributions, but they are exceptional.

by professors and newspaper reporters, persons to whom $25 is a wad of money, and it is doubtful that they achieve a sophisticated comprehension of the motivation, attitudes, and expectations of persons who can blithely throw $5,000 in the pot to help elect old Joe, a college classmate, a drinking companion, and a fellow Rotarian, without being any the poorer. Moreover, meaningful speculation is hampered by a paucity of facts. Politicians talk at length about where the money comes from, but usually the closer they are to the facts the more disposed they are to discuss sources in vague terms.

One proposition about the sources of campaign funds seems clear enough: in a region predominantly agricultural the funds for gubernatorial and senatorial campaigns come mainly from business and finance. In Mississippi one hears of substantial campaign gifts from delta planters and in Arkansas goodly sums can be raised from the eastern plantation operators. Elsewhere undoubtedly prosperous farmers pitch in to help local campaigns for their favorites for governor and Senator, but farmers are not important as a source of campaign funds. An Arkansas campaign manager of long experience, for example, usually tries to raise 25 per cent of his fund in driblets from outside Little Rock. The outstate solicitation is more to get many persons psychologically committed to the candidate by a small contribution than for the cash itself. Three-fourths of the fund comes from Little Rock, where few farmers reside, and it is doubtful that much of the money from the rest of the state originates with farmers.

The burden of supporting political activity falls mainly on men with ready cash in considerable sums, most of whom are businessmen. But there are businessmen and businessmen and there are campaigns and campaigns. Contributions by different sorts of businessmen in different sorts of campaigns have different meanings, perceptible without imaginative reconstruction of the impulses and rationalizations that percolate through the mind of the contributor.

Businessmen can be classified broadly from the standpoint of their importance in campaign finance into two groups: those who want to do business with the state and those who are concerned with state regulatory and tax policy. The behavior of these two groups in political financing sometimes differs sharply. And all the members of each group do not act uniformly in all types of campaigns.

A campaign which draws fairly clearly the issue over broad governmental policies—a race between a neo-Populist or a New Dealer and a conservative—tends to direct the flow of money from businessmen concerned primarily with governmental regulatory and tax policy to the more conservative candidates. A determined and ably led movement to expand governmental services—to build more roads, to expand educational services, to increase aids to the needy—tends to unite this class of businessmen, whatever their line may be, by a common concern over taxation. The candidate of such a movement is also apt to sponsor regulatory measures. When the issue thus becomes one of a broad philosophy of government and the outcome is uncertain, businessmen of our second category can be easily induced—sometimes frightened—into contributing generously. Often the individual contributor concerns himself not at all with what he might get out of the campaign in the way of particular action or inaction affecting his enterprise alone. The concern is rather with a generally safe, sound, and conservative type of governmental policy.

The campaign that draws clearly such issues is infrequent, and, hence, business solidarity in high degree is not the invariable rule. But this sort of campaign has been more frequent since the New Deal. The Jester-Rainey gubernatorial race of 1946 in Texas, the Folsom-Ellis contest for the governorship of Alabama in 1946, the Jones-Long rivalry in Louisiana, the 1938 Georgia senatorial race, the two races of Ralph Mc-Donald for governor of North Carolina in 1936 and 1944, and the Hill-Simpson Alabama senatorial race of 1944 could be classed in this category. The grand issue of the scope and nature of governmental activity in each instance was more or less clearly drawn. In none of these instances did the liberal candidate campaign on a shoestring, but a common concern about taxation and spending imparted considerable unity to the business community. The type of businessmen who contribute to such campaigns varies with the composition of business in each state. In Texas the natural resource industries—principally petroleum—overshadow all others in their generosity as contributors and in their sensitivity to tax policy. In Louisiana to oil and gas is added fairly extensive lumbering operations. In South Carolina it is the textile mills. In Alabama mining, iron, and allied industries play a role. In an earlier day in Virginia tobacco manufacturers furnished the money but currently sources seem to be diversified.

The situation in which the businessman is moved to contribute, not for particular advantage but, as he sees it, to save the capitalist system from the communists, is most apt to occur in those states with a dual factionalism or with a political system that occasionally permits fairly clear class alignments. A dual factionalism stimulates the raising of issues —for the sake of challenging the organization in power, if for no other. In turn a successful faction in such a situation attracts the financial support of those attached to the status quo. Businessmen of Virginia, for example, rarely contribute to candidates opposing the Byrd organization. In Tennessee, at least until the revolution of 1948, businessmen interested in a regime that would not rock the boat supported Crump candidates.

From the business community generally one must except those who want to do business with the state, the most important of whom are highway contractors and related construction supply and road-machinery firms. Printers, wholesale grocers, textbook publishers, bond houses, insurance firms, and surety companies are smaller fry. The extent to which contractors and vendors contribute apparently varies greatly from state to state. When they contribute, they, of course, often throw their money in the same direction as business generally, but the contractor-donor is more concerned with whether a candidate will win than with his ideology. The consequence is that "radical" gubernatorial candidates frowned on by the vast majority of businessmen sometimes attract substantial financial support.[14] In Alabama and Louisiana contractors are said to have supported gubernatorial candidates not regarded as sound by the majority of businessmen. In Tennessee during the war years anti-Crump leaders bemoaned the fact that contractors at "outs" with the state were so surfeited with Federal business that they had no incentive to finance opposition campaigns. In senatorial races, the relations between the late Senator Bilbo and war contractors have been made a matter of record. In another state the informed political gossip is that a construction firm which had had large Federal contracts and hoped for more, provided the wherewithal for the campaigns of a couple of New Deal senatorial candidates. At times these arrangements involve no gain to businessmen and no loss to the state. Thus, to meet the deficit of the losing gubernatorial candidate whom it had supported one state administration gave the state's insurance to a co-operative agent. When the administration surrendered the seals of office, the insurance commissions had not completely paid off the deficit. The new administration, however, agreed to leave the insurance as it had been placed until the deficit of the vanquished was paid off.[15]

In campaigns in which issues are imperceptible the so-called business community tends to divide in its financial affections. Recent Florida gubernatorial campaigns provide an illustration. Each first primary race

[14] After describing an instance in which a highway contractor had contributed $3,000 to pay the "Strawberry Pickers," Governor Folsom's hillbilly band, a special committee appointed by Governor Folsom made the following observations: "It has come to the attention of the Committee that there is an established custom in Alabama, over a long period of years, for highway contractors to make sizeable donations to political campaigns. . . . While all of the contractors before the Committee denied that there was any advantage in being on the successful side in a political campaign, or close to an administration, yet the highway contractors are striving desperately to gain such a position. . . .

"One contractor stated to the Committee that the donations that he had made to political campaigns were charged in his overhead and were considered as a part of the overhead in making estimates on new jobs. Other contractors admitted that they had made political donations but had not charged them in their overhead. . . . This is a deplorable condition and a shameful practice, even though it has been going on for a long number of years and custom and usage has apparently condoned it."—Report of August 18, 1948. Similar observations would be applicable in several, if not all, southern states, and probably nonsouthern as well.

[15] It is easy enough to cover the deficit of a victorious candidate. Managers of gubernatorial winners mention that after the great day, many offers come in of help to cover the campaign deficit. The original stockholders resent such offers to buy in at the last minute and often insist that they take care of the deficit themselves.

ordinarily has several candidates, among whom differences in broad philosophy of government are not great. Each candidate who has any chance of getting into the second primary appears to have no great difficulty in attracting enough financial support to make a fairly respectable campaign. The sources of the funds of each candidate seem to depend in large measure on his past connections and friendships.

Especially in campaigns in which the chips are not down, personal acquaintance, friendship, and band-wagon considerations move contributors. A man with plenty of free cash happens to have a friend running for governor. Another gets a taste of politics and likes the notion that the state might have a governor who would call him John and who would consult him. But always, in the absence of broad issues, the band wagon plays a role. Thus, an experienced South Carolina politician refuses to worry about money for his campaigns. It was his observation that the purpose of the contribution was not usually to obtain a specific commitment but to keep open an avenue to government. If a candidate cannot raise enough money to win he will not win anyway. Money is almost automatically available to a candidate in proportion to his strength. One has to have money to campaign but one gets it because he has a chance to win; he does not win necessarily because he gets the money. This sort of pattern, however, seems to occur principally when deep issues are not drawn. When a straight-out conservative-liberal battle occurs, the big money concentrates on the right.

The uncertainty of politics leads to the hedging contributor who gives his major support to one candidate, but places a small bet on another by way of insurance. The multiple-giver, however, seems to be most in evidence when the differences among the candidates are least. Thus, an unsuccessful, better-element gubernatorial candidate in Georgia recalled that a corporation which gave generously to his opponent offered him a small contribution which he rejected. In another campaign, it is related, the vice-president of a major bank brought over $1,000 in cash as an anonymous contribution from the bank. It was accepted with some resentment because of the belief that the bank undoubtedly had shipped much larger sums over to the enemy. In Florida, practicing politicians indicate that road contractors contribute heavily and manage to get money to the fund of every candidate with a chance of winning. One experienced manager seemed puzzled about their motives because, insofar as he knew, individual contractors received no preference. His only explanation was that probably the state could do more construction by "force account," i.e., through its own employees rather than by contract— and that the state probably "took a beating" because it did not do so. In Arkansas it is said that road contractors and machinery concerns often give to all candidates, although in this state the affirmation is not so often heard that the tradition of making awards to the low bidder is firmly established.

In another contribution pattern particular types of business are immediately concerned with specific public policy in contrast with the right and left cleavage over broad philosophy of government. Railroads, electric utilities, motor transport, insurance, and petroleum provide specific examples. In each of these types of industry particular concerns have immediate and direct interest in specific legislative and administrative actions. Public utilities have, of course, won a great reputation as campaign financiers. The commonly published report, for example, is that the Georgia Power Company generously finances gubernatorial candidates not unfriendly to its interests, and many Georgians firmly believe this to be true. A governmental agency with far superior facilities for investigation than professors writing books went over the company records with a fine-toothed comb and took no action under legislation prohibiting political contributions. Of the influence of Georgia Power in the state's politics there seems to be no question, but that contributions are made directly from corporate funds does seem to be questionable. Surprisingly enough, persons closely connected with campaign finance minimize the significance of power utility contributions. These observations are widely at variance with popular notions on the subject, but in several states the denial comes from credible sources. Even some utility critics agree and cite alternative means by which power companies can assert influence, such as by contributions of their executives, through their networks of attorneys on retainer many of whom happen to be legislators, and through their extensive programs for the cultivation of public good will.

Campaign contributions of businesses subject to intimate governmental regulation sometimes resemble a shake-down as much as a bribe. A former member of a utility commission, for example, indicated that in his state utilities had most definitely made campaign contributions. "All their officials have practically unlimited expense accounts, you know," but even under these unlimited conditions in this state $5,000 was thought to be a large utility donation. On the commission were two men vigorous in their anti-utility views, one sincerely so and the other was "trying to work himself into a position" where he would not have to do much work the rest of his life. The misdeeds of the utilities make them suspect and fair game for those who would take advantage of the latent public prejudice against them. In this instance, the majority of the commission objected to the principal utility's tactics of bringing pressure on the commission through every conceivable channel. It finally got across to the utility the idea that the commission was interested in facts and arguments and resentful of pressure. And when the commission insisted that particular negotiations be cleared with the utility's top executive, it found him much more considerate of the public interest than were the corporate attorneys.[16] Our ex-commissioner in all his experience found only one utility which was not fair when given a chance to be.

Conflicting political interests of different types of business sometimes disperse business contributions among candidates and factions. In Texas in the 1930's the railroads set out to strangle truck transport by legislative limitation of load and by other means. The battle waxed warm, and motor transport leaders levied on truck operators for a fund for offense and defense. "Why, even the operator of one old bob-tailed truck would chip in $100," a legislator recalled. The same legislator, when heckled on the floor of the House by questions whether he had received campaign funds from truckers, replied, "Hell, yes; they gave me $2,000." His hecklers perhaps had been in touch with the railroads.

In the adverse interests of different businesses and the consequent disunity within the business community is found one solution of the problem of financing competing candidates. It may be, however, that over the past 40 or 50 years the forces unifying business—the labor movement and the expansion of governmental services and costs—have introduced into business generally a discipline that represses political expression of its inner conflicts of interest. The trade association, combinations, interlocking arrangements that permit banker arbitration of business differences rather than political settlement all may contribute to business unity. If such is the trend, the problem of financing a competitive politics becomes more critical as the business and financial community solidifies. Whether the nature of the one-party system contributes to the financial unity of business is a neat question. Scraps of evidence about the financing of the Rainey-Jester campaign in Texas in 1946 and the Folsom-Ellis campaign in Alabama in the same year suggest that perhaps the one-party system, in its more fluid form at least, facilitates the coalition of business interests of all types when broad issues seem to be involved. Campaign finance may take on a different form than when individuals have become traditionally known as Democrats or Republicans. Not even such sentimental attachments as the fact that a man's grandfather was a Copperhead obstructs economic calculus in the allocation of campaign donations.

Under such circumstances the financing of candidates in opposition to the dominant cluster becomes a matter of chance. The two chief angels of the Texas Rainey campaign were said to be oil men, both persons of progressive inclinations. One of them is said to have been a devout person who was attracted by Rainey's sincerity, earnestness, and religious beliefs. This donor incidentally took the view that an enlightened capitalism is

---

[16] One of the incidental curses of the corporate form of business is that in dealings with government corporation representatives are almost always by definition agents rather than principals. The code that must guide agents—fidelity to their principal—often converts what by any other standard might be thievery or at least bad citizenship into the work of a good and faithful servant.

apt to last longer than one that squeezes the last possible cent out of lesser peoples. In other instances in other states the chief financiers of some campaigns have been persons of great wealth, with no apparent ax to grind save the desire to be kingmakers. Such angels are not numerous, and, consequently, the financing of campaigns of candidates opposing a business coalition tends in no small degree to depend on contractors and others unmoved by ideological considerations who think they see a winner.

In another respect campaign finance under one-party conditions may take on peculiar forms. Mention has been made of huge business enterprises with a great stake in politics, such as public utilities. They may be, the remarks of practicing politicians indicate, far more concerned with legislative races than with the governorship. By judicious investments in legislative candidacies far-flung enterprises may obtain friendly legislators and, by the threat of financing opposition, they may give sitting legislators pause. The practice in most one-party states by which legislative candidates run independently of any gubernatorial candidate or statewide factional ticket may enhance the financial power of special interests. The lone legislative candidate must win or lose by his own efforts. He cannot call on a state party headquarters for help when he is in trouble. Nor does he benefit from the general Republican or Democratic trend, as does such a candidate in a two-party state. No party organization exists to function as a counterpoise to special financial interest. The possibilities are suggested by the surprise a labor leader in one southern state expressed about the ease with which he had stimulated a goodly number of successful legislative candidacies by persons friendly to labor. A trip around the state, a word of encouragement here and there, produced results. Others, of course, learned the trick long before labor. All this is not to suggest that there are no bagmen beating the bushes for friendly legislative candidates in two-party states, but the speculative surmise is plausible that a difference of degree exists when there is no party machinery, no ties of party loyalty, nothing save the individual candidate standing without defense against all the financial pressures that can be brought to bear. Moreover, isolation of all southern races from the trends and forces of national politics accentuates the necessity of individual self-reliance by the candidate. He does not stand to benefit from the great groundswells of national sentiment, which at times are too powerful to be modified by the amount of money spent.

The intimacy of the relation that often exists between contributor and candidate under one-party conditions may be another difference of degree. Often campaign collectors shield the candidate for governor from too intimate knowledge of the sources of funds. One said, for example, that he "accepted" a contribution approaching $25,000 in size, put it in his safe, and returned it to the donor after the campaign to avoid committing his governor and at the same time to deprive the opposition of the cash. Nevertheless, some gubernatorial candidates, perhaps most of them, know in detail where the cash comes from. Possibly the highly personal financial nexus between candidate and contributor inevitable in a loose factionalism creates a special sense of obligation and expectation. Thus, one gubernatorial candidate of long political experience observed that he had declined all contributions in excess of $1,000. He figured that if faced by indefensible demands, he could always raise a thousand dollars and refund the contribution. A difference of degree may exist, too, when contributions from many sources are pooled in a party war chest and expended indiscriminately in support of all candidates on the party ticket. The financing of the party as an institution may differ in degree in its effects from the financing of individual candidates.

The liquor industry warrants special mention. Subject to discretionary governmental control, it is extremely responsive to fund solicitation and is, of course, not indisposed to take the initiative in seeking out favorable candidates. The distribution of liquor money, however, takes on a peculiar pattern in each state, varying with the allocation of authority over the industry. In Arkansas, liquor wholesalers and retailers are said by the political gossip to be perhaps the second or third most important source of campaign funds, trailing the highway contractors.[17] Their interest extends to the gubernatorial race and the consensus is that their money usually finds its way to all major contenders. The governor appoints the revenue commissioner, the liquor licensing authority, whose unfettered discretion makes the liquor industry desirous of having in that post a man not inclined to abuse his power. The threat of a system of state liquor stores in Arkansas also keeps the industry on its political toes. Tennessee is another state in which liquor has the reputation of being an important source of funds. In Alabama—with its system of state liquor stores—the distillers who wish to sell to the state appear to provide most of the liquor money for state campaigns, although licencees to sell by the drink are also beholden to state authority and at times bear their share. South Carolina's retail liquor dealers are regarded as an important source of funds for candidates who stand right on what is called in South Carolina "law enforcement." In Mississippi, a dry state, the bootleggers are chiefly interested in the election of sheriffs rather than in state-wide races.[18]

[17] Exceptional seems to be the instance of a single liquor wholesaler in a gubernatorial race in another state who contributed about 65 per cent of the cost of a campaign costing upwards of $100,000. The candidate had kept the donor out of the penitentiary, and the gift was ascribed to gratitude rather than to hopes of future favors.

[18] Gambling seems to have significance as a source of funds chiefly in local rather than state races. In Florida, for example, gambling interests appear to play no inconsiderable role in some county and city campaigns. A manager for a recent candidate for governor, however, indicated that he had watched carefully to keep clear of gambling money. The gambling people, he says, want to give to any candidate who will take their

The ancient custom of assessing public employees to finance campaigns exists in the South and is given unusual character by one-party factionalism. Use of supervisory power to induce employee contributions assumes that those in power have a candidate to succeed themselves. In some states with impermanent factional structures the administration simply has no faction, no candidate for the succession to the governorship; hence, the conditions essential for routine and repetitive assessment of employees do not exist.

In states with factional continuity such as Tennessee and Louisiana assessment has been routine, although Governor Earl Long pledged himself not to use the "dee-duct" system.[19] The Virginia press is credited with stamping out systematic assessments some years ago. In North Carolina, employees are assessed to help finance the Democratic general election campaign, departmental quotas being set by the Democratic state chairman. That this type of assessment should prevail only in North Carolina is explained, of course, by that state's Democratic-Republican rivalry, unique in the South.[20] In almost every state, the custom prevails of re-electing minor statehouse officials for many terms. In such situations, the "administration" has a candidate to succeed itself and the political assessment of employees of departments headed by such officials seems to be the general rule, with, of course, exceptions here and there.

Employee assessments supposedly relieve the candidate of obligation to the special interests. A few spectacular candidates use other means to solicit small contributions. They usually provide entertainment at their political rallies and pass the hat for contributions. "Big Jim" Folsom passed the "suds bucket" at his rallies. Although the total take is unknown, apparently the "suds bucket" yielded at least enough to cover the traveling costs of the candidate and his entourage. In Texas W. Lee O'Daniel's hillbilly band entertained the audience which had a chance to drop cash into a "flour barrel"; O'Daniel had a few solvent backers, too, whose individual contributions bulked larger in his campaigns. In 1948 in Arkansas "Uncle Mac" MacKrell was accompanied in his vote-

money, which is proffered because of the unusual disciplinary powers over local officials possessed by Florida's governor. Florida race-track gambling interests also take a keen interest in legislative races. Gambling interests are of political importance in Louisiana and are, or have been, in scattered localities in other states, such as Hot Springs, Arkansas.

[19] The etiquette of assessment is, of course, usually observed. Thus, in 1948 the Tennessee press reported that state employees had been coerced into contributing 10 per cent of their monthly salary checks for a few months preceding the primary. Governor McCord denied the charge of coercion: "These charges are absolutely false. No employee of the state government is in any danger of losing his job thru failure or refusal to make a campaign contribution. Only voluntary contributions will be accepted."—*Memphis Press-Scimitar,* May 6, 1948.

[20] Indicative of the reality of the general election campaign are reports filed by the Democratic state executive committee showing an expenditure of $53,000 in the 1944 general election campaign and $46,000 in 1946.

getting tour by his gospel musicians and the hat was passed. "Uncle Mac's" pastoral experience gave him exceptional skill in the extraction of contributions. Hard-boiled politicians almost wept when they saw the collections.

Labor contributions do not bulk large in campaign finance as a whole, but particular candidates, especially congressional candidates, have in scattered instances leaned heavily on this source. The AFL is infrequently mentioned by southern politicians as a source of funds, although occasionally a local helps in a minor race. The CIO-PAC has a wider reputation as a campaign donor, but its total contributions are difficult to estimate. The national CIO-PAC may make a donation, the state CIO-PAC, and scattered locals may also pitch in on a single race, and not even the CIO-PAC knows exactly how much it has spent. CIO-PAC contributions look small alongside those of such groups as highway contractors and the liquor business. A gift of from $1,000 to $5,000 to a gubernatorial candidate, an expenditure of $1,000 to $2,000 in scattered congressional races are typical. Occasionally in a metropolitan county expenditures on several races in two primaries may aggregate $15,000. On the whole, however, labor contributions have been small potatoes. Insofar as can be determined from good sources, the conclusion seems quite safe that labor expenditures have been grossly exaggerated. Businessmen find it easy to persuade themselves that the CIO is throwing a quarter of a million dollars into a senatorial race. Fund collectors do not discourage such beliefs, for they simplify solicitation no end.

Prohibition of trade-union political funds has subjected union leaders to the inconvenience of collecting special political funds and probably reduced the significance of labor as donor. About the only part of American corrupt practices acts that anyone makes a show of enforcement is that relating to union contributions. If it is assumed that the maintenance of a competitive politics in the South is desirable, the wisdom of limitations on unions is questionable. The extraordinary difficulty of financing an opposition faction or candidate under some circumstances is apparent. Only an innocent or a hypocrite would contend that statutes limiting business contributions have a far-reaching effect. Experience of 40 to 50 years has shown that ample funds will be forthcoming to assure that business has a political champion. A labor special interest may be quite as undesirable as a business special interest, but a noncompetitive politics may be more undesirable than either.

3. Invitation to Perjury

Southern states are equipped with the usual laws to regulate campaign finance. These statutes differ in the degree of their approach to technical perfection. Alabama's corrupt practices act reflects relatively skillful legislative drafting; that of Georgia is more primitive. In neither state does the law have practical bearing on the amounts of expenditures, the sources of funds, or the extent to which the voters are informed about the nature of campaign finance. The chances are about 99 to 1 that not a single serious race for state-wide office in any southern state (or any other state) during the past 20 years has been unaccompanied by perjury, morally if not legally, either by the candidate or his managers in reports of campaign receipts and expenditures.

Legislation to control expenditures came from the resolve that swept the country 35 or 40 years ago to clip the political wings of the special interests. The firmness of that resolve has weakened over the years, and state corrupt-practices acts have become in no small degree dead letters, if not objects of ridicule. Candidates for the Texas House of Representatives, for example, are limited to an expenditure of $300, four-fifths of which may be spent in the first primary campaign and the remainder in the second. A candidate in a central Texas county once presented to the county clerk a sworn, itemized report of expenditures totaling $350. The clerk declined to receive the report, "Don't you know that the law puts a $300 ceiling on your campaign expenses?" The candidate, surprised by this news, replied, "No." Nevertheless, he took his report away and returned with a revised, sworn report, which stated that total outlay had been $198.50. The clerk laughed heartily and accepted the second report. Even the candidate's opponent, when he heard the story, was amused and refused to use the incident against him in the run-off campaign.

Quite apart from the levity with which corrupt-practices acts are regarded, literal adherence to some of the state laws would make a state-wide campaign almost impossible. Florida, for example, fixes a top limit of $15,000 on the amount to be spent "in the furtherance" of candidacies for governor and for the United States Senate. This maximum includes "all expenditures by the candidate himself or his campaign manager or committee." Perhaps expenditures by persons other than the candidate, his campaign manager or committee would not come strictly within the limitation, but it is safe to say that no governor has been elected in Florida in 20 or 30 years "in the furtherance" of whose candidacy less than $15,000 was spent.

In other states a more realistic upper limit is placed on expenditures. Mississippi allows its candidates for governor and Senator to spend $61,-000 plus the salary of the state campaign manager. This total consists of $15,000 plus $1,000 for each county of 40,000 or more population and $500 for each county of less population. These county sums, however, must be spent from contributions "made by qualified electors of the particular county," and, as one state campaign manager observes, it is difficult to obtain such a distribution of contributors. At any rate $15,000 plus the campaign manager's salary is a small state-level expenditure; experienced managers consider $50,000 woefully inadequate. Nevertheless, candidates who make a fairly respectable showing may occasionally keep within the limits.

In other instances, when limitations apply only to the candidate or to expenditures for certain purposes, there is no difficulty in keeping within the legal ceiling because it has no real meaning. Arkansas, for example, limits the amount to be spent by a candidate for governor to $5,000, exclusive of his personal traveling and hotel expenses. No ceiling applies to the candidate's campaign committee. "The only person restricted is the actual candidate, which is like passing a law providing that a bullfrog can't fly," opines "Spider" Rowland, the *Arkansas Gazette's* philosophical paragrapher. "A candidate generally doesn't spend two-bits out of his own pocket. In the first place, the tariff is so high the candidate couldn't afford to take the job if he had to personally foot the bills and, second, some of the candidates in the recent race couldn't spend $5,000 of their own lettuce if their lives had depended on it. Anybody who can get to town and back knows what the candidates spend personally, if anything, doesn't amount to a drop in the bucket." [21]

Limitations on total expenditures were fixed on the theory that candidates with access to huge sums of money enjoy a special advantage and that by their acceptance of such sums they assumed obligations contrary to the public interest.[22] Moreover, the notion still has currency that large expenditures in themselves involve an attempt to corrupt the electorate. Though neither proposition is invariably true, efforts to limit total expenditures have proved futile,[23] and the necessity of raising large sums to finance campaigns undoubtedly gives great advantage to those

[21] "The High Cost of Politicking," *Arkansas Gazette* (Little Rock), August 27, 1948.

[22] "Spider" Rowland, whose *Arkansas Gazette* observations have been quoted earlier, expresses the prevailing view: "Right's right and wrong's wrong and right doesn't wrong anybody, but any citizen with gumption enough to wind a watch knows there's something wrong as a two-foot yard stick when a quarter of a million coconuts are spent to get a 10,000 slug a year job for a guy. I don't profess to have any more sense than the law allows but this same situation crops up every time we have a gubernatorial election and even a guy who would flunk in a diploma mill would wake up that there is something rotten much closer than Denmark."—"The High Cost of Politicking," *Arkansas Gazette* (Little Rock), August 27, 1948.

[23] In 1948 Martin Dies made motions toward running for the Senate from Texas but withdrew after exchanges with the attorney general about the statute limiting expenditures. The limitation for a senatorial race is $10,000 plus additional sums which can be raised and expended within each county. "I want to know," Dies said, "if it is all right for me and my friends to violate" the law. "I'd like to run but I wouldn't want to go up to the Senate a criminal. Why the statute is just as plain as the hog-theft law and you could go to the pen for stealing a hog." The attorney general could see no way around the law, which he thought, "should either be enforced or changed by the legislature." Dies withdrew, saying, "There is no way that I or any other law-abiding citizen can run for the Senate that I have discovered."—*Dallas Morning News*, May 19, June 5, 6, 1948.

candidates with access to wealthy donors. Protection against plutocratic interests rests, not in corrupt-practices legislation, but in the fact that candidates with little or no money but wide popular appeal can from time to time overcome the moneybags. And money is sensitive to trends of sentiment. If wealth cannot elect the candidate of its own choice, it is apt to be willing to contribute to the next best bet. An old-time North Carolina politician once of great prominence, thus, expressed the greatest impatience with these young fellows who consider running for governor and try to budget out everything in advance. "Get out and champion the rights of the people and the money will take care of itself. Sure, you have to have money but you don't need to act like a business man and let it control you in everything you do." Money may as often pick as make a winner.

Most students of campaign finance concede the futility of attempts to set ceilings on expenditures and argue that the necessities of democracy can be met by removing limits and by assuring publicity on the sources of funds and on the objects of expenditure. They assume that politicial equity will be served if the electorate knows what interests are backing whom and with what. In effect, the Alabama statute attempts to meet this prescription. Personal expenditures by a candidate for governor or Senator are limited to $10,000, and few candidates spend this much out of their pockets. A candidate must, however, designate a campaign committee, on whose expenditures there is no limit. The law prescribes that "all contributions, donations and subscriptions" on behalf of the candidate are to be made to the committee which is obliged, by the law at least, to make all expenditures on his behalf. Expenditures by any other person or committee are illegal. In principle the statute thus provides for a centralization of information on campaign finance to make possible the filing of complete reports with the proper public authority. It can be said with complete assurance that this arrangement provides the Alabama electorate with no more enlightenment on campaign finance than do the laws of more backward states.

Many contributors manifest a reticence about public identification with campaign funds. If their candidate loses, there may be reprisals. Often money goes through several hands before it reaches a candidate's committee or manager. In several states one hears of shadowy and mysterious individuals, often not in the public eye, who more or less make a profession of serving as a go-between linking the principal sources of funds and campaign committees. One of these men was actually run to ground and he explained, cheerfully enough, his role. A lot of businessmen felt the urge to do their bit, he explained, but did not know how to go about it and in some instances preferred to have no dealings with politicians. It had become the custom in his state for him to serve as a channel for contributions. By the time the campaign manager received the cash, the identity of its original source was lost.[24]

Few candidates or managers of campaigns for major office regard the reporting requirements with awe. In any state the most cursory inspection of the reports on file reveals prima facie violations. The requirement of itemization of receipts may be, for example, ignored. A Virginia senatorial candidate reported receipts of less than $4,000, "all from residents of Virginia." A Texas gubernatorial candidate lumped his as coming from "Friends of a Greater Post-War Texas." A weak Mississippi gubernatorial contender reported $5,000 from "friends of Meridian" and $1,000 from "friends in Jackson." The Mississippi incident, in itself not extraordinary, precipitated a most unusual action. The secretary of state advised the candidate that he should list the names of his friends.[25] Usually the reports are merely filed and that is the end of it.

The reporting process conveys no meaningful information to the electorate. The sketchy reports that are filed usually receive some publicity in the press, but it is doubtful that these newspaper items attract wide attention. The fact is that even with complete disclosure by campaign managers the reports would mean nothing unless subjected to analysis to identify the economic affiliations of the principal contributors and to indicate the nature of the relation of government to their interests. The voters might then, as one politician said, "know who owns you." Obviously this type of analysis is impossible on the basis of false reports. Further, a fluid factional system makes doubly difficult effective publicity. Presidential campaign reporting requirements have probably produced a fairly clear identification in the public mind of the general character of the groups which, campaign after campaign, support the Republican and Democratic parties. By repetition through many channels the idea

[24] If the truth could be known, the conclusion might well be that no small percentage of campaign cash sticks to the hands through which it must pass from donor to ultimate expenditure in its sub rosa travels through a vale bordering on illegality. The collection and channeling of funds provides for some individuals a way of making money. In one state politicians regale the visitor with the yarn, which has probably grown in the telling, about Mr. A, an active politician known to be as smart as a whip and thought to be as crooked as a ram's horn. Some years ago Mr. A arranged for a group of cement makers to contribute $25,000 to a campaign fund. He put one Mr. B on the train to go to Atlanta to pick up the cash. Then, Mr. A took a plane to Atlanta, all this in the days when one did not fly at the drop of a hat, and picked up the $25,000 himself. Mr. B arrived, called on the cement people. They told him that they had given the cash to Mr. A, whom B insisted he had left back home. He called them all the names in his vocabulary and they almost had to put him in jail to quiet him. Mr. A returned home, delivered $1,500 to the campaign fund; the cement people to this day swear that the packet contained $25,000. Mr. A's only comment after the incident was that B had always been a little slow.

[25] *Memphis Press-Scimitar*, July 10, 1947. The legal duties of secretaries of state usually extend only to receiving the reports as filed. These officials indicate in conversation that they do not consider it their proper function to examine reports to determine conformity with the law. Nor do they look for trouble by seeking an enlargement of their functions.

may finally get across to the voter that steel makers are not a major source of Democratic campaign funds. However, in states without factional continuity even this meager opportunity for voter identification of who's who does not exist.

Some southern states prohibit political contributions from certain sources, sources supposedly under special temptation to corrupt candidates and in a position to profit in especial degree from governmental favoritism. Thus, in North Carolina all corporations are prohibited from participating in a campaign. Mississippi prohibits contributions by common carriers and telegraph and telephone companies. Texas makes corporate and labor union contributions illegal. Alabama's prohibition of corporate contributions extends also to persons or trustees owning or holding a majority stock in specified types of corporations engaged in business clothed with a public interest, such as utilities, banks, and insurance companies. The legislation in most southern states limiting sources of funds would not be thought up to standard by those persons who attribute importance to such laws. Corporate contributions, for example, are permissible in several states. Prohibition of corporate contributions does not prevent adequate financial representation of the corporate viewpoint in campaigns, although the law may provide corporate officers and directors a defense against extortion.

All in all, legislation regulating money in politics has had little or no effect in the South; yet its futility is no greater there than anywhere else. The laws are significant only as a legislative recognition of a belief that something ought to be done to restrict the influence of wealth in government. In that endeavor little faith can be placed in corrupt-practices acts.

PART | FOUR

Southern Voters

I N THE discussion of southern politics a prominent place is given to the low levels of voting in the region. Although the facts are often misrepresented and the consequences of nonvoting exaggerated, widespread nonparticipation in voting remains an extremely significant characteristic of the politics of the South. The one-party system both contributes to low levels of citizen-interest and in turn perhaps is perpetuated in part by citizen disinterest. Nonvoting not only sets the South off from the rest of the Union, but also places it in an even more notable position. Among the great democracies of the world, the southern states remain the chief considerable area in which an extremely small proportion of citizens vote. While low popular interest in elections is commonly attributed to Negro disfranchisement, as a matter of fact, only a small proportion of the white population regularly votes.

The copybook maxim reads that people govern themselves through electing their governors. In reality, men of ability, of substance, and of sharp wit assume leadership and manage the affairs of the state with the consent, with the tolerance, or simply by the acquiescence of those who have to earn a living and cannot afford to devote their time to politics. In the governing of peoples, a few always hold power; it is exercised, however, subject to the influence of the governed which may be almost imperceptible or it may be irresistible. It makes itself felt in diverse ways, although in democratic systems popular influence characteristically exerts itself through voting.

Obviously the make-up of the body of voting citizens and the way in which they use their franchise determine, within limits, the character of governing groups and the manner in which they exercise their power. In the growth of democratic systems the right to vote has been gradually extended. Generally, the more extensive the body of citizens entitled to vote, the greater the concern that governments must manifest for the welfare of the mass of people. If one group of leaders does not cater to the people's needs, another, yearning for the power and perquisites of office, will.

Certainly, with a restricted electorate, benevolent despotism is possible. With universal suffrage, virtual dictatorship is possible. Yet over the long pull, governments that must win the consent of the masses will differ from those that can hold on to power by the support of an extremely small proportion of the people. If our general proposition is correct, the low level of electoral interest in southern states has had and now has a profound influence on the ways of state governments and of representatives of the South in national affairs. And this influence can, in a sense, be separated from the race question. Depressed civic interest among southern whites has far-reaching consequences quite apart from Negro disfranchisement.

Speculation on the significance of low levels of zeal in voting needs to be founded upon an adequate basis of facts on variations in voting interest. With these preliminary observations on the consequences of varying degrees of citizen-interest in elections, an expedition may be led, with adding machine and calculator, through the jungle of southern voting statistics. A first objective will be to determine the proportion of potential southern voters that actually vote. The size of the southern electorate takes on meaning, of course, only in contrast to electoral interest in other areas, and appropriate comparisons with the voting records of other states will be introduced. A second matter, of great importance and more difficult of determination, is the identification of the characteristics of the limited southern electorate. Do those who vote simply constitute a cross section of the entire potential voting population? Or do some groups of citizens vote in high degree, others in low degree? Are some classes of citizens in effect removed from the body politic by nonvoting?

Chapter Twenty-three

THE SIZE OF
THE SOUTHERN ELECTORATE

IN propaganda about the politics of the South, figures on the proportion of southerners who vote are thrown about with abandon. Estimates of levels of voting are derived often from figures chosen to lead inevitably to preordained conclusions. By any standard precious few southerners exercise the rights of citizens in a democracy. The estimate of how few depends on what figures are used; there are many from which to select.

If estimates of electoral enthusiasm in the South are based on participation in Democratic primaries, a different finding results than if general election returns are used. Or if an analyst carefully selects primaries or elections to serve as a measure, he can "prove" high or low interest among voters as he desires, for electoral turnout varies from time to time. Again, since the vote on different offices varies, conclusions about the level of voting may be determined by whether the test is the vote on county surveyor or that on United States Senator.

To escape all these pitfalls, reliance can be placed on no single calculation to provide a measure of the size of the active electorate. To avoid the peaks or troughs of interest in particular elections, calculations in the pages that follow are derived from voting data extending back to 1920. In a sense there are no elections in the South: the matter is settled when the Democratic party makes its nominations. The vote in Democratic

primaries, therefore, is used as a gauge of the size of the voting population. In the main, because of the availability of data, votes on offices filled
by state-wide elections, such as governor, rather than votes on local offices
are used.

1. Voting for Governors

Most of the startling and well-publicized conclusions about southern
electoral apathy are derived from the easily accessible figures on votes in
presidential elections and in elections of United States Senators and Representatives. To critics who hammer them with these figures, southerners
reply that if one looks at the Democratic primaries, an entirely different
picture of citizen-interest will emerge. In fact, an extremely small part of
the potential voting population controls Democratic nominations, although the primary vote usually exceeds that in the general elections.
The turnout at the primaries almost never reaches the level of participation in general elections in two-party states.

Usually less than 30 per cent of all citizens 21 years of age and over
vote for governor in Democratic primaries in most southern states; in
four states—Virginia, Georgia, Tennessee, Alabama—the rate of participation averages less than 20 per cent. In five states—Louisiana, Florida,
Mississippi, Texas, and South Carolina—the average hovers around 30
per cent. The average percentages of the citizen population 21 years of
age and over voting in the Democratic gubernatorial primaries of the
southern states from 1920 through 1946 are shown in Figure 57. For
comparative purposes the chart also shows the average turnout at elections of governors in New York and Ohio over the same period.[1] The
use of an average of the rates for a series of elections, of course, conceals

---

[1] The population figures used as a base for computing percentages of adults voting
in the years between censuses were obtained by interpolation, that is, by assuming that
one-tenth of the increase in population during the decade between censuses occurred
each year. In estimates so crude it was considered a labor of supererogation to interpolate
to the month or day of the primary. Thus, the population interpolation for an election
held five years after a census would be made on the assumption that the voting occurred
exactly midway between two censuses when in fact it might have been held five years
and three months or four years and ten months after the last census. The population
figures for the years since 1940 are based on the census estimates of civilian population
published in *Current Population Reports, Population Estimates*, Series P-25, No. 2
(1947). It was assumed that in each year since 1940 the proportion of the total civilian
population, as estimated, included the same percentage of whites 21 and over and of
Negroes 21 and over as in 1940. Probably in most southern states the resulting figures
overestimate the Negro population and understate the white population owing to a
higher rate of Negro than white migration since 1940. Obviously any calculation of
voter-interest for the years since 1940 must be taken with reserve both because of errors
in the population estimates and from assumptions about the age and race composition
of the estimated total population. The vote in the first primary was used.

variations in turnout from election to election, a matter that will be explored later.

The most extreme contrast demonstrated by the chart is that between Virginia and Ohio and New York. In Ohio and New York about five times as large a proportion of the electorate votes for governor in the general elections as participates in the Democratic primaries for governor in Virginia. But the Virginia situation is exceptional. A less-marked contrast is presented by New York and Texas: the New York rate is only about twice as high as that of Texas.

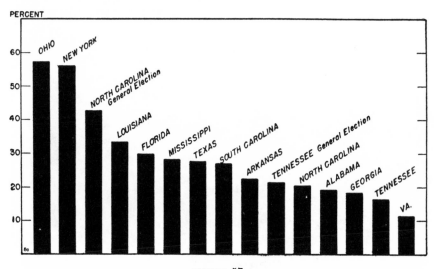

FIGURE 57

Ohioans Outvote Southerners from Two-to-One to Five-to-One: Average Percentage of Citizens 21 and over Voting for Governor in General Elections in New York and Ohio, and for Candidates for Democratic Nominations for Governor in Southern States, 1920–46

Striking differences between southern and northern states are apparent from the chart; among the states of the South contrasts are no less striking. Mississippi, South Carolina, and Louisiana, even with their large nonvoting Negro populations, maintain high voting records in comparison with those of Virginia, Georgia, Tennessee, and Alabama. Texas and Florida similarly have high participation rates; Florida is characterized by a degree of political consciousness not present in more typically "southern" states. The relatively small Negro population in Texas accounts in large part for a voting rate higher than that of Georgia and Alabama.

Earlier warnings about the ease with which a case may be made by the adroit selection of figures are re-enforced by the data on North Carolina in the chart in Figure 57. Average participation rates for both the Democratic primaries and the general elections appear in the chart. The primary figures convey an idea of how narrowly political power is held within the population, for the Democratic primary invariably controls the choice of governor. Yet the turnout at the general election invariably exceeds that in the primary; the Republicans of North Carolina poll enough of a vote to compel the Democrats to wage an active campaign for their candidates.

The dangers of wholesale invidious comparisons between the South and the rest of the nation appear from an examination of graphs in

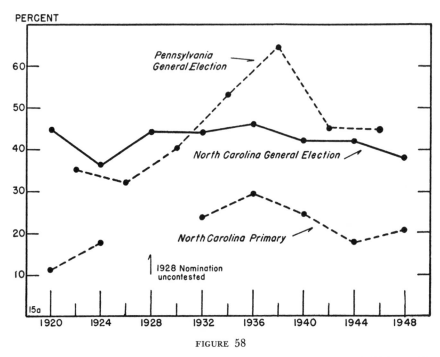

PERCENT

FIGURE 58

The Conclusions Depend on the Figures You Use: Percentage of Citizens 21 and Over Voting for Governor in General Elections and in North Carolina Democratic Gubernatorial Primaries, 1920–46

Figure 58, which shows the percentage of adult citizens voting for governor in general elections in Pennsylvania and North Carolina since 1920. In the 'twenties, when the Republicans ruled Pennsylvania without challenge, the voting rate in North Carolina actually exceeded that of Pennsylvania. On the other hand, as the chart shows, when the Pennsylvania Democrats are not moribund, the Pennsylvania turnout far exceeds that of North Carolina. One factor affecting the Pennsylvania and North Carolina comparison is that North Carolina gubernatorial elections are held in the years of presidential contests, a fact that stimulates the vote for governor, while Pennsylvania chooses its governors in off-years when the turnout invariably slumps. The level of citizen-interest in general elections in North Carolina far exceeds that of other southern states, a feature that good North Carolinians might conclude parallels other characteristics of a progressive and enlightened area.

All these comparisons are based on the proportions of all citizens 21 and over participating in primaries and elections. The comparisons, it may be argued, are unfair, since they do not take into account the peculiar southern institution of Negro disfranchisement. Perhaps the level of voting interest of southern whites matches that of citizens generally elsewhere. It is impossible, of course, to determine precisely how many votes are cast by whites and how many by Negroes; the records are not kept that way. For the years 1920–46, the vote may be considered as having been cast almost entirely by whites, and participation rates calculated by a determination of the percentage that total votes are of the white citizen population 21 years of age and over. The overestimate of the voting rate of whites is not great.

The results arrayed in the chart in Figure 59 may be both astonishing and dismaying. Clearly the electoral lethargy of the citizens of Virginia, Tennessee, Georgia, Alabama, and Texas, revealed in Figure 59, cannot be attributed to Negro disfranchisement. The whites of these states simply do not vote in nearly so high degree as do all citizens of two-party states. On the average, at least 85 per cent of the adult whites of Virginia do not vote for governor in the Democratic primaries. The proportion of all adult citizens of New York that vote for governor in general elections is about twice as great as the proportion of whites participating in the Democratic gubernatorial primaries in Alabama, Arkansas, Georgia, and Texas. Almost four times as many New Yorkers, in proportion, vote as do white Virginians.

Mississippi, South Carolina, and Louisiana depart markedly from the general pattern of participation in the South. About twice as great a proportion of whites vote in the Mississippi and South Carolina Democratic gubernatorial primaries as in those of Alabama or Georgia. Louisiana likewise has a high level of white participation in the primaries. In Louisiana and Mississippi the percentage of whites voting in the Democratic primaries almost equals the average participation rate of all citizens in New York or Ohio general elections.

The reasons for the high levels of electoral participation by whites in these three southern states are not readily apparent. A partial explanation is the fact that Negro disfranchisement removes from the potential electorate many of the poor and thus leaves an electorate of relatively high economic status, that is, high within these states. Wherever detailed analyses have been made,[2] they reveal an increase in voting interest as economic status rises. Perhaps this factor accounts to some extent for the

[2] Herbert Tingsten, *Political Behavior* (London: P. S. King & Sons, 1937), chap. 3.

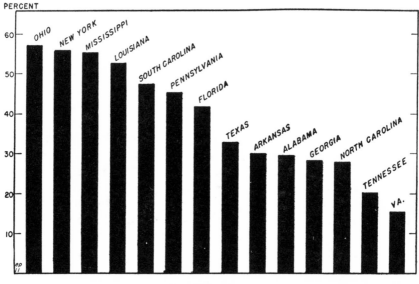

FIGURE 59

Negro Nonvoting Accounts for Part, but only Part, of Southern Electoral
Apathy: Average Percentages of *All* Citizens 21 and Over Voting for Governor
in General Elections in Pennsylvania, Ohio, and New York and Estimated Percentages of *White* Citizens 21 and Over Voting for Governor in Southern Democratic Primaries, 1920–46

higher level of white participation in those states with high proportions
of Negro population.

2. Voting for United States Senators

Interest of voters in the choice of United States Senators usually does
not equal that shown in the election of governors. Popular interest tends
to be focused on chief executives rather than legislators. The South is no
exception to the rule. The rates of electoral participation in Democratic
primaries for the nomination of United States Senators from southern
states are usually lower than the levels of voting in gubernatorial primaries. On the whole the difference in voter-interest in the two types of
offices tends to be greater in southern states than in states with a genuine
two-party system.

The level of participation, again in averages of the percentage of
citizens 21 years of age and over voting, in southern senatorial primaries
1920–46, is shown in Figure 60. For purposes of comparison participation
rates for New York and Ohio senatorial elections over the same period

are shown.[3] The contrasts apparent from the chart almost make comment superfluous; the meanings hidden within the percentages may be inferred from a few calculations. In 1928 Kenneth McKellar won the Democratic nomination in Tennessee, with 120,000 votes of 190,000 cast. If the Tennessee electorate had been as active in that year as that of New York, Mr. McKellar would have had to poll 521,000 votes to win by the same percentage margin. The nomination of Walter F. George, of Georgia, for the Senate in 1944 furnishes another like example. George won the nomination in a walk by polling 211,000 of 245,000 votes. With a partici-

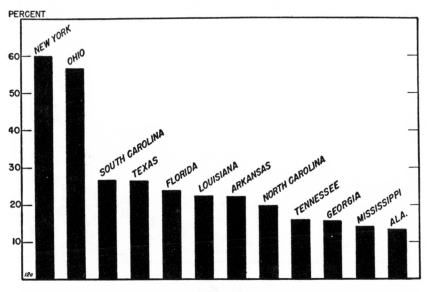

FIGURE 60

Even Fewer Southerners Vote for Senator than for Governor: Average Percentage of Citizens 21 and Over Voting for United States Senator in Southern Democratic Primaries and in Ohio and New York General Elections, 1920–46

pation rate the same as that of Ohio in the same year, Mr. George would have had to receive the support of about 955,000 of his fellow Georgians to win by the same percentage margin.

Comparison of the chart on senatorial voting with the chart on interest in gubernatorial primaries reveals that the differences among southern states are about the same with respect to voting on the two offices. One striking exception, however, occurs: in Mississippi about twice as large a proportion of the citizenry bestirs itself to vote for governor as for senatorial candidates. Politicians in Mississippi explain the

[3] The omission of Virginia from the chart is explained by the fact that unopposed nominations deprive the data of meaning.

differential in interest by the state's election calendar. The primaries for the two offices take place at different times. The gubernatorial primary is held at the same time that county officials are elected. The intense concern over the selection of local officials causes the vote for governor to be markedly higher than that for Senator.

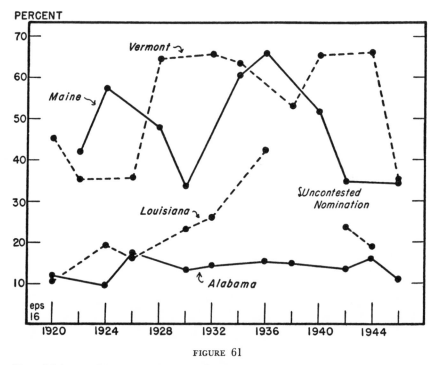

FIGURE 61

Even Maine and Vermont Outvote the South: Percentages of Citizens 21 and Over Voting for United States Senator in Maine and Vermont General Elections and in Louisiana and Alabama Democratic Primaries, 1920–26

The appearance of Southern electoral apathy, it may be said, is exaggerated by the use of New York and Ohio as yardsticks. In these states both parties campaign energetically to get out the vote. One ought to place the record of the South alongside that of northern states that are virtually one-party states. Even in Maine and Vermont, however, senatorial campaigns are fought with enough verve to bring out a vote that far exceeds the usual southern vote. The record since 1920 for Maine, Vermont, Louisiana, and Alabama is presented in Figure 61. The Maine and Vermont turnout fluctuates widely, in part because when senatorial races coincide with presidential elections the number of voters is swollen by the excitement of the national campaign. The White House sweepstakes, on the other hand, do not affect the voting curves for southern primaries.

The record of Louisiana, as it appears from the chart, incidentally suggests the dangers of unqualified assertions about low levels of voting in the South. The peak Louisiana turnout rate in a senatorial primary during the period covered by the chart exceeded the lowest turnout rates of Maine and Vermont. The Louisiana peak occurred under exceptional circumstances: the Long regime activated the Louisiana electorate to an extraordinary degree. The tremendous fluctuation in Louisiana, as it appears in the chart, is far from characteristic of the political behavior of southern states.

The upshot is that northern one-party states exceed the South in electoral interest only in lesser degree than do two-party states. The significant difference between northern and southern one-party states seems to be that in the South there is a ceiling on voter-turnout. The northern one-party states at some elections moves down to the southern level, but when citizens of a northern one-party state have the inclination to vote they turn out in about as large numbers as do voters in two-party states.

3. Voting for United States Representatives

The South sets no higher record in voting for Representatives than for its governors and Senators. The data are not complete because often southern states do not collect at a central place the primary vote on nominations of Representatives. Hence, only scattered returns are conveniently available, and they show that voter-interest in congressional races usually drops slightly below that in gubernatorial and senatorial primaries. More complete information probably would not change the finding.

Sample calculations, made on the basis of availability of figures rather than through a refined process of sampling, give an adequate notion of the level of participation in Democratic primaries. The graphs in Figure 62 contrast voter participation in Democratic primaries to nominate United States Representatives in Alabama from 1920 through 1946 with that in New York elections of Representatives for the same period. On the average, throughout the period, the participation rate in New York was four times that of the Alabama electorate. If the potential white electorate of Alabama alone were to match the participation record of New York, more than twice as many whites would have to turn out at the polls than has been the custom. The Alabama rates are reduced by the fact that many candidates are unopposed and the vote in such districts is presumably less than the total would have been had the nomination been contested. This factor introduces an element of noncomparability between the New York and Alabama figures, but the reduction of the vote through lack of opposition for some seats is small.[4]

An incidental but striking feature of the voting tendencies demonstrated by Figure 62 is that the voters of neither Alabama nor New York became greatly exercised about the choice of United States Representatives. The peaks in the New York saw-tooth graph occur in the years of presidential elections. The hullabaloo over the Presidency brings the

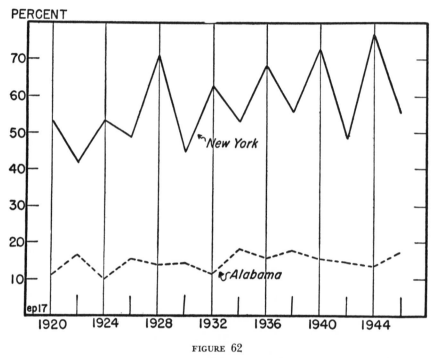

FIGURE 62

Presidential Campaigns Stimulate Voting for Representatives in Two-Party States: Percentage of Population 21 and Over Voting for United States Representatives in New York Elections and in Alabama Democratic Primaries, 1920–46

voters to the polls and while they are about it, they vote for a House candidate. In Alabama, on the other hand, the peak vote for Representatives comes usually at the primaries in the middle of each presidential term. At this time Alabama chooses its governor and the campaign for

[4] The effect of the lack of opposition may be suggested by a comparison of the rate of participation in selected Alabama districts in which nominations were made without opposition and for the state as a whole in 1940. In that year, 15.6 per cent of all citizens 21 and over registered a choice in Democratic primaries for the selection of House nominees. In districts in which the nomination was made without opposition the rates were: First, 13.8; Third, 15.8; Fifth, 25.2; Sixth, 17.5; Ninth, 11.3. Among these districts variations in the proportions of nonvoting Negroes in the population introduces an element of noncomparability.

this office pulls the voters to the polls. The fact that New York has a presidential campaign and Alabama does not accounts for part of the difference in the electoral enthusiasm of the two states.

Further sample votes in the choice of Representatives are shown in Table 53. The Georgia averages run only slightly below voting in gubernatorial primaries over the period 1928–44. In primaries on House nominees the average of the state-wide vote for the eight elections, in percentage of citizen population 21 years of age and over, was 17.5; over the same period the average for the gubernatorial primaries was 18.0. Table 53 contains also state-wide participation figures of a few states for selected years. The Texas figure for 1942, 25.6 per cent of total population 21 and over, is almost the same as that for the gubernatorial primary of the same year. The 1936 Louisiana figure of 42.1 per cent of total (and 65.3

TABLE 53

Voter Participation in Selected Democratic Congressional Primaries

| | | TOTAL VOTE AS PERCENTAGE OF | |
| | | TOTAL CITIZEN POPULATION 21 | WHITE CITIZEN POPULATION 21 |
STATE	COVERAGE OF FIGURES	AND OVER	AND OVER
Alabama	State, average, 1920–44	14.5	22.5
Georgia	State, average, 1928–44	17.5	26.8
Louisiana	State, 1936	42.1	65.3
Arkansas	State, 1938	26.3	35.2
Texas	State, 1942	25.6	30.0
New York [a]	State, average, 1920–44	55.4	
	State, 1940	73.2	
	State, 1922	41.7	

[a] General election rather than primary figures.

per cent of white) voting population is slightly below participation in the gubernatorial primary of that year. The 1936 Louisiana turnout, the year of the battle of the Long succession, marked a peak of interest in Louisiana primaries.

The level of participation in primaries for the nomination of Representatives must be interpreted against the background of the one-party system and associated restrictions on the suffrage. It is evident that the higher voting levels on Representatives in two-party states reflect in considerable degree the vote brought to the polls by the presidential contest rather than a sharper interest in the selection of Representatives as such. Furthermore, within one-party primaries competition for the post of Representative is far less keen than that for senatorial and gubernatorial places. To a high degree nominations for Representative go by default, a condition that contributes to low electoral interest and also reflects the southern awareness of the advantages to be gained through representation by Congressmen with seniority.[5]

4. Voting in Presidential Elections

That few southerners vote in presidential elections is no news. The absence of a battle for the electoral vote of southern states—coupled with other factors—results in an extraordinary low turnout of voters in presidential elections. The level of voting in these elections gives an

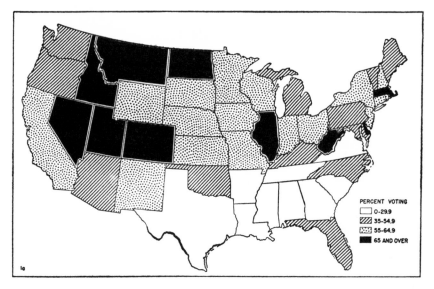

FIGURE 63

The South Marks Itself Out by Nonvoting in Presidential Elections: Percentage of Citizens of 21 and over Voting for President, 1948: By States

erroneous notion of the degree of citizen participation in politics in the South—as the preceding figures on Democratic primaries make plain—but, for completeness, the record ought to be shown.

The political South defines itself through its electoral inactivity in the map in Figure 63, showing the percentages of citizens 21 and over that voted in each state in the 1948 presidential election. Less than 25 per cent of those of voting age went to the polls in Arkansas, Mississippi, Alabama, Georgia, South Carolina, and Virginia, in contrast with a national percentage of 52. While other southern states did better, they were far below the national rate. The percentages for those exceeding the 25 per cent mark were: Louisiana, 28; Texas, 26; Tennessee, 30; Florida,

[5] On the extent of nomination without contest, see above, pp. 381–82.

39; North Carolina, 39.[6] In 10 nonsouthern states more than 65 per cent of the potential voters filed through the polling places.

The meaning of the levels of participation may be suggested by a few calculations based on the 1940 turnout. If the citizens of South Carolina had gone to the polls to the same degree in 1940 as did those of New Hampshire, almost 800,000 would have turned out instead of the 99,830 who voted. Or if Texas had flocked to the polling booths with the same enthusiasm as the voters of Illinois, more than 2,000,000 additional votes would have been cast in the Lone Star State. Had Mississippians been

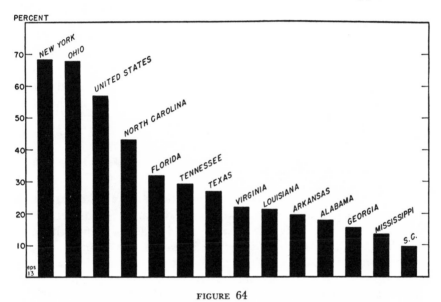

FIGURE 64

Percentages of Persons 21 and Over Voting in Presidential Elections: Averages 1920–44 for Southern States, Ohio, and New York

under the same compulsion to vote as Ohioans, 879,000 ballots would have been marked instead of 175,000.

The difference between the South and the remainder of the country in the 1940 presidential election was not, of course, exceptional. The geographical pattern of participation varies but little from election to election. On the day after a presidential election the returns regularly show that South Carolina had the distinction of the lowest percentage turnout of all the states in the Union, with Mississippi usually a close second. In the bar chart in Figure 64, averages are shown of the percentages of citizens 21 and over voting in the presidential elections, 1920–44. Essentially the same picture emerges as that revealed by the map (Figure 63), but the data for a longer period assure us that 1948 variations in

[6] The figures in the text were based on census estimates of 1948 voting population.

state participation did not differ markedly from those in preceding elections. The figure also shows participation in the United States as a whole and in New York and Ohio, to furnish a contrast with that in the South. It may be noted, incidentally, that southern participation in presidential elections shows no substantial increase over the period, 1920–44. The rate fluctuates slightly in the South, generally in consonance with the ups and downs of participation in the nation but in swings of narrower amplitude at a much lower level.

Turnout rates at presidential elections, when compared with the earlier data on voting in Democratic primaries, indicate that commentators on southern politics have not committed gross libel in relying on the readily accessible data on voting in presidential elections as indicators of southern electoral interest. In particular states, however, erroneous inferences may be drawn from the presidential figures. Mississippi and South Carolina, for example, have an extremely low presidential vote, but in keeping with their tempestuous politics, they rank much higher in voting to nominate state officers.

5. Nonvoting: Extent, Causes, Significance

Our reconnaissance of the southern political terrain knocks into a cocked hat the prevalent notion that a drab uniformity characterizes the South's politics. Variety, in fact, abounds and is reflected even in the mute election statistics. Although electoral apathy in the South generally assumes colossal proportions, it differs greatly from state to state. The political activation of Louisiana by Huey Long produced an average turnout at the Democratic gubernatorial primaries about twice as high as that of Tennessee; North Carolina, with an arrangement approaching a two-party system, has a vote at its general elections sometimes higher than that in Pennsylvania, a reputedly less-benighted state; South Carolina and Mississippi, even with their huge Negro populations, have such lively political battles that their turnout rate more than doubles that of Virginia.

The percentages of *all* citizens 21 and over voting on the average in Democratic primaries to nominate Senators and governors from 1920 to 1946 are brought together (from the earlier charts) for convenience in comparison:

STATE	GOVERNOR	SENATOR
North Carolina	42.8 *	35.3 *
Louisiana	33.5	22.7
Florida	29.9	23.9
Mississippi	28.3	14.1
Texas	27.8	26.6
South Carolina	27.1	26.9

Arkansas	22.6	22.6
Tennessee	21.6 *	18.1 *
North Carolina	20.6	19.9
Alabama	19.2	13.6
Georgia	18.4	15.8
Tennessee	16.5	16.1
Virginia	11.6	
New York	56.1 *	60.0 *

* General elections.

Another general conclusion flowing from our broad analysis is that the low level of participation in southern voting can by no means be attributed entirely to Negro disfranchisement. Nonvoting by Negroes does not alone produce the low turnout percentages; in most states of the South the rate of participation by whites falls far below the rates for the total voting population in two-party states. Mississippi, Louisiana, South Carolina have average rates of white voting not far below the rates of two-party states for comparable offices, but they are exceptional. Below are shown the averages of the total vote in Democratic primaries as a percentage of the *white* population 21 and over. This procedure yields a rate that is slightly higher than the actual level of voting by whites because the total vote invariably includes some votes cast by Negroes. The consequent overestimate of white participation rates probably is greatest in North Carolina, Tennessee, and Virginia. Averages of the percentages are as follows:

STATE	GOVERNOR	SENATOR
North Carolina	58.5 *	48.4 *
Mississippi	55.6	27.6
Louisiana	52.6	35.8
South Carolina	47.3	46.2
Florida	41.9	35.7
Texas	32.9	31.5
Arkansas	30.3	30.6
Alabama	29.6	21.0
Georgia	28.4	24.5
North Carolina	28.1	27.2
Tennessee	26.8 *	22.3 *
Tennessee	20.3	20.0
Virginia	15.4	

* General elections.

Percentage figures such as those above may convey no real meaning. The record can be translated into another form that may by sheer incredibility be more comprehensible. Instead of looking at the level of voting let us attempt to estimate the number of nonvoters. Here the results depend on the standard that is used. The total number of persons who actually do not vote is an impressive figure, but a more realistic and more modest estimate of nonvoting can be obtained by calculating how many additional southerners would have to vote to bring the turnout rate up to that prevailing in nonsouthern states.

If the citizens of the South, black and white, had manifested the same interest in their 1940 Democratic gubernatorial primaries as the voters of the median nonsouthern state in the presidential election of that year, viz., a 75 per cent participation, about 8,500,000 more southerners would have voted. If the whites alone had matched the record of the voters of the median nonsouthern state, about 4,900,000 more southern whites would have voted. To meet the voting level of the median nonsouthern state, the southern voters would, of course, have had to have better turnout records than half the nonsouthern states. For the southern rate to have equaled that for the nation as a whole in the presidential election of 1940 (63 per cent), about 6,350,000 more southerners would have had to vote. For the whites alone to match the national rate, over 3,300,000 more of them would have had to go to the polls.[7] A figure of 8,500,000 nonvoters, like the amount of the national debt, does not mean much, but it takes on some reality when it is considered that this number about equaled the vote cast in the 1940 presidential election in Arizona, Colorado, Connecticut, Delaware, Idaho, Indiana, Iowa, Kansas, Maine, Maryland, Montana, Nebraska, New Mexico, Rhode Island, and South Dakota combined.

With only a cursory analysis of electoral interest in its broadest outlines, one of the significant immediate causes of the low level of voting interest in the South becomes discernible. The South, in its voting on state officials, suffers by contrast with nonsouthern states, but it is quite evident that the higher level of voting in nonsouthern states for state officials is in considerable measure a by-product of high citizen-interest in presidential elections. In states in which the presidential campaign is contested the voters come to the polls in large numbers and incidentally indicate a choice of candidates for state officers elected at the same time. In the South, the electorate is not usually stirred by a presidential campaign; the turnout at primaries for the choice of governors and Senators is fixed by the popular interest in those offices alone.

The poll tax, the white primary, and other suffrage qualifications and disqualifications undoubtedly play a part in restricting turnout in the South; another major factor is the isolation of the South from presidential campaigns. The identification of this element points to a condi-

[7] The Southern voting and nonvoting figures were based on the total vote in the Democratic primaries for governor in 1940 or 1938 if no primary was held in 1940. The choice of these years avoided the war years of abnormally low participation. For North Carolina, the total vote cast for governor in the general election was used.

tion of fundamental importance in the determination of the nature of the politics of the South. The prevailing theory among southerners is that the South can be Democratic nationally, but can fight out issues on state affairs within the Democratic party in about the some manner as two parties would contest for power. The contrary thesis can be more plausibly defended, viz., that a genuine competition for power is not likely to be maintained for state purposes unless the state is also a battleground between national parties in the presidential campaign. The Presidency is a powerful organizing influence in American politics. Interests concerned with great national issues of public policy array themselves on one side or the other of the fight for control of this office. The tremendous stakes hinging on control of the Presidency permit no party to stand idly by and see its organization go completely to pieces in any state that it must win to gain the Presidency. The party machinery in any state may be stimulated by outside help—financial and otherwise.

The play of all these outside forces aids in maintaining a two-party system in a state; they help to keep a minority alive. Outside the main streams of national politics, the southern states are not subject to the forces that drive toward the maintenance of dual political organizations, each a means for developing and nurturing political leaders, each anxious to gain control of the state government. In these isolated principalities the more or less natural tendency toward the liquidation of organized opposition and the consolidation of all the significant elements of society into a single ruling party can proceed without outside interference. The minority, weak in these states perhaps because of the homogeneity of interest of those persons of consequence in society, is weakened further by the absence of external allies. The maintenance of an organized competition for power in state affairs becomes extremely difficult, in part because of the South's inert role in presidential politics.

Yet a further consequence of isolation from national politics may be noted. The political sterilization of large numbers of people, through the effects of this isolation, profoundly influences the nature of the factional struggle within the Democratic party for control of state and local offices. In effect, low participation slices from the electorate the persons who would form the basis for a large faction or, in a two-party state, the basis for a party. By custom and by law this sort of surgery has been accomplished on the southern body politic. In some areas of the South the electorate resembles, for example, what the upstate New York electorate would be with the disfranchisement of a large proportion of those people not disposed to vote Republican. This result flows from the fact that a decline in electoral interest generally operates to a much higher degree among the less prosperous than among the more substantial elements of the community.

Low citizen-interest in voting in the South is both a cause and an effect. Absence of a presidential contest, the nature of suffrage restrictions, and Negro disfranchisement result in a low turnout of voters. The habit of nonvoting grows and the electorate by custom becomes limited. The limited electorate, in turn, influences the nature of factional politics within the Democratic party by practically eliminating from the voting population substantial blocs of citizens whose political interests and objectives, if activated, would furnish the motive power for important political movements and demands.

Of the broad political significance of nonvoting, nothing would need to be said in a democratic regime with unwavering faith in its ideology. The South is not without its antidemocratic theorists who frankly insist that the ballot should be a privilege enjoyed only by the "better" element. The simple fact is that a government founded on democratic doctrines becomes some other sort of regime when large proportions of its citizens refrain from voting. The marking of the ballot, an act by which a citizen can participate in the choice of his rulers, epitomizes and symbolizes the entire democratic process.

The moral significance of the vote in a society attached to democratic ideals can be noted and conceded; a cold-blooded determination by more or less scientific methods of the consequences of the restricted suffrage in the South presents a question of another order. The most plausible assumption is that if certain groups or classes of citizens habitually do not vote their interest will be neglected in the actions and policies of governments. The problem of analysis then becomes one of determining whether nonvoting is more prevalent among some groups of citizens than others.

Chapter Twenty-four | C O M P O S I T I O N   O F

THE SOUTHERN ELECTORATE

To make an intelligent guess about the effects of low levels of voting in the South requires an identification of those who vote and of those who do not vote. What classes or groups vote and thereby gain whatever influence in public affairs that goes with the ballot? What classes or groups do not vote and thereby may be ignored by candidates and perhaps given little recognition in the actions of government? Or, do all classes and groups perchance participate in elections to about the same degree, with the result that a low voting level simply means that those who vote constitute a miniature of the potential electorate?

Identification of those who vote and of those who do not vote can be accomplished in only the crudest fashion. The simplest method of estimating the composition of the group of citizens who vote is the sampling technique made familiar by the Gallup poll. A representative sample of the potential electorate is interviewed, their characteristics are noted, and calculations are made to show what proportion of particular classes voted. Since it was impracticable to make the Gallup-poll type of analysis of participation in southern primaries, indirect methods had to be used. Election returns are available on a county-by-county basis. Rates of voting vary enormously from county to county. From the census it is possible to determine differing characteristics of the population from county to county. By comparing county rates of electoral interest with other characteristics of county population, one may identify characteristics of the population associated with varying degrees of electoral enthusiasm. Thus, if the proportion of adults that vote increases, from county to county, with an increase in the proportion of white population, the relationship coincides with what was known all along, viz., that Negroes do not vote in substantial numbers.

By the foregoing method of analysis it is possible to make rough tests to determine whether the southern electorate behaves like voters elsewhere. Analyses of voting made in many parts of the world demonstrate a remarkable uniformity of voting behavior: almost everywhere larger proportions of men vote than of women; larger percentages of the well-to-do, than of groups lower down the economic scale; smaller proportions of the young and of the aged, than of persons in the middle years. While the evidence indicates that the same general tendencies prevail in the South, the southern electorate also possesses peculiarities growing out of its population composition, traditions, and suffrage regulations.

1. Politics Flourishes at the Forks of the Creek

In a predominantly agrarian land the rural and small-town population inevitably has a governing voice in politics. Despite rapid urbanization, the South remains predominantly rural. In 1940 only one of the eleven southern states—Florida—was more than 50 per cent urban, by the census definition. Scattered over the 11 states were 42 cities of more than 50,000 population. In 1940 three states—Arkansas, Mississippi, and South Carolina—had no city of over 100,000 population; and the entire South could boast of only 17 such cities.

Small though the city population may be, it constitutes a substantial proportion of the total potential vote in most southern states. Yet urbanites minimize their influence in state politics by maintaining a much lower degree of interest in voting than prevails in the rural, agricultural counties. City dwellers everywhere normally manifest a lower degree of electoral interest than do farm and small-town people. In the larger cities of the South a remarkably high degree of nonvoting is the rule. The spread in electoral zeal between city and country in the South far exceeds that in nonsouthern states whose voting records have been inspected. The depressing effect of urbanism on voting interest is most marked in cities of over 100,000, but levels of voting are extremely sensitive to urbanization. In some areas a county with a city of 10,000 population is almost certain to have a lower level of participation than surrounding rural counties.

The proportion of the adult population that votes in rural counties is often twice as great as that in the large cities of the South. In Table 54 are contrasted the turnout rates for counties with cities of over 100,000 population with the rates for rural counties with about the same proportion of Negro population.[1] The table also shows the voting rate for the county with the largest city of each of the three states that have no city of over 100,000.

Typically from one and one-half to twice as many rural citizens vote, proportionately, as do urbanites. The differentials, as may be seen from the table, vary from state to state. The cities of North Carolina, Tennessee, and Virginia rank well alongside their rural areas. Perhaps the relatively effective factional organizations of Tennessee and North Carolina raise their urban rates, while Virginia's turnout rate is so low that chance factors may affect the comparisons. The ratios in the table, however, should be regarded as only a suggestive comparison of rural and urban participation. In each instance choice of another rural county for comparative purposes would produce another ratio, somewhat higher or lower. Nevertheless, metropolitan counties almost invariably have a substantially lower degree of voter-interest than rural counties, other things being equal.[2]

Urban political indifference is not a matter only of statistical interest. It gives freer play to those forces that well up from the rural areas and sometimes determines the outcome of elections. The possibilities are suggested by the victory of W. Lee O'Daniel in the 1942 Texas senatorial primary, with 51.0 per cent of the total popular vote. If the state rate of participation had prevailed in the four big-city counties the total state vote would have been swollen by slightly over 100,000 or almost 10 per cent. Dallas, Fort Worth, Houston, San Antonio, and every county with any considerable city turned in majorities for former Governor James V. Allred. If voters of the four big cities alone had turned out in the same degree as those of the state as a whole, O'Daniel's lead would have been reduced to about 6,000 votes, on the assumption that additional votes would have been divided in the same way as those cast. If the city vote generally had been activated, the chances are that O'Daniel would have been retired to private life.

The explanation for the metropolitan-rural differential rests on several factors. The low voting record of the larger cities—and probably of the smaller as well—comes in large measure from nonvoting by wage

---

[1] The reason, of course, for comparison of the metropolitan county with a rural county with like proportions of Negro population is to hold constant the factor of Negro nonvoting. A rural county with relatively fewer Negroes than the metropolitan county would show a much higher rate of voting not because of its ruralism but because of its fewer nonvoting Negroes.

[2] The findings of the above analysis were confirmed by another approach, viz., a comparison of metropolitan rates of adult white participation with the same rate for the entire state. The rates for the metropolitan counties were in almost all cases lower than the state rates. The metropolitan-state differential was far wider than the same differential in selected northern states.

TABLE 54

Comparisons of Percentages of All Adults Voting in Metropolitan Counties and in Rural Counties with Similar Percentages of Negro Population [a]

METROPOLITAN COUNTY	PER CENT VOTING	RURAL COUNTY	PER CENT VOTING	RATIO OF RURAL TO URBAN RATE
Fulton (Atlanta)	14.1	Evans	32.4	2.30
Hillsborough (Tampa)	28.3	Charlotte	64.6	2.28
Bexar (San Antonio)	23.5	Franklin	53.0	2.25
Dade (Miami)	30.6	Okeechobee	67.8	2.21
Dallas (Dallas)	18.1	Tyler	38.1	2.10
Jefferson (Birmingham)	14.7	Elmore	30.0	2.04
Harris (Houston)	21.3	Chambers	43.0	2.01
Duval (Jacksonville)	31.6	Citrus	62.8	1.99
Tarrant (Fort Worth)	25.1	Calhoun	49.5	1.97
Pulaski (Little Rock) [b]	17.9	Lonoke	34.2	1.91
Orleans (New Orleans)	42.7	Caldwell	53.5	1.77
Charleston (Charleston) [b]	31.7	Hampton	55.0	1.73
Caddo (Shreveport) [b]	24.5	Plaquemines	42.4	1.73
Davidson (Nashville) [c]	14.1	Trousdale	21.8	1.55
Hinds (Jackson) [b]	18.8	Amite	28.2	1.50
Knox (Knoxville) [c]	28.2	McNairy	39.0	1.38
Mecklenburg (Charlotte) [c]	36.8	Lee	40.3	1.09
Hamilton (Chattanooga) [c]	20.9	Crockett	21.9	1.05
Richmond	10.8	Culpepper	9.3	0.86
Shelby (Memphis) [c]	24.8	Hardeman	18.9	0.76
Norfolk	9.6	King George	6.5	0.67

[a] With exceptions to be noted, the 1940 Democratic gubernatorial primary turnout as a percentage of *all* citizens 21 and over was used as a measure of voting-interest. For the states having no 1940 primary the gubernatorial primaries of the following years were used: Virginia, 1941; Alabama, 1938; Mississippi, 1939; South Carolina, 1938. In each instance a completely rural county with approximately the same proportion of Negro population as the metropolitan county was chosen for comparison.

[b] Counties containing cities of less than 100,000 population in 1940.

[c] North Carolina computations based on 1940 general election for governor. Tennessee computations based on 1940 senatorial general election. In all instances Republican strength in rural counties was about the same as in metropolitan counties; differentials in turnout, therefore, presumably could not be attributed to varying intensity of party competition.

earners. CIO unions in scattered localities report checks of their membership to determine the degree to which the workers are qualified to vote. In every instance, an astonishingly small proportion of their membership had paid the poll tax or observed other rituals necessary to qualify. It is likely that the poll tax disqualifies a larger proportion of urban than of rural voters. With scattered exceptions, the political organization and leadership of southern cities have made little headway in integrating the mass of urban dwellers into the practices of democracy. And this failure extends even into the smaller cities. The mayor of a Mississippi city of less than 5,000 souls lugubriously opined, for example, that two groups in his city showed greatest activity in politics: the wealthy citizens and the bootleggers. Men owning $20,000 homes wanted to have them assessed for taxation at $5,000, and the bootleggers had an obviously different concern.

Rural dwellers are subject to influences not felt strongly in cities. Farmers have a direct interest in such matters as local roads under the jurisdiction of the county commissioners or of other local elective authorities. They have an immediate concern with schools. Moreover, the rural citizen, especially in the smaller and more sparsely settled counties, is subject to a far higher degree of political stimulation than is the citizen of the larger city. Few southern cities have elaborately organized machines to get out the vote. On the other hand, when 30 or 40 candidates for local office take to the hustings in the smaller counties, almost every farmer is solicited for his vote by several candidates for offices from public weigher to probate judge.[3] Unlike city dwellers, rural citizens are voting for or against some person whom they know, not a name that they see in the newspapers.

2. Black-Belt Whites

In the South urbanization appears to be associated with a low level of civic participation; however, voting rates are not uniformly higher in all types of rural areas than in urban centers. In several states markedly higher proportions of whites vote in rural counties with large proportions of Negro population than in counties with comparatively few Negroes. To the extent that keen political awareness prevails among black-belt whites, it maximizes the strength of the groups most immediately concerned in the maintenance of white dominance. The hillbilly is popularly supposed to be most fearful of the black, most disposed to participate in lynching bees, most responsive to exhortations against the black man. Yet the whites of the black belt have the most pressing and most intimate concern with the maintenance of the established pattern of racial and economic relations.

[3] The smaller the county in population the more importunate and intense voter solicitation probably becomes. There is some evidence that participation increases with a decline in the number of voters within a county (when other things are equal). In some western Texas counties with less than a thousand voters, extremely high rates of participation prevail.

State rates of white electoral participation do not uniformly increase from state to state as the proportion of Negro population increases; other factors also influence levels of electoral interest. It is probably significant that the highest rates of white participation in gubernatorial primaries occur in Mississippi, Louisiana, and South Carolina, all states with high proportions of Negro population. The relation of a high percentage of Negro population to white electoral interest becomes apparent only by inspection of county voting rates.

Alabama manifests most clearly a heightened political consciousness of whites in its black-belt counties in contrast with its areas of few Negroes. Although the rate of voting does not decline uniformly from county to county with a decline in the proportion of Negro population, the highest rates of voting by whites tend to occur in counties with high percentages of Negro population. The relation between the concentration of Negro population and the concentration of counties with high white voting rates in the 1938 Democratic governor's primary is shown in the maps in Figure 65. In that primary the counties with the 17 highest white participation rates (about the first quartile of the counties) included 12 of the 17 counties with the highest percentages of black population.[4] The white participation rates in these counties ranged from one-third more than the state rate to twice that rate.[5]

The high level of political interest among black-belt whites in Alabama takes on a special significance since this region tends to support a conservative or reactionary candidate when the issues are drawn on progressive-conservative lines.[6] Whether the high level of electoral zeal of the whites in this area is attributable entirely to the presence of Negroes in large numbers is open to doubt. The whites of the black belt are better educated and better off economically than the rural whites of other regions and these differentials are usually accompanied by differentials in electoral interest.[7] Furthermore, the high level of political interest in

[4] It is unlikely that the method of computation of participation rates—dividing the total Democratic primary vote for governor by the number of whites 21 and over—exaggerated the rates for counties with large numbers of Negroes. It is in these counties, usually rural, that Negro voting is least likely to occur.

[5] The participation rates underlying the statement were: Lowndes County, 66.7; Lamar County, 41.8; the state, 30.3. The rates were based on the 1938 primary vote and 1940 population figures, a procedure which understated slightly the absolute rates of participation in 1938 but does not reduce the value of the figures for comparative purposes. Lest this primary be thought exceptional, it should be noted that in general variations in participation rates, even in small areas, show a remarkable persistence. Thus, in Alabama ten counties with high Negro population percentages placed themselves in the first quartile of counties in white participation in the primaries of 1930, 1938, and 1942. These counties were: Lowndes, Bullock, Wilcox, Clarke, Hale, Choctaw, Marengo, Greene, Sumter, and Perry.

[6] See above, chap. 3.

[7] Detailed study of the two maps will reveal the effect of other influences on voting. Thus, Dallas County is included among the first 17 counties in Negro population percentage but not among those ranking high in white voting-interest. This county has

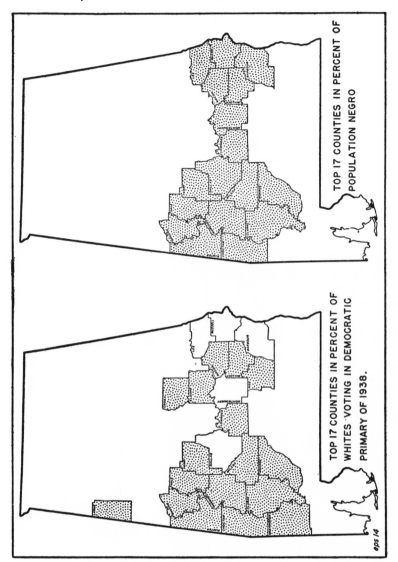

TOP 17 COUNTIES IN PERCENT OF
POPULATION NEGRO

TOP 17 COUNTIES IN PERCENT OF
WHITES VOTING IN DEMOCRATIC
PRIMARY OF 1938.

FIGURE 65

Black-Belt Electoral Zeal: Alabama Counties with 17 Highest Percentages of Negro Population
and Counties with 17 Highest Rates of Voting by Whites in 1938 Gubernatorial Primary

the black belt probably flows in part from a long tradition of cohesion and potency in state politics—a regional consciousness not so apparent in comparable areas of other states of the South.

In no other state is there so marked a variation in electoral interest of the whites of the black- and non-black-belt areas as in Alabama. Yet almost everywhere the figures suggest that when other conditions are the same the presence of a substantial Negro population brings with it a higher level of white voting. In South Carolina, for example, the rate of white participation in Democratic primaries does not increase uniformly with the proportion of Negro population, but at the extremes—counties with the lowest and the highest Negro population percentages—marked differences in electoral interest prevail. Thus, the median percentage participation of whites in counties with over 65 per cent Negro population in one gubernatorial primary was 76.2, while in counties with less than 25 per cent Negro population the median participation rate was 51.0. Relatively about 50 per cent more whites voted in the predominantly black counties than in those of lighter hue. The details appear in Table 55.

TABLE 55

Participation Rates in South Carolina Counties with Highest and Lowest Percentages of Black Population: Vote in First Gubernatorial Primary, 1938, as a Percentage of 1940 Adult White Population

COUNTIES OVER 65 PER CENT NEGRO			COUNTIES UNDER 25 PER CENT NEGRO		
COUNTY	PER CENT NEGRO	PARTICI-PATION RATE	COUNTY	PER CENT NEGRO	PARTICI-PATION RATE
Calhoun	73.1	71.2	Lexington	24.8	55.5
Allendale	72.2	89.0	Spartanburg	23.9	47.9
Clarendon	71.7	76.2	Cherokee	23.4	61.3
McCormick	67.9	80.9	Greenville	22.3	42.5 [a]
Beaufort	67.1	47.7 [b]	Oconee	15.8	36.7
Williamsburg	66.5	72.5	Pickens	13.2	54.1
Lee	65.5	91.5			
Median	67.9	76.2		22.8	51.0

[a] Greenville County contains the city of Greenville, and the factor of urbanism may account in part for the depressed participation rate in the county. No such ready explanation occurs for the eccentric rate of Oconee County which was consistently low over a series of elections.

[b] The participation rate of Beaufort, a coastal county, is lower than would be expected on the basis of comparison with other counties of high Negro populations. The low rate occurs over a series of elections. The Paris Island Marine Base is located in the county, and the Beaufort population figures may include many persons unqualified or for other reasons inactive in local politics.

within its borders Selma, a city of some 20,000 souls, and the element of urbanism depresses its vote below the level that would be expected in a rural county with a like Negro population percentage. The same influence probably depressed the vote in Montgomery County, site of the state capitol.

The black-belt counties do not uniformly vote in higher degree over the entire South, although the sample analyses presented suggest that under certain conditions the presence of large numbers of Negroes is associated with intense political consciousness. The reason for that electoral zeal may not be the Negro; the South Carolina table suggests that ruralism may be the underlying cause. Whatever the cause, the black-belt counties gain whatever influence comes from a higher degree of voting. The inflation of the political potency of black-belt whites by their high zeal for voting pales into insignificance, of course, in comparison with the ballooning of their political strength through systems of representation based on total population. In our earlier analyses it became clear that from the black belts there is most likely to come those legislators and leaders who are generally most reactionary—and most vocal about white supremacy. From the hills and from the cities there sometimes comes a more progressive sort of political leader less obsessed by the race question. The black-belt whites, because Negroes are counted in giving them representation, have their point of view blown up into dimensions that distort the views of the South through legislatures, the House of Representatives, and party machinery.

3. Negro Voters and Nonvoters

So few have been Negro voters in the South that to estimate their number seems futile. It is worth while, however, to identify the points of low resistance to Negro participation in politics: they may indicate future trends. Estimation of the quantity of Negro voting is fraught with hazard. It must be mainly impressionistic. Estimates of supposedly informed persons on the extent of Negro voting in their own communities are highly unreliable, though such sources serve adequately to identify the places where Negroes vote and generally the kinds of Negroes who vote.

While Negro nonvoting reflects the general system of race relations, its effects go beyond color. Negro disfranchisement completely excludes from the ballot a large proportion of the lower half of the southern economic structure. Negro disfranchisement has about the same effect in the South as would result in Chicago, for example, if the entire population of from five to twenty-five of that city's least prosperous wards were removed from the electorate. In 1939, about 70 per cent of southern urban Negro families received an annual income from wages and salaries of less than $1,000, as may be seen in Table 56. The remaining white electorate is by no means economically well off, yet it is largely made up of persons better off than the nonvoting Negro population. Elimination of voters on racial grounds removes worrisome problems stirred up by the agitation of economically depressed classes in political campaigns.

Quantitative estimates of Negro voting in the South are subject to a wide range of error, although certain generalizations about geographical variations in Negro voting can be made. The Negro votes least in Mississippi, South Carolina, Louisiana, and Alabama. In Arkansas he encounters obstacles to voting yet manages to vote to a greater extent than in the first group of states. Larger proportions of Negroes vote in Tennessee, Virginia, North Carolina, Texas, Georgia, and Florida. In all these states except Georgia the number of Negro voters, both in primaries and general elections, has gradually increased over a period of years without

TABLE 56

Southern Urban Families Classified According to Wage and Salary Income, 1939 [a]

FAMILY WAGE OR SALARY INCOME	PER CENT OF ALL FAMILIES	PER CENT OF NONWHITE FAMILIES
None	18.8	14.2
$1 to $999	36.4	69.3
$1,000 to $1,999	25.1	12.7
$2,000 to $2,999	10.8	1.6
$3,000 to $4,999	5.5	0.4
$5,000 and Over	1.7	0.1
Not reported	1.7	1.7
Total	100.0	100.0

[a] A condensation of tables in the 16th Census, *Population and Housing, Families General Characteristics*, pp. 47–48. The data cover only income from wages and salaries; the original tabulation includes an indication of whether income was received from other sources but no indication or distribution of the amounts. The census definition of "The South" includes the District of Columbia, West Virginia, Delaware, Maryland, and Oklahoma in addition to the 11 states covered by this study.

much commotion. Georgia's great upsurge of Negro voting in the 1946 Democratic primary aroused intense controversy.

Within all states of the South, Negro voting occurs most in the larger cities and least in the rural agricultural areas. Apparently Negroes vote least of all in those rural counties that have high proportions of black population. Further, extremely sharp differences prevail in voting among Negro classes. Teachers, tradesmen, lawyers, businessmen, doctors, landowners compose a much larger proportion of Negro voters than of the Negro population. In point of time, Negro voting has grown quite rapidly since the decision of the Supreme Court holding the white primary invalid in April, 1944. These increases, however, have been irregular over the South. In fact, the white-primary rule had never been applied with absolute uniformity, and even before the Supreme Court action a few Negroes in scattered localities regularly voted in white primaries.

Louisiana authorities compile and publish figures on the number of "colored" persons registered as voters. While not all registrants vote, these figures, which follow, indicate that the top limits on Negro voting in Louisiana are insignificant:

DATE	MALE	FEMALE
March 21, 1936	1,737	270
October 8, 1938	1,003	120
October 5, 1940	791	95
October 3, 1942	788	169
October 7, 1944	1,284	388
October 5, 1946	5,521	2,040

The adult Negro population of the state in 1940 was approximately 473,000. Of the Negroes registered, about three-fourths are usually in New Orleans and Baton Rouge. In 1944, local registrars reported that no Negroes were on the voting lists in 45 of the 64 parishes of the state, and three parishes had only one Negro registrant each. In 1946, 36 parishes reported no Negro registrants.

Florida experienced a sharp increase in Negro registration after 1944. Registration tabulations by the secretary of state showed 32,280 colored Democrats and 15,877 colored Republicans qualified to participate in the 1946 primaries. Around 13 per cent of the state's Negroes of voting age were registered. Thirty per cent or more of the total population of voting age participates in Democratic primaries. No Negroes were registered in four counties, all primarily rural counties with heavy colored populations in the northern section of the state. Less than 20 Negroes were registered in each of another eight counties.

Top limits can be placed on the numbers of Negro voters in Virginia from data on poll-tax payment by Negroes carefully compiled by Luther P. Jackson, Professor of History at Virginia State College, for the Virginia Voters League. Dr. Jackson's figures, collected from local tax officials, show that the following numbers of Negroes have met the three-year cumulative poll-tax requirement in recent years:

1941	25,411
1942	28,845
1943	32,504
1944	41,579
1945	44,051
1946	48,448
1947	57,796 [8]

[8] From annual reports on *The Voting Status of Negroes in Virginia* (Petersburg, Va.: Virginia Voters League).

Not all Negroes who pay their poll taxes register as voters. In rural areas Negroes often pay their poll taxes as one item in a tax bill, including taxes on personal and real property, without knowing that they have satisfied one of the voting requirements. Dr. Jackson estimates that a maximum of 30,000 Negroes registered in 1946 and 48,000 in 1947. He guesses that 15,000 voted in the senatorial primary of 1946. With an adult Negro population of 365,000 in 1940, a vote of 15,000 constitutes no great menace to white supremacy.

Most voting by Virginia Negroes occurs within the cities and is especially notable in contests in which there is a Negro candidate. Negro candidates for the state legislature and city council have stimulated Negro voting in recent years in Charlottesville, Danville, Lynchburg, Norfolk, Portsmouth, and Richmond. In 1947 a Negro candidate for the general assembly from Richmond finished eighth in a campaign to fill seven posts. In 1948 the same man was elected to the Richmond city council.

Outside Florida, Louisiana, and Virginia estimates of the top limits of Negro voting must be on the surmises of more- or less-informed persons. The best guesses seem to be that in North Carolina from 60,000 to 75,000 Negroes (of a 1940 adult total of 254,000) are registered as voters and that a somewhat smaller number actually votes. Negro registration and voting tend to be higher in cities than in rural counties with high percentages of colored population. Concentrations of Negro voters are found in Durham, Charlotte, Raleigh, Greensboro, and Winston-Salem.

In Alabama, estimates of the number of Negroes voting in 1946 run from 3,000 to 5,000. Of these about 1,450 were in Birmingham, 350 in Montgomery, and 700 in Mobile. The number of Negroes 21 and over in Alabama in 1940 was 521,000.

In 1946 the voting status of Georgia Negroes changed radically. In the race between Talmadge and Carmichael for the Democratic gubernatorial nomination, Negro leaders, with the encouragement of the Carmichael forces, conducted an energetic campaign to increase the registration of Negroes. The Talmadge organization, in those counties in which it could manage to do so, challenged the registration of Negroes and succeeded in purging some thousands from the rolls. Plausible estimates put the number of Negro registrants in 1946 at about 110,000 after the purge, with 85,000 or slightly more voting in the primary. The 1940 adult Negro population of the state was 580,000. If the estimates are approximately correct, Georgia in 1946 had by far the highest rate of Negro participation of the southern states. In the 1948 primary between 65,000 and 75,000 Negroes are reliably reported to have voted.

Mississippi Negroes make up half the state's population yet only an infinitesimal proportion of them votes. For years isolated individuals have voted usually in the general election and occasionally in the Democratic primary. A colored Confederate veteran of Yazoo County, who has long since departed this earth, won the right to vote in the Democratic primary by carrying a musket against the enemy. A sharp rise in Negro participation has come since 1944, but the total vote remains exceedingly small. Percy Greene, Negro leader and editor of Jackson, estimates that from 2,000 to 2,500 Negroes voted in the Democratic senatorial primary of 1946.[9] Most Negro voting takes place in Jackson, the capital and the largest city of the state, and the remainder of the colored voters are to be found chiefly in Greenville, Meridian, and Clarksdale.

Arkansas, like most southern states, has no election or registration statistics worthy of the name, and one must rely for estimates of Negro voter participation on impressions. Estimates of voting in the 1946 Democratic primaries made by Negro leaders run from 3,000 to 7,000 out of more than a quarter of million potential voters. Since that time in scattered local campaigns Negroes have participated in increased numbers. Interviews with many leading politicians reveal a marked lack of concern about the prospect of continued increase in Negro voting. In substantial areas of the state there are comparatively few Negroes, and this attitude among white politicians is not a matter for surprise. The urban Negro— Little Rock, Pine Bluff—has been most active in voting; Negro voters in the black delta counties have been few indeed. Even in these counties some white plantation potentates view the prospect without alarm. "We're going to follow the law, but I don't care if they vote or not. If they do, they'll vote the way I want 'em to. It doesn't matter to me."

The most reliable estimate places the number of Negroes voting in the 1946 Texas Democratic primary at about 75,000.[10] Texans seem to have accepted the Supreme Court's decision in the Allwright case with better grace than states of the Deep South. Negroes constitute a relatively small proportion of the population, a factor that produces a general political situation far different from that of Mississippi, for example. Consequently, with a few scattered local exceptions, Negroes voted without hindrance in the 1946 Democratic primaries.

To supplement the state-wide estimate of Negro voting in Texas, a few informed guesses on Negro participation in scattered areas may be

[9] Estimates of the number of Negro voters vary enormously. Thus, the chairman of the Washington County, Mississippi, Democratic committee stated that he did not think that more than 200 Negroes had voted in his county in the 1946 primaries. On second thought, he felt that he had better check the figure and called a couple of persons who assured him definitely that only 25 Negroes had voted in the entire county, 23 in Greenville and 2 in Leland. A few days later the mayor of Leland stated that 5 or 6 Negroes had voted in Leland. The president of the Mississippi Progressive Voters League reported that in 1946 forty Negroes voted in the Democratic primary in Oxford, "with no trouble at all—just as the white folks voted." The circuit clerk in Oxford assured us that only two Negroes presented themselves at the polls; one was not registered and the other was successfully challenged. The only moral is that most estimates of the number of Negro voters must be taken with a grain of salt.

[10] D. S. Strong, "The Rise of Negro Voting in Texas," *American Political Science Review*, 42 (1948), pp. 510–22.

cited. In San Antonio, from 4,000 to 6,000 Negroes regularly vote; their participation in municipal elections, and from time to time in Democratic primaries, extends back perhaps to 1900. In 1946, about 4,500 Negroes in Travis County (Austin) qualified to vote and about three-fourths of them actually voted in the primary, according to a careful estimate by a Negro political leader. In Harris County (Houston) between 16,000 and 18,000 Negroes voted in the 1946 primary, as estimated by R. R. Grovey, Negro political leader and president of the Third Ward Civic Club.[11] In Dallas the secretary of the local chapter of the Progressive Voters League estimated that from 4,000 to 5,000 Negroes participated in the 1946 Democratic primaries. The consequences of the 1944 white-primary decision are illustrated by the report of an election judge of Fort Worth that 113 Negroes voted in his precinct in 1946, whereas no more than five had ever voted in the precinct before.

Negroes in urban centers of Texas, as elsewhere in the South, both encounter less serious obstacles in voting and manifest keener interest in politics than do rural Negroes. A Texas Negro leader explains that this difference stems in part from the fact that urban Negroes are organized into lodges, fraternal, and social organizations to a greater extent and are therefore easily reached for political purposes. The rural Negro, on the other hand, lives in greater isolation. Further, there is the practical fact that, in Texas at least, the superiority of police protection in cities makes Negro political activity more practicable than in the country. Within the cities, according to a white Waco politician, chiefly school teachers and the "smarter Negroes in general" are the ones who vote.

Electoral participation of Tennessee Negroes follows the usual southern pattern: higher degrees of voting in the cities than in the rural areas. In the two or three rural counties in southwest Tennessee in which Negroes form a large proportion of the population they approach the ballot box with the same infrequency and the same hesitancy as in Mississippi and Louisiana. In Memphis, the blacks, like the whites, have been voted as the Crump organization saw fit. In Nashville, Negroes vote relatively freely.

Negroes have encountered stubborn opposition to even a gradual admission to Democratic primaries in South Carolina. The last vestige of the white primary was stricken down by court action in that state in 1948.[12] Prior to that time virtually no Negroes voted in the primaries. About 35,000 are reported to have cast ballots in the 1948 primary.[13]

---

[11] Mr. Grovey was the appellant in *Grovey v. Townsend*, one of the earlier Supreme Court decisions on the white primary.

[12] See below, pp. 628–32.

[13] Two recent estimates of the number of Negroes qualified to vote are available. The NAACP (in its *Bulletin*, November 1946) made such estimates for 1946 and Luther P. Jackson made similar estimates for 1947 ("Race and Suffrage in the South Since 1940," *New South*, June–July, 1948). The Jackson estimates are probably more

4. Political Tension, Voter Turnout, and Composition of the Electorate

Analyses of voters generally show that the composition of the voting population changes with its size. Under American conditions at least, large increases in voter participation tend to be associated with much larger increases in participation by the lower half economically. The low levels of voting in the South, therefore, lay the basis for an assumption that the lower half is represented in unusually low degree in the voting population. In part, the small size of the southern electorate (and its distorted composition) flows from the fact that the issues of one-party politics do not impress those classes of the citizenry from which an increased turnout would come as matters of importance. A general rule of politics is that the closer the vote between two candidates is expected to be, the greater the turnout will be. Observation of southern politics suggests that the theory needs to be amended to take into account the fact that unless potential voters feel deeply about the issues, they will display a vast indifference no matter how close a race is predicted. It is practically impossible under the one-party system to formulate issues and to maintain political organization that will activate the electorate to the extent that a two-party system does.

The extraordinary Louisiana voting record demonstrates the effect on voter-interest of issues that touch people deeply. During the rule of the Long machine, voting by whites in Louisiana reached a peak unmatched in the recent history of any other southern state. The Kingfish aroused bitter opposition, and conflict stirs interest. In other southern states campaigns often become heated without affecting appreciably the level of voter-interest. Something more than intense conflict influenced the Louisiana voting record, shown in Figure 66. Huey Long's program benefited voters previously untouched and unconcerned by governmental

---

reliable. The two sets of figures follow with a computation of the proportion of the adult Negro population qualified to vote according to the Jackson estimate:

	1946 NAACP NUMBER	1947 JACKSON NUMBER	PER CENT
Alabama	10,000	6,000	1.2
Arkansas	16,000	47,000	17.3
Florida	50,000	49,000	15.4
Georgia	150,000	125,000	18.8
Louisiana	7,000	10,000	2.6
Mississippi	5,000	5,000	0.9
North Carolina	75,000	75,000	15.2
South Carolina	5,000	50,000	13.0
Tennessee	55,000	80,000	25.8
Texas	200,000	100,000	18.5
Virginia	50,000	48,000	13.2

services. Outsiders proclaimed him a dictator and a buffoon, but within Louisiana his works were not all sound and fury. His concrete achievements in governmental action, as well as the hopes and aspirations he stimulated, aroused the long-dormant political consciousness of great numbers of people. The peak of political interest came in 1936, with the battle to determine whether the Long machine would outlive its founder. Factors other than the birth of an aroused public spirit, of course, boosted electoral participation. Long's critics would have us believe that election fraud swelled the vote; perhaps it did, but the number of voters of a state

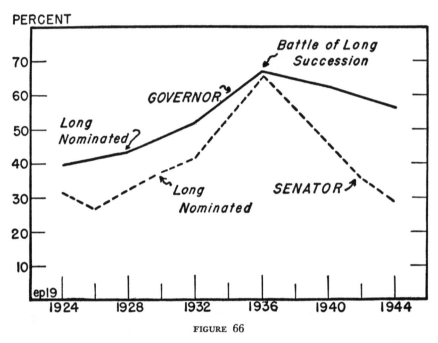

FIGURE 66

Long and the Louisiana Voter Turnout: Percentage of Whites 21 and over Voting in Louisiana Gubernatorial and Senatorial Primaries, 1924–44

is not doubled or tripled by fraud. Although the repeal of the poll tax in 1934 helped bring more voters out to the polls, the extraordinary increase in the number of voters must be attributed chiefly to the issues, leadership, and organization that Long introduced.

The moral of Louisiana may be that when leaders raise issues that concern the mass of people, the turnout will rise. On the other hand, leaders perhaps refrain from raising issues because the mass of people does not vote. The spirit of North Carolina politics differs from that of Louisiana, yet North Carolina provides another instance of the relation between competition and voter-turnout. The progressive tendencies of the North Carolina Democracy is not unconnected with the Republican threat; the Republican-Democratic competition in turn stimulates a high turnout in the general elections and probably gives the North Carolina electorate a composition unlike that of a state with a lower degree of political participation. Electoral turnout in North Carolina general elections tends to increase from county to county as the strength of the Republican candidate increases. In the 1940 general election, for example, less than 30 per cent of the adult population voted in the 32 counties that gave the Republican candidate for governor less than 10 per cent of the total vote. Where the race was closer, the participation rate jumped sharply. Of the 16 counties with a Republican strength of from 40 to 59.9 per cent, all but one had rates in excess of 50 per cent, and 13 of them exceeded 60 per cent. The detailed information is presented in Table 57.[14]

TABLE 57

Relation between Republican Percentage of Vote for Governor in North Carolina Counties in 1940 General Election and Percentage of Adult Population Voting

COUNTIES WITH PARTICIPATION PERCENTAGES OF—	NUMBER OF COUNTIES WITH REPUBLICAN PERCENTAGES OF—							
	0–9.9	10–19.9	20–29.9	30–39.9	40–49.9	50–59.9	60–69.9	70–79.9
80.0–89.9				1	1			
70.0–79.9					4	2		
60.0–69.9			1	7	5	1		
50.0–59.9			4	6	2		1ᵃ	1ᵃ
40.0–49.9		5	4	3		1ᵇ		
30.0–39.9	16	8	4					
20.0–29.9	16	6	1ᶜ					

ᵃ These counties, Mitchell and Avery, were so heavily Republican that the turnout presumably was reduced in the same way that the certainty of the outcome in sure Democratic counties brought a low turnout.

ᵇ Sampson County, a county with 34 per cent Negro population and a comparatively heavy Republican vote. Negro nonvoting probably resulted in a lower participation rate by the total adult population than would be anticipated on the basis of the closeness of the vote. Substantial Republican strength is extremely unusual in counties with 34 per cent Negro population. The atypical voting behavior of Sampson County, which also reveals itself in other types of analysis, is locally explained by the fact that the county was the home of the great Populist leader, Marion Butler. Elected to the United States Senate as a Populist in 1895, he affiliated with the Republican party after the demise of the Populists and carried with him a substantial vote in his home county. In scattered counties over the South a better-than-average Republican vote persists to this day as a historical residue of the decision of local groups of Populists to turn Republican rather than go back to the Democratic fold.

ᶜ Halifax County, another county with a comparatively high Republican vote and a high percentage of nonvoting Negroes and, therefore, a low rate of participation for the county as a whole.

High electoral turnouts can occur when there is no contest. Witness the extraordinary level of electoral participation in the plebiscites of the

[14] To some extent the correlation in the table is spurious in that Negroes, chiefly nonvoters, are concentrated in counties heavily Democratic. Participation rates based on total adults produce a low rate. Separate analysis of counties with less than 20 per cent Negro population showed also that for these counties participation rates tended to rise with Republican percentages to the point where Republican predominance resulted in electoral indifference.

dictatorships. Yet under American conditions high levels of participation occur when the issues run deeply enough or when massive party machines labor assiduously to bring out the electorate. Broad shifts in voting levels are almost invariably associated with significant changes in the composition of the active electorate. The tremendous decline in voting levels in the South since the days of the Populist battles with the Democrats in the 1890's has paralleled a repression of issues. When a Huey Long comes on the scene with both a program and a propaganda to appeal to the lower half of the population a boost in electoral interest occurs. And as the level of voting interest rises under such a stimulus the class composition or the distribution of the active electorate among classes is altered. And, if the class composition of the electorate is altered, the nature of the candidates, campaign issues, and ultimately of government itself, will change.

5. Voting Differentials and Their Consequences

The influence of levels of citizen-interest on the nature of the politics of an area is by no means a spectacular phenomenon. Low levels of popular participation rather constitute a conditioning influence that over the years makes itself felt in unobtrusive ways. The effect may be regarded as somewhat like that of the gorge that guides a raging stream, an ever-present and controlling but immobile influence. The size and composition of the South's voting population determine the matrix within which the struggle for political power is carried on. The character of the voting population possesses more significance that its size. A small body of active citizens almost invariably results in a working electorate that is a caricature of the potential electorate, but the particular distortions in the active electorate of the South have peculiar significance.

The methods feasible in this survey yield only an unsatisfactory answer to the question of what classes of citizens vote in higher degree than others. Yet certain characteristics of the southern voting population emerge plainly from the analysis. They include the following:

City dwellers—that is, persons living in cities of 25,000 and over— vote in lesser degree than do rural citizens. Depressed electoral participation becomes quite marked in most southern cities of over 100,- 000. Rural electoral interest exceeds that of urbanites elsewhere, but southern city people lag farther behind the state average than do city dwellers in the North.

In most states, most notably Alabama, a high proportion of Negro population in rural counties is closely associated with a high level of participation in Democratic primaries by whites. More refined methods of statistical analysis would probably show a more widespread relation between Negro population concentrations and white electoral interest than is revealed by the relatively crude methods of measurement used here.

Few southern Negroes vote, a fact that required no investigation to establish. They vote in higher degree in cities than in rural areas; they probably voted in Georgia in 1946 in higher degree than at any time in the South in this century; over a longer period North Carolina Negroes have exercised the suffrage in higher degree than in other southern states. Over the entire South a marked upturn in Negro voting has taken place since 1944. In general, voting by the better-educated and economically more important Negroes is markedly higher than among other classes of blacks.

Differentials in electoral interest along economic lines, perhaps the most important type of distortion of the potential electorate, are identified in our analysis only by inference. The southern electorate is probably no exception to the general rule that electoral participation increases from group to group up the economic ladder. The most telling evidence on this point is that widespread Negro nonvoting means that this economically depressed group is virtually removed from the electorate of which it constitutes from one-seventh to one-half. Even if all whites voted, the active electorate would consist mostly of persons better off than the nonvoting Negro population. Low electoral interest in the larger cities undoubtedly reflects in large measure a low level of electoral participation among urban workers. High participation by whites in the black belt, where it occurs, probably reflects in part the fact that these whites are relatively better off than whites in areas predominantly white.[15]

Such are the facts, or at least the approximate facts, about group differences in voting and nonvoting. What is their significance, if any? The blunt truth is that politicians and officials are under no compulsion to pay much heed to classes and groups of citizens that do not vote. One needs only to mention the status of the Negro. In those limited areas in which the Negro votes as a matter of course politicians demonstrate a profoundly different attitude toward him than in areas where the race issue is bitter, and where voting, if it occurs at all, takes place in an atmosphere of conflict. A group of voters does not have to be a majority

---

[15] A line on the relation between economic status and electoral participation could have been obtained, it might be supposed, by comparison of county voting percentages with per-capita indices of economic status. No satisfactory index of economic status of whites is available. In most economic indices, for example, the per-capita status of the population of black-belt counties is extremely low. The average is depressed by the status of Negroes. A fairly high degree of negative correlation prevails in Alabama between the number of white pupils per teacher in the public schools and the percentage of whites voting. That is, from county to county the white turnout rate declines as the number of pupils per teacher increases. If the teacher-pupil ratio is a satisfactory index of white economic well-being, the relationship could be taken as an indicator of increase in electoral interest with increase in economic status.

to command deference; a few votes may deflect the course of a political career, a fact of which the politician is keenly aware.[16]

The singular governmental neglect of the Negro can be matched by parallels among white groups. It seems evident that poorer rural whites vote in low degree, at least in most states of the South. Their elementary legal rights—the rights of agricultural tenants, for example—are weak indeed. Contrast the status of the southern white tenant and sharecropper with that of the northern industrial worker who is unquestionably more active politically. While the status of the lower third of the South's agricultural population cannot be traced entirely, of course, to political inactivity, electoral inertness is a contributory factor.

Public policy relative to southern industrial labor likewise is partially explained by the political abdication of a larger proportion of southern wage earners than of other classes. The psychology of the political situation reveals itself in a statement by Horace Edwards, former state Democratic chairman and holder of various elective offices in Virginia. He spoke about a study that showed that 2 per cent of Richmond street railway workers and 78 per cent of city employees voted. "Mr. Edwards said," the press reported, "he did not understand until he made the study why, when he was running for office, he didn't get up at 6 a.m. and go to the car barns to speak as he did to address city workers at the city stables." [17] The stout defense by southern Congressmen of child labor, in an earlier day, and, more recently, of regional wage differentials with southern workers on the short end, illustrates the indifference of southern politicians toward their nonvoting laboring constituents. Groups other than Negroes, workers, and farm tenants gain from their more active role and greater power in political affairs. Obviously, whites govern and win for themselves the benefits of discriminatory public policy.[18] Among classes of whites, it would be fairly accurate to conclude that public policy discriminates in favor of the most prosperous, rural landowners.

[16] Amusing instances occur in which white politicians, in deference to the dominant sentiment, make sonorous public statements in support of white supremacy and simultaneously attempt to assure the Negro, by way of the grapevine, that they are really his friends.

[17] Richmond *News Leader*, May 15, 1945.

[18] Moreover, discrimination in favor of whites tends to increase roughly as Negroes are more completely excluded from the suffrage. The following figures for 1930, showing the per cent that instructional expenditures per Negro pupil enrolled in public schools was of the per-capita white pupil expenditure, illustrate the point: Mississippi, 15.7; South Carolina, 17.7; Louisiana, 24.1; Georgia, 26.5; Alabama, 30.3; Florida, 30.5; Texas, 41.3; North Carolina, 44.2; Virginia, 44.4; Arkansas, 45.8; Tennessee, 51.8; Maryland, 68.6; Kentucky, 98.6. Furthermore, within the South the tendency was for per-capita Negro pupil expenditure to increase from county to county as the percentage of Negro population declined. Negro voting is most restricted where Negroes constitute the highest percentage of the local population. The data on expenditure are from Charles S. Johnson and others, *Statistical Atlas of Southern Counties* (Chapel Hill: University of North Carolina Press, 1941).

PART | FIVE

Restrictions on Voting

THE one-party system and the absence of contest for southern electoral votes do not account entirely for low levels of electoral interest in the South. A circular relation of cause and effect exists in which these factors bring about electoral disinterest, which, in turn, contributes to the maintenance of the one-party system. Voting is further depressed by constitutional and statutory limitations on the suffrage, anachronisms in a modern democracy. Designed originally to circumvent the Federal constitutional rule on Negro voting, their main significance now is the disfranchisement of whites.

The present suffrage regulations originated chiefly in the period from 1890 to 1908, although experimentation in disfranchisement occurred earlier. The south-wide movement for revision of its constitutional rules on the suffrage coincided with radical agrarian stirrings and thus generated the theory that suffrage limitation was deliberately calculated to disfranchise the poor white as well as the Negro. Regardless of whether the Bourbons—as the conservatives of the time were called—conspired to clip the political wings of the back-country farmer, examination of events surrounding the adoption of limitations on voting can aid in a comprehension of the southern suffrage system.

The disfranchisement movement developed a variety of ingenious contrivances to inconvenience the would-be voter. The analysis that follows aims to determine, insofar as practicable, the significance of these voting limitations. The grand purpose of suffrage limitation and of the one-party system is, of course, to maintain an interracial equilibrium consistent with the dominant ideology of the South. It is erroneous, however, to speak of "The South" in this context; the southern suffrage system represents rather the success of black-belt whites in rallying the entire South to aid them in maintaining supremacy in those parts of the South where the Negro is concentrated. Fundamentally the doctrine of white supremacy, as embodied in suffrage rules, came about in the same manner as secession: a comparatively small minority of whites succeeded in winning the support of the majority.

Southern interracial equilibrium rests not alone on success in amalgamating white groups, some of which are essentially indifferent about the fate of whites in black counties. It depends also on success in parrying the demands of a national constitutional system hostile to traditional southern arrangements. Southern concern over Negro voting may serve only a symbolic function; if the whole business were forgotten, the consequences might not be so grave as advocates of white supremacy predict. Nevertheless, many whites believe that the southern political order would be overturned by free suffrage for the Negro. Hence, by outlawing the white primary in 1944 the Supreme Court precipitated a veritable constitutional crisis.

Chapter Twenty-five	# SOUTHERN SUFFRAGE RESTRICTIONS: BOURBON COUP D'ETAT?

Persons impatient with the South's political health today may be equally impatient with an inquiry into the circumstances surrounding the adoption of suffrage restrictions half a century ago. They want reform here and now; yet recommendations for action are wrong unless based on a correct diagnosis of the effect of suffrage limitations. And one way to make that diagnosis is to go back to the beginning.

The evolution of suffrage restrictions differed from state to state, and for some, perhaps even for all, southern states the thesis could be argued plausibly that formal disfranchisement measures did not lie at the bottom of the decimation of the southern electorate. They, rather, recorded a fait accompli brought about, or destined to be brought about, by more fundamental political processes.

The case of Texas serves as an instructive introduction to the history of disfranchisement. In that state, which limited itself to the comparatively mild device of the poll tax, all the effects usually attributed to it were felt before the tax itself came into force: the Negro had been persuaded to stay away from the polls; the Populist specter had been laid; and the actual electorate had been whittled down to less than half its former size.

The relevant political history of Texas is compressed into graph form in Figure 67, which will bear reflective inspection. The graph shows the percentage of the potential voters that came to the polls at each gubernatorial election from 1880 to 1944. Voting zeal of Texans reached an all-time peak in 1896. The bitterness of the Bryan-McKinley struggle attracted many voters to the polls. The Populist candidate for governor in that year polled the highest vote of any candidate in the party's history, 44.2 per cent of the total.

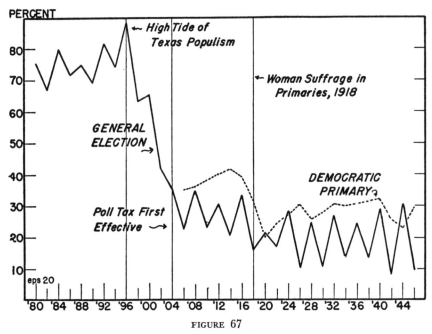

FIGURE 67

Nonvoting Came Before the Poll Tax: Percentage of Potential Texas Electorate Voting for Governor in General Elections and Democratic Primaries, 1880–1946

The sharp drop in Texas electoral participation immediately following the 1896 campaign requires careful observation in the interpretation of the consequences of suffrage restrictions. In that campaign the Democratic presidential candidate appropriated the Populist policies, and over the nation the agrarian movement rapidly lost strength. In Texas the disillusionment of the Populists and their desertion by many of their leaders were accompanied by a drop in electoral interest. The race question, of course, had no bearing on the subsidence of Populism nationally, but in Texas the Populists and Democrats had bid for Negro votes. The fear, fancied or real, that the Negroes would gain and hold the balance of power if the whites continued to divide among themselves was played upon. The slogan of white supremacy aided in closing the ranks of the whites, and the burning issues, fought with religious fervor by the Populist leaders, disappeared from campaigns. The turnout at the 1902 election was less than half that of the peak of 1896. The drop occurred *before* the effect of the poll tax was felt; that tax, adopted by constitutional amendment in 1902, first influenced an election turnout in 1904.[1]

By the time the Texas poll tax became effective not only had Negroes been disfranchised but a substantial proportion of the white population had begun to stay away from the polls. Party conflict had been repressed; Populists leaders had almost completely given up the battle. Conservative Democratic forces and whites of the black-belt counties had joined forces to kill off dissent. Should the poll tax be held responsible for low levels of voting interest consistently maintained since 1904? Apparently the poll tax merely reflected a fait accompli; opposition had been discouraged and suppressed. The solidification of economic power, characteristic of the one-party system, had been accomplished and the electoral abdication of a substantial part of the white population signed and sealed.

In other southern states the process toward monopolization of political control by a small proportion of the white population did not precisely parallel the Texas pattern; nevertheless Texas experience points to the necessity of discriminating interpretation of disfranchisement systems in their bearing on citizen-interest in elections.[2]

1. Legalization of Fait Accompli: Disfranchisement Within the Limits of the Fifteenth Amendment, 1890–1908

Oddly enough those who urge an institutional change to enable them to gain power usually first win virtual control without benefit of the procedural or organizational advantage they seek. Law often merely records not what is to be but what is, and ensures that what is will continue to be. Before their formal disfranchisement Negroes had, in most states, ceased to be of much political significance and the whites had won control of state governments. If disfranchisement merely anchored in power those already in control, the crucial issue in the interpretation of the disfranchisement movement lies in the identification of the groups pushing it, for by no means were all whites united on the issue. To lay the ground work for such an analysis requires a record of the chronology of Negro disfranchisement.[3]

Triumph of Radical Republicans in Congress over the moderates

[1] The total vote in the general election of 1896, 539,000, was not reached again until the Democratic primary of 1918 when 678,491 votes were polled. At that primary woman suffrage—for the primaries—became effective and the state also had a heated gubernatorial campaign.

[2] For instance, voter-turnout in Georgia reached a peak of 221,750, in the gubernatorial race of 1894, a level not again equaled, it appears from available figures, until the Democratic primary of 1920 despite a steady population growth.

[3] The exclusion of the Negro from general elections preceded and underlay his exclusion from the Democratic primaries in the later period of unchallenged one-party dominance. For treatment of the white primary, see below, chap. 29.

led to Negro enfranchisement under the Reconstruction Act of 1867. That act, in effect, made the establishment of southern state governments conditional upon the formation of new constitutions by delegates elected by male citizens "of whatever race, color or previous condition." During Reconstruction Negroes were organized, led, and exploited by Radical Republican politicians who had facilities for electoral agitation in the Freedmen's Bureau, the Union League, and other types of official and semi-official agencies. A few white leaders annexed most of the Negro votes to the Republican party. In the 'seventies whites regained control of the state governments. The withdrawal of Federal troops knocked the props from under the Radical Republicans, but the fatal blow to the Negro-white combination ruling the South was struck by whites organized to capture control by force, if necessary. Presently, most Negroes realized that it was wiser not to attempt to vote. Moreover, their inclination to vote weakened when their white leaders found it safer to reside outside the South.

As whites regained control of the states in the 'seventies a first stage in disfranchisement got into motion. Legislators contrived devious electoral procedures to nullify the efforts of blacks who still had the inclination to vote.[4] In addition, in all southern states during the 'seventies and 'eighties mild and unexceptionable electoral qualifications and procedural requirements were adopted to discourage Negro voting.[5] Virginia, for example, in its legislative session of 1875–76 made petit larceny a disqualification for voting.[6] All these disfranchising measures, of course, contributed nothing to the power of the whites. Force and threat of force had put the whites in power. Within 10 or 15 years after 1867 the premature enfranchisement of the Negro was largely undone, and undone by veritable revolution.[7]

In almost every state from time to time white factions competed for the remaining Negro vote. They rarely used fair methods of political competition: bribery and coercion served at times as instruments to enlist Negro support for one white faction; intimidation and fraud, as means by which one white faction might offset Negro support of the other.

In most states intense competition between white factions for Negro votes preceded the second stage of disfranchisement, viz., the contrivance

---

[4] W. A. Dunning, "The Undoing of Reconstruction," *Atlantic Monthly*, 88 (1901), pp. 437–49.

[5] For a running summary of actions in the various states, see S. B. Weeks, "The History of Negro Suffrage in the South," *Political Science Quarterly*, 9 (1894), pp. 671–703.

[6] At a Negro convention in Richmond in 1875 a delegate remarked, "It is hard that a poor Negro cannot take a few chickens without losing his right to vote."

[7] The revolution interpretation is that of S. S. Calhoon, President of the Mississippi Constitutional Convention of 1890, "The Causes and Events that Led to the Calling of the Constitutional Convention of 1890," *Publications of the Mississippi Historical Society*, VI (1902), pp. 104–10.

after 1890 of methods of disfranchisement compatible with the Fifteenth Amendment of the Federal Constitution. Circumvention of that amendment demanded ingenious legal sophistry; it reads as follows:

> Section 1. The right of citizens of the United States to vote shall not be denied or abridged by the United States or by any State on account of race, color, or previous condition of servitude.
>
> Section 2. The Congress shall have power to enforce this article by appropriate legislation.

Mississippi, South Carolina, and Louisiana invented the principal techniques for voiding the Constitution by constitutional means, although not all states adopted such drastic limitations as these three. In 1890 Negroes made up more than 50 per cent of the population of each of these states. Mississippi's constitutional convention of 1890 first contrived ways to disfranchise the Negro without formal violation of the Fifteenth Amendment. The convention, however, moved with trepidation; it was breaking new ground. The possibility remained of Federal intervention to protect the Negro; the month before the convention gathered the national House of Representatives had passed Senator Lodge's "force bill" to provide Federal supervision of congressional elections. The convention's action had to bear all the earmarks of constitutionality. Moreover, it had to disfranchise Negroes and at the same time leave a loophole for all whites to vote. The counties with few Negroes had been reluctant to concur in the calling of a convention that might, by some such qualification as the educational test, take the ballot from many whites.

The solutions evolved by the Mississippi convention, which were widely imitated, can be summarized as follows:

> *Residence.* A residence requirement of two years in the state and one year in the election district or in the incorporated city or town. The lengthy residence requirement was expected to bear more heavily on Negroes because of their supposedly peripatetic habits.
>
> *Poll tax.* A cumulative poll tax as a prerequisite for voting. The rate was fixed at $2 per year for state purposes, and county authorities could levy up to $1 additional. Persons offering to vote were required to produce satisfactory evidence that they had paid "all taxes" legally required of them "for the two preceding years." The poll tax in itself was calculated to discourage Negro voting; the requirement that evidence of payment be presented to election officials presumably discriminated by reason of the absence among Negroes of a predilection for the preservation of records.
>
> *Literacy and the alternative of "understanding."* The crowning achievement of the convention was the "understanding" clause. The new constitution required that every elector shall "be able to read any section of the Constitution of this State; or he shall be able to understand the same when read to him, or give a reasonable interpretation thereof." By this clause the fears of illiterate whites were

to be quieted. If a white man could not read, he could certainly "understand" or give a "reasonable interpretation" of a section of the constitution to a white registration official, whereas it was not expected that sophistication on constitutional matters would be general among Negroes.

Registration. Registration four months before an election was made a necessary qualification to vote.

Disqualification. Conviction for certain crimes operated as a disqualification. They were: bribery, burglary, theft, arson, obtaining money or goods under false pretenses, perjury, forgery, embezzlement or bigamy. The list was not so long as that adopted in other states, and this method undoubtedly occupied a relatively insignificant place in the calculations of the constitution framers.

All the suffrage provisions of the Mississippi constitution were phrased to exclude from the franchise not Negroes, as such, but persons with certain characteristics most of whom would be Negroes. A Mississippian, writing in 1902, explained, presumably with a straight face, how the convention kept within the limitations of the Fifteenth Amendment:

> Every provision in the Mississippi Constitution applies equally, and without any discrimination whatever, to both the white and the negro races. Any assumption, therefore, that the purpose of the framers of the Constitution was ulterior, and dishonest, is gratuitous and cannot be sustained.[8]

In 1895 a South Carolina constitutional convention promulgated a constitution whose suffrage provisions resembled in most respects those of Mississippi. The principal South Carolina contribution to the technique of disfranchisement was the contrivance of additional alternatives to literacy by which whites might qualify to vote. A person unable to read and write a section of the constitution might qualify by showing that he owned and had paid taxes during the previous year on property assessed at $300 or more. The new Louisiana constitution, put into effect without popular vote in 1898, was notable for the "grandfather clause," a device that had been rejected in South Carolina because of doubts about its constitutionality. The clause was not, of course, in itself a method of Negro disfranchisement. It was an exception to the literacy test which could be taken advantage of only by illiterate whites. The Louisiana clause provided that

> no male person who was on January 1st, 1867, or at any date prior thereto, entitled to vote under the Constitution or statutes of any State of the United States, wherein he then resided, and no son or grandson of any such person not less than twenty-one years of age at the date of the adoption of this Constitution, . . . shall be denied the right to register and vote in this State by reason of his failure to possess the educational or property qualifications. . . .

[8] Frank Johnston, "Suffrage and Reconstruction in Mississippi," *Publications of the Mississippi Historical Society,* VI (1902), p. 228.

The right to register under the clause was temporary; it had to be exercised prior to September 1, 1898.

The Mississippi, South Carolina, and Louisiana constitutions contained the basic techniques that were incorporated in various combinations in other state constitutions.[9] In 1900 North Carolina established an educational qualification for all save those who could register under the grandfather clause. The usual poll-tax and extended-residence qualifications were added. In 1901 Alabama adopted a new constitution framed primarily with a view to disfranchising the Negro. Virginia followed in 1902. Georgia, which had long had a poll tax, in 1908 adopted a constitutional amendment prescribing a literacy test. In general, suffrage qualifications were most stringent in those states with the largest percentages of Negro population. States with fewest Negroes limited themselves, insofar as formal legal action was concerned, to the poll tax. These states, with the dates of action, were: Florida (1889), Tennessee (1890), Arkansas (1893), and Texas (1902).

Outside the formal modes of disfranchisement an extralegal method developed that was to prove more effective than the formal ones. This was the "white primary." As the Democratic party succeeded in liquidating Republican and Populist opposition it became possible by private party action—presumed not to be in violation of the Fifteenth Amendment since it was not state action—to limit participation in the Democratic primary to whites.

2. Forces in the Drive for Disfranchisement

Why, after white supremacy had been generally re-established, did southern states set to work to effect legally what had already been accomplished more or less outside the law? It was suggested earlier that the explanation might be found by the identification of forces driving for disfranchisement. While those elements and their avowed motives differed from state to state, several common features characterized the agitation in all states.

Most interpretations of disfranchisement movements give great weight to the American constitutional mores that place a high value on legality and regularity in government. Illegal, irregular, and informal practices, according to this argument, produced painful conflicts with inherited notions of propriety in government. The efficacy of the inner urge toward constitutionality can be debated, but undoubtedly pressures external to the South re-enforced whatever compulsion toward legality

[9] This is the conclusion of York Willbern, *The Adoption of Legal and Constitutional Devices for the Disfranchisement of the Negro in the South, 1870–1910* (M. A. Thesis, University of Texas, 1938).

that existed. The House of Representatives, in seating Representatives from southern districts frequently examined the legality of elections. From 1874 to 1900, for example, in 16 of the 20 Virginia elections contested before the House, fraud was the basis for contest.[10] Furthermore, fear of Federal intervention to police elections remained. In 1889 President Harrison advocated such a measure in his message to Congress and the House passed the Lodge "force bill," around which centered a bitter debate that "served only to stir up past memories and to increase the solidarity of the South against the aggressiveness of Northern Republicans."[11]

Politicians, newspaper editors, and other leaders of opinion emphasized the demoralizing effects upon the whites of the methods used to disfranchise Negroes. Numerous practices, none of them quite cricket, were employed to dissuade the black man from voting and to nullify his ballot when he did vote. Gerrymandering, trickery in election administration, fraud in casting and counting ballots were tactics that pricked sensitive consciences. Moreover, these methods could be, and were, used against whites as well as blacks.

Although protestations of revulsion against corrupt electoral practices were frequent, the principal drive for Negro disfranchisement in most states came from those areas in which Negroes constituted a majority of the population. Negro disfranchisement was not a question of "the South" disfranchising "the Negro." The problem of interracial conflict for power occurred in its most acute form in connection with local government and legislative representation in those counties and cities with black majorities, which areas were by no means the entire South.

The whites in the black counties occupied a most insecure position. It is the custom to speak of the Negro question as a minority problem. In these counties the whites were the minority. Nor could the whites gain a balance-of-power position between competing Negro factions, for the blacks did not split politically. In racial solidarity they clung to their savior, the Republican party. Under these circumstances in black localities, "With universal negro suffrage, the logical alternatives were between negro government on the one hand and illegal election contrivances on the other."[12]

The whites in the black counties had to win support of the white counties. Only by that means could the Negro be disfranchised to the end that white supremacy could be assured in local governments of the black counties. In a sense the managers of the disfranchisement agitation

[10] R. C. McDanel, *The Virginia Constitutional Convention of 1901–1902* (Baltimore: Johns Hopkins Press, 1928), p. 11.

[11] R. L. Morton, *The Negro in Virginia Politics, 1865–1902* (Charlottesville: University of Virginia Press, 1918), p. 130.

[12] Johnston, "Suffrage and Reconstruction in Mississippi," p. 205.

were up against the same problem as that of the ante-bellum slaveowners. Nonslaveholding whites had no burning zeal for the South's peculiar institution; the slaveholding minority, territorially segregated in a small part of the South, had sufficient political skill to rally southerners generally to their cause. Similarly, in the disfranchising movement the generating force came fundamentally from whites in the predominantly black counties, and one of their chief motives was the preservation of white control of local government. To assure this end, like the slaveocracy, they had to rally to their cause the white counties less immediately concerned about white supremacy.

After 1876, as an interim arrangement, the traditional practices of local self-government were radically subverted in many states to assure white control in black counties. Instead of electing county and city officials, several states vested their appointment in the governor. With white control of the governorship assured, it could confidently be expected that whites would be appointed to local offices.

Of great practical significance in some states in setting off the movement for disfranchisement was the fact that in the agrarian movement informal restraints on Negro participation in politics had weakened. The Farmers Alliance and the Populist party generated a dispute among whites whose outcome was of such deep concern that both factions breached the consensus to keep the black from the polls. Both Democrats and Populists were willing to bid for Negro support. According to southern tradition Negroes were in a position to hold the balance of power between white factions. The degree to which Negroes actually voted *en bloc* and participated in the elections of the agrarian uprising has never been adequately investigated, and the difficulties of finding the facts would be formidable. Nevertheless, the Populists, either alone or in combination with Republicans, threatened Democratic supremacy, and a situation emerged in which the plea for white supremacy could be made effectively. The pattern of events varied. In some states, the disfranchising constitutions came immediately on the heels of "agrarian trouble"; in others, as in Texas, the Populist specter had been laid before suffrage limitations became effective.

The sequence of events in which disfranchisement usually followed divisions among the whites has spawned the legend that the whites, seeing the error of their ways, united to take the vote from the Negro lest he enjoy forever a pivotal position in southern affairs. In later days a contrary interpretation has been advanced, viz., that the conservative or, as they were known at the time, Bourbon Democrats, took the lead in disfranchisement, with the intent of depriving many agrarian radicals of the vote along with the Negro. An inkling of the validity of these conflicting hypotheses can be obtained from the record of agrarian revolt and disfranchisement.

3. A Scheme to Disfranchise Whites Too?

A fact not often recalled is that southern whites were bitter in division rather than united on the disfranchisement question. In all the states—even in Mississippi—formal disfranchisement of the Negro was opposed. While other factors entered, always a major objection was that by whatever means the Negro was disfranchised a goodly number of whites would also be kept from the polls. And those whites who would be most affected were the poorer whites and those resident in Republican areas (which areas in most states were also the principal centers of Populist strength).

In the state legislatures proposals to call a convention, or to submit the question of calling a convention to a popular vote, invariably had to overcome substantial opposition. In Alabama a bill to submit such a question to the people was passed by the house but defeated by the senate in the session of 1896–97. "The bitterest and most determined opposition came from those senators representing the predominantly white counties. They feared the disfranchisement of their poor white constituents." [13] The press joined in the debate, and, in the hyperbole of the day, the Tuscaloosa *American* expressed anxieties about disfranchisement:

> Past history teaches us that the rule of the so called "virtuous and intelligent," the rule of the rich and the favored ones of the earth has ever been of the most tyrannical and despotic character. Under such rule but two classes exist, the master and the slave, but two kinds of homes, the splendid palace and the miserable hovel. True manhood's ambition is crushed out of the toiling masses while the rich revel in vice and splendor. This is no fancy picture. A constitutional convention insures the disfranchisement of the great masses of the toiling people.[14]

Once the advocates of suffrage restriction hurdled the legislative obstacle, they carried the popular vote only against strong opposition in most states. The popular votes on the question are set out in Table 58 for these states that submitted the issue for determination by the people. Only in Louisiana were more than 61 per cent of the voters in favor of calling a convention and this vote was at a special election in 1898, an element of tactics probably helpful to the proponents.[15] Two years earlier, however, the Louisiana electorate had rejected disfranchising amendments. The figures in the table indicate the strength of opposition to the convocation of constitutional bodies to limit the suffrage. In the

[13] M. C. McMillan, *A History of the Alabama Constitution of 1901* (M. A. Thesis, University of Alabama, 1940), p. 61.

[14] July 28, 1898. Quoted by McMillan, *Alabama Constitution*, pp. 67–68.

[15] The special election in January, 1898, attracted to the polls only 44,748 voters; 101,127 votes expressed choices on presidential candidates the preceding November.

main, the opposition was not moved by zeal for the right of the Negro to vote; the nay ballots voiced a fear that the dispossessed white man was also about to be disfranchised.

Whether the proponents of disfranchisement plotted to sterilize politically the lowly agrarian whose vagaries had caused the mighty to quaver in their seats of power presents a question difficult of proof or disproof. Their avowed purpose was to disfranchise the Negro. The annals of conventions and legislatures abound with candid declarations of the intent to accomplish an end forbidden by the Constitution of the United States—denial of suffrage on account of color. Few open expressions of intent to disfranchise the troublesome Populists (along with a goodly number of white Republicans) are to be found in the official

TABLE 58

Popular Votes on Calling Constitutional Conventions to Deal Primarily with the Question of Negro Franchise

STATE	YEAR OF VOTE	FOR CONVENTION	AGAINST CONVENTION	PER CENT FOR
Alabama	1901	70,305	45,505	60.7
Louisiana	1898	36,170	7,578	82.7
South Carolina	1894	31,402	29,523	51.5
Virginia	1897	38,326	83,453	31.5
Virginia	1900	77,362	60,375	56.2

proceedings and debates of the conventions.[16] Yet, remarks by contemporaries suggest that this objective was by no means absent from the minds of convention leaders.[17]

From the debate of the time it is plain that considerable numbers of whites were expected to be disfranchised and that this expectation was

[16] Mr. McIlvaine, a delegate to the Virginia convention, observed: "The need is universal, not only in the country, but in the cities and towns; not only among the blacks, but among the whites, in order to deliver the state from the burden of illiteracy and poverty and crime, which rests on it as a deadening pall. . . . It is not the negro vote which works the harm, for the negroes are generally Republicans, but it is the depraved and incompetent men of our race, who have nothing at stake in government, and who are used by designing politicians to accomplish their purposes, irrespective of the welfare of the community."—*Proceedings and Debates of Constitutional Convention of Virginia*, 1901–02, p. 2998.

[17] Francis G. Caffey, a lawyer who was practicing in Montgomery at the time of the Alabama convention, stated in 1905: "How to get rid of the venal and ignorant among white men as voters was a far more serious and difficult problem than how to get rid of the undesirable among the negroes as voters. While it was generally wished by leaders in Alabama to disfranchise many unworthy white men, as a practical matter it was impossible to go further than was done and secure any relief at all. . . . To rid the state eventually, so far as could possibly be done by law, of the corrupt and ignorant among its electorate, white as well as black, the poll tax and vagrancy clauses were put into the Constitution."—"Suffrage Limitations at the South," *Political Science Quarterly*, 20 (1905), pp. 56–57.

voiced most loudly by those whites—both leaders of opinion and rank and file voters—who had cast their lot with the Republicans and Populists. Contrariwise, it is not a dubious inference that Bourbon Democratic leaders had the same expectations without regret but said little about them publicly. In the divisions among whites on the disfranchisement issue a remarkable similarity prevailed over most of the South; with few exceptions, from state to state the same groups were found in support of disfranchisement and the same groups in opposition.

In Alabama the battle over the adoption of the constitution of 1901 arrayed on opposite sides the predominantly white counties and the black-belt counties. Only 52.7 per cent of those voting favored ratification of the constitution. The proportion of the vote for the constitution increased roughly from county to county as the Negro proportion of the population increased. The 10 counties with the highest percentages in favor of the constitution and the 10 counties with the lowest are listed in Table 59. All 10 high counties, save one, had more than 50 per cent Negro population; eight of them were 75 per cent or more Negro. In most of them Reuben Kolb, the 1892 Populist gubernatorial candidate made a poor showing. On the other hand, the 10 counties with the lowest percentage in favor had a low percentage of Negro population and most of them had been hotbeds of Populism in the early 'nineties. Territorially the pros centered in a belt across the south center of the state, with the antis in northern and southeastern Alabama,[18] a pattern of sectionalism that reappears even now when state politics organizes itself around a class issue.

In North Carolina disfranchisement by constitutional amendment followed a brief period of control of the state by a Republican-Populist coalition. In contrast with several other states, this Republican-Populist fusion received the support of the bulk of voting Negroes. To regain power the Democrats appropriated Populist doctrines, rekindled the embers of race prejudice, and supplemented these weapons with fraud and intimidation. During the campaign of 1898, in which Democrats recaptured the legislature, some Populist leaders foresaw a necessity of Negro disfranchisement to deprive the Democrats of a powerful weapon of propaganda.[19] Following their triumph the Democrats submitted a dis-

---

[18] The opposition areas had also been coolest in their enthusiasm for secession. See C. P. Denman, *The Secession Movement in Alabama* (Montgomery: Alabama State Department of Archives and History, 1933) and Lewy Dorman, *Party Politics in Alabama from 1850 through 1860* (Montgomery: Alabama State Department of Archives and History, 1935). See also above, chap. 3.

[19] One such person, in a letter to Marion Butler, Populist Senator, concluded: "The Negro, as I hold, is a factor in our politics, and has been under Democratic rule, and I firmly believe was kept so by Democrats for the sole purpose of demoralizing and corrupting them and to use as a bugbear to scare white ignorant men, thereby solidifying them into the perpetuation of Democratic machine rule. I believe the time has come to force the white man idea in such a way as to compel the Democrats, should they be

TABLE 59

Counties with Highest and Lowest Percentages of Popular Vote for
Adoption of Alabama Constitution of 1901; Relation to Negro Percentage of Population and to Populist Vote for Governor in 1892

	PER CENT FOR ADOPTION OF CONSTITUTION OF 1901	PER CENT NEGRO IN 1900	PER CENT FOR KOLB, POPULIST, 1892	PER CENT FOR CALLING CONSTITUTIONAL CONVENTION
10 High Counties				
Hale	98.0	81.7	35.5	97.2
Perry	97.3	78.5	29.3	98.2
Dallas	97.2	83.0	13.3	96.6
Wilcox	96.3	80.4	12.1	98.5
Sumter	94.6	82.7	43.0	95.4
Greene	91.4	86.3	32.3	98.7
Chambers	89.3	53.5	55.7	86.5
Marengo	85.1	76.9	40.4	90.1
Limestone	79.3 ª	43.9	75.0	53.5
Macon	75.0	81.6	63.7	55.4
Median	93.0	81.0	37.95	96.0
10 Low Counties				
Franklin	29.8	13.1	59.6	32.2
Clay	28.6	11.0	55.4	42.3
Marion	26.7	5.4	39.2	45.5
Cherokee	26.1	14.3	64.5	22.3
Cullman	23.6	0.1	56.8	27.1
Shelby	20.4	29.6	51.4	37.4
St. Clair	19.8	17.7	68.9	25.4
Chilton	19.1	19.8	71.2	22.6
Jackson	18.0	11.9	41.6	43.5
Marshall	15.3	6.4	62.2	21.9
Median	22.0	12.5	58.2	29.6
The State	52.7	45.2	47.5	60.7

ª This figure looks odd in view of the county's earlier vote on the calling of
the convention, the high Populist vote, and the comparatively low Negro population percentage. This county in ante-bellum days had much larger Negro
population and had many great plantations. Mr. Erle Pettus, a delegate to the
constitutional convention from Limestone county, explained the deviation to
us as the result of an energetic campaign in support of ratification conducted
by himself and another delegate.

franchising amendment to be voted on in 1900. The Populist executive
committee opposed the amendment and predicted that it would "dis-

successful in securing the legislature, to disfranchise the Negro."—W. A. Mabry, *The
Negro in North Carolina Politics Since Reconstruction* (Durham: Duke University Press,
1940), p. 51.

franchise approximately as many white men" as Negroes. The Republicans likewise opposed it.

In their campaign for the amendment the Democrats had to overcome opposition based on the expectation that the literacy test and poll tax would disfranchise the poor and illiterate whites. To offset this opposition proponents of the amendment included a proviso that illiterates could register for their lifetime before December 1, 1908. In the effectuation of the poll tax, however, there would be no delay. Spokesmen of the black-belt counties and Democratic leaders exerted themselves to persuade enough voters in the white counties that the peril of the white in the black belt should be regarded sympathetically by the people of the western uplands and of the eastern coastal fringe where the Negro did not flourish.

Advocates of the amendment were able to muster only 58.6 per cent of the popular vote. The map in Figure 68 shows the counties that returned majorities against the amendment and those that produced a bare majority in its support. No county with more than 50 per cent Negro population had a majority against the amendment; and, on the contrary, no county with a majority against the amendment had as much as 50 per cent Negro population. Most of the counties with opposition majorities were predominantly white counties in the western half of the state, the mountain strongholds of peasant Republicanism and Populism.

In Virginia the chronology of disfranchisement and the cleavage on the issue resembled the situations in Alabama and North Carolina. In the 1900 vote on calling a convention,[20] 52 counties returned majorities against and 48 favored the convention as did all of the 18 independent cities. All save seven of the 32 counties west of the Blue Ridge voted against the convention. Its support was strongest in those counties with the highest proportions of Negroes. In the western and southwestern areas of opposition white Republicans were numerous and Negroes were few. Only in the "counties where the negro was found to constitute a menace to white control or an excuse for election fraud was there a real desire to disfranchise him legally." [21]

The split in the vote on the convention closely paralleled the cleavages that prevailed during the Readjuster movement, Virginia's forerunner of Populism. The Readjuster party had been "essentially the party of the poor man." [22] It urged adjustment of the public debt and when in power in the early 'eighties adopted a "multitude" of measures tending "to subserve the interests of the masses and to break the power

---

[20] After considerable controversy the convention decided not to submit the new constitution for popular ratification but to put it into effect by promulgation.

[21] McDanel, *Virginia Constitutional Convention*, p. 18.

[22] Ibid., pp. 6–7.

of wealth and established privilege." [23] Its chief source of strength was the poorer agricultural areas where Negroes were fewest, in the south and southwest, but it also won in the eastern counties where Negroes under Republican leadership could vote.

In Louisiana disfranchisement quickly followed conflict among

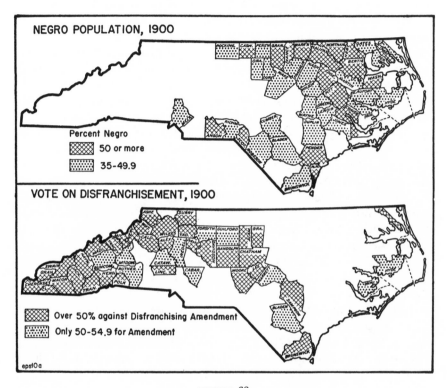

FIGURE 68

The Black Belt and Disfranchisement: Relation between Distribution of Negro Population and of Popular Vote for North Carolina Disfranchising Amendment, 1900

whites that resembled the general pattern of agrarian disturbance. [24] Republicans and Populists fused in 1896 and competed for the Negro vote in the April gubernatorial election. The Democrats won the governorship, but disfranchising amendments sponsored by them failed of adoption. The great Populist stronghold was in "the hill parishes of north-

[23] C. C. Pearson, *The Readjuster Movement in Virginia* (New Haven: Yale University Press, 1917), p. 146.

[24] It was not entirely by coincidence that Winn parish, which nurtured the Louisiana Populist movement, was also the birthplace in 1893 of a boy who was later to create some disturbance in Louisiana politics. His name was Huey Long.

western Louisiana, peopled mainly by small white farmers. . . . Populism never gained much of a foothold in the cotton parishes of the delta, or in the sugar parishes; and it was never strong in the cities." [25] Two years later a call for a convention was approved at a special election.

In most southern states the leadership of the disfranchisement movement came from the conservative Democratic faction, and the center of its strength, at least outside the towns and cities, was in black-belt counties. In South Carolina and Georgia, however, the radical wing of the party sparked the movement. The Populists, as Populists, got nowhere politically in South Carolina; rather, the agrarians, under the leadership of Pitchfork Ben Tillman, captured the Democratic party. Tillman, the moving spirit in disfranchisement, feared that his conservative opponents would use the Negro vote against him. His nomination for governor by the Democrats in 1890 aroused dissatisfaction in the conservative element of the party and A. C. Haskell, a lawyer and bank president, bolted to run against him as an independent. Haskell "appealed to the Negroes for their support and promised them 'fair play.' " [26]

In 1894 Tillman, as king-maker, campaigned for a candidate for governor and also for approval of a proposed constitutional convention to deal with Negro suffrage. Some conservatives threatened not to accept the verdict of the Democratic convention and to carry the fight against the Tillman candidate into the general election, a strategy that would inevitably lead to an appeal for the Negro vote. Tillman warned: "If these people want to warm this black snake into life, . . . we are ready to meet them and give them the worst drubbing they have ever had in their lives."

In the campaign on the convention referendum, white leaders, restive under Tillman domination, organized Negro opposition; Tillman charged "an unholy alliance between the independents and the negroes." Not only Negroes opposed the convention; upcountry whites, who gave Tillman his most steadfast support, could not readily see how the Negro could be disfranchised without simultaneously taking the ballot from many whites. The convention project involved, it was charged, a conspiracy to disfranchise "thousands of honest but poor and uneducated Anglo-Saxon voters." Opponents of the convention nearly carried the day; they mustered 48.45 per cent of the votes.[27]

The Georgia disfranchisement amendment, like the South Carolina constitution, came into existence under radical auspices. Its adoption

[25] M. J. White, "Populism in Louisiana during the Nineties," *Mississippi Valley Historical Review*, 5 (1918), p. 15.

[26] W. A. Mabry, "Ben Tillman Disfranchised the Negro," *South Atlantic Quarterly*, 37 (1938), pp. 170–83.

[27] Based on the account by Francis Butler Simkins, *Pitchfork Ben Tillman* (Baton Rouge: Louisiana State University Press, 1944), pp. 278–82.

was preceded by a long period of political turbulence perhaps unexcelled in any other southern state. In the 'seventies the Independent Democrats, from their strongholds in the hills of North Georgia, threatened the hegemony of the black-belt planters, the brigadiers, and the new industrialists and financiers. Vanquished in the late 'seventies as Independents, the untrammeled yeomanry rose again in another incarnation, the Farmers' Alliance, in the late 'eighties and, at least in their own territory, ousted the guardians of the status quo. In the counties chiefly Negro the conservatives held their ground.[28]

The Populists, in the 'nineties, represented only another episode of the antecedent ebb and flow of radicalism and conservatism. The groups in opposition followed patterns already familiar from their occurrence in other states. The Populists won relatively few adherents in the towns and cities; in the rural area their strength was concentrated in counties having the lowest proportions of Negroes, with the exception of the territory in the vicinity of the home of Tom Watson, the great Populist leader.[29]

In the conservative-radical battles in Georgia, the specter of a black balance of power was invariably raised and, with about the same invariability, the conservative Democrats garnered or neutralized the Negro vote. In 1880, in the Bourbon-Independent battle, the "bulk of the colored vote seems to have been brought by various means to the support of the straight Democracy." [30] In 1892 Republican leaders "were unable to swing the negro vote en masse" to the Populist candidates.[31]

Tom Watson, at this time, fought for a reconciliation between white and black. He argued that "the accident of color can make no difference in the interests of farmers, croppers, and laborers." [32] Yet his conservative Democratic opponents in his own district committed colossal frauds against him through their control of the colored vote. Probably over the entire South, as in Georgia, the Negro, by economic status and interest, was drawn toward the radical movements that preached equity for the downtrodden and the dispossessed. Yet almost everywhere that conservative Democrats controlled election machinery they seemed to be able to enlist the Negro vote, through superior organization and resources, or to counteract it, through election irregularities.

Populism subsided and a more placid politics ruled until the 1906 campaign when Hoke Smith, an anticorporation and antirailroad leader,

[28] A. M. Arnett, *The Populist Movement in Georgia* (New York: Columbia University Press, 1922), p. 129.

[29] Ibid., p. 184.

[30] Ibid., p. 43.

[31] Ibid., p. 153.

[32] Quoted by C. Vann Woodward, *Tom Watson: Agrarian Rebel* (New York: Macmillan, 1938), p. 221.

sought the Democratic nomination for governor on a platform that also demanded Negro disfranchisement. Smith feared that "the conservatives would not abide by the result of the primary, but would carry the fight into the general election and try to win with the aid of the Negro vote." [33] The amendment was approved by 66.5 per cent of the popular vote in 1908.

Enough cases have been examined to indicate that in the adoption of the disfranchising arrangements southerners were not of one mind. In part, the dispute on the issue arose from technical obstacles to the invention of a constitutional test that would disfranchise Negroes without at the same time affecting whites. Literacy tests, fairly applied, would disfranchise a larger proportion of blacks than of whites, but it was not expected that they would be applied fairly to blacks, and tests that could be applied in a spirit of discrimination against blacks could also be used to disfranchise whites.[34]

It would be a mistake, however, to presume that opposition to disfranchisement came solely or even primarily from the illiterate. In view of the large popular vote against amendments and constitutions, it is certain that a great many highly literate, even solvent, persons opposed the contraction of the electorate. Opposition was rooted deeper. It was strongest from those areas in which slaves had been few, enthusiasm for The War had been coolest, relatively few Negroes resided, the rich were least numerous, and white Republicans were respectable.

It is reasonable to assert that the battle for suffrage contraction was not solely a question of the Negro's position. Although the Bourbon Democrats of the black belt were usually in the vanguard and probably expected a degree of disfranchisement of the poor whites, the exceptions of South Carolina and Georgia make it difficult to defend a general theory of conspiracy to disfranchise the lesser whites. Perhaps the sounder generalization is that the groups on top at the moment, whatever their political orientation, feared that their opponents might recruit Negro support. Tillman presumably thought that his constitution would disfranchise relatively few whites, a small price for protection against the voting of the blacks by his Charleston enemies. In Georgia the radical Democrats feared that the conservatives would appeal to the Negroes for support in the general election. The progressives had special reason for disfranchising Negroes; the Bourbon element usually had the longer purse to meet the cost of the purchaseable vote.

[33] W. R. Smith, "Negro Suffrage in the South," *Studies in Southern History and Politics* (New York: Columbia University Press, 1914), p. 244.

[34] Of the native white males of native parentage of voting age, the percentage illiterate in 1900 ranged from 5.3 per cent in Texas to 20.3 per cent in Louisiana. For colored males of voting age the illiteracy percentage ranged from 39.4 in Florida to 61.3 in Louisiana. The 1900 census defined illiterate persons as those "who can neither read nor write, or who can read but not write."

4. Developments beyond the Constitution and Laws

Suffrage limitations alone do not account for southern disinterest in voting. If that conclusion is correct, one must go beyond the theory that these limitations resulted from a conspiracy to disfranchise whites as well as blacks to explain the sharp decline in white voting that followed the adoption of constitutional limitations. The one-party system (or perhaps the absence of the two-party system) contributes in large degree to the low electoral interest in the South. Its development paralleled the evolution of suffrage limitations, whose adoption, in a sense, marked the demise of tendencies toward the re-establishment of a two-party system.

A lively two-party competition prevailed in the South before The War. The Whigs, the party of the larger planters and the urban mercantile and financial interests, opposed the Democrats, who, in the Jeffersonian and Jacksonian tradition, drew their major support from the small farmer and the back-country areas.[35] Regions of rich soil, large plantations, large slaveholders were Whig strongholds. When The War approached, party lines became blurred as southerners aligned themselves on opposite sides of the secession issue. Yet at the final showdown on secession, splits within the southern states tended to parallel earlier party divisions. In every state the people of the hills, those who had few slaves, and those who had been little blessed in the distribution of this world's goods, manifested restrained enthusiasm for secession.

The explanation of both suffrage restrictions and the one-party system must come from a valid theory of why the pre-Civil War bipartisanism did not succeed in re-establishing itself after The War. That failure came fundamentally from the operation of two forces: first, social discipline tending to bind a large proportion of the whites, especially the whites of substance and property, to the Democratic party; second, measures and actions calculated to repress those opposed to the dominant, "respectable" coalition.

These forces operated approximately from 1870 to 1900. During this era in every southern state the cleavage between big planter and small farmer emerged from time to time only finally to be defeated by the combined forces of discipline and repression, which made themselves felt in at least two phases, not always sharply separated chronologically, but clearly distinguishable in substance. The first stage included the period of Reconstruction and the restoration of white and southern supremacy that immediately followed; the second phase included the agrarian revolt, which reached its climax in most states in the 'nineties yet smoldered both earlier and later.

[35] See A. C. Cole, *The Whig Party in the South* (Washington, 1913).

Reconstruction and the restoration of home rule in the South generated powerful social forces that brought into the Democratic party most southerners of substance and reduced the Republican party to virtual impotence. Social discipline almost invariably tightens when external danger threatens. The people of an occupied land bury their differences and join forces to repel the alien. The occupier, unless he is to restore the ancien regime, must discriminate against all those who once held positions of prestige, against those of talent, against those of technical, professional, and managerial ability. Thus it was in the South; Radical Republican rule, a regime dependent fundamentally on military support, made Democrats of almost everyone of consequence.

As local control of state governments was re-established, discipline had its counterpart in repression and coercion of opposition. Fraud and intimidation in elections weakened the Republicans, who symbolized the potentiality of Federal intervention. Republicanism and Negro rule became synonymous; racial antipathies and hostility toward the outsider were compounded in hatred of Republicans. An opposition party cannot flourish without leaders; most potential Republican leaders had been drawn into the Democratic party. Those who dared to oppose the dominant cluster of interests met social ostracism, economic coercion, electoral chicanery. Few could withstand the scorn attached to the epithets "scalawag," "carpetbagger," "nigger lover," "Republican."

In the long period of economic deflation following The War the farmer—and especially the small back-country farmer—bore the brunt of economic readjustment. In consequence the latent political cleavages implicit in the southern economy began to find expression in unorthodox political movements and candidacies. Though generally on a small scale, these early eruptions foreshadowed the nature of the coming Populist upsurge of the 'nineties. The "independency" movement in Georgia in the 'seventies formed a pattern that came to be reproduced in almost every southern state. Revolt against Georgia's ruling coalition of black-belt planters, brigadiers, and railroad promoters first appeared in the northern part of the state.

> A region of small farmers, for the most part isolated and primitive, and always strongly opposed to any "ruling class," it offered fertile soil for the spread of opposition to the town politicians. The percentage of negroes was too small for appeals to the necessity of white solidarity to carry the same force as in other parts of the state. Outside a few of the larger towns such as Athens and Rome, social conditions and standards were too crude for the masses to place much value upon that type of respectability to which unfailing support of the regular Democracy was elsewhere regarded as essential . . . most of them had formerly opposed secession . . .[36]

[36] Arnett, *Populist Movement*, pp. 33–34.

As agrarian discontent spread, and the Farmers' Alliance and the Populist movement took hold in other states, the pattern of contention took a similar form. And with the long continuance of agricultural deflation economic deprivation affected once-richer persons who came to ally themselves with those farmers, and workers as well, who had always been poor. The Populist heresies were met by a coalition of the more prosperous black-belt whites and townspeople. The ante-bellum conflict of yeoman and planter could scarcely be resumed in its old form. A new ingredient had been added: the planter found new allies in the growing industrial and financial classes. In Georgia, the coalition had unusually high visibility since several men made themselves prominent both in Democratic politics and in railroad promotion.

The Populist episode brought into play new social sanctions to reenforce the taboo against insurgency inherited from Reconstruction. To maintain an opposition party based on the dispossessed is a difficult political feat; it can be kept alive only if it has enough men of economic independence and substance to provide a continuing leadership. The story is not well documented, yet it is apparent from scattered evidence that the Bourbon Democrats, to liquidate the opposition, must have applied with savagery all the social and economic sanctions available. The "better," the "respectable" classes were threatened, and no fastidious regard for legality or morality checked the use of any measure that would contribute to their defense. "There is record," says Woodward, "of Populists' being turned out of church, driven from their homes, and refused credit because of their beliefs. . . . A Southern Populist leader told a Western writer, 'The feeling of the Democracy against us is one of murderous hate. I have been shot at many times. Grand juries will not indict our assailants. Courts give us no protection.'" [37] Not only were Populist leaders subjected to these pressures. In Augusta, Georgia, for example, the " 'Job-lash' was used . . . to force mill employees, white and black, to vote 'regular.' Some who refused to heed the warning were discharged." [38] All the techniques of private economic coercion and intimidation came into play to weaken the rebel ranks—armies that are by their nature poorly disciplined.

In some states at least, and perhaps in all, the formal limitation of the suffrage was the roof rather than the foundation of a system of political power erected by a skillful combination of black-belt whites, financial and trade interests, and upper-class citizens of the predominantly white counties. First, the resentment against Radical Reconstruction bound most whites together and provided a powerful taboo against political insurgency. Added to this was the organization of white attitudes against blacks; and, finally, the system of social discipline was re-enforced by

[37] *Tom Watson: Agrarian Rebel* (New York: Macmillan, 1938), p. 223.
[38] Ibid., p. 154.

invocation of the power of property and of status against the challenge of discontent.

Undoubtedly the cumulative effects of these parallel sanctions contributed mightily to the creation of the one-party system. Moreover, their effects live on. It is impossible to speculate on the nature of political behavior without attributing to events long past their profound influence in the establishment of current habits of action. Yet the piling up of compulsions toward conformity within the South happened to be fortuitously supplemented by events on the national political scene. The nomination of Bryan, in 1896, and the Democratic theft of Populist principles, left the southern Populists high and dry. Their alternative was to return to the Democratic party, which was controlled locally by their natural political antagonists, or to join the Republican party, also controlled by their natural political antagonists, northern business and finance. The return of the Populists to the Democratic fold and the inability of the Republican party to build a southern wing threw all political debate into the Democratic party. One-party politics, re-enforced by suffrage limitations, cannot arouse the electoral interest that accompanies two-party politics.

Chapter Twenty-six | **THE LITERACY TEST:**
FORM AND REALITY

Tʜᴇ disfranchisement movement of the 'nineties gave the southern states the most impressive systems of obstacles between the voter and the ballot box known to the democratic world. Yet these suffrage limitations have been more impressive in theory than in practice. The fundamental bases of Negro disfranchisement have been informal rather than legal. Nonvoting has constituted but one element in a system of race relations maintained by a variety of informal sanctions, illegal and extralegal.

The southern system of suffrage qualifications has included several principal components. The literacy test and allied requirements have provided legal means of accomplishing illegal discrimination. The poll tax has served as an additional element of the system in some states; in others, it has been the only unusual suffrage requirement. Until its nullification by the Supreme Court in 1944, the white primary was a more important component of the system than formal limitations on the right to vote. Negroes were excluded as Negroes from the party primary; they could be legally excluded from the general election only by indirection. Invalidation of the white primary, therefore, brought again into prominence the literacy test and other methods of disfranchisement by indirection.

Since their adoption literacy tests have undergone alteration in de-

555

tail. That evolution need not be traced, but the present status of these requirements needs to be outlined. Literacy tests may be radically different in their application from their form. A report of impressions of the administration of literacy tests will incidentally provide opportunity to indicate the nature of procedures for the registration of voters. Reserved for later treatment are the poll tax and the white primary.

1. Literacy Requirements and Their Alternatives

Drafters of southern suffrage requirements set out to establish standards that would admit whites to the electorate but would exclude Negroes without mentioning race or color. At the time of the disfranchisement movement illiteracy was much more prevalent among blacks than whites; hence, the literacy test seemed an obvious method of discrimination between the races in fact but not in form. Yet to fulfill their promises to disfranchise no whites, constitution drafters had to contrive alternatives to the literacy requirement that would take care of the illiterate white. The "grandfather clause" was one such loophole, but it was only a temporary expedient.[1] The Mississippi convention invented the "understanding clause" as an alternative to the literacy test. A person who could not "read" any section of the constitution might qualify as an elector if he could "understand" and give a "reasonable interpretation" thereof when it was read to him. The assumption was that registrars would find that illiterate whites had the capacity to "understand" and "interpret" the constitution.

In addition, to the "understanding" alternative to literacy, a few states provided other alternatives. Georgia authorized registration of illiterates "of good character" who could show that they understood "the duties and obligations of citizenship under a republican form of government." The same state adopted a property-owning requirement as another alternative to literacy. A person owning 40 acres of land on which he resided or property in the state assessed for taxation at $500 or more might qualify although unable to meet the literacy test. Alabama, until

[1] The grandfather clauses about which some misconceptions prevail deserve only brief mention. Their effect was to permit certain classes of individuals, defined so as to exclude Negroes, to register permanently within a specified period without the necessity of meeting literacy or other tests. The individuals who might claim the right to register under these clauses differed from state to state. The 1898 Louisiana clause permitted the registration of males who were entitled to vote in any state on January 1, 1867, or prior thereto, the sons and grandsons of such persons, and male persons of foreign birth naturalized before January 1, 1898. Applicants for registration were required to have five years' residence in the state. The clause spread to several other states, but was finally held unconstitutional in 1915 in litigation arising in Oklahoma. By this time the period had expired in which permanent registration could be accomplished under the grandfather clauses. Apart from its bearing on the Oklahoma constitution, the principal effect of the court decision was to prevent revival of the clause.

1946, permitted those to register who owned 40 acres of land on which they resided, or real estate or personal property in the state assessed for taxation at $300 or more. The Louisiana constitution of 1898 contained a similar provision.

The trend since the adoption of the disfranchising constitutions has been toward the elimination of alternatives to literacy.[2] Thus, the "understanding" alternative remains in its original form only in Mississippi. Georgia retains a "good character" alternative. The property-owning alternative has disappeared in Louisiana and Alabama. In states with property alternatives Negroes have found it easier to register under this provision than to meet the literacy test; an application for registration based on property ownership cannot be so easily denied as can an application under a literacy clause. The spread of property ownership among Negroes enabled more of them to qualify under the property alternative, which in 1948 existed only in Georgia and South Carolina.[3]

Alabama, Georgia, Louisiana, Mississippi, North Carolina, South Carolina, and Virginia have a literacy requirement in one form or another.[4] The nature of the current requirements and their alternatives, if any, are presented in Table 60, except those of Alabama and Louisiana, which do not readily lend themselves to tabular treatment.

The tendency to tighten the literacy requirement by eliminating understanding and property-owning alternatives has been paralleled by the establishment of requirements supplemental to literacy. With the gradual reduction of illiteracy among Negroes, the requirement of literacy, if fairly administered, would not exclude nearly so large a proportion of persons of color as in 1900. In Louisiana and Alabama literacy has not been thought enough. Additional tests, readily susceptible of discriminatory application, have had to be met by the applicant for registration.

[2] The statement of constitutional and statutory suffrage requirements in this chapter analyzes the situation as of January 1, 1949. It seemed probable that 1949 legislatures would make statutory changes and propose constitutional amendments, not all of which could be taken note of by proof changes.

[3] Several states, including Georgia and Mississippi, have had requirements that in order to vote persons should have paid all taxes assessed against them. These suffrage standards were not a requirement that a person be a taxpayer to vote but that he should have paid taxes levied against him. The great depression killed off these requirements; many leading citizens, temporarily in straitened circumstances, were delinquent in paying their taxes. Property ownership, however, remains a requirement for voting in local referenda on bond issues and related questions in several southern states.

[4] Whether the South Carolina test has ever been of significance in application to whites is doubtful. Before the recent repeal of its laws relating to primaries, South Carolina legislation empowered political parties to prescribe "requirements and safeguards" for the conduct of primaries except that no party should enact "rules or regulations based upon an educational or property qualification as a requisite for voting in a primary. . . ."—*South Carolina Civil Code, 1932*, Title 24, sec. 2369. After the repeal of all South Carolina statutes governing the primary, the party rules were amended to provide that enrollment in Democratic clubs should be conditioned, among other things, on ability "to read and write and interpret the Constitution of the State of South Carolina."

TABLE 60

TABLE 60

Literacy Tests for Registration and Alternatives [a]

STATE	TEST OF LITERACY	UNDERSTANDING ALTERNATIVE	PROPERTY ALTERNATIVE
Georgia [b]	Correctly read in English "any paragraph" of State or U. S. Constitution and "correctly write the same" when read to him	Only those unable to read or write because of "physical inability" may qualify if they can "understand" and give a "reasonable" interpretation when "read" to them	40 acres of land in the state on which elector resides or property in the state assessed for taxation at $500
Mississippi	"Read" any section of state constitution	"Understand" any section when read to him and give a "reasonable interpretation" thereof	
North Carolina	"Read and write" any section of constitution to the "satisfaction of the registrar"		
South Carolina	"Read and write" any section of state constitution		Ownership and payment of taxes for previous year on property in state assessed at $300 or more
Virginia	Apply to registrar "in his own handwriting" stating name, age, date and place of birth, residence, occupation, etc.		

[a] Presumably in the states that had grandfather clauses a few persons still vote by virtue of permanent qualification under other alternatives to literacy set out in the clauses.

[b] Still another alternative to literacy is open to applicants for registration in Georgia: a person may be registered if he "be of good character, and understand the duties and obligations of citizenship under a republican form of government." For 1949 changes, see note 26, p. 577.

The Louisiana suffrage requirements are formidable, at least in language. To register a person must be (a) of "good character," (b) "understand the duties and obligations of citizenship under a republican form of government," and (c) be able "to read and write." To establish the ability to write an applicant must fill out an application blank stating the qualifications for voting "without assistance or suggestion from any person or any memorandum whatever." He must also "be able to read any clause" in the state or national constitution; and (d) be able to "give a reasonable interpretation" of any clause in either constitution. A person unable to read and write may qualify to vote, but he shall be "a person of good character and reputation, attached to the principles of the Constitution of the United States and of the State of Louisiana and shall be able to understand and give a reasonable interpretation of any section of either constitution when read to him by the registrar, and he must be well disposed to the good order and happiness of the State of Louisiana and of the United States and must understand the duties and obligations of citizenship under a republican form of government." Lest it be thought that few citizens of Louisiana meet these qualifications, it may be noted that thousands of Cajuns have qualified under tests that would fluster a Supreme Court justice.

In 1946 Alabama adopted a constitutional amendment setting up standards for registration similar to those of Louisiana. In March, 1949, the Supreme Court ruled that the amendment was unconstitutional. The requirements of the Alabama amendment were, in brief, that an applicant for registration be able to "read and write" *and* "to understand and explain" any article of the Constitution of the United States in English. Furthermore, unless physically unable to work, a person must have "worked or been regularly engaged in some lawful employment, business, or occupation, trade, or calling for the greater part of the twelve months" preceding his application for registration. Finally, the amendment provided that no "persons shall be entitled to register as electors except those who are of good character and who understand the duties and obligations of good citizenship under a republican form of government."

The Alabama amendment of 1946 was designed, according to its proponents, to apply only to future applicants for registration. Those already on the permanent lists of electors would not have to meet the new qualifications unless the legislature ordered a re-registration and compel all citizens to meet the new requirements. In any event, persons moving from county to county and applying for re-registration would have to meet the new tests.[5]

[5] In addition to the suffrage tests peculiar to the region, southern states have the usual requirements of citizenship, age, residence, and the like. In some instances these conventional requirements have been formulated in a manner to limit Negro voting, but they deserve only brief mention.

Residence. Four states—Alabama, Louisiana, Mississippi, and South Carolina—

2. Machinery for Registration

A solemn recapitulation of the formal literacy and understanding requirements verges on the ridiculous. In practice literacy and understanding have little to do with the acquisition of the right to vote. Whether a person can register to vote depends on what the man down at the courthouse says, and he usually has the final say. It is how the tests are administered that matters. Qualifications of would-be voters are generally determined before election day by application to the cognizant public authorities who prepare lists or registers of those qualified to vote. Some jurisdictions have permanent registration of voters, i.e., a person's name remains on the list until he dies, moves from the jurisdiction, or otherwise becomes disqualified. In others, registration is periodic, i.e., the voter must register at annual, biennial, quadrennial, or other intervals. With few exceptions a person may not vote if his name is not on the list prepared in advance.

Registration thus becomes a function basic to the operation of a democratic regime. Conducted efficiently it establishes a list of persons legally qualified to vote. Registration, properly managed, permits the maximum number of citizens to register with minimum inconvenience. Conducted inefficiently or corruptly it results in lists containing names of unqualified or nonexistent persons and thereby provides a means for fraud on election day. By creating an additional step in the voting process any registration system reduces the number of voters, but at times the procedure seems to have been deliberately designed to make it impracticable for many persons to register.

In the South registration assumes special importance because of the peculiar regional suffrage qualifications. Registration authorities determine whether applicants meet literacy and understanding tests and thus have functioned as the principal governmental agency for Negro disfranchisement. The southern registration process is important not only

---

require residence of two years in the state to qualify to vote. Elsewhere, only in Rhode Island must residence be so long. The other southern states require a year's residence; none reduces the period to six months as do 11 nonsouthern states. Unusually long residence requirements were thought to discriminate against the Negro, supposedly more of a wanderer than the white. Recent studies of farm tenancy indicate, however, that Negro tenants are more stable than white tenants.

Age. The only breaches in the usual requirement of 21 years have been made in the South. In 1943 Georgia lowered the voting age to 18. The slogan was, "Fight at 18, Vote at 18." In 1946 the South Carolina Democratic party admitted those over 18 to its primaries, but it returned to the normal standard in 1948.

Disqualification for Crime. In common with other states, those of the South deny the vote to persons convicted of specified crimes. The only regional peculiarity of these disqualifications is that several states disqualify for petty crimes supposedly committed more frequently by Negroes than whites.

for this reason. Nearly everywhere the management of registration and elections is a backward art; southern registration practices match the primitiveness of those anywhere else in the United States.

Nine southern states have systems of voter registration, although Tennessee does not require registration in all parts of the state.[6] The other two—Arkansas and Texas—prepare voting lists as an incident to poll-tax collection. Neither state surrounds its tax-collection procedures with the safeguards of a well-ordered registration system, yet presumably the fact that a poll tax must be paid for each name deters padding of the lists.[7]

Southern registration machinery is probably not much worse in its design and personnel than registration machinery elsewhere. It is peculiar, however, in the extent to which it is centralized and in the absence in most states of bipartisan participation in the registration process. In several states county registration authorities are state-appointed. In Alabama an ex officio board consisting of the governor, the commissioner of agriculture and industries, and the auditor appoints for each county a board of registrars of three "reputable and suitable persons." In Mississippi the circuit clerk functions as county registrar but an ex officio state board of elections appoints boards of county election commissioners, which hear appeals from denials of registration and purge the lists of deadwood. The governor of South Carolina appoints for each county three "competent and discreet" persons to serve as a board of registration; county Democratic committees, however, conduct a separate registration for voting in Democratic primaries.[8]

North Carolina's state board of elections appoints bipartisan county boards of elections which in turn designate registrars for townships, wards, or districts. In Tennessee the state-appointed county election commissioners name the registrars for wards or other local units used for registration purposes. Virginia arrangements permit state control of regis-

[6] The Tennessee statutes require registration in counties with 50,000 population or more in all cities, towns, and civil districts of 2,500 inhabitants or more. Local legislation modifies the general rule for particular localities. The state board of supervisors of elections must by law maintain a list of all counties, towns, cities, and civil districts "which are under the laws pertaining to the registration of voters." The chairman of the board, when interviewed, was mildly astonished to learn that it had this duty.

[7] The Arkansas constitution has prohibited the adoption of a registration requirement, in memory of Reconstruction when registration meant the disfranchisement of good Confederates. An amendment to permit registration, proposed in contemplation of repeal of the poll tax, was adopted in 1948.

[8] Quite commonly a separate registration is required to vote in southern municipal elections. In some South Carolina cities the good citizen must register four times, viz., once with the city Democratic committee to vote in municipal primaries; once with the city registration board to vote in municipal elections; once with his precinct or ward Democratic club to vote in state and county primaries; and finally with the county board of registration to vote in general elections.

tration personnel in the final analysis. The circuit or corporation judge, chosen by the legislature, designates the county electoral board which in turn appoints district registrars.

State concern over registration usually ends with the act of appointment. The local registrars are on their own and are subject to no prodding or inspection by state officials. Nor do they receive any sort of assistance, advice, or guidance from state authorities except in North Carolina and Virginia. They are left alone and unaided, guided by complex and often incomprehensible election laws, provided usually with the most archaic records, paid miserable pittances, and expected to do a good job. And some of them do.

The usual interpretations of state appointment of registration officials are twofold. It assures Democratic control in all localities even in those counties, once more numerous, with Republican majorities; and white control in all counties, even in those with Negro majorities. While at one time Democrats may have made it difficult for Republicans to register, inquiries among Republican leaders bring no complaint of current discrimination. Sometimes Republicans are counted out, but they are not barred from the ballot box by arbitrary decisions of registrars.[9] Discrimination against the Negro is, of course, another story. It may be significant in speculating about administrative origins to note that states with the most unlimited state power of appointment—Mississippi, South Carolina, Alabama—are states with high proportions of Negro population. In reality, of course, state control is now illusory because state authorities rely on local political potentates for counsel in appointing registrars.

In three states appointment of registrars is local in form as well as in fact. Louisiana's parish registrars are appointed by the policy jury; the governor appoints the New Orleans registrar. An ex officio state board of registration (the governor, Lieutenant-governor, and speaker) may remove local registrars.[10] The most prevalent arrangement in Florida is for the county to elect a supervisor of registration. Georgia's county tax collectors function as registrars in the first instance, but each county has a board of registrars, of three "upright and intelligent" citizens appointed by the judge of the superior court. The board's main job is to purge the names of unqualified persons from the list. In most states special arrangements deviating from that prescribed by general law exist for particular localities.

[9] In Florida Negroes and Republicans relate that a favorite device of registrars has been to register Negroes as Republicans, an action equivalent to disfranchisement. When the white-primary rule was in effect, registrars automatically enrolled Negroes as Republicans and the habit persists. In North Carolina, on the other hand, Republicans complain without intense feeling that Democratic registrars sometimes refuse to enroll Negroes as Republicans.

[10] See Alden L. Powell, *Registration of Voters in Louisiana* (Baton Rouge: Bureau of Government Research, Louisiana State University, 1940).

Commonly the statutes attempt to vest finality of decision in the local registration officials and make appeals from their decisions difficult. In states whose suffrage qualifications involve wide discretion in their application, this finality of decision may re-enforce abuses of discretion. In Alabama, for example, an applicant must "establish by evidence to the reasonable satisfaction" of the board that he is qualified to register. Appeal lies to the circuit court within 30 days after denial of registration. In practice, to make doubly sure of the finality of their action, local boards sometimes do not notify applicants of denial until more than 30 days after their action. In any case, few persons, black or white, of so lowly a status that a board would dare deny them registration have the spare cash to hire a lawyer to take an appeal to the circuit court. In 1948 the Birmingham Bar Association scale of minimum fees fixed $100 for filing a suit in circuit court and $150 for court attendance in such a suit. Mississippi's county board of election commissioners hears appeals from the county registrar. The board's decisions are final on questions of fact, but appeal lies to the circuit court, within two days, on questions of law. South Carolina provides appeal from the board of registration to the court of common pleas and from thence to the supreme court. All these and other such appeals procedures provide recourse from arbitrary action, but they are little used.

3. Glimpses at Registration in Practice

The local registration official gives specific meaning to the grandiloquent phraseology of constitutional suffrage requirements. Actual practice is, of course, impossible of determination without extensive local investigations. Every local registration officer is a law unto himself in determining the citizen's possession of literacy, understanding, and other qualifications. No state agency knows what these officials do or how they interpret the requirements. In only Louisiana and Florida do state authorities even know the number of registered voters. Interviews with scattered local registrars and with others familiar with registration practices indicate the widest diversity in administration within individual states. Florida, Louisiana, and isolated counties in other states give promise of developing effective registration systems; over most of the South, however, the simple business of preparing a list of names of voters seems to be relatively untouched by clerical efficiency and unmarred by record-keeping techniques of a vintage later than 1850.

The administration of voter registration differs, at least in principle, in three groups of states with different types of suffrage requirements. Those in one group—Georgia, Mississippi, North Carolina, South Carolina, and Virginia—require literacy to vote and the constitution usually

fixes the test for its determination. In a second group, Louisiana and
Alabama have required, in addition to literacy, capacity to understand
or explain the constitution and an understanding of the duties of citizenship, as well as good character. Evaluation of these higher faculties and
abstract qualities presumably presents a problem of greater intricacy
than the determination of literacy alone. The states of a third group—
Tennessee and Florida—impose on their registrars only the duty of determining whether the would-be voter meets such requirements as age
and residence. All the states have, of course, in common the problem of
maintaining accurate and usable records of voters and of purging from
the lists those who lose their right to vote.

In the first group—those with literacy tests alone—is Virginia with
its simple requirement that persons apply for registration in their own
handwriting. Negroes complain only infrequently of discrimination in
the application of this test. Persons informed about Virginia practices
report that in most counties and cities literate Negroes have no trouble.
In some places, chiefly rural counties, with many Negroes, denial of
registration is often accomplished by such genteel and courteous tactics
that complaint is forestalled. A favorite device for rejecting Negro applicants is built on the requirement that the applicant "make application . . . in his own handwriting, without aid, suggestion or memorandum, in the presence of the registration officers stating therein his name,
age, date and place of birth, residence and occupation at the time and
for one year next preceding and whether he has previously voted, and if
so, the State, county, and precinct in which he voted last." Obviously if
the constitutional mandate were regarded seriously a great many whites,
respectable and otherwise, would fail the test.[11] Some registrars, in violation of the constitution, provide a blank to be filled in by the applicant.[12]
A Negro may be presented with a blank piece of paper and told to write
thereon the information required by the constitution. On the other hand,
in Richmond blacks and whites alike are given printed application forms;
if they can read and write well enough to fill out the form, they are
registered. In the rural areas registrars at times manifest complete ignorance of the legal requirements. One registrar, for example, questions
the applicant about the items of information required in the application
and writes down the answers himself.

[11] Until 15 or 20 years ago, it was not uncommon for registrars to superimpose an
"understanding" test on the constitutional literacy requirement. The courts held, in a
case arising in Hampton, that registrars had no authority to deny registration because
a person could not answer questions unrelated to the suffrage requirements prescribed
by the constitution. Apparently the local registrar had examined applicants to determine
their knowledge of picayune governmental forms and procedures, a test entirely beyond
the law.—*Davis* v. *Allen*, 160 S. E. 85, 157 Va. 54.

[12] In 1948 J. Lindsay Almond, Jr., became the third attorney general to declare the
practice illegal. He went further, however, and asserted that it was the duty of the
registrar to tell the applicant orally what questions he should answer.

Virginia's permanent registration makes essential a frequent purging of the lists.[13] Yet a clerk in one registrar's office for several years recalls no purge. Court clerks, the law says, must report to the registrars the names of persons convicted of crimes which disqualify for the franchise, and it is the duty of the registrar to strike such names from the lists. Our clerk's office has received no reports from court clerks in accord with the statute. No use has been made of the health department's records of deaths. In fact, in this city, the law on the purging of the lists is utterly without effect.

A high degree of finality in determination of right to register is vested in precinct registrars of North Carolina. Although the state board of elections has exerted itself more in the improvement of elections than in the betterment of registration processes, little rumor and complaint are heard of electoral abuses hinging on registration weaknesses. North Carolina's handling of Negro registration resembles that of Virginia. Negroes register freely in most cities; discrimination occurs chiefly in the eastern rural counties with high proportions of Negro population.

The registrar has discretion by the fact that the applicant must "read" and "write" any section of the constitution "to the satisfaction of the registrar." This phraseology permits some registrars to graft on to the literacy requirement a test of "understanding." An applicant may read and write the section, and the registrar may then follow up with questions to determine whether, as one registrar is said to have put it, the applicant can "interrupt" the constitution. It is reported that in one county more than 50 per cent of the obviously qualified Negro applicants are arbitrarily rejected on the basis of the writing test. Variations in administration within the state are suggested by the statement of one registrar that he never requires demonstration of ability to write but that he requests the applicant to read a passage from the state constitution. When the applicants are not in his judgment obviously intelligent and educated citizens, he asks them questions about the state and Federal governments. Further, this registrar states that he considers somewhat the general character of the Negro applicant as, for example, whether his vote will be purchaseable. On the other hand, in some larger cities of the state registration officials even come out to Negro meetings to facilitate registration.

In North Carolina, as in other states with permanent registration,

[13] An incomprehensible phenomenon of a civilization that has developed remarkedly efficient office procedures and prides itself on its great organizing ability is the dispute over permanent versus periodic registration. Completely stumped by the problem of striking from the registers persons who have died or lost the right to vote, some argue that the only way to produce clean lists is to compel the electorate—hundreds of thousands or even millions of citizens—to troop to the registration offices every year or two or four, fundamentally because registration officials are either lazy or stupid. The Virginia legislature in its proposed constitutional amendment repealing the poll tax, to be voted on in 1949, substitutes an annual registration for permanent registration.

the purging of the lists seems to be an unsolved problem. The county board of elections can order a complete re-registration. Beyond this means of clearing up the rolls, the precinct registrars have the duty of purging the lists but the decentralization of work to them makes awkward the direction of routine flows of relevant information, such as death certificates. Thus, one registrar says that the only purging that he does is of names of registrants who he knows have died. His books, he says, are loaded with the names of persons who have moved away and with people who have probably died but whose death he does not know about. The statute provides for purging by challenges from interested citizens. Our registrar says that he faithfully goes to the high school with his registration books on the days prescribed for challenges and sits there all day reading for pleasure. No one has ever come in to make a challenge. If a challenge should be made, he supposes that he would call up the Democratic county chairman to find out what he ought to do.

Mississippi's circuit clerks function as registrars, subject to the supervision of the board of county commissioners of elections. Visits to the offices of a few clerks reveals what might be expected all along, viz., that some clerks do a sloppy job and that others are meticulous in the performance of their duties. Mississippi registrants must be able to "read" any section of the constitution. It seems doubtful that any test of this ability is actually administered to whites, although the act of signing the registration book and of filling in the data on residence, age, and so forth constitutes a simple test of literacy.

In rural counties registration is a casual process. One registrar, for example, simply has the person sign the registration book and fill in the required items of information. She does not require him to swear to the oath printed at the top of the page. She gives no reading test nor does she require proof of residence. She knows most of the persons who come in because they are her neighbors. If a stranger came in, she would make a more particular inquiry. The law forbids a person to register twice, she says, and, hence, there is no chance of duplicate registration. Another clerk indicates that she requires no proof of a registrant's qualifications. Each registrant takes an oath that appears at the top of the page and when he swears to that, full responsibility rests on him and not on her. She feels free to register anyone who will take the oath.

Few Negroes apply for registration except in two or three of the most urbanized counties. One of the gentler techniques of dissuasion in the rural counties is illustrated by the practice of the registrar of a county with over 13,000 Negroes 21 and over, six of whom were registered in 1947. The registrar registers any qualified person, black or white, if he insists. When a Negro applies, however, she tells him that he will be registered if he insists, but she gives him a quiet, maternal talk to the effect that the time has not yet come for Negroes to register in the county.

The people are not ready for it now and it would only cause trouble for the Negro to register. Things move slowly, she tells the applicant, but the day will come when Negroes can register just as white people. Almost always, she says, the applicant agrees with her and departs in peace.

Another registrar says that sometimes she asks questions of the applicant, questions on the "constitution and similar things." Still another registrar requires Negroes to present poll-tax receipts for registration, a procedure unauthorized by law. He frequently requires Negroes to read the constitution and to answer questions, "sometimes questions which are very hard," says a local Negro leader. Thus, in Mississippi the reading requirement tends to be supplemented by an informal "understanding" requirement.

Removal of deadwood from Mississippi's permanent lists seems to be on the basis of information that comes personally to the attention of the registrar or the election commissioners. As a last resort the commissioners may order a new registration. In one county the registrar says that the board of election commissioners does little purging of the lists. "Oh, if they happen to know that some individual has died they will probably take his name off the books." A person must present a couple of poll-tax receipts when he votes anyway, it is argued, so the accuracy of the lists matters little. Election officials do not invariably demand presentation of the receipts, but one hears little gossip in Mississippi of election frauds based on inaccurate rolls.

Mississippi registration laws, enacted in the era of horse transport, require the registrar to spend a day at specified intervals in each voting precinct to receive applications for registration. This year, one of the circuit clerks said in 1947, she spent a day in each of two dozen precincts and did not receive more than a dozen applications. If for any reason she particularly desires to get a person registered, she must look him up individually.

South Carolina has maintained a dual registration system. To register for the general election a person must be able to "read and write" any section of the state constitution. Few people vote in the general election, anyway, and, hence, the Democratic party's enrollment system for primary voters is of more practical importance. Party rules require that club members shall be able to "read and write and interpret the Constitution of the State of South Carolina." The nature of the requirement may be deduced from a sharp denial by one politician that such a requirement existed. When the rules were shown to him, he conceded the point, but insisted that the only real requirement was that one be white.

Party officials who are aware of the existence of the reading, writing, and interpreting requirement indicate that it is generally ignored. Further, usually the "administration" of party enrollment is loose. In some counties the enrollment books are deposited in grocery stores, filling stations, and similar places. Usually the proprietor is supposed to be in charge of the book, but anyone who wishes can go in and write his name on the list, and as many other names as he wishes. This sort of "absentee enrollment" does not prevail in the enrollment conducted by the city Democratic club of Columbia, which also makes an effort to purge duplicate names from the books. In Charleston and Columbia, factional workers are said to check the lists and by their surveillance to contribute to the accuracy of the rolls.

The county board of registration—three "competent and discreet" citizens—registers applicants for participation in the general elections and determines their ability to "read and write" any section of the state constitution. Although this test is not uniformly applied to white applicants, Negro leaders make remarkably little complaint about refusals of registration to Negroes who can "read and write." Their chief grievance has been exclusion from the Democratic primaries, a matter rectified by court decision in 1948. Insofar as registration to vote in the general elections, their grievances relate to a few local situations. For instance, one registrar, a white woman, is said to require Negroes, or at least some of them, to read the entire state constitution and then to write it. Her prescription arises from the constitutional mandate that the applicant be able to read and write "any" section. In another locality the chairman of the board sought to discourage a group of Negroes who showed up to register by absenting himself. The leader of the Negroes said that he guessed he would go down to Columbia and see the NAACP about it. The news traveled over the white grapevine to the chairman of the board who turned up at the office to register the colored applicants.[14] But these are isolated instances. At the opposite extreme is the 1948 case of Negro leaders of a community about 30 miles from the county seat who approached the board and told them that people in their community intended to register and wanted to know precisely what the requirements

[14] The Progressive Democratic party, a Negro organization, distributes to its county leaders photostatic copies of a letter from an Assistant Attorney General of the United States which probably eases the way. The letter acknowledges information about discriminatory practices in registration. "All otherwise qualified citizens have a federally secured right to register for voting and any interference with that right because of race or color is a matter of federal concern." The Department of Justice, the letter goes on to say, "will promptly act upon any specific information that you will provide on this subject. Please furnish the names and addresses of the complainants, the officials involved, and the full circumstances surrounding the denial of the right to register." State leaders carefully instruct Negroes in the procedures and etiquette of registration. A broadside, for example, warns that the registrar has the right to "refuse to register you" and "to punish you if you cause a disturbance." "If you are not allowed to register . . ., do not argue. Ask the registrar for a statement telling why you were refused, and if possible get names and addresses of witnesses to the refusal. Have an affidavit (sworn statement) prepared and send it to the S. C. Conference, NAACP, Box 1145, Columbia, South Carolina."

were. The board responded by saying that if the Negroes would pay for their gas and oil the board would go over to their town and save them the trip to the county seat. The board went over and registered 360 Negroes, a number equivalent to the entire supply of registration certificates taken along.

Although for 50 years general elections have had no importance in South Carolina, increased registration of Negroes in recent years has stimulated whites to counter measures. For example, in three or four counties of the coastal plain, the boards of registration are said to have stimulated registration by whites, i.e., they have written out registration certificates for all unregistered whites whose names they could lay their hands on, mailed the certificates to them, and thereby saved them the trouble of a personal appearance.

A registrant in Georgia must be able to "read" correctly "any paragraph" of the state or Federal Constitution and "correctly write the same," with certain exceptions.[15] Tax collectors maintain "voters' books" for each militia district of their counties, and the law directs them to permit only those persons with the qualifications to vote to sign the "voters' books."[16] After the closing of a collector's books several months in advance of the election, he transmits lists of new names to the county board of registrars for addition to the existing permanent list of voters. The board has the duty of purging the lists. Any voter may examine the lists and challenge names of persons thought to be unqualified.

Tests of ability to read and write constitutional passages seem to be given rarely. Nor are Negroes even uniformly required to demonstrate literacy. At times, however, literacy tests are enforced against Negroes in a discriminatory fashion,[17] and in some instances apparently a test of understanding is added to that of literacy, all in violation of the constitu-

---

[15] An alternative to literacy is "good character" and an understanding of the duties and obligations of citizenship. Registrars' books provide blanks for indication of whether a voter qualified under the literacy clause, or the good character, or property holding alternatives. Registrars, however, often make no notation of how a registrant qualified.

[16] In practice not all voters have to sign the book. Thus, Bunche reports the case of a tax collector who requires all registrants to sign the book in person "unless it's a wife, or a sister or somebody like that" or a person registering for close kin "if you know them."—*Political Status of the Negro* (mss.), p. 237. This manuscript, prepared for the Myrdal survey, is available in microfilm at the Library of Congress.

[17] Thus, in a southwest Georgia county in 1946 Negroes had to demonstrate ability to read and write. Mrs. D. and her cook went down to vote on election day, and the cook was turned away on the ground that her name was not on the lists. Mrs. D. went around to see "the man" to ask the reason. His answer was that the cook had not demonstrated her ability to read and write. The undisputed retort was that her cook could read and write better than a great many of the white people who were voting that day and that probably many of the whites flushed out of the swamps to vote that day could not read and write at all. The chairman of the board of registrars gave the cook a card entitling her to vote. Not all Negroes have white friends who will go to bat for them in this way.

tion and laws.[18] Scattered evidence suggests that some tax collectors register about anyone and everyone whom they know not to be obviously disqualified and then leave it to the board of registrars to cleanse the rolls.[19] These boards, as in Alabama, are part-time boards and are not always competently manned.[20]

Thorough purging of the lists by boards of registrars appears to be exceptional. The principal use of the power to purge has been to harass Negroes. In 1946, following the closing of the registration books, the Talmadge forces organized a campaign to purge the rolls of Negroes in those counties in which it would be to their advantage to do so. Estimates of the number removed from the lists run from 15,000 to 25,000. In some counties all Negroes were removed from the rolls. The anti-Talmadge forces resisted the purge by slowdown tactics. They employed lawyers to represent Negroes before the boards and argued each purge as if it were a court trial. Thus, in Fulton County slowdown tactics limited review of challenges to about 250 in the period in which the registration authorities had to act. In one county the "defense" lawyer stretched out the argument so that only four or five cases were completed per day.

In the 1947 legislative session Talmadge leaders attempted to revise the registration laws to substitute biennial for permanent registration, to require a complete re-registration, to levy a $1 registration fee, and to alter the procedures in other respects, but the bill failed of enactment. The proposals were made again in 1949, with better prospects of passage.

The states mentioned in the foregoing pages require as one condition for voter registration literacy, although in some instances alternative routes to registration are available. In Alabama and Louisiana registration requirements—at least on paper—have been more formidable. In addition to literacy, applicants have been required to understand, interpret, or explain the constitution and to meet other standards which registration authorities may apply with wide discretion.

Administration of Alabama's registration requirements rests in three-member county boards of registrars. The board itself is supposed to examine each applicant for registration. Board members, except those in the more populous counties, receive $7.50 a day when actually engaged in their duties. The level of compensation tends to restrict board membership to widows, others in necessitous circumstances, and to public-spirited citizens given to self-sacrifice.

[18] A tax collector for 10 years was unable to recall that he had ever refused to register a white person. He once started to do so when a man wanted to register his brother who was known by the tax collector to be *non compos*. The collector did not refuse because he did not want to tell "this on him right here in front of everybody."— R. J. Bunche, *Political Status of the Negro*, p. 242.

[19] Tax collectors under general legislation, modified for particular localities by special legislation, receive 5 cents per name added to the voters' books.

[20] In Haralson County in 1948 all three of the registrars were past 70 years of age. —*Atlanta Journal*, April 11, 1948.

Before the adoption of more stringent registration requirements in 1946, practices of the boards varied from place to place. Ability to read and write was usually considered established if a person could fill out an application for registration. Few Negroes applied for registration and even fewer were registered in the predominantly Negro counties, although they fared better in cities and in the northern counties of the state. Some boards apparently set up quotas; they decided to accept five or ten Negroes at a session of the board. The first five or ten applicants would be notified promptly that they had been accepted, but other Negro applications would go unanswered. In Montgomery, Negroes properly identified as the cook or the butler of white citizens of standing would be registered, but generally hostility toward Negro registration prevailed. Qualified Negro applicants in Mobile encountered no insuperable obstacles, although slowdown tactics in the examination of applicants limited the number of registrants. In Anniston, in northern Alabama, discriminatory application of the literacy test apparently constituted no part of the mechanisms of disfranchisement.

One of the most serious procedural obstacles to Negro registration in Alabama has been a requirement by some local boards that applicants be "vouched for" by two white men. At some places, it is reported, politicians "hang around" registration offices on registration day to vouch for applicants, but in other communities only the leading citizens in the Negro community can produce vouchers with ease.[21]

In 1946 Alabama adopted the "Boswell Amendment" to the state constitution which set up new suffrage standards and lodged in the boards of registrars of broad discretion akin to that long exercised by Louisiana registration officials. The boards became petty tribunals to determine whether would-be voters could "read and write, understand and explain any article of the constitution of the United States," whether they were of "good character," and whether they understood "the duties and obligations of good citizenship under a republican form of government." It was this wide latitude granted to the boards and the demonstrated discriminatory use of it against Negroes that led a Federal district court in 1949 to enjoin permanently the Mobile County board of registrars from enforcing the requirements of the amendment. The court noted that 57 Negroes had been rejected because they were unable to "understand and explain" the constitution, whereas during the same period only 11 whites had been denied registration, and they for other reasons than the standards set by the amendment.

No instance has come to our attention in which a board of registrars

---

[21] The defense of the voucher requirement has been that both whites and blacks were required to have their applications supported by persons able to give evidence that the applicants met such requirements as those of residence.—*Mitchell* v. *Wright*, 62 F. Supp. 580 (1945), 154 F. (2d) 924 (1946), 69 F. Supp. 698 (1947).

has formulated objective tests of ability of applicants to meet the suffrage requirements. Rather, the board of "three reputable and suitable" persons decides each case on its merits, usually after an examination of the applicant in private. In Jefferson County (Birmingham) the board consisted in 1948 of a former house detective of the Tutwiler Hotel whose home county had had no high schools when he was growing up, a former rural school teacher who had not been graduated from high school but had won a teaching certificate by attending a normal school, and a clerk of the elections commission who had quit high school before graduation to attend a business college. These three persons sat to determine their fellow citizens' understanding of the constitution, their good character, and their acquaintance with the duties and obligations of good citizenship.

Douglas L. Hunt, of the *Birmingham News,* inquired into the functioning of the board and discovered wide variations and inconsistencies in its practices. Some persons were questioned at length; others were registered without inquiry. The questions ranged far and wide.[22] The board had no announced policy toward Negroes but it subjected them to closer questioning than whites and discouraged them by dilatory tactics. Charges of discrimination against whites were made by the Birmingham Federation of Labor which felt that two members of the board found a good many workingmen unable to comprehend the constitution and the duties and obligations of citizenship.

In Birmingham, a goodly number of Negroes is registered, but in rural counties with heavy Negro populations a stiffer policy tends to be followed. In 1946, the Macon County (81 per cent Negro) board of registrars resigned, no other citizen to whom appointment was offered would accept, and for approximately two years the county registration machinery did not function for either blacks or whites. The explanation offered was that a Tuskegee Negro had sued board members for damages because of denial of registration. Registrars at $7.50 a day could not afford the risk of damage suits.

Aside from the question of Negro registration, Alabama registration procedures suffer from defects common to many states. Although registration is permanent, the process is discontinuous. The board of three sits only on prescribed days. Applicants have to line up and wait to file individually before the board for examination. In effect a person has to take a day off from work to register. The Mobile Building and Construction Trades Council protested without success the refusal of the

---

[22] Dr. Hunt's series of articles in the *News* (February 11, 13, 18, 20, 1948) constitutes a valuable case study. Of interest are some of the questions asked by the board: How many state senators are there? In what congressional district do you live? Who is the sheriff of Jefferson County? What do we mean by UN? How old are your wife's father and mother? Why have you never registered before? Who is in charge of street inprovements in Birmingham?

Mobile board in 1948 to schedule night sessions for applicants who could not conveniently appear during the day. The labor spokesmen wanted a larger number of qualified voters so they would be able "to combat the Mobile County political machine."

Outside a few of the more populous counties of Alabama the purging of the permanent lists seems to be treated casually. In Birmingham the clerk of the board receives reports of deaths and reports of convictions for disfranchising crimes and makes other checks of the lists. In rural counties less systematic purging is apt to prevail. Thus a rural official observed that their list of 6500 included the names of about 250 persons who were dead, some of them for 20 years. "It would be awful to make a mistake and call somebody dead who really isn't," he explained. The Alabama poll tax provides some check against inadequate purging, since the registration list is supposed to be checked against the poll-tax list in the preparation of voter lists for each election. The procedure, however, has a loophole as broad as a barn door. The check does not affect those exempt from the tax, which include all veterans among others.

Alabama's registration laws, in common with those of many other states, are cluttered with archaic provisions. Special legislation gives the more populous counties discretion to use modern records procedures, but the general law for most counties abounds with references to that great classic of American local government law, "a well-bound book." Thus, the board of registrars in a rural county meets at the beginning of the month for a session and reports its handful of new registrants to the probate judge in a "well-bound book" about 20x20 inches and one and one-half inches thick. Or the statutes require that a list of qualified voters be transmitted to the secretary of state, and some registrars actually comply, but to what end no one has ever been able to figure out.

Louisiana's battery of literacy, understanding, and character requirements antedate those of Alabama. It seems obvious that for the white population these tests mean absolutely nothing. They exist only as a bar to Negro registration, and they do not have to be utilized frequently, for the general tradition of nonparticipation by Negroes results in few Negro applicants. Most Negro registrants reside in urban centers. In rural counties without Negro registrants the constitutional arrangements have little to do with the absence of blacks from the lists of voters. Thus, in a rural parish with a high proportion of Negro population a local politician reported that some 15 years ago 18 Negroes presented themselves at the registrar's office. A deputy sheriff was called, and he "cracked the head of one of the niggers open with a pistol butt. Oh, it didn't injure him permanently."

In those localities in which Negroes can register, apparently Louisiana's formidable constitutional requirements mean little or nothing. In New Orleans, for example, the policy in 1947 was to register all persons, black or white, who could satisfactorily fill out the application blank required by the constitution. The act of filling out the blank constituted a demonstration of ability to read and write, but the tests of "good character" and comprehension of the "duties and obligations of citizenship under a republican form of government" were applied to neither blacks nor whites.[23] The completion of the application blank, however, is not a simple task, and opportunity exists for discrimination. The constitution forbids any assistance to the applicant who is coping with the blank, and while registration clerks maintain correct legal neutrality with respect to blacks they often aid whites in dealing with the tricky questions. For example, the applicant must compute his exact age in years, months, and days. Once a Negro surmounts the application hurdle, he is usually registered without regard to the nonsense about "interpreting" the constitution and "understanding" the duties and obligations of citizenship.[24]

Sample inquiries suggest that in rural parishes greater use is made of the understanding and interpretation clauses as a basis for the denial of registration than is the practice in the urban centers. It is scarcely necessary to note that few Negroes are registered under the alternative clause by which illiterates may qualify to vote. In October, 1946, the voting lists included 49,603 white voters who had "made their mark" instead of writing their names while two Negroes had "made their mark."

Two states—Florida and Tennessee—are handicapped neither by literacy tests nor by the understanding and interpreting mumbo-jumbo. Registration is required only in localities of prescribed sizes in Tennessee. Some counties, notably those with large cities, have set up systems of permanent registration under special legislation, but elsewhere biennial or quadrennial registration is required. There is a marked lack of uniformity in procedures within the state.

Inquiries at a few Florida registration offices yielded the impression that Florida's political atmosphere in this respect, as in others, is unlike that of states of the Deep South. Its registration laws, on the whole, seem to make sense, and the few registrars interviewed appeared to know what they were about, to be concerned with efficient performance of their duties, and to be motivated by pride in their work.

The operations of a supervisor of registration of a county with a

[23] A 1946 circuit court decision brought about a discontinuance by the local registrar of reliance on tests of "understanding" and of ability to interpret the constitution to exclude Negroes. The registrar had refused to permit an applicant to fill out the application blank, after he had correctly identified the judicial district in which he resided but admitted that he did not know the number of his senatorial district. See *Hall* v. *Nagel*, 154 F. (2d) 931 (1946).

[24] A New Orleans Negro political leader reported that he knew of only two instances in recent years of the use of the "understanding" clause against Negroes. In these cases the applicants had already fouled up two application cards, and, he says, the registrar's office was probably simply trying to get rid of them quickly.

city of around 20,000 population provide an illustrative case. Her tenure extends back 18 years, although she had had opposition in every primary save one. She takes great pride in the system of loose-leaf records in use in her office. She designed it, sold the plan to her county commissioners, and obtained special legislation to permit its use instead of the archaic "well-bound books" prescribed by general laws.

Registration at her courthouse office is continuous; she makes no effort to limit registration to the times prescribed by statute. Applicants are asked to show their driver's license or some other evidence of the length of their residence in the county. They do not actually raise their right hand and swear to the oath, but they are asked to read it and sometimes they say that they can't sign it because they lack a month or so of having the required residence.

The law applicable to this county requires registration in the precincts during specified periods in advance of the primary and the election. Our registrar instructs the precinct registrars, whom she appoints, and visits them at intervals during their work to advise with them. She does not insist that precinct registrars limit themselves to the prescribed office hours; she tries to have as precinct registrars the sort of person who will drum up trade at church suppers and other gatherings, on the theory apparently that registrars should work for the voters and not the voters for the registrars.

In this county the law provides for permanent registration and hence transfers and purging of the lists takes on importance. Our registrar receives reports of deaths and reads the papers and pulls the cards containing the names of the deceased. Her greatest difficulty is keeping check on persons who move from the county; yet the sources of information available to women are manifold, and she thinks that she keeps track of people who move away and of those who move from precinct to precinct. Her loose-leaf system permits her to make intracounty transfers easily. While she receives no formal reports of convictions for disfranchising crimes, the court clerk upstairs is a great friend of hers and keeps her informed.

Our registrar speaks with great enthusiasm of her attendance at the sessions of the association of supervisors of registration. Though the desire to obtain legislation raising the pay of registrars contributes to the association's vitality, at its meetings they trade ideas, thrash out their problems, and agree on legislation to improve registration practices. Occasionally, their proposals are enacted. She pays her own expenses to the meetings of the association.

The registrar of a rural county with a small population presents a different picture. An elderly storekeeper, who functions as supervisor of registration for $50 a month, demonstrates less clerical virtuosity than our urban registrar but conveys the same impression of integrity and interest in his job. On his desk is a well-worn copy of the election laws, and he is intimately familiar with its contents. For the law he has a genuine respect. He requires all applicants to raise their right hand and take their oath to the facts qualifying them for registration. Yet for the convenience of the citizenry he registers people out of the prescribed hours, though he is strict about not registering on Sunday. He does not bother about instructing his precinct registrars; he gives them the books and tells them to go to it; while some are better at going to it than others, there are few registrants in the precincts anyway.

In purging the books our rural registrar relies on his personal information to know who should be stricken from the books. The county commissioners also participate and pool their knowledge with that of the registrar. In this county the general laws prescribe the use of "well-bound books" and about every 15 or 20 years the records get in such a mess that the county has the legislature pass an act requiring a completely new registration.

4. Literacy and an Enlightened Electorate

No matter from what direction one looks at it, the southern literacy test is a fraud and nothing more. The simple fact seems to be that the constitutionally prescribed test of ability to read and write a section of the constitution is rarely administered to whites. It is applied chiefly to Negroes and not always to them. When Negroes are tested on their ability to read and write, only in exceptional instances is the test administered fairly. Insofar as is known, no southern registration official has utilized an objective test of literacy. In some states, of course, the constitution prescribes the method for testing, but in other states it would be legally possible to employ a simple objective test similar to that used by some northern states that prescribe literacy as a voting prerequisite.

A literacy test fairly administered would even now exclude large numbers of Negroes from the suffrage and relatively few whites. It would also enable literate Negroes now excluded from the electorate to qualify to vote. Illiterate persons, black and white, uniformly show a much lower degree of interest in voting than do persons higher up the educational scale. Yet if competing whites should scheme to vote blocs of illiterate blacks, such a test would be a deterrent. The largest proportions of illiterate Negroes are to be found in those rural, agricultural, black-belt counties which are supposed to be threatened by Negro domination. And it is, of course, in these counties that the Negro shows least interest in voting. A fair literacy test would exclude the few black and white illiterates who applied for registration, a matter of no great consequence one way or another. Yet a fairly conducted literacy test would have great propaganda value for those who wish to defend before the nation the

South's right to take care of its own problems in its own way.[25] Rather than advocate a defensible limitation that would permit some Negroes to vote, short-sighted politicians have stood for methods of arbitrary exclusion that may be used to prevent all Negroes from voting.

Of the tests supplementary to literacy—ability to understand, explain, or interpret the constitution, and understanding of the duties and obligations of citizenship—little more can be said. Born of a union of constitutional fraud and political ineptitude, they have served only to make the South's position even more untenable before the nation and to postpone the facing of realities. The understanding and explaining clauses must in their nature be cloaks for the arbitrary exclusion of voters or tests of the possession of useless knowledge. It would be possible to reduce them to fairly administered tests. In fact, if any test of understanding were applied at all to any substantial number of citizens of status, the registrars would be hanged to the nearest lamp post and no grand jury could be found that would return a true bill. Suffrage requirements that cannot be made at least to appear nondiscriminatory in their application will sooner or later fall before the constitutional ban on racial discrimination.

Apart from the problem of discriminatory application of literacy and other tests, southern registration systems have difficulties common to registration in all states. Registration administration in the South, as elsewhere, is on the whole primitive. There are bright spots here and there, but there is a long way to go to achieve the simple objective of clean lists of persons eligible to vote. Undoubtedly in many rural communities and small towns, ineffectiveness of registration administration results in no fraud, but lists cluttered with deadwood are a standing invitation to fraud. Southern registration policies in some respects provide a sound foundation on which to build a good voter-registration system, given the will. The general acceptance of the principle of permanent registration, for example, is in accord with the best practice. The general absence of a custom of bipartisan administration by party hacks also clears the way for the development of a system manned by persons with a professional interest in the improvement of registration and election administration.[26]

[25] Albert B. Saye, of the University of Georgia, advocates for Georgia a test of educational attainment. He would have applicants for registration show that they have completed the seventh grade or have passed an examination based on this level of education administered by the state department of education.—"The Elective Franchise in Georgia," *Georgia Review*, 2 (1948), pp. 434–46.

[26] The 1949 legislature overhauled Georgia's registration machinery and requirements. To establish "understanding," as an alternative to ability to read and write, the applicant must answer correctly 10 of 30 questions specified by law. The legislature ordered a complete re-registration, but declined to abolish permanent registration. It also voted down a proposed $1 registration fee.

| # THE POLL TAX:

VARIATIONS IN FORM AND APPLICATION

Seven southern states require the payment of a capitation tax as a prerequisite to voting. Four others at one time or another had the poll tax but abolished it. Thus, the poll tax has had a wider vogue than the literacy test. The tax, which was in most instances adopted during the disfranchisement movement,[1] remains in effect in Mississippi, Tennessee, Arkansas, South Carolina, Alabama, Virginia, and Texas. Florida, Louisiana, North Carolina, and Georgia have abolished the tax as a prerequisite for voting.[2] In Tennessee, Texas, and Arkansas, the tax constitutes the principal formal barrier between the voter and the ballot box, while it is a requirement in addition to that of

[1] Dates of adoption were: Florida, 1889; Mississippi, 1890; Tennessee, 1890; Arkansas, 1893; South Carolina, 1895; Louisiana, 1898; North Carolina, 1900; Alabama, 1901; Virginia, 1902; Texas, 1902. Georgia's tax long antedated the period of general disfranchisement. Virginia first amended its constitution to require the poll tax in 1876, but the provision was repealed in 1882 under the leadership of the Readjusters, the "radical" agrarian party of the day.

[2] Abandonment of the tax occurred as follows: North Carolina, 1920; Louisiana, 1934; Florida, 1937; Georgia, 1945. Virginia's legislature in 1946 and 1948 took steps to submit a repealing amendment to the voters in 1949. In 1948 Arkansas voters amended their constitution to permit the adoption of a registration system in contemplation of possible federal action on the poll tax. In 1949 Governor Sid McMath requested the legislature to consider submission of a constitutional amendment to repeal the poll tax. It did not submit such an amendment. In 1949 the Tennessee legislature exempted women and veterans from the tax.

literacy in Mississippi, South Carolina, Alabama, and Virginia.[3] On the other hand, South Carolina in one sense is not a poll-tax state, for payment of the tax is not required for participation in the Democratic primaries, where the decisions of the electorate are actually made. In 1949 Tennessee adopted the South Carolina plan.

In northern discussion of southern politics, the poll tax often plays the role of the chief villain. Southern Congressmen, according to commentators, are reactionary because of the poll tax. The Democratic party controls the South because of the poll tax. Negroes suffer because of the poll tax. Poor whites are poor because of the poll tax. The Bourbons, the "big mules," and the delta planters can rule unchecked because of the poll tax. In short, all the ills of a region of many ills have been attributed to the poll tax. All this sort of discussion does the poll tax too much honor; it is simply one, and not the most important one, of a battery of disfranchising devices.[4]

Unquestionably the poll tax contributes to a reduction of popular participation in primaries and elections. Originally designed chiefly to discourage Negro participation, it became obsolete for that purpose, with the invention of the white primary. It became simply a tax on voting by whites and nothing more. Yet poll taxes are by no means uniform from state to state; some forms are more restrictive of the suffrage than others. Before examining the effects of the poll tax in barring the potential voter from the polls, a survey of its variations in form and application is necessary.

1. Rates, Coverage, and Time of Payment of Tax

Although its defenders often justify the poll tax as a means for raising revenue, it cannot be regarded seriously as a revenue source.[5] It yields an infinitesimal proportion of state and local income. Payment of

[3] In Tennessee, primaries for the designation of candidates for county offices are held at the option of local party authorities, who also determine whether to require the poll tax as a prerequisite for participation. Such primaries are held separately from those for state-wide candidates, and for the state-wide primary the poll tax was until 1949 required by statute. The number of county party committees requiring payment of the tax has declined in recent years. In some Tennessee municipalities a city poll tax is a prerequisite to participation in city elections.

[4] Illustrative of misconceptions about the effects of the poll tax is its treatment in *The Report of the President's Committee on Civil Rights* (Washington, 1947), p. 38. A graphic presentation contrasts a turnout of 18.3 per cent of the potential voters in states with poll taxes in the 1944 presidential election with a rate of 68.7 per cent for the other states. The implication that the difference in turnout could be attributed to the poll tax is both naive and misleading.

[5] Proceeds of the tax in all states are earmarked for educational purposes, except that Texas permits the use of 50 cents of its $1.50 tax for general revenue purposes, while Virginia permits the city or county where the tax is collected to apply 50 cents of the $1.50 tax for such purposes as are locally desired.

the tax is, in effect, optional with the taxpayer. Efforts to enforce its collection are exceptional, and are in some states prohibited. The tax must be treated for what it is—a condition for exercise of the suffrage.

Poll-Tax Rates. The amount that a citizen has to pay to vote varies from state to state and, in some states variations even exist or are permissible among counties. Always a single rate is levied uniformly over the entire state by state statute or constitution, and in four of the seven states local governments may add a surcharge. The annual state rate in three states is $1.00; in three others, $1.50; and in one, $2.00.[6]

These more or less nominal rates do not tell the whole story. In estimating its effects on voting, the most significant aspect of poll-tax form is whether the tax is cumulative or noncumulative. In four states—Arkansas, South Carolina, Tennessee, Texas—the tax is noncumulative; that is, although it is an annual tax, the taxpayer need pay it only for the year of the election or primary in order to qualify to vote. Consequently the tax can be avoided in the off years, a fact testified to by the sharp oscillations in yield.

The cumulative tax—i.e., a tax that must be paid for each of a series of years in order to qualify to vote—exists in Alabama, Mississippi, and Virginia, and, before 1945, prevailed in Georgia. Alabama's cumulative provision is the most severe. The period of cumulation extends from age 21 to 45 or from the date that a person moving to the state after age 21 first becomes liable to the tax until age 45. A person over 45 is exempt from the payment of the tax, but in order to vote he must show that he paid the tax for each year for which he was liable before reaching that age. A person who had lived in the state from the age of 21 to 45 would have to prove payment of the poll tax for 24 years; thus, the maximum cumulative liability, at the Alabama rate of $1.50 per year, is $36

Virginia and Mississippi have much less extended periods of cumulation than Alabama. A Virginian who has been lax in meeting his poll-tax payments and wants to qualify to vote will have to pay for three preceding years or a total of $4.50 exclusive of penalties and whatever levy is made by local authorities. In Mississippi the cumulative feature differs for the general election and for the primary. For the general election the tax may cumulate for only two years to a total of $4.00, exclusive of county surcharges (and few, if any, counties levy the permissible additional $1.00 per year) and penalties. To qualify to vote in primaries the elector must

---

[6] Information on the extent to which counties and cities take advantage of their authority to levy a charge additional to the state rate has not been accumulated. In Mississippi, persons familiar with local government matters report that they know of no county that levies the surcharge. Similarly, no local levies were encountered in Virginia. In Tennessee agitation of the poll-tax issue brought in 1941 the abandonment of the one-dollar local levy in about one-third of the counties.—Jennings Perry, *Democracy Begins at Home* (Philadelphia: J. B. Lippincott, 1944), chap. 7. In Texas the permissible county surcharge is usually levied.

conform to a peculiar statutory twist. He must have paid the tax for each of two years at the time it was due, that is, before February 1, of the year of the primary and of the preceding year.[7] The Mississippi tax as applied to primary voting, thus is not cumulative in the conventional sense, yet probably its effect in reducing the number of qualified voters is more severe than would be an ordinary two-year cumulative tax. The details on poll-tax rates are set forth in Table 61.

TABLE 61

Poll-Tax Rates

STATE	ANNUAL STATE RATE	CUMULATIVE PROVISION	MAXIMUM STATE CUMULATION [a]	MAXIMUM ADDITIONAL TAX AT OPTION OF LOCAL AUTHORITIES
Alabama	$1.50	For entire period of liability	$36.00 [b]	None
Arkansas	$1.00	None		None
Mississippi	$2.00	Two years preceding election	$4.00 [b]	$1.00, Counties
South Carolina	$1.00	None		None
Tennessee	$1.00	None		$1.00, Counties
Texas	$1.50	None		$0.25, Counties $1.00, Cities
Virginia	$1.50	Three years preceding election	$4.50	$1.00, Counties, cities, towns

[a] Exclusive of penalties. Usually payment of both cumulative and noncumulative taxes after the due date involves a penalty. In the case of the cumulative tax the penalty increases the total sum that may cumulate and must be paid to qualify to vote.

[b] See textual explanation of cumulation in Alabama and Mississippi.

The cumulative feature of the tax undoubtedly contributes to the low record of participation in elections in those states that utilize it. The chairman of the Alabama state Democratic executive committee remarks:

I consider the maintenance of the cumulative feature of the poll tax law all-important. You let one of these citizens, whether he be white or black, fail to pay his poll tax for two or three years and get to the point where he owes $4.50, $6.00, or $7.50 in back poll taxes, then you have mighty near eliminated this person as a voter, and while, as I have already stated, there are many exceptions to the rule, yet in the vast majority of cases the persons so eliminated are persons

[7] *Laws*, 1936, chapter 320.

who would not take enough interest in their government to cast an intelligent ballot even if they were given the privilege of voting.[8]

Georgia, before the repeal of its poll-tax law, had a policy of cumulation similar to that of Alabama. The maximum liability, including penalties, amounted to $47. The Alabama and Georgia cumulative provisions probably constitute important elements in accounting for the low rates of participation in elections in those states in comparison with most other poll-tax states. Although Virginia, with a less-stringent cumulative rule, maintains a record of even lower voter-interest than Alabama or Georgia, other factors as well as the poll tax contribute to its impressive record of political inactivity.

Liability for the Tax. In several states the exemption of certain groups from the poll tax mitigates its effects. Those most commonly relieved from the tax are aged persons, although most states exempt at least some small classes, such as the maimed, blind, or disabled.[9] Three states exempt those over 60; one, those over 50. Alabama exempts those over 45 years of age, as well as veterans of World War I, who in 1922 were relieved from payment both future poll taxes and those for which they were previously liable under the cumulative feature of the tax. In 1944 the same exemption was extended to veterans of World War II. The Alabama tax thus bears in a discriminatory fashion on persons without military service; few women can escape the tax through the military exemption. In 1949 Tennessee exempted veterans of both World Wars.

Most poll-tax laws were amended during World War II to grant temporary exemption to service personnel, usually for the period of their service and for a specified period thereafter. Some states have continuing arrangements for the exemption of citizens serving in the National Guard or in the United States military services.

TABLE 62

Persons Liable for Payment of Poll Tax

STATE	PERSONS LIABLE	PERSONS EXEMPT [a]
Alabama	Persons over 21 and under 45	1. Persons over 45 years of age [b] 2. Those permanently and totally disabled from following any substantially gainful occupation with reasonable regularity, whose taxable property does not exceed $500

[8] Statement to legislative committee, Feb. 9, 1945.

[9] The disability exemption is sometimes interpreted liberally. In recognition of such practices the Alabama exemption for disability is tighter than it once was.

TABLE 62 (*Continued*)

Persons Liable for Payment of Poll Tax

STATE	PERSONS LIABLE	PERSONS EXEMPT [a]
		3. Officers and enlisted men of Alabama State Guard during active membership and all who have served 21 years
		4. Persons with honorable military service between January 1, 1917 and November 11, 1918, between September 16, 1940 and December 8, 1941, or at any time past, present or future, when the United States was, is, or shall be at war with any foreign state
Arkansas	Men over 21 Women over 21 desiring to vote	1. Women not desiring to vote 2. Persons who became 21 since assessing time next preceding election 3. Any citizen while serving in U. S. Armed forces
Mississippi	Persons over 21 and under 60	1. Persons over 60 years of age 2. Persons who are deaf and dumb or blind or who are maimed by loss of a hand or foot
South Carolina	Men over 21 and under 60	1. Women 2. Men over 60 3. Confederate soldiers over 50 4. Persons incapable of self support from being maimed or any other cause
Tennessee	Men between 21 and 50	1. Persons over 50 2. Those blind, deaf, dumb or incapable of labor and of earning a livelihood

TABLE 62 (*Continued*)

Persons Liable for Payment of Poll Tax

STATE	PERSONS LIABLE	PERSONS EXEMPT [a]
		3. Members of Tennessee National Guard, except for tax of 50¢ for the use of state
		4. Women
		5. Veterans of World Wars I and II
Texas	Persons between 21 and 60	1. Persons over 60 years of age
		2. Indians not taxed, persons insane, blind, deaf, or dumb, those who have lost a hand or foot, those permanently disabled, and all disabled veterans of foreign wars where such disability is 40% or more
		3. Persons who become 21 after January 1 before the following election
		4. Officers and men of state militia except for $1.00 tax for schools
		5. Persons in armed forces during war or within one year after close of calendar year in which war terminates; and persons who were in forces within 18 months prior to such election
Virginia	Persons over 21	1. Civil War veterans and their wives or widows
		2. Persons pensioned by the state for military services
		3. Members of the U. S. armed forces in time of war

[a] Temporary exemptions for service personnel adopted for the duration of World War II and for short periods thereafter are not noted.

[b] Persons over 45, however, must have paid taxes for which they were liable before reaching that age.

South Carolina exempts all women from the tax, an exemption that loses significance since neither men nor women must pay the tax to vote in that state's Democratic primaries. Arkansas makes only those women "desiring to vote" liable to the tax, a provision that is, of course, no exemption at all. In reality in all the states only those "desiring to vote" must pay the tax. Tennessee in 1949 exempted women from the tax.

Any assessment of the effects of the poll tax ought to include an estimate of the magnitude of the exemptions. In Texas exemption of persons over 60 gives a "tax-free" vote to about one-eighth of the potential voting population. In Tennessee, 29.4 per cent of the potential voting population, those 50 and over, is not subject to the poll tax.[10] The figures on the several states are set out in Table 63, which includes no estimate for Alabama. In that state "exemption" begins at 45, but since taxes for which liability accrued before that age must have been paid, the proportion of the electorate affected by the exemption cannot readily be determined.[11]

Time of Payment of Tax. Defenders of the poll tax refer to it as a nominal levy and assert that any citizen can afford to pay the dollar or two required. The shiftless, the irresponsible, and others not interested enough in civic affairs to pay the small tax ought not to be entitled to vote anyway, the argument runs. Yet many persons to whom the dollar or two is no burden do not pay the tax because of conditions surrounding its collection. One factor is the requirement that the tax be paid long in advance of the primary or election. When the tax is due six months or more in advance of a campaign, before the candidates have announced and before political interest is aroused, the natural result is a smaller degree of payment than would occur if collection continued until a shorter time before the voting. The restriction of the electorate is of the same type as that effected by variations in the period between registration and election in nonpoll-tax states.

[10] The exemption because of age may have less effect on voting than might be expected for unless a person becomes habituated to electoral participation before age 50, he is not likely to become suddenly interested in politics at that time. The proportion of the potential Tennessee electorate voting for governor in both Democratic primaries and general elections is usually less than the proportion exempt from the poll tax because of age. The exemption of women in 1949 increased to about 65 per cent the proportion of Tennessee adults not liable for the tax.

[11] In 1940, 36.1 per cent of adult citizen population was over 45 years of age, which figure sets top limit on the proportion of persons that might qualify for voting without current payment of the tax because of the age exemption. The military exemption, which covers both past and current taxes, probably has more real effect. From the state, Selective Service inducted 210,599 persons in World War II, a figure equal to 13.5 per cent of the 1940 population of voting age. If one includes World War I veterans, well over 50 per cent of the population of voting age is exempt from current payment of the tax. Yet the chances are that the cumulative feature, for nonveterans and women, makes the tax an effective bar to voting. The state collects no statistics on tax payment or registration, but the figures for one county may suggest the situation. In Madison County in 1948, about 12,500 voters were qualified; 2,543 paid poll taxes.

The tax has to be paid ten months before the Democratic gubernatorial primary in Arkansas; in Alabama and Virginia, three months before
the primary; in Texas, six months in advance of the primary. Mississippi's
requirement is unique and is an element of the cumulative form of her
tax. To vote in the general election, it is necessary only that the two years'
tax be paid by February 1 before the election in which a person votes.
For participation in the primary, however, the annual tax must have
been paid on or before the first day of each of the two preceding Feb-
ruarys. The first of the two taxes must have been paid about 18 months
in advance of the primary.

Discouragement of participation is not always the only objective in
fixing the period between the date of payment and the day of the bal-

TABLE 63

Persons Exempted from Poll-Tax Payments under Provisions Relieving
Aged of Liability

STATE	POPULATION 21 AND OVER, 1940	POPULATION EXEMPT FOR AGE [a]	PER CENT 21 AND OVER EXEMPT BE- CAUSE OF AGE
Mississippi	1,197,617	173,137	14.4
South Carolina	481,576 [b]	61,804	12.7
Tennessee	1,707,760	502,965	29.4
Texas	3,861,721	533,431	13.8

[a] That is, those 60 and over, except in Tennessee where exemption begins
at age 50.
[b] Men 21 and over; all women are exempt from the tax. In 1940, 51.4 per
cent of the potential voting population was female. Of the total population of
voting age, 57.7 per cent was exempt from the tax on account of age and sex
exemptions.

loting. In Arkansas, for example, if one wishes to vote in the primary he
must hold a receipt issued before October 1 of the preceding year. If he
wishes to vote in the general election, he must pay the tax before October 2 of the election year or four or five weeks preceding the election.
Before the statute took this form, payment before October 2 of odd years
qualified for both the primaries and general elections of the even years.
To raise additional revenue the statute was amended in the late 'thirties
to stimulate double payments by persons desiring to vote in both primaries and general elections. The change reduced the period between tax
payment and the general election, but, of course, required that persons
pay the tax in both odd and even years to vote in both the primary and
general election of an even year. The statutory change reduced the
biennial fluctuations in collections.

In most states the payment date was deliberately fixed far in advance
of the voting to reduce the number of voters. Typical of comments in

TABLE 64

Poll-Tax Payment Dates

STATE	DUE DATE	APPROXIMATE PE-RIOD BEFORE GUBERNATORIAL PRIMARY [a]
Alabama	Payable only between October 1 and February 1	3 months
Arkansas	Before October 1 of year before primary	10 months [b]
Mississippi	On or before February 1	18 months [b]
Tennessee	60 days before election [c]	
Texas	Before February 1	6 months
Virginia	6 months before general election	3 months

[a] The exact length of time before the primary that the tax must be paid varies slightly because of the method of fixing the date of the primary. Thus, in Virginia, the primary is held on the first Tuesday in August preceding the November general election. In South Carolina, the poll tax is not a prerequisite for voting in the primary. The state constitution specifies that the tax shall be paid 30 days before the general election, but the registration statute demands payment six months in advance of the election as a condition for registration, which is decennial.

[b] See textual discussion for qualifying details on these states.

[c] Tennessee's poll tax may be paid up to the day before the primary.

the discussion of this feature was the conclusion of a member of the Alabama constitutional convention of 1901:

> I was going to say that the negro and the vicious element will not pay two months ahead of time a dollar and a half in order to exercise this privilege, but if the business man knows he is liable for the tax, although he will not give a dollar and a half to vote or exercise the franchise, he will put it on the list of liabilities like he does everything else and tell his clerk to pay it when it is due, and will not wait until the first of February, but will pay it between October and February, along with the balance of his bills, and he will, as a matter of business, qualify himself to vote, and there will be no incentive on the day of election for him to refuse to vote on account of the extra burden; whereas, when the day of election comes, and purchasers come around (and nobody will buy a tramp or a Negro ahead of time) or when the politician comes around two weeks before election and wants to buy, lo and behold! the first day of February has passed and he has no vote to sell.[12]

Proof of Payment at the Polls. Accounts of the poll tax usually record that poll-tax proponents had the notion that if persons offering to vote were required to present tax receipts to the election officials, the effect would be to disfranchise Negroes, who were unaccustomed to the preservation of records. The theory, of course, has had little or nothing

[12] *Official Proceedings,* p. 3374.

to do with nonvoting by Negroes, but the necessity of establishing the fact of payment creates a nuisance for both voters and election officials.

The method of proof of payment of the tax differs from state to state. In Virginia and Alabama, both states with cumulative taxes, tax collectors notify registration officials of payment. The official list of voters then serves as evidence that the tax has been paid, and no presentation of evidence by the voter is required. In Texas the receipt must be presented at the polls or an affidavit made in writing that it has been lost. In Arkansas the tax receipt or other evidence of payment must be presented. To vote in the South Carolina general election the receipt, or a certificate from the tax collecting authority in lieu thereof, must be presented at the polls. In Tennessee, in the absence of the tax receipt, the fact that a voter's name is on the list certified by the tax collector constitutes satisfactory evidence of payment. In Mississippi the requirement of presentation of the receipt appears to be most rigid. The receipt, or a certified copy, must be presented at the primary election; at the general election the voter must only produce "satisfactory evidence" of payment.[13]

A word is in order about the fact that the poll-tax system serves as a substitute for a system of voter registration in Texas and Arkansas. Neither state has, unlike other southern states, systematic procedures for the preparation of lists of qualified voters in advance of the election. The poll-tax receipt serves at least as presumptive evidence that the person applying to vote is a qualified elector. In Texas persons exempt from the tax are required to obtain "exemption certificates" and present them on the day of election in lieu of the tax receipt. At the time of voting the election officials are required to stamp the receipt or certificate to indicate the fact that it has been "voted" and may not be used to vote again.

The Texas poll tax, according to persons active in politics at the time of its adoption, was designed primarily as a registration system to prevent fraudulent voting rather than to disfranchise the Negro.[14] Its continuance in that state has been defended on the ground that it serves as a system of registration. Unlike registration records that include the voter's signature, it provides no ready and easy means of voter identification as a preventive of fraud. As an annual tax that has to be paid at least

[13] The practice is indicated by the published announcement of the Mississippi secretary of state in 1946: "Secretary of State Walker Wood said yesterday that voters in Mississippi will not be required to show their poll tax receipts at the special and general elections on Tuesday, November 5."—*Clarion-Ledger* (Jackson, Miss.), October 27, 1946.

[14] Old-time Texas politicians, their memories refreshed by current rationalizations of the tax, recall that the tax was adopted expressly as a registration system. That may have been a consideration, but debate at the time of adoption paralleled that in other states. The remnants of the Populists opposed a scheme to "rob" the laboring people "of their liberties." Union labor voted against the poll-tax amendment and large majorities were recorded for it in the black-belt counties. See Laura Snow, *The Poll Tax in Texas: Its Historical, Legal, and Fiscal Aspects* (Mss., M. A. Thesis, University of Texas, 1936), pp. 47–51.

biennially if one wishes to vote, it is the equivalent of a crude biennial system of registration.

2. The Tax in Application

Beyond the form of the poll tax are questions of the manner of its administration and of local customs and usages embellishing and supplementing the statutory form. To what extent do tax administrators make it convenient for the taxpayer to pay the tax? What sorts of systematic programs to stimulate tax payments are carried on by partisan groups? By other civic organizations? To what extent do political leaders pay the tax for their followers? Is the tax inherently conducive to electoral corruption? On all these matters a confusing variety of custom prevails and only the results of sample borings here and there over the South can be presented, with the warning that one must generalize warily.

The manner of poll-tax administration has a bearing on the number of qualified voters just as the nature and management of a system of registration influence the number of registrants. Entirely apart from the fiscal burden of the tax as a deterrent, the methods of its collection may result in short voters' lists. The greater the inconvenience associated with paying the tax, the smaller will be the number of people who pay it. If the poll tax were in reality levied to produce revenue rather than to limit voting, questions of convenience to the citizen might not arise. Tax collectors usually find ways and means to make it inconvenient for the citizen not to pay his taxes; if the poll tax were treated as a tax, probably larger proportions of the citizenry would qualify to vote under it than do in jurisdictions where registration is a purely voluntary act. But the tax is not a tax in the ordinary sense of the word. In most states the citizen exercises an option whether to pay it. It is paid by those persons who have an interest in politics and public affairs and, in some areas, it is paid by such persons for others.

Like many long-established governmental institutions and practices, the poll tax finds an urban environment uncongenial. In a rural community composed largely of small landowners who had to go to the county courthouse occasionally to pay their property taxes and to transact other business, the payment of the poll tax was merely incidental to such visits. With urbanization and the rise of rural tenantry, a different administrative situation prevails. The necessity of taking a half day off to make a trip to the courthouse to pay the poll tax probably disfranchises more urban wage and salaried workers than does the disinclination to part with the dollar or so for the tax.

Over the South generally, tax collectors have done little to adapt tax administration to the conditions of urban life. They leave it to the taxpayer to go to the courthouse to pay the tax. In some urban localities, however, tax administrators take special measures to make payment convenient. For example, the Jefferson County (Birmingham), Alabama, tax collector in January, 1947, established 19 booths at points throughout the county for the convenience of taxpayers, and as the February 1 deadline for payment approached he set up additional places in department stores in the downtown Birmingham area at which the tax might be paid.

In some urban communities tax collectors have exercised ingenuity to make tax payment convenient within the limits of law. In Knoxville in 1947 the tax trustee authorized church groups, unions, factory managers, and civic groups to accept payment and to give temporary receipts. The tax could be paid on almost any street corner. The salesmen of temporary receipts would then deliver the list of names and the sums collected to the trustee who mailed the official receipt to the voter. This manner of collecting public funds is, of course, not without its dangers and is exceptional in Tennessee. The trustee of another Tennessee county, distrustful of his fellow man, observed that the Knoxville method of collection would be utterly impossible in his county. Unless the taxpayer came to the courthouse, the money might never reach the county treasury: "All of the bonds in Tennessee would be necessary to protect the procedure."

In their efforts to simplify tax payment Tennessee union leaders have induced some county trustees to send deputies to plants, at times publicized in advance, to make collections. Other trustees may let a union man take along a poll-tax receipt book and sell receipts to anyone he likes. In Memphis, it is reported, there has been selective door-to-door collection, i.e., collections by house-to-house canvass of faithful supporters of the Crump organization. In some localities, the county trustee will accept a list of names and a sum adequate to cover their taxes from anybody who turns up at his office; he assumes that the taxpayer has sent the money by a messenger. Other trustees insist that the taxpayer appear in person at the courthouse. Others will accept payment by mail. Within the same county tax-collection practice may vary from year to year, depending on the expectations of the political leaders about the effects of collection procedures on the next election. Thus, prior to the 1948 primary a controversy raged in Memphis over the refusal of the county trustee to accept payment by mail, a practice permitted in earlier years. Opponents of the Crump machine, who thought that their candidates would benefit from an expanded voting list, were vociferous in support of tax payment by mail.

In a few Texas cities tax collectors use temporary deputies to facilitate payment. In Houston the collector even appointed over a score of

Negro deputy collectors, one of whom set up headquarters in the barber shop of R. R. Grovey, of the noted white-primary case, *Grovey* v. *Townsend,* and collected 7,000 poll taxes. In Dallas, in 1947, the collector likewise appointed Negro deputies, who went from door to door, and also set up collection booths in retail stores. It should not be supposed that the Dallas County tax collector drew the color line in the facilitation of tax payment; in 1948 he deputized seven leaders of the local Federation of Women's Clubs to receive poll-tax money and to issue certificates of exemption from the tax. Such arrangements for the convenience of the taxpayer are exceptional. And in Dallas they caused difficulties. The tax officials eventually discovered that receipts had been sold to apparently nonexistent persons, and they revised their procedure to permit only sale of applications which might be checked to determine whether the taxpayer gave a vacant lot as an address.

Arkansas taxpayers may authorize an agent to pay the tax for them, and in many localities those interested in increasing the vote volunteer to collect the tax and serve as "agents." In Little Rock, liquor stores customarily have on their counters blank forms for their customers to use in authorizing the payment of poll taxes. In a single transaction one may buy a bottle of liquor, pay a dollar to cover his poll tax, sign an authorization, and within a few days he will receive his poll-tax receipt through the mail. The liquor stores are not alone in rendering this public service; civic clubs set up collection booths in the department stores. In Washington County—and presumably the practice is not limited to this county— beer parlors accept tax payments. Some beer licensees, in their enthusiasm to facilitate the performance of civic duty, even place signs on the front of their establishments announcing that poll-tax receipts may be purchased there. They theorize that anyone who pays his poll tax in a beer parlor will probably vote wet in the next local option election. Factional leaders, as would be expected, also serve the voter by taking his dollar down to the tax collector.

Informalities in tax administration carry with them special hazards in Arkansas and Texas where the poll-tax system serves as a system of registration. The bearer of a poll-tax receipt, unless challenged at the polls, is presumed to possess the qualifications for voting. In other states the would-be voter establishes these qualifications through the registration machinery. In Arkansas, from time to time it is charged that poll-tax receipts are issued to fictitious persons, to dead persons, to nonresidents; holders of the receipts have the same basis for electoral fraud as do machine operators who pad registration lists under conventional systems of election management. Thus, in a battle between the Hot Springs machine and a GI group in 1946, a Federal court voided 1,607 tax receipts insofar as their use in a congressional primary was concerned. About half of them had been issued to a Negro proprietor of a gambling house on the basis of "signatures" to authorizations to purchase receipts copied from an old poll book.[15]

All in all, southern tax authorities make it neither convenient for the tax to be paid nor embarrassing for it not to be paid. Although for most states the number of persons liable for the tax and the number who actually pay it are not known—an extraordinary commentary in itself—it is clear that a large proportion of those subject to the tax escape payment. In Texas in 1940, for example, 3,328,290 persons fell within the age group subject to the tax; 1,259,878 tax receipts were issued. Thus 62.2 per cent of those liable were tax dodgers. The proportion of Texans not paying the tax is considerably larger in nonelection years. In 1940 approximately 60 per cent of those liable paid the tax in South Carolina; the collection rate betters that of Texas probably because women are exempt from the South Carolina tax.[16]

Legal measures for poll-tax collection are exceptional. In Alabama, the constitution provides that there shall be no legal process or any fee or commission for collection. Mississippi's constitution allows no criminal proceedings to enforce the tax, but in South Carolina nonpayment is a misdemeanor punishable by a fine not in excess of $10 and costs. The enforcement of this criminal statute appears not to be draconian.

In general, tax-assessing and -collecting arrangements make it more probable that owners of real property will pay the poll tax than will persons possessed only of personal property. In those states requiring that the poll tax be assessed before payment, it is assessed more or less as a matter of course when a person's real property is put on the rolls. Taxation of personal property always tends to be hit or miss and, hence, those persons liable only for personal property taxes are not so likely to pay the poll tax as an incident to the settlement of their general tax obligations. It is reported that occasionally Arkansas tax collectors illegally use the poll tax as leverage to collect property taxes by refusing to accept poll taxes unless accompanied by payment of property taxes. In Arkansas it is thought, and probably the same is true elsewhere, that many persons decline to pay their poll tax on the ground that to do so would assure their being assessed for personal property taxes, a levy that is never applied with equity and that is perhaps impossible of such application. Arkansas in 1947 abolished assessment of the poll tax and permitted the taxpayer to go directly to the tax collector to pay his poll tax. He thereby

[15] *Arkansas Gazette,* November 3, 1946. The machine-controlled party authorities proceeded to rule that the voided receipts could be voted in a primary in which only state and local candidates were chosen, all of which incidentally illustrates one of the advantages of separating state and local primaries and elections from Federal elections.

[16] Data on the proportion of those liable who paid the tax in Arkansas and Texas over a period of years appear in Figures 69 and 70, below, pp. 601–602.

avoids routine assessment of personal taxes at the time of assessment of the poll tax.

In poll-tax administration—as in the administration of other taxes —fraud can occur. The effect may be the same as that of fraud in the registration of electors but with fiscal overtones; or the operation may be the same as financial fraud with electoral consequences. If, as sometimes happens, voting officials do not require proof of payment of the tax, it becomes a dead letter in the community. Or, under the cumulative tax for Alabama the matter of determining whether a new resident of a county has paid his earlier cumulative tax in another county is a nuisance. Obviously it would be expecting meticulous administration to suppose that this fact is always ascertained by the officials of the county of new residence. Or, under the system of assessment prevailing in Arkansas, the voter had to appear in person for the assessment and payment of his tax or furnish written authorizations to others to take care of these matters. In a few localities the local political organizations ignored these requirements and, without written authorization, assessed taxes and issued receipts in large blocks. In most states, payment of the tax must be made long in advance of the primary or election. In Mississippi, it is reported that the sheriff not infrequently holds out tax receipts and issues them to his supporters after the deadline for payment.

Of all the practices associated with the poll tax, that of block payment by political leaders has been most criticized. This custom involves the assumption of the tax by the political candidate, boss, or leader who arranges, legally or illegally, to pay the taxes for blocks or groups of voters. Block payment increases the candidate's financial burdens, leads often to the purchase of votes, and sometimes moves gradually into the issuance of receipts to fictitious names in states that rely on the tax rolls for a list of the qualified voters. The degree to which block payment prevails cannot be determined with precision. To judge from conversations with politicians in all the poll-tax states, the custom is far less prevalent than one might be led to believe from the propaganda of antitax organizations. Often political leaders or candidates merely function as collectors and messengers in the payment of the tax, a practice different from the actual assumption of the tax itself. Among the poll-tax states, if the volume of rumor, of first-hand evidence, and of talk about the subjects offers a gauge at all reliable, Arkansas excels all the states in the extent of block payment by political leaders.

Conversations with Arkansas political leaders suggest that block payment of poll taxes by candidates and would-be candidates is fairly widespread over the state. The atmosphere of the situation may be indicated by a few scattered reports. In explanation of most curious gyrations of total tax payments in an eastern Arkansas county a local political leader related that in one year a sheriff, short in his accounts, was opposed in an extremely hot race by a young Turk. Both sides bought poll-tax receipts for everyone that they thought would support them and thereby produced the odd peak in collections that appeared in the statistics. The same informant reported that in earlier years when the tax did not have to be paid so long before the primaries as now, local leaders could obtain subventions from gubernatorial candidates to purchase blocks of receipts. With the deadline for payment now long in advance of the primaries, state subventions are less frequent. Even now, however, according to a one-time gubernatorial candidate, a state administration may put a thousand dollars or so into a county a day or two before the October 1 deadline to cover poll taxes. The holder of the poll-tax receipt is, of course, given to understand that he will support the administration candidate the following year.[17] A newspaper editor in a western Arkansas county estimated that candidates for local offices usually spend from $200 to $1000; their largest item of expenditure is for poll-tax receipts. In an Ozark county, in which Republican-Democratic rivalry prevailed, a judge indicated that Republican and Democratic candidates had formed pools to buy tax receipts in a recent year, a report given a color of authenticity by an extraordinarily high peak in tax collections for the county. A person familiar with county finances over the state reported that block-buying often resulted in the issuance of duplicate tax receipts for the same individual. In the rush before the deadline politicians would bring in long lists of persons for whom the tax was to be paid. Following the deadline, a check of payees would reveal from 100 to 150 duplications in a county. "As an accommodation," the tax collector would usually refund $1 in exchange for one of the duplicate receipts and void it.

In Virginia it has been common practice for political leaders to make block payment of poll taxes to qualify their faithful adherents, especially in the rural counties, yet the general impression prevails that the practice has declined since investigations by the state comptroller's office in the 'thirties. The burden of payment of taxes for the faithful is said to be borne by the county leaders and candidates unassisted by subsidy from the state Democratic organization. The strength of the Byrd organization is greatest in the rural counties, where block payment of taxes is reputed to be most common. Payment of poll taxes places a heavy financial burden on local political organizations; the burden became so serious in the 'thirties that county treasurers eased the limitations on the suffrage and the strain on the organization treasury by marking as paid the taxes of loyal supporters of the county organizations without the formality of collection. Investigations by the state comptroller's office revealed shortages.

---

[17] Our informant opines that this is "a damned fool practice because you usually have to buy the votes again the following year anyway."

Mississippi politicians conclude that block payment of poll taxes has declined since the adoption in 1935 of a requirement that each of the two annual payments of the cumulative tax be paid in the year in which it becomes due. The practice, however, is reported to prevail yet on a large scale in a few counties. In such counties an officeholder may inspect the list of those who have not paid their poll tax on the last day for payment. He picks out 150 or 175 people "he can handle" and writes a check for their taxes. With the tax receipts in his possession, he has an effective instrument for the solicitation of votes when the campaign rolls around.

Rumor and remark about block payment of poll taxes seem less general in Texas than in other southern states. In the Rio Grande Valley the story goes that local potentates buy poll-tax receipts in blocks for Mexican-Americans. In some instances the voters are rounded up, given $1.75 each with which to pay the tax, and herded through the tax collector's office. As they file out, they deliver the receipt to their benefactor who retains it until the day of voting at which time it is "voted," sometimes by the person to whom it was issued. It is also reported, not on the best authority, that in some of these counties tax collectors will sell pads of poll-tax receipts in blank. In San Antonio, the local tradition goes, a former Negro leader ordinarily "owned" 3,000 "poll taxes." The process of payment resembled that reported to prevail in the Mexican-American counties; the leader retained the tax receipts in his safe for use by trustworthy individuals on the day of voting. With the exception of these local practices, discussion of block payment of taxes is not a prominent subject in the shop gossip of Texas politicians.

Block payment of poll taxes in Tennessee appears, from discussions with political leaders scattered over the state, to be localized. In a few East Tennessee machine counties candidates are reported to get together a fund with which to buy poll-tax receipts. In other parts of the state the practice, when it exists, is said to prevail only on a limited scale.

In Alabama, local politicos aid in the administration of the tax laws by paying the poll taxes of persons who may be counted on to vote for them. In Marion County it is reported to be accepted practice to make "blanket" payment of poll taxes, which is the Alabama equivalent of block payment. In one North Alabama County in 1940 the political situation became warm and $25,000 in tax collections flowed in; the greatest previous annual yield had been $9,474. Over $10,000 was paid on the day before the deadline, most of which came from "agents" financed by candidates.[18] The nature of the custom is suggested by the pleas of a legislator for the abolition of the poll tax in a committee hearing. He based his argument on the cost to elective officials, especially legislators, who have

[18] George C. Stoney, "Tool of State Machines," in *The Poll Tax* (Southern Conference for Human Welfare), 1940, p. 11.

to pay $200 to $300 in poll taxes before each election. Candidates do not universally bear the burden without assistance. For example, in a northern Alabama county in which Republicans run candidates for local office, county political leaders apply a crude version of the ability-to-pay principle. Republican and Democratic leaders touch their more affluent fellow partisans for contributions to cover the poll taxes of party members in less-prosperous circumstances.

The ethics of poll-tax paying can be deduced from the experience of an Alabama teacher who, on offering to pay his poll tax, found that it had already been paid. A few days after the election, a knock came at his door and a defeated candidate appeared for whom the teacher had not voted. The candidate said that he had gone to the trouble and expense of paying the teacher's poll tax and the teacher had not even had the courtesy to vote for him. Under the circumstances, the unsuccessful candidate thought it not unfair to request reimbursement of his expenditure.[19]

This survey of blanket payment of poll taxes makes relevant reference to the sweeping allegations about the relation of the tax to the corruption of the electorate. It is often declared that votes are controlled through payment of the tax and that the existence of the tax encourages corruption. In scattered local areas where block payment of taxes has been systematically practiced the tax is of far greater significance as a tool for management of voters than as a suffrage restriction. Generally, of course, the tax creates the opportunity for a pecuniary nexus between the candidate and the voter; it cries out to those disposed to take advantage of the chance to curry favor by relieving the taxpayer of his burden, nominal though it may be. Yet it is extremely doubtful that the tax is a prime cause in electoral corruption. In areas disposed toward electoral irregularity the poll tax merely gives a peculiar twist to improbity that would probably exist anyway.

Campaigns to persuade voters to qualify to vote by paying the poll tax and actual assumption of the tax by political leaders are not unexpected concomitants of political warfare. These practices parallel efforts of political organizations in other jurisdictions to get voters' names on the registration lists. The fact that comparatively so few persons in the poll-tax states meet the taxpaying qualification undoubtedly reflects in considerable measure, not the tax deterrent, but the weak and rudimentary nature of political organization in these states. The existence of party organizations in genuine competition for power would undoubtedly be accompanied by a substantially higher degree of poll-tax payment, both by and for the voters.

Beneficiaries of the prevailing distribution of political power have no great enthusiasm for an increase in the size of the effective electorate, and it is left to those challenging the existing power-holders to stimulate

[19] It should be said that secrecy of the ballot is not assured in Alabama.

an increase in the number of qualified voters. In recent years the most important drives for poll-tax payment have come from the NAACP, or closely associated Negro organizations, and CIO unions. The antilabor attitude of many southern members of Congress set in motion efforts by the CIO to qualify its members to vote, while nullification of the white primary by the Supreme Court gave the Negroes hope that they might now participate in politics.

The CIO has attempted in various states to become, in effect, a sort of poll-tax collection agency and has worked out means, of varying degrees of legality, by which it can either collect the tax from its members, or loan them the money, and act as their agent in the payment of the tax. In one Alabama county the local industrial council maintains a record of the poll-tax status of members of its affiliated locals and keeps payments current. The council collects the taxes from union members and, if necessary, makes loans for payment of taxes. The union practice succeeded an earlier custom by employers in the same area who insisted on poll-tax payment as a condition of employment. A change in Alabama's election laws introduced a somewhat higher degree of secrecy into the ballot; simultaneously labor became more politically conscious. The company, unable to control votes, lost interest in encouraging payment of poll taxes.

In one Alabama locality, however, a large employer, by agreement with the union, operates a check-off from wages for the collection of funds for payment of poll taxes. The union pays the taxes of its 1500 members and is then reimbursed by the mill. This instance appears to be unusual; proposals for the introduction of the same practice were rejected by some large employers in Birmingham on legal grounds that probably happily coincided with political preference.

In Alabama systematic collection of poll taxes from union members does not prevail except in isolated areas. The burden on the union of maintaining what is in effect a system of tax administration is not inconsiderable. In Virginia labor groups have set up poll-tax collection systems in several industrial centers of the state. The system operates with a regard for legality; the union member signs a card that amounts to a power-of-attorney authorizing a union official to pay his tax for him. The union either collects from the member or advances money for payment. Activities in the stimulation of voter qualification assume great importance in a state with an extraordinarily small electorate; the hold of the Virginia machine is apparently strong but in fact precarious. In one Virginia locality an increase of 400 in the number of qualified voters through a union tax-collection campaign persuaded a legislator generally unfriendly to labor not to seek re-election.

Recent campaigns by Negro organizations to induce their members to pay the poll tax suggest mention of its role in Negro disfranchisement. In the past the significance of the tax in this respect has been slight: white primary, literacy tests, and related requirements have been far more important. Only with the crumbling of the white primary have Negroes gained any incentive to pay the tax. Over most of the South tax collectors show no unwillingness to accept poll-tax payments from Negroes, although occasionally Negroes have difficulty in persuading tax officials to accept payment. Thus, in an Alabama black-belt county an educated Negro, a former agricultural extension agent, appeared to pay his tax. He was told that the office had no receipts and could not accept his money that day. The next time he went in he took his check and the collector refused to accept it. A third time he came to the office, left the exact change for his taxes on the collector's counter, and announced that he would appreciate a receipt when they got the office in order to accept poll taxes. A receipt was mailed to the persistent taxpayer.[20]

In Arkansas the law has required that poll taxes be "assessed" in the same manner as property taxes prior to payment. In the discussion of a bill that eliminated this requirement, a representative from eastern Arkansas opposed the bill on the ground that it would encourage Negroes to vote. "We just don't assess Negroes in Mississippi County, so they can't vote," she declared.[21] Whether the assessment procedure was of genuine effect in preventing Negroes from qualifying to vote, citizens of eastern Arkansas thought so. Western Arkansas leaders regarded the assessment procedure as a nuisance: " 'We' have been looking out for you on this thing long enough and we feel in our part of the state that the assessment provision is just too much trouble."

The fiction has prevailed that the poll tax deters Negro participation, but the tax has counted for little in comparison with other restraints.[22] The poll tax, insofar as it has deterred voting, has operated primarily to keep whites away from the polls. The extent of nonvoting attributable to the poll tax, however, raises questions requiring extended analysis to arrive at even a rough estimate. The following discussion is directed toward a measurement of the effect of the poll tax in disfranchisement.

[20] In 1948 in one of the recurring political fracases of East Tennessee some 400 would-be poll taxpayers marched on the Polk County courthouse demanding that their taxes be accepted. The charge was that Burch Biggs, long time Democratic boss of the county, had decreed that no poll taxes be accepted from Republicans. Biggs explained that some work had to be done on the tax books before tax receipts could be sold and that not even his own men had tax receipts. The tax officials began accepting payments after a court order had been issued.

[21] *Arkansas Gazette* (Little Rock), February 20, 1947.

[22] A gauge of popular sentiment about the effects of the tax is provided by the popular votes in North Carolina and Louisiana on proposals for its abolition. The counties returning majorities for retention were counties with heavy concentrations of Negro populations.

Chapter Twenty-eight

THE POLL TAX:

DISFRANCHISING EFFECTS

Iᴛ is impossible for me to believe," said the late Thomas Lomax Hunter, "that anybody is denied a vote through inability to pay his poll tax." [1] Mr. Hunter's deprecation of his ability to believe may be set against equally exaggerated estimates of the effects of the poll tax. Certainly the tax weighs less as an element in southern electoral apathy than the complex of factors that make up the one-party system, of which the tax itself may be one. With equal certitude, it may be said that the tax keeps some people from voting. To determine how many, though, is another matter. The poll tax is only one of many influences on electoral participation. The assignment of a weight to one of these influences—the poll tax—is somewhat like trying to decide what proportion of the score of a football team can be attributed to the efforts of any one player.

While several simple approaches show that the poll tax exerts a restraining influence on the potential voter, they produce only estimates of the outside limits of its effect. One method is the comparison of changes in the proportion of the people who pay the tax with shifts in general economic conditions; the hypothesis is that as times get hard, a smaller proportion of the potential electorate will pay the tax. Other methods are to contrast rates of voting participation before and after the repeal of the tax in those states that have abolished it; to compare the voting

[1] *Richmond Times-Dispatch,* August 3, 1947.

participation of states with and without the tax; and to contrast payment rates in counties of different social and economic characteristics within the same state. By all these techniques the results are the same. The poll tax keeps people from voting, certainly by the hundreds of thousands but scarcely by the millions as some persons would have us believe.

1. Poll-Tax Payment and Changing Economic Conditions

The most persuasive demonstration of the effects of the poll tax comes from a comparison of fluctuations in economic conditions with the ups and downs in the proportion of people who actually pay it. Insofar as the evidence goes, the tax-payment rate generally fluctuates with significant changes in economic conditions. The story for Texas is told in Figure 69. The unbroken curve represents the percentage of population age 21 to 60 paying the tax during the election or even years from 1922 to 1940. The broken curve shows the fluctuations in the price of cotton, which serves as a rough measure of changes in the general level of prosperity.[2]

During the period 1922–40 each time the price of cotton declined, the tax-payment rate also took a dip. With one exception, each time the price of cotton moved upward, the proportion of those liable who paid the tax also shifted in the same direction. Fluctuations in poll-tax payment, however, were much smaller than those in cotton prices. Yet the variations in payment rates were not inconsiderable. At the peak year 1924, 48.7 per cent of those 21 to 60 paid the levy, while at the bottom in 1932 the rate was only 35.4 per cent. Thus, 13.3 per cent of those liable in 1932, who did not qualify to vote, would have done so at the 1924 level of prosperity, if it is assumed that this was the causal factor in the variation. To put the matter in another way: in 1932, about 398,000 more persons would have paid the tax had the 1924 rate of payment governed.

In the interpretation of the chart, factors other than economic fluctuations cannot be ignored, for they undoubtedly enter into the changes in tax-payment rates. The chart shows for example, a long-term decline in poll-tax payments paralleled by a similar general trend in cotton prices. During this 20-year period urbanization, with its political sterilization of the population, proceeded apace and may have contributed to the downward trend in payment. Moreover, year-to-year movements in the payment curve probably are influenced by the nature of the campaign

---

[2] One feature of the chart requires explanation. The curve on poll-tax payments is based on the number of receipts issued by January 31 of each of the years indicated. The tax must be paid by that time to qualify to vote in primaries and elections during the year. The tax-paying season, however, begins shortly after the harvest of the cotton crop for the preceding year. Therefore, the rate of tax payment is aligned in the chart with the cotton price for the preceding year.

in prospect, just as are participation rates. In the peak payment year, 1924, for example, Texans were wrought up by crusades for and against the Ku Klux Klan and by the activities of the colorful Ferguson family, "Pa" and "Ma." Or, it will be noted that from 1926 to 1928 the price of cotton rose, but the level of poll-tax payment declined slightly. In 1928 Texans were tranquil; Dan Moody was scheduled to seek a second term as governor, and in Texas a second term usually goes to a governor as a matter of course.[3]

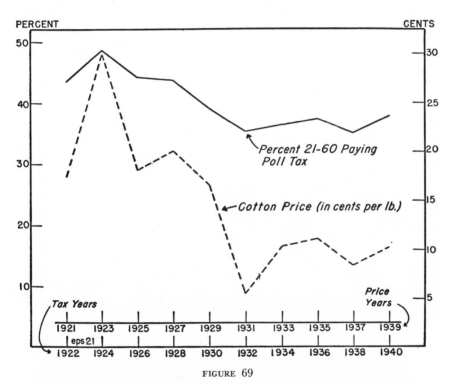

FIGURE 69

Cotton-Price Declines Reduce Poll-Tax Payments: Percentage of Texans 21–60 Paying Poll Tax and Cotton-Price Fluctuations, 1922–40

Rates of payment by those liable to the Arkansas poll tax[4] are related to fluctuations in average per-capita income in the state for the years 1929–46 in Figure 70. Here the sharp drops in payment in the off years, which also occur in Texas, are shown on the chart. Again, during the early depression years tax-payment rates declined. With the improvement of economic conditions the payment ratio began a return toward

[3] The data are not carried into the war years because of complications in calculations caused by military exemptions.

[4] Technically only those women "desiring to vote" are liable for payment of the tax, but in the computations for the chart the percentages are of all citizens 21 and over.

the level that prevailed in prosperity. The variations in payment have not followed so closely changes in income as shifts in the Texas ratios followed the ups and downs of cotton prices. On the whole, however, a sharp decline in Arkansas per-capita income is apt to bring with it a drop in the proportion of the people qualified to vote through payment of the poll tax. It is also apparent, as in Texas, that variables in addition to that of per-capita income influence the level of tax-payment.[5] It should not be supposed that nonpayment always prevents voting. In the depression some Arkansas counties and townships ignored the poll-tax law and threw the polls open.

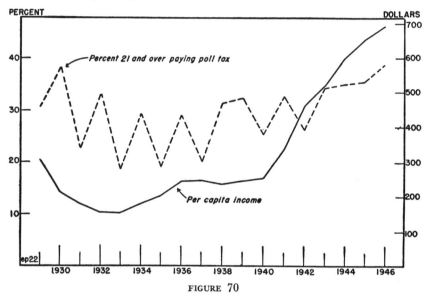

FIGURE 70

Percentages of Citizens 21 and Over Paying Poll Tax and Changes in Per-Capita Income in Arkansas, 1929–46

The facts are not available to make comparable analyses for other states, but the Texas and Arkansas records make it apparent that a substantial deterioration in economic conditions is likely, other things remaining constant, to bring a decline in the proportion of potential voters paying the poll tax.[6] It should be added, however, that invariably fewer

[5] The shift of the biennial peak to the odd years in 1939, as shown on the chart, followed a change in the law that required payment in odd years to vote in the primary of the following even year. No ready explanation is at hand for the smoothing of the curve following 1943, although challenges to primary nominees in the general elections may have boosted tax payments in the even years.

[6] The query may well be raised whether the proportion of the potential voting population registered to vote in states without the poll tax tends to decline with a drop in per-capita income. Or to put the question in another way: If Texas had not had the poll tax but had been equipped with a registration system from 1922 to 1940, would the proportion of potentials registered have varied in the same way that the ratio of tax payment fluctuated?

people vote than pay the poll tax. It does not follow, however, as has been argued, that the tax does not restrict the number of qualified voters.[7]

2. Before-and-After Analyses

A common method of analyzing the effects of the poll tax is to compare the turnout of voters before and after its repeal.[8] Usually the turnout curve rises steeply after the repeal of the tax. This upturn usually has been caused by several forces striking concurrently with the lifting of the tax. In fact, repeal ordinarily comes with some political movement that brings with it a rise in voting interest before the removal of the tax. The records of three states present trends in participation that illustrate these propositions.[9]

Louisiana repealed its poll tax in 1934 on the recommendation of Huey Long. Organized labor supported the proposal of a constitutional amendment to abolish the tax, while it is reported that sugar, oil, and lumber interests through their representatives in the legislature opposed repeal and gave the Kingfish a tough fight. Long heaped scorn on those who defended the tax on the ground that a person indisposed to pay a dollar for the support of the schools should not be allowed to vote. He spoke contemptuously of those who favored a school system supported by such a trifling form of taxation. The repeal move is regarded by old Long men as a logical part of his program: free bridges, free schoolbooks, free votes, all appealed to the common man. Others suggest that repeal was calculated to increase Long's popular vote. Centers of opposition remained in parishes where sheriffs paid the poll taxes of large numbers of voters who felt obliged to vote the sheriffs' anti-Long ticket. The Kingfish, it is said, wanted to free these voters from their ties to their local bosses, free them so that they would be able to vote for the Kingfish.

Whatever its motivation, the repeal proposal carried by popular vote in 1934. The record of voting—both in totals and in estimated percentages of adult whites participating in the Democratic gubernatorial primaries before and after repeal—is set out in the graphs in Figure 71.

[7] South Carolina accumulates no data on the number of persons paying the poll tax, but figures on annual yield indicate that the proportion of those liable paying the tax fluctuates with broad shifts in levels of prosperity.

[8] The data cannot be easily accumulated to compare turnout rates before and after adoption. The Texas data in Figure 67, page 535, show that the sharp drop in turnout occurred before the tax became effective and was therefore attributable to other causes.

[9] No meaningful before-and-after analysis of the fourth state to repeal the tax, North Carolina, can be made. Its repeal of the tax as a voting prerequisite occurred in 1920 concurrently with the grant of woman suffrage. The turnout rate for the enlarged electorate declined. Presumably it would have declined even more had the tax not been lifted, but how much more is a question that cannot be readily answered.

Judgments about the effects of repeal rest on the interpretation of the trends shown in the chart. Participation rose from 51 per cent of white adults in 1932 to 66 per cent in 1936. Can this increase be attributed entirely to the removal of the poll tax? It is plain that other elements contributed to the rise in participation. The turnout rate climbed from 1924 to 1928, when Long first won the governorship. From 1928 to 1932 the upward movement continued. In 1936, after the assassination of Long the battle over the succession brought an extremely bitter campaign and a peak in turnout. The total vote rose from 379,000 in 1932 to 540,000

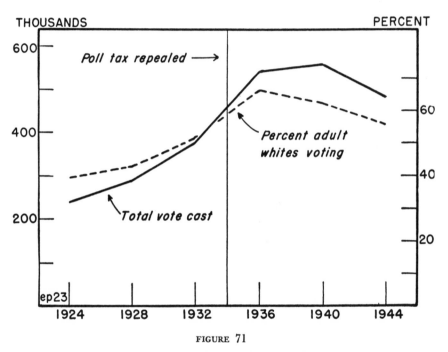

FIGURE 71

Before and After Poll-Tax Repeal: Vote in Louisiana Gubernatorial Primaries, 1924–44

in 1936. The Long program, with its powerful appeal to people accustomed to receiving few benefits from government, together with the intensive organization work by the Long and anti-Long factions, swelled the number of voters. Yet the upward trend began before the repeal of the tax; it continued afterwards to the 1936 peak, which was probably higher than it would have been had the tax remained in effect. Participation declined in 1940 and still further in 1944. The 1944 level undoubtedly reflected in part the general voting slump associated with war, but it also resulted from the return of a less-turbulent politics. Longer operation without the tax may enable a better estimate of the effect of repeal on participation, but probably as good a guess as any is that under Louisiana conditions the abolition of the tax cannot be credited with bringing an additional turnout of more than 10 per cent of the adult whites. Given a low level of participation, such an addition to the number of voters is, of course, not inconsiderable.

Florida revoked its poll-tax legislation in 1937. As in Louisiana the interpretation of the boost in turnout rates immediately following the repeal is fraught with hazard since other events in motion concurrently contributed to a heightened interest in voting.[10] The vote, both in total number and as a percentage of the adult white citizen population,[11] before and after repeal in the gubernatorial and senatorial primaries, appears in the graphs in Figure 72. The senatorial voting curve is influenced, of course, by the southern custom of often re-electing Senators and Representatives without genuine contest. The participation curve in gubernatorial primaries probably furnishes a better measure of the general trend in political interest. Participation in the senatorial primary of 1938 exceeded that of preceding primaries; the vote in the 1940 gubernatorial primary moved to an even higher level. After 1940 both rates declined, doubtless in large measure from wartime influences.

How much of the sharp increase in turnout in 1938 and 1940 resulted from enfranchisement by poll-tax repeal? In the senatorial campaign of 1938, Claude Pepper, who had been a consistent supporter of New Deal measures ranging from Supreme Court packing to wages and hours legislation, opposed Ex-Governor Sholtz, who styled himself a friend of the President, and Representative Wilcox, a conservative Democrat. The White House intervened in the primary, and Pepper emerged from a heated campaign as the victor. The Florida campaign came early in the series of 1938 primaries in which the President, as party leader, sought to purge his enemies and to give aid and comfort to his friends.[12] Both poll-tax repeal and the nature of the campaign contributed to the increase in turnout. The nature of the campaign may have contributed quite as much as repeal of the tax to the peak turnout in 1938. With other factors constant, poll-tax repeal might be credited with bringing

[10] Repeal of Florida's poll tax does not seem to have been accompanied by much fireworks. The legislature that lifted the requirement made a record as a liberal legislature, but the drive for repeal was spearheaded by Senator Ernest Graham, of Miami. His immediate concern was that the racing and gambling interests opposing him were quite able to purchase poll-tax receipts for their supporters. Labor organizations advocated repeal as did some metropolitan newspapers. Converts to the cause, it is said, included local politicians, heavily burdened in paying poll taxes for their followers in the depression years. The legislators recorded against came principally from northern and western Florida, the sections of the state with a spirit of the Old South.

[11] Translation of the total vote into a percentage of the adult white population results in an overestimate of white participation rates. Negroes have participated more freely in Florida Democratic primaries than in those of Louisiana.

[12] See J. B. Shannon, "Presidential Politics in the South," *Journal of Politics*, 1 (1939), pp. 151–52.

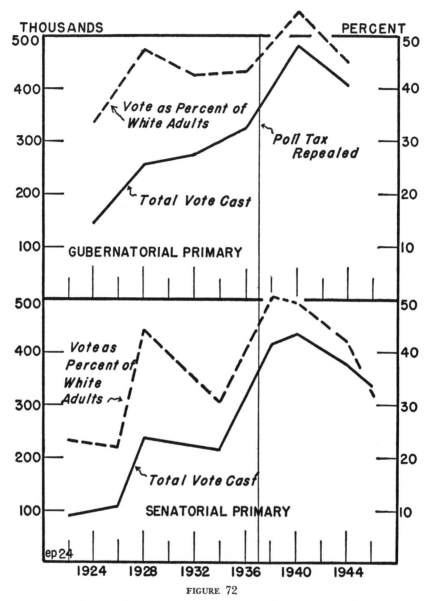

FIGURE 72

Before and After Poll-Tax Repeal: Vote in Florida Gubernatorial and Senatorial Primaries, 1922–46

immediately an additional number of voters to the polls equal to little
more than 5 per cent of the adult whites.[13]

Spectacular increases in turnout followed Georgia's 1945 elimination

[13] The 1936 gubernatorial primary turnout was equal to 43.1 per cent of the adult
whites; the 1938 senatorial rate, 50.7 per cent; the 1940 gubernatorial rate, 54.9 per cent.

of the poll tax, but again repeal alone did not account for the rise. In the middle 'thirties political interest, as may be seen from Figure 73, moved to a plateau above that of the 'twenties. In the 1936 gubernatorial primary Ed Rivers championed the New Deal against a candidate backed by Eugene Talmadge, and the vote shot up 44 per cent above that of 1934. Even more striking increases followed poll-tax repeal in 1945. The turnout at the 1946 primary, in which Talmadge battled Carmichael for the nomination, totaled 691,000, more than double the 1942 vote of 303,000. Poll-tax repeal cannot be credited entirely with the boost. In 1944 the Supreme Court invalidated the white primary, and in 1946

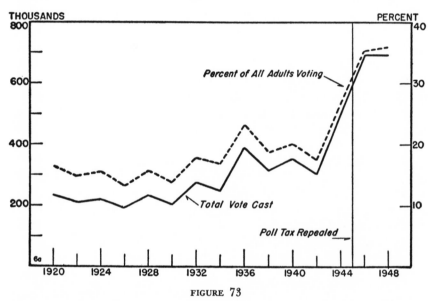

FIGURE 73

Before and After Poll-Tax Repeal: Vote in Georgia Gubernatorial Primaries, 1920–46

Negroes were encouraged to register. The Carmichael forces negotiated for Negro support, and Talmadge, always a vote stimulator, called all and sundry to the balloting to stave off a threat to white supremacy. In addition to being fattened by the combustible issues of the 1946 campaign, the total turnout benefited from the reduction of the voting age to eighteen.[14]

The post-repeal period in Georgia has been too short to determine the long-run effects of the abolition of the poll tax on electoral participation. *A priori* it would be supposed that the Georgia tax, which was

[14] The percentage turnout in the chart for 1946 is, of course, computed on the basis of the estimated number of citizens 18 and over. The estimated percentages of citizens of voting age participating in the primaries were: 1936, 23.5; 1938, 18.4; 1940, 20.0; 1942, 17.7; 1946, 35.4.

cumulative in form, would restrict the electorate more severely than a noncumulative tax. For the period 1920–44 Georgia and Alabama have extremely low records of voter participation in comparison with other southern states, perhaps their cumulative poll-tax systems have contributed significantly to that result. If this assumption is correct, it would follow that removal of the Georgia tax would have a more substantial consequence than did repeal in Louisiana and Florida.

What conclusions can be drawn from the analysis of voting before and after poll-tax repeal? The analysis yields only an estimate of the outside limits of the effects of repeal. The natural history of repeal appears to include prior to repeal a period of sharpened political interest that manifests itself in higher levels of voting. This broader concern with elections probably itself stimulates repeal, and, after repeal, a further sharp increase in participation occurs. The post-repeal increase, however, in the instances analyzed has been brought about in part by conditions that would have increased voting, although not to the same degree, even had the tax remained in effect. Probably a fair estimate is that in the states with a noncumulative tax, repeal in itself has brought out not more than an additional 5 to 10 per cent of the potential white electorate within a short time after the change.

It should be emphasized that these are estimates of short-term effects of repeal. Long-term consequences may turn out to be considerably greater. Moreover, the significance of the short-term increases in turnout should not be underestimated. Comparatively small increases, in terms of the proportion of the potential voting population, amount to substantial expansions of the actual electorate.

3. Interstate Comparisons

Exaggerated estimates of the effects of the poll tax are often drawn from comparisons of the voting participation rates in poll-tax states and in nonsouthern two-party states. The differences between the turnout rates of such states so obviously flow in large measure from factors other than the poll tax that the method of analysis and the conclusions it produces warrant only the briefest attention. Plainly only a small part of the difference in voting enthusiasm of Texans and New Yorkers is to be explained by the Texas poll tax which is only one of many factors that keep Texans away from the polls in droves.

A contrast of Tennessee and Kentucky voting in presidential election, presented by Jennings Perry,[15] as a measurement of the effects of the poll tax, illustrates the method of analysis. In Figure 74 the proportions of the potential electorates of Tennessee and Kentucky voting in

[15] Jennings Perry, *Democracy Begins at Home* (Philadelphia: J. B. Lippincott, 1944), p. 215.

presidential elections from 1872 to 1940 are shown. Through 1888 the turnout rates in the two states were at about the same level. After Tennessee enacted the poll tax in 1890 its voting rate began a long decline and leveled off at a point substantially below that of Kentucky, which had no poll tax. The two states, side by side, were, Perry argued, practically alike save for the Tennessee poll tax. Therefore, it was reasoned, the lower participation rate in Tennessee could be blamed on the tax.

Part of the difference in political participation in the two states can be credited to the poll tax, but in all likelihood the major portion of the

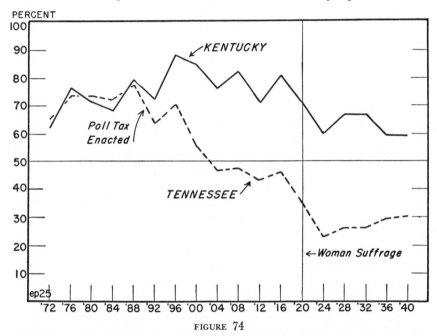

FIGURE 74

Voting in a Poll-Tax State and a Nonpoll-Tax State: Turnout in Presidential Elections as a Percentage of Total Adult Citizen Population in Tennessee and Kentucky, 1872–1940

contrast arises from other factors. The greater strength of the Republican party in Kentucky, for example, undoubtedly accounts in a measure for higher turnout in that state. Interpretation of the difference between the two states would require an intensive comparative political analysis; a single-factor interpretation—the poll tax—should be taken with great reserve.

4. Intercounty Contrasts

Although state-by-state contrasts yield only implausible conclusions on the effects of the poll tax, the same method of comparison applied to different counties within the same state produces significant findings. A question of importance is whether some classes of people pay the tax in lesser degree than do others. Light is thrown on this question by comparison of payment rates of counties of different social characteristics. The application of the method, however, is limited by the fact that only two states—Arkansas and Texas—collect data on the number of persons paying the tax in each county. The Texas records are by far the more useful because the large number of counties in that state makes it possible to examine many different groups of counties with common characteristics save for a single variable. By this sort of comparative analysis the Texas figures for 1940 permit rough estimates of differentials in payment of the tax by various classes of persons.[16]

Among Texas counties the proportion of persons 21 to 60 paying the tax differs enormously. In 1940 in 13 counties 70 per cent or more of those aged 21–60 paid the tax; in one county the number of tax receipts reached the remarkable figure of 100.8 per cent of those 21–60. At the other extreme, 13 counties had payment rates below 30 per cent. In half the counties of the state the rate of payment exceeded 45 per cent. The distribution of all counties according to the proportion of those 21–60 liquidating their poll-tax obligations appears in Table 65.

How are these wide variations in propensity to pay the poll tax to be explained? Let us examine the top 26 counties in rate of tax payment, that is, those counties with payment rates of 65 per cent or higher. They were predominantly rural counties, each with relatively few Negroes in its population, not many foreign-born whites, and only a small total population. On the average, they had a large number of motor vehicles registered in relation to their population, and all of them were west of the 98th meridian, i.e., west of Austin.[17]

Twenty-three of the 26 counties had no urban population. The county with the highest proportion of Negroes in its population was only 3.7 per cent colored; 17 counties had less than one per cent Negro population. In 23 counties less than 5 per cent of the population were foreign-born white; in one county, a most unusual local political situation or a clerical error in the tax figures, the percentage of foreign-born white was 17.2. Twenty-one counties had less than 5,000 population each, ten had less than 2,000, while the largest county had only 10,670. Small rural counties develop among their citizens a keener civic interest and perhaps

---

[16] 1940 was the last year for which census data were available at the time of the analysis.

[17] The 26 counties, with their rates of tax payment, were as follows: Andrews, 75.8; Armstrong, 77.7; Bandera, 73.2; Blanco, 72.9; Borden, 66.8; Briscoe, 71.1; Brooks, 65.9; Cochran, 68.0; Edwards, 65.6; Gillespie, 75.0; Hartley, 69.6; Hemphill, 66.4; Irion, 73.0; Kendall, 69.8; Kimble, 66.9; King, 71.2; Loving, 80.5; McMullen, 100.8; Mason, 66.5; Menard, 70.9; Ochiltree, 65.6; Oldham, 74.2; Roberts, 68.7; Sterling, 65.1; Throckmorton, 68.3; Zapata, 73.2.

a more integrated political community than do larger political units. Smallness of population may also facilitate tax administration. If ownership of motor vehicles indicates prosperity rather than simply transport necessity in sparsely settled territory, citizens of the 26 counties were relatively well off. The median in number of persons per registered motor vehicle for the 26 counties was 2.95; for all 254 counties, the median was 3.625.

If payment of the poll tax tends to be most general in the rural county of small population, perhaps it will be lowest in metropolitan counties. Inspection of the counties at the lower end of the scale for the entire state immediately reveals that counties with major cities rank low in rates of poll-tax payment. The statistics do not permit computation of rates for city dwellers alone, but the rates for counties at least half of

TABLE 65

Texas Counties: Distribution According to Percentage of Persons
21–60 Paying Poll Tax, 1940

PERCENTAGE PAYING TAX	NUMBER OF COUNTIES
80 and over	2
70–79.9	11
60–69.9	29
50–59.9	56
40–49.9	78
30–39.9	65
20–29.9	13

whose population consists of persons residing in cities of 20,000 or over are presented in Table 66.

It is plain that the people of the great cities lag in the payment of the poll tax. Seven of the 16 counties in the table fall among the lowest 10 per cent of the counties of the state in rate of payment; the county of the group with the highest rate—Travis—contains the state capital whose citizens presumably have a high interest in politics. Yet the rate for this county—41.1—is below the median for all counties of the state. While nonpayment of poll taxes by citizens of the larger cities is most striking, urbanization on a smaller scale also depresses the payment rate. When rates are laid out on a map, counties with cities of 10,000 almost invariably command attention because their payment rates are lower than those of the surrounding rural counties.

An important question is whether the low degree of qualification for voting in cities can be attributed to certain urban characteristics rather than to the poll tax. Although the answer can be only conjectural, several hypotheses suggest themselves. Obviously the rudimentary character of political organization in Texas cities contributes negatively; forces activating the electorate operate at relatively low pressure. Further, the chances are that urban workers find it more troublesome to pay the tax than do farmers, whose routine may be more likely to take them to the county courthouse.

Even among the counties with large cities considerable variation in rate of tax payment occurs; therefore, it is plain that factors other than urbanization have a bearing on poll-tax payment. Yet when allowance

TABLE 66

Percentages of Population 21–60 Paying Poll Taxes in Texas Counties in 1940 Whose Population Consisted 50 Per Cent or More of Residents of Cities of 20,000 or More

COUNTY	PRINCIPAL CITY	POPULATION OF CITY	PER CENT PAYING TAX
Harris	Houston	384,514	32.5
Dallas	Dallas	294,734	27.8
Bexar	San Antonio	253,854	35.2
Tarrant	Fort Worth	177,662	32.6
El Paso	El Paso	96,810	24.2
Travis	Austin	87,930	41.1
Galveston	Galveston	60,862	34.0
Jefferson	Beaumont	59,061	34.3
	Port Arthur	46,140	
Nueces	Corpus Christi	57,301	31.3
McLennan	Waco	55,982	33.5
Potter	Amarillo	51,686	29.1
Wichita	Wichita Falls	45,112	39.9
Webb	Laredo	37,374	33.3
Lubbock	Lubbock	31,853	33.1
Taylor	Abilene	26,612	38.0
Tom Green	San Angelo	25,802	38.0
Median of Counties Listed			33.4
Median County of State			45.0
The State as a Whole			37.9

is made for other factors,[18] it appears that the mere massing of people in cities brings with it a lower rate of payment. It is plausible to suppose that the obstacles to the integration of the individual into the political life of the larger community account in no small degree for the inferiority of the great cities in poll-tax performance over that of small rural counties.

[18] The proportion of Negro population, for example, may result in a lower rate of poll-tax payment, but counties with major cities have lower payment rates than do counties without cities of 10,000 and with comparable proportions of Negroes. Of the counties in Table 66, Dallas, McLennan, Travis, and Harris counties fall within the range of 15–19.9 per cent Negro population. Their tax-payment rates are 27.8, 33.5, 41.1, and 32.5 respectively. The average rate of the eleven counties without cities of 10,000 in the same Negro population range was 42.6.

Variations in the degree of urbanization obviously do not account entirely for the differences among Texas counties. The generally low record of payment in the eastern half of the state, in which the Negro population is principally concentrated, suggests that Negroes, as might be expected, qualify to vote in smaller proportions than do whites. The payment rate tends roughly to decline from county to county with an increase in the proportion of Negro population, although the decline by no means occurs in every instance nor is it so great as might be expected on the basis of the proportion of Negro population.

To indicate the relation of the proportion of Negro population to tax-payment rates, groups of completely rural counties, with less than 5 per cent foreign-born white population,[19] are contrasted in Table 67. On the average, the counties with higher proportions of Negro population

TABLE 67

The Negro and the Poll Tax: Payment Rates in Rural Texas Counties, Predominantly Native-Born, with Varying Proportions of Negro Population [a]

COUNTY AND COUNTY GROUP	PER CENT OF PER- SONS 21–60 PAYING POLL TAX
Average payment rate in 58 counties with less than 5 per cent Negro population	61.6
Counties 20–29.9 per cent Negro	
Austin	45.9
Chambers	50.3
Lee	50.8
Polk	37.0
Rockwall	47.8
Sabine	45.4
San Augustine	46.2
Trinity	45.4
Average payment rate for group	45.9
Counties 30–39.9 per cent Negro	
Burleson	42.1
Cass	30.1
Colorado	48.1
Madison	34.6
Morris	37.6
Average payment rate for group	37.1
Average payment rate for six counties with more than 40 per cent Negro population	36.3

[a] Counties analyzed had no urban population and less than 5 per cent foreign-born white population.

[19] As will be shown shortly the presence of a high proportion of foreign-born whites in the population of a county depresses its tax-payment rate.

have lower tax-payment rates than do the predominantly white counties. The differences that emerge from the contrast, however, probably cannot be attributed solely to variations in Negro population. The group of counties predominantly white consists mainly of sparsely populated counties and presumably their payment rate is boosted by whatever effect a small integrated community may have. Further, the predominantly white counties are, on the whole, more prosperous and their relative well-being, rather than their whiteness, may account for some of the difference.

Areas with high proportions of population of Mexican origin have conspicuously low poll-tax payment rates. Although data on the number of persons of Mexican origin are not available for 1940, census figures on foreign-born whites serve to identify the counties of high Mexican-American population. The tax-payment rates of a group of such counties, together with the rates of another group of counties comparable save for the element of foreign-born white population, are set out in Table 68. Native-white counties on the average have better records of tax payments than do counties with considerable Mexican-American population. Yet it is evident from the data that other elements enter into the performance of the Mexican-American counties.[20]

It seems clear that the size of the political community, the degree of urbanization, the proportion of Negroes, and the proportion of foreign-born whites all have some relation to the rate of poll-tax payment. Another factor—that of economic status of the people—may also enter into the variations. No satisfactory measure of the economic status of the people of a county is to be had. One measure of economic prosperity is automobile ownership; it may be presumed that a higher level of economic well-being prevails in a county with a high number of automobiles in relation to population than in another with a lower automobile-population ratio. To apply this measure of economic status to the poll-tax payment problem simply requires the segregation of counties approximately alike save for the factor of automobile ownership.

Those rural counties with less than 5 per cent foreign-born and with from 30–34.9 per cent Negro population related to the automobile-ownership ratio present the following picture:

COUNTY	TAX-PAYMENT RATE	PERSONS PER MOTOR VEHICLE
Colorado	48.1	3.68
Madison	34.6	5.49
Cass	30.1	6.08

The conclusion might be that, with other things equal, the proportion of persons paying the poll tax declines with an increase in poverty.

[20] The two groups of counties are on the whole on different levels of economic well-being. The counties with less than 1 per cent foreign-born white have a higher ratio of motor vehicle ownership than the counties with substantial numbers of foreign-born whites.

TABLE 68

The Mexican-American and the Poll Tax: Comparison of Poll-Tax Payment Rates in Rural Counties with More than 5 Per Cent Foreign-Born White Population and in Rural Counties with Less than 1 Per Cent Foreign-Born White [a]

	COUNTIES WITH OVER 5 PER CENT FOREIGN-BORN			COUNTIES WITH LESS THAN 1 PER CENT FOREIGN-BORN	
COUNTY	PER CENT 21–60 PAYING TAX	PER CENT FOREIGN-BORN WHITE	PER CENT ADULTS ALIEN [b]	COUNTY	PER CENT 21–60 PAYING TAX
Zapata	73.2	17.2	25.9	Andrews	75.8
Brooks	65.9	7.3	7.7	Briscoe	71.1
Culberson	58.5	6.0	8.3	Cochran	68.0
Jim Hogg	57.4	10.8	17.2	Borden	66.8
Terrell	52.4	10.4	17.3	Crane	61.8
Crockett	46.8	6.8	0.5	Dickens	61.8
Medina	46.2	8.6	12.3	Castro	61.4
Hudspeth	44.1	14.6	24.2	Coke	59.7
Kenedy	41.6	5.4	8.2	Carson	59.7
Atascosa	42.1	5.5	5.9	Bailey	57.9
Dimmit	37.7	16.6	21.9	Donley	56.1
Starr	26.8	8.0	12.0	Callahan	49.8
Average	49.4				62.5

[a] To limit the comparison, insofar as practicable, to the factor of the influence of the foreign-born, the two groups of counties were selected in the following way: The counties with over 5 per cent foreign-born white population include all such counties except those with any population classified as urban or with more than 5 per cent Negro population. The other group also includes only rural counties with less than 5 per cent Negro population; this group consists of the first counties in the alphabetical listing meeting this specification and having less than one per cent foreign-born white population.

[b] Computed on the basis of the number reported as alien, which probably underestimates the proportion of noncitizens. Some of those of unreported citizenship are probably also alien.

The limits of the conclusion, however, are illustrated by another group of counties, those meeting the specifications of the first group, but with from 20–24.9 per cent Negro population. The relation follows:

COUNTY	TAX-PAYMENT RATE	PERSONS PER MOTOR VEHICLE
Chambers	50.3	2.82
Trinity	45.4	7.45
Sabine	43.5	7.14

Such small groups of counties provide no basis for generalization. A larger group of counties needs to be examined. The relation between rates of poll-tax payment and motor vehicle registration is shown in Figure 75 for the 28 rural counties with less than 5 per cent foreign-born white population, less than 5 per cent Negro population, and under 2500 persons from 21 to 60.[21] By this selection of counties we hold constant at least a number of factors bearing on variations in tax-payment rate. It is evident from the scatter-diagram in Figure 75 that factors other than

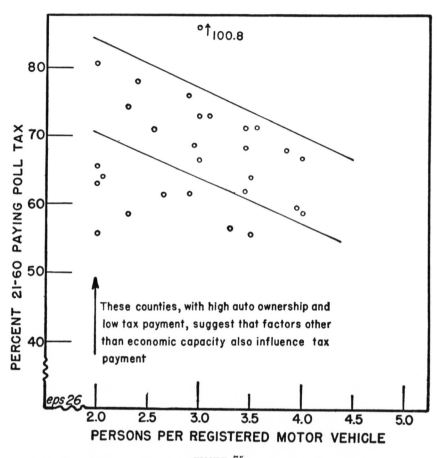

FIGURE 75

Relation between Motor Vehicle Ratio and Rates of Poll-Tax Payment in Rural Counties with Less than 5 Per Cent Foreign-Born White Population, Less than 5 Per Cent Negro Population, and Under 2500 Persons Aged 21–60

economic status (as and if measured by ratios of motor vehicle registration) influence rates of payment, although there is a slight tendency for rates of tax compliance to decline with a rise in the motor vehicle ratio. The scatter-diagram suggests, as do the preceding analyses, that the tax-

[21] These counties are: Andrews, Armstrong, Blanco, Borden, Briscoe, Castro, Cochran, Coke, Crane, Glasscock, Hansford, Hemphill, Irion, Jeff Davis, King, Loving, McMullen, Menard, Moore, Ochiltree, Oldham, Reagan, Real, Roberts, Schleicher, Sherman, Somervell, Throckmorton.

payment rate is influenced by factors not susceptible to quantification, such as local political traditions, the intensity of local political contests, the efficiency of tax collection, and so forth.

County-by-county analysis of poll-tax payment in Texas suggests that the highest rate of tax payment is associated with a complex of factors including ruralism, prosperity, predominance of native-white population, and smallness of political unit. At the low end of the scale, the political indifference of citizens of the larger cities emerges as the most striking finding. The wide spread between small rural counties and metropolitan centers undoubtedly comes in large degree from differences in organization and intensity of political activity. A similar abstention by urbanites probably would occur if they had only to register and not pay the tax.

5. Summary Estimate of Effects of Poll Tax

Any measure of the effects of the poll tax punctures the broad claim that differences in voting interest in states with and without the tax can be attributed entirely to it. On the other hand, assertions that the tax has absolutely no disfranchising effect are likewise false. The chances are that, if other things remain equal (and they rarely do), elimination of the poll tax alone would increase voting in most southern states by no more than from 5 to 10 per cent of the potential number of white voters. The evidence suggests, however, that the disfranchising effect of the tax is greater at the trough of the business cycle and that taxes cumulative over long periods of time—as the Alabama tax and the now repealed Georgia tax—have more severe effects than does a noncumulative tax.

Even if these estimates of the effects of the tax are correct, its consequences are by no means negligible. In some states the addition of 5 or 10 per cent of the potential white electorate to the voting population brings a substantial increase—a third or a fourth—in the number of voting citizens. A complex of factors, of which the tax is only one, accounts for the low level of voting in the South. Probably the tax would constitute a far more serious deterrent to voting than it now does if some of the allied obstacles to high electoral interest were removed. If, for example, party machinery developed in the South and attempted to perform its conventional function of getting out the vote, the tax bar would become more real as the party functionaries labored to bring a larger and larger proportion of the potential electorate to the polls. An increase of the voting population must almost inevitably be accomplished by bringing into the active electorate persons who, with each increment of participation, would be less able to pay the poll tax. Thus, the chances are that the restrictive effects of the tax are much less when other factors produce a working electorate comprised of a small proportion of the total electorate than when various pressures cumulate in an urge toward high participation. If, for example, all other restraints on Negro voting disappeared overnight, the economic burden of the tax would be a real obstacle to voting by poorer Negroes.

From one standpoint the degree of disfranchisement effected by the poll tax is totally irrelevant. On principle there may be objection to a tax of any sort as a condition for voting. While this view may be expressed with great eloquence and force, the fact remains that the immediate consequences of the removal of the tax are not apt to be so great as is often supposed. North Carolina, Louisiana, Georgia, and Florida have eliminated the tax, and no great social upheaval has resulted.

The poll tax has had little or no bearing on Negro disfranchisement, the object for which it was supposedly designed. On the contrary, those kept from voting by the tax have been the whites. Negro disfranchisement has been accomplished by extralegal restraints and by the white primary. And it has been the judicial undermining of the white primary that has produced a crisis in southern suffrage policy and caused many states to reconsider the policy and methodology of Negro disfranchisement.

Chapter Twenty-nine │ **THE WHITE PRIMARY**

DISFRANCHISEMENT of the Negro by statutory and constitutional means—the literacy test, understanding requirements, poll taxes, and the like—had to be accomplished by methods appearing to comply with the Federal Constitution. The color line could not be drawn outright; other lines that might happen to coincide with it had to be the basis for discrimination. The conspiracy of events, however, that threw most whites into the Democratic party and made it dominant opened the way for explicit exclusion of the Negro from the franchise. The Constitution prohibited the state from denying the vote on account of color; the Democratic party, a private association, might, according to legal theory, discriminate on whatever line it chose. At least it could until 1944 when the Supreme Court nullified the white primary. The Court's about-face stimulated search for a legal substitute for the white primary and precipitated a crisis in southern politics.

The origins of the white primary are not easily traced. The constitutional and statutory suffrage restrictions are duly engrossed on the records, but the actions of state and local party committees in excluding Negroes from the Democratic councils were not put down in readily accessible places. It seems probable, however, that the white primary originated in the South about as early as the direct primary method of nomination. The reduction of the Republican party to impotence in

619

the counterattack against the Populist revolt carried with it the virtual necessity for adoption of the direct primary. Otherwise Democratic nominations and, in reality, elections would have been determined by conventions, with only limited popular participation in the choice of public officials.

In the post-Reconstruction period Negroes adhered, almost to a man, to the Republican party, and the Democratic party, as the white man's party, had no occasion to admit Negroes to its councils. As direct primary nominations came into effect, the white primary rule was but a continuation of the practices of the Democracy: Negroes were all Republicans anyway. In local primaries and elections, understandings between white factions had the effect of excluding Negroes,[1] and as the direct primary came to rest on statute rather than party rule, local and state party committees were empowered to prescribe qualifications for voters in the primaries. At times by state party rule, at times by county party rule, participation in the Democratic primaries over most of the South came to be formally limited to whites.[2]

Eventually the white primary prevailed over the entire South, although there were localities where the formal rule was never adopted, and there were many more local departures in practice from the formal rule that existed. Lewinson in 1930 found that all states of the South barred the Negro from the primary by state party rule except Florida, North Carolina, and Tennessee. In Virginia the state party rule remained on the books, but it had been nullified by a decision of a lower Federal court that had not been appealed. A few counties in Florida had no white-primary rule; Negroes were permitted to participate in the primaries in some western North Carolina counties; and only a few Tennessee counties had rules that kept Negroes from the Democratic primaries.[3]

White-primary rules have always been violated here and there over the South. In county after county instances are called to our attention in which a few Negroes have voted for many years in Democratic primaries conducted under white-primary rules. These breaches seem to have occurred chiefly in cities and in counties with relatively small proportions of Negro population. Thus, a Negro businessman of Anniston, Alabama, remarked in 1946 that qualified Negroes had been permitted to vote in the Democratic primary in his county for 24 years, the state rule to the contrary notwithstanding.

Negro organizations have been attacking the legality of the white primary for two decades. Particular arrangements have been struck down

[1] For one such instance, see A. F. Raper, *Tenants of the Almighty* (New York: Macmillan, 1943), pp. 128–29.

[2] See O. Douglas Weeks, "The White Primary," *Mississippi Law Journal,* 8 (December, 1935), pp. 135–53.

[3] *Race, Class and Party* (New York: Oxford University Press, 1932), Appendix III.

by the courts, but white Democratic leaders until recently have always been able to adjust the situation to meet the legal necessities. After many legal skirmishes in which the white primary suffered only temporary setbacks, in 1944 the institution met with disaster. The Supreme Court, by a long sequence of cases, was led to consider the realities of the white primary in the light of the Constitution and handed down a decision that weakened the Democratic party as an instrument of white supremacy. Whether the consequences of the court's action were even potentially as great as spokesmen for white supremacy thought, drastic steps were taken in several states in another effort to make the primary system fit both the exigencies of white supremacy and the niceties of constitutional exegesis.

1. The Supreme Court and the White Primary

The white primary offered a means by which the Negro, as Negro, could be disfranchised without bruising constitutional consciences. The Constitution prohibited discrimination by the state against the Negro. Theoretically the party acted as a purely private organization. So long as the fiction of party as private association could be maintained, all could agree on the legality of its exclusion of the Negro from the Democratic primary.

In 1944, in the case of *Smith* v. *Allwright* the Supreme Court came to grips with the facts and held the white primary unconstitutional. A tortuous process of litigation led to this decision. The Texas legislature in 1923 made legal attacks on the white primary possible. The white primary had existed in the state by party rule, although in a few areas white factions relied on the Negro vote in primaries. In San Antonio, the Democratic faction that did not benefit from Negro support agitated for legislation to prohibit Negro participation in primaries. In the belief that an earlier decision by the Supreme Court placed party primaries beyond Federal control, the legislature in 1923 enacted a law providing:

> In no event shall a negro be eligible to participate in a Democratic primary election held in the State of Texas, and should a negro vote in a Democratic primary election, such ballot shall be void and election officials shall not count the same.

Subsequently, Dr. L. A. Nixon, an El Paso Negro, attempted to vote in the Democratic primary. After election officials denied his request to vote, Nixon sued one Herndon, an election judge, for damages. He challenged the legislature's exclusion act on the grounds that it violated the Fourteenth and Fifteenth Amendments of the Federal Constitution. In a brief opinion the Supreme Court did not consider the validity of the act under the Fifteenth Amendment, which prohibits denial of the right to vote on account of race or color, but held the act void as a denial of the equal protection of the laws guaranteed against state action by the Fourteenth Amendment. The Court found it "hard to imagine a more direct and obvious infringement" of the Fourteenth Amendment, which was adopted "with a special intent to protect the blacks from discrimination against them." [4] The Court, however, avoided the question whether party primaries were generally within reach of Federal regulation.

To circumvent the decision the Texas legislature in 1927 repealed its statute barring Negroes and simply authorized "every political party in this State through its State Executive Committee . . . to prescribe the qualifications of its own members." Under this grant of power the state executive committee of the Democratic party adopted a resolution "that all white Democrats who are qualified under the constitution and laws of Texas . . . and none other, [shall] be allowed to participate in the primary elections." Again Dr. Nixon was denied the ballot at a primary and again he sued for damages.

Defenders of the party action argued that the rule under which Nixon had been excluded was an act of the party; that the prohibition of denial of equal protection of the laws by the Fourteenth Amendment applied only to the state; hence, the party rule was not in violation of the equal-protection clause. The Supreme Court refused to say whether the party could exclude Negroes. It observed that the state executive committee possessed no inherent power to exclude Negroes or any other group from the party. "Whatever power of exclusion has been exercised by the members of the committee has come to them, therefore, not as delegates of the party, but as the delegates of the state." The committee had acted under authority granted by the state legislature. They became, therefore, "organs of the state itself, the repositories of official power." In effect, a private association was not discriminating against Negroes; the state, through the executive committee of the party, discriminated. Therefore, the Court concluded, the action constituted a denial of the equal protection of the laws by the state and fell under the constitutional prohibition.[5]

The rebuff by the Supreme Court stimulated Texas lawyers to contrive another way to deal with the problem. In 1932 a new rule limiting participation in the direct primaries to whites was adopted, not by the legislature, not by the state executive committee of the party, but by the state convention of the party. The wheels of justice grind slowly but perpetually and in 1935 the issue came before the Supreme Court again. Was the action of the party through its convention the action of a pri-

---

[4] *Nixon* v. *Herndon,* 273 U. S. 536 (1927).
[5] *Nixon* v. *Condon,* 286 U. S. 73 (1932).

vate voluntary association, or was it the action of an instrumentality of the state and as such an infringement of the equal-protection clause? The Court examined the legal nature of political parties in Texas. It observed that parties were compelled by law to use the direct primary method of nomination, but that the primary was a party primary. The expenses of the primary, in contrast with the practice in many other states, were borne by the members of the party seeking nomination, the ballots were furnished by the party, and the votes were counted and returns made by agencies of the party. Furthermore, the Court looked to the 'decisions of the Texas courts for their views on the nature of parties in that state. The highest state court had held that parties "are voluntary associations for political action, and are not the creatures of the state"; that the party "by its representatives assembled in convention, has the power to determine who shall be eligible for membership and, as such, eligible to participate in the party's primaries." As a private association, the Supreme Court concluded, the party might exclude Negroes from its primaries without violating the equal-protection clause, which applied only to state action.[6]

The ways of courts and lawyers are awesome, and to catch the next episode of the white-primary litigation requires a jump to New Orleans to look at a different legal angle. It will be recalled that the original Texas white-primary law had been based on the assumption that the Supreme Court had held party primaries to be beyond regulation by the Federal Government. By 1940 a lot of water had gone over the political dam and the Supreme Court had acquired some new members. A case came up from New Orleans, a place where election frauds are said to occur from time to time. Election officials charged by Federal authorities with fraud in a direct primary for the nomination of a United States Representative defended themselves by arguing that direct primaries were beyond Federal regulation. Under the Constitution, so the argument ran, Federal power extended only to general elections. In layman's language, the issue before the Court was whether the United States Government could stand by and see members of its Congress chosen in direct primaries in which fraud was committed by state officials. In technical verbiage, the question was more involved. It was argued that the constitutional language, directing that members of the House of Representatives should be "chosen . . . by the people in the several States," created a right for the voter to participate in that choice, a right that might be protected by Federal action. The primary was in reality, at least in Louisiana, the election. Therefore, a primary election official could be punished under a Federal law making it an offense to deprive a citizen of any right or privilege under the Constitution. The Court accepted this argument and said: "Where the state law has made the

[6] *Grovey* v. *Townsend*, 295 U. S. 45 (1935).

primary an integral part of the procedure of choice, or where in fact the primary effectively controls the choice, the right of the elector to have his ballot counted at the primary is . . . included in the right protected" by Article I, section 2, of the Constitution, just as it is in an election.[7]

After this detour to New Orleans and its case of election fraud, we can get back to the white primary. If the power of the Federal Government extended to the protection of United States citizens against fraud in primaries for the nomination of Congressmen, probably Negroes could not be discriminated against by exclusion from primaries either by the party or by the state. In 1944, over 20 years after the beginning of the round of law suits, the Supreme Court, in *Smith* v. *Allwright*,[8] again had the question before it. On the basis of its New Orleans decision, the Court held unconstitutional the exclusion of Negroes from the Texas Democratic primary as a violation of the Fifteenth Amendment's prohibition of discrimination in the right to vote because of color. The Court reasoned that the primary in Texas was an integral part of the machinery for choosing officials. Although the Democratic state convention had acted on its own authority and not as an agent of the state in excluding Negroes from the primary, in other respects the primary was regulated by state law and the state provided procedure by which the party certified its nominees for inclusion on the general election ballot. By such action the state itself endorsed and enforced the party's discrimination against Negroes. Under these circumstances, discrimination by the party had to be treated as discrimination by the state.

Unlike other white-primary states, Virginia did not have to await the end of the almost interminable litigation before the Supreme Court to have the question decided. A Federal District Court in 1929 held the white-primary rule, in the form that prevailed in Virginia, invalid and the Circuit Court upheld the decision the following year.[9] The matter was not further contested and Negroes came to be permitted to vote in Democratic primaries on about the same basis as in the general election. The Democratic party rules, however, continued in form to limit participation in the primaries to whites. They so provided even in 1947. At a recent convention the removal of the dead proscription from the party rules was considered by the leaders, who concluded that it would be preferable not to raise the issue. It would have created an opportunity for intolerant elements to sound off, unnecessarily and undesirably opening the whole race issue, which is little discussed in Virginia politics. Responsible party leaders counseled such action; meanwhile Negroes sat as members of the convention and participated in primaries.

[7] *United States* v. *Classic,* 61 Sup. Ct. 1031 (1941).
[8] 321 U. S. 649 (1944).
[9] *West* v. *Bliley,* 33 F. (2d) 177; 42 F (2d) 101 (1930).

2. New Ways Around the Supreme Court?

The Supreme Court's 1944 decision compelled the admission of Negroes to the Democratic primaries, although it affected actual Negro voting but little until the 1946 primaries. Some state Democratic authorities amended their rules to remove the limitation of participation to whites; others let the rules stand but allowed Negroes to participate. In some instances further litigation was necessary to make certain that the principle of *Smith* v. *Allwright* applied to the form of the primary existing in a particular state; in others, litigation was required to induce party authorities to heed the court decision.[10]

The extreme white-supremacy advocates were not disposed to accept the Supreme Court decision without exploring the possibilities of circumvention. The white primary, since it drew the color line sharply and cleanly, appealed more strongly to the defenders of white supremacy than did literacy and understanding tests. The latter, applied with even a modicum of fairness, would permit many Negroes to vote, whereas the white-primary rule, in principle, could exclude all Negroes from participation in political affairs, given the one-party system.

Squawks about the white-primary decision resounded over Dixie, but close inspection reveals that concrete measures to negate its spirit were confined mainly to the Deep South. Mississippi, Alabama, and South Carolina adopted measures of various sorts to preserve, in effect if not form, the white primary. Georgia reacted violently and only by chance failed to take positive action in 1947. In these states, the states with the highest proportions of Negro population, the irreconcilables were most potent and most vocal. The states around the rim of the Deep South accepted the new order more or less as a matter of course. Diehards in Florida,[11] Texas,[12] Tennessee, North Carolina, and Virginia expressed

[10] In one southern state the Justice Department, according to report, agreed not to prosecute party authorities for denial of the vote to Negroes in 1944 on condition that they abide by the Supreme Court decision in the 1946 primaries. The collection of evidence in support of such prosecutions was handicapped by the fact that Negroes, like whites under similar circumstances, feared reprisals. For example, a Negro mortician, denied the right to vote in the 1944 primary, refused to make an affidavit to that fact. He had a contract with the city to handle the bodies of Negroes accidentally killed.

[11] A proposal to follow the South Carolina plan of severing the state from the primary failed in 1945. In 1947 it failed again and apparently few persons other than the sponsor regarded the proposal seriously. Not only the CIO and AFL but about everyone else opposed the idea including the State Association of County Supervisors of Elections. The 1947 session also voted down, by a narrow margin, a proposed literacy test. The literacy test was attacked on the state senate floor as "nothing more than a white primary bill with another suit of clothes on." By the time the white-primary bill and related measures came to a vote, their sponsor was so dispirited that he an-

dissent, chiefly for the record, but these states made no institutional changes to offset the decision. Arkansas adopted measures in confusion and avoidance; but her heart was not in it. The next Arkansas legislature repealed the principal act calculated to overcome the decision. Louisiana, a state with a relatively large Negro population took no counteraction, perhaps because its existing "good character," "understanding," and literacy requirements for voting were felt to be adequate to cope with the situation.[13]

In the geographical concentration of the most positive reaction against the principle of *Smith* v. *Allwright,* perhaps we have a clue to profound changes taking place within the South. The decision had its most agitated reception in the states containing the largest proportions of counties with Negro majorities. The pattern recurs thematically from act to act in the history of the adjustment of racial relations. Contrariwise, in the states around the edge of the Deep South the more rapid growth of white population, and perhaps also some attrition of attitude, come gradually to produce a less-excitable social situation.

The first plan contrived to avoid the effects of the Supreme Court decision was the "South Carolina Plan." This scheme consisted in the repeal of all state laws relating to the primary, which left completely to party authorities the management of nominations. To understand this action it is necessary to backtrack to the earlier reasoning of the court. It had declared, in the *Classic* case involving fraud in New Orleans primaries, that the constitutional right to participate in elections extended to primaries under two conditions: first, where "the state law has made the primary an integral part of the procedure of choice"; and, second, "where in fact the primary effectively controls the choice."

The decision in *Smith* v. *Allwright* hinged on the finding that state law had made the primary "an integral part of the procedure of choice." as did the ruling in the *Classic* case. Judges who write opinions throw in views not essential to settlement of the case and these observations, called *obiter dicta* in the trade talk of the lawyer, are not necessarily law. South Carolinians concluded that the standard of effective control of choice, as uttered in the *Classic* opinion, was a side remark of a learned jurist and, therefore, that by wiping primary laws off the books the situation could be met. By this means, the state would no longer make the primary "an integral part of the procedure of choice," and the primary, or whatever other means of nomination the party used, would be

nounced to the senate: "I don't care what you do with them."—*Florida Times-Union* (Jacksonville), May 14, 1947.

[12] On Texas, see D. S. Strong, "The Rise of Negro Voting in Texas," *American Political Science Review,* 42 (1948), pp. 510–22.

[13] For a summary of actions following the white-primary decision, see O. Douglas Weeks, "The White Primary: 1944–1948," *American Political Science Review,* 42 (1948), pp. 500–10.

beyond reach of the Federal constitutional prohibition of discrimination by a state.

After the *Smith* v. *Allwright* decision in April, 1944, South Carolina acted quickly to preserve the white primary. Within two weeks, Governor Olin D. Johnston summoned the legislature and when it convened he outlined the course of action.

> After these statues are repealed, in my opinion, we will have done everything within our power to guarantee white supremacy in our primaries of our State insofar as legislation is concerned. Should this prove inadequate, we South Carolinians will use the necessary methods to retain white supremacy in our primaries and to safeguard the homes and happiness of our people.
>
> White Supremacy will be maintained in our primaries. Let the chips fall where they may!

The legislature repealed all state laws on the primary, and in November, 1944, the voters approved a constitutional amendment erasing all mention of it from the state constitution. After repeal of the primary laws the Democratic state convention met and adopted a set of regulations for the organization of Democratic clubs and for the conduct of primaries. Included in the regulations was a statement of qualifications for club membership and for participation in the primaries:

> The applicant for membership, or voter, shall be 18 years of age, or shall become so before the succeeding general election and be a white Democrat. He shall be a citizen of the United States and of this State, and shall be able to read or write, and interpret the Constitution of this State. No person shall belong to any club or vote in any primary unless he has resided in the State two years and in the county six months prior to the succeeding general election and in the club district 60 days prior to the first primary following his offer to enroll: Provided, That public school teachers and ministers of the gospel in charge of a regular organized church shall be exempt from the provisions of this section as to residence, if otherwise qualified.[14]

The South Carolina plan left the party entirely responsible for the conduct of primaries and for the maintenance of honesty in nominations. Fraud no longer was an offense against the state. After the first primary conducted under party authority, complaint arose about fraud. The Charleston *News and Courier* observed that the only hope of protecting the primary was through the "honor system." "Unless the chieftains, the candidates, the managers, the voters shall conduct primaries as gentlemen conduct elections in the colleges, the white man's party as a voluntary association similar to literary societies or congregations of churches, will be afflicted with internal combustion and blow up." [15]

[14] *Rules of the Democratic Party of South Carolina,* adopted by the Democratic State Convention, Holden at Columbia, May 15, 1946, p. 2.

[15] September 23, 1946.

Attacks against the South Carolina plan on constitutional grounds were not long in forthcoming. In 1947, under the sponsorship of a Negro citizen's committee and the NAACP, suit was instituted against the Richland County (Columbia) Democratic executive committee in the name of a Negro for damages because he had been denied the right to vote in the 1946 Democratic primary. The plaintiff sought to bring the South Carolina arrangements under the second inhibition of the *Classic* case, viz., that the primary effectively controlled choice. It was stipulated by the parties that since 1900 every Governor, member of the General Assembly, United States Representative, and United States Senator for the state had been a nominee of the Democratic party. If 47 years was enough, the Democratic primary indubitably controlled the choice. The only question was whether that control brought a privately conducted primary within the prohibition against discrimination on account of race.

The case came to trial before United States District Judge J. Waties Waring, a Charlestonian of impeccable South Carolina connections. He found that the South Carolina plan fell before the Constitution, and in his opinion admonished his fellow South Carolinians to mend their ways. He dismissed the contention that the Democratic party should be regarded as a private club: ". . . private clubs and business organizations do not vote and elect a President of the United States, and the Senators and members of the House of Representatives of our national congress; and under the law of our land, all citizens are entitled to a voice in such selections." He thought that the argument that there was any material difference between the situation before and after repeal was "pure sophistry." Further, all other states permitted Negroes to vote in the primary: "I cannot see where the skies will fall if South Carolina is put in the same class" with other states. He concluded: "It is time for South Carolina to rejoin the Union. It is time to fall in step with the other states and to adopt the American way of conducting elections." [16] Early in 1948 the Circuit Court affirmed Judge Waring's decision, and the Supreme Court declined to review that action.

In a confused state of mind South Carolina Democrats met in convention in 1948 to decide what to do, now that their plan for evading the Supreme Court decision had failed. The *Columbia Record* pronounced as "beneath the dignity of the party and of the state" proposals for further equivocation. It pointed to a May, 1948, municipal election in Columbia in which 47 Negro voters participated; 16 voted Republican and 31 Democratic. "Here is concrete evidence for the fearful-and-trembling South Carolina Democratic party misleaders that the Negroes of South Carolina are not of one mind, but are divided as all other voters are divided on issues and on personalities. And this, of course, is what

[16] *Elmore* v. *Rice,* 72 F. Supp. 516 (1947).

every intelligent person expected." [17] The same journal at the opening of the convention advised it to follow "the only one logical course for the party to adopt." That was to "admit Negroes to the party primaries and to the party membership." The editor asked: "Why should the Democratic party of South Carolina find itself forced to run around like a hound dog with a can tied to his tail seeking a way to do what every member of the party, every party leader knows must be done—if not today, then tomorrow?" [18]

The party convention rejected all such advice and insisted on emulating the hound dog with a can tied to his tail. It proposed to admit only whites to membership in the party but to permit Negroes who were qualified electors to vote in the Democratic primary. The qualification for membership in the party was stated as follows:

> The applicant for membership shall be twenty-one (21) years of age, or shall become so before the succeeding general election, and be a white Democrat, who subscribes to the principles of the Democratic Party of South Carolina, as declared by the State Convention.

In addition, he was required to meet the qualifications of citizenship, literacy, and so forth, as stated in the 1946 rule quoted above. Negroes, if qualified electors, were to be permitted to vote in the primary if they presented their certificate of registration and took the oath required of voters in the primary. That oath, whose adoption aroused no little furor, came out of the convention in the following form:

> I do solemnly swear that I am a resident of this club district, that I am duly qualified to vote in this primary under the rules of the Democratic Party of South Carolina, and that I have not voted before in this primary, and that I am not disqualified from voting under Section 2267 of the South Carolina Code of Laws, 1942, relating to disqualifying crimes.
>   I further solemnly swear that I understand, believe in and will support the principles of the Democratic Party of South Carolina, and that I believe in and will support the social, religious, and educational separation of races.
>   I further solemnly swear that I believe in the principles of states' rights, and that I am opposed to and will work against any F. E. P. C. law and other federal law relating to employment within the states.
>   I further solemnly swear that I will support and work for the election of the nominees of the primary in the ensuing general election and that I am not a member of any other political party.[19]

[17] *Columbia Record* (Columbia, S. C.), May 15, 1948.

[18] Ibid., May 19, 1948.

[19] The principles to which the voter was required to swear belief as adopted by the 1948 convention were as follows:
  WE BELIEVE in the fundamental principles of constitutional government enunciated by Thomas Jefferson and followed throughout the years by the Democratic Party of South Carolina.
  WE BELIEVE in the time honored and cherished traditions and customs of

"The more you study the plan," the *Columbia Record* concluded, "the more foolish and futile it appears." Negroes would be admitted to vote only if they subscribed to principles with which they presumably disagreed and in the formulation of which they had no voice, since they were excluded from party membership. And party conventions chose delegates to the national convention to nominate presidential candidates; Negroes as nonmembers were excluded from participation in the process.[20] The oath also drew fire. Roman Catholics and Episcopalians objected to the requirement that they swear belief in, and support of, religious separation of races in order to vote. The party executive committee met and tinkered with the language of the oath, although how an executive committee found authority to undo the work of the sovereign convention was not made plain. The revised paragraphs of the voter's oath read as follows:

> I further solemnly swear that I believe in and will support the principles of the Democratic Party of South Carolina, and that I believe in and will support the social and educational separation of races.
> I further solemnly swear that I believe in the principles of States'

the South and are opposed to any legislation, movement, or policy which seeks to destroy or impair them.

WE BELIEVE in States' Rights and local self-government and are opposed to the Federal government assuming any powers except those expressly granted it by the States in the Federal Constitution.

WE BELIEVE in the social and educational separation of races.

WE BELIEVE in the American system of free enterprise and private initiative.

WE BELIEVE in the right of labor to bargain collectively and in just and fair labor laws whereby the rights of the public, the employee and the employer are adequately and equally protected.

WE BELIEVE in a governmental system of adequate social welfare and aid for the aged, helpless, infirm, and needy.

WE BELIEVE in reasonable and adequate educational facilities for all citizens, and for facilities for the care of the mentally and physically infirm.

WE BELIEVE in equal opportunities to all and special privileges to none, and in strong, decentralized National and State governments, with their roots firmly planted in the people and fully accountable to the people.

WE BELIEVE in adequate National defense.

WE BELIEVE in the adequacy of the natural resources and the citizenship of South Carolina to continue to carry our State forward economically and industrially, with greater opportunities for all its citizens.

WE BELIEVE we are honor bound to support the nominees of the Democratic Party of South Carolina in the ensuing general election.

WE OPPOSE any Federal legislation which seeks to usurp the sovereign rights of the States to regulate and govern their internal affairs and to determine the qualifications of electors.

WE OPPOSE any Federal legislation setting up the proposed so-called F. E. P. C. law.

WE OPPOSE Communism, Socialism, Fascism, Totalitarianism, Nazism, and all forms of dictatorship.

WE FAVOR just and adequate laws to protect the public from abuses by majority or minority groups.

[20] *Columbia Record* (Columbia, S. C.), May 24 and 27, 1948.

Rights, and that I am opposed to the proposed Federal so-called F. E. P. C. law.[21]

The redoubtable *Columbia Record* returned to the fray. Tinkering with the oath was not enough. "The idea of the 'thought-control' oath is repugnant to free men and there is only one way to get rid of it and that is to exterminate it root and branch." [22] Local Democratic executive committees, principally in the upcountry in repetition of a familiar pattern of geographical division of sentiment,[23] resolved in favor of a new convention to clear up the muddle. The same committees proceeded, in violation of the convention rules, to permit white and black to enroll as party members without discrimination in accordance with the spirit of the court decision. "Our lawyers," the Richland county chairman advised the state chairman, "seem to think that we may be cited for contempt of court, if we fail to allow Negroes to enroll." He thought the court's ruling to be "poor law, yet, nevertheless, it is the law of the land, which should be respected by all." [24]

The state party authorities temporized, and, as was inevitable, on the basis of denials of enrollment, the whole question found its way back to court. The NAACP brought action against the state executive committee and against those county committees that were operating in accord with party rules. Judge Waring, evidently by now impatient with disregard of the authority of the Federal judiciary, laid down the law in no uncertain terms. "The time has come when racial discrimination in political affairs must stop," he declared. He had a good word for those counties that had obeyed his earlier decision. "Thank God for Greenville, Laurens, Pickens and Jasper counties for some men who put their feet on the ground and said we are going to obey the law. It's a disgrace and a shame that you have to come into court and ask a judge to tell you to be American citizens. The law of the land is supposed to be obeyed." He promised that further violations of his orders would be punishable by imprisonment.[25] His order prescribed an end to discrimination on the basis of race in party enrollment and the elimination of all the voters' oath except those sections relating to residence, to the fact that the voter had not voted before, and to the pledge to support nominees of the primary. Candidates in the senatorial campaign at the time talked of impeachment of Judge Waring, but the *Columbia Record* scolded them. They were "acting like children." The party had had its

---

[21] *Rules of the Democratic Party of South Carolina*, 1948, sec. 36.

[22] *Columbia Record*, May 29, 1948.

[23] See above, pp. 135–42.

[24] *Columbia Record*, June 1, 1948.

[25] Ibid., July 16, 1948. Judge Waring had sharp words about the obvious effort to evade the spirit of the *Elmore* decision: ". . . the law was clearly and succinctly stated and anyone who can read the English language must have known what it meant."—*Brown* v. *Baskin*, 78 F. Supp. 933 (1948).

chance, but had invited "the Negroes to sue and be damned." And by that policy the party had "magnified the attractions of voting to the Negroes, who feel that they must get something for the energy and money they have had to spend, something for the victory they have won." [26]

South Carolina's ill-considered action in 1944 to offset the decision of *Smith* v. *Allwright* preceded action in other southern states. In 1946 Alabama, instead of repealing its primary laws, tightened voting qualifications. Democratic leaders rejected the South Carolina plan. Without regulation of the primaries, Gessner T. McCorvey, chairman of the state Democratic executive committee, said that he did not "know how such elections could be properly policed." If the primaries were conducted under private auspices, he said, "then we will just have a loose-knit organization where unprincipled politicians could simply get by with murder, and know that there was no punishment awaiting them." [27] Mr. McCorvey thought that the white primary decision would not "make so much difference" at least for the time being. Few Negroes had registered and paid their poll taxes. "My own idea," he said, "is that the way to handle the situation with which we are confronted is to see that only properly qualified persons are permitted to register."

To see that "only properly qualified persons" were permitted to register, the voters of Alabama in November, 1946, adopted the "Boswell amendment" to their constitution, so called from the name of its initiator in the legislature. In brief, before the adoption of the amendment the following persons were eligible to register as voters:

> 1. Those able to read and write any article of the United States Constitution in English provided that they were physically unable to work or had worked or been regularly employed for the greater part of the year preceding their application for registration.
> 2. Persons unable to read and write if this disability was due solely to physical disability.
> 3. Persons who owned (or whose husband or wife owned) forty acres of land, or real estate assessed at $300, or personal property assessed at $300 or more.

Thus, a person could qualify to vote either by demonstrating literacy or by the ownership of property. By the adoption of the amendment, an applicant for registration, with an exception for the physically disabled, had to show that he had:

> 1. Ability to read and write;
> 2. Ability to "understand and explain" any article of the Constitution of the United States in English;
> 3. Worked or been regularly engaged in lawful employment or occupation for the preceding twelve months; and

[26] *Columbia Record*, July 24, 1948.
[27] Statement before legislative committee, February 9, 1945.

4. "Good character" and an understanding of "the duties and obligations of good citizenship un'der a republican form of government."

The amendment eliminated the possibility of qualification by property ownership. Added to literacy was the requirement that an applicant "understand and explain" the Constitution and meet the test of "good character" and comprehension of "the duties and obligations of good citizenship."

Leaders in the campaign for the adoption of the Boswell amendment beat the drums for white supremacy, although it was improbable that under the prevailing standards for registration any real threat to white supremacy existed. Any proposal to assert white supremacy gains great support or at least people are fearful to dissent, whether it has connection with white supremacy in the world of reality. In support of the amendment, Mr. Horace Wilkinson, a leader of the Alabama bar, defended the doctrine of the superiority of white to black and contended that the suffrage should never be conferred upon those who by nature or racial constitution were not fitted for the kind of co-operation upon which democracy must rest. Further, he argued that "education causes the Negro to seek political equality because political equality leads to social equality and social equality leads to intermarriage." [28]

Mr. McCorvey, the state Democratic chairman, contended that the new measure was needed because the situation had radically changed since the adoption of the literacy test in 1901: ". . . under our compulsory education statutes there are only a few hundred negroes of voting age in Alabama who cannot read and write." [29] Registrars, he asserted, are "in effect required to register practically everyone, both black and white, who are over twenty-one, regardless of their ability to vote intelligently." He thought that unless the amendment was adopted not a white county officer would be elected in 18 or 20 black-belt counties. As in the days of secession the problem of political strategy was to rally the voters of the white counties to the support of the black belt.. "We should give relief to these good people," said Chairman McCorvey.

Opponents of the amendment were by no means advocates of racial equality. They ridiculed as hysterical those who saw Negroes taking possession of the courthouses. Richard T. Rives, a Montgomery lawyer and one of the chief opponents of the amendment, was willing, if the neces-

[28] *Birmingham News,* September 18, 1946.
[29] Granting the accuracy of Mr. McCorvey's estimate of the number of illiterate Negroes, the Alabama Negro has demonstrated a remarkable capacity for self-education. The census takers in 1940 counted 62,151 Negroes 25 years of age or over who had not completed one year of schooling. Another 181,134 had completed only from one to four years of schooling. Over 50 per cent of all Negroes 25 years of age or over in 1940 had either never completed a year of school or had not gone beyond the fourth year, and a "year" in a rural Alabama Negro school may amount to very little in schooling.

sity should arise in the future, to increase the educational requirement perhaps to that of a high school education. He proposed impartial administration of registration tests and the registration of qualified Negroes. He argued: "The problems presented by two races living so closely together will be with us through this generation and through generations to come. Those problems, if approached in a Christian spirit by men of good will in both races, can, I believe, be solved, but the kind of arbitrary power sought by this Amendment will destroy confidence and be an effective hindrance to any just and lasting solution."

The campaign over the amendment was fought out mainly, not on the issue whether Negroes should be allowed to vote, but on the question whether the amendment might be used to disqualify whites. The arbitrary power that a board of registrars would have to determine whether a person could "understand and explain" a section of the Constitution or whether he possessed "good character" and understood the "duties and obligations" of citizenship aroused fears.

The division on the measure resembled progressive-reactionary cleavages in many other campaigns in the state. Further, the sectional pattern of Alabama politics—which has persisted since before The War —appeared. Proponents of the measure were strong in the black-belt counties, while the opposition centered in the cities and in northern and southern Alabama. Among the supporters of the amendment were the state Democratic executive committee, a body controlled by party conservatives; the principal political-corporation lawyers of the state, suggestive if not evidential of the black-belt-big-mule combination in Alabama politics; and such prominent conservative leaders as Chauncey Sparks and Frank Dixon.

In opposition to the amendment were the Alabama State Federation of Labor, Senator Lister Hill, Governor-elect Jim Folsom, the Republican party, the Committee for Alabama, Negro organizations of all sorts, and progressive groups generally. Protestant ministers divided on the matter, but Mobile's Catholics, who are numerous, were reported to have been advised by the Church to vote against the amendment. The cleavage on the issue by no means followed economic lines. Many substantial citizens, including the editors and publishers of the principal dailies of the state, opposed the amendment in part on the ground that it was the wrong way to deal with the race question.

Pronouncements of the advocates of the amendment lent credence to the charge by Senator Hill that the aim of the amendment was to prohibit voting by those whom "the Big Mules do not approve." Chairman McCorvey replied that "no so-called 'Big Mule' had ever suggested to" him the advisability of adopting the amendment. McCorvey was by way of being something of a little "Big Mule" himself and the most prominent lawyers of the "Big Mules" were fighting for the amendment. Their rationalizations in its support no doubt fell not unpleasantly on "Big Mule" ears. Chairman McCorvey thought it "absurd and ridiculous" to permit "a man, whether he be black or white," to register as a qualified voter "merely because he or his wife might own some junky, second-hand, rattletrap automobile assessed at $300.00." Horace Wilkinson supported the amendment because, he said, "I am not an equalitarian." "The theory of equality," he avowed, "is a communistic theory. It reaches all to a dead level. The general idea of equality is a leveling down that is harmful to individuals, to nations, and to races. It is a philosophy of negation. Nature knows no equality. The philosophy of equality is fatal to those who aspire. Democracy does not mean equality."

The amendment carried by 89,163 to 76,843; it thus received the support of 53.7 per cent of those voting upon it, a statistic that those who regard all southerners as alike may ponder well. The counties with high percentages of Negro population were generally most enthusiastic for the amendment. Of counties with more than 40 per cent Negro population, only two turned in majorities against the amendment and one of these was Montgomery County, an urban center as well as a stronghold of Senator Hill. Of the 43 counties with less than 40 per cent Negro, 24 reported majorities against the amendment. Of the large cities, only Birmingham supported the amendment; the swanky residential districts gave it thumping majorities.

The effectiveness of the Alabama scheme necessarily depended on systematic discrimination against Negroes in administration by the boards of registrars. On the other hand, obviously the plan had potentialities. By a judicious enfranchisement of the "better" element in the Negro population the whites, if they had the wit to see it, had an instrument by which they might temper the intensity of dissatisfaction among the blacks. The boards did not have the wit; they arbitrarily denied registration to blacks and to some whites. In January, 1949 a special three-judge Federal district court (composed entirely of Alabama native sons) saw what everyone knew: ". . . that this amendment was intended to be, and is being used for the purpose of discriminating against applicants for the franchise on the basis of race or color." It was, therefore, "both in its object and the manner of its administration," unconstitutional. The Supreme Court declined to overrule the lower court decision.[30]

The battle in Georgia over the white-primary, like that in Alabama, demonstrated that even the people of the Deep South are far from unanimous in the notion that the white man must commit political hari-kari to keep the Negro in his place. In 1946 Eugene Talmadge, idol of the "wool hat" boys and a rabble-rouser of no mean talents, won the Democratic nomination on an out-and-out white-supremacy platform. He won, however, only because of the county-unit system, which gives the rural

[30] *Davis* v. *Schnell*, 81 F. Supp. 872 (1949), 69 S. Ct. 749 (1949).

counties a disproportionate weight in nominations; his popular vote was less than that of his principal opponent, James V. Carmichael. Negroes voted relatively freely in the primary and few of them supported Talmadge. "We Democrats," Talmadge said in a telegram to the state Democratic convention following the primary, "who believe in the democracy of our forefathers, believe that a Democratic white primary should be restored in our Southland." [31] He asserted that one of his opponents had "received 99 per cent of the Negro vote." "Such block voting by an uneducated group," he continued, "does not further the cause of good government and is not in accordance with the wishes of Georgia Democrats." The convention in its platform deemed it "necessary and proper that all appropriate steps be taken" to preserve the white primary.

After the death of the senior Talmadge before inauguration, his son, Herman, by an assertion of legality and a show of force, grasped the governorship. His adherents determined to push through the legislature a bill to divorce the party from the state in the South Carolina manner, a scheme for which they thought there was constitutional hope. They set forth their purpose explicitly in the title of the bill: "An act to revise the election laws and to repeal all laws or parts of laws providing the method and manner of holding primary elections by any political party . . . by striking all sections in which any reference is made to primary elections and rewriting the same leaving out such reference to primary elections, so as to completely divorce the State of Georgia from having anything to do in any manner, shape, or form, with the holding of primary elections. . . ."

During the "governorship" of Herman Talmadge the legislature debated the bill to repeal primary laws and after a bitter fight adopted it. The split over the bill was between the progressive Arnall faction and the white-supremacy crowd led by Talmadge. In the lower house, most opponents of the measure were members from the northern part of the state who had support from Savannah representatives and from a few scattered far south Georgia counties. The passage of the bill and its approval by Herman Talmadge came to naught when the state supreme court declared Melvin E. Thompson to be governor. He vetoed the measure, he said, not because he was against the white primary, but because he thought the same end might be attained by means that would be neither an invitation to fraud nor of doubtful legality. He suggested, without effect, that the legislature tighten educational requirements for voting and provide separate voting booths for whites and Negroes.

In the gubernatorial primary of 1948 Herman Talmadge, exponent of white supremacy, won over Thompson. High on the agenda of the 1949 session of the Georgia legislature was the Talmadge program to minimize the Negro vote.

[31] *Atlanta Journal*, October 9, 1946.

Arkansas reaction against the white-primary decision produced another variant in methods of avoiding the decision, the double primary. A clumsy scheme, it was soon abandoned, and the general tenor of Arkansas attitude on the question was muted in contrast with that of Georgia. The initiative for the double primary came from a few counties in eastern Arkansas where Negroes are numerous. Legislators from the remainder of the state went along but without enthusiasm. Moreover, the action occurred against a background of comparatively bland party policy toward Negroes. In 1928 Negro leaders had campaigned for Al Smith for President with the understanding, according to them, that they would subsequently be admitted to the Democratic primaries. The agreement, if it existed, was not honored, though here and there Negroes voted in the Democratic primary, particularly in the cities, the white-primary rule to the contrary notwithstanding.

Arkansas sought to meet the situation raised by the white-primary decision by two methods: (1) separating primaries for the nomination of state officers from those for the nomination of Federal officers, on the theory that the suffrage protected by the Federal Constitution extended only to the choice of Senators and Representatives; (2) permitting state party authorities to establish standards of membership, not in terms of color, but in terms distasteful to persons of color, on the assumption that Negroes would refuse to subscribe to the principles of the party and could thereby be excluded from its primaries.

In 1945 the legislature authorized separate primaries, both "preferential" and "regular" (Arkansas terminology for first and second primaries), for the selection of candidates for Federal offices and prescribed that no citizen should be denied the right to vote in any such primary "on any ground prohibited by the Fifteenth Amendment to the Federal Constitution." [32] As a consequence of the new law in 1946 primaries fell in four successive weeks: first and second primaries for the nomination of candidates for state and local office and first and second primaries for the nomination of candidates for Federal office. Even with the double primary specifically designed to exclude Negroes, observers and participants report that Negroes with a poll-tax receipt could vote in all four Democratic primaries of 1946—save in the plantation principalities of eastern Arkansas. The correct interpretation may be that Arkansas reaction against the white-primary decision was to a considerable extent ceremonial.

After the 1946 trial of the quadruple primary, it was agreed on all sides that the scheme was foolish, and in 1947 the legislature repealed the law with alacrity. The repealer was the first bill passed by the Senate. The succession of primaries—one a week for four weeks—was too much for the good citizens of Arkansas, who could not take off so much time

[32] Acts of 1945, No. 107.

from their plowing to man the polls. After 1946 experience with the quadruple primary the Arkansas County Judges Association urged repeal of the law because the counties had to pay the cost of the Federal primaries, whereas candidates had traditionally financed the primaries. Candidates for Congress sought repeal of the scheme even before it had been tried, doubtless in fear of erratic results that sometimes flow from the small turnout inevitable with the multiplicity of primaries produced by the Arkansas law.

The other leg of Arkansas' effort to offset the Supreme Court decision consisted in the definition of standards for membership in the Democratic party and for participation in its primaries. The legislature in 1945 granted each organized political party "the right to prescribe the qualifications for its own membership, and to prescribe the qualifications for voting in its party primaries." [33] In this the legislature, in effect, ratified resolutions adopted by the Democratic state convention in September, 1944.

Under the 1944 resolutions of the Democratic convention, a person need not be a party member to vote in its primaries but he must meet certain tests. No person would be permitted to vote in the primary who had not "openly declared his allegiance to and sympathy with the principles and policies of the Democratic Party of Arkansas." These principles were stated as follows:

> The purpose and objective of the Democratic Party in Arkansas is to maintain inviolate those fundamental principles of the Party, as well as the practical application thereof in Governmental affairs, which were established by the founding fathers, and which the Party, as originally organized and presently existent, has caused to be written into the constitution and statutes of the State. Among the most important of these principles which the Party is organized to promote and perpetuate are:
> (1) The constitutional principle relating to the separation of Governmental powers into the Legislative, Executive and Judicial branches; and the prevention of encroachment by Executive directives and administrative tribunals on the legislative and judicial processes.
> (2) The preservation of the right of local self-government not to be encroached upon, nor in any wise impaired by, Federal authority.
> (3) Preservation of existing laws relating to the segregation of races in schools, public conveyances and other lawfully designated places.
> (4) Legal prohibition of intermarriage of persons of White and African descent.
> (5) Preservation of the constitutional provision which requires payment of a poll tax as a qualification of an elector.[34]

[33] Acts of 1945, No. 108.
[34] *Rules of the Democratic Party in Arkansas*, January 15, 1946, p. 3.

Judges of election were authorized to question a person offering to vote about his fealty to party principles and to decide finally whether he was in accord with them and had the right to vote.

Although Negroes, if willing to subscribe to the party principles, are not excluded from the primary, membership is limited to "legally qualified White electors who have openly declared their allegiance to, and are in good faith in sympathy with, the fundamental principles, objectives and practices of the Party. . . ." No persons not a member of a party may be a candidate of the party for any public office. "Nor shall any person not a member of the Party act as a party official or serve on the membership of any committee of the Party, or participate in any Party convention." Thus, by a circuitous method Arkansas Democrats attempted to exclude Negroes from public and party office. The later South Carolina decisions would seem to make unconstitutional the Arkansas attempt to exclude Negroes from party candidacy and membership on party committees.

Arkansas party policy, insofar as it concerned primary voting by Negroes, appeared more draconian than it was. Where Negroes sought to vote, the test seems to have been rarely applied. Negroes voted in 1946, and the chairman of the Democratic state committee said in 1947 that he had heard of no instances in which Democratic county committees had required even Negroes to subscribe to the party principles. He did not believe that the opportunity to require the voter to swear to the party principles had been exercised at all.[35] Where Negroes did not seek to vote, their electoral reticence undoubtedly sprang from factors other than the formal party policy.[36]

Early in 1947 the Mississippi legislature met in a special session called to preserve the white primary. Two or three thousand Negroes had voted in the 1946 primaries, and early in the session the legislators were hell bent toward the adoption of the South Carolina plan. Level-headed Mississippians got the wild-eyed members of the legislature under control. The threat of Negro voting, it was argued, was not so portentous as it had been made to seem. Repeal of state laws governing the primary would open the door to fraud. Few Negroes would vote anyway; nothing was to be gained by action with no effect save the stimulation of external criticism. The South Carolina plan might turn out to be unconstitutional anyway.

[35] Other interviews in Arkansas with Negroes and whites turned up no person with any knowledge of insistence by election judges that the voter swear to the party principles.

[36] It should be noted that Virginia, Louisiana, and Mississippi have, at least in part, separate primaries for state and local officials and for Federal officials. In all three states gubernatorial primaries are held at separate times from those for the nomination of Representatives and Senators.

The upshot of the legislative give-and-take was the adoption of a scheme essentially the same as the Arkansas plan. The legislature made ineligible to participate in party primaries persons not "in accord with the statement of the principles of the party holding such primary, which principles shall have been declared not less than" 60 days before the primary by the state executive committee. The state committee met in Jackson in May, 1947, and adopted the following creed (with its pointed omission of reference to Franklin D. Roosevelt):

> The Democratic Party of the State of Mississippi adopts and reaffirms as its party principles those fundamental principles of constitutional government advocated by George Washington, Thomas Jefferson, Andrew Jackson, Grover Cleveland and Woodrow Wilson.
>
> We believe in the Democratic version of a constitutional representative republican form of government of the people, by the people and for the people.
>
> We stand for equal opportunities to all, with special privileges to none.
>
> We are opposed to strong centralized government, national or state.
>
> We believe in state rights and local self-government, and are unalterably opposed to any encroachment upon the rights of the states by the federal government and upon county and municipal rights by the state government.
>
> We believe in the three separate and distinct departments of government as set forth in the federal and state constitutions, namely, legislative, judicial and executive, and oppose the encroachment upon or usurpation of the functions of one by either of the others.
>
> We believe in free enterprise and private initiative.
>
> We are opposed to any legislation, federal or state, setting up what is known as a Fair Employment Practice Committee, commonly known as "F. E. P. C."
>
> We favor fair and just labor laws, whereby the rights of the public, the employee and employer, are adequately and equally protected.
>
> We are opposed to Communism, Socialism, Fascism, and all other forms of Totalitarianism.
>
> We are opposed to any legislation on the part of Congress which attempts to usurp the right of the states to regulate and govern their internal affairs.
>
> We are opposed to the enactment by the Congress of the United States of a so-called anti-poll tax measure as being in violation of the rights of the states to fix the qualifications of electors and in violation of the provisions of the Constitution of the United States. We favor the poll tax and are opposed to any attempt to abolish it either by federal or state legislation.
>
> We are opposed to lynching, mob rule and other forms of violence and lawlessness, and favor adequate state laws to deal with and suppress such crimes, but we are opposed to any so-called federal anti-lynching law as being an attempt to usurp the soverign powers of the states to regulate and govern their internal affairs.

We believe in the time honored and cherished traditions of the South and oppose any legislation, movement or policy which would do violence to or destroy them.

We believe in an honest, sound, economic and efficient government and are opposed to dishonesty, inefficiency and extravagance in government.

We believe in supporting the nominees of our party for the offices for which they are nominated, and, as members of the party, pledge ourselves to vote and support them in the general election.

We favor just and adequate laws to protect the general public from abuses by majority or minority groups.

We hold as a prerequisite to voting in this Democratic Primary the voter has hereby repudiated his affiliation with any other party whatsoever and affirmed his allegiance to the Democratic Party.

The statute provided that persons could be challenged at the polls and caused to "answer, under oath, questions relating to his qualifications and whether or not he is in accord with the principles of the party. . . ." A loophole, however, made the requirement of belief in principles applicable only to new voters, black or white. Any person who had voted in three primaries without being challenged could not be challenged on grounds of disbelief in party principles. Moreover, the act was not to "be construed as preventing a candidate from announcing and advocating any platform. . . ."

The first application of the Mississippi arrangement came in the gubernatorial primary of August, 1947. Even before the primary top officials of the Democratic party expected adherence to the principles to be required, if at all, of only a few Negroes in a few places. Leaders of the Mississippi Progressive Voters' League, a Negro organization, underwent some intellectual discomfort in seeking a rational position on the question of swearing allegiance to the party principles. The League advised Negroes to agree to the party principles: ". . . we believe, as the party believes, in States' rights. We believe that such things as the FEPC, poll tax and lynching law should be left to the States." Moreover, Mr. T. B. Wilson, President of the League, stated: "I don't know what obstacles may be met at the polls, but our members are being advised to create no disturbance if their vote is challenged and they are turned away." [37]

In only scattered instances in the 1947 primary were the tests applied. The president of the Progressive Voters' League had reports of its application in only one county, Washington, in the heart of the Delta where about 15 out of 50 Negroes offering to vote declined to subscribe to the principles. One Democratic county chairman before the primary observed that so few Negroes had registered in his county that there was no need to require adherence to the party principles. In a few places fore-

[37] *Clarion-Ledger* (Jackson, Mississippi), August 5, 1947.

handed whites of good will arranged that voting by the few Negroes who would come to the polls would be conducted to minimize friction. Thus, one Democratic county chairman advised the chairman of the local chapter of the Progressive Voters' league not to let the Negroes vote "in blocks" —by which he meant that they should go to the polls not in large groups but only two or three at a time so that they would not be conspicuous. In Pass Christian the party tests were applied. Two would-be Negro voters approached the polls to vote. Party officials subjected them to the catechism of party orthodoxy:

Q. How do you intend to vote, Democratic or Republican?
A. Democratic.
Q. Do you believe in Communism or Fascism?
A. No.
Q. Are you in favor of F. E. P. C.?
A. Yes.

The judgment followed: "You boys are disqualified." [38]

In its 1948 session the Mississippi legislature returned to the problem of tightening restrictions on Negro voting. It first decided to propose to the electorate for ratification in November, 1948, a constitutional amendment to change a single word, "or" to "and," in the suffrage requirements. Instead of ability to read "or" interpret the constitution ability to read "and" interpret would be required, which change would have converted the "interpreting" alternative into a supplementary requirement.[39] The legislature, however, had a second thought, changed its mind, and proposed an amendment to require simply that the applicant for registration "sustain a good moral character." Proponents said the test would keep Negroes from voting. Ninety per cent "of them live in bigamy and adultery" and "you know that the election officials will never attack the character of a white man." An elderly legislator in opposition to the scheme declared: "We call ourselves Jeffersonian Democrats. How in the name of God can we be Jeffersonian Democrats and pass an amendment of this kind?" [40] The good people of Mississippi agreed with him and defeated the amendment by about five to one. In so doing they provided another case for those who contend that the people have better sense than their legislatures. Their action also disconcerts those who contend that southerners blindly accept any anti-Negro proposal. Perhaps the voters of Mississippi knew that all this sort of legal folderol has little bearing on nonvoting by Negroes.

The white primary has to be written off the books as a valid avoid-

[38] *Journal and Guide* (Norfolk, Va.), August 16, 1947.

[39] The same legislature voted down a proposal that the State Textbook Commission furnish high schools with copies of the state constitution to be used as a part of the curriculum. "Opponents complained it would make more Negroes eligible to vote."— *Birmingham News*, March 25, 1948.

[40] *Birmingham News*, March 28, 1948.

ance of the Federal Constitution. South Carolina Democrats played out all the possibilities to the bitter end. Other states have been ingenious in the contrivance of other methods of disfranchisement, all of them resting ultimately on arbitrary administrative action and all of them, therefore, subject to judicial invalidation should an effort be made to apply them. In one respect, and a most important aspect, the response of the South to the *Allwright* decision is more significant for what has not occurred than for the means that have been devised to circumvent the Constitution. The states around the rim of the Deep South did not react violently and concretely to re-establish the form of the white primary. The reality in no small measure remained everywhere, but the area of maximum intensity of reaction was more circumscribed than it would have been 40 years ago. Yet the hard fact remained that nullification of formal rules could have only long-run effect in altering the fundamental system of caste and attitude of which the primary-exclusion rules were a manifestation. Nevertheless, invalidation of the white primary puts the suffrage issue to the South in a new form. It is as if the courts were saying: "We have winked at constitutional evasions for three-quarters of a century. Three-quarters of a century is enough. You must work out a solution that will stand the test of constitutionality in fact as well as in form."

Chapter Thirty

CRISIS OVER THE SUFFRAGE:
FERMENTS AND FEARS

THE white-primary decision and its aftermath were but one phase of the suffrage crisis of the 1940's. The southern political system was attacked from both without and within. A steady criticism of disfranchisement came from nonsouthern liberal groups, not only on ground of principle but also for the reason that southern political arrangements were thought to produce conservative Senators and Congressmen. The House of Representatives several times passed a bill to outlaw the poll tax but southern Senators exercised their right of veto by filibuster. All these bills undoubtedly contained an element of demagoguery: many of their supporters were seeking votes outside the South rather than actual changes in suffrage rules within the South.

While outside pressure for change served to unite most of the South against suffrage reform by Federal action, outside criticism strengthened the hands of southerners opposed to the prevailing suffrage restriction and increased their number. Regional liberals fought the battle from within and on occasion gained the support of earthy, practical politicians whose immediate interests might be promoted by suffrage reform. By such means the poll tax fell in Louisiana, Florida, and Georgia and was endangered in Virginia, Arkansas, Texas, and Tennessee.[1] It seemed only a matter of time, a comparatively few years, until the poll tax would disappear.

[1] In 1943 the Tennessee legislature repealed the poll tax, but the state supreme court, in an extraordinary decision, held the repeal unconstitutional.—*Biggs* v. *Beeler,*

The movement within the South for loosening suffrage restrictions was only a part of the nation-wide social movement associated with the New Deal. About once a generation a great wave of political sentiment sweeps the United States, sentiment that stirs deeply the masses of the people and gives hope that the promise of American democracy can be fulfilled. These great groundswells do not leave the South untouched. The New Deal affected the masses of the South as had no political movement since the Populist uprising. Its program reached down to the grass roots and actually had some bearing on the course of human events. The southern voter had long been accustomed to a politics that consisted mainly of oratorical fulmination steeped with cadence and pompous promise but with little effect on the world of reality. In the New Deal, oratory came to life, something to cause even the most cloddish poor white to blink, perhaps languorously, in amazement. Here was a politics that was more than speakings, more than barbecues, more than hillbilly bands.

The New Deal aroused the political interests and the political hopes of classes of people left unmoved by traditional southern politics. Negro leaders also began to see advantage in shedding their inherited Republicanism. Progressive southern whites took heart. Insofar as there was a labor movement in the South, it began to rouse itself politically. Southern governors, Senators, and Representatives were not unmoved by these currents; many adjusted their sails to the new direction of the wind. On every hand, leaders of groups stimulated politically by the progressive temper of the times thought themselves handicapped by existing suffrage restrictions.

Moves to lighten suffrage restrictions and to intensify political interest threatened the structure of political power in the South. The dominant groups in the South, since they had downed the Populist menace, had been, on the whole, not seriously challenged in the enjoyment of their perquisites. They had bought their politicians—those that had to be bought—as they bought plantation provisions, saw mills, and oil well derricks. They had lost the habit of tolerating and dealing with political opposition and criticism. They became perhaps more fearful than the weak forays against the established order warranted.

1. The Negro Again

In the suffrage crisis of the 1940's, the central subject of discussion, although perhaps not always the real issue, was the Negro. The question

---

173 S. W. (2d) 1944 (1943). See H. N. Williams, "The Poll Tax and Constitutional Problems Involved in Its Repeal," *University of Chicago Law Review*, 2 (1944), pp. 177–83.

of white supremacy was debated in the same terms as it had been 40 or 50 years before. As with the discussion of all inflammable social issues, little or no attention was given to the fact that changes of great significance had occurred since the last great debate on the question. Nor can it be said that much effort was dedicated towards a realistic estimate of what the consequences of Negro voting might be.

"White supremacy" is a watchword of no exact meaning. Broadly it includes the practice of residential segregation, the custom of social separation, the admonition of sexual isolation, the reality of economic subordination, and the habit of adherence to the caste etiquette of black deference toward white. When applied to politics white supremacy in its most extreme formulation simply means that no Negro should vote. In this sense the phrase is used for its symbolic potency rather than in its literal connotation, for in no state would Negro voting produce "black supremacy."

In a sense the issue of Negro suffrage is a question not of white supremacy but of the supremacy of which whites. In the 1940's the question of Negro suffrage became in large part one of whether a goodly number of persons would be permitted to vote who were disposed to support New Dealish candidates. In 1946 and 1948 Negro groups were prominently allied with such candidates. In Virginia many Negro leaders active in movements to increase Negro registration were also working in support of candidates opposing the Byrd organization. In Georgia, in 1946 and 1948 Negroes voted almost solidly against the Talmadges and in favor of candidates backed by Ellis Arnall. In Alabama, the few Negroes who participated in the Democratic primary of 1946 in the main supported "Big Jim" Folsom. In Texas, Rainey, the progressive candidate for the gubernatorial nomination, drew most of the Negro vote.

Rarely, however, did opponents of wider political participation by Negroes base their position on the tendency of Negroes to support candidates committed to programs of more adequate public services. They relied, rather, on the frightening specter of mass registration and block voting by Negroes. In support of their fears they pointed to the activities of Negro political associations that sprang up at about the time of the white-primary decision.

These associations dedicated their efforts to the establishment of the right of the Negro to vote and to leading him to vote for candidates not hostile toward the race. They also exerted themselves mightily to induce the Negro to vote. The fact that such exertions were necessary to bring the Negro to the polls should have allayed fears that Supreme Court decisions could quickly produce large-scale Negro voting. Negroes presumably have all the reasons that southern whites have to be apathetic about politics. To the pervading electoral disinterest common to both races is added in the case of the Negro special taboos. All these ingrained restraints made predictions of immediate mass voting improbable. As a realistic Mississippi politician said to us, "It's hard enough to get the whites to vote." [2]

The Negro groups that exerted themselves to get the Negro to vote were led largely by southern Negro lawyers, newspapermen, educators, businessmen. They usually acted with the aid and counsel of the National Association for the Advancement of Colored People, an association with headquarters in New York, a fact that lays it open to the charge of Yankee meddling in southern affairs. The association upholds the hand of local Negro leadership which, otherwise, might be unable to withstand the pressures brought to bear on it. The association's legal staff has also aided in the recurring law suits in which Negroes have challenged efforts to exclude them from the electorate.

In all these efforts to increase Negro political activity, the NAACP has maintained its traditional nonpartisan role. The officers of its local conferences and branches, however, have frequently formed parallel, shadow organizations to support candidates. The form of the Negro political leagues has varied from state to state. The local units are sometimes purely political in character, with such names as progressive voters' league or citizens' Democratic club. At other times a businessmen's club, a social organization, a civic club has assumed a political role. In some states local clubs have been organized into a state league, in others they have been only loosely associated if at all. The pool of aggressive Negro leadership in southern communities is so small that persons of ability and energy frequently turn up as the moving spirits of all going organizations. This integration of leadership often makes available for political efforts all the channels of communication provided by the religious, fraternal, and professional groups of the Negro community.

The formation of exclusively Negro organizations for political action has been a consequence of the necessity to overcome suffrage barriers. In no area where the Negro has become newly enfranchised has the Democratic party attempted to assimilate him into the normal party operations. Extreme exclusiveness has prevailed in South Carolina where resistance to the admission of Negroes to the Democratic primaries resulted in the formation of a separate Negro party. In a few instances old-time Negro Republican organizations have been transformed into political associations whose members vote in Democratic primaries. It might be noted that promoters of Negro political action often meet opposition from Negro Republicans with an ineradicable allegiance to the Great

---

[2] He continued, more or less literally, as follows: The Negro will not vote in the South if he is left alone even if there are no suffrage barriers. The fear of mass Negro voting is a bunch of poppycock if a lot of attention is not called to the subject and people do not go out and deliberately try to get him to vote. The number of Negroes voting in Mississippi in 1946 was greatly increased by Senator Bilbo's speeches on the subject.

Emancipator and from patriarchs who concluded in a long-gone day that the Negro gets along best when he "keeps his place."

Whites have been on sounder ground in predicting block voting by Negroes than in forecasting wholesale exercise of the suffrage. The basis of block voting, of course, has been the white man's denial of the right of participation in civic affairs. So long as the right of Negroes to vote is itself an issue, Negroes will overwhelmingly support candidates who do not challenge this elementary right.[3] In addition, if the calculus of self-interest has any bearing on voting, a tendency toward Negro solidarity would be expected in that as members of an economically disadvantaged group blacks would support candidates pledged to provide large-scale services.[4] In such matters, the drive toward small-scale objectives in local politics often gives the Negro community the same kind of political cohesiveness found among similarly situated groups of whites. This cohesiveness stems directly from discrimination in local governmental services. Candidates for municipal office are finding it easier and easier to understand the plea of Negro leaders (with a block of dependable votes at their command) for improved street lighting, paving, or sewerage facilities in the Negro section of town. Demands for improved school and recreation facilities and for Negro policemen are other political objectives for which Negroes rally with a fair degree of unanimity if one candidate will promise them and another is indefinite.[5]

[3] They do not, however, exclusively support such candidates. Strange as it may seem a few Negroes voted for both Eugene and Herman Talmadge and in 1946 even Senator Bilbo attracted Negro votes.

[4] Thus, the president of one voters' league in reporting on activities in his locality said: "The Negro vote has in every election been cast solidly for the liberal candidate. Much attention has been given to training him for the necessity of voting in a block. We have taught him to vote for candidates who believe in social legislation and actually vote for it when the time comes."

[5] Many Negro leaders impress on their race the grave importance of responsible use of the ballot. A Florida leader in a communication to his fellow Negro citizens in 1948 observed: "Since Negroes now have the privilege of helping to elect somebody, we shall be approached by numerous candidates seeking our support. Some will offer us money or a few drinks of liquor in an effort to get our votes. Some will come to us with soothing words and vain promises while others will try to reach us through their Negro 'friends.' But we must not be too easily swayed. We cannot afford to sell our votes for a few dollars or a few drinks. We must be concerned about the general welfare of the masses of our people. . . . Fellow citizens, this is our opportunity to remove some of these evils. Let us consider carefully the records and attitudes of our candidates, and let us help to put in office people who are inclined to give Negroes a fair deal."

After the 1948 primaries the same leader admonished his flock: "There also is a tendency on the part of some Negroes to be bought over by such flimsy benefits as free fish frys, free drinks, and free rides to the polls. Our votes are more valuable than this, and we must seek more lasting benefits. Another grave danger facing us is the tendency of some Negro leaders to 'sell out' to the politicians. Such leaders have little interest in group welfare, and they are concerned primarily with getting dollars for their own pockets. They are ready to sacrifice principles for money. This is one big mistake that was made by our fathers during the Reconstruction Period, and we cannot afford to repeat it now. We must be on the lookout for these 'sell-out' leaders and be ready to expose them."

Experience of the past decade, limited though it has been, indicates that like supports like and that only a Negro candidate can stir deeply the political enthusiasm of Negroes. However, the possibility of victories by Negro candidates is limited to a few counties and city wards. Negro leaders, moreover, recognize that to draw the line between a white and Negro candidate would only bring grief to the group as a whole and restrain Negroes from running for office except in a few localities prepared to accept Negro representation on local governing boards. In the instances of election of Negroes to office no disturbance has resulted. A Negro is a city councilman of Winston-Salem. Another was elected to the Richmond council with the help of white votes. A Negro has been elected to the governing board of a junior college in San Antonio.

In localities that have accepted Negro voting for many years, principally cities of Tennessee, North Carolina, and Virginia, Negroes seem to manifest less solidarity than in those areas where the right to vote is less firmly established. They divide in the manner of whites. Crump has controlled both his Negro and white constituents. Local Negro groups have played ball with local outposts of the Byrd organization in various Virginia cities. In Nashville, Charlotte, and Raleigh the Negro vote has splintered much as the white electorate.

Although there had been some experience to judge from, the dyed-in-the-wool white-supremacy advocates in the suffrage debates of the 'forties did not bother themselves much about calculating the probable effects of opening the polls to Negroes. To them, a single Negro vote threatened the entire caste system. They continued to talk as they had talked in 1890 and 1900. Horace Wilkinson, of Birmingham, in 1946, for example, averred:

> If it was necessary to eliminate the Negro in 1901, because of certain inherent characteristics, it is even more necessary now because some intellectual progress makes the Negro more dangerous to our political structure now than he was in 1901.
> The Negro has the same disposition to live without working that his ancestors had in the jungle 10,000 years ago.[6]

Most advocates of white supremacy needed no theories of racial superiority to bolster their beliefs. Thus, a member of the Mississippi state Democratic executive committee: "Right or wrong, we don't aim to let them vote. We just don't aim to let 'em vote." And that was about the long and the short of it. Nor did he concede that gradual extension of the suffrage would be a solution: "The time to stop a fire is when it is small."

For the white-supremacy extremist, to permit the Negro to vote is to take the first step toward allowing him to run for office. If he runs, he may be elected. If he is elected, he will govern whites. The late Eugene Talmadge voiced this fear:

[6] *Birmingham News*, September 18, 1946.

I do not have to be a prophet to predict that just as day follows night in from 4 to 8 years if Arnall, Wallace, Cox, Carmichael and others of their like have their way, you will see negro Mayors, negro School Superintendents, negro Congressmen, negro Judges, and negro Sheriffs and negro Jailers in that part of the state where the negroes predominate. Negro Solicitors will try white people before negro Judges and white men and white women prisoners will be subject to the orders of the negro Sheriffs and their negro Jailers.[7]

Some southerners pay little heed to abstractions about racial superiority and racial equality and devote themselves to the contrivance of some working arrangement that may conform to no particular theory or ideal but will meet the practical necessities. They realize that the theorists of racial superiority have all the anthropologists against them, but they well know that the anthropological conclusion has no utility in dealing with the work-a-day problem of the Negro and politics. Even if it is conceded that the Negro's capacities are equal to those of the white, those capacities have not been developed. The Negro is poorer than the white, more plagued by disease, less literate, less trained in manual and professional skills, less experienced in the management of group affairs. Whether all these characteristics flow from inherent incapacity or simply from environmental oppression, they are there and have to be faced in dealing with the question of the Negro and the suffrage.

Negroes, as well as whites, differ enormously among themselves. As a consequence one block of southern whites takes the position that the vote should gradually be extended to Negroes as their level of achievement rises. That is, permit, even encourage, Negro doctors, lawyers, ministers, businessmen, and upper-class Negroes to vote and such others as are known to be "responsible" citizens. Persons of this view advance gradualism as an alternative to sudden, large-scale voting by Negroes inexperienced in political life. The fact is that southern whites have a bear by the tail and don't know what to do about it, but they contend that gradualism postpones the full consequences of enfranchisement and offers a workable approach. Even this position is, of course, taken publicly with hesitation by southern whites. It concedes the entire argument on the question of racial superiority and looks toward the eventual assimilation of the Negro into the political life of the community. And the execution of the doctrine of gradualism requires patience, good will, and good faith—on both sides.[8]

In effect, North Carolina practices the doctrine of gradual enfranchisement. It is nowhere written into the regulations, but it seems to be

[7] *The Statesman* (Hapeville, Ga., Editor: The People; Associate Editor: Eugene Talmadge), June 13, 1946.

[8] The doctrine of gradual enfranchisement might appear to conflict with the requirements of the Constitution and laws. We proceed on the assumption that the rulings of the Supreme Court on this question will mean in practice not much more than the dominant white groups of the region are willing to have them mean.

the guiding principle of state authorities in their informal advice to local registration and election officials. And North Carolina has moved a long way from the Deep South in coping with race relations. The same policy seems to prevail in Virginia, where the race question has been consciously and firmly played down in political campaigns by responsible white leaders. Oddly enough, many upper-class Negroes feel the same way about the suffrage as the white gradualists. They say, not for quotation, that some qualification ought to be erected to fence from the polls the poor and illiterate. Thus, a Georgia Negro leader believes that the quality of electoral performance would be greatly increased by higher standards of an educational or economic sort. He opposes such restrictions only because they would be administered to the disadvantage of Negroes.

A potent factor in the gradual initiation of the Negro into public affairs is the expectation of local officials and candidates that they may gain Negro votes. Thus, in a North Carolina town a Negro businessman approached the white registrar of the Negro ward to discuss the denial of registration to all save a few Negroes. The registrar opined that politics was white man's business and that his visitor could best serve his race by telling his fellow blacks to stay on their side of town and be good Negroes. The Negro businessman expounded the usual views about justice and fairness, and then inquired whether the registrar had ever thought about what the Negroes could do for him. The registrar was, in the view of his Negro visitor, being used by the dominant political people in the community and kept in the lowly status of registrar. The political leaders were trying to keep apart the fellows down at the bottom of the ladder, like the registrar and the Negroes. On reflection, the registrar concluded that this was the most sensible talk he had heard in a long time. Gradually more Negroes were added to the list, but only gradually. After three years our registrar ran for alderman, was elected, and has served happily ever since. Or, similarly, in a west Alabama county, a member of the board of registrars permitted over a period of years several hundred Negroes to register. When the member happened to run for office, the Negroes caucused to agree on candidates to support and naturally decided to cast their ballots for the registrar.

The chances are that in the long run the most effective force for the promotion of Negro participation in politics is the actions of white men who think that they need and can win Negro votes. When whites split among themselves and seek Negro support, the way may be opened for the Negro to vote. While the results are not always pretty,[9] breaches of

[9] Consider the remarks of W. Earl Hotalen, Executive Secretary, Alabama Temperance Alliance, in the *Alabama Christian Advocate*, March 28, 1946, p. 5: "All day long on Monday, March 18, wet campaign workers hauled negro war veterans into Tuscumbia, herded them into the courthouse and registered them for the next day's voting. As discharged soldiers they were exempt from payment of poll tax, of course. Drys watched in amazement as hundreds of these negroes, shepherded by bootleggers,

this sort in the wall against Negro political participation have been made all over the South.

In this reconnaissance of southern attitude on Negro voting, we have passed in review the standpat advocates of white supremacy and the gradualists. A few persons feel that a Negro cannot be taught to swim by letting him wade: you throw him into the water. The way to teach him to become a responsible citizen is to let down the bars. Persons with these views usually find it convenient to express them outside the South. Finally, a great many southerners are indifferent about the whole business. They live in those parts of the South where there are only few Negroes. Southwestern Virginia, western North Carolina, northern Georgia, northern Alabama, eastern Tennessee, northwestern Arkansas, and western Texas are areas of comparatively sparse Negro population and there the whites are less immediately concerned about Negro suffrage.

Intensity of white opposition to Negro voting seemed in the 'forties, as in the 1890's, to be keenest in the areas in which Negroes formed the highest proportion of the population. These areas furnished the driving power in the original disfranchisement movements and in them opposition to Negro voting centered 40 years later. In such areas whites feared the possibility of Negro control of city, county, and other local governments. Throughout, the whites in such areas have furnished the main strength of the movement to keep the Negro out of politics.[10] Their strategy has been to win enough support from those whites less immedi-

---

would-be honky-tonk owners and wet politicians, were herded like cattle for registration purposes.

"In this way the Wets piled up a total of 1,131 votes in Sheffield's six boxes. Drys polled only 491 votes in the same boxes.

"With a 640 vote majority counted at Sheffield, plus the wet majority in Brick Beat, the liquor forces of Colbert County met and overcame the drys' majority of nearly 500 votes in the rest of the county.

"Preachers of six different denominations stationed themselves at the polls and watched the voting all day long. They, and other Dry campaign workers, talked to a few of the negro GI voters. Some of the expressions made to them by Negro voters were very disturbing. One burly negro muttered: 'We got de balance o'power now; from now on we'll be de boss.' One negro was asked: 'How much did they pay you to vote wet?' He answered, 'Don't know yit; we don't git paid till after we votes.' Still another, when asked for whom he will vote for governor, 'Ah don't know exactly; de man ovah yondah will tell me de right candidate'; and the 'man ovah yondah' to whom he pointed was one of Handy Ellis' most energetic leaders and vote-getters in Colbert County."

It should be noted that the drys did not get out the white vote. The total vote in the local option election was 5,416. The county had a population of voting age of 18,707 in 1940, of whom 14,000 were white.

[10] It is imperative to bear constantly in mind that there are deep divisions among southern whites, even within localities of high Negro concentration, over the solution of the "race problem." This division is only slightly less marked over demands of Negroes for political rights than over their demands for greater social justice and greater economic opportunity. All across the South, one finds newspaper editors, lawyers, educators, laborers, businessmen, even planters, who see the inevitability and preach the necessity of an orderly and impartial admission of Negroes to full citizenship.

ately concerned to carry the day. Perhaps the hope of the South lies in the long-run decline in the number of units of local government in which Negroes constitute the majority.

Even in areas of concentrated Negro population white-supremacy orators exaggerated the immediate threat. Agitation to stir the Negro to political activity was confined mainly to urban centers, where Negroes are on the whole better educated and where leaders of Negro opinion and most Negroes of the business and professional classes live. Even in cities the Negroes, in addition to the habit of nonparticipation in elections, shared with whites of the poorer classes a comparatively low interest in politics. In the rural areas agitation was weak and participation almost negligible. In fact, even a fairly administered literacy test under existing constitutional and statutory provisions would exclude from the polls a substantial proportion of the Negroes in the rural agricultural counties of heavy black populations. Illiteracy remains high among rural Negroes. In South Carolina, in 1940, 67.9 per cent of rural-farm Negroes 25 and over had either not completed a year of schooling or not finished more than four years.

In areas of both heavy and light concentrations of Negroes even those who could look at the suffrage issue with least emotion were troubled by their expectations about the nature of Negro voting behavior. In the 'nineties it was argued that Negro participation in elections insured electoral corruption. Whites bid against each other for the support of the blacks. To prevent wrongdoing by whites it was essential to deprive the Negro of the vote. The same contention appeared again in the 'forties. In all probability by this time the purchaseability of the Negro vote had decreased sharply, at least for those elections that were dramatic enough in their issues for either white or black to know what the debate was all about.[11]

In issueless local campaigns Negroes might still be prone to sell their votes; whether more so than whites of like economic status is another question.[12] Yet scattered examples of startling departures from the folk picture of Negro vote-selling were to be found. Thus, in San Antonio a Negro leader, accustomed to delivering a considerable vote to the candi-

[11] In San Antonio at the 1946 primary a white woman ardently campaigning for Rainey was annoyed by the sight of Negro women handing out Jester campaign literature around the polls. When she could restrain herself no longer, she said to a young Negro woman: "I don't understand why you are doing this. Don't you realize that Rainey is the man you should be voting for?" The reply was: "Oh, we've already voted for Dr. Rainey. We're just doing this because we need the money."

[12] In all our conversations in the South not a single person referred to the fact that it is illegal for a white man to buy a black vote. In any state of the South the right fifty or a hundred men, banded together, could stamp out vote-buying by organizing opinion, by thorough investigation, by merciless prosecution. The possibility of dealing with the matter in this way is so revolutionary that it seems never to have occurred to anyone.

dates backed by the local machine, in 1946 found himself in the embarrassing position of having to back Rainey for governor, both against his own personal inclinations and in opposition to the white machine leaders. To have done otherwise would have lost him the confidence of his own followers.

The receptivity of Negro ministers to contributions in return for promises to throw the vote of their people is traditional.[13] The inclination has not disappeared. A well-posted informant, for example, estimates that 65 per cent of the colored men of the cloth sold out in the 1946 Savannah municipal elections, but their flocks did not follow. One minister expressed the old notion that the black man would not benefit from the controversy whichever side won and that he might as well get what he could out of it: "big money and I mean big money." Perhaps the political influence of the ministry, black as well as white, is on the decline. In some communities in North Carolina Negro political groups have organized a sort of combination in restraint of bribery. Responsible leaders of the race deliver the vote, or a substantial portion of it, but white politicians who attempt to buy votes are disciplined, and the delivery of the vote is on the basis of issues.[14] In some cities of North Carolina Negroes have had a longer experience in politics and greater opportunity to develop a responsible community leadership than they have in, for example, Mississippi. Colored conspiracies in restraint of bribery are also reported in Florida.

Not a few Negro leaders are keenly conscious of the necessity that their group establish its cause by the most upright behavior. The development of able Negro leaders of integrity (white, too, for that matter) is a long and arduous process. Given their white counterparts as models, the growing Negro upper class may quite as likely become exploiters as humane leaders of their people. Consider the colored landlord in a Mississippi city who, much to the admiration of some of his white brethren, invented a new mode of eviction. He removed the windows from the homes of delinquent Negro tenants in mid-winter to speed their departure.

Although the gradual emergence of a responsible Negro leadership gave grounds for optimism, elements remained in the southern caste in-

[13] In fairness it should be reported that candidates often have the opportunity to help a white congregation paint its church edifice or buy a new piano.

[14] A political advertisement by a Negro political club before a 1947 primary included the following passage: "The Negro vote will play a large part in the election of candidates for office in the coming primary. The Political Club believes in clean politics, and will re-act against anyone who will seek to purchase votes, or appoint markers without the consent of the body. Our chief interest lies in the fact that much improvement needs to be done in our district, such as street improvements, water, lights, and sewage—even our school is without an auditorium or gymnasium, and athletic activities have to be carried on any where we can find a place."

heritance that were inadequately pondered on all sides. A basic principle of the social system is that the black man does what the white man says. This ingrained habit undoubtedly gives the Negro vote (not so much as it is, but as it might be on a larger scale) a high degree of organizability, which would probably be more marked in rural than in urban communities. The problem of transforming the Negro's habit of obedience into a capacity for independent and responsible exercise of the suffrage appears far simpler when viewed from Boston than when seen from Atlanta. Yet even this matter of political exploitation of an organizable vote comes down to a question of white rather than of black morality.

2. What about the Whites?

Although electoral interest varies tremendously from state to state, in sheer quantity nonvoting whites outnumber the voteless Negroes of the South as a whole. It is not strictly correct to speak of southern whites as "disfranchised." While complex registration systems, the poll tax, and other suffrage requirements undoubtedly keep many whites from the polls, most politically sterilized whites derive their civic indifference from other and deeper causes. To get to the bottom of the matter one must delve into the nature of the social structure of the South, which is reflected in all its aspects in the one-party system. If in no other way the one-party system, by its insulation of the South from national campaigns, deprives the southern electorate of the stimulation of most grand questions of public policy.

Beyond such obvious matters the one-party system builds on fundamental elements of class structure and attitude that depress political interest. Among these social characteristics is an impressive solidarity of the upper economic classes that disciplines without mercy, where it can, those who would arouse and rise to power with the votes of the lower third. Those who cannot be disciplined are bought without hesitation and without remorse. Further, the presence of the black provides a ready instrument for the destruction of tendencies toward class division among the whites. The specter of Reconstruction, of Negro government can still be used to quell incipient rebellion by discontented whites. In addition, within white society there is only the faintest awareness of the possibilities of political power in lifting the lower half by its bootstraps. This unawareness of the potentialities of politics flows from many factors. A low level of education; a high degree of insulation from the main stream of ideas; the siphoning off into the governing classes of men of ability by a social system still remarkably fluid; a religious tradition of acceptance as divine purpose of whatever comes; all these and doubtless many other elements contribute toward political ignorance or indifference, if not defeatism, among a substantial proportion of the southern white population.[15]

Great significance must be attached to a pair of interconnected elements in the structure of the southern political system in the production of mass indifference. These are upper-class solidarity and the related, probably consequent, weakness of political leadership of mass movements. Upper-class solidarity interacts with the one-party system which facilitates amalgamation of men of substance and ability. Yet from such men must come leadership of political movements to improve the lot of the people. The mass of nonvoting whites will not arouse on their own motion; they must have a leadership drawn in the main from the upper brackets. The mechanisms of upper-group discipline are powerful enough to hold the line. Few men with the necessary ability and cash dare, even if they are so disposed, to play the role of the progressive. And it is only leaders of such persuasion who can stir people to political participation. Whenever an able candidate with a progressive program appears, the curve of voter participation inevitably rises. By progressive is not meant radical. By regional standards any person who looks even a bit beyond the needs of tomorrow can be considered a progressive.

Perhaps the small size of the South's economic elite aids in the maintenance of its unity; at any rate, its powers of self-discipline are impressive. In consequence, the leadership in the movement of the 'forties to bring the mass of southern whites to life politically has been in the main of a capacity that often commanded no great respect in the upper brackets of the community. In general, the movement to bring about registration and voting to a greater extent by whites drew its inspiration from New Dealish organizations, labor unions, and a few progressive persons with political ambitions. And, as is often the case with leaders of such movements, many of them were of less ability than those persons who had established niches for themselves within conservative groups.

It is inevitable, of course, that a movement for the induction of the mass of southern whites into citizenship must be a movement of the "outs." It will, therefore, have a tinge of unrespectability in the eyes of the respectable classes of the community. The policy objectives of those concerned with the increase of white voting aroused fears and anxieties among conservatives for the same reasons that the move to enfranchise the Negroes aroused anxieties. Most of the new white voters would be workers, small farmers, and others who, once politically aroused, might upset applecarts. Groups that had enjoyed their status for decades with-

---

[15] A public health expert wryly observes that malnutrition may explain the political lassitude of many southern whites. They accept their lot because they do not have the energy either to recognize or to rebel against the intolerable.

out serious political disturbance naturally viewed the prospect with alarm.

It would be a mistake, however, to interpret southern skirmishes over the poll tax and other suffrage restrictions solely as a conflict of classes or a battle of ideologies. The lines crossed and crisscrossed in a confusing manner. Many small cliques and rings in control of local governments here and there believed that their rule would be ended by repeal of the poll tax. Nevertheless, the nature of some of the prominent sources of opposition to suffrage restrictions gave a color of truth to the view that the end objective was to upset applecarts. One of the more conspicuous agencies in exciting the electorate was the Southern Conference for Human Welfare. Through its state affiliates in several states, the conference organized campaigns to propagandize prospective voters to register and to vote and was usually in sympathy with factions opposed to traditional southern Democratic conservatism. Its leadership was drawn generally from middle-class groups: educators, clergymen, lawyers, reformers, and the like.

Another, and in the long run more important, element striving toward the elimination of suffrage restrictions and toward greater participation was the CIO. In 1946, it launched a drive to unionize the South, a crusade for the "political and economic emancipation" of southern wage-earners. The CIO nowhere enjoyed the sympathy of the upper classes; in the South it was even less popular. This animosity was in large part an automatic response to the press and other leaders of opinion, but people who knew what they were about saw in the CIO invasion an ultimate threat to the balance of political power. Unionization invariably increases labor's political awareness, and urban labor has been probably the most inert element of the population politically.

The intensity and extent of the activities of CIO Political Action Committees (organized by individual unions, local industrial union councils, and state industrial union councils) varied tremendously from state to state. Even in Mississippi, where organizable labor is scarce, a couple of local PAC's were formed, and in Laurel the committee did some work in 1947 to induce white unionists to pay their poll taxes and to qualify to vote. In Alabama, in one or two localities the CIO advanced funds to its members for the payment of taxes and organized a systematic campaign to see that unionists qualified as voters. In Georgia, in the 1946 primaries the CIO almost certainly brought about the defeat of Representative M. C. Tarver, a member of Congress for over 20 years. In North Carolina local Political Action Committees were negligible in number and in effect. The Virginia CIO Political Action Committee conducted probably the most effective campaign to collect poll taxes and to register unionists. The press carried such reports as this: "Textile unionists are now flocking to Chatham to pay their poll taxes so as to be in a position to vote." [16] In Danville it was expected that a higher vote would be cast in the special election for Mayor and in the August primary "than ever before." Moreover, "many of those who recently have perfected qualifications have been people of the working class," it was reported.[17]

It ought to be noted that there is also an AFL. Shortly after the CIO announced its "Operation Dixie" the AFL started a drive to organize the South. The AFL, with local exceptions, exerts itself much less energetically to increase voting by workers than the CIO. Its inactivity flows in part from the fact that the AFL membership includes a larger proportion of skilled workers, who are probably already registered as voters in higher degree than CIO members. Yet the AFL in the South suffers in political effectiveness from the same policies that weaken it elsewhere. It leaves its state and local officials free to make whatever deals they wish with local political groups, a policy that puts the AFL with some strange political bedfellows. The campaign against the Taft-Hartley Act drew the AFL and CIO closer together, but it was an uneasy alliance. Prior to 1948 AFL high policy frowned on local AFL-CIO alliances to promote or defeat candidates. William Green's southern regional representative had the duty of destroying such coalitions when they came officially to his attention, a procedural ritual that provided some elasticity of policy.

In bringing their members to political life, both the AFL and CIO came up against the race issue. To maximize union influence, in both the usual realm of economic bargaining and in that of politics, union leaders here and there were driven to try to ameliorate interracial frictions. In many localities—although the total effect may not have been great— union leaders preached the doctrine that their members had a community of interest, be they black or white, and urged black and white without discrimination to vote for that interest.

Weak as the southern labor movement is, it increased the political consciousness of its members and won victories here and there. It was not alone labor's interest in bringing its members to the polls that frightened the southern old guard; almost everywhere labor groups, Negro organizations, and progressive societies collaborated not only in trying to break down suffrage restrictions and in exciting the political interests of the habitual nonvoter but also in supporting candidates against southern Bourbons. It is not astonishing, then, that agitation for the repeal of the poll tax was at times labeled as communistic.

The interrelation of streams of protest against suffrage restrictions and movements against conservative ruling cliques is illustrated by the

---

[16] *Richmond Times-Dispatch*, January 14, 1947.
[17] Ibid., April 30, 1947.

case of Virginia. In 1940 the Southern Electoral Reform League commenced a campaign for repeal of the Virginia poll tax. It drew support from all classes of people and had affiliated with it several labor unions. Its director served as campaign manager for Moss Plunkett, anti-Byrd candidate for governor in 1945. Local branches of the NAACP and labor unions undertook campaigns to increase the number of citizens voting. In 1947 a "Committee for Democracy in Virginia" issued a manifesto calling for voting by all "literate adults." The manifesto was signed by Martin Hutchinson, unsuccessful opponent of Byrd for the senatorial nomination in 1946, and by Francis P. Miller, anti-Byrd leader who was destined to run for governor in 1949.

Although the results of the movement to increase the vote were not on the whole impressive, in some localities sharp increases in the vote occurred. Entrenched officeholders viewed the agitation with alarm and leaders of the Byrd organization foresaw a decline in its share of the popular vote if the total number of voters rose. In some areas local officials exhibited a new respect for the "labor vote."

The first step toward poll-tax repeal had been taken in 1940 by Governor James H. Price, a governor of progressive tendencies for whom the Byrd hierarchy had no burning enthusiasm. He asked the Virginia Advisory Legislative Council to study the question. A subcommittee of the Council, headed by Professor Robert K. Gooch, unequivocally recommended repeal of the tax as a prerequisite for voting. In the course of its report the subcommittee made Jeffersonian observations scarcely in keeping with the dominant tone of Virginia politics.

"In proposing the removal of the poll tax as a prerequisite for voting in Virginia, the Subcommittee is prompted primarily by the conviction that the basis of political democracy ought to be restored in the Commonwealth. . . .

"Whether instinctive or articulate, opposition to removal of the poll-tax stipulations or, in other words, support of the present stipulations seems to the Subcommittee to be founded on disbelief in political democracy as the basis of government and on the distrust of the operation in practice of . . . . . . government so based. . . .

"When the suffrage in Virginia has been placed upon a democratic basis, popular government will be restored. As has been suggested, nothing else is worthy of the true Virginia tradition. What the concrete results of popular government will be depends, of course, as the term *popular government* implies, on the people. There again, Virginia should be satisfied with nothing less than such dependence on the people.

"But there is a more fundamental answer to the contention that Virginia is so well governed that its suffrage requirements should be left unexamined and unaltered. It is that the contention misses the whole point. The question is not one primarily of good government but of free government. And, as the late Elihu Root once observed, good government is never a substitute for free government. This is the essential point. . . .[18]

The Byrd machine keeps its ears to the ground. Eventually the machinery for repeal got into motion. In 1946, the legislature proposed a constitutional amendment to remove the poll tax, to set up a system of annual registration. In 1948, in conformity with Virginia's amending procedure, the legislature again passed the amendment and submitted it to a popular vote in 1949. In scheduling the vote for 1949 rather than for 1948 when a much larger turnout would have occurred, the organization may have been trying to stave off the evil day when it would have to fight for its life.

Movements for increased voting by whites and blacks were interconnected; in turn, an antidemocratic attitude existed that would have further limited the suffrage of both black and white. That Negroes should be kept from the polls was a matter on which many whites agreed. In addition, many individuals went a step further and contended that the ballot should be reserved to the more responsible whites. Rationalizations for limitation of civic rights to the so-called better element, while not always publicly uttered, were widespread. These arguments had an anachronistic character; they could have been uttered in 1800 and the years afterwards when tax-paying and property-holding qualifications for voting were being wiped away. Even in the 1940's the South had its anti-Jacksonians.

It is only a short step from the contention that the Negro has not the qualifications for citizenship to the position that whites of similar economic and social status likewise lack the judgment requisite to vote. In fact, among many upper-class whites with a benevolent attitude towards the Negro the sentiment is not so much that Negroes should not vote as a distrust of the less-accomplished citizens of the community, which group includes most of the Negroes. Even in areas of Negro concentrations such views are found. Some big economic operators hold the view that only the more intelligent, better educated, best citizens should elect public officials and that the color line is inadequate for sifting out the incompetent. Rationalizations for the exclusion of the Negro from the suffrage lead also to the conclusion that only selected whites should have the right to vote. Gessner T. McCorvey, chairman of the Alabama state Democratic committee, in discussing the suffrage issue in 1945 stated:

Merely because a man, white or black, has reached the age of 21 years is in his case no indication whatever that he is qualified intelligently to take part in the government of his country. He should be able to understand the constitution of our country and fully realize

[18] "Report of the Subcommittee (of the Virginia Advisory Legislative Council) for a Study of Constitutional Provisions Concerning Voting in Virginia" (1942?) (mimeographed).

and appreciate the duties of its citizens before he should be entrusted with the ballot.

I am not in favor of requiring too high a standard of education or the ownership of too much property but certainly the power should be vested in somebody—and the board of registrars is the proper party—for passing upon the qualifications of a participant to become a qualified voter with full protection afforded the voter to prevent any abuses of discretion that might be vested in a board of registrars.[19]

The opinions expressed by the late Thomas Lomax Hunter, of Virginia, fell pleasantly on many ears:

The fact that Virginians are not boiling up to the ballot box is a sign that they are filled with faith, hope and charity. Being of a sympathetic soul, I sorrow with those who sorrow because they cannot make us discontented enough to take our sorrows to the polls. Take off the capitation tax. Let the paupers vote. They will always vote for greater largesse. Having no wealth to distribute, they favor the redistribution of wealth. What neighbor State votes more than we do? North Carolina? Her greater vote registers her larger discontent with the government she is getting. I believe she has enfranchised her paupers.[20]

Again, in Mississippi, a state legislator from the Delta feels that it would be entirely satisfactory for Negroes to vote if they were educated and competent citizens. It is not possible for a man who cannot run his own business to be asked to help to run someone else's. It would be wise to have a property qualification for the suffrage. An intelligence test, also, should be employed so that persons who vote can do so on the basis of some understanding of the community's problems. Any qualifying test, intelligence, property, or other, should be applied without discrimination to all applicants whatever their hue may be.

3. A Test of Leadership

Obviously the conversion of the South into a democracy in the sense that the mass of people vote and have a hand in their governance poses one of the most staggering tasks for statesmanship in the western world. The suffrage problems of the South can claim a closer kinship with those of India, of South Africa, or of the Dutch East Indies than with those of, say, Minnesota. Political leadership in the State of New York or California or Ohio simmers down to matters of the rankest simplicity alongside those that must be dealt with in Georgia or Mississippi or Alabama. Men of moderate endowments—like Messrs. Bricker and Dewey—win national renown for taking over and running going party organizations

[19] *Birmingham News*, February 9, 1945.
[20] *Richmond Times-Dispatch*, April 4, 1947.

and state governments supported by a prosperous citizenry. Such assignments could be regarded by southern politicians as strictly minor league.

Solution of the suffrage issue and of the attendant problems of democratization place a severe strain not only on political leadership—narrowly defined as candidates, party functionaries, and the like—but on the entire body of public and private citizens who set the pace. The economic elite and the upper orders generally are obliged, if progress is to be made, to exercise the utmost restraint in the amelioration of social frictions and to sacrifice what they may regard as their own short-term interests.

The ticklish business of contriving a new sort of interracial adjustment demands the broadest conception of responsibility for long-term community welfare from those of the southern upper strata. In the short run it may be profitable to maintain the status quo. Responsible southerners see that a readjustment is inevitable in the long run and that without the most intelligent and unselfish leadership the new equilibrium may be reached only at great cost.

Hodding Carter, editor of the *Delta Democrat-Times*, of Greenville, Mississippi, states the problem, after saying that it is important to "put off the time when large numbers of Negroes may vote in primary elections in Mississippi."

> Before that time comes, two things ought to be achieved. One is genuine education of Negroes for citizenship, so that intelligently voting Negroes will recognize an identity of economic interests with the intelligently voting white men. The other is proof by the Negro, especially in those counties like ours, where he outnumbers the white, that he will not vote by color and for color. The white man must be as responsible for avoiding this tragic result as must the Negro, and there is only one way we can meet this responsibility. That is by proving by our acts that the Negro can receive equal legal justice, fair economic treatment, adequate schools, and decent health and housing facilities without resorting to political division by race in an attempt to achieve these proper objectives.
>
> Unless these things can be accomplished only tragedy can come. It will take time to accomplish them. Thus, the legal tactics of delay have a long-range purpose with which we agree. . . . [21]

Sustained effort to improve the Negro's economic and political status costs money, and upper-class southerners, like upper-class nonsoutherners, dislike to part with cash, although the only possible long-run outcome of increasing the productivity of the Negro would be to make rich whites richer and more whites rich. The almost overwhelming temptation, especially in areas with many Negroes, is to take advantage of the short-run opportunity to maintain the status quo by using, or tolerating the use of, the race issue to blot up the discontents of the lesser whites. By this means

[21] *Delta Democrat-Times* (Greenville), August 6, 1947.

the governing classes can kill off or minimize pressures for improved governmental services from whites and find support for low public outlays for the benefit of the Negro. It is naive, of course, to interpret southern politics as a deliberate conspiracy among the better-off whites to divide the mass of people by tolerating Negro-baiting. Nevertheless, with a high degree of regularity those of the top economic groups—particularly the new industrialists—are to be found in communion with the strident advocates of white supremacy. In the political chaos and demoralization that ensue alert men with a sharp eye for immediate advantage take and count their gains. The requirements thus are for a remarkably enlightened leadership that is at the same time tough enough to maintain a hard-boiled discipline within its own ranks. Only by such means can a social situation with volcanic potentialities be kept under control.

Chapter Thirty-one

IS THERE A WAY OUT?

A DEPRESSINGLY high rate of self-destruction prevails among those who ponder about the South and put down their reflections in books. A fatal frustration seems to come from the struggle to find a way through the unfathomable maze formed by tradition, caste, race, poverty. In view of this record, for reasons of personal comfort, if for no other, the inclination to look for a ray of hope in the prospects of the South is strong. Actually, despair need not be the only outcome of a reconnaissance of the southern political scene. Although the question of race overshadows all other factors conditioning the politics of the South, even on the question of race the unity of the region has been greatly exaggerated in the national mind. Nor do the conventional stereotypes of southern politics convey any conception of the diversity of political attitude, organization, and tradition among the southern states. The term "southern" conjures up notions that have little resemblance to reality. Strangely enough, southerners themselves fall prey to the same sort of misconceptions as do northerners. Not only is there diversity within the South; the region is also changing. Its rate of evolution may seem glacial, but fundamental shifts in the conditions underlying its politics are taking place. All these changes drive toward a political system more completely in accord with the national ideas of constitutional morality.

664

1. The Solid South

Southern political regionalism derives basically from the influence of the Negro. Other factors, to be sure, contribute to sectional character, but in the final analysis the peculiarities of southern white politics come from the impact of the black race. Common concern with the problems of a cotton economy forms a foundation for regional unity, although perhaps to a lesser extent than several decades ago. A white population that is predominantly native-born, Anglo-Saxon is bound together by a sentiment of unity against those sections whose people include many recent immigrants. A rural, agricultural people views with distrust the urban, laboring classes of the North. The almost indelible memories of occupation by a conqueror create a sense of hostility toward the outsider. Yet most of these nonracial bonds of unity differ little from those factors that lend political cohesion, for example, to the wheat states or to the corn belt.

Southern sectionalism and the special character of southern political institutions have to be attributed in the main to the Negro. The one-party system, suffrage restrictions departing from democratic norms, low levels of voting and of political interest, and all the consequences of these political arrangements and practices must be traced ultimately to this one factor. All of which amounts to saying that the predominant consideration in the architecture of southern political institutions has been to assure locally a subordination of the Negro population and, externally, to block threatened interferences from the outside with these local arrangements.

While these objectives have molded southern political institutions, it would be incorrect to say that the problem of race relations is a constant preoccupation of politicians or a matter of continuous debate. Campaign after campaign is waged in which the question of race is not raised; in campaign after campaign candidates most unrestrained in Negro baiting find themselves defeated when the votes are counted. The situation is, rather, that the struggles of politics take place within an institutional framework fixed by considerations of race relations, a framework on the order of a mold which gives shape and form to that which it contains. It is chiefly when the equilibrium in race relations is threatened that the issue of the Negro comes to the fore in political discussion.

It is, of course, no news to conclude that the Negro gives the South its special political color. Yet our analyses indicate that the influence of race is more complex than might be supposed from the usual notions derived from white-supremacy oratory and from fictional pictures of the South. In fact, the effects of race are such that the participants in politics are not always conscious of them. Much less are outside observers aware of the precise nature of the consequences of race and, indeed, in many instances it is most difficult to estimate their significance although their general nature may be divined.

The mechanisms of race and regionalism are identified if attention is focused on those counties of the South with large proportions of Negroes in their population. With almost monotonous regularity, no matter from what angle the politics of the South is approached, the black belt stands out as the hard core of the political South. It is in this relatively small part of the South that attitudes thought to be universal in the South occur with highest intensity. The black-belt counties [1] can be regarded as a skeleton holding together the South. They have, in a sense, managed to subordinate the entire South to the service of their peculiar local needs.

If any single thread runs through most of the preceding chapters, it is that of the association of a special set of political attitudes or at least attitudes of high intensity with the black-belt counties. In the period of the disfranchisement movement, the black-belt counties, with a relatively high degree of uniformity, turned in by far the highest popular majorities in favor of proposals to tighten suffrage restrictions for the purpose of excluding the Negro from the suffrage and perhaps also incidentally to make it inconvenient for lesser whites to vote. This cleavage between the white and the black counties had appeared even earlier, with varying degrees of sharpness, in the return to power of the old Whigs who were reincarnated as Conservative Democrats and gradually became the exclusive bearers of the true Democratic faith. By the time of the Populist revolt, in state after state the lines were fairly clearly drawn between the black belts and the white areas. The black belts allied themselves with the conservative forces of the cities and towns to beat down the radicals who flourished in the hills where there were few Negroes. The division was not, of course, governed solely by the distribution of Negroes; the areas of heavy Negro concentrations have tended to possess a peculiar economic structure based on large-scale agricultural operations.

Although the differences between the lowlands and the uplands, between the delta and the hills, and between other such regions have become less, far less, bitter with the passage of time, in several states the black belt continues to play a major role in state politics. By the overrepresentation of rural counties in state legislatures, the whites of the black belts gain an extremely disproportionate strength in state law making. By the political alertness of their people, an alertness growing perhaps out of necessity, they also gain strength. While the black belts have a significant place in state politics, the lines are often blurred and in some states the black belts are too small to exert a controlling influence.

[1] See above, Figure 1, p. 6.

The role of the black belts in giving cohesion to the South appears with most clarity in national politics. At times when the unity of the South is strained the black belts are etched out sharply as the backbone of the South. In the presidential election of 1928 by and large the voters of the black-belt counties showed greatest resistance to the appeal of the Republican candidate. In the white counties Democratic loyalties were not nearly so strong. The whites in these counties could vote their convictions on prohibition and religion. They had far less concern about the maintenance of a solid Democratic front as a means for the long-run preservation of the racial equilibrium. The black-belt counties may have been immediately governed by a more potent partisan tradition than by conscious calculations about party and race, yet that tradition itself rested ultimately on such considerations. In the Dixiecrat revolt of 1948, on the other hand, the most serious defections from the Democracy occurred in the black-belt counties. In the white counties the traditional attachment to the Democratic party coincided with a generally liberal viewpoint and Mr. Truman polled his strongest vote in these counties. The black-belt counties, most immediately and most deeply concerned about civil rights proposals, had most reason to support the Dixiecratic candidates. In both 1928 and 1948 there were many departures in individual localities from the cleavage along white-black lines, yet in general divisions fell along those lines.

In presidential voting at moments of strain the roots of southern solidarity are defined by the split in the popular vote. In the South's representation in Congress, however, no such split occurs, at least on the race issue. The solidarity of southern spokesmen in Congress reflects in part the success of the black belts in converting the entire South to their will and in part a regional aversion to external interference on any question. Yet it is only on the race question that the South presents a solid front in Congress. In the Senate to a relatively greater extent than in the House the factional differences within the Democratic party of each southern state are projected into the voting on nonracial matters. In the House, however, it appears that one of the serious consequences of the one-party system is a much higher degree of solidarity on all kinds of questions than in the Senate. Yet in both House and Senate it is the race issue that evokes the highest degree of southern solidarity. This phenomenon contributes additional support to the proposition that the Negro gives the South its peculiar political characteristics.

This summary may seem to overstate the role of the black belts because the many qualifications enumerated in earlier chapters cannot be included. Nevertheless, the general point is valid that the most profound conditioning of white political behavior by the Negro occurs in the areas of heavy Negro population concentrations. It does not, of course, follow as a matter of political therapy that the South could be remade politically by converting its black belts into mandated territories or non-self-governing semi-colonial areas. Such a move would not isolate and sterilize intransigence completely, for the black-belt attitude spills over into other territory. Moreover, the black belts have powerful political allies in the cities among conservative groups unconcerned about race policy, such as urban industry and finance.

2. The South Divided

In congressional politics, southern cohesiveness in the resistance of proposals to repeal the poll tax, to punish lynching, and to enact other race legislation conveys a false impression about the political homogeneity of the South. There is, to be sure, a high degree of solidarity in congressional politics on a limited range of issues. The black belts manage to control almost the entire southern congressional delegation in opposition to proposals of external interference. Yet in intrastate politics, even on issues of race, uniformity of attitude by no means prevails. Departures from the supposed uniformity of southern politics occur most notably in those states with fewest Negroes and in those sections that are predominantly white. The unknown political South is in a sense the obverse of the Solid South; it consists in the main of those areas outside the black belt.

Outside the black belts southern political behavior often takes on a tone distinctly at odds with the planter-financier stereotype. The area outside the black belt in several states consists largely of the highlands which have been marked by an unbroken strain of political rebelliousness. Opposition to The War was most intense in the uplands. Afterwards the Republican party won strength in the hills as did the Populists. In the disfranchisement movement the people of the piedmont and the hills manifested a coolness toward schemes to restrict the suffrage. Through the years in state campaigns radical or progressive candidates generally have been accorded their most enthusiastic support in these regions. In Alabama, Hugo Black and Jim Folsom came out of the hills to harry the "big mules." Louisiana's northwestern red hills gave Huey Long to the world, and Mississippi's hills unwaveringly supported Bilbo. Virginia's southwestern uplands nurtured John Flannagan, a thorn in the side of the Byrd machine. Tennessee's mountain country sent Estes Kefauver to Congress, while Ellis Arnall came from the Georgia piedmont. Olin Johnston built on a mill following in South Carolina's piedmont, while North Carolina's progressivism must be attributed in considerable measure to the spirit of the uplands. Throughout the South in the presidential campaign of 1948 it was in the hills that Truman's support tended to be strongest.[2] Although the uplands constitute the area of most striking deviate political behavior, similar departures from the supposed southern norm occur in other areas with few Negroes. Along the coast in almost every state there are tidewater counties, too poor in soil to develop a plantation agriculture, that often join hands with the hills against the black belt.

Within individual states the areas predominantly white stand out as centers of political ferment. Similarly among the states those with fewest Negroes seem most disposed toward deviation from the popular supposition of how the South behaves politically. It is the custom to speak of the border states. It is more accurate to speak of the states around the rim of the South. Texas, Arkansas, and Florida seem destined to develop in the long run a nonsouthern sort of politics. The extraordinary growth of industry and trade in Texas and the decline in the proportion of Negro population conspire to create a new variety of politics not much concerned about the Negro. Florida similarly has enjoyed a tremendous population growth. While the state has a relatively large number of Negroes, the whites of the newly settled areas do not seem to be governed by a Negrophobia to the same extent as the long settled agricultural areas of the Old South. To a less marked degree Arkansas politics seems to be moving toward an emancipation from the Negro question; large areas with few Negroes are gaining rapidly in population and shifting the balance of power away from the plantation principalities of the eastern part of the state. Tennessee, Virginia, and North Carolina are other states of the southern rim, and all of them manifest a considerably higher degree of freedom from preoccupation with the race question than do the states of the Deep South.

Although there can be no exact measure, the apparent variations in intensity of reaction to the Supreme Court decision outlawing the white primary define the rim of the South. Texas, Arkansas, Tennessee, Virginia, North Carolina, and Florida seemed to accept the new state of affairs with the least effect on their political temperatures. There were, to be sure, outbursts here and there in which orators recited the conventional orotundities, yet on the whole political leaders in these states did not exhibit the irreconcilability so manifest in South Carolina, Georgia, Alabama, Mississippi, and, to a lesser extent, in Louisiana. Indeed, around the rim of the South there was less reason for concern, for there were fewer Negroes.

By the types of anaylsis employed in this study the people of the areas with few Negroes show striking departure from the political attitudes of the black belt. Perhaps more significant for the long pull is the

[2] The significance of the uplands in southern politics has been emphasized by H. C. Nixon, "Politics of the Hills," *Journal of Politics,* 8 (1946), pp. 123–33.

differential in attitudes of the larger urban centers. In many ways the cities differ from rural areas with like proportions of Negro population. It is in the cities that the obstacles to Negro political participation are least formidable. It is mainly in the cities that a Negro is now and then elected to a minor office. In the cities, too, the white vote is conditioned to a much less degree by the Negro than in the rural counties. Urban Representatives in Congress free themselves to a much higher degree from the black-belt-conservative coalition than even Representatives from white rural districts. In the cities there is, to be sure, gross discrimination in public services, but the conditions of city life compel a much greater concern for the colored population than generally prevails in rural counties. The causes of the different racial equilibrium of the cities are difficult to discern. Perhaps the physical conditions of urban life permit the development of more or less autonomous, parallel communities. The organization of authority is more institutionalized, less personal, and the Negro may exercise, for example, the right of petition without great fear of illegal or extralegal retaliation against him as an individual. It should be remembered, however, that the institutional arrangements of the South prevent the exertion of the full strength of the cities in politics. Gerrymandering against the urban centers takes on special significance in that it gives heavy weight to those areas in general the most conservative and in particular the most irreconcilable on the Negro issue. And in Georgia, of course, even in gubernatorial politics the cities are practically disfranchised.

The prominent place of the plantation counties in the conservative wing of the southern Democratic party makes it almost impossible for the conservative wing to take the leadership in moves to ameliorate race problems. That leadership goes to the liberal wing which draws its heaviest popular support ordinarily from the areas of white dominance and from the cities. And southern liberalism is not to be underestimated. Though southern conservatism is not entirely a myth, as W. G. Carleton has argued,[3] fundamentally within southern politics there is a powerful strain of agrarian liberalism, now re-enforced by the growing unions of the cities. It is not always perceptible to the outsider—or even to the southerner—because of the capacity of the one-party system to conceal factional differences. Yet an underlying liberal drive permeates southern politics. It is held in check in part by the one-party system which almost inevitably operates to weaken the political strength of those disposed by temperament and interest to follow a progressive line. Moreover, if the Negro is gradually assimilated into political life, the underlying southern liberalism will undoubtedly be mightily strengthened, for the Negro, recent experience indicates, allies himself with liberal factions whenever they exist.

[3] "The Conservative South—A Political Myth," *Virginia Quarterly Review*, 22 (1946), pp. 179–192.

The potentialities in national politics of a South freed from the restraint of the Negro and of the one-party system are extremely great. On the contrary, the maintenance of the degree of conservatism that prevails depends ultimately on ability to frighten the masses with the Negro question or the winning over of the growing Negro vote to the conservative wing of the Democratic party. The latter alternative is not open; hence, the long-run prospect for southern reaction can be considered only as dark unless the Negro issue can be raised in a compelling manner. The Dixiecrats beat the drums of racial reaction in 1948 without impressive results; the Dixiecratic movement may turn out to have been the dying gasp of the Old South.[4]

In the combination of economic conservative and Negro baiter against economic liberal and Negro there occurs a coalition at odds with political folklore about the South. Upper bracket southerners habitually attribute all the trouble with the Negro to the poorer whites. Yet it is the poorer whites who support candidates favoring governmental policies for the reduction of racial discriminations and for the alleviation of racial tensions. The line is by no means, of course, sharply drawn between rich and poor, but the economic conservatives are by interest thrown on the side of those who wish to maintain discrimination, to keep alive racial antagonisms. Such policies accrue to the short-term advantage of the economic conservatives.

3. Portent of Trends

The foregoing interpretation may overestimate the significance of the Negro in southern politics. Certainly the Negro is not in the normal course in the forefront of the debate. Rather the presence of the Negro has created conditions under which the political process operates. Those conditions in many respects were fixed long ago and they make themselves felt now although participants in current politics are not always aware of the influences under which they act. Yet there are within the South underlying trends that probably will in due course further free it from the

[4] Kenneth C. Royall, a North Carolinian and Secretary of the Army, put the matter bluntly and with insight in a Jackson Day speech at Jackson, Mississippi, early in 1949: "From a long range standpoint there is no room in this country for a provincial party, whether it be a provincialism of occupation or of race or of religion. Nor will America long support a party of prejudice—prejudice for or prejudice against any particular group. There will always be some who will hearken to the arguments of bitterness and bigotry, but the fundamental common sense and the essential spirit of fairness of the American people will ultimately bring failure to any class party or any party of intolerance. This American spirit is what brought failure—failure even in our Southland —to a recent effort to create a Southern party—a party which at least acquired the reputation of being a party of prejudice. There were a great many sincere men in this new party—many of them friends of mine and of yours—but they misjudged the temper of the American people. And they underestimated the South's breadth of vision."

effects of the Negro on its politics. Some of these trends are changes in public attitudes; others, perhaps more significant in the long run, are changes in the composition and distribution of the population and in the nature of economic organization and endeavor. These changes are altering the shape of the mold that influences, if it does not fix, the shape of southern politics.

TABLE 69

Number of Counties with 50 Per Cent or More Negro Population, by States: 1900, 1920, 1940 [a]

STATE	1900	1920	1940	TOTAL COUNTIES IN EACH STATE, 1940
Alabama	22	18	18	67
Arkansas	15	11	9	75
Florida	12	5	3	67
Georgia	67	58	46	159
Louisiana	31	22	15	63
Mississippi	38	34	35	82
North Carolina	18	12	9	100
South Carolina	30	32	22	46
Tennessee	3	2	2	95
Texas	12	4	3	254
Virginia	36	23	18	100
Total	284	221	180	1108

[a] Bureau of the Census, Population—Special Reports, Series P-45, No. 3, March 29, 1945.

Not of the least significance in altering the conditions of southern politics is the gradual decline of the relative position of the Negro population. Since 1900 the colored proportion of the population has decreased in each state. In several states the Negro population percentage dropped sharply from 1900 to 1940. In Florida the percentage fell from 44 to 27; in Louisiana, from 47 to 36; in South Carolina, from 58 to 43. Of equal or greater importance is the fact that over the same period the areas with high proportions of Negro population contracted, again sharply in some states. It is these areas that constitute the backbone of southern intransigence on the race question. In Virginia, for example, the number of counties over 50 per cent Negro dropped from 36 to 18; in Louisiana the decline was from 31 to 15. The changes in all the states are shown in Table 69. The shrinkage of the black belt is probably of greater importance than the simple decline in Negro population percentages for entire states. It is not to be supposed, of course, that a reduction in the Negro population ratio brings with it immediately a shift in white political attitudes. That change comes only gradually; an alteration of population composition, however, creates a new political setting that will eventually make itself felt.

The growth of cities contains the seeds of political change for the South. In almost every type of analysis urban political behavior differs significantly from that of the rural areas. Apart from other political consequences of urbanism, cities seem to be less dominated in their political behavior than rural areas by consideration of the race question. The Negro himself meets less rigid obstacles to political participation in the cities; the whites, in turn, appear to be less bound by Reconstruction tradition and free to vote without the same regard for the maintenance of the racial system that governs the whites of the rural counties with high proportions of Negro population. If the consequences of urbanization are conceded, the important question then is whether the extent and rate of city growth are great enough to be of significant effect. The South has lagged behind the remainder of the nation in urbanization, and the chances are that urban-rural population readjustment will continue to occur in the region. Nevertheless, striking shifts in population have already taken place. In 1900 the 11 southern states had only seven cities with over 50,000 population; by 1940, this number had grown to 41. Doubtless the 1950 census will show a larger number of cities within the category of 50,000 and over. Another measure of the magnitude of population redistribution is provided by the urban-rural division of the Negro population. In 1900, 14.7 per cent of the Negro population of the South was urban; in 1940, 33.7 per cent. The southern Negro may migrate to Detroit and Chicago but he also moves to Houston, Atlanta, and Birmingham, and migration internal to the South has somewhat the same political effect as movement to points outside the South. With a continuation of improvement of agricultural technology, an acceleration of population shifts may be expected.

Apart from its effects on the race question, urbanization is, of course, an accompaniment of other changes of profound consequence for political behavior. The development of industry and trade in a region hitherto more completely dedicated to agriculture has had and will continue to have far reaching influences in several directions. The growth of urban labor already has had considerable effect and will undoubtedly have further consequences. In all the recent movements for the abolition of the poll tax and for the mitigation of other suffrage restrictions labor unions have played a prominent role. In the factional struggles of particular states organized labor has come to play a controlling role at times. In states such as Texas and Florida, for example, labor organizations in recent years have exerted a rapidly increasing influence. The political activation of urban labor has proceeded less rapidly than the growth of the laboring population. As obstructions to urban political activity are overcome, a significant expansion of labor influence may be expected.

Nor must the South become completely urbanized or industrialized to a high degree for union political strength to become formidable. It is virtually a law of our politics that any considerable minority, if it becomes highly vocal, can command a remarkable deference from political leaders. The southern urban dweller has scarcely begun to speak politically.[5]

Concurrently with the growth of the number of urban workers there are coming into being, of course, industrial and financial interests that have a fellow feeling with northern Republicanism. A continuing growth of industry and a continued leftward veering of the Democratic party nationally would place a greater and greater strain on the Democratic loyalties of rising southern big business. At each recent presidential election the results of that strain have been perceptible in the open support of Republican presidential candidates by southern personages formerly of prominence in Democratic councils. In the building of a party within most southern states the Republicans work under the handicap that a large proportion of their existing popular following has little reason to be enthusiastic about Republican policies nationally. The Dixiecrats rather than the hill Republicans are the natural allies of northern Republicanism. Moreover, the strength of the Democratic loyalties of most southern voters is not to be underestimated. In fact, partisan loyalties of Americans wherever they live have an extraordinary persistence. Southerners are no exception to the rule and Republicans have no easy task in making converts among the mass of southern voters. Of course, Republicans make little effort over most of the South to win votes. The development of an opposition party in the South will probably depend more on events outside the South than on the exertions of native Republicans. If the balance of power becomes one that clearly requires a Republican fight for southern votes to win the Presidency, presumably the national party could no longer tolerate its ineffective southern leadership.[6] If and when Republicans make a real drive to gain strength in the South, they will find, if present trends continue, a larger and larger group of prospects susceptible to their appeal.

The decline in the Negro population, the growth of cities, and the dilution of an agricultural economy by the rise of industry and trade occur only slowly and their influences on the political system occur even more slowly. Moreover, it is not to be supposed that these fundamental trends automatically bring political change. They only create conditions

[5] On the growth of manufacturing labor in the South, see Bureau of Labor Statistics, *Labor in the South* (Bulletin No. 898, 1947).

[6] Obviously the adoption of the proposal to split each state's electoral vote in the same proportion as its popular vote in the presidential election would revolutionize southern politics. Such a change would give a powerful stimulus to southern Republican efforts in presidential campaigns. A strengthened Republicanism would inevitably interest itself also in state and local politics.

favorable to change that must be wrought by men and women disposed to take advantage of the opportunity to accelerate the inevitable. In every state of the South there are many such persons and their efforts are bringing results to an extent not commonly appreciated outside the South. Yet the hard fact has to be recognized that their labors bear fruit most readily in those localities where the underlying population movements and economic developments create the most favorable surrounding circumstances. The way is hard and progress is slow. Yet until greater emancipation of the white from the Negro is achieved, the southern political and economic system will labor under formidable handicaps. The race issue broadly defined thus must be considered as the number one problem on the southern agenda. Lacking a solution for it, all else fails.

INDEX

Absentee voting, abuses of, 454–57
Acuff, Roy, 80
Adams, Arthur L., 333
Adkins, Homer, 187, 188, 191, 402
Agrarianism, *see* Populism
Alabama: absentee-ballot abuse, 456n, 457;
agrarianism in, 46; anti-bolters 1948,
332; black belt, 42–43; Boswell amendment to constitution 1946, 632; conduct
of primaries in, 446; county machines,
53–54; delegation to national convention
1948, 335; Democratic electors 1948, 340;
direct-primary voting requirements,
427–48; distribution of Negro population, 42; Dixiecrats, 332–33, 340; Extension Service and politics, 55–56;
factionalism, 17, 37, 45, 47, 49–52, 57,
67, 365, 367; Farm Bureau in, 55; farm
population, 85; Heflin excluded from
1930 primaries, 435; illiteracy, 161; labor
unions and politics, 56; legislative apportionment, 308n; localism, 37–41, 48,
149; Negro voting in, 520; one-party
system in, 44–45; party loyalty of candidates, 433–35; per-capita income, 85;
personal machines, 50; political process
in, 37; poll tax in, 580, 595; presidential
electors 1948, 435; presidential vote
1928, 324–25; probate judge, 53; run-off
primary 1948, 332; sectionalism, 41–42,
45, 67, 544–45; tone of politics, 36; registration boards, 571–72; registration eligibility, 632–33; registration procedures,
559, 571–73; secession and party realignment, 45; selection national convention
delegates, 393; state executive committee
leadership, 398–99; urban population,
85; vote on adoption 1901 constitution,
542; voter-interest, 1920–46, 500–501;
voting qualifications 1946, 632–34; white
voting rates, 514–16; Winston County
and secession, 282–83; *see also* Democratic party; one-party system
Alabama Education Association, 57
Alabama League of Municipalities, 55
Albright, Mayne, 214–16

Aldrich, Ransom, 230n
Alexander, H. M., viii, 418n, 434n, 439n
Allred, James, 268
Almond, J. L., Jr., 564
American Federation of Labor, 658; *see
also* Labor
Andrew, C. Blythe, 290–91
Arkansas: Adkins faction, 187; Bailey faction, 187; Bond's machine, 203; campaign
finance, 198n; campaign issues 1948, 194;
civil rights program, 191; county machines, 196–98, 204; county vote 1928,
325; delta counties vote 1946, 197–98;
Democratic party principles, 638–39;
Dixiecrats in, 338–39; educational association in politics, 192n; election fraud
in, 200–203, 443; electoral behavior, 197;
factionalism in, 17, 185–93, 200; Farm
Bureau, 192n; farm population, 85;
farm tenancy in, 185; first-primary gubernatorial vote 1948, 192–93; Free Enterprise Association, 197; gambling and
politics, 202; general election 1946, 202;
GI's in politics, 198, 201–204, 436–37; 453,
460–61, gubernatorial primary (1944,
1946), 199, (1948), 189; illiteracy in, 161;
issueless politics, 186; localism, 187, 192–
93, 198; local and rural leaders, 194–99;
machine counties, 198; McLaughlin machine, 192, 201–202; national and state
convention delegates, 393; Negro voters,
521; nonsecrecy of ballot, 458–59; one-
party politics in, 183–84; party loyalty
of candidates, 433–34; party membership, 426–27; personal politics, 194–200;
per-capita income, 85; poll-tax administration, 591–92, 598; poll-tax payment,
594, 601, 610; presidential Republicans,
279–80; press in politics, 185; public
utilities in politics, 192n; race issue in,
194, 426–27; Republican party in, 296–
97; run-off primary, 193, 195, 418; sanctions against bolting, 437; state Democratic chairman, 399; urban population,
85; vote for Thurmond 1948, 344; white-
primary decision in, 637–39

i

A NOTE ON THE TYPE

THE TEXT OF THIS BOOK was set on the Linotype in Baskerville. Linotype Baskerville is a facsimile cutting from type cast from the original matrices of a face designed by John Baskerville. The original face was the forerunner of the "modern" group of type faces.

John Baskerville (1706–75), of Birmingham, England, a writing-master, with a special renown for cutting inscriptions in stone, began experimenting about 1750 with punch-cutting and making typographical material. It was not until 1757 that he published his first work, a Virgil in royal quarto, with great-primer letters. This was followed by his famous editions of Milton, the Bible, the Book of Common Prayer, and several Latin classic authors. His types, at first criticized as unnecessarily slender, delicate, and feminine, in time were recognized as both distinct and elegant, and his types as well as his printing were greatly admired. Four years after his death Baskerville's widow sold all his punches and matrices to the Société Littéraire-typographique, which used some of the types for the sumptuous Kehl edition of Voltaire's works in seventy volumes.